Texts in Theoretical Computer Science
An EATCS Series

Editors: W. Brauer G. Rozenbe

On behalf of the European Associatior
for Theoretical Computer Science (EATCS)

D. Bjørner

with contributions from Christian Krog Madsen

Software Engineering 2

Specification of Systems and Languages

With 151 Figures and 27 Tables

 Springer

Author

Prof. Dr. Dines Bjørner
Computer Science and Engineering
Informatics and Mathematical Modelling
Technical University of Denmark
2800 Kgs. Lyngby, Denmark
bjorner@gmail.com
db@imm.dtu.dk

Series Editors

Prof. Dr. Wilfried Brauer
Institut für Informatik der TUM
Boltzmannstr. 3
85748 Garching, Germany
brauer@informatik.tu-muenchen.de

Prof. Dr. Grzegorz Rozenberg
Leiden Institute of Advanced
Computer Science
University of Leiden
Niels Bohrweg 1
2333 CA Leiden, The Netherlands
rozenber@liacs.nl

Prof. Dr. Arto Salomaa
Turku Centre of
Computer Science
Lemminkäisenkatu 14 A
20520 Turku, Finland
asalomaa@utu.fi

Library of Congress Control Number: 2006920552

ACM Computing Classification (1998): D.1, D.2, D.3, F.3, F.4, G.2.0, K.6.3, H.1, J.1

ISBN-10 3-540-21150-0 Springer Berlin Heidelberg New York
ISBN-13 978-3-540-21150-1 Springer Berlin Heidelberg New York

Springer is a part of Springer Science+Business Media
springer.com

© Springer-Verlag Berlin Heidelberg 2006

Cover Design: KünkelLopka, Heidelberg
Typesetting: Camera ready by the Author
Production: LE-TEX Jelonek, Schmidt & Vöckler GbR, Leipzig

Printed on acid-free paper   45/3100/YL   5 4 3 2 1 0

Charlotte, Camilla and Caroline

Am I grateful? You bet! Am I a happy father? Also your doing!

Two roads diverged in a yellow wood,
And sorry I could not travel both
And be one traveler, long I stood
And looked down one as far as I could
To where it bent in the undergrowth;

Then took the other, as just as fair,
And having perhaps the better claim,
Because it was grassy and wanted wear;
Though as for that the passing there
Had worn them really about the same,

And both that morning equally lay
In leaves no step had trodden black.
Oh, I kept the first for another day!
Yet knowing how way leads on to way,
I doubted if I should ever come back.

I shall be telling this with a sigh
Somewhere ages and ages hence:
Two roads diverged in a wood, and I —
I took the one less traveled by,
And that has made all the difference.

Robert Frost: The Road Not Taken (1915) [121]

Preface

The present volume is the second of three volumes on the engineering principles and techniques of software engineering. We refer to the Preface of Vol. 1, as well as to Chap. 1 of that same volume, for a proper preface and overall introduction to all volumes in this series. We assume that the reader has studied Vol. 1.

Overview

The present volume focuses on principles and techniques for specifying languages and systems. It uses the abstraction and modelling principles, techniques and tools covered in Vol. 1, and it supplements those principles, techniques and tools with additional ones. In particular the present volume emphasises the following four aspects:

"UML"-ising Formal Techniques

Some notable features should be emphasised here. The concurrency aspect, Chaps. 12–14, also illustrates diagrammatic specifications, as does Sect. 10.3 (UML class diagrams). Together this material illustrates that popular features of the Unified Modeling Language (UML [59, 237, 382, 440]) can simply and elegantly be included, i.e., used, with RSL. Christian Krog Madsen is the main author of Chaps. 12–14.

The RAISE Specification Language: RSL

As in Vol. 1, we use RSL extensively in the present volume. Hence we insert, in Chap. 1, an RSL Primer — and otherwise refer to the RAISE URL: http://www.iist.unu.edu/raise/.

Acknowledgments

The preface of Vol. 1 contained an extensive acknowledgment section.

Combining RSL with Petri nets (Chap. 12), with message or live sequence charts (Chap. 13), and with statecharts (Chap. 14) is due primarily to Christian Krog Madsen [316, 317]. Very many and dear thanks are therefore extended to Christian. Combining RSL with UML-like class diagrams (Sect. 10.3) is due primarily to Steffen Holmslykke [9, 10]. Similar thanks are therefore graciously extended to Steffen. Martin Pěnička is likewise dearly acknowledged for having provided Examples 12.8 (Sect. 12.3.4), 14.7 (Sect. 14.4.1) and 14.8 (Sect. 14.4.2).

Colleagues at the National University of Singapore, Andrei Stefan and Yang ShaoFa, studied and proofread Chaps. 12–15. It was with Yang ShaoFa, as the leading person, that I decided to work out the model of CTP (Communicating Transaction Processes) of Sect. 13.6. Their comments and work are much appreciated.

A main source of academic joy has been the 30 years I have been at the Technical University of Denmark, 1976 till now.

Last, but not least, I acknowledge the tremendous support received from the Springer editor, Ronan Nugent.

Brief Guide to Volume 2

This volume has several chapters. The chapters are grouped into parts. Figure 2 abstracts a precedence relation between chapters. It is one that approximates suggested sequences of studying this volume.

- Chapter 1 is considered a prerequisite for the study of any chapter.
- We group some parts into the dash-circled groups $A - E$.
- Group A consists of Chaps. 2–5 that can be studied in any order.
- Group B consists of Chaps. 6–9 that should be studied in order 6, 7, 8 and 9.
- Group C consists of Chaps. 10–11 that can be studied in any order.
- Group D consists of Chaps. 12–15 that can be studied in almost any order. Chap. 14 does contain an example which requires having studied Chap. 13 first.
- Group E consists of Chaps. 16–19 that should be studied in order 16, 17 and 18. Chap. 19 can be studied in-between, before, or after. Preferably after.
- Groups $A - E$ can be studied in any order. But it might be useful to have studied Chap. 5 before Chap. 15, and Chap. 10 before Chap. 18, and to have studied Group B before Group E.
- It is no harm to study Chap. 20.
- Appendix A contains an overview of our naming convention.

Within most chapters many sections can be skipped. Typically those with larger examples or towards the end of the chapters.

In this way a teacher or a reader can compose a number of suitable courses and studies. Some such are suggested in Fig. 1.

Advanced Abstraction & Modelling	Languages	Concurrent Systems
Chaps. 1–5, 10, 11	Chaps. 1, 6–9, 16–18	Chaps. 1, 12–15, 19

Fig. 1. Alternative courses based solely on Vol. 2

Dines Bjørner
Technical University of Denmark, 2005–2006

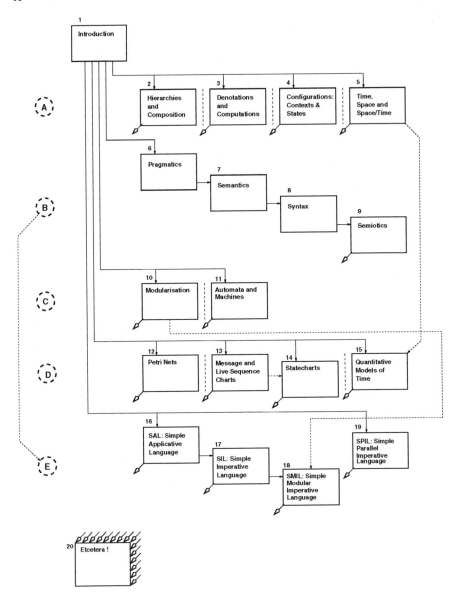

Fig. 2. Chapter precedence graph

Contents

Part IV LINGUISTICS

Part V FURTHER SPECIFICATION TECHNIQUES

Part VI CONCURRENCY AND TEMPORALITY

Christian Krog Madsen is chief author of this chapter

Part VIII CLOSING

Part IX APPENDIXES

Part I

OPENING

1

Introduction

- The **prerequisite** for studying this chapter is that you have read and understood Vol. 1 of this series of textbooks on software engineering.
- The **aims** are to motivate why the present volume is written, to motivate why you should read it by outlining what it contains and how it delivers its material, to explain the notion of formal methods "lite", and to briefly recall the main specification language of these volumes, RSL.
- The **objective** is to set you firmly on the way to study this volume.
- The **treatment** is discursive, informal and systematic.

1.1 Introduction

Volume 2 continues where Vol. 1 left off. Having laid the foundations for discrete mathematics, Vol. 1, Chaps. 2–9, abstraction and modelling, Vol. 1, Chaps. 10–18, and specification programming, Vol. 1, Chaps. 19–21, which we consider the minimum for the pursuit of professional software engineering, we need now to expand, considerably, the scope of areas to which we can apply our abstraction, modelling and specification skills.

This chapter has two main sections: First we outline the justification for and contents of this volume as well as how the material in this volume is presented. Then we give an ever-so-short primer on RSL: the syntactic constructs, very briefly their "meaning" and their pragmatics, that is, which "main" uses with respect to abstraction and modelling they serve to fulfill. The primer can, of course, be skipped.

1.1.1 Why This Volume?

It is one thing to learn and be reasonably fluent in *abstraction and modelling* as covered in Vol. 1 of this series. It is another thing to really master the principles, techniques and tools. With the present volume our goal is to educate

you to the level of a professional software engineer in: (i) specifying complicated computing systems and languages, (ii) being aware of major semiotics
principles (pragmatics, semantics and syntax), (iii) being well acquainted to
means of handling concurrency, i.e., parallel systems, and real-time, and (iv)
formally conceiving reasonably sophisticated systems and languages.

1.1.2 Why Master These Principles, Techniques and Tools?

Why master these principles, techniques and tools? Because it is necessary.
Because, to be a professional in one's chosen field of expertise, one must know
also the formal techniques — just as engineers of other disciplines also know
their mathematics. Just as fluid mechanics engineers handle, with ease, their
Navier–Stokes Equations [83, 496], so software engineers must handle *denotational* and *computational semantics*. Just as radio communications engineers
handle, with ease, *Maxwell Equations* [245, 502], so software engineers must
handle *Petri nets* [238, 400, 419–421], *message sequence charts* [227–229], *live
sequence charts* [89, 195, 268], *statecharts* [174, 175, 185, 193, 197], the *duration
calculus* [557, 559], *temporal logics* [105, 320, 321, 372, 403], etc. We will cover
this and much more in this volume.

The above explanation of the "why" is an explanation that is merely a
claim. It relies on "Proof by authority"! Well, here is the longer, more rational argument: Before we can *design software*, we must understand its *requirements*. Before we can *construct requirements*, we must understand the
application *domain*, the area of, say human, activity for which software is
desired. To express domain understanding, requirements and software designs
we must use language. To claim any understanding of these three areas the
language used must be precise, and must be used such as to avoid ambiguities, and must allow for formal reasoning, i.e., proofs. This entails formal
languages. To cope with the span from domains, via requirements, to designs
the languages must provide for abstraction, and refinement: from abstract to
concrete expressibility. The principles, techniques and tools of these volumes
provide a state-of-the-art (and perhaps beyond) set of such methods.

The complexities of the computing systems that will be developed in the
future are such that we cannot expect to succeed in developing such computing systems without using formal techniques and tools, such as covered and
propagated in these volumes.

1.1.3 What Does This Volume "Contain"?

Volume 1 covered basic abstraction and modelling principles, techniques and
tools. The major tool was that of the RAISE Specification Language (RSL).
The major new, additional tools of this volume will be those of the *Petri
nets*: condition event nets, the place transition nets, and the coloured Petri
nets [238, 400, 419–421]; the *sequence charts* (SCs): the message SCs (MSCs)
[227–229] and the live SCs (LSCs) [89, 195, 268]; the *statecharts* [174, 175,

$185, 193, 197$]; the *interval temporal logic* (ITL) and the *duration calculus* (DC) [557, 559].

The major principles and techniques of abstraction and modelling covered earlier were: *property-* (sorts, observers, generators, axioms) and/versus *model-oriented abstraction* in general, and the model-oriented techniques of *set, Cartesian, list, map* and *function*, including *type abstractions;* and *functional, imperative* and *concurrent* (parallel) *specification programming techniques* in particular.

The new, additional principles and techniques of abstraction and modelling in this volume fall along five axes:

1. An advanced abstraction and modelling axis, covering hierarchical and compositional modelling and models, denotational and computational semantics, configurations: contexts and state, and time and space concepts. This axis further extends the techniques of Vol. 1. The time concepts will be further treated along axis (4).
2. A semiotics axis, covering pragmatics, semantics and syntax. This axis treats, along more systematic lines, what was shown more or less indirectly in Vol. 1 and previous chapters of Vol. 2 (notably Chap. 3). Axis (5) will complete our treatment of linguistics.
3. A structuring axis, briefly covering RSL's scheme, class and object concepts, as well as UML's class diagram concepts. This "short" axis, for the first time in these volumes, brings other notational tools into our evolving toolbox. This "extension" or enlargement of the variety of notational tools brings these volumes close to covering fundamental ideas of UML. The next axis, (4), completes this expansion.
4. A concurrency axis, covering *qualitative* aspects of timing: the *Petri nets* [238, 400, 419–421], the *sequence charts*, SCs, message SCs (MSCs [227–229]) and live SCs (LSCs [89, 195, 268]), the *statecharts* [174, 175, 185, 193, 197], and *quantitative* aspects of timing in terms of the *interval temporal logic* (ITL) [105, 320, 321, 372, 403], and the *duration calculus* (DC) [557, 559]. These specification concepts, available in some form in UML, will complete these volumes' treatment of, as we call it, *"UML-ising"* Formal Techniques.
5. A language development axis, covering crucial steps of the development of concrete interpreters and compilers for functional (i.e., applicative), imperative (i.e., "classical"), modular, and parallel programming languages. This axis completes our treatment of programming language linguistics matters. The chapters in axis (5) will cover important technical concepts of run-time structures for interpreted and compiled programs, compiling algorithms, and attribute grammars.

1.1.4 How Does This Volume "Deliver"?

The previous section outlined, in a sense, a *didactics* of one main aspect of software engineering.

So this *didactic* view of software engineering as a field of activity whose individual "tasks" can be "relegated" to one, or some simple combination, of the topics within one or, say, two axes, as listed above offers one way in which this volume "delivers". That is, the reader will be presented with these topics, more or less in isolation, one-by-one, but the practicing software engineer (and the reader as chapter exercise solver) is expected to merge principles and techniques of previous topics and tools when solving problems.

Another way in which this volume delivers is in the manner in which each individual (axis) topic is presented. Each topic is presented by means of many examples. Their "story" is narrated and the problem is given a formal specification. Where needed, as for the qualitative and quantitative aspects of concurrency,[1] a description is given of (i) their notational apparatus, (ii) the pragmatics behind them, (iii) their syntax and (iv) their informal semantics. Method principles and techniques are then enunciated. A heavy emphasis is placed on examples. References are made to more theoretical treatments of, in particular, the concurrency topics.

A third way in which this volume delivers is by presenting a "near-full" spectrum of principles, techniques and tools, as witnessed, for example, by the combination of using the RSL tool with those of UML's class diagrams, the Petri Nets, the (Message and Live) Sequence Charts, the Statecharts, the Interval Temporal Logic and the Duration Calculus.

This can also be seen in the span of abstraction topics: hierarchy and composition, denotation and computation, configurations (including contexts and states), temporality (in various guises) and spatiality, and both qualitative and quantitative aspects of concurrency. Volume 3 covers further abstraction principles and techniques. Finally this is also witnessed by the span of application topics: real-time, embedded and safety critical systems, infrastructure components (railways, production, banking, etc.), and programming languages: functional, imperative, modular, and parallel. Volume 3 covers further application topics.

1.2 Formal Techniques "Lite"

Although we shall broach the subject on several occasions throughout this volume, when we cover formal techniques we shall exclusively cover formal specification, not formal proofs of properties of specifications.

That may surprise the reader. After all, a major justification of formal techniques, i.e., formal specifications, is that they allow formal verification. So why do we not cover formal verification? First, we use, and propagate

---

[1]The qualitative aspects of concurrency are expressible when using the Petri Nets, the Message and Live Sequence Charts and the Statecharts. The quantitative aspects of concurrency are expressible when using the Interval Temporal Logic and the Duration Calculus.

the use of, formal techniques in the "lite"[2] manner. That is, we take formal specification rather seriously. And hence we focus on principles and techniques for constructing effective specifications, i.e., pleasing, elegant, expressive and revealing specifications. We find (and have over more than 30 years found) that systems developed in this manner come very, very close to being perfect!

Second, we find that principles and techniques for theorem proving or proof assistance or model checking, even today (2005) are very much "bound" to the specific notational system (i.e., specification language), and to its proof system of rules and tools. And we also find that there is much less a common consensus on whether proofs should be done in one way or in another way.

For a good introduction to a number of leading approaches to software verification we refer to the following papers:

1. J. U. Skakkebæk, A. P. Ravn, H. Rischel, and Zhou Chaochen. *Specification of embedded, real-time systems.* Proceedings of 1992 Euromicro Workshop on Real-Time Systems, pages 116–121. IEEE Computer Society Press, 1992.
2. Zhou Chaochen, M. R. Hansen, A. P. Ravn, and H. Rischel. *Duration specifications for shared processors.* Proceedings Symp. on Formal Techniques in Real-Time and Fault-Tolerant Systems, Nijmegen 6-10 Jan. 1992, LNCS, 1992.
3. A. P. Ravn, H. Rischel, and K. M. Hansen. *Specifying and verifying requirements of real-time systems.* IEEE Trans. Software Engineering, 19:41–55, 1992.
4. C. W. George. *A theory of distributing train rescheduling.* In FME'96: Industrial Benefits and Advances in Formal Methods, proceedings, LNCS 1051,
5. C. W. George. *Proving safety of authentication protocols: a minimal approach*, in International Conference on Software: Theory and Practice (ICS 2000), 2000.
6. A. Haxthausen and X. Yong. *Linking DC together with TRSL.* Proceedings of 2nd International Conference on Integrated Formal Methods (IFM 2000), Schloss Dagstuhl, Germany, November 2000, number 1945 in Lecture Notes in Computer Science, pages 25–44. Springer-Verlag, 2000.
7. A. Haxthausen and J. Peleska, *Formal development and verification of a distributed railway control system*, IEEE Transaction on Software Engineering, 26(8), 687–701, 2000.
8. M. P. Lindegaard, P. Viuf and A. Haxthausen, *Modelling railway interlocking systems*, Eds.: E. Schnieder and U. Becker, Proceedings of the 9th IFAC Symposium on Control in Transportation Systems 2000, June 13–15, 2000, Braunschweig, Germany, 211–217, 2000.
9. A. E. Haxthausen and J. Peleska, *A domain specific language for railway control systems*, Sixth Biennial World Conference on Integrated Design

---

[2] "Lite" is an "Americanism", and, as many such, is a nice one that indicates that we take certain things seriously, but not necessarily all that "seriously".

and Process Technology, (IDPT 2002), Pasadena, California, Society for Design and Process Science, P. O. Box 1299, Grand View, Texas 76050-1299, USA, June 23-28, 2002.

10. A. Haxthausen and T. Gjaldbæk, *Modelling and verification of interlocking systems for railway lines*, 10th IFAC Symposium on Control in Transportation Systems, Tokyo, Japan, August 4–6, 2003.

One runs a danger by adhering too much to the above "liteness" principle (perhaps it is one of lazy convenience?). That danger is as follows: Formulating which property is to be verified, of a specification, or, respectively, which correctness criterion is to be verified "between" a pair of specifications, and carrying through the proofs often helps us focus on slightly different abstractions than if we did not consider lemmas, propositions and theorems to be verified, or verification itself. And sometimes these proof-oriented abstractions turn out to be very beautiful, very much "to the point" and also "just", specification-wise!

So what do we do? Well, we cannot cover everything, therefore we must choose. These volumes have made the above choice. So, instead, we either refer the reader to other seminal textbooks on correctness proving [20, 97, 151, 205, 206, 363, 429], even though these other textbooks pursue altogether different specification approaches, or to two books that pursue lines of correctness development very much along the lines, otherwise, of this book: Cliff Jones' book [247], which uses VDM, and the RAISE Method book [131].

1.3 An RSL Primer

This is an ultrashort introduction to the RAISE Specification Language, RSL.

1.3.1 Types

We refer the reader to Vol. 1, Chaps. 5 and 18.

The reader is kindly asked to study first the decomposition of this section into its subparts and sub-subparts.

Type Expressions

RSL has a number of *built-in* types. There are the Booleans, integers, natural numbers, reals, characters, and texts. From these one can form type expressions: finite sets, infinite sets, Cartesian products, lists, maps, etc.

Let A, B and C be any type names or type expressions, then:

```
—————————————————————— Basic Types ——————————————————————

type
  [1] Bool
```

[2] **Int**
[3] **Nat**
[4] **Real**
[5] **Char**
[6] **Text**

            Type Expressions

[7] A-**set**
[8] A-**infset**
[9] A × B × ... × C
[10] A*
[11] A$^\omega$
[12] A $\overrightarrow{m}$ B
[13] A → B
[14] A $\overset{\sim}{\to}$ B
[15] (A)
[16] A | B | ... | C
[17] mk_id(sel_a:A,...,sel_b:B)
[18] sel_a:A ... sel_b:B

The following are generic type expressions:

1. The Boolean type of truth values **false** and **true**.
2. The integer type on integers ..., –2, –1, 0, 1, 2, ...
3. The natural number type of positive integer values 0, 1, 2, ...
4. The real number type of real values, i.e., values whose numerals can be written as an integer, followed by a period ("."), followed by a natural number (the fraction).
5. The character type of character values $''a''$, $''b''$, ...
6. The text type of character string values $''aa''$, $''aaa''$, ..., $''abc''$, ...
7. The set type of finite set values.
8. The set type of infinite set values.
9. The Cartesian type of Cartesian values.
10. The list type of finite list values.
11. The list type of infinite list values.
12. The map type of finite map values.
13. The function type of total function values.
14. The function type of partial function values.
15. In (A) A is constrained to be:
    - either a Cartesian B × C × ... × D, in which case it is identical to type expression kind 9,

- or not to be the name of a built-in type (cf., 1–6) or of a type, in which case the parentheses serve as simple delimiters, e.g., (A $\overrightarrow{m}$ B), or (A*)-**set**, or (A-**set**)list, or (A|B) $\overrightarrow{m}$ (C|D|(E $\overrightarrow{m}$ F)), etc.

16. The postulated disjoint union of types A, B, ..., and C.
17. The record type of mk_id-named record values mk_id(av,...,bv), where av, ..., bv, are values of respective types. The distinct identifiers sel_a, etc., designate selector functions.
18. The record type of unnamed record values (av,...,bv), where av, ..., bv, are values of respective types. The distinct identifiers sel_a, etc., designate selector functions.

Type Definitions

Concrete Types

Types can be concrete in which case the structure of the type is specified by type expressions:

```
─────────────────────── Type Definition ───────────────────────

type
    A = Type_expr
```

Some schematic type definitions are:

```
─────────────────── Variety of Type Definitions ───────────────────

[1]  Type_name = Type_expr /* without |s or subtypes */
[2]  Type_name = Type_expr_1 | Type_expr_2 | ... | Type_expr_n
[3]  Type_name ==
          mk_id_1(s_a1:Type_name_a1,...,s_ai:Type_name_ai) |
          ... |
          mk_id_n(s_z1:Type_name_z1,...,s_zk:Type_name_zk)
[4]  Type_name :: sel_a:Type_name_a ... sel_z:Type_name_z
[5]  Type_name = {| v:Type_name' • P(v) |}
```

where a form of [2–3] is provided by combining the types:

```
─────────────────────── Record Types ───────────────────────

    Type_name = A | B | ... | Z
    A == mk_id_1(s_a1:A_1,...,s_ai:A_i)
    B == mk_id_2(s_b1:B_1,...,s_bj:B_j)
    ...
    Z == mk_id_n(s_z1:Z_1,...,s_zk:Z_k)
```

Subtypes

In RSL, each type represents a set of values. Such a set can be delimited by means of predicates. The set of values b which have type B and which satisfy the predicate $\mathcal{P}$, constitute the subtype A:

```
───────────────────────── Subtypes ─────────────────────────
type
    A = {| b:B • P(b) |}
```

Sorts — Abstract Types

Types can be (abstract) sorts in which case their structure is not specified:

```
───────────────────────── Sorts ─────────────────────────
type
    A, B, ..., C
```

1.3.2 The RSL Predicate Calculus

We refer the reader to Vol. 1, Chap. 9.

Propositional Expressions

Let identifiers (or propositional expressions) a, b, ..., c designate Boolean values. Then:

```
───────────────────── Propositional Expressions ─────────────────────
    false, true
    a, b, ..., c
    ~a, a∧b, a∨b, a⇒b, a=b, a≠b
```

are propositional expressions having Boolean values. $\sim$, $\wedge$, $\vee$, $\Rightarrow$, $=$ and $\neq$ are Boolean connectives (i.e., operators). They are read: *not, and, or, if then* (or *implies*), *equal* and *not equal.*

Simple Predicate Expressions

Let identifiers (or propositional expressions) a, b, ..., c designate Boolean values, let x, y, ..., z (or term expressions) designate non-Boolean values and let i, j, ..., k designate number values, then:

─────────────── Simple Predicate Expressions ───────────────

false, true
a, b, ..., c
~a, a∧b, a∨b, a⇒b, a=b, a≠b
x=y, x≠y,
i<j, i≤j, i≥j, i>j, ...

---

are simple predicate expressions.

Quantified Expressions

Let X, Y, ..., C be type names or type expressions, and let $\mathcal{P}(x)$, $\mathcal{Q}(y)$ and $\mathcal{R}(z)$ designate predicate expressions in which x, y and z are free. Then:

─────────────── Quantified Expressions ───────────────

∀ x:X • $\mathcal{P}(x)$
∃ y:Y • $\mathcal{Q}(y)$
∃ ! z:Z • $\mathcal{R}(z)$

---

are quantified expressions — also being predicate expressions. They are "read" as: For all x (values in type X) the predicate $\mathcal{P}(x)$ holds; there exists (at least) one y (value in type Y) such that the predicate $\mathcal{Q}(y)$ holds; and there exists a unique z (value in type Z) such that the predicate $\mathcal{R}(z)$ holds.

1.3.3 Concrete RSL Types

We refer the reader to Vol. 1, Chaps. 13–16.

Set Enumerations

We refer the reader to Vol. 1, Chap. 13, Sect. 13.2.
Let the below a's denote values of type A, then the below designate simple set enumerations:

─────────────── Set Enumerations ───────────────

$\{\{\}, \{a\}, \{a_1, a_2, ..., a_m\}, ...\} \in$ A-set
$\{\{\}, \{a\}, \{a_1, a_2, ..., a_m\}, ..., \{a_1, a_2, ...\}\} \in$ A-infset

---

The expression, last line below, to the right of the ≡, expresses set comprehension. The expression "builds" the set of values satisfying the given predicate. It is highly abstract in the sense that it does not do so by following a concrete algorithm.

```
_____ Set Comprehension _____

type
    A, B
    P = A → Bool
    Q = A ⇸ B
value
    comprehend: A-infset × P × Q → B-infset
    comprehend(s,𝒫,𝒬) ≡ { 𝒬(a) | a:A • a ∈ s ∧ 𝒫(a) }
```

Cartesian Enumerations

We refer the reader to Vol. 1, Chap. 14, Sect. 14.2.

Let e range over values of Cartesian types involving $A, B, \ldots, C$ (allowing indexing for solving ambiguity), then the below expressions are simple Cartesian enumerations:

```
_____ Cartesian Enumerations _____

type
    A, B, ..., C
    A × B × ... × C
value
    ... (e1,e2,...,en) ...
```

List Enumerations

We refer the reader to Vol. 1, Chap. 15, Sect. 15.2.

Let a range over values of type A (allowing indexing for solving ambiguity), then the below expressions are simple list enumerations:

```
_____ List Enumerations _____

{⟨⟩, ⟨a⟩, ..., ⟨a1,a2,...,am⟩, ...} ∈ A*
{⟨⟩, ⟨a⟩, ..., ⟨a1,a2,...,am⟩, ..., ⟨a1,a2,...,am,... ⟩, ...} ∈ Aω

⟨ ei .. ej ⟩
```

The last line above assumes e_i and e_j to be integer-valued expressions. It then expresses the set of integers from the value of e_i to and including the value of e_j. If the latter is smaller than the former, then the list is empty.

The last line below expresses list comprehension.

```
─────────────── List Comprehension ───────────────
type
   A, B, P = A → Bool, Q = A →̃ B
value
   comprehend: Aʷ × P × Q →̃ Bʷ
   comprehend(lst,𝒫,𝒬) ≡
      ⟨ 𝒬(lst(i)) | i in ⟨1..len lst⟩ • 𝒫(lst(i)) ⟩
```

Map Enumerations

We refer the reader to Vol. 1, Chap. 16, Sect. 16.2.

Let a and b range over values of type A and B, respectively (allowing indexing for solving ambiguity), then the below expressions are simple map enumerations:

```
─────────────── Map Enumerations ───────────────
type
   A, B
   M = A ⇸ₘ B
value
   a,a1,a2,...,a3:A, b,b1,b2,...,b3:B

   [], [a↦b], ..., [a1↦b1,a2↦b2,...,a3↦b3] ∀ ∈ M
```

The last line below expresses map comprehension:

```
─────────────── Map Comprehension ───────────────
type
   A, B, C, D
   M = A ⇸ₘ B
   F = A →̃ C
   G = B →̃ D
   P = A → Bool
value
   comprehend: M×F×G×P → (C ⇸ₘ D)
```

comprehend(m,$\mathcal{F}$,$\mathcal{G}$,$\mathcal{P}$) $\equiv$
[$\mathcal{F}$(a) $\mapsto$ $\mathcal{G}$(m(a)) | a:A • a $\in$ **dom** m $\wedge$ $\mathcal{P}$(a)]

Set Operations

We refer the reader to Vol. 1, Chap. 13, Sect. 13.2.

――――――――――― Set Operations ―――――――――――

value
  $\in$: A $\times$ A-**infset** $\rightarrow$ **Bool**
  $\notin$: A $\times$ A-**infset** $\rightarrow$ **Bool**
  $\cup$: A-**infset** $\times$ A-**infset** $\rightarrow$ A-**infset**
  $\cup$: (A-**infset**)-**infset** $\rightarrow$ A-**infset**
  $\cap$: A-**infset** $\times$ A-**infset** $\rightarrow$ A-**infset**
  $\cap$: (A-**infset**)-**infset** $\rightarrow$ A-**infset**
  $\setminus$: A-**infset** $\times$ A-**infset** $\rightarrow$ A-**infset**
  $\subset$: A-**infset** $\times$ A-**infset** $\rightarrow$ **Bool**
  $\subseteq$: A-**infset** $\times$ A-**infset** $\rightarrow$ **Bool**
  $=$: A-**infset** $\times$ A-**infset** $\rightarrow$ **Bool**
  $\neq$: A-**infset** $\times$ A-**infset** $\rightarrow$ **Bool**
  card: A-**infset** $\xrightarrow{\sim}$ **Nat**

――――――――――― Set Examples ―――――――――――

examples
  a $\in$ {a,b,c}
  a $\notin$ {}, a $\notin$ {b,c}
  {a,b,c} $\cup$ {a,b,d,e} = {a,b,c,d,e}
  $\cup${{a},{a,b},{a,d}} = {a,b,d}
  {a,b,c} $\cap$ {c,d,e} = {c}
  $\cap${{a},{a,b},{a,d}} = {a}
  {a,b,c} $\setminus$ {c,d} = {a,b}
  {a,b} $\subset$ {a,b,c}
  {a,b,c} $\subseteq$ {a,b,c}
  {a,b,c} = {a,b,c}
  {a,b,c} $\neq$ {a,b}
  card {} = 0, **card** {a,b,c} = 3

- $\in$: The membership operator expresses that an element is a member of a set.
- $\notin$: The nonmembership operator expresses that an element is not a member of a set.
- $\cup$: The infix union operator. When applied to two sets, the operator gives the set whose members are in either or both of the two operand sets.
- $\cap$: The infix intersection operator. When applied to two sets, the operator gives the set whose members are in both of the two operand sets.
- $\setminus$: The set complement (or set subtraction) operator. When applied to two sets, the operator gives the set whose members are those of the left operand set which are not in the right operand set.
- $\subseteq$: The proper subset operator expresses that all members of the left operand set are also in the right operand set.
- $\subset$: The proper subset operator expresses that all members of the left operand set are also in the right operand set, and that the two sets are not identical.
- $=$: The equal operator expresses that the two operand sets are identical.
- $\neq$: The nonequal operator expresses that the two operand sets are not identical.
- card: The cardinality operator gives the number of elements in a finite set.

The operations can be defined as follows ($\equiv$ is the definition symbol):

──────────── **Set Operation Definitions** ────────────

value

$\quad$ $s' \cup s'' \equiv \{\, a \mid a{:}A \bullet a \in s' \lor a \in s'' \,\}$

$\quad$ $s' \cap s'' \equiv \{\, a \mid a{:}A \bullet a \in s' \land a \in s'' \,\}$

$\quad$ $s' \setminus s'' \equiv \{\, a \mid a{:}A \bullet a \in s' \land a \notin s'' \,\}$

$\quad$ $s' \subseteq s'' \equiv \forall\, a{:}A \bullet a \in s' \Rightarrow a \in s''$

$\quad$ $s' \subset s'' \equiv s' \subseteq s'' \land \exists\, a{:}A \bullet a \in s'' \land a \notin s'$

$\quad$ $s' = s'' \equiv \forall\, a{:}A \bullet a \in s' \equiv a \in s'' \equiv s{\subseteq}s' \land s'{\subseteq}s$

$\quad$ $s' \neq s'' \equiv s' \cap s'' \neq \{\}$

$\quad$ **card** $s \equiv$

$\quad\quad$ **if** $s = \{\}$ **then** 0 **else**

$\quad\quad$ **let** $a{:}A \bullet a \in s$ **in** $1 + $ **card** $(s \setminus \{a\})$ **end end**

$\quad\quad$ **pre** s /$*$ is a finite set $*$/

$\quad$ **card** $s \equiv$ **chaos** /$*$ tests for infinity of s $*$/

Cartesian Operations

We refer the reader to Vol. 1, Chap. 14, Sect. 14.2.

```
─────────────────── Cartesian Operations ───────────────────

type                                    (va,vb,vc):G1
  A, B, C                               ((va,vb),vc):G2
  g0: G0 = A × B × C                    (va3,(vb3,vc3)):G3
  g1: G1 = ( A × B × C )
  g2: G2 = ( A × B ) × C       decomposition expressions
  g3: G3 = A × ( B × C )           let (a1,b1,c1) = g0,
                                           (a1′,b1′,c1′) = g1 in .. end
value                                let ((a2,b2),c2) = g2 in .. end
  va:A, vb:B, vc:C, vd:D             let (a3,(b3,c3)) = g3 in .. end
  (va,vb,vc):G0,
```

List Operations

We refer the reader to Vol. 1, Chap. 15, Sect. 15.2.

```
─────────────────────── List Operations ───────────────────────

value
  hd: A^ω ⇾̃ A
  tl: A^ω ⇾̃ A^ω
  len: A^ω ⇾̃ Nat
  inds: A^ω → Nat-infset
  elems: A^ω → A-infset
  .(.): A^ω × Nat ⇾̃ A
  ^: A* × A^ω → A^ω
  =: A^ω × A^ω → Bool
  ≠: A^ω × A^ω → Bool
```

```
─────────────────────── List Examples ───────────────────────

examples
  hd⟨a1,a2,...,am⟩=a1
  tl⟨a1,a2,...,am⟩=⟨a2,...,am⟩
  len⟨a1,a2,...,am⟩=m
  inds⟨a1,a2,...,am⟩={1,2,...,m}
  elems⟨a1,a2,...,am⟩={a1,a2,...,am}
  ⟨a1,a2,...,am⟩(i)=ai
```

$$\langle a,b,c \rangle \widehat{\ } \langle a,b,d \rangle = \langle a,b,c,a,b,d \rangle$$
$$\langle a,b,c \rangle = \langle a,b,c \rangle$$
$$\langle a,b,c \rangle \neq \langle a,b,d \rangle$$

- **hd**: Head gives the first element in a nonempty list.
- **tl**: Tail gives the remaining list of a nonempty list when Head is removed.
- **len**: Length gives the number of elements in a finite list.
- **inds**: Indices gives the set of indices from 1 to the length of a nonempty list. For empty lists, this set is the empty set as well.
- **elems**: Elements gives the possibly infinite set of all distinct elements in a list.
- $\ell(i)$: Indexing with a natural number, i larger than 0, into a list ℓ having a number of elements larger than or equal to i, gives the ith element of the list.
- $\widehat{\ }$: Concatenates two operand lists into one. The elements of the left operand list are followed by the elements of the right. The order with respect to each list is maintained.
- $=$: The equal operator expresses that the two operand lists are identical.
- $\neq$: The nonequal operator expresses that the two operand lists are *not* identical.

The operations can also be defined as follows:

─────────── **List Operation Definitions** ───────────

value
    is_finite_list: $A^\omega \to$ **Bool**

   len q $\equiv$
       case is_finite_list(q) **of**
          true $\to$ **if** q = $\langle\rangle$ **then** 0 **else** 1 + **len tl** q **end**,
          false $\to$ **chaos end**

   inds q $\equiv$
       case is_finite_list(q) **of**
          true $\to$ { i | i:**Nat** • 1 $\leq$ i $\leq$ **len** q },
          false $\to$ { i | i:**Nat** • i$\neq$0 } **end**

   elems q $\equiv$ { q(i) | i:**Nat** • i $\in$ **inds** q }

   q(i) $\equiv$
       if i=1
          then
             if q$\neq\langle\rangle$
                then let a:A,q':Q • q=$\langle$a$\rangle\widehat{\ }$q' **in** a **end**

     else chaos end
    else q(i−1) **end**

 fq $\hat{}$ iq ≡
  ⟨ **if** 1 ≤ i ≤ **len** fq **then** fq(i) **else** iq(i − **len** fq) **end**
  | i:**Nat** • **if len** iq≠**chaos then** i ≤ **len** fq+**len end** ⟩
  pre is_finite_list(fq)

iq$'$ = iq$''$ ≡
 inds iq$'$ = **inds** iq$''$ ∧ ∀ i:**Nat** • i ∈ **inds** iq$'$ ⇒ iq$'$(i) = iq$''$(i)

iq$'$ ≠ iq$''$ ≡ ∼(iq$'$ = iq$''$)

Map Operations

We refer the reader to Vol. 1, Chap. 16, Sect. 16.2.

―――――――――――――――― Map Operations ――――――――――

value
 m(a): M → A $\overset{\sim}{\to}$ B, m(a) = b

 dom: M → A-**infset** [domain of map]
  dom [a1↦b1,a2↦b2,...,an↦bn] = {a1,a2,...,an}

 rng: M → B-**infset** [range of map]
  rng [a1↦b1,a2↦b2,...,an↦bn] = {b1,b2,...,bn}

 †: M × M → M [override extension]
  [a↦b,a$'$↦b$'$,a$''$↦b$''$] † [a$'$↦b$''$,a$''$↦b$'$] = [a↦b,a$'$↦b$''$,a$''$↦b$'$]

 ∪: M × M → M [merge ∪]
  [a↦b,a$'$↦b$'$,a$''$↦b$''$] ∪ [a$'''$↦b$'''$] = [a↦b,a$'$↦b$'$,a$''$↦b$''$,a$'''$↦b$'''$]

 \: M × A-**infset** → M [restriction by]
  [a↦b,a$'$↦b$'$,a$''$↦b$''$]\{a} = [a$'$↦b$'$,a$''$↦b$''$]

 /: M × A-**infset** → M [restriction to]
  [a↦b,a$'$↦b$'$,a$''$↦b$''$]/{a$'$,a$''$} = [a$'$↦b$'$,a$''$↦b$''$]

 =,≠: M × M → **Bool**

$$\circ: (A \xrightarrow{m} B) \times (B \xrightarrow{m} C) \rightarrow (A \xrightarrow{m} C) \text{ [composition]}$$
$$[a{\mapsto}b,a'{\mapsto}b'] \circ [b{\mapsto}c,b'{\mapsto}c',b''{\mapsto}c''] = [a{\mapsto}c,a'{\mapsto}c']$$

- $m(a)$: Application gives the element that a maps to in the map m.
- **dom**: Domain/Definition Set gives the set of values which *maps to* in a map.
- **rng**: Range/Image Set gives the set of values which *are mapped to* in a map.
- †: Override/Extend. When applied to two operand maps, it gives the map which is like an override of the left operand map by all or some "pairings" of the right operand map.
- ∪: Merge. When applied to two operand maps, it gives a merge of these maps.
- \: Restriction. When applied to two operand maps, it gives the map which is a restriction of the left operand map to the elements that are not in the right operand set.
- /: Restriction. When applied to two operand maps, it gives the map which is a restriction of the left operand map to the elements of the right operand set.
- =: The equal operator expresses that the two operand maps are identical.
- ≠: The nonequal operator expresses that the two operand maps are *not* identical.
- °: Composition. When applied to two operand maps, it gives the map from definition set elements of the left operand map, m_1, to the range elements of the right operand map, m_2, such that if a is in the definition set of m_1 and maps into b, and if b is in the definition set of m_2 and maps into c, then a, in the composition, maps into c.

The map operations can also be defined as follows:

──────── Map Operation Redefinitions ────────

value
  rng m ≡ { m(a) | a:A • a ∈ **dom** m }

  m1 † m2 ≡
    [a↦b | a:A,b:B •
        a ∈ **dom** m1 \ **dom** m2 ∧ b=m1(a) ∨ a ∈ **dom** m2 ∧ b=m2(a)]

  m1 ∪ m2 ≡ [a↦b | a:A,b:B •
                a ∈ **dom** m1 ∧ b=m1(a) ∨ a ∈ **dom** m2 ∧ b=m2(a)]

  m \ s ≡ [a↦m(a) | a:A • a ∈ **dom** m \ s]
  m / s ≡ [a↦m(a) | a:A • a ∈ **dom** m ∩ s]

$$m1 = m2 \equiv$$
$$\mathbf{dom}\ m1 = \mathbf{dom}\ m2 \land \forall\ a{:}A \cdot a \in \mathbf{dom}\ m1 \Rightarrow m1(a) = m2(a)$$
$$m1 \neq m2 \equiv \sim(m1 = m2)$$

$$m°n \equiv$$
$$[\ a{\mapsto}c \mid a{:}A,c{:}C \cdot a \in \mathbf{dom}\ m \land c = n(m(a))\ ]$$
$$\mathbf{pre\ rng}\ m \subseteq \mathbf{dom}\ n$$

1.3.4 λ-Calculus+Functions

We refer the reader to Vol. 1, Chaps. 6, 7 and 11.

The λ-Calculus Syntax

We refer the reader to Vol. 1, Chap. 7, Sect. 7.2.

———————————————— λ-Calculus Syntax ————————————————

type /∗ A BNF Syntax: ∗/
⟨L⟩ ::= ⟨V⟩ | ⟨F⟩ | ⟨A⟩ | (⟨A⟩)
⟨V⟩ ::= /∗ variables, i.e. identifiers ∗/
⟨F⟩ ::= λ⟨V⟩ • ⟨L⟩
⟨A⟩ ::= (⟨L⟩⟨L⟩)
value /∗ Examples ∗/
⟨L⟩: e, f, a, ...
⟨V⟩: x, ...
⟨F⟩: λ x • e, ...
⟨A⟩: f a, (f a), f(a), (f)(a), ...

Sections 8.4–8.5 cover the notion of BNF grammars in detail.

Free and Bound Variables

We refer the reader to Vol. 1, Chap. 7, Sect. 7.3.

———————————————— Free and Bound Variables ————————————————

Let x, y be variable names and e, f be λ-expressions.

- ⟨V⟩: Variable x is free in x.
- ⟨F⟩: x is free in $\lambda y \cdot e$ if $x \neq y$ and x is free in e.
- ⟨A⟩: x is free in $f(e)$ if it is free in either f or e (i.e., also in both).

Substitution

We refer the reader to Vol. 1, Chap. 7, Sect. 7.4. In RSL, the following rules
for substitution apply:

---------------------- Substitution ----------------------

- **subst**($[N/x]x$) ≡ N;
- **subst**($[N/x]a$) ≡ a,
    for all variables a≠ x;
- **subst**($[N/x](P\ Q)$) ≡ (**subst**($[N/x]P$) **subst**($[N/x]Q$));
- **subst**($[N/x](\lambda x \cdot P)$) ≡ λ y•P;
- **subst**($[N/x](\lambda$ y•P)) ≡ $\lambda y \cdot$ **subst**($[N/x]P$),
    if x≠y and y is not free in N or x is not free in P;
- **subst**($[N/x](\lambda y \cdot P)$) ≡ $\lambda z \cdot$**subst**($[N/z]$**subst**($[z/y]P$)),
    if y≠x and y is free in N and x is free in P
    (where z is not free in (N P)).

α-Renaming and β-Reduction

We refer the reader to Vol. 1, Chap. 7, Sect. 7.4.

---------------------- α and β Conversions ----------------------

- α-renaming: λx•M
  If x, y are distinct variables then replacing x by y in λx•M results in
  λy•**subst**($[y/x]M$). We can rename the formal parameter of a λ-function
  expression provided that no free variables of its body M thereby become
  bound.
- β-reduction: (λx•M)(N)
  All free occurrences of x in M are replaced by the expression N provided
  that no free variables of N thereby become bound in the result. (λx•M)(N)
  ≡ **subst**($[N/x]M$)

Function Signatures

We refer the reader to Vol. 1, Chaps. 6 and 11. For sorts we may want to
postulate some functions:

---------------------- Sorts and Function Signatures ----------------------

type
    A, B, C
value
    obs_B: A → B,

obs_C: A → C,
gen_A: B×C → A

Function Definitions

We refer the reader to Vol. 1, Chap. 11, Sects. 2–6. Functions can be defined explicitly:

```
_____ Explicit Function Definitions _____

value
    f: A × B × C → D
    f(a,b,c) ≡ Value_Expr

    g: B-infset × (D ⇸ C-set) ⥲ A*
    g(bs,dm) ≡ Value_Expr
    pre 𝒫(bs,dm)

comment: a, b, c, bs and dm are parameters of appropriate types
```

or implicitly:

```
_____ Implicit Function Definitions _____

value
    f: A × B × C → D
    f(a,b,c) as d
    post 𝒫₁(a,b,c,d)

    g: B-infset × (D ⇸ C-set) ⥲ A*
    g(bs,dm) as al
    pre 𝒫₂(bs,dm)
    post 𝒫₃(bs,dm,al)

comment: a, b, c, bs and dm are parameters of appropriate types
```

The symbol ⥲ indicates that the function is partial and thus not defined for all arguments. Partial functions should be assisted by preconditions stating the criteria for arguments to be meaningful to the function.

1.3.5 Other Applicative Expressions

Let Expressions

We refer the reader to Vol. 1, Chap. 19, Sect. 19.2.
Simple (i.e., nonrecursive) **let** expressions:

────────── Let Expressions ──────────

let a = $\mathcal{E}_d$ **in** $\mathcal{E}_b$(a) **end**

is an "expanded" form of:

$(\lambda a.\mathcal{E}_b(a))(\mathcal{E}_d)$

Recursive **let** expressions are written as:

────────── Recursive **let** Expressions ──────────

let f = λa:A • E(f) **in** B(f,a) **end**

is "the same" as:

let f = **YF in** B(f,a) **end**

where:

F ≡ λg•λa•(E(g)) and YF = F(YF)

Predicative **let** expressions:

────────── Predicative **let** Expressions ──────────

let a:A • $\mathcal{P}$(a) **in** $\mathcal{B}$(a) **end**

express the selection of a value a of type A which satisfies a predicate $\mathcal{P}$(a) for evaluation in the body $\mathcal{B}$(a).

Patterns and *wild cards* can be used:

────────── Patterns ──────────

let {a} ∪ s = set **in** ... **end**
let {a,_} ∪ s = set **in** ... **end**

let (a,b,...,c) = cart **in** ... **end**
let (a,_,...,c) = cart **in** ... **end**

let ⟨a⟩^ℓ = list **in** ... **end**
let ⟨a,_,b⟩^ℓ = list **in** ... **end**

let [a↦b] ∪ m = map **in** ... **end**
let [a↦b,_] ∪ m = map **in** ... **end**

Conditionals

We refer the reader to Vol. 1, Chap. 19, Sect. 19.5.
 Various kinds of conditional expressions are offered by RSL:

―――――――――――――――――― Conditionals ――――――――――――

if b_expr **then** c_expr **else** a_expr **end**

if b_expr **then** c_expr **end** ≡ /* same as: */
    if b_expr **then** c_expr **else skip end**

if b_expr_1 **then** c_expr_1
elsif b_expr_2 **then** c_expr_2
elsif b_expr_3 **then** c_expr_3
...
elsif b_expr_n **then** c_expr_n **end**

case expr **of**
    choice_pattern_1 → expr_1,
    choice_pattern_2 → expr_2,
    ...
    choice_pattern_n_or_wild_card → expr_n
end

Operator/Operand Expressions

We refer the reader to Vol. 1, Chap. 19.

―――――――――――― Operator/Operand Expressions ――――――――

⟨Expr⟩ ::=
        ⟨Prefix_Op⟩ ⟨Expr⟩
        | ⟨Expr⟩ ⟨Infix_Op⟩ ⟨Expr⟩
        | ⟨Expr⟩ ⟨Suffix_Op⟩
        | ...

$\langle$Prefix_Op$\rangle$ ::=
  $-$ | $\sim$ | $\cup$ | $\cap$ | **card** | **len** | **inds** | **elems** | **hd** | **tl** | **dom** | **rng**
$\langle$Infix_Op$\rangle$ ::=
  $=$ | $\neq$ | $\equiv$ | $+$ | $-$ | $*$ | $\uparrow$ | $/$ | $<$ | $\leq$ | $\geq$ | $>$ | $\wedge$ | $\vee$ | $\Rightarrow$
  | $\in$ | $\notin$ | $\cup$ | $\cap$ | $\setminus$ | $\subset$ | $\subseteq$ | $\supseteq$ | $\supset$ | $\widehat{\ }$ | $\dagger$ | $^{\circ}$
$\langle$Suffix_Op$\rangle$ ::= !

1.3.6 Imperative Constructs

We refer the reader to Vol. 1, Chap. 20.

Often, following the RAISE method, software development starts with highly abstract-applicative constructs which, through stages of refinements, are turned into concrete and imperative constructs. Imperative constructs are thus inevitable in RSL.

Variables and Assignment

We refer the reader to Vol. 1, Chap. 20, Sects. 20.2.1–20.2.2.

———————————— Variables and Assignment ————————————

0. **variable** v:Type := expression
1. v := expr

Statement Sequences and skip

We refer the reader to Vol. 1, Chap. 20, Sects. 20.2.5 and 20.2.4.

Sequencing is expressed using the ';' operator. **skip** is the empty statement having no value or side-effect.

———————————— Statement Sequences and **skip** ————————————

2. **skip**
3. stm_1;stm_2;...;stm_n

Imperative Conditionals

We refer the reader to Vol. 1, Chap. 20, Sects. 20.2.6 and 20.2.8.

```
———————————————— Imperative Conditionals ————————————

   4. if expr then stm_c else stm_a end
   5. case e of: p_1→S_1(p_1),...,p_n→S_n(p_n) end
```

Iterative Conditionals

We refer the reader to Vol. 1, Chap. 20, Sect. 20.2.7.

```
———————————————— Iterative Conditionals ————————————

   6. while expr do stm end
   7. do stmt until expr end
```

Iterative Sequencing

We refer the reader to Vol. 1, Chap. 20, Sect. 20.2.9.

```
———————————————— Iterative Sequencing ————————————

   8. for b in list_expr • P(b) do S(b) end
```

1.3.7 Process Constructs

We refer the reader to Vol. 1, Chap. 21, Sect. 21.4.

Process Channels

We refer the reader to Vol. 1, Chap. 21, Sect. 21.4.1.

Let A and B stand for two types of (channel) messages and i:KIdx for channel array indexes, then:

```
———————————————— Process Channels ————————————

   channel c:A
   channel { k[i]:B • i:KIdx }
```

declare a channel, c, and a set (an array) of channels, k[i], capable of communicating values of the designated types (A and B).

Process Composition

We refer the reader to Vol. 1, Chap. 21, Sects. 21.4.4–21.4.7.

Let P and Q stand for names of process functions, i.e., of functions which express willingness to engage in input and/or output events, thereby communicating over declared channels.

Let P() and Q(i) stand for process expressions, then:

```
———————————————— Process Composition ————————————————

    P() ‖ Q(i)    Parallel composition
    P() [] Q(i)   Nondeterministic external choice (either/or)
    P() ⊓ Q(i)    Nondeterministic internal choice (either/or)
    P() ‖‖ Q()     Interlock parallel composition
```

express the parallel (‖) of two processes, or the nondeterministic choice between two processes: either external ([]) or internal (⊓). The interlock (‖‖) composition expresses that the two processes are forced to communicate only with one another, until one of them terminates.

Input/Output Events

We refer the reader to Vol. 1, Chap. 21, Sect. 21.4.2.

Let c, k[i] and e designate channels of type A and B, then:

```
———————————————— Input/Output Events ————————————————

    c ?, k[i] ?     Input
    c ! e, k[i] ! e  Output
```

expresses the willingness of a process to engage in an event that "reads" an input, and respectively "writes" an output.

Process Definitions

We refer the reader to Vol. 1, Chap. 21, Sect. 21.4.3.

The below signatures are just examples. They emphasise that process functions must somehow express, in their signature, via which channels they wish to engage in input and output events.

```
———————————————— Process Definitions ————————————————

value
    P: Unit → in c out k[i] Unit
    Q: i:KIdx → out c in k[i] Unit
```

$$P() \equiv ...\ c\ ?\ ...\ k[i]\ !\ e\ ...$$
$$Q(i) \equiv ...\ k[i]\ ?\ ...\ c\ !\ e\ ...$$

The process function definitions (i.e., their bodies) express possible events.

1.3.8 Simple RSL Specifications

Often, we do not want to encapsulate small specifications in schemes, classes, and objects, as is often done in RSL. An RSL specification is simply a sequence of one or more types, values (including functions), variables, channels and axioms:

─────────────── Simple RSL Specifications ───────────────

type
...
variable
...
channel
...
value
...
axiom
...

1.4 Bibliographical Notes

The main references to RSL — other than Vol. 1 of this series — are [130,131].

Part II

SPECIFICATION FACETS

- The **prerequisites** for studying this part are that you possess some familiarity with abstraction and modelling, property- and model-oriented specifications (à la RSL), and applicative, imperative and parallel specification programming.
- The **aims** are to introduce along an axis of model structuring and contents the concepts of hierarchies and compositions (of development as well as of presentation of description documents), to introduce denotational and computational semantics and to introduce the concepts of configurations in terms of the concepts of contexts and states.
- The **objective** is to make the serious reader versatile in an important complement of abstraction and modelling principles and techniques.
- The **treatment** is systematic to formal — with Chaps. 2–4 readable in any order.

Introduction

In earlier chapters of this volume and of Vol. 1 of this series we covered a number of abstraction and specification programming concepts: property- and model-oriented abstractions, that is, algebraic abstractions, respectively set-theoretic abstractions (sets, Cartesians, lists, maps and functions). In later chapters we shall cover specification programming, that is, applicative, imperative and concurrent (i.e., parallel) specifications. In this part we shall first, however, apply the property- and model-oriented abstraction and the specification programming principles and techniques to tackle additional abstraction and modelling principles and techniques.

Categories of Abstraction and Modelling

Our decomposition, so far, into property- and model-oriented specification programming, and modularisation abstraction principles and techniques, represents a deliberate choice. We shall in subsequent chapters introduce further abstraction principles and techniques. We can say that the sum total of these methodological concerns represents a categorisation, which we shall later justify. Suffice it, for now, to motivate it: One motivational impetus is that of *separation of concerns*. We believe that the various categories represent more or less orthogonal concerns. Another motivational impetus is that of pedagogics. We are "carving", as it were, the seemingly complex "web" of principles and techniques into manageable pieces. A final impetus is that of didactics. It is, of course, related to the issue of 'separation of concerns'. The various categories represent different theories.

Structure of Part II

There seem to be several axes of description and presentation. Let us briefly review three of these axes. One axis is of separable, but orthogonal means of developing and/or expressing abstractions, that is, *hierarchically* versus *compositionally*, *denotationally* versus *operationally*, *configurationally*, in terms of *contexts* and *states*, and *temporally* and *spatially*. We will cover the above in this part. Another axis is of structuring the development and presentation into *modules* such as, for example, offered in RSL: possibly *parameterised schemes*, consisting of possibly nested *classes*, and instantiating schemes and classes into *objects*. We shall cover *modularisation* in Chap. 9.

Discussion

In Vol. 1 of this series we paraphrased and treated in some detail the main abstraction and modelling approaches to both property- and model-oriented specifications. Chap. 12 of Vol. 1, in particular, surveyed these abstraction and modelling approaches. In these volumes we strive to bring to the readers what we consider the main principles, techniques and tools for methodological software development. In the present part we shall further identify numerous principles and techniques. Most of these, as were some of the previous, are presented for the first time in textbook form. Please take time to study them carefully. Please think about them as you proceed into your daily software development. Many have found them useful before you. These techniques all attest to the intellectual vibrancy of our field: so rich in strongly interrelated concepts, so full of opportunities for intellectual challenges and enrichment. Indeed, it is fun to develop software.

2

Hierarchies and Compositions

- The **prerequisite** for studying this chapter is that you have studied and understood, to a reasonable extent and depth, Vol. 1 of this series of textbooks on software engineering.
- The **aims** are to introduce the development principles of hierarchical and compositional specification developments, as well as the hierarchical and compositional presentation of such specifications.
- The **objective** is to make you able to choose an appropriate development as well as an appropriate presentation strategy: hierarchical and/or compositional.
- The **treatment** is from systematic to semi-formal.

> Hierarchy: Any system of persons or things in a graded order.
> A series of successive terms of descending rank.
> Composition: Relative disposition of parts.
> *The Random House American Everyday Dictionary. 1949–1961* [485]

2.1 The Issues

The main issues of this chapter are those of non-atomic parts: the relation of parts to wholes, whether viewed first as a whole, hierarchically, or first viewed from basic parts, compositionally.

The above was itself a hierarchical (i.e., a meta-) view. Now to a compositional meta-view of the problem being addressed: The derived issues are those of [de]compositionality, that is, the operations of composing and decomposing wholes from, respectively into, parts; and of expressing relations between parts and wholes.

2.1.1 Informal Illustrations

Scientists, engineers, managers and many others like to present complex ideas diagrammatically. A category of such graphic presentations is in the form of trees, which have roots and subtrees.

Example 2.1 *Hierarchical Presentation: Trees:*

1. A tree has a labelled root and a possibly empty set of uniquely labeled sub-trees.
2. Subtrees are trees.
3. Roots are further unexplained quantities.
4. Root and subtree labels are further undefined.

∎

In programming languages we speak of values.

Example 2.2 *Compositional Presentation: Values:*

1. There are record field identifiers and there are natural number vector indices starting from index 1.
2. There are simple, scalar values: Booleans, integers, and characters.
3. Scalar and compound values can be composed into compound values:
   (a) Flexible vector values, which consist of an indefinite collection of consecutively indexed values of the same type
   (b) Record values, which consist of a finite collection of field identified values
4. Scalar and compound values are values.

∎

2.1.2 Formal Illustrations

Example 2.3 *Compositional Model of Trees:* We refer to Example 2.1:

type
[0] N, L
[1] Tree = N × (L $\overrightarrow{m}$ Tree)

Here line [0] corresponds to items 3–4 of Example 2.1, and line [1] corresponds to items 1–2. Thus they are in reverse order to one another: compositional ↔ hierarchical!

∎

Example 2.4 *Hierarchical Model of Values:* We refer to Example 2.2. The correspondence between lines of Example 2.2 and of the formulas below is: Line [1] corresponds to item 4 above; line [2] corresponds to item 3 above; line

[3] corresponds to item 3(b) above; line [4] corresponds to item 3(a) above; line [5] corresponds to item 2 above; and line [6] corresponds to item 1 above.

type
[1] VAL == com(c:CmpVAL) | sca(s:ScaVAL)
[2] CmpVAL == rec(r:RecVAL) | vec(v:VecVAL)
[3] RecVAL = Fid ⇾ VAL
[4] VecVAL = VAL*
[5] ScaVAL == bv(b:**Bool**) | iv(i:**Int**) | cv(c:**Char**)
[6] Fid

Line [6] contains only a specification relevant to records. Line [6] does not contain a specification part corresponding to the mention of natural number indices in Example 2.3. That "mentioning" is implied in the use of the RSL list type in formula line [4].   ∎

Thus the two definitions are, line-wise, basically in reverse order of one another. That is, compositional ↔ (where ↔ means versus) hierarchical!

2.2 Initial Methodological Consequences

2.2.1 Some Definitions

The definition of trees (Example 2.1) started with recursively composing trees from roots and the defined concept. It then went on to define the "lesser", i.e., the component subsidiary notions. The *recursive descent* from the root of a tree towards its leaves, or — vice versa — the *recursive ascent* from leaves towards the root, are powerful concepts, both in processing (presenting, reading, understanding or mechanically interpreting) and in constructing (developing) treelike structures. Among such structures we may have the kinds of systems that we wish to describe and the descriptions themselves.

We say that a tree represents a hierarchy. We may describe the hierarchy by explaining the roots, the branches of a(ny) subtree and the leaves. We may thus liken or "equate" a system (a domain, a set of requirements or a software design) by a tree. We may choose to develop the tree structure from the root towards the leaves (also, colloquially, "in the vernacular", known as "top-down"), or we may choose to develop the tree structure from the leaves towards the root (colloquially known as "bottom-up"[1]). By "developing the tree" we here mean: *constructing a description of the system.*

---

[1]Obviously those who coined the terms "top-down" and "bottom-up" first, had a two-dimensional, "vertical", picture in mind; and second, drew or imagined trees with roots "uppermost" and branches "lowermost"!

Hierarchical Abstraction

Characterisation. By a *hierarchical abstraction* we mean a description (or a development) which initially emphasises the overall structure of the phenomenon or concept ("thing", system, language) being described (or developed) as decomposable into parts and which then proceeds to emphasise the further decomposition of parts into subsidiary such, etc., descending towards a final emphasis on the atomic parts of the phenomenon or concept.   ∎

"Top-down"

We colloquially refer to a development or a presentation which primarily emphasises hierarchical abstraction as a "top-down affair".

Compositional Abstraction

Characterisation. By a *compositional abstraction* we mean a description (or a development) which initially emphasises (i.e., presents or develops) the atomic parts of the phenomenon or concept being described (or developed) and which then proceeds to emphasise the composition of concepts from atomic parts, etc., ascending towards a final emphasis on the whole phenomenon or concept as composed from parts.   ∎

"Bottom-up"

We call a development or a presentation which primarily emphasises compositional abstraction a "bottom-up affair".

2.2.2 Principles and Techniques

Principles. A *presentation* of a description of a phenomenon or concept may be either hierarchical or compositional.   ∎

Principles. A *development* of a description of a phenomenon or concept may be either hierarchical or compositional.   ∎

Principles. *Development and Presentation:* Development of a description of a phenomenon or concept may be performed in one way, and it may be presented in the "reverse" way.   ∎

Principles. *Hierarchical development* can take place only if the developers already have a good grasp of the development universe of discourse: Overall concepts to be decomposed must already be basically understood before decomposition can take place.   ∎

Principles. *Compositional development* takes place if the developers do not already grasp the development universe of discourse: From "smaller", i.e., less composite, but well-understood parts, one composes "larger", now "more" composite, and, by now, well-understood parts.   ∎

Techniques. *Hierarchy Development:* Having chosen, or by necessity been forced to conduct, hierarchical development the developer selects the phenomena and concepts to be decomposed, decomposes them into suitable compositions, determines the constituent phenomena or concepts, and hence models, and records these: developing types of entities, signatures (and possibly also definitions) of functions (including predicates and behaviours), and determining whether process (i.e., behavioural) models are relevant, including channels and events. Then the developer decides whether to present the development hierarchically or compositionally.   ∎

Techniques. *Composition Development:* Having chosen, or by necessity been forced to conduct compositional development, the developer selects the basic phenomena and concepts of concern and composes them into possible suitable compositions, determines their new "the whole is more than the parts" phenomena or concepts and hence models, and records these: developing types of entities, signatures (and possibly also definitions) of functions (including predicates and behaviours), and determining whether process models are relevant, including channels and events. Then the developer decides whether to present the development hierarchically or compositionally.   ∎

Some observations or disclaimers are in order:

- We are not claiming that one can "ideally" abstract (develop and/or present descriptions of) phenomena and concepts (i.e., specifications) purely hierarchically or purely compositionally.
- But we are claiming that it may be a good idea that the developer consciously consider the issue of to what "degree" shall a hierarchical, respectively a compositional, development or presentation approach be contemplated.
- A specification may be basically compositionally developed, but hierarchically presented.

Why are we claiming that hierarchical and compositional abstraction indeed represent abstraction? The answer is that in either we abstract certain concerns. In hierarchical abstraction we postpone consideration of certain details ("smaller" parts) till a subsequent decomposition of the "larger" parts. And in compositional abstraction we abstract from how we later are to compose the "lesser" parts.

2.3 The Main Example

In the next four examples (Examples 2.5–2.9) we show what may be considered both an example development as well as an example presentation. The subject of our concern, i.e., our domain, is railway nets. In keeping with our principle of describing domains (prescribing requirements and specifying software designs) both informally and formally, and in preferably doing so in that order, the next four examples constitute two pairs: An informal and a formal description of the "syntax", i.e., the "statics", of rail nets, respectively an informal and a formal description of some of the "semantics", i.e., of some of the "dynamics", of rail nets.

2.3.1 A Hierarchical, Narrative Presentation

Before we embark on the example let us bring in an abstract picture of a railway net. See Fig. 2.1.

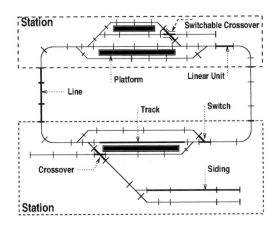

Fig. 2.1. A "model" railway net

Example 2.5 *Rail Nets I — A Hierarchical Presentation, Narrative:* Figure 2.1 suggests a railway net with lines and stations. Lines contain linear rail units while stations additionally may contain crossover and switch (i.e., point) units.

We shall attempt to give a precise narrative description of such nets. We introduce the *phenomenological concepts* of railway nets, lines, stations, tracks, (rail) units, and connectors. (See end of example for explanation of the term *phenomenological concept.*)

1. A railway net consists of one or more lines and two or more stations.

2. A railway net consists of rail units.
3. A line is a linear sequence of one or more linear rail units.
4. The rail units of a line must be rail units of the railway net of the line.
5. A station is a set of one or more rail units.
6. The rail units of a station must be rail units of the railway net of the station.
7. No two distinct lines and/or stations of a railway net share rail units.
8. A station consists of one or more tracks.
9. A track is a linear sequence of one or more linear rail units.
10. No two distinct tracks share rail units.
11. The rail units of a track must be rail units of the station (of that track).
12. A rail unit is either a linear rail unit, or is a switch rail unit, or is a simple crossover rail unit, or is a switchable crossover rail unit, etc.
13. A rail unit has one or more connectors.
14. A linear rail unit has two distinct connectors. A switch (a point) rail unit has three distinct connectors. Crossover rail units have four distinct connectors (whether simple or switchable), etc.
15. For every connector of a net there are at least one and at most two rail units which have that connector in common.
16. Every line of a railway net is connected to exactly two distinct stations of that railway net.
17. A linear sequence of (linear) rail units is an acyclic sequence of linear units such that neighbouring units share connectors.

By a *phenomenological concept* we mean a concept that directly abstracts a phenomenon. A phenomenon is something that one can point to, i.e., is a value. The immediate abstraction (i.e., the phenomenological concept) is the type of all the intended values being described.   ■

Figure 2.2 suggests the four different kinds of rail units as mentioned above.

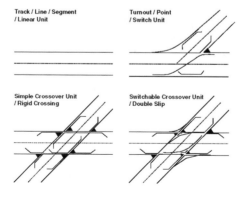

Fig. 2.2. Example rail units: details

Figure 2.3 shows simple line drawing abstractions of the four different kinds of rail units used in Fig. 2.1 and individually detailed in Fig. 2.2.

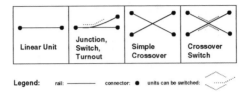

Fig. 2.3. Example rail units: icons

Notice how, in the above narrative description, we have used such technical terms as *consists of*, *is a*, *share*, *acyclic*, *sequence* and *neighbouring*. These terms are not defined, they are assumed understood. That is, there is another task at hand: to properly define an ontology (of "systems", "parts", "composition", "decomposition", "consists of", "is a", "share", "acyclic", "sequence", and "neighbouring"). In any case, the formalisation of the above "embodies", in the semantics of the formula texts, a formalisation, albeit maybe a convoluted one, of these latter terms, as well as, of course, the railway net terms.

Statement 15, i.e., axiom 15, really is a very strong one. It amounts to presenting the whole syntax for any topology, i.e., any "layout" of any railway net in one single phrase!

2.3.2 A Hierarchical, Formal Presentation

Example 2.6 *Rail Nets II — A Hierarchical Presentation, Formalisation:*

type
    N, L, S, Tr, U, C
value
    1.   obs_Ls: N $\rightarrow$ L-set
    1.   obs_Ss: N $\rightarrow$ S-set
    2.   obs_Us: N $\rightarrow$ U-set
    3.   obs_Us: L $\rightarrow$ U-set
    5.   obs_Us: S $\rightarrow$ U-set
    8.   obs_Trs: S $\rightarrow$ Tr-set
    12. is_Linear: U $\rightarrow$ **Bool**
    12. is_Switch: U $\rightarrow$ **Bool**
    12. is_Simple_Crossover: U $\rightarrow$ **Bool**
    12. is_Switchable_Crossover: U $\rightarrow$ **Bool**
    13. obs_Cs: U $\rightarrow$ C-set
    17. lin_seq: U-set $\rightarrow$ **Bool**

lin_seq(us) ≡
    ∀ u:U • u ∈ us ⇒ is_Linear(u) ∧
    ∃ q:U* • **len** q = **card** us ∧ **elems** q = us ∧
      ∀ i:**Nat** • {i,i+1} ⊆ **inds** q ⇒ ∃ c:C •
      obs_Cs(q(i)) ∩ obs_Cs(q(i+1)) = {c} ∧
      len q > 1 ⇒ obs_Cs(q(i)) ∩ obs_Cs(q(**len** q)) = {}

Some formal axioms are now given, but not all!

axiom

1. ∀ n:N • **card** obs_Ls(n) ≥ 1 ∧ **card** obs_Ss(n) ≥ 2

3. ∀ n:N, l:L • l ∈ obs_Ls(n) ⇒ lin_seq(l)

4. ∀ n:N, l:L • l ∈ obs_Ls(n) ⇒ obs_Us(l) ⊆ obs_Us(n)

5. ∀ n:N, s:S • s ∈ obs_Ss(n) ⇒ **card** obs_Us(s) ≥ 1

6. ∀ n:N, s:S • s ∈ obs_Ls(n) ⇒ obs_Us(s) ⊆ obs_Us(n)

7. ∀ n:N,l,l':L•{l,l'}⊆obs_Ls(n)∧l≠l'⇒obs_Us(l)∩ obs_Us(l')={}

7. ∀ n:N,l:L,s:S•l ∈ obs_Ls(n)∧s ∈ obs_Ss(n)⇒obs_Us(l)∩ obs_Us(s)={}

7. ∀ n:N,s,s':S•{s,s'}⊆obs_Ss(n)∧s≠s'⇒obs_Us(s)∩ obs_Us(s')={}

8. ∀ s:S • **card** obs_Trs(s) ≥ 1

9. ∀ n:N, s:S, t:T • s ∈ obs_Ss(n) ∧ t ∈ obs_Trs(s) ⇒ lin_seq(t)

10. ∀ n:N, s:S, t,t';T •
    s ∈ obs_Ss(n) ∧ {t,t'} ⊆ obs_Trs(s) ∧ t≠t'
    ⇒ obs_Us(t) ∩ obs_Us(t') = {}

15. ∀ n:N • ∀ c:C •
    c ∈ ∪ { obs_Cs(u) | u:U • u ∈ obs_Us(n) }
    ⇒ 1 ≤ **card**{ u | u:U • u ∈ obs_Us(n) ∧ c ∈ obs_Cs(u) } ≤ 2

16. ∀ n:N,l:L • l ∈ obs_Ls(n) ⇒
    ∃ s,s':S • {s,s'} ⊆ obs_Ss(n) ∧ s≠s' ⇒
    let sus = obs_Us(s), sus' = obs_Us(s'), lus = obs_Us(l) **in**
    ∃ u,u',u'',u''':U • u ∈ sus ∧ u' ∈ sus' ∧ {u'',u'''} ⊆ lus ⇒
    let scs = obs_Cs(u), scs' = obs_Cs(u'),
      lcs = obs_Cs(u''), lcs' = obs_Cs(u''') **in**
    ∃ ! c,c':C • c ≠ c' ∧ scs ∩ lcs = {c} ∧ scs' ∩ lcs' = {c'}

end end

The reader is encouraged to follow, axiom by axiom of this example the same numbered statements of Example 2.5. ∎

Notice how the relatively simple informal wording of statement 16 almost "explodes" into a not very simple axiom (16). That axiom has to express a lot: "connected to", "exactly two" and "distinct". It is, however, the "connected to" part of the phrase that causes the problem. Remember our note, above, about a need for a "system" ontology and its formalisation. Since we did not formalise the term "connected to" we have to do it implicitly, through the RSL formula of axiom 16. Had we introduced a formal predicate connect, then axiom 16 might look like the axiom shown in Example 2.7.

Example 2.7 *Rail Nets II, Revisited:*

value
   connect: $N \times L \times S \times S \to$ **Bool**
   connect(n,l,s,s') $\equiv$
      let sus = obs_Us(s), sus' = obs_Us(s'), lus = obs_Us(l) **in**
      $\exists$ u:U • u $\in$ sus, u':U • u' $\in$ sus', u'',u''':U • {u'',u'''} $\subseteq$ lus •
      let scs = obs_Cs(u), scs' = obs_Cs(u'),
        lcs = obs_Cs(u''), lcs' = obs_Cs(u''') **in**
      $\exists$! c,c':C • c $\neq$ c' $\land$ scs $\cap$ lcs = {c} $\land$ scs' $\cap$ lcs' = {c'}
      end end
      pre l $\in$ obs_Ls(n) $\land$ {s,s'} $\subseteq$ obs_Ss(n) $\land$ s$\neq$s'

axiom
16. $\forall$ n:N,l:L • l $\in$ obs_Ls(n) $\Rightarrow$
    $\exists$ s,s':S • {s,s'} $\subseteq$ obs_Ss(n) $\land$ s$\neq$s' $\Rightarrow$ connect(n,l,s,s')

∎

But we might wish a much stronger connect predicate, one that "connects" not only lines with distinct stations in a net, but, say reinforced concrete beams with floors in a building, etc. This is really what an ontology should do: abstract from the details of *what connects what with what in which context*.

Notice that the above statements say nothing about whether a railway net is connected, that is, whether a railway net "falls" into two or more "disjoint", i.e., "smaller" railway nets. Such a situation, as is hinted at in the previous sentence, would be the case for the railway net of, say a railway company, where the railway net is "spread out" over several islands not connected by railway bridges. There is a lot more the above does not "reveal" — and some of that will now be revealed!

Trains "run" on railway nets, along lines and through stations. To properly guide train traffic we need to introduce a number of concepts. That is, the new "things" are more like concepts than phenomena. Rail units, lines, stations and tracks could be phenomenologically sensed by the human sensory apparatus. As could connectors. Even though we may abstract them into physical "things" of no volume, i.e., like points in space. These new concepts, to be revealed below, must be defined. Hence, if they are to be of relevance to, that is, related to, railways, the most basic of these concepts must be definable in terms of the basic phenomena described above.

2.3.3 A Compositional, Narrative Presentation

To appreciate the concepts being introduced in the next example, let us consider Figs. 2.4–2.5. Those figures suggest that rail units can be in either of a number of states.

Fig. 2.4. States of linear rail units

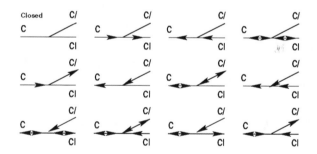

Fig. 2.5. States of simple switch rail units

The arrows are intended to show the direction in which a train may move through the units.

Example 2.8 *Rail Nets III — A Compositional Presentation, Narrative:* We introduce defined concepts such as paths through rail units, states of rail units, rail unit state spaces, routes through a railway network, open and closed routes, trains on the railway net, and train movement on the railway net.

18. A path, $p : P$, is a pair of distinct connectors, (c, c'),

19. and of some unit.[2]
20. A state, $\sigma : \Sigma$, of a unit is the set of all open paths of that unit (at the time observed).[3]
21. A unit may, over its operational life, attain any of a (possibly small) number of different states $\omega : \Omega$.
22. A route is a sequence of pairs of units and paths such that the path of a unit/path pair is a possible path of some state of the unit, and such that "neighbouring" connectors are identical.
23. An open route is a route such that all its paths are open.
24. A train is modelled as a route.
25. Train movement is modelled as a discrete function (i.e., a map) from time to routes such that for any two adjacent times the two corresponding routes differ by at most one of the following:
    (a) a unit path pair has been deleted (removed) from one end of the route;
    (b) a unit path pair has been deleted (removed) from the other end of the route;
    (c) a unit path pair has been added (joined) from one end of the route;
    (d) a unit path pair has been added (joined) from the other end of the route;
    (e) a unit path pair has been added (joined) from one end of the route, and another unit path pair has been deleted (removed) from the other end of the route;
    (f) a unit path pair has been added (joined) from the other of the route, and another unit path pair has been deleted (removed) from the one end of the route;
    (g) or there has been no change with respect to the route (yet the train may have moved);
26. and such that the new route is a well-formed route.

We shall arbitrarily think of one end as the "left end", and the other end as the "right end" — where "left", in a model where elements of a list are indexed from 1 to its length, means the index 1 position, and 'right' means the last index position of the list.

∎

The two parts, Examples 2.5–2.7 and Examples 2.8–2.9, further illustrate the application of a principle:

Principles. *From Phenomena to Concepts:* Since we wish to construct theories of domains and requirements, since domains initially and usually are manifested through physical phenomena, and since requirements — or just the theories in general — are conceptualisations of such phenomena, there is

---

[2] A path, (c, c'), of a unit designates that a train may move across the unit in the direction from c to c'. We say that the unit is open in the direction of the path.

[3] The state may be empty: The unit is closed.

a principle to be applied, namely that of "converting" (classes of manifest) phenomena into (similar) concepts.   ∎

Techniques. *From Phenomena to Concepts:* The "conversion" alluded to in the above principle can be effected as follows: First "lift" any one phenomenon to a class of like phenomena. When, as here, the phenomena are entities, we can model such classes as suitably constrained abstract types, i.e., sorts. Now define, usually in the form of concrete types, and usually from the most atomic kinds of types.   ∎

2.3.4 A Compositional, Formal Presentation

Figure 2.6 suggests the full variety of train movements with respect to the "leaving" and/or "capturing" of rail units.

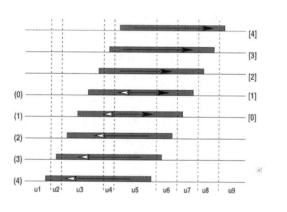

Fig. 2.6. A discretised "picture" of possible train movements wrt. rail unit

Example 2.9 *Rail Nets IV — A Compositional Presentation, Formalisation:* The formalisation of the above narrative now follows:

type
18. P = {| (c,c′):(C×C) • c≠c′ |}
20. Σ = P-**set**
21. Ω = Σ-**set**
22. R ={| r:(U×P)* • wf_R(r) |}
24. Trn = R
25. Mov = {| m:(T $\overrightarrow{m}$ Trn) • wf_Mov(m) |}
value
20. obs_Σ: U → Σ
21. obs_Ω: U → Ω

axiom

    ∀ u:U • **let** ω = obs_Ω(u), σ = obs_Σ(u) **in** $\sigma \in \omega \wedge$

19. **let** cs = obs_Cs(u) **in** ∀ (c,c′):P • (c,c′) ∈ ∪ ω ⇒ {c,c′} ⊆ obs_Cs(u)

    end end

22. wf_R: (U×P)* → **Bool**

    wf_R(r) ≡

        len r > 0 ∧ ∀ i:**Nat** • i ∈ **inds** r **let** (u,(c,c′)) = r(i) **in**

        (c,c′) ∈ ∪ obs_Ω(u) ∧ i+1 ∈ **inds** r ⇒

            let (_,(c″,_)) = r(i+1) **in** c′ = c″ **end end**

23. open_R: R → **Bool**

    open_R(r) ≡ ∀ (u,p):U×P • (u,p) ∈ **elems** r ∧ p ∈ obs_Σ(u)

25. wf_Mov: Mov → **Bool**

    wf_Mov(m) ≡ **card dom** m ≥ 2 ∧

      ∀ t,t′:T • t,t′ ∈ **dom** m ∧ t < t ∧ adjacent(t,t′) ⇒

        let (r,r′) = (m(t),m(t′)), (u,p):U×P • p ∈ ∪ obs_Ω(u) **in**

25(a. (l_d(r,r′,(u,p))   ∨ 25(b. r_d(r,r′,(u,p))   ∨

25(c. l_a(r,r′,(u,p))   ∨ 25(d. r_a(r,r′,(u,p))   ∨

25(e. l_d_r_a(r,r′,(u,p)) ∨ 25(f. r_d_l_a(r,r′,(u,p)) ∨

25(g. r=r′) ∧ wf_R(r′)

        end

The last line's route well-formedness ensures that the type of Move is maintained.

value

    adjacent: T × T → **Bool**

    adjacent(t,t′) ≡ ~∃ t″:T • t″ ∈ **dom** m ∧ t < t″ < t′

    l_d,r_d,l_a,r_a,l_d_r_a,r_d_l_a: R × R × P → **Bool**

    l_d(r,r′,(u,p)) ≡ r′ = **tl** r   **pre len** r>1

    r_d(r,r′,(u,p)) ≡ r′ = fst(r)   **pre len** r>1

    l_a(r,r′,(u,p)) ≡ r′ = ⟨(u,p)⟩⌢r

    r_a(r,r′,(u,p)) ≡ r′ = r⌢⟨(u,p)⟩

    l_d_r_a(r,r′,(u,p)) ≡ r′ = **tl** r⌢⟨(u,p)⟩

    r_d_l_a(r,r′,(u,p)) ≡ r′ = ⟨(u,p)⟩⌢fst(r)

    fst: R $\overset{\sim}{\to}$ R′

    fst(r) ≡ ⟨ r(i) | i **in** ⟨1..**len** r−1⟩ ⟩

If r as argument to fst is of length 1 then the result is not a well-formed route, but is in (U×P)*.   ■

Notice that we have not specified, in either Example 2.8 or in Example 2.9, that moves must involve only open routes.

2.4 Discussion

Models may be developed hierarchically, i.e., from "larger" phenomena or concepts by decomposing these into constituent, "smaller, contained" phenomena or concepts. Furthermore models may be presented or communicated hierarchically. Models may be developed compositionally, i.e., from "smaller" phenomena or concepts by composing these into composed, "larger" phenomena or concepts. Similarly models may be presented or communicated compositionally. Any combination of the two may be used: compositional development, hierarchical documentation, etc.

Principles. *Choosing Compositional Development and/or Presentation:* Usually compositional development (respectively presentation) is chosen when the phenomenon or concept being modelled is unfamiliar to the developer (respectively to the reader). And usually hierarchical development (respectively presentation) is chosen when the phenomenon or concept being modelled is familiar to the developer (respectively to the reader). ∎

2.5 Bibliographical Notes: Stanisław Leshniewski

The main issues of this chapter were those of non-atomic parts: the relation of parts to wholes, whether viewed first as a whole, hierarchically; or first viewed from basic parts, compositionally.

The Polish mathematical logician Stanisław Leshniewski studied, amongst other things, the subject of mereology. Mereology is the theory of part-hood relations: of the relations of part to whole and the relations of part to part within a whole. As a formal theory of part-hood relations, however, mereology made its way into modern philosophy mainly through the work of Franz Brentano and of his pupils, especially through Husserl's third *Logical Investigation* (1901). The latter may rightly be considered the first attempt at a rigorous formulation of the theory, though in a format that makes it difficult to disentangle the analysis of mereological concepts from those of other ontologically relevant notions (such as the relation of ontological dependence). It was not until Leshniewski's *Foundations of a General Theory of Manifolds* (1916, in Polish) that the pure theory of part-relations as we know it today was given an exact formulation. And because Leshniewski's work was largely inaccessible to non-speakers of Polish, it was only with the publication of Leonard and

Goodman's *The Calculus of Individuals* (1940) [294] that this theory became a chapter of central interest for modern ontologists and meta-physicists.[4]

We refer to [313, 348, 481, 482, 495] for some coverage of the works of Stanisław Leshniewski.

2.6 Exercises

Exercise 2.1 *Document Development, Narration and Formalisation.* This exercise is about written, possibly electronic, documents. Presently it emphasises their syntactic structure.

Select one document type among the following: mathematics, or physics, or biochemistry, or some other natural sciences textbook. Now (develop and) present narrative descriptions and accompanying formalisations of the syntactical structure of your selected type of book. Remember that textbook chapters, sections, figures and formulas are usually consecutively numbered, and can be referenced anywhere. Present your developments separately in both of two ways: hierarchically and compositionally, first one, then the other. Which presentation do you prefer?

Exercise 2.2 *Part Assemblies.* This exercise is about how certain kinds of (for example, civil engineering, mechanical engineering and woodcrafting) artifacts are put together: A house from floors/ceilings, walls, roofs, windows, doors, etc., and these again from beams, plates, planks, frames, glass, etc. A steel bridge or tower is assembled from steel beams, screw/nut assemblies, etc. A chair is assembled from legs, seat, back and arm rests, etc.

Some analysis of the above should show that one can identify spatially distinct and non-overlapping atomic parts, and that all other parts are assembled from these without changing the parts being put together. Glue and nails (or screws), as in the case of building or woodcraft constructions are thus claimed not to "change" the parts they "connect" (the nail or screw holes [the latter as for mechanical assemblies] can be claimed to have been properties of the parts being assembled).

Now, describe, in general (i.e., generic) terms, the syntax of assemblies. Take into account that in-going parts have spatial extents and result in parts, likewise with spatial extents, and thus that parts cannot be assembled if somehow their in-going spatial extents and the orientation of their being put together conflict (in trying to force "spatial overlaps"). You have to figure out what we may mean by this yourself.

As in Exercise 2.1, (develop and) present your model in both of two ways, separately: hierarchically and compositionally. Which presentation do you prefer?

---

[4]The above paragraph is based on J.J. O'Connor and E.F. Robertson's Internet essay on Stanisław Leshniewski: http://www-gap.dcs.st-and.ac.uk/~history/-Mathematicians/Leshniewski.html

Exercise 2.3 *City Road Nets — Streets and Intersections. Narrative:* A city road net consists of street segments and intersections. A segment provides a connection between one or two intersections. That is, there may be cul-de-sacs ("inside" the city) or (not further described) roads leading out of the city. Intersections may connect three or more street segments (those with arity: 3 or more). Sequences of one or more (intersection-connected — but acyclic) street segments have unique names. That is, street segments have exactly one name with several having the same name. Street segments are either one-way or two-way traffic streets. It is always possible to get from any street segment to any other street segment. Such a possible sequence of street segments is called a route. (Thus a route is a more general concept than a street, which is a route all of whose segments have the same name.)

Questions: Define the abstract types of road nets, street segments and intersections. Give the signature of functions that observe street segments and intersections, and their properties, from respectively nets, street segments and intersections. Also define the concrete types of routes. Define functions which generate all routes between any pair of streets such that all segments allow traffic in the direction of the route: from first segment to last. Express necessary and sufficient axioms that properly constrain road nets.

References: This exercise continues in Exercise 4.1 in Chap. 4 and in Exercise 5.3 in Chap. 5.

Exercise 2.4 *Air Traffic Route Nets: Air Lanes and Airports. Narrative:* An air traffic route net consists of airports and air lanes. Each air lane connects exactly two airports. There may be several air lanes between any two airports. Air lanes are either one-way or two-way. The air traffic route net is such that it is possible to find a sequence of air lanes, i.e., a route, between any two airports in the net and such that each adjacent pair of air lanes allows traffic in the direction from the "from airport" of the first air lane to the "to airport" of the second air lane.

Air lanes have length. Airports accommodate one or more aircraft. An airport is characterised by the maximum number (i.e., capacity) of aircraft that may be parked on the airport tarmac.

Questions: Define the abstract type of air traffic route nets, airports, and air lanes. Define observer functions that observe airports and air lanes from the net, airport capacity and air lane length. Axiomatise suitable air traffic route nets.

References: This exercise continues in Exercise 4.1 in Chap. 4 and in Exercise 5.4 in Chap. 5.

Exercise 2.5 *Shipping Nets: Lanes and Harbours. Narrative:* A shipping transport net consists of shipping lanes and harbours. A shipping lane connects exactly two harbours. Shipping lanes have length and are all to be considered two-way sailable. (We ignore such phenomena as canals.) Two or more shipping lanes may, over long stretches, share geographical positions

(but nevertheless be distinguishable). A harbour consists of uniquely identified *mooring buoys* and *quay berths* (the former at sea, the latter at public
cargo working areas and container terminals). In addition, a harbour may provide holding areas where ships that cannot be berthed or moored because of
a full harbour may wait. It is always possible from any holding area, mooring
buoy or berth of any harbour to come to any holding area, mooring buoy or
berth of any (other or the same) harbour. A sea voyage is characterised by
a sequence of alternating shipping lane sailings and harbour visits, starting
and ending with harbour visits. Each harbour visit is characterisable by zero
or more holdings, moorings or berths with at least one of these. Ships are
implicitly introduced: A holding area may hold up to a maximum capacity
of ships; a buoy or a quay berth may hold at most one ship. A shipping lane
may, for all practical purposes, hold any number of ships.

Questions: Define the abstract types of shipping transport nets, shipping
lanes and harbours. Define observer functions that observe shipping lanes,
respectively harbours of a net, and any other needed observations. Define
suitable axioms or invariant functions over net and/or harbours expressing
appropriate constraints.

References: This exercise continues in Exercise 4.1 in Chap. 4 and in Exercise 5.5 in Chap. 5.

Exercise 2.6 *Robots.* This exercise takes Exercise 2.2 for granted. That is,
we shall not, in the present exercise, be bothered by the 'part assembly' issues
of that former exercise. Our problem is, in a sense, orthogonal and additional
to the part assembly problem. It is about the structure of robots: How their
base, their links, their grippers and the joints that connect links into arms —
how all that — ends up being a robot.

Consult a suitable book on robotics, any of [337, 374, 392, 445, 447, 550].
Try understand the notions of robot base, joints links, and grippers. A robot
base is that part of the robot from which one or more links ("first") emanate.
Either the base is stationary, or it is mounted on a movable platform with
respect to which it is fixed. A link is a rigid body, a single whole. A joint
is the connection between two or more links. A gripper (a robot hand) is a
"last" link, from which no further links emanate, i.e., to which, by a joint, no
further link is connected.

An arm is a chain of links, from the base to a gripper. A joint permits the
orientation and position of the two links it connects to change. A joint may
either be a rotating (revolute) joint or a linear (prismatic) joint. A rotating
joint defines an axis around which the two connected links may revolve. A
linear joint allows one link to slide with respect to the other link. A link,
being rigid, maintains a fixed relationship (length and twist) between its two
joints. A link has a length, which is the perpendicular distance between the
two axes supported by the link, i.e., of its two joints. A link twist is the
angle between the projections of the two axes on a plane perpendicular to
the abstract link: the length line. Two adjacent links define a joint with a

common axis. The link offset is the distance along this common axis from one link to the other. Offsets can be measured as the distance between the two perpendiculars of the two links, one with respect to the predecessor link, the other with respect to the successor link. A prismatic joint allows link offsets to change. A joint angle describes the rotation, at any moment, about the common axis of a first link with respect to a second link. A revolute joint allows the joint angle to change. A joint variable is either a joint angle or a link offset. The link parameters are therefore the fixed link length and twist, and the one variable: Either the joint angle or the link offset.

Links are usually ordered. A 'straight' robot, with just one arm, has the links totally ordered, from base to gripper. A 'closed' robot, i.e., a robot where three or more links form a cycle (when links are considered undirected), has its links ordered by imposing a direction on the links, "away" from the base, "towards" gripper(s). In a closed robot links can only be partially ordered. Given any link we can speak of the next (a unique next) link, which may be a gripper. Normally a link has one or more, but, of course, a small, finite number of predecessors. Links emanating from the base have no predecessor link. A robot geometry can now be completely described by giving, for each link, the link parameters, and how these links are ordered with respect to one another.

Now describe, informally and formally, the way in which robots are put together, i.e., the geometry of the robot.

As for previous exercises, possibly (develop and) present your model in both of two ways, and separately: hierarchically and compositionally. Which presentation do you prefer?

3

Denotations and Computations

- The **prerequisite** for studying this chapter is that you have studied and understood, to a reasonable extent and depth, Vol. 1 of this series of textbooks on software engineering.
- The **aims** are to introduce the model concepts of denotational and computational semantics, to informally relate how one might "transform" a denotational semantics model into a computational semantics model, and to (thus) introduce some classical concepts of computing science.
- The **objective** is to enable you to choose an appropriate model type (of the two presented in this chapter): either denotational or computational.
- The **treatment** ranges from systematic and semi-formal to formal.

> One of the real highlights of software engineering is denotational semantics. For the software engineer to think "denotationally", i.e., of "things" expressed in words as denoting mathematical functions, can often in actual practice prove very beneficial.

3.1 Introduction

Conventionally, many programmers perceive of their programs as executing:[1] *The program first does this, then it does that!* In this chapter we shall take a more "refined" view of programs than that espoused in the previous sentence. And we shall claim, and later chapters shall illustrate the point, that not just computer programs but also actual world phenomena and concepts can be viewed, as we shall here present it, denotationally.

---

[1]More properly, programs as prescriptions for computations. Programs do not do anything. They are mere syntactic markers on a screen or on paper, as in a book. If we speak of programs as doing this or that, then we are anthropomorphising programs, that is, we are giving them human qualities.

3.1.1 Computations and Denotations

Saying: *"The program first does this, then it does that!"* — besides being an unfortunate anthropomorphisation — reflects an operational view: The computational abstraction. Since the 1960s, that is, from almost the very start of software engineering, the denotational view has gained currency. Typically an imperative program, viz., a Java program [8, 15, 146, 301, 465, 513] or an Eiffel program [344, 345], denotes a mathematical function from initial program states and program inputs to final program states and program outputs. We shall now cover "bare-bone" essentials of denotational and computational semantics.

3.1.2 Syntax and Semantics

Syntax is what we write down and say. Semantics is what we mean by what is written or said. Pragmatics is why we wrote or said it. Formal syntactic structures may be given formal semantic meaning. Such meaning definitions may either be denotational, or computational, or other! Thus semantics may be formally definable, whereas we seem not to be able to capture pragmatics formally. In this chapter we shall contrast two extreme semantics styles. Chapters 16–19 will provide a smoother, stepwise-related spectrum of intermediate semantics, including specifying compiling algorithms.

3.1.3 Characterisations

Characterisation. By a *denotational semantics*, $\mathcal{M}$, of a language or a system we shall understand a semantics which to each atomic syntactic construct, s_a, (of the language or system) associates a simple mathematical function, $\mathcal{M}(s_a) = \phi_{s_a}$, and which to each composite syntactic construct $s_c : (c_1, c_2, \ldots, c_n)$ associates a mathematical function, $\mathcal{M}(c_a, c_2, \ldots, c_n) = \psi$, which result from the semantics, $\mathcal{M}(c_i)$, of the syntactic components by simple function composition $\mathcal{F}: \mathcal{M}(c_1, c_2, \ldots, c_n) = \mathcal{F}(\mathcal{M}(c_1), \mathcal{M}(c_2), \ldots, \mathcal{M}(c_n))$.   ∎

We shall in this chapter explain the denotational concept while giving examples and providing abstraction and modelling techniques.

Characterisation. By a *computational semantics* of a language or a system we shall understand a semantics which to each atomic syntactic construct (of the language or system) associates a state transition, and which to each composite syntactic construct associates a sequence of state transitions.   ∎

We shall likewise in this chapter explain the computational concept while giving examples and providing abstraction and modelling techniques.

3.2 Denotational Semantics

One of the major schools of semantics specifications is that of denotational semantics. In this section we shall introduce the essentials of the engineering construction of a denotational semantics. Denotational semantics is classically used in defining the semantics of applicative as well as imperative and procedure-oriented programming languages. But denotational semantics can be used for other application areas: the "languages" of banking transactions, database management system command languages, rules and regulations in railway systems, etc. In defining the semantics of, for example, a program of a programming language the denotational principle states:

Principles. *Denotational Semantics:* Associate with every identifier (user-chosen or built-in literal or operator name) of the given (syntactic) text, a denotation, usually a function; then express the semantics of composite program constructs as a function of the semantics of its constituents. ∎

3.2.1 A Simple Example: Numerals

We start with a very simple example.

Example 3.1 *Denotational Semantics of Numerals:* Numerals are names of numbers. Thus numerals represent syntactic values. And numbers represent, i.e., are, semantic values. Syntactically numerals are composite structures: either as a single digit, or as a numeral paired with a ("trailing") digit.

type
    Num = NilNum × Digit
    NilNum == nil | mk_Num(n:Num)
    Digit == zero|one|two|...|nine

value
    M: Num → **Nat**,
    D: Digit → **Nat**,
    C: **Nat** × **Nat** → **Nat**

    M(n) ≡ **case** n **of** (nil,d) → D(d), (mk_Num(n'),d) → C(M(n'),D(d)) **end**
    D(d) ≡ **case** d **of** zero → 0, one → 1, two → 2, ... , nine → 9 **end**
    C(i,j) ≡ 10*i + j

Annotations. If a numeral *num* consists of just the digit *d* then its meaning, actually, its value, is the meaning (the value) *D* of that digit. If, instead, the numeral in addition has a proper numeral part, i.e., denotes a larger number, then the meaning (the value) of that proper numeral part must be multiplied by ten and added to the meaning (value) of the digit part.

∎

Observation. The meaning of a simple numeral is the simple meaning of that simple case. The meaning of a composite numeral is a function (above it was the C function) of the meanings (values) of the parts of the composition. This observation is now formalized.

3.2.2 The Denotational Principle

There are two steps to the construction of a denotational semantics. No matter whether it is for some source language (whether a programming language, a database model, an operating system (command language), or other), or for some other notions (as we shall later see) — there are just two steps!

Primitive Phrases: First the meanings, $\mathcal{M}(e)$, of the primitive, i.e., elementary, constructs e of the source language are established; and these meanings are usually given as functions.

Compound Phrases: Then the meanings of composite source language constructs are expressed as functions, $\mathcal{F}$, of the meaning of the immediate constituent constructs, such that also the resulting meanings are functions.

The former step is "truly" denotational: in it we establish the denotation of primitive symbols such as, for example, operators (add , or , :=, ...), and of identifiers.

The second step is more of an algebraic principle. It expresses a *homomorphism* ($\mathcal{F}$). Let "$c_1, c_2, \ldots, c_n$" designate a composite construct. The semantic (generic) function which ascribes meaning to any construct then reads:

$$\mathcal{M}(c_1, c_2, \ldots, c_n) = \mathcal{F}(\mathcal{M}(c_1), \mathcal{M}(c_2), \ldots, \mathcal{M}(c_n))$$

In both cases denotational semantics usually ascribe functions as meanings. In so doing denotational semantics differ from, for example, algebraic semantics — which ascribe algebras, but which otherwise adhere to the homomorphic principle. We shall take a very liberal view and accept any semantics definition which satisfies the two parts of the denotational principle as enunciated above — without necessarily ascribing functions to all primitives (i.e., identifiers) — as a denotational definition.

In the next two sections we bring in two large examples. One illustrates the denotational principle on simple expression evaluation. The other illustrates the principle on interpretation of imperative programs with labels and GOTOs.

3.2.3 Expression Denotations

First, we present a simple expression semantics example. The point of this next example is to exemplify that syntactic constructs denotationally stand for functions. The first point of denotations, being that their construction implied the use of the homomorphism principle, has already been exemplified above.

Example 3.2 *Denotational Semantics of Simple Expressions:*
Our example source language consists, syntactically, of expressions. Expressions are either constants, identifiers or pre- or infix operator/operand expressions. Constants are (for simplicity) integers. Identifiers are just that. Prefix expressions have two parts: a monadic operator and an expression. Infix expressions have three parts: a dyadic operator and two expressions. Monadic (dyadic) operators are "plus", "minus", "factorial", etc. (and "add", "subtract", "multiply", etc.):

type
    Token
    Ex == mk_intg(i:**Int**)
       | mk_iden(id:Token)
       | mk_prefix(o:Mo,e:Ex)
       | mk_infix(le:Ex,o:Do,re:Ex)
    Mo == minus | fact
    Do == add | sub | mpy | ...

(The above equations display, or exhibit, almost negligible representational abstraction; little room is given in this example for doing abstraction!)
We observe how expressions have been recursively defined — just as would be expected in a standard, concrete BNF grammar definition.[2]
Only constants have been representationally abstracted: instead of specifying numerals, we (directly) specify the integer numbers denoted.
Identifiers occurring in expressions are bound to integer values, in something we shall call an environment:

type
    ρ:ENV = Token $\overrightarrow{m}$ **Int**

The primitives of the language are constants, identifiers and operators. Constants denote themselves. Identifiers denote integers, with their denotation being recorded in the environment. Operators denote certain arithmetic functions:

value
    O: Mo → **Int** → **Int**
    O: Do → **Int** × **Int** → **Int**

---

[2]By a BNF grammar we mean a Backus–Naur Form context-free syntax. The Glossary (Appendix B) of Vol. 1 defines these and related terms. We also refer to Sects. 8.4–8.5 of this volume.

$O(o) \equiv$
    case o **of**:
        minus $\rightarrow \lambda$ x:**Int** $\bullet$ $-$x,
        fact $\rightarrow \lambda$ x:**Int** $\bullet$ x!,
        add $\rightarrow \lambda$ x,y:**Int** $\bullet$ x+y,
        sub $\rightarrow \lambda$ x,y:**Int** $\bullet$ x$-$y,
        mpy $\rightarrow \lambda$ x,y:**Int** $\bullet$ x$*$y,
        ...
    end

In order that the semantic function can find the meaning (i.e., value) of an identifier it must refer to an environment which is therefore an argument to the semantic function.

Without much ado, we present the semantic function which, since expressions were recursively defined, itself is recursively defined.

value
    V: Ex $\rightarrow$ ENV $\overset{\sim}{\rightarrow}$ **Int**
    $V(e)\rho \equiv$
        case e **of**
            mk_intg(i) $\rightarrow$ i,
            mk_iden(t) $\rightarrow \rho$(t),
            mk_prefix(o,e') $\rightarrow O(o)(V(e')\rho)$,
            mk_infix(le,o,re) $\rightarrow O(o)(V(le)\rho,V(re)\rho)$
        end

The functions $\mathcal{M}$ and $\mathcal{F}$ alluded to in the introduction can now be stated: $\mathcal{M}$ is *Val-Expr* when the syntactic construct is an expression, and is O when it is an operator. $\mathcal{F}$ is functional composition for the case of prefix expressions:

$$F(O(m),V(e)\rho) = O(m \underbrace{\quad)(\quad}_{\text{function composition}} V(e)\rho)$$

$\mathcal{F}$ is the composite of the "pairing" function with functional composition when the composite is an infix expression:

$$F(V(l)\rho,O(d),V(r)\rho) = O(d \underbrace{\quad)(\quad}_{\text{function composition}} V(l)\rho \underbrace{\quad,\quad}_{\text{pairing}} V(r)\rho)$$

That is, we view the prefixing of an expression with a monadic operator, respectively the infixing of two expressions with a dyadic operator as (syntactic) operators — not explicitly written. And we then assign the meaning:

$$\lambda f.\lambda x.f(x)$$

to the (invisible) prefixing operator, and:

$$\lambda x.\lambda f.\lambda y.f(x,y)$$

as the meaning of the (invisible) infixing operator.

Instead of "juggling" around with the O function and with what to us are rather convolute formulas of V, we syntactically sugar Vr while factoring O into the new V.

value
   V(e)ρ ≡
      case e **of**
         mk_intg(i) → i,
         mk_iden(t) → ρ(t),
         mk_prefix(o,e′)
            → **let** v = V(e′)ρ **in**
               case o **of**: minus → −v, fact → v! **end end**
         mk_infix(le,o,re)
            → **let** rv = V(re)ρ, lv = V(le)ρ **in**
               case o **of**:
                  add → lv+rv, sub → lv−rv, mpy → lv∗rc, ...
               end end
      end

We are finally ready to summarize the type of the denotation of expressions, whether constants, identifiers or operator/operand expressions. That general type can be read directly from the type of the semantic function. The type of the meaning of an expression, [e]:[E], i.e., its semantic type, is that of a function from environments to integers:

$$[\,Ex\,]:\ ENV \overset{\sim}{\to} \mathbf{Int}$$

The function is partial in that expression identifiers not in the domain of the environment lead to undefinedness. For a constant, *mk_intg(i)*, expression the function is the constant function which "maps" any environment, ρ, into i. For an identifier, *mk_iden(t)*, expression, e, the function maps any environment, ρ, into the integer, $\rho(e)$, which that identifier is associated with in those environments. If the identifier is not in the environment, **chaos** is yielded. For the remaining expressions we refer the reader to the formulas from which we also read the meaning functions of the two previous sentences.

An Extension

For the sake of making the computational semantics example a bit more interesting than it would otherwise be with the present source language of expressions, we extend this language. The extension amounts to the introduction of conditional expressions:

type
    Ex == ... | mk_cond(b:Ex,c:Ex,a:Ex)

value
    V(mk_cond(b,c,a))ρ ≡
        let bv = V(b)ρ **in**
        if bv **then** V(c)ρ **else** V(a)ρ **end end**

Thus $\mathcal{F}$ of a conditional expressions' semantics is that of "delaying" the evaluation of either the consequence or the alternative expression till the value of the test expression has been obtained. More precisely:

$$M(b, c, a) = F(M(b), M(c), M(a))$$
$$= \lambda\rho.(\textbf{if } M(b)\rho = 0 \textbf{ then } M(c)\rho \textbf{ else } M(a)\rho \textbf{ end})$$

whereby $\mathcal{F}$ is expressible as:

$$\lambda\rho.\lambda m_b.\lambda m_c.\lambda m_a. \textbf{if } m_b(\rho) = 0 \textbf{ then } m_c(\rho) \textbf{ else } m_a(\rho)\textbf{end}$$

where m_b, m_c and m_a are now the "meanings" of the "correspondingly" named syntactic objects b, c and a. Observe how the delay is afforded by the "encapsulation" of final evaluations of c and a.   ∎

Do not take offense that the meaning of the source language's "if ... then ... else ... end" expression is explained in terms of RSL's similarly looking **if ... then ... else ... end** clause. The latter has already been given an axiomatic semantics. Thus it can be applied since it is not applied self-referentially, that is, to itself.

The emphasis of the above definitions — which the reader is kindly asked to review — is on ascribing mathematical functions as meanings of syntactic quantities. From now on we shall often have occasion to think in that way: That syntactic things denote functions. Rather than thinking of the syntactic quantities operationally, by what they may prescribe in the way of computations, we "lift" up to the denotational principle.

3.2.4 GOTO Continuations

In Example 3.2, the denotation of expressions with free variables were functions from environments to values — where the environments bound the free variables to values. In Example 3.3, we not only introduce an imperative language with assignable variables, but also labels and GOTO statements.

The presence of assignable variables mean that we conveniently need a storage (STG). Storages bind locations to values. Since the language to be illustrated also features nested blocks with possible reintroduction of variable names we conveniently need environments (ENV) which bind variable names to locations. Because of labels and GOTOs we conveniently model labels in terms of continuations (CON) — and these are seen as functions from storage transformations to storage transformations.

In all we find that syntactic constructs of this kind of programming language denote functions from environments to functions from continuations to functions from storages to storage, that is continuations, indeed, higher-order denotations:

type
$$ENV = Id \xrightarrow{\sim}_{m} (LOC \mid CON)$$
$$STG = LOC \xrightarrow{\sim}_{m} VAL$$
$$CON = STG \xrightarrow{\sim} STG$$
value
[syntactic construct]: ENV $\xrightarrow{\sim}$ CON $\xrightarrow{\sim}$ CON

There are several ways of developing denotational models. And there are syntactic quantities which, at first glance seem to defy being definable denotationally. An example is GOTOs and labels.

The continuation semantics definition style was first proposed by either F. Lockwood Morris in [366] (privately circulated notes) or by Christopher Strachey [490].

We shall illustrate the continuation style[3] of semantics definitions on imperative programs with labels and GOTOs.

Example 3.3 *A Continuation Model of Labels and GOTOs:*
We assume that the reader is familiar with the classical concept of imperative programming languages permitting statements to be labelled and to have statements that effect transfer of control from the GOTO program point to the GOTO target label's program point:

```
la1: stmt_1 ;
la2: stmt_2 ;
la3: stmt_3 ;
la4: IF tst_exp THEN GOTO la2 ;
la5: stmt_5 ;
```

That is, assume that interpretation of the above program text starts at program point la1 and proceeds by interpreting statements stmt_1 ; stmt_2 ; stmt_3 ; . Having reached program point la4 the interpreter decides that the value of the Boolean test expression tst_exp is true. If so the next statement to be interpreted is that of stmt_2; whereupon the interpreter continues, sequentially, from there on!

---

[3]The notation used in expressing the continuations semantics is a tiny subset of RSL, one for which it makes sense to write the formulas. The full RSL would not do: Its semantics does not allow the kind of reflexive types, or recursively defined interpretation functions, that a continuation-style semantics often implies.

The Problem

The problem with the semantic functions we presented earlier (in Vol. 1, Chap. 20, Sect. 20.6), and which we basically repeat below, is that those semantic functions (repeated below) only know how to interpret a linear sequence of statements. From the beginning to the end — no exceptions. Once, and that's it:

type
    Stmt, ...
    ENV, Σ
value
    I_s: Stmt $\overset{\sim}{\to}$ ENV $\overset{\sim}{\to}$ Σ $\overset{\sim}{\to}$ Σ
    I_sl: Stmt* $\overset{\sim}{\to}$ ENV $\overset{\sim}{\to}$ Σ $\overset{\sim}{\to}$ Σ

    I_sl(stl)(ρ)(σ) $\equiv$
        if stl = ⟨⟩ **then** σ **else** I_sl(**tl** stl)(ρ)(I_s(**hd** stl)(ρ)(σ)) **end**

We could operationalise the interpreter by giving it a cue, in the form of the index of the statement to be interpreted next, in the statement list:

type
    Stmt == mkCGo(e:Exp,la:**Nat**)
    Stmt_list == mkStl(stl:Stmt*)
    Lbl, Exp, ...
    ENV, Σ
    VAL = **Bool** | ...
value
    I_s: Stmt $\overset{\sim}{\to}$ ENV $\overset{\sim}{\to}$ Σ $\overset{\sim}{\to}$ Σ
    I_sl: Stmt* $\overset{\sim}{\to}$ **Nat** $\overset{\sim}{\to}$ ENV $\overset{\sim}{\to}$ Σ $\overset{\sim}{\to}$ Σ
    V_e: Exp $\overset{\sim}{\to}$ ENV $\overset{\sim}{\to}$ Σ $\overset{\sim}{\to}$ VAL

    I_sl(sl)(i)(ρ)(σ) $\equiv$
        if i>**len** stl
            then σ
            else
                case sl(i) **of**
                    mkCGo(exp,idx) $\to$
                        if V_e(exp)(ρ)(σ)
                            then I_sl(sl)(idx)(ρ)(σ)
                            else I_sl(sl)(i+1)(ρ)(σ) **end**,
                    _ $\to$ I_sl(sl)(i+1)(ρ)(I_s(sl(i))(ρ)(σ))
        end end

But — although it works for simple, straightforward statement lists — it does not look elegant, and it "violates" the denotational principles by being rather operational. And then the above formula must be modified if we were to allow statements to be blocks consisting of (thus embedded) statement lists — and then what if we allowed GOTOs to target a statement in some surrounding block's statement list?

So we try an altogether different approach. That other approach, the 'continuation' approach, does satisfy the denotational principle. It ascribes denotations to labels (i.e., program points) — they had no denotation above! And it works for arbitrary kinds of GOTOs.

The idea of the continuation approach can be illuminated by considering the ordinary, non-GOTO, semantic function for statement lists:

I_sl(stl)(ρ)(σ) $\equiv$
   if stl = $\langle\rangle$ **then** σ **else**
   I_sl(**tl** stl)(ρ)(I_s(**hd** stl)(ρ)(σ)) **end**

In the above, the order of interpretation is, of course, right, but it "looks *round-about* or backwards". If a statement is a GOTO statement, whether conditional, as shown, or unconditional (not shown), then we end up in a situation where the last line above gets to look like:

I_sl(**tl** stl)(ρ)(I_s(mkCGo(esp,idx))(ρ)(σ))

And then what? In I_sl(**tl** stl)(ρ)(...), what is (...) going to be such that no interpretation takes place of "the rest of the statement list" **tl stl**, but that, instead, computation is resumed "as from the program point designated by lbl!

By "twisting things a bit" we could list, left-to-right, the syntactic components in the order of their "normal" occurrence — such as we informally see it when typed on paper:

type
   $\Theta = \Sigma \to \Sigma$
value
   I_s: Stmt $\overset{\sim}{\to}$ ENV $\overset{\sim}{\to}$ Θ $\overset{\sim}{\to}$ Σ $\overset{\sim}{\to}$ Σ

   I_sl: Stmt* $\overset{\sim}{\to}$ ENV $\overset{\sim}{\to}$ Θ $\overset{\sim}{\to}$ Σ $\overset{\sim}{\to}$ Σ
   I_sl(stl)(ρ)(θ)(σ) $\equiv$
      if stl = $\langle\rangle$ **then** $\theta(\sigma)$ **else**
      I_s(**hd** stl)(ρ)(I_sl(**tl** stl)(ρ)(θ))(σ) **end**

Then perhaps it was easier to "avoid" I_sl(**tl** stl)(ρ)(θ) by simply ignoring that part if **hd stl** was a successful GOTO! But then two identical questions are: What is this $\theta : \Theta$ that allows us to do so, and does it work? This is what we shall show next.

Syntactic Types

First, we narrate a description of the language of programs, statements, blocks, assignments, conditional GOTOs, labels, etc. We will do so, in a strict style, such that the text below corresponds, phrase-by-phrase, to the formalisation further on.

A program is a block statement. A block statement consists of a set of variables declaration part, and a list of labelled statements part. A labelled statement consists of a label part and a statement part. Statements are either assignment, block, while loop or conditional GOTO statements. An assignment statement consists of a variable part and an expression part. A while loop statement has an expression part and an unlabelled statement list part.

(If the programmer wishes to have labelled statements in the simple statement list part of a while loop, then the programmer should reduce the list to a singleton list whose only statement is a block, which then otherwise obeys the rules for GOTOs and labels.)

A conditional GOTO statement consists of (what is known as) a test-expression part and (what is known as a target) label part. Variables, expressions and labels are further undefined quantities. No two labels of a list of labelled statements of any block statement are identical. That is, a list, ℓ, of labelled statements may contain (what will be known as embedded) block statements and these may contain labels that are identical to a label of some statement of what will be known as the surrounding block list, ℓ. Similarly for variables: They may also be redeclared in embedded blocks.

type

    Pgm == mkPgm(b:Blk)

    Blk′ == mkBlk(svs:Var-**set**,ssl:LaS*)

    LaS == mkLaS(l:Lbl,s:Stm)

    Stm = Blk | Asg | StL | While | CGo

    Asg == mkAsg(v:Var,e:Exp)

    StL == mkStL(sl:Stm*)

    Whi == mkWhi(b:Exp,sl:StL)

    CGo == mkCGo(e:Exp,l:Lbl)

    Var, Exp, Lbl

    Blk = {| blk:Blk′ • wf_Blk(blk) |}

value

    wf_Blk: Blk′ → **Bool**

    wf_Blk(_,ℓ) ≡

        $\forall$ i,j:**Nat** • {i,j}⊆**inds** ℓ∧ i≠j ⇒

            let mkLaS(li,_)=ℓ(i), mkLas(lj,_)=ℓ(j) **in** li≠lj **end**

        assert: card{l(ls(i))|i:**inds** ℓ}=**len** ℓ

Etcetera.

Semantic Types

Distinct variables denote distinct locations. Variable declarations give rise to the allocation of fresh locations, to the binding of the variables (i.e., variable names) to these locations in an environment ρ:ENV, and to the association of locations to values in a storage $\sigma : \Sigma$:

type
    LOC, VAL
    ENV = Var $\underset{\overrightarrow{m}}{}$ LOC
    Σ = LOC $\underset{\overrightarrow{m}}{}$ VAL

Distinct labels denote distinct state-to-state transformation functions, also known as *continuations*. A continuation, $\theta : \Theta$, is that state-to-state transformation that would be effected by an execution as prescribed from that label (when in any one state) and to the program exit, i.e., to and including the last statement of a program — where we hope that if that statement is a conditional GOTO statement that it itself will eventually lead to a no-GOTO to the target label being effected. Variables of a block denote locations, so labels of a block denote continuations, and these bindings are both kept in the block environment:

type
    LOC, VAL
    ENV = (Var $\underset{\overrightarrow{m}}{}$ LOC) $\bigcup$ (Lbl $\underset{\overrightarrow{m}}{}$ Θ)
    Σ = LOC $\underset{\overrightarrow{m}}{}$ VAL
    $\Theta = \Sigma \to \Sigma$

The $\bigcup$ is not "standard" RSL. It denotes a type operation that takes two map types A $\underset{\overrightarrow{m}}{}$ B and C $\underset{\overrightarrow{m}}{}$ D and yields the type of all maps from A elements into B elements, and from C elements into D elements. It so to speak "merges" the values of two kinds of maps into one map, for all maps.

The Main Semantic Functions

Programs

We assume that evaluation of expressions is without "side effect", that is, does not change the state (σ). Semantic function types are almost as usual, except that we have now "inserted" a continuation argument:

value
    V: Exp $\overset{\sim}{\to}$ ENV $\overset{\sim}{\to}$ Σ $\overset{\sim}{\to}$ VAL
    I: Pgm $\overset{\sim}{\to}$ Σ
    I: Stm $\overset{\sim}{\to}$ ENV $\overset{\sim}{\to}$ Θ $\overset{\sim}{\to}$ Σ $\overset{\sim}{\to}$ Σ

$$I(\text{mkPgm}(\text{blk})) \equiv$$
$$I(\text{blk})([\,])(\lambda\theta{:}\Theta\bullet\lambda\sigma{:}\Sigma\bullet\sigma)([\,])$$

To interpret a program, $I(\text{mkPgm}(\text{blk}))(\rho)(\sigma)$, is to interpret the block that it is in a continuation, which, to keep the above explanation of what continuations are, stands for the state-to-state transformation denoted by "the rest of the program" after the block (that it is). Since there is no more program text for the interpreter to obey, that state-to-state transformation function is the identity function on states: $\lambda\theta{:}\Theta\bullet\lambda\sigma{:}\Sigma\bullet\sigma$. The interpretation of a program is assumed to take place in the context of an empty environment, [], and hence in the context of an empty state, []. One could as well have chosen to initially assume some "link and load" nonempty environment and storage that would bind free identifiers of the program text to locations or continuations that represented, say, database values, respectively operating system program points.

Blocks

Below is a proper definition of the interpretation of a block. It is usual continuation-style specification. But it may be somewhat convoluted to understand it by just reading it now. Therefore, skip to the annotation following, and then refer back to the formula below. Further into the below annotation is then a schematic of what really goes in in the $\delta\rho\theta$ clause below, the most "novel" kind of specification:

value
$$I(\text{mkBlk}(\text{vs},\text{lsl}))(\rho)(\theta)(\sigma) \equiv$$
[1]   **let** ls:LOC-set •
[2]   **card** ls=**card** vs $\wedge$ ls $\cap$ **dom** σ={} **in**
[3]   **let** $\delta\rho$:ENV • **dom** $\delta\rho$=vs $\wedge$ **rng** $\delta\rho$=ls,
[4]   **let** $\rho' = \rho \dagger \delta\rho \dagger \delta\rho\theta$,
[5] $\delta\rho\theta = [\ \text{l}(\text{lsl}(i)) \mapsto$
[6]   **let** $\theta' =$ **if** i=**len** lsl
[7]   **then** θ **else** $\rho'(\text{s}(\text{lsl}(i{+}1)))$ **end**
[8]   **in** $I(\text{s}(\text{lsl}(i)))(\rho')(\theta')$ **end**
[9] | i **in** $\langle 1..\textbf{len}\ \text{sls}\rangle\ ]$ **in**
[10]   **let** $\delta\sigma$:Σ • **dom** $\delta\sigma = $ ls **in**
[11] $(\rho'(\text{s}(\text{lsl}(1))))(\sigma \cup \delta\sigma)$
            end end end end

Let us now explain what is going on here. Our explanation will be given as if the I function describes an interpreter rather than, as we originally saw it, assigning semantics (i.e., higher-order functional meanings) to syntactic texts.

To interpret a block, $I(\text{mkBlk}(\text{vs},\text{lsl}))(\rho)(\theta)(\sigma)$, shall be first understood as follows: (i) ρ is the environment of the "surroundings" of the block, one that establishes the bindings of variables and labels in effect when, i.e., *before*, entering the block interpretation. (ii) θ is the continuation: the state-to-state transformation to be effected *after* having interpreted the block (see the note following). (iii) σ is the state of the program execution at entry to block interpretation. Thus two arguments, the configuration (ρ, σ), designate one on entry to the block, whereas the continuation designates one of "the rest of the program", if any, *after* the block.

Note. It is this roundabout *after* that it takes a little time to get used to. But we remind the reader: A label denotes the state-to-state transformation to be effected as from the program point of the label and to the very end of the program in which it is embedded.

Block interpretation "proceeds", i.e., the definition of its "body" is obeyed as follows: Upon entry, as part of what we would call, during block prologue, we must establish allocation of fresh, distinct locations, one for each declared variable, i.e., we must establish an increment environment, $\delta\rho$, for those variable bindings. We must also establish denotations for all the labels of that block's statement labels.

To properly, and perhaps intuitively more easily understand, let us show schematically what is going on in the $\delta\rho\theta$ clause ([5–9]):

$$\delta\rho\theta =$$
$$[\ \text{lbl}_1 \mapsto \theta_1,$$
$$\text{lbl}_2 \mapsto \theta_2,$$
$$\ldots$$
$$\text{lbl}_{n-1} \mapsto \theta_{n-1},$$
$$\text{lbl}_n \mapsto \theta_n\ ]$$
$$\textbf{where}$$
$$\text{lbl}_i = l(\text{lsl}(i)) \wedge$$
$$\theta_i = I(s(\text{lsl}(i)))(\rho)(\theta_{i+1}) \textbf{ for } i{<}n \wedge$$
$$\theta_n = I(s(\text{lsl}(n)))(\rho)(\theta)$$
$$\textbf{where } 1 \leq i \leq \textbf{len lsl}$$

That is, the label of the ith statement denotes the continuation which is obtained from finding the meaning of the rest of the program, as a continuation, that is, without "applying" the "current" state. This is achieved by interpreting the ith statement in the same environment as that in which all the block statements are interpreted, and the continuation denoted by the next label. For the last label, that "next" continuation is, of course, that which is in effect "after" block interpretation.

Once the block prologue has also set up a proper storage extension, $\delta\sigma$, in which we do not care what values the local allocations are bound to, we, in a sense, "obey" the first statement of the block statement list by finding the continuation of its label, and by applying this continuation to the current state. And that's it. All of it!

A Profound Problem

But there is a problem: The above cannot be defined in RSL at all! RSL does not allow the kind of recursive construction of higher-order functionals as is implied by the construction of $\delta\rho\theta$. The semantics of RSL would not yield the desired fix points.

So what do we do? We fake it! For the example, as just given, we say that it is not defined in RSL, but in exactly the sublanguage of RSL that you see actually used. Almost; one also has to "linearise" the allocation of storage so as to leave out any nondeterminism. As it is now we specify any nondeterministic choice of locations and bindings. We will not go into details here but refer to standard textbooks on semantics [93, 158, 432, 448, 499, 533].

Further Remarks on Example 3.3

There are some comments to attach to the block definition given above. If you "lift" the above block interpretation function by abstracting away from storage states $\sigma : \Sigma$, then we can simplify the above semantic function for blocks and focus on the essence:

value
   I(mkBlk(vs,lsl))(ρ)(θ) $\equiv$
      let $\rho' = \rho$ †
        [l(lsl(i)) $\mapsto$
            let θ' = **if** i=**len** lsl **then** θ **else** ρ'(s(lsl(i+1))) **end in**
            I(s(lsl(i)))(ρ')(θ') **end** | i **in** $\langle$1..**len** sls$\rangle$] **in**
      ρ'(s(lsl(1)))
      end

We shall leave it with the above for the reader to ponder. We urge the reader to seek further understanding on the topic of semantic continuations from the standard textbooks which, in addition to examples like those basically presented here, also carefully explain the mathematics needed to properly denote and define such continuations [93, 158, 432, 448, 499, 533].

The Remaining Semantic Functions

Assignments

To interpret an assignment statement is to apply the continuation (as from "after" that statement) to an update state. The state update is that of re-defining the binding of the location of the assignment variable to the value of the expression of the assignment statement found in the current environment and current state.

value
   $I(mkAsgn(v,e))(\rho)(\theta)(\sigma) \equiv \theta(\sigma \dagger [\rho(v) \mapsto V(e)(\rho)(\sigma)])$

Statement Lists

To interpret a statement list is now to interpret the first statement of the list in the context of the continuation for "the rest" of the program from "after" the first statement. We find that continuation by interpreting the remaining part of the statement list in the context of the continuation for the rest of the program "after" the statement list. If the statement list is empty the argument continuation is applied to the current state. That is, the state-to-state transformation for the "rest" of the program "after" the statement list is applied to the current state to thus yield the final state.

   $I(mkStL(stl))(\rho)(\theta)(\sigma) \equiv$
      if stl=$\langle\rangle$ **then** $\theta(\sigma)$ **else** $I(\mathbf{hd}\ stl)(\rho)(I(mkStL(\mathbf{tl}\ stl))(\rho)(\theta))(\sigma)$ **end**

Conditional GOTOs

To interpret a conditional GOTO is to evaluate its Boolean-valued expression. If it is true then the continuation for the label is yielded — which is that of the "rest" of the program from that label "onwards". If it is false the continuation "as from after" the GOTO statement is yielded. In any case, either of these continuations is applied to the current state, yielding the final state.

   $I(mkCGo(e,l))(\rho)(\theta)(\sigma) \equiv (\mathbf{if}\ V(e)(\rho)(\sigma)\ \mathbf{then}\ \rho(l)\ \mathbf{else}\ \theta\ \mathbf{end})(\sigma)$

While Loops

To interpret a while loop is to yield a continuation and apply it to the current state. The continuation to be yielded is either that of the "rest" of the program ("after" the while loop statement) if the Boolean expression evaluates to **false;** or it is that which is yielded after interpreting the composition of the while loop statement list with the entire while loop statement if the Boolean expression evaluates to **true.** This corresponds to the equivalence first listed below:

axiom
   $\forall$ e:Exp,stl:Stm* •
      $I(mkWhi(e,stl)) \equiv$
         if $V(e)$ **then** $I(mkStL(stl\char`^\langle mkWhi(e,stl)\rangle))$ **else** $I(\langle\rangle)$ **end**
value
   $I(mkWhi(e,stl))(\rho)(\theta)(\sigma) \equiv$
      $(\mathbf{if}\ V(e)(\rho)(\sigma)$
         then $I(mkWhi(e,stl))(\rho)(I(stl)(\rho)(\theta))$
         else θ **end**$)(\sigma)$

The axiom determines the formulation of the semantic function.   ▪

Discussion

It is time to conclude. Above we have mostly explained the semantics function definitions using an operational approach. But it should not be forgotten that the function's main purpose is to ascribe higher-order denotations, i.e., functions as meanings to syntactic quantities.

3.2.5 Discussion of Denotational Semantics

We have presented two styles of denotational semantics definitions: the "direct" and the continuation styles. The former, in the realm of programming languages, suffices to achieve adherence to the denotational principle for programs with "linear" flow of computation, while the latter is a good way of achieving adherence for programs with "nonlinear" flow on control. We assume that the reader understands the terms "flow of computation", "flow of control", "linear" and "nonlinear".

But basically, the two flows refer to the same thing: "Execution" order. Linearity refers to whether the flow follows the syntactic phrase structure of the program text, or not (nonlinearity). In the above examples we have often read the semantic function definitions as those of interpreters. And we have stated, in their conclusions, that these semantic function definitions ascribe denotational meanings to syntactic constructs. They do so as follows: by suitably reading the definitions, moving the semantic arguments away from the argument list position "across" the $\equiv$ definition (actually equivalence) symbol, thereby "lifting" the semantic function definition body to become bodies which define functions over these semantic arguments to other semantic values.

But there is a third way of reading these semantic function definitions. We will treat that third way in more, and necessary, detail in Sections 7.6 and 16.6. But for now let is just "lift the veil". When a semantic formula defines:

$$M(syn) \equiv text\_2 \ ... \ M(f(syn)) \ ... \ text\_2$$

then we can indeed claim that a (third) meaning of the definition of M is like that of a compiler: If one is given the syntactic text: syn, in some source language, then M defines it compiled into the syntactic RSL text text_2 ... $M(f(syn))$ ... text_2. The embedded "call" of $M(d(syn))$ leads to further "translation", i.e., compilation, into additional RSL texts. We shall later return to this, as we shall call it, *macro-expansion* view.

● ● ●

Denotational semantics will become a cornerstone in our abstraction of many facets, of languages and of systems.

Principles. *Denotational Semantics:* The principle of denotational semantics is basically as follows: In trying to find suitable abstractions for syntactic constructs consider ascribing mathematical functions as the meaning of these syntactic constructs, and consider expressing, that is, constructing, the denotations homomorphically: That is, the denotation of simple syntactic constructs, i.e., atomic parts, are assigned simple functions; and composite constructs have their semantics be a homomorphic function of the denotation of the parts.   ∎

Techniques. *Direct and Continuation Semantics:* The denotational semantics of systems or languages with "relative" static and "relative" dynamic semantic concepts are classically modelled in terms of environments, storages and possibly continuations. By relative statics we mean names that are bound to constant values over large program fragments, or within specific subsystems, i.e., statically. By relative dynamics we mean names whose binding changes within considered subsystems, or are prescribed to so change within smaller program fragments, i.e., dynamically. In summary, remaining modelling techniques are implied by respective semantic function signatures:

type
  [Syntactic Value Types]
    Id, Lbl, Stmt, Expr
  [Semantic Value Types]
    VAL, LOC
    $\text{ENV} = (\text{Id} \xrightarrow{m} (\text{VAL}|\text{LOC})) \bigcup (\text{Lbl} \xrightarrow{m} \text{CON})$
    $\text{STG} = \text{LOC} \xrightarrow{m} \text{VAL}$
    $\text{CON} = \text{STG} \xrightarrow{\sim} \text{STG}$
value
[1] eval_pure_Expr: $\text{Expr} \xrightarrow{\sim} \text{ENV} \xrightarrow{\sim} \text{VAL}$
[2] eval_ord_Expr: $\text{Expr} \xrightarrow{\sim} \text{ENV} \xrightarrow{\sim} \text{STG} \xrightarrow{\sim} \text{VAL}$
[3] elab_impure_Expr: $\text{Expr} \xrightarrow{\sim} \text{ENV} \xrightarrow{\sim} \text{STG} \xrightarrow{\sim} \text{STG} \xrightarrow{\sim} \text{VAL}$
[4] int_Stmt: $\text{Stmt} \xrightarrow{\sim} \text{ENV} \xrightarrow{\sim} \text{STG} \xrightarrow{\sim} \text{STG}$
[5] int_Stmt: $\text{Stmt} \xrightarrow{\sim} \text{ENV} \xrightarrow{\sim} \text{CON} \xrightarrow{\sim} \text{CON}$

The semantic functions that ascribe denotation to "pure" expressions, i.e., expressions with no assignable variable identifiers, usually are called [e]valuation functions. They ascribe the denotational type shown in line [1] above.

The semantic functions that ascribe denotation to "ordinary" expressions, i.e., expressions with assignable variable identifiers but whose evaluation cannot cause any storage change, are also called [e]valuation functions. They ascribe the denotational type shown in line [2] above.

The semantic functions that ascribe denotation to "impure" expressions, i.e., expressions with not only assignable variable identifiers but also with such embedded constructs whose elaboration may cause storage changes, are usually called elaboration functions. They ascribe the denotational type shown in line [3] above.

The semantics functions that ascribe denotation to statements are usually called interpretation functions. They ascribe the denotational types shown in lines [4–5] above.   ∎

3.3 Computational Semantics

3.3.1 The Issues

Denotational semantics definitions are abstract, but are relatively easy to grasp. Denotational meanings are functions. Hence denotational semantics definitions cannot usually be the direct basis for executions, as conventional computers and programming languages cannot handle such higher-order values, but must be refined into more concrete prescriptions. Computational semantics definitions "unravel" recursive function definitions into iterative (loop) prescriptions, and recursive (syntactic) data structures into linear (list-oriented) data structures. In doing so recursion is "converted" into stacks and iteration. Computational meanings are sequential compositions of simple state changes. Computational semantics definitions are concrete, but relatively difficult to grasp.

3.3.2 Two Examples

We follow up on the two denotational semantics examples of Sect. 3.2 (Examples 3.2 and 3.3). In Example 3.4 — first put forward by Peter Landin [284] around 1964 — we exemplify a mechanical interpreter for the expression language of Example 3.2. The example belongs to the folklore of computing science.

3.3.3 Expression Computations

The example now given is a forerunner of what became known as the SECD interpreter: the Storage, Environment, Control and Dump machine. In the computational semantics for expressions we shall not illustrate the dump part. That part will be prominent in the computational semantics for the imperative language with labels and GOTOs exemplified in Example 3.5.

Example 3.4 *Mechanical Evaluation of Expressions:*
    The basic idea of this example is that of realising the recursion of V by means of *stacks*, that is, of recursion removal. Many realisations of the recursion of V are possible. We will, rather arbitrarily, select one.

Before proceeding into a description of which stacks to create and how they are used we note that our stacks are not to be used for sorting out precedence of operators. Since we work only on abstract syntactic objects, all such precedence has already been resolved and is "hidden" in the (invisibly) parenthesized subexpressions.

Thus we remove recursion in the function definition of V by introducing one or more stacks. At the same time, we change our definitional style from applicative to imperative. This is not an intrinsic consequence of choosing stacks, but a pragmatic one. In doing so we can, at the same time, simply change the recursive function definitions into iterative. The imperative/iterative nature of the resulting definition further gives it an air of being "mechanical".

A Computational State

One stack is the *value stack*. It is motivated by the "stacking" of temporaries. Here we make explicit the implicit stacking of intermediate or temporary results, as expressed in the denotational semantics definition through its recursive invocation of semantic elaboration functions.

Another stack is a *control*, or *operator/operand expression* stack. It is motivated by recursion over syntactical expression objects. Here we make explicit the recursion in terms of stacks. The two kinds of recursion intertwine.

Thus we make two decisions: first to state the model imperatively, in terms of some globally declared variables. Then to express the computational semantics in terms of two stack variables and a constant environment.

type
    ite
    MDEi = Mo|Do|Ex|ite
    SE = MDEi*
variable
    opestk:SE := $\langle \rangle$
    valstk:**Int*** := $\langle \rangle$
value
    env:ENV

Note that *env* will be referred to below, as a global constant.

Why we made these two, and not other, among quite a few other possible, decisions will not be explained much further! In our computational semantics, as imperatively stated, we must necessarily choose an elaboration order for operand expressions of infix expressions. This order was left "unspecified" by V.

Motivating the Control Stack

The idea of the operator/operand stack is now that the topmost element is either an expression to be evaluated, or an operator to be applied to either the operator/operand or to the value stack.

If the top of the operator/operand stack is an expression then it is either elementary or composite. If it is elementary, i.e., a constant or an identifier then the associated value is pushed onto the value stack, while the expression is being popped off the operator/operand stack. If it is composite, i.e., a prefix, infix or conditional expression, then those expressions are decomposed, with the decomposition replacing it on the operator/operand stack. Hence the control stack will consist of a sequence of operators and their operands, in what turns out to be some variant of a *postfix* or *reverse Polish* notation:

1: A *prefix expression* is replaced by two elements on this stack: the monadic operator and the (sub)expression (on top).
2: An *infix expression* is replaced by three elements: the dyadic operator and the two (sub)expressions (in some order, on top).
3: A *conditional* expression is replaced by four elements, in order from top towards bottom: the test expression, a metaoperator ite (for if then else), and the consequence and alternative expressions — the latter two in arbitrary, but fixed, order. The idea of the ite operator will be explained in item 6 below.
4: If the top of the operator/operand stack is a *monadic operator*, then the denoted operation is applied to the top of the value stack. (Thus if the operator is minus the top of the value stack is replaced by its complemented (negative) value.) It follows from the operator/operand stack manipulations that the value stack top is the value of the expression to which the monadic operator was once prefixed.
5: If the top of the operator/operand stack is a *dyadic operator*, then the denoted operation is applied, in an appropriate way, to the two topmost values of the value stack — with the result replacing these values.
6: Finally, if the operator/operand stack top element is ite then it means that the value of the test expression of the conditional expression, whose manipulation gave rise to this ite operator, is on the top of the value stack. If it, the latter, is 0 then we compute only the consequence expression, otherwise we compute only the alternative expression. These are the next two elements on the operator/operand stack. The appropriate one is thrown away together with the value stack top.

The Elaboration Functions

Computation proceeds based, as always, on the top element of the operator/operand stack. And computation proceeds as long as there are elements on the operator/operand stack. When it becomes empty the computed value is the top value of the value stack. The function informally described in this paragraph is called Compute. It is defined formally below.

Let us call the function which transforms the system state dependent on the top of the operator/operand stack for Transform, then:

value
Compute: Ex → **read,write** opestk,valstk **Int**
Compute(e) ≡
    opestak := ⟨e⟩;
    while opestak ≠ ⟨⟩ **do** Transform() **end**;
    hd valstk

To facilitate the statement of *Transform* we define four auxiliary stack functions:

PopO: **Unit** $\overset{\sim}{\to}$ **read,write** opestk MDEi
PopO() ≡ **let** oe = **hd** opestak **in** opestk := **tl** opestk; oe **end**

PopV: **Unit** $\overset{\sim}{\to}$ **read,write** valstk **Int**
PopV() ≡ **let** v = **hd** valstk **in** valstk := **tl** valstk; v **end**

PushO: SE $\overset{\sim}{\to}$ **read,write** opestk **Unit**
PushO(oel) ≡ opestk := oel ⌒ opestk

PushV: **Int** $\overset{\sim}{\to}$ **read,write** valstk **Unit**
PushV(v) ≡ valstk := ⟨v⟩ ⌒ valstk

Now to the main function.

value
Transform: **Unit** → **Unit**
Transform() ≡
    let oe = PopO() **in**
    case oe **of**:
        mk_intg(i) → PushV(i),
        mk_iden(t) → PushV(env(t)),
        mk_prefix(o,e) → PushO(⟨e,o⟩),
        mk_infix(le,o,re) → PushO(⟨re,le,o⟩),
        mk_cond(be,ce,ae) → PushO(⟨be,ite,ce,ae⟩),
        minus → PushV(−PopV()),
        ... → ...,
        add → PushV(⟨PopV()+PopV()⟩),
        ... → ...,
        ite → **let** bv = PopV(), ce = PopO(), ae = PopO();
                PushO(⟨**if** bv=0 **then** ce **else** ae **end**⟩) **end**,
    end end

Recall that *env* was a globally defined constant.   ∎

Discussion

The recursive definitions of the semantics functions of Examples 3.1 and 3.2 have been replaced by a combination of two stacks, push and pop operations on both of these stacks and iteration. The control stack resembles the compile-time translation of structured, for example, infix, expressions to reverse *Polish* notation. The value stack resembles the run-time interpretation of code for intermediary values of subexpressions. Thus we may say that the computational semantics gives hints as how to develop an interpreter, or even a compiler, from a denotational semantics definition. We shall take this topic up in Chap. 16.

3.3.4 Computational Semantics of GOTO Programs

In Example 3.5, first put forward by John Reynolds [427, 428], we exemplify a mechanical interpreter for the jump language of Example 3.3. This example also belongs to the folklore of computing science.

Example 3.5 *Mechanical Evaluation of a Statement Language:*

The Syntax

We start by presenting a syntax for an almost conventional imperative and block structured language. The "twist" in this language is that we allow expressions to be labels, that variables may store label denotations, and that GOTOs can refer to label variables.

type
    Var, Lbl
    Block == mkBlock(defns:(Var $\overrightarrow{m}$ Type),cl:Cmd*)
    Type == label | ...
    Cmd == mkCmd(p:PPt,s:Stmt)
    PPt == Lbl | nil
    Stmt = Asgn | GOTO | Block | ...
    Asgn == mkAsgn(v:Var,e:Expr)
    GOTO = VGOTO | LGOTO
    VGOTO == mkVGOTO(v:Var)
    LGOTO ==mkLGOTO(l:Lbl)

    ...
    Expr == mkLbl(Lbl) | mkVar(Var) | ...

Some Semantic Observations

Observation 1

The "newcomer" is label variables, and hence label values. The question therefore is: What is the denotation, in a computational semantics model, of a label? We now argue our answer to this question. To see, in a language like that of this examplem that labels cannot just denote themselves we perform the following experiment. We let a program "schematically" look like:

```
1.  begin
2.     dcl lv type label ;
3.     l : statement-A ;
4.     lv := l ; ... ; GOTO lv ; ...
5.     begin
6.        l : statement-B ; ...
7.        lv := l ; ...
8.        GOTO lv ; ...
9.     end ; ...
10. end
```

The GOTO in (4) is (clearly) intended to transfer flow of control to that statement whose label, "l", was most recently assigned to "lv", and likewise for the GOTO in (7). Assume, in (4), that "lv's" content at the point of GOTO is the "l" of (3), then transfer is to (3). Assume, in (8), that "lv's" content is the "l" of (3), then transfer is to (3). Assume, instead, in (8) that (7) was most recently executed, then transfer should be to (6). The question is therefore this: How to distinguish between the "l" of the outer and inner blocks (now that it is allowed to have redefinition of "l's")?

Observation 2

There is, however, another problem: Assignment of local labels of two disjoint blocks to a common, global variable may raise problems:

```
1.  begin
2.     dcl lv type label ;
3.     begin
4.        l_1: stmt ; ... ; lv := l_1 ; ...
5.     end ;
6.     ...
7.     begin
8.        l_2: stmt ; ... ; lv := l_2 ; ... ; GOTO lv ; ...
9.     end ; ...
10. end
```

If at the point of executing the GOTO in (6) "lv's" value is not that (possibly conditionally) assigned "earlier" in (6), but that resulting from and bound in line (4), then an attempt is seemingly being made to jump into block (3–5) — something which was otherwise deemed illegal statically.

Semantic Types

As before, we formulate the semantics around an SECD structure: storage, environment, control and dump. The state of the computational model thus consists of four components: (i) a **storage**, as usual; (ii) an **environment**, which is as usual, only we keep it in a global variable; (iii) a **control**, which contains the statements of the block currently being executed; and (iv) a **dump**.

The dump records the state of computation at the point of entry to a block exclusive of that block. That is, the dump contains a triple: (ii) the **environment** of the block embracing the block being entered (i.e., *env* or ρ of earlier models), (iii) the list of commands, i.e., **control**, following the block being entered (i.e., a concretisation of I_sl(sl)(i)(ρ)(σ) (cf. Example 3.3) for some i where sl(i-1) is the block being entered); and (iv) the **dump** at the point of entering a block.

Leaving a block means restoring the ("top") dump element to the respective global **environment**, **control** and **dump** variables.

A label **value** is a dump.

"Going to" a labelled statement means taking the label value and letting its component replace the current environment, control and dump values.

type
    STG = LOC $\rightarrowtail$ VAL
    ENV = (Var $\rightarrowtail$ LOC) $\bigcup$ (Lbl $\rightarrowtail$ DMP)
    DMP = ENV × CTL × Dmp
    Dmp == DMP | null
    CTL = Cmd*

variable
    Stg:STG := [],
    Env:ENV := [],
    Ctl:CTL := $\langle\rangle$,
    Dmp:DMP := null;

Interpreter Functions

We assume a program, p, to be a block (or a command list). We define a function, **Iterate**, which "executes" a statement at a time, and otherwise iterates until control is empty ($\langle\rangle$), and dump is likewise (null):

value
    Iterate: Block → **write** Ctl **read** Dmp **Unit**
    Iterate(b) ≡ Ctl:=b; **while** (Ctl≠⟨⟩∧Dmp≠null) **do** Transform() **end**

    Transform: **Unit** → **write** Stg,Env,Ctl,Dmp **Unit**
    Transform() ≡
      if Ctl≠⟨⟩
        then
          let mkCmd(,s) = **hd** Ctl **in** Ctl := **tl** Ctl ;
          Compute_Stmt(s) **end**
        else
          let (env,ctl,dmp) = Dmp **in**
          (Env:=env ‖ Ctl:=ctl ‖ Dmp := dmp) **end**
      end

Compute_Block (i.e., Compute_Stmt for Blocks) prepares a new environment, dumps the old environment, control and dump on the dump, and initialises the control to the block command list.

value
    Compute_Stmt: Stmt → **write** Stg,Ctl,Env,Dmp **Unit**
    Compute_Stmt(mkBlock(vars,cl)) ≡
      let $\delta\rho$ = [v↦Alloc()|v:Var•v ∈ **dom** vars]
          † [l↦makeDump($\delta\rho$,(l,cl))|l:Lbl•mkCmd(l,)∈ **elems** cl] **in**
      Dmp := (Env,Ctl,Dmp) ;
      (Env := $\delta\rho$ ‖ Ctl := cl)
      end

Alloc allocates storage space for declared variables.

    Alloc: **Unit** → **write** Stg LOC
    Alloc() ≡
      let loc:LOC • loc∉ **dom** Stg **in**
      Stg := Stg ∪ [loc↦undefined] ;
      loc **end**

makeDump prepares a dump for each label of a block command list.

    makeDump: ENV × (PPt × Cmd*) **read** Dmp DMP
    makeDump(ρ,(lbl,cmdl)) ≡
      let cl = ⟨cmdl(i)|i **in** ⟨j,**len** cmdl⟩•j ∈ **inds** cmdl∧lbl=p(cmdl(i))⟩
      in (ρ,cl,Dmp) **end**

Compute_Assign looks up the assignment left-hand variable, evaluates the right-hand expression, and updates storage.

value
   Compute_Stmt(mkAssign(var,lbl_or_expr)) ≡
   let loc = look_up(var)(Env,Dmp),
       val = Compute_Expr(lbl_or_expr) **in**
   Stg := Stg † [loc ↦ val]
   end

look_up first searches the local environment, then, if needed, successively dumps "surrounding" environments.

value
   look_up: (Lbl|Var) → Env × Dmp → **read** Dmp **Unit** (DMP|LOC)
   look_up(lv)(ρ,δ) ≡
     if lv ∈ **dom** Env
       then env(lv)
       else
          let (env,,dmp) = Dmp **in**
          look_up(lv)(env,dmp) **end**
     end

Compute_Expr evaluates an expression. That expression may either be a variable, a label or something else.

value
   Compute_Expr: Expr → **read** Env,Dmp **Unit** VAL
   Compute_Expr(e) ≡
     case e **of**
       mkLbl(l) → look_up(l)(Env,Dmp),
       mkVar(v) →
          let loc = look_up(v)(Env,Dmp) **in**
          Stg(loc) **end**
     end

Compute_GOTO computes the label valued expression of its argument, throws the current dump away (entirely, yes!), and distributes the components of the retrieved dump over the control, environment and dump variables.

value
   Compute_Stmt(mkGOTO(var_or_lbl)) ≡
     let le =
       case var_or_lbl **of**
          mkVGOTO(var) → mkVar(var),
          mkLGOTO(lbl) → mkLbl(lbl)
       end in
     let (env,ctl,dmp) = Compute_Expr(le) **in**
     (Env := env || Ctl := ctl || Dmp := dmp)

end end

We remind the reader that the above constitutes one of the major models of computing science.   ∎

3.3.5 Computational Semantics of Coroutine Programs

Example 3.5 forms the background for this small section — mostly taken up by a "pseudo-example". That pseudo-example illustrates an important programming technique, that of coroutines. The pseudo-example challenges the reader to formalise the syntax and semantics of the illustrated coroutine language. That syntax and semantics, obviously, is expected to follow very much the solution given in Example 3.5.

Example 3.6 *Coroutines:* By a coroutine we mean a program block that can be called, i.e., whose interpretation can be "commenced" as from a first declaration. We also mean one whose interpretation can be "temporarily" suspended, and whose interpretation can be resumed as from any designated (internal) program point. Finally, we mean one whose interpretation can be "ended" by normal interpretation of an ordinary last statement of that coroutine block.

Let us consider the "Coroutine" Program Text I below[4].

"Coroutine" **Program Text I**

```
      begin                                      start
         variables: lva,lvb, v1,v2,...,vn ;       +
         l1: st1 ;                                 +
         l2: st2 ;                                 +
         l3: begin                                 +
            variables: ... ;                       +
            l31: st31 ;                            +
            l32: lva := l34 ;                      +
            l33: GOTO l4 ;                         +
            l34: st34 ;                            |    |  -> +
            l35: GOTO lvb                          |    |     +
               end                                 |    |     |
         l4: st4 ;                                 +    |     |
         l5: begin                                 +    |     |
            variables: ... ;                       +    |     |
            l51: st11 ;                            +    |     |
            l52: lvb := l54 ;                      +    |     |
            l53: GOTO lva ;                        + -> |     |
            l54: st14                                         +
               end                                           +
         l6: st6                                             +
      end                                         out
```

---

[4]Disregard for the moment the +s, the |s, the -s and the >s of the right-hand side of text.

According to the computational semantics of the language of this example, the following execution sequence — mentioning only the labels of statements actually computed, omitting the assumed block prologue allocation of variables — is possible: 11, 12, 13, 131, 132, 133, 14, 15, 151, 152, 153, 134, 135, 154, 16! We attempt to illustrate this sequence by the *trace* shown by the +'s, the |'s and the ->'s of the right-hand side of the "Coroutine" Program Text. The +'s designate statements (etc.) being interpreted. The |'s designate "transfer of control" to a next statement (etc.) being then interpreted. The ->'s likewise, i.e., as for the |'s. Naturally, the dynamics of execution is "diagrammed" by the *program trace* "winding its way down and up and down again".

That is, the blocks labeled 13 and 15 can be considered coroutines.

Of course, instead of the possibly haphazard, i.e., error prone, assignment of labels to variables, one can design a language whose syntactic forms more appropriately indicate call, suspend, resume and terminate.

A proposal is given in the Coroutine Program Text II next:

Coroutine Program Text II

```
begin                         start
   variables: v1,v2,...,vn ;    +
   COROUTINE ca:                |    | -> +
      begin                     |    |    +
         variables: ... ;       |    |    +
         la1: st31 ;            |    |    +
         la3: CALL cb ;         |    |    +
         la4: st34 ;            |    |    |    | -> +
         la5: RESUME cb         |    |    |    |    +
      end ca ;                  |    |    |    |    |
   COROUTINE cb:                |    |    +    |    |
      begin                     |    |    +    |    |
         variables: ... ;       |    |    +    |    |
         lb1: st11 ;            |    |    +    |    |
         lb3: RESUME ca ;       |    |    + -> |    |
         lb4: st14 ;            |    |         |    +
         lb5: TERMINATE         |    |         |    +
      end cb ;                  |    |         |    +
   l1: st1 ;                    +    |         |
   l2: st2 ;                    +    |         |
   l3: CALL ca ;                + -> |         |
   l6: st6                                     +
end                                          out
```

We leave it to the reader to decipher the latest Coroutine Text (II), to compare the two Coroutine Texts (I–II), and to design a proper imperative, "toy" coroutine programming language.

3.3.6 Discussion

It is time to conclude. Above we presented a computational semantics for a slight variation of the GOTO language otherwise denotationally defined in Example 3.3. The variation has been that of allowing assignable variables to be assigned "the value of a label", and to let GOTO statements identify the target label as the value contained in such label variables.

Two kinds of comments are in order: one on the modelling of labels, and one of "the power" of the current variant of GOTO languages.

On the Mechanisation of Continuations

Labels denote continuations. So it was in the denotation semantics modelling of GOTOs. Labels denoted dumps: records of environments, controls (i.e., program fragments) and dumps. So it was in the computation semantics modelling of GOTOs. In other words: dumps offer one form of implementation of continuations.

The latter gives us the hint that labels, in such GOTO languages as here illustrated (with label variables etc.), be implemented in terms of references to environments, program points and references to dumps.

In Chaps. 16–18, we shall base developments towards compilers for functional, imperative and modular languages upon this insight.

On the "Power" of GOTOs via Label Variables

GOTOs are usually considered harmful. It was the late (and illustrious) computer scientist Edsger Wybe Dijkstra [101] who pointed out undesirable possibilities when using GOTOs in programming. But used judiciously, and perhaps only after steps of refinement where earlier stages did not use GOTOs, such may be useful. As also pointed out, eloquently, by Donald E. Knuth [274].

But, as shown in Example 3.5 and hinted at in Example 3.6. GOTOs can be made very useful. In any case, our hardware computers "feature" them, extensively!

On Computational Semantics

We observe that the above example definitions do not satisfy the denotational principle. This is because we have decomposed ("compiled") composite expressions (resp. statements) into, in this case, postfix-like sequences of immediate expression and operator components (etc.). Instead we should get a rather operational "feeling" for how one might mechanically pursue an evaluation of expressions (resp. interpretation of statements) — resulting, after some iterations rather than recursions, in their value (resp. side-effect).

3.4 Review: Denotations and Computations

In denotational semantics meaning is abstracted as functions. In computational semantics meaning is concretised as computations. Denotational semantics functions express homomorphisms. Computational semantics functions express sequences of state changes. Recursions, say in denotational definitions, are, in computational definitions expressed in terms of stacks and iterations. Denotational semantics over recursively defined syntactic structures are expressed in terms of recursively descending functions which functionally compose meanings from embedded parts.

Computational semantics typically encodes (i.e., translates) recursive structures into linear data structures as a result of either pre- or post-order traversals of the original, recursively defined (treelike) structures. The recursive to linear, i.e., syntax-to-syntax, translation is expressed in terms of stacks as is the linear syntax to semantics computation.

Principles. The principle of *denotations versus computations* is one of abstraction: If you seek an abstract, yet model-oriented abstraction "try" to formulate a denotational semantics. If you seek to explain, albeit abstractly, how a computation over some program text can occur, then "go for" a computational semantics.   ∎

3.5 Some Pioneers of Semantics

There are many pioneers of semantics. Besides mathematicians, there are a number who, in the era of computing, i.e., from the mid-1950s onwards, have contributed significantly to providing a theoretical and a practical basis for expressing the semantics of programming languages. Two will be mentioned in this section: John McCarthy and Peter Landin. Others, really, should be mentioned in other end-of-chapter biographies. Some of these are: people from the IBM Vienna Laboratory group of the 1960s and early 1970s (Hans Bekič, Peter Lucas and Kurt Walk [30, 31, 33–37, 248, 305–312, 565]), and from the Oxford University Computing Laboratory, also of the 1960s and early to mid-1970s: Dana Scott and Christopher Strachey [157, 355, 452–463, 489–491].

3.5.1 John McCarthy

John McCarthy's work in relation to semantics is of decisive importance. He has also contributed significantly to the area of artificial intelligence (AI). Here we shall just concentrate on a few years of McCarthy's work in relation to programming language semantics. In particular to references [329–331, 333, 334] which we show, and briefly comment on, below as items 1–5.

1. John McCarthy. Recursive Functions of Symbolic Expressions and Their Computation by Machines, Part I. *Communications of the ACM*, 3(4):184–195, 1960.

This was the original paper on LISP. Part II, which never appeared, was to have had some LISP programs for algebraic computation.

2. John McCarthy, Paul W. Abrahams, Daniel J. Edwards, Timothy P. Hart, and Michael I. Levin. *LISP 1.5 Programmer's Manual*. The MIT Press, Cambridge, Mass., 1962.

The LISP 1.5 list-oriented programming language is defined in terms of a set of recursive equations. The style of the definition, the LISP 1.5 interpreter, can be read as being operational (i.e., computational).

3. John McCarthy. Towards a Mathematical Science of Computation. In C.M. Popplewell, editor, *IFIP World Congress Proceedings*, pages 21–28, 1962.
4. John McCarthy. A Basis for a Mathematical Theory of Computation. In *Computer Programming and Formal Systems*. North-Holland Publ. Co., Amsterdam, 1963.

These two papers figure among the great classics of computer science. The latter extends the results of the former paper. The first paper was presented in 1961 at the Western Joint Computer Conference and in 1962 at a symposium sponsored by IBM in Blaricum, Netherlands. Among other things, it includes a systematic theory of conditional expressions, a treatment of their recursive use and the method of recursion induction for proving properties of recursively defined functions.

The latter paper introduced the term abstract syntax — and maybe the first occurrence of the idea — as it also, briefly, covered the notion of semantics.

5. John McCarthy and James Painter. Correctness of a Compiler for Arithmetic Expressions, in J.T. Schwartz. *Mathematical Aspects of Computer Science, Proc. of Symp. in Appl. Math.* American Mathematical Society, Rhode Island, USA, 1967, pages 33–41, 1966 [451].

This paper seems to have contained the first proof of correctness of a compiler. Abstract syntax and Lisp-style recursive definitions kept the paper short.
We quote from the introduction:

This paper contains a proof of the correctness of a simple compiling algorithm for compiling arithmetic expressions into machine language. The definition of correctness, the formalism used to express the description of source language, object language and compiler, and the methods of proof are all intended to serve as prototypes for the more complicated task of proving the correctness of usable compilers. The expressions dealt with in this paper are formed from constants and variables. The only operation allowed is a binary + although no change in method would be required to include any other binary operations. The computer language into which these expressions are compiled is a single address computer with an accumulator, called ac, and four instructions: li (load immediate), load, sto (store) and add. Note that there are no jump instructions. Needless to say, this is a severe restriction on the generality of our results which we shall overcome in future work. The compiler produces code that computes the value of the expression being compiled and leaves this value in the accumulator. Again because we are using abstract syntax there is no commitment to a precise form for the object code.

3.5.2 Peter Landin

> *Most papers in computer science describe*
> *how their author learned what someone else already knew.*
>
> Peter Landin

Peter Landin's scholarly career started at the end of the 1950s. He was much influenced by McCarthy and started to study LISP when the most common language was FORTRAN. LISP was very different from the other contemporary languages because it was based on a functional calculus rather than being procedural in nature.

References [284–291] are listed below.

• [284] Peter J. Landin. The Mechanical Evaluation of Expressions. *Computer Journal*, 6(4):308–320, 1964.

We quote, from the abstract of Olivier Danvy's [90]:

> Landin's SECD machine was the first abstract machine for the λ-calculus viewed as a programming language. Both theoretically as a model of computation and practically as an idealized implementation, it has set the tone for the subsequent development of abstract machines for functional programming languages.

Olivier Danvy's abstract continues:

> However, and even though variants of the SECD machine have been presented, derived, and invented, the precise rationale for its architecture and modus operandi has remained elusive. In this article, we deconstruct the SECD machine into a λ-interpreter, i.e., an evaluation function, and we reconstruct λ-interpreters into a variety of SECD-like machines. The deconstruction and reconstructions are transformational: they are based on equational reasoning and on a combination of simple program transformations — mainly closure conversion,

transformation into continuation-passing style, and defunctionalization. The evaluation function underlying the SECD machine provides a precise rationale for its architecture: it is an environment-based *eval-apply* evaluator with a callee-save strategy for the environment, a data stack of intermediate results, and a control delimiter. Each of the components of the SECD machine (stack, environment, control, and dump) is therefore rationalized and so are its transitions. The deconstruction and reconstruction method also applies to other abstract machines and other evaluation functions. It makes it possible to systematically extract the denotational content of an abstract machine in the form of a compositional evaluation function, and the (small-step) operational content of an evaluation function in the form of an abstract machine.

- [285] Peter J. Landin. A Correspondence Between Algol 60 and Church's Lambda-notation (in 2 parts). *Communications of the ACM*, 8(2–3):89–101 and 158–165, Feb.–March 1965.

These two papers were very influential in demonstrating the importance (i) of the λ-calculus in practice, (ii) as a tool to understand programming language semantics, and (iii) of the functional programming paradigm.

The next two papers:

- [288] Peter J. Landin. Getting Rid of Labels. Technical Report, Univac Systems Programming Research Group, N.Y., 1965.
- [286] Peter J. Landin. A Generalization of Jumps and Labels. Technical Report, Univac Systems Programming Research Group, N.Y., 1965.

although — at the time not widely spread — did indeed have some rather substantial influence. They clearly show Landin's canny ability to deal with complicated "phenomena" in elegant ways. Landin handles control by way of a special form of closure, giving a statically scoped form of control, namely in terms of the J operator.

Later authors have analysed these papers: [430, 433, 500, 501]. In [292] Landin reviews his work of the 1960s and draws lines into the years after.

Further reports and papers were:

- [287] Peter J. Landin. An Analysis of Assignment in Programming Languages. Technical Report, Univac Systems Programming Research Group, N.Y., 1965.
- [289] Peter J. Landin. A Formal Description of Algol 60. In T.B. Steel. *Formal Language Description Languages*, IFIP TC-2 Work. Conf., Baden. North-Holland Publ. Co., Amsterdam, 1966, pages 266–294, 1966 [484].
- [290] Peter J. Landin. A Lambda Calculus Approach. In L. Fox, editor, *Advances in Programming and Non-numeric Computations*, pages 97–141. Pergamon Press, 1966.

The final paper in our listing:

- [291] Peter J. Landin. The Next 700 Programming Languages. *Communications of the ACM*, 9(3):157–166, 1966.

introduced the concept of ISWIM: I See What I Mean.
We quote from FOLDOC [118]:

> ISWIM is purely functional, a sugaring of lambda-calculus, and the ancestor of most modern applicative languages. An ISWIM program is a single expression qualified by 'where' clauses (auxiliary definitions including equations among variables), conditional expressions and function definitions. ISWIM was the first language to use lazy evaluation and introduced the offside rule for indentation.

3.6 Exercises

Exercise 3.1 *Denotational Semantics: Case Expression Extension.* We refer to Example 3.2. Extend that expression language with case expressions, say like:

```
case expr of
    expr_1v → expr_1c,
    expr_2v → expr_2c,
    ...
    expr_nv → expr_nc
end
```

where evaluation of expr is compared for equality, in turn, with expressions expr_iv, from i=1 to i=n. For the first i=j for which there is equality, the value of the whole case expression is the value of expression expr_jc. If no equality is yielded, then **chaos** is yielded!
This exercise continues in Exercise 3.2.

Exercise 3.2 *Computational Semantics: Case Expression Extension.* We refer to Example 3.4 and to Exercise 3.1. You are to reformulate the semantics of the case expression as a computational semantics — as per the ideas expressed in Example 3.4.

Exercise 3.3 *Denotational Semantics: A Simple Bank.* Narrative: A much simplified bank is configured into a context $\rho : R$, which records client $c : C$ account numbers $k : K$, and a state $\sigma : \Sigma$, which records balances on accounts. That is, clients are named $c : C$, and so are accounts $k : K$. Two or more clients may share accounts. Clients may "hold" more than one account. All accounts have clients.
    The bank accepts the following transactions: create account, close account, deposit into an account, withdraw from an account, transfer monies between

accounts and deliver a statement (of a client's transactions since either the last time a statement transaction from that client was honoured, or since the opening of the identified account). These transactions amount to syntactic commands. They appropriately name client and account names as well as money amounts, as needed.

The bank state also records the bank's own profit (interest income) and fee (income) accounts. The bank charges the customer a fixed fee, say $d : \$$, for certain transactions (open, close, statement and transfer), a fixed daily interest, say $i : I$, on negative accounts, and offers a fixed, lower yield, $y : Y$, on positive accounts. Thus the transactions also need to record the day on which a transaction is issued. We assume all such day identifications to be natural numbers, as from day 0, the opening of the bank, till any other day after that. In other words, whenever a deposit, withdrawal, transfer or closing transaction takes place, the bank computes the interest or yield to be withdrawn from, respectively added to, the appropriate account(s): the clients' as well as the bank's.

Questions: First formalise the abstract types (i.e., sorts) of client names and account identifiers. Then formalise the concrete types of banks (contexts and states). Then define, still in RSL, the semantic functions which assign denotational meaning to transactions and to transaction sequences (the latter likely to relate to different clients).

References: This exercise continues into Exercise 3.4 immediately below.

Exercise 3.4 *Denotational Semantics: A Simple Banking Script Language.* Reference: This exercise continues from Exercise 3.3.

Narrative and problem: Now, from your definition of the semantics of transactions, devise a simple script language, that is, a simple exercise and conditional (if–then–else) statement and expression language in which the bank can itself define the semantics of transactions in the form of scripts. A script is just a sequence of simple exercise and conditional (if–then–else) statements. Define the syntactic and semantics types of this language as well as denotational functions that ascribe meanings to scripts.

Hint: Scripts are like small programs. Variables of these programs are the finite set of two bank variables, **context** and **accounts**, the finite set of two bank constants, **interest%** and **yield%**, a finite set of (how many?) client name, account number, statement accumulation, and period computation (from date of last interest or yield computation, to current date) variables, etc.

Exercise 3.5 *Denotational (Continuation) Semantics: Language with Storable Label Values.* References: References are made to Examples 3.3 and 3.5. The imperative GOTO language, for which a denotational continuation semantics is sought, had its syntax defined in Example 3.5 (which is basically also the syntax of the language of Example 3.3).

The Problem: The problem to be solved is now, instead of the computational (cum operational) semantics of Example 3.5 to define a denotational (cum mathematical) semantics using continuations like those shown in Example 3.3. Hint: Let continuations be storable values!

Exercise 3.6 *Denotational (Continuation) Semantics: A Proper Coroutine Programming Language.* **Reference**: Reference is made to Example 3.6.

The Problem: You are to come up with a denotational continuation semantics for a proper, imperative coroutine language. In this exercise you also are to first make precise a narrative description of the syntax and semantics of this language. The below text only gives a rough sketch of the language. That is, you are to "fill in the details"!

Narrative: The imperative coroutine language, to be given a formal definition is like a block structured imperative language as given in several examples so far in these volumes. Programs, besides (syntactically) being blocks that allow the introduction of variables, also allow the definition of routines, <u>routine</u> r = "block" and <u>call</u> r statements, where r is the name of a defined routine. Routines are parameterless, but named procedures, which, syntactically speaking are otherwise like blocks, but where routine blocks allow two new kinds of statements: <u>call</u> r, a routine (named r), and <u>resume</u> r, where it is assumed that some routine r is currently suspended. Speaking operationally, when a routine is invoked (i.e., called) from within a routine then that routine's activation is said to be suspended, and at that point. Resumption then reactivates the most recently suspended routine (named r) as from that point onwards. Routines are "exhausted", i.e., terminate, when there are no more statements to execute, i.e., when they "reach the end of their body of statements". At that time an implicit "resumption" takes place: Transfer of execution control occurs to the routine or the program — whichever invoked (i.e., called) the present routine activation.

Comments: We leave it to you to guess the rest — and hence to first narrate a precise, informal description, before formally defining the syntactic and semantic types and the semantic functions.

4

Configurations:
Contexts and States

- The **prerequisite** for studying this chapter is that you have studied and understood, to a reasonable extent and depth, Vol. 1 of this series of textbooks on software engineering.
- The **aims** are to introduce the model (and configuration modelling) concepts of contexts and states, and to exemplify and discuss these configuration concepts from a variety of viewpoints.
- The **objective** is to enable you to choose an appropriate balance between a "decomposition" of configurations into contexts and states.
- The **treatment** is systematic and semi-formal — with an important state concept (automata and machine) being covered in Chap. 11.

On Notions of State

By *the state of affairs* we generally mean how the *universe of discourse* (which we are observing) is composed, and, for each of the atomic components, what their values are, at any time.

- Thus we can take a look at that *universe of discourse* at a very detailed level: Considering all the values as they change, continuously over time. This is the classical control-theoretic view point [16, 104, 120]. There are now infinitely many states, and they typically form various continuities.
- Or we can "summarise" certain value ranges as being significant. That is, we can impose one or another equivalence relation and thus "divide" the typically infinite space of values (for each observable) component into a finite number of "adjacent" ranges (intervals). Each interval now denotes a state (of a given component, i.e., a sub-state of the system of components). And permissible combinations of components and their respective ranges designate a state. Again, if there are a finite number of components and, for each, a finite number of relevant value ranges (to be observed), then we have, essentially, a finite state system — albeit that there may be many, many states.

- Or the *universe of discourse* presents itself as a discrete system, that is, as a composition of components, each of which "takes on" a value from a finite, discrete set of values.
- So the notion of state is the same, only we may treat it differently from one *universe of discourse* to another *universe of discourse*!
- In this chapter we shall take the last view: That the system to be considered, i.e., the *universe of discourse*, is already — or has already been abstracted into — a system of discrete states.
- That is, in the present chapter we shall take a state to designate something *stable*.
- In all cases, *states represent summaries of past behaviour*.

4.1 Introduction

We shall, in this section, treat notions of contexts and states[1], as we have come to be familiar with them in computing. As a whole, i.e., viewed as a pair, we shall refer to these as configurations. We do so by first treating these notions as we claim they occur in "the real world"!

But first, we present some examples from computing. In computing, *environments* are associations of names (identifiers) with their values (including denotations). And in computing, *states* are aggregates of named values of assignable and control variables when a model is imperatively expressed, or of a (usually named) structure of applicatively 'passed' and 'returned' values (of immutable[2] variables) when a model is functionally expressed.

Example 4.1 *Applicative and Imperative States:*

value
    fact: **Nat** $\to$ **Nat**
    fact(n) $\equiv$
        if n=0
           then 1
           else n∗fact(n−1) end

variable
    r:**Nat** := 1;
value
    fact: **Nat** $\to$ **read** r **write** r **Nat**
    fact(n) $\equiv$
        for i in ⟨1..n⟩ do r := r∗i end; r

In the applicative definition, above left, the state of the described computation is represented partly by the decreasing formal parameter (i.e., argument) value, n, partly by the accumulating expression value n∗fact(n−1). In the

---

[1]Usually what we here call 'context' is, in connection with programming language semantics, called 'environment'. Similarly what we here call 'state' is, in connection with programming language semantics, called 'storage'.

[2]Immutable: Not capable of or susceptible to change.

imperative definition, above right, the state of the described computation is represented by the value of assignable variable r and the value of the control variable counter i.

∎

Contexts summarise which name/value associations are in effect. States summarise past computations. Actions effect state changes and take place in a context. States and actions "go together". Contexts are bindings of user-defined identifiers and their denotations. Contexts and bindings "go together". States reflect the dynamics of program execution. Contexts reflect the statics of program planning. User-defined identifiers (i.e., names) have a scope and a span. The scope determine where an identifier can be used. The span of a user-defined identifier determine a largest computational interval[3] encompassing those of the scope of that identifier.

Contexts and states thus are relevant for programming. In this chapter we shall see that contexts and states are relevant for understanding domains and for expressing requirements as well.

Example 4.2 *Context and Bindings:* For the applicative case (cf. Example 4.1 left part) each recursive invocation of fact binds n to a new value in the environment. For the imperative case (cf. Example 4.1 right part) the context, i.e., the environment associates program variable or control identifiers to their storage locations, respectively values (viz.: r,i).

For both cases: The scope is that of the block, i.e., the function definition, excluding contained blocks (and function invocations)[4]. The span is the (allocation) computation interval of the variable.

∎

With computing, the concepts of environments and their bindings, and of states (storages) and actions (statements, i.e., operations on states), have become central notions.

In the world of computing a state is a summary of a computation and is represented by the value of a number of variables. In that same world an action is something that changes the value of some variables, i.e., the state.

---

[3]Usually the literature uses the term 'lifetime' where we use the term 'computational interval'. The distinction may be subtle: The fact that computation takes time usually has no influence on the values, the results, being computed. That is, it does not, or should not have any bearing on the computation and hence its result. Therefore, to speak about lifetime when the notion of time is not material may be a bit misleading. At this stage we prefer to be more precise and say 'computation interval' with the meaning: *A span of computations, stretching from a first action to a last action.*

[4]The block and the function definition (function name, formal parameter list and body) concepts are basically the same and are motivated by the pragmatic desire to group names and their meaning into "localities", into contexts — thus enabling us, the developers and readers of these texts, to focus our attention on small pieces of specification and program texts.

A context is something that prescribes which names (identifiers) are relevant, and with which values (denotations), at a certain step of a computation.

In the world of applications — say one in which we need not necessarily speak of computing — a state (viz.: "a state of affairs") is also represented by the values of a number of components of that "actual" world. An action is still that "something" which changes the values of these components. A context, finally, is that which focuses on which — of many — components are worth our attention.

There are two dualities "buried" here [(i–ii)]. There is the obvious one that relates the two worlds just sketched. That is, (i) the duality of what goes on "inside the computer" vis-à-vis what goes on "out there, in an 'actual' world"; (ii) and the duality of states and computations: of states as summaries of past computations. That is, we can capture "whole" or "part" computations in states, as values — and vice versa. That is the duality. In this section we shall explore both dualities.

We have a few words to say about the latter duality:

- The number zero can be thought of as a function. Whenever applied, it returns the value zero:

$$z = \lambda x.0$$

We could claim that this function is data: the value 0.

- Any natural number, n, can now be thought of as an appropriate composition of successor functions:

$$s = \lambda x.x + 1, \underbrace{s^\bullet s^\bullet s^\bullet \cdots {}^\bullet s}_{n-1}$$

We could claim that this function stands for a computation: one that computes n.

Other illustrations will be made in due time.

The example shows that the decision of what is "put into a state" versus "what is put into a computation" (over such a state) is a pragmatic one. That is, there are no absolutes here.

Computations occur in "time"[5]-space: Actions take "time" to execute, and actors require resources that occupy physical space. Computational states can therefore be associated with a *dynamic*, i.e., *temporal* notion of change of the values of the computing resources. These latter are the actors that are implied by the program texts which prescribe computations. In contrast, computational contexts (environments) are usually associated with a *static*,

---

[5] When we put double quotes around terms we are trying to communicate something "half" meant, "half" intimated. Above, we really do not mean 'time', but rather computation sequence or interval: one after the previous! It is not that any one of them "takes time to execute"; they may well do. But the exact time of whether one execution time is longer than another is immaterial.

i.e., a *syntactic* notion of program prescriptional texts. Colloquially speaking, we can say that states change "more frequently" than contexts, the former in response to single statements, the latter in response to blocks of statements. That is, the syntactic notion of a block (of program text) is, and has been, introduced — from the very early days of computing, the late 1950s — in order to "bundle" into contexts the naming and use of such resources as identifiers denoting values or variable locations. Thus the notion of a context is a practical or pragmatic notion. The notion of state is more often forced upon us by necessities, by the semantics of an "actual world" and of computing.

The delineations attempted above are indeed attempts: The characterisations are approximate. Since the computational concepts are man-made, and since computing, as of 2005, is "hardly" 50 years old, the concepts — as we discuss them in this introductory part of this chapter — cannot be made fully concise.

Later in this chapter we shall impose our own, stricter characterisations, but the reader should be prepared to accept other, albeit not that different, characterisations of the *state* and **context** notions. Also, the reader may have observed that we seem to "waver" between using the term 'context' and the term 'environment'. The latter, as we shall use it in these volumes, has been in use since around 1960, and then rather specifically in connection with the explanation of programming language semantics. We have additionally introduced the term 'context' in these volumes in order not to fall into a simple trap of reducing every "actual world" phenomenon to that of a programming (or, more widely, to that of a specification) language concept.

4.2 The Issues

We summarise, in a terser, enumerative form, the concepts mentioned in the introductory part of this section. The following concepts are important for our understanding, i.e., represent an essence of the combined notions of states and actions (hence actors), contexts and bindings (hence binders):

- We shall use the term **state** in two senses. One is *syntactic*; the other is *semantic*.
  - ⋆ By a **state** we syntactically mean the structuring of a number of components (i.e., variables) into "the state" — that which we choose to consider (versus that which is left out or not considered).
  - ⋆ By a **state** we semantically mean the value of these components (i.e., variables).

  The decision as to which components to put into the state is usually the result of a longer analysis. Volume 3, Chap. 10 will (additionally) consider a number of these analysis principles.
- **Computation**: a sequence of state changes afforded by an execution as prescribed by a sequence of statements.

- **Sequential process**: A term which we use alternatively to designate a computation, i.e., a sequence of actions (in the real world).
- **Event**: an atomic phenomenon. An event is something which either spontaneously or deliberately "happens": *an overflow upon addition inside a computer, the reaching of the end of a road; the breakdown of a motor, the synchronisation and communication between two (or more) processes (a [broadcast] rendezvous)*, etc. Events usually cause consequential (sometimes remedial) actions to happen, or to be required to happen.
- **Action**: a term which we use alternatively to designate an atomic step of computation, often the effect of (viz. "triggered" by) an event.
- **Actor**: that which carries out an action, the computer (in the world of computing) or some agent (in the "actual world"). Actors of some "imagined, i.e., perceived real world" are resources like machines, people, "Mother Nature", etc. Again, in Vol. 3, Chap. 10, we shall systematically cover some so-called dynamic domain characteristics of an actual world and the actions and actors of this dynamics.
- **Statement**: a statement is a piece of text which prescribes an action to be carried out by some actor.
- **Context**: statements usually contain identifiers which refer to entities ("things", phenomena, concepts, components) — from a class of such. A context identifies which of several alternative, but specific phenomena is being referred to.
- **Binding**: a binding associates identifiers (names) with their designated phenomena. A binding establishes (i.e., 'is') an identification.
- **Allocation**: actors represent resources, *a vehicle (train, airplane)*, a computer, *a storage location*. In order for an action to take place an actor must be allocated to it. Allocations thus serve as placeholders of actors.
- **Freeing**: when an actor is no longer required it may be freed, made available to carry out other actions.
- **Binder**: a binder is a piece of text which prescribes a binding to be "in force" over some span of activity.

4.3 "Real-World" Contexts and States

We continue to put double quotes around the term "actual (or real) world". The reason is, of course, that we will never "really know" what that world is: We perceive it; several people can agree on a number of observations made about it; but they must also agree that their perception is an abstraction. That is, their perception has focused on certain properties while "suppressing" other properties. From now on we shall be less discursive about our subject, and more definitive. We shall impose certain views, while hoping that these views are generally applicable and broadly acceptable.

4.3.1 A Physical System: Context and State

We will illustrate some issues of physical system context and state modelling using just one example (Example 4.3). Later we shall illustrate similar modelling issues for a man-made system.

Example 4.3 *A Liquid Container System (I): Context and State (1):* This example will be continued, as Example 4.5.[6] It is important for the reader to distinguish between what the examples are about and what the examples attempt to illustrate wrt. methodological principles and techniques. The latter are currently, in these volumes, the important aspect. The former are, although not entirely accidental, only "carriers": The specific formulas (including axioms and calculations) are just "school" examples.

The liquid container system (Fig. 4.1) consists of a container (a tank), an intake pipe with a valve, an outtake pipe also with a valve, an overflow pipe (without a valve), and some liquid fluid. The cross-sectional area of the tank is fixed and is area A. The intake and overflow pipes are both placed with their lower level at height hi over the container bottom. The outtake valve is placed with its lower level at height lo over the tank bottom. The valves can either be in a fully open or in a fully closed position.[7] When open, an intake valve will supply the container with s (s: supply) units of volume measure of liquid per unit of time. When open, an outtake valve will withdraw w (w: withdraw) units of volume measure of liquid per unit of time from the tank. The overflow pipe withdraw capacity, o (o: overflow), "matches" or exceeds ($o \geq s$) the intake pipe supply capacity. A capacity meter senses the current height of liquid fluid in the container.

In modelling this system we choose the following context and state: context: the tank measures area A, maximum height H, the in- and outflow capacities s, o, and w, and the in- and outtake pipe positions hi and lo. State: the current height h ("implements" the capacity measure meter), and the two controllable valves, each with their open, closed status. Comments: We need not model all the other facets of the liquid fluid container system — the liquid content, the amount of change of liquid content as valves open and close, etc. — as their values are governed by laws of nature.   ∎

4.3.2 Configurations of Contexts and States

The borderline between *when to consider something as part of a context,* and *when to consider it part of a state* is "soft", i.e., is one of pragmatics. We shall introduce the term 'configuration' to stand for the model component that combines the context and the state components (of a physical or a man-made phenomenon, or, inter alia, of a man-made intellectual concept).

---

[6]The liquid container system example will be further continued in Example 11.1.

[7]For the purposes of this example it is not necessary to consider intermediate opening and closing valve positions.

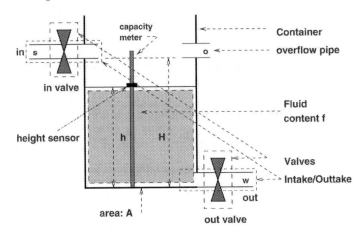

Fig. 4.1. A liquid container system: the physics

type
    Config = Context × Σ

Usually configurations will be the only semantic arguments to the function definitions that otherwise specify model behaviour.

4.3.3 Nonphysical System: Context and State

The next example illustrates notions of context and states of man-made systems. The idea is to show that the same pragmatic abstraction delineations (context and state) apply.

Example 4.4 *A Bank System Context and State:*

The Context

We focus in this example on the demand/deposit aspects of an ordinary bank. The bank has clients k:K. Clients have one or more numbered accounts c:C. Accounts, a:A, may be shared between two or more clients. Each account is established and "governed" by an initial contract, ℓ:L ('L' for legal). The account contract specifies a number of parameters: the yield, by rate (i.e., percentage), y:Y, due the client on positive deposits; the interest, by rate (i.e., percentage), i:I, due the bank on negative deposits less than a normal credit limit, n:N; the period (frequency), f:F, between (of) interest and yield calculations; the number of days, d:D, between bank statements sent to the client; and personal client information, p:P (name, address, phone number, etc.).

The State

Above we focused on the "syntactic" notion of a client/account contract and what it prescribed. We now focus on the "semantic" notion of the client account. The client account a:A contains the following information: the balance, b:B (of monies in the account, whether debit or credit, i.e., whether positive or negative), a list of time-stamped transactions "against" the account: establishment, deposits, withdrawals, transfers, interest/yield calculation, whether the account is frozen (due to its exceeding the credit limit), or (again) freed (due to restoration of balance within credit limits), issue of statement, and closing of account. Each transaction records the transaction type, and if deposit, withdrawal or transfer and the amount involved, as well as possibly some other information.

A Model

We consider contract information a contextual part of the bank configuration, while the account part is considered a state part of the bank configuration. We may then model the bank as follows:

type
   K, C, Y, I, N, D, P, B, T
   [Bank: Configuration]
   Bank = $\Gamma \times \Sigma$
   [Γ: Context]
   Γ = (K $\underset{m}{\rightarrow}$ C-set) × (C $\underset{m}{\rightarrow}$ L)
   L == mkL(y:Y,i:I,n:N,f:F,d:D,p:P)
   [Σ: State]
   Σ = C $\underset{m}{\rightarrow}$ A
   A = {free|frozen} × B × (T × Trans)*
   Trans = Est|Dep|Wth|Xfr|**Int**|Yie|Frz|Fre|Stm|Sha|Clo
   Dep == deposit(m:**Nat**)
   Wth == withdraw(m:**Nat**)
   Xfr == toxfer(to:C,m:**Nat**) | fmxfer(fm:C,m:**Nat**)
   Sha == share(new:C,old:C)

Bank is here the configuration.[8] Γ is the context. Σ is the state.   ∎

4.3.4 Discussion, I

The banking system so far outlined is primarily a dynamic, programmable system: Most transactions, when obeyed, change the (account) state $\sigma{:}\Sigma$. A

---

[8]But, the bank configuration could, in more realistic situations, include many other components not related directly to the client/account "business".

few (to wit: establish, share) change the context $\gamma:\Gamma$. Establishment occurs exactly once in the lifetime of an account. Initially contracts, from which the $\gamma:\Gamma$ configuration component is built, are thought of as specifying only one client. Hence the share transaction, which "joins" new clients to an account, could as well be thought of as an action: one changing the state, rather than the context. We have arbitrarily chosen to model it as a context changing "action"! All this to show that the borderline between context and state is "soft": It is a matter of choice.

4.3.5 Discussion, II

Notice that, although time enters into the banking model, we did not model time flow explicitly. Here, in the man-made system model, it is considered "outside" the model. We claim that the concepts of context and state enter, in complementary ways, into both physical systems and man-made systems. Before proceeding with more detailed analysis of the configuration (cum context $\oplus$ state) ideas, let us recall that these concepts are pragmatic.

4.4 First Summary: Contexts and States

4.4.1 General

The (system and language semantics) configuration concepts of contexts and states intertwine. Decisions on what to include in the context and what to include in the state (i) influence one another, (ii) depend on our ability to state laws that relate values of context and state components and (iii) is otherwise an art!

Characterisation. By the *context* of a system, or of the evaluation of a program, or of a specification in some programming, respectively some specification language, we usually understand an aggregation, a structuring, of those components whose values remain fixed. That is, we understand those components whose values can be considered constant over some "sizable" ("macro") time interval, or over the sequence of many events or actions (operations), or over the evaluation of a sizable textual, so-called block part of a program or of a specification.   ∎

So a context is modelled by an abstract or concrete type and has a value. It is usually syntactically determined: "one half" of the context, the identifiers (the names) being associated, is fully determined statically by some prescription text. The decision as to what to relegate to the context influences what to "put in" the state, and vice versa.

Characterisation. By the *state* of a system or of the evaluation of a program or of a specification in some programming, respectively some specification language, we usually understand an aggregation, a structuring, of those components whose values change (i) over time, or (ii) over the sequence of one or more events, or (iii) as the result of actions (operations), or (iv) over the evaluation of any textual part of a program or a specification — no matter how close in time, and how many such events and actions there are.   ∎

So a state is modelled by an abstract or concrete type and has values. It is usually semantically determined; it depends on the "course", the behaviour of computation. The full force of abstraction plays an important role in the design of the context and the state of a system model.

Characterisation. By a *configuration* we mean a pair of contexts and states appropriate for a consistent and complete elaboration of a system or a syntactic text.   ∎

Model Versus Specification States

Let us remind ourselves that we construct specifications to model some phenomenon — including the modelling of a notion of state of that phenomenon while at the same time using a specific specification language such that an evaluation of a specification in that language gives rise to a state. The former is the model state; the latter is the specification state. The two are (thus) not the same. But, in a good specification, they relate. We shall keep this in mind in the following and point out which are the model states, which are the specification states, and their relationships.

4.4.2 Development Principles and Techniques

Principles. *Context and State:* In any programming or specification language, and in any system, determine early in the domain analysis phase whether separable concepts can be "equated" with context and state notions. If so, follow the modelling techniques outlined below.   ∎

Techniques. *Context Design:* In analysing a system, or in analysing a (specification or programming) language, determine which names or which identifiers are being used, i.e., stand for statically knowable entities. That is, determine which names remain "constant" during the lifetime of the system, respectively during the elaboration of well-delineated parts of the specification or program text. Earmark those name designations to be part of the context.   ∎

Techniques. *State Design:* In analysing a system, or in analysing a (specification or programming) language, determine which names or identifiers are being used, i.e., stand for dynamically changing entities. That is, determine which names "vary" in value or even number (quality, respectively quantity) throughout the lifetime of the system, respectively during the elaboration (i.e., computation interval) of even well-delineated parts of the specification or program text. Earmark those name designations to be part of the state. ∎

4.5 Programming Language Configurations

In Vol. 1, Chap. 20, we gave examples of three formal definitions of a block structured, but otherwise simple imperative programming language. In those definitions environments, binding variable identifiers to locations, served the role of contexts, and storages, binding locations to values, served the role of states. We modelled the semantics of this one language in three ways: We first modelled both contexts and states applicatively, then we modelled contexts applicatively and states imperatively and finally we modelled both contexts and states imperatively. All three examples illustrated the concept of contexts and states. All we shall do presently, in this section on configurations is to remind the reader that we have already covered the subject somewhat extensively. The reader is thus encouraged to go back to study Vol. 1, Chap. 20.

4.6 Concurrent Process Configurations

By a concurrent process model we mean a model which expresses multiple concurrent behaviours. This is in contrast to a sequential model, which expresses a single behaviour. Recall that models of sequentiality can be expressed in the applicative or in the imperative style, or in combinations thereof. The same goes for concurrent models.

4.6.1 The Example

It may be a bit far-fetched to claim, as we now do, that we can model the concepts of context and state by means of processes. So, let us turn it around and say instead: *How would the concepts of context and state be expressed in a process-oriented model?* We will illustrate this style of modelling through Example 4.5 which is a continuation of Example 4.3.

Example 4.5 *A Liquid Container System, II: Context and State:* We continue Example 4.3. The present example will find another formulation in Example 11.9.

The present example consists of three parts: a domain analysis, a requirements and a software design. Some preliminary comments on these parts are:

The domain analysis is somewhat extensive; the requirements is somewhat "loose", being short; and the design is formalised.

The purpose of this extended example is to show the interplay between the *context* and the *state* concepts. We shall, in this second step of the development of the *liquid tank system*, take the view that the system is a *dynamic reactive* system (cf. Volume 3, Chap. 10).

Domain Analysis: Text

Figure 4.5[A]–[D], mentioned in this section, have been put at the end of this section for technical reasons.

When studying a domain we usually *domain-analyse* its behaviour before *narrating* (and *formalising*) possible *requirements*. We shall therefore in this section devote quite some space to a systems analysis.

To get an idea about how the *liquid container system* might behave when subjected to arbitrary open and closed positions of valves, please consider Fig. 4.5[A].

In Figs. 4.5[A]–[B] we assume that the contextually determined s and w relate as s = 2*w. Setting the valve openings as shown then, illustratively, results in the state behaviour as shown. Between times t_2 and t_3 and times t_9 and t_{10} the overflow valve is in use. Between times t_5 and t_6 the outflow valve is unnecessarily open: The tank has already been emptied. As from time t_{11} and onward (that is, beyond time t_{12}) the container content remains constant.

To get an idea about how the *liquid container system* might behave when subjected to controlled open and closed positions of valves, please consider Fig. 4.5[B].

Figure 4.5[B] reflects an experiment set up so that valves will not be unnecessarily open. That is, there will not be overflows: no open inflow valve with full tank, and no empty tank with open outflow valve. To get an idea about how the *liquid tank system state* might behave for different relations between the *contextually determined inflow (s) and outflow (w) capacities, please consider Fig. 4.5[C].

We briefly comment on Fig. 4.5[C]. If we open both valves for s=w in an initial state with an empty tank, then the tank will remain empty (this case is not shown). Cases 4 and 5 show the effect of "similar controls" for different relations between s and w.

To get an idea about how to control the settings of the intake and outtake valves in order to "fit" the actual filling (or emptying) of the *liquid container system* to a given, desired curve, let us consider Fig. 4.5[D].

In Fig. 4.5[D] we assume that there is a smallest time interval between (OPEN/CLOSED) valve settings. Let this interval be designated Δ. Then we see that, for some desired curves, shown with dashed, slanted lines, there are two (or more) ways of achieving the curve. The particular cases shown illustrate, in *experiments 1* and *3*, that a curve can be approximated by repeated

OPEN/CLOSED settings, while in *experiments 2* a curve can, probably in statistically "rare" cases, be achieved by a more "constant", though time-limited, simultaneous setting of the two valves.

A Word of Warning

The reader should, by now, be aware that we are stepping onto "dangerous" ground if we believe we can just simply argue our way into the software engineer deciding on the control algorithm for the valve opening and closing to achieve arbitrary curves. This is not computer or computing science "stuff"; this is a control theory and control engineering subject. So we shall leave it with that — and bring in the example only to show: (i) the need, in most software development cases, for joint collaboration with other engineering professionals, and (ii) how that collaboration is faced with both control theoretic problems and software development problems. Determining proper Δ's, for example, is a deep problem of control theory in the realm of sampling theory.

Domain Analysis: Figures

Comments on the Semantics of Fig. 4.5[A]

The upper part of Fig. 4.5[A] shows the simple ON/OFF values of the indicated two valves and as a function of time. A shaded area means ON; no shading means OFF. The lower part of Fig. 4.5 shows the liquid height of the container as a function of time. When the intake valve is ON, the outtake valve is OFF, and the height is less than the maximal height, then the contents are rising, and so on.

Comments on the Semantics of Fig. 4.5[B]

Note in Fig. 4.5[B] that when both valves are open and the height is less than maximal, then either the height is rising slower than when the outtake valve is closed, for s<w, or is falling, for w>s.

Comments on the Semantics of Fig. 4.5[C]

The "semantics" of Fig. 4.5[C] is the same as for Figs. 4.5[A] and 4.5[B],

Comments on the Semantics of Fig. 4.5[D]

The upper part of Fig. 4.5[D] has same semantics as for the related previous figures. The lower half only indicates some properties that are dealt with in the text.

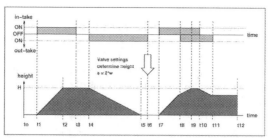

[A] Time trace of monitored system behaviour, s=2*w

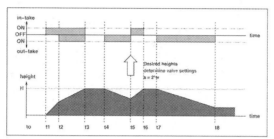

[B] Time trace of controlled system behaviour, s=2*w

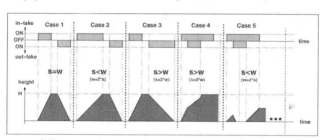

[C] Time trace of controlled system behaviours

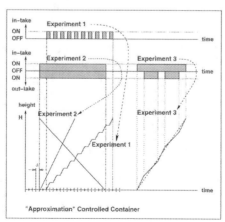

[D] Time trace of curve-fitting controlled system behaviours

Fig. 4.2. The liquid container system traces

Requirements

We are now ready to specify possible requirements to a *liquid tank control system:* given a desired filling curve, and an initial setting of valves and an initial height of liquid in the container, to control valve settings so as to achieve a reasonable fit of actual filling state (i.e., height) to desired curve. The above formulation is "loose" in the sense that questions could be raised as to the precise meaning of a number of its terms and phrases. We will leave this (albeit serious, objectionable) aspect of the requirements to be resolved by techniques that are systematically covered in Vol. 3, Chaps. 17–24 (Requirements Engineering). Instead, we assume that the form of the desired curve is presented to the (required) *control system* such that it can compare the *dynamic state behaviour* to the *static prescription* (i.e., the desired curve), and from this comparison draw its conclusions as to which valve settings to change or leave unchanged at the end of each time interval.

A Software Design

We see the overall *liquid tank system* monitoring and control software process as consisting of four component processes: the system process, two valve processes and the height-metering process (Fig. 4.3).[9]

These processes are connected by input/output channels, as shown in Figure 4.3. The valve processes contain both sensors and actuators. Only the height metering process is autonomous: It contains just a sensor.

We suggest a formalisation:

type
    Supply, Withdraw, Height
    Curve_Script
    Valve == open | closed
channel
    rh:Height, riv,rov,wiv,wov:Valve
variable
    $\sigma{:}\Sigma$

---

[9]Figure 4.3 shows as four rounded corner boxes four processes. Tracing the box outline in the direction of their arrows designates a process behaviour. Thus the processes are here all seen as cyclic. Imagine a token passing around the box outline. At any point it designates a process point. The four fat dots designate process starting points. The arrows that connect two processes designate channels, and the directions indicated by the arrows designate which process outputs and which process inputs (arrowhead) a message. When two processes have reached the program points where one channel intersects respective box outlines, then a rendezvous between the two processes can take place: They are synchronised and can communicate a value. The Δ designates a Δ time unit delay. Bracketed numerals ([0], [1], [2], [3] and [4]) are program point labels and refer to program points in the formal text.

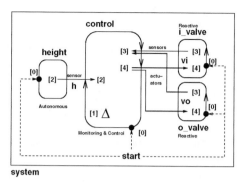

Fig. 4.3. A liquid container system: a process model

value
  s:Supply, w:Withdraw, H:Height

  system: Valve×Valve×Curve_Script×Time → **Unit**
  system(ioc,ooc,cs,it) ≡ i_valve(ioc)∥o_valve(ooc)∥control(cs,it)∥height()

  i_valve: Valve → **read** iv **out** iv **Unit**
  i_valve(ioc) ≡ [0] **variable** vi:Valve := ioc;
    while true do [3] riv!vi; [4] vi := wiv? **end**
  o_valve: Valve → **read** iv **out** iv **Unit**
  o_valve(ooc) ≡ [0] **variable** vi:Valve := ooc;
    while true do [3] rov!vo; [4] vo := wov? **end**

  control: Curve_Script × Time → **read** σ **write** σ **Unit**
  control(cs,it) ≡ [0] **variable** tv:Time := it;
    while true do
        wait Δ;
        let (i,o) = calc((s,w,H),cs,(tv,[1]rh?,[2]riv?,[2]rov?)) **in**
        [3] (wiv!i∥wov!o) **end**; tv := tv + Δ
    end

  calc: (Supply × Withdraw × Height)
          × Curve_Script
              × (Time × Height × Valve × Valve)
                  → **read** σ **write** σ Valve × Valve

We comment on the *software design* model: We use an imperative version of
the RSL process concept as introduced in Vol. 1, Chap. 21. Time is rather
crudely modelled as a variable of the *system* process. The valve settings are
modelled as variables of respective *valve* processes. Valve sensors are modelled

as the reading (riv?,rov? [1,2]) of valve settings. Valve actuators are modelled as the writing (wiv!,wov! [3]) of valve settings. The height sensor is modelled as a further unexplained reading (rh? [1]) from the autonomous *height* process. The regular sensing and actuation at Δ time intervals is modelled by a **wait** Δ time period extension to RSL [132, 204] (Sect. 15.4). We assume that computation time around the system loop is modelled reasonably accurately by the Δ time period.

We do not further specify the calc algorithm by means of which new valve settings are computed other than specifying that it is calculated on the basis of the following values: the three **contextual** values (i–ii) supply and withdraw capacities (s,w), and (iii) the maximum height (H). (iv) The desired curve script (cs): The three **contextual** values (i–iii) are intended to be stable, i.e., to remain unchanged over a long time, or over many different uses of the same or different curve scripts. The curve script is intended to be relatively stable, i.e., to remain unchanged over some time, or over many different uses (of that same script). Thus a curve script is a relative context quantity, as are the four **state** values: (v) current time (tv), (vi) current height (rh?) and (vii viii) the current valve settings (riv?,rov?). calc accumulates, in a global variable, $\sigma : \Sigma$, the past history of the curve fitting so as to find an optimal tactic for setting the switches.

The software design model just presented is idealistic. It assumes perfectly functioning channel communications, sensors and actuators. Although the calc state (σ) could remember the previous valve settings we have included their sensing anyway — in preparation, it is here suggested, for a sensor/actuator (etc.) system that may fail. ■

4.6.2 Summary

We have seen a first example of the process modelling of a system. We shall often have occasion to illustrate such system process models. We have modelled what appears to be physically separably identifiable and more or less independently operating components as processes: One process per component. The *phenomena shared* between two or more such components have been modelled by **channels**. We have defined some of these processes, but only given signature to others (here just the height process). The physical world of dynamic system sensors and actuators — and their sensing and actuation — have, in the design specification presented here, been abstracted as state variables that are read, respectively written. Because of the process decomposition, these readings and writings occur as the result of **channel** events: pairs of output/inputs (!/?).

One can combine process modelling with either the applicative or the imperative style model. Here we have used the applicative context and the imperative state style.

Characterisation. By a *process context* we understand a concept of context which has been modelled either as a global constant (thus trivially accessible from a process function definition), or as a process function definition argument that is passed unchanged to possibly recursive invocations of the designated process.   ∎

Characterisation. By a *process state* we understand a concept of state which has been modelled either as a global variable (thus trivially accessible and update-able from a process function definition), or as a process function definition argument that is usually (i) passed to possibly recursive invocations of the designated process with changed values, or (ii) is a local, imperative process definition variable.   ∎

Techniques. *Process Context:* Two possibilities offer themselves: If use of (access to) process context values can be restricted to a single, or a few function invocations — within a single, or a few process function definitions — and hence their respective function definition(s), then the model context can be [exceptionally, and as shown in Example 4.5] modelled as global values. Otherwise the process context values should be modelled as arguments passed to relevant functions: initially as formal parameters of an initial system invocations, and otherwise unchanged to subsequent functions.   ∎

Principles often have the fate of never being strict. The above is an example.

Techniques. *Process State:* Three possibilities offer themselves: If use of (i.e., access to/reading of, or update of/writing to) process state values can be restricted to a single process function (definition), then the model context can either be modelled by (a) global or by (b) local variables. Otherwise, (c) the process state values should be modelled as arguments passed to relevant functions: initially as formal parameters of an initial system invocations, and otherwise, possibly [and usually] changed, to subsequent functions.   ∎

4.7 Second Summary: Contexts and States

We have, as mentioned earlier in this chapter and in three examples of Vol. 1, Chap. 20, shown three styles of modelling contexts and states.[10] Usually, in particular when abstracting domains, we start a sequence of developments with applicative style models, then we proceed to change state models from the applicative to the imperative style. Sometimes, when introducing process-oriented models, a stage and stepwise development is advised, one which goes

---

[10]We remind the reader: In modelling block-structured, procedural programming languages, we can model contexts applicatively or imperatively, and we can model storages (i.e., states) applicatively or imperatively. It seemed to not be a good idea to model contexts imperatively, but states applicatively!

from an applicative (nonprocess) to an applicative process model, and only from there to a process model with imperative states. It does not seem to be a reasonable style to model contexts imperatively and states applicatively. The process style seems a most relevant first step of requirements or software design abstraction when the system being modelled is dynamic reactive, as shown in Example 4.5.

4.8 Information States and Behaviour States

So far we have presented two views of states: states as information summaries, and states as behaviour summaries.

States as Information or Data Summaries: In the real world we have at any time gathered some information and we have discarded some of that information. That is, we have an information state. In analogy: In a computation we have a state of the variables, that is, a data state.

States as Behaviour or Process Summaries: In the real world the usually complex phenomena are at any time at some point in their concurrent and stepwise behaviour. That point represents a state in analogy to the state of the computation process: The program point at which execution control presently resides.

In this section we wish to show that the two views are not that different, just two sides of the same coin.

4.8.1 Program Flowcharts as State Machine Data

Every program flowchart can instead be represented as a finite state machine (Fig. 4.4). Diamond-shaped boxes with Greek letter labels designate predi-

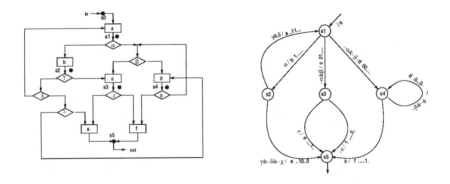

Fig. 4.4. "Equivalent" flowchart and finite state machine

cate decisions. A left exit from the diamond-shaped box can be, but is not, annotated with that label; whereas a right exit can be, but is likewise also not, labeled with its negation. Rectangular boxes with Roman letter labels designate actions. We can associate a state (labelled *s1–s5*) with the first in arrow to a sequence of one or more decision boxes. Initial and final states are then associated with the initial and final starting actions. Finite state machine transitions are now the pairs of sequences of decision box (left or right exit) annotations and action labels.

4.8.2 Flowcharts ≡ Machines

The predicates $\alpha, \beta, \ldots, \omega$ evaluate either to **true** (1) or **false** (0). Generally all have to be evaluated in each state, but some values are ignored (.) [i.e., are "don't care" values]. In Fig. 4.4 this is shown by the seven symbol-long ('0', or '.', or '1') character sequences next to each action label. These $\langle \alpha, \beta, \gamma, \delta, \epsilon, \phi, \xi \rangle$ "Boolean" vectors (including dotted "don't care" designations) are listed as if there were ten different symbols. But that is only conceptually so. The vector $\langle 1.....\rangle$ is, for example, contained in any of the vectors $\langle .0...0.\rangle$, $\langle ....1..\rangle$, $\langle .....0.\rangle$, $\langle ..10..0\rangle$ and $\langle .....1.\rangle$. The idea of predicate vector $\langle \alpha, \beta, \gamma, \delta, \epsilon, \phi, \xi \rangle$ values is best expressed, we believe, by using this seemingly ambiguous shorthand.

Should an action box contain just a simple, i.e., a direct, recursive "invocation of flowchart", then a stack is added to the finite state machine representation, the current state pushed onto that stack (etc.), and a new "image" of the finite state machine started in the initial state. Reaching a final state of such a recursive flowchart then results in popping any stacked states and resuming as from such a state in a thus recovered finite state control.

The "moral" is: Every program flowchart can be represented as a possibly stack-oriented state machine.

4.8.3 Flowchart Machines

Thus the consequence is: Any program can be converted (transformed) into a normalised program of program schematic form. That of our conceptual example becomes:

```
variable s := s0;
let fsm = ... in
a: actions_a;
while s ≠ s5 do
    let input = Eval(α,β,γ,δ,ε,φ,ξ) in
    let (s',act) = fsm(s,input) in
    case act of
        b → actions_b,
        c → actions_c,
        d → actions_d,
```

    e → actions_e,
    f → actions_f
  end ;
  s := s'
end end end end

Here a, b, c, ..., f stand for encoded action labels, and actions_a, actions_b, actions_c, ..., actions_f for corresponding actions. The Eval function expresses that the decision box predicates are evaluated and lead to one of the input vectors of $\langle \alpha, \beta, \gamma, \delta, \epsilon, \phi, \xi \rangle$ "Boolean" values. They are not "quite" Boolean in that we additionally allow "don't care" (dot [.]) values. The state machine of Fig. 4.4 (right) can be presented in tabular form:

A Finite State Machine									
↓ states inputs →	..11...	1......	01.....	00.....	.0...0.	....1..	......0.	.....1.	..10..0
s1		(s2,b)	(s3,c)	(s4,d)					
s2	(s1,a)								(s5,e)
s3						(s5,e)	(s5,f)		
s4					(s4,d)			(s5,f)	

The input column dots (.) denote $\{0|1\}$ (either 0 or 1). Thus we really are dealing with a 2^7 character input alphabet shown in compressed form. Blank entries of the table are never encountered, and are thus left unspecified.

4.8.4 Observations

The conceptual program, i.e., the program schema above is also a flowchart, and corresponds to a one-state *flowchart machine* (Fig. 4.5).
This machine "mirrors" the way hardware (i.e., computers) has microprogrammed the control flow and instruction interpretation of compiled programs. Thus the conversion of an arbitrary flowchart program to normalised program schema form is really that of translating the arbitrary flowchart program to a microprogram for a software machine.

4.8.5 Conclusion

Computations based on flowcharts, i.e., on ordinary program text, as delivered by a programmer, operate with two state notions: a state of the ordinary program variables (the data), and the state of execution (the locus of control — the program pointer). Computations based on flowchart machines operate with two state notions: the data state, as before, and the computation state — which is now made into a control data state encompassing the finite state machine data (fsm) and the state control variable s. It is thus we see that the two state notions meet in the limit: The information (data) state and the

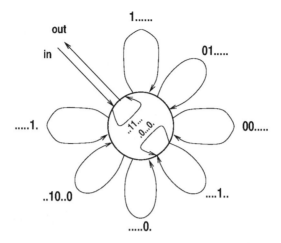

Fig. 4.5. A normalised [micro-] program flowchart machine

behaviour (computation, control) state are one and the same! We can "trade" one for the other.

Flowchart machines provide a normalised representation wherein every arbitrary program (via its flowchart) can be converted into a flowchart machine program. Thus a flowchart machine program is a specialised program that is "molded" over one "template".

The transformation of ordinary programs to machines is "folklore" [172]. The specific transformation, as indicated here, from regular flowcharts to machines is treated in [42]. The transformation from recursive flowcharts is indicated in both [42] and [43]. Chapter 11 treats the important engineering subject of state machines in some detail.

4.9 Final Summary: Contexts and States

The specification concepts of configurations, contexts and states are development concepts. As such they are meta-concepts. They are brought into consideration when abstractly modelling phenomena and actual concepts of the universe of discourse under investigation. Contexts model more or less static, i.e., syntactic — structural — attributes or properties. States model more or less dynamic, i.e., temporal — varying — attributes.

It is important, however, to observe that we are normally confronted with a "smooth" spectrum from more or less static to more or less dynamic attributes: For ordinary (non-GOTO) imperative programming languages with nested block structures, we have a relatively simple notion of contexts (i.e., ENVironments) and states (i.e., SToraGes):

value

M: Syntax $\overset{\sim}{\to}$ ENV $\overset{\sim}{\to}$ STG $\overset{\sim}{\to}$ STG

For imperative programming languages with nested block structures and GOTOs we have a slightly more composite notion of contexts (i.e., ENVironments), CONtinuations, and states (i.e., SToraGes):

value

M: Syntax $\overset{\sim}{\to}$ ENV $\overset{\sim}{\to}$ CON $\overset{\sim}{\to}$ STG $\overset{\sim}{\to}$ STG

For systems[11] we can have an even finer graduation:

value

M: Command $\overset{\sim}{\to}$ Ψ $\overset{\sim}{\to}$ Γ $\overset{\sim}{\to}$ Θ $\overset{\sim}{\to}$ Σ $\overset{\sim}{\to}$ Σ

Here we may think of Ψ defining a type of values of some constant *syntactical structuring* attributes, Γ defining a type of values of some, for example, seasonally regulated *tabular* attributes, Θ defining a type of values of some *continuation*-like attributes, and Σ as defining some type of values of *dynamic state* attributes.

Principles. *Configurations — Contexts and States:* In analysing any phenomenon, any concept, examine to which extent static and dynamic attributes determine overall behaviour. Then partition these phenomena and concepts into an appropriate spectrum from contextual to state attributes.   ■

Techniques. *Configurations — Contexts and States:* If the principle of configurations, contexts and states applies, then model the appropriate types in the spectrum and reflect these in the type of all relevant functions.   ■

4.10 Exercises

Exercise 4.1 *Traffic Nets: Configurations, Contexts and States.* References: We refer to earlier exercises:

- Exercise 2.3: *Road Net: Streets and Intersections*
- Exercise 2.4: *Air Traffic Route Net*
- Exercise 2.5: *Shipping Nets: Lanes and Harbours*

as well as to exercises in the next chapter:

- Exercise 5.3: *Road Traffic*
- Exercise 5.4: *Air Traffic*
- Exercise 5.5: *Sea and Harbour Traffic*

---

[11] We shall, in Sect. 9.5, more systematically discuss the notion of languages and systems.

Comment: To answer the present exercise you have to first have read the problem formulations of Exercises 2.3–2.5.

The Problem: For each of those exercises (i.e., 2.3–2.5) please identify configurations, contexts and states. If need be, try to restructure your type formalisations so as to, as clearly as possible, separate contexts from states.

Exercise 4.2 *Supermarkets (I).* You are asked to narrate and formalise a concept, such as you see it, of a supermarket, with shelves, price-tagged merchandise on shelves, a backup store from where near-empty or empty shelves can be replenished, consumers being in the supermarket, selecting merchandise from shelves and checking these out at a check counter. Assume each shelf to be typed with the merchandise it displays or is supposed to display.

What of the above, i.e., which entities of your model, constitute a (daily) context, and which constitutes the current state?

This exercise is continued in Exercise 5.1.

Exercise 4.3 *Manufacturing (I).* The Problem: The production "floor" of a metal-working and machine assembly factory (a manufacturing plant) consists of a fixed number of machines, $m_1, m_2, \ldots, m_\mu$ (lathes, drills, saws, cutters, etc.), a fixed number of trucks, $t_1, t_2, \ldots, t_\tau$ (that collect machine parts from a supply store, or from machine out-queues, and bring them to the in-queues of other machines or to a product store), and the two stores. Any machine consists of one in-queue, one out-queue and the machine tool (possibly robotic) itself.

A daily production plan, PP, describes a number of separate production scenarios: one for each product to be produced that day. For simplicity we assume sequential productions: One or more parts are brought from the supply store by an available truck to a specific machine, m_k, and processed by its tool. Then the result, which is to be considered one partial or completed, product, p_i, is brought to a next machine, $m_{k'}$, or to the product store. In the latter case that ends the production scenario. To that next machine, $m_{k'}$, may also be brought other supply parts and/or partial products, $p_{i_1}, p_{i_2}, \ldots, p_{i_m}$, to be processed together with p_i, etcetera.

The Question: Now formalise the above: the shop floor (machines and trucks), the stores and the production plan. Your model of a machine should include what is in its in- and out-queues, and whether a set of one or more parts is being processed, i.e., is "in" the tool. Similarly, your model of a truck should model where it is: in a store, at a machine, between the supply store and a machine, between two machines, or between a machine and the product store, and which parts it carries. Finally, your model of a production plan should, besides the production scenarios, also model which of the implied productions have yet to start, which have been completed, and, for the productions "in between", where they have come to in the production process.

What of the above, i.e., which entities of your model, constitutes a (daily) context, and which constitutes the current state?

This exercise is continued in Exercise 5.2.

Part III

A CRUCIAL DOMAIN AND COMPUTING FACET

In this short part, which comprises one chapter,

- we investigate a simple view of the concepts of **time, space** and **time/space**;
- we bring in some axiomatisations of these concepts; and
- we present some principles and techniques according to and using which we model phenomena of the **time** or **space** or **space/time** attribute.
- The simple view emphasises *quantitative* aspects of time.

In Part VI we will bring in separate, additional chapters on not only *qualitative* aspects of time:

- Petri Nets, Chap. 12,
- Message and Live Sequence Charts, Chap. 13,
- Statecharts, Chap. 14,

but also in Chap. 15 on *quantitative* aspects of time:

- Interval Temporal Logic (ITL),
- Duration Calculus (DC) and
- Timed RSL (TRSL).

5

Time, Space and Space/Time

- The **prerequisites** for studying this chapter are that you are thoroughly familiar with the abstraction and modelling principles and techniques covered so far, but that you have realised that issues of timing and space, and their combination, require special attention.
- The **aims** are to cover abstraction and modelling principles and techniques for some temporal or spatial phenomena, and for some combinations of these, while seeking some deeper understanding of time in particular.
- The **objective** is to make you reasonably competent in modelling time and space.
- The **treatment** is discursive, systematic, and formal, while at times additionally bordering on epistemological concerns.

Time and space are fundamental concepts. They enter into many aspects of domain and requirements models and into software design. Time has, since antiquity, been an almost philosophical problem. Space seemed, from the days of Euclid on, somehow easier to grasp — until Nikolai Lobachevsky introduced the notion of non-Euclidean geometries. Understanding space/time, as from Einstein, became rather more of an "exotic" undertaking.

In this chapter we shall take a look at these notions: Time, space, and space/time. Our coverage — here and in Chaps. 12–15 — restricts itself to the ways in which these notions, based on our experience, enter into our modelling processes and into our models.

In the present chapter we shall also introduce the notions of discrete and continuous (dense) time, and (dense) space. We will also examine events as changes in or occurrences of time, space or space/time, or — by analogy — events as changes in or occurrences of non-physical "measures". Finally we will look at behaviour as discrete or continuous traces (sequences) of physical (time, space, space/time) or nonphysical events.

Later chapters will then cover additional specification principles and techniques for special cases of temporal and concurrent phenomena.

5.1 Time

> (i) a moving image of eternity;
> (ii) the number of the movement
> in respect of the before and the after;
> (iii) the life of the soul in movement as it passes
> from one stage of act or experience to another;
> (iv) a present of things past: memory,
> a present of things present: sight,
> and a present of things future: expectations.
>
> *(i) Plato, (ii) Aristotle, (iii) Plotinus, (iv) Augustine; [17].*

5.1.1 Time — The Basics

Three of the above quotes refer to temporal notions, hence are circular, and hence are useless to our discussion of time. But they put our mind in the right direction — and poetically so. Still, we need to more precisely "encircle" concepts of time. "*Time* is the dimension of *change*, a fact which distinguishes it from the three dimensions of *space*" [216]. In Vol. 3, Chap. 10 we summarise time as a dynamic, active, autonomous domain. For the present chapter we wish to consider time from various other viewpoints.

Characterisation. For our mundane purposes we shall take a simplistic view of *time* as a totally (i.e., linearly) ordered dense point set.　　　　　∎

Time-Varying Entities = Dynamic Entities

Entities are of types and have values. The entities now considered do not have time as values. By a time-varying entity we mean an entity whose value may change with time.

Example 5.1 *Informal Examples of Time-Varying Entities:* The weather changes all the time, by itself, autonomously. A railway train timetable changes only when railway planners explicitly update it. (Such timetables are inert.) The state of a computer changes for every computer clock cycle, programmably.　　　　　∎

We shall take a closer look at some specific cases of time-varying entities.

Example 5.2 *Rail Unit States:* We remind the reader of our — by now — long sequence of examples that model one or another facet of railway systems. We saw earlier that a unit could be in either one of possibly several states: $\sigma \in \omega$. State changes occur over time. Thus we can "lift" our view of units from being units to being functions from time to (those previous kinds of) units:

type
  T, U, C
  UF = T → U
  Σ = (C × C)-**set**
  Ω = Σ-**set**
value
  obs_Cs: U → C-**set**
  obs_Σ: U → Σ
  obs_Ω: U → Ω
  reset_Σ: U → U

The above formalisation is one way of expressing things. Here is another way, which is a narrative: There is a set of time values of type T. There is a set of unit values of type U. There is a set of unit connector values of type C. A unit state (σ : Σ) is a set of paths, i.e., a set of pairs of connectors "through" a unit. Over a lifetime a unit can be in any one of possibly several states ω : Ω. From a unit we can observe its connectors, its state and its possible state space. The reset_Σ function "closes" a rail unit. That is, leaves it in a state with no paths open, but of the same state space:

value
  $\mathcal{D}$: (A $\xrightarrow{\sim}$ B) → D-**infset**, $\mathcal{R}$: (A $\xrightarrow{\sim}$ B) → B-**infset**
axiom
  $\forall$ u:U • obs_Σ(reset_Σ(u)) = {} $\wedge$ obs_Ω(u) = obs_Ω(reset_Σ(u)) $\wedge$ ...
  $\forall$ uf:UF,u,u':U • {u,u'}$\subseteq$$\mathcal{R}$uf $\Rightarrow$ reset_Σ(u)=reset_Σ(u')
      assert: obs_Ω(u)=obs_Ω(u')
  $\forall$ uf:UF,u,u':U • {u,u'} $\subseteq$ $\mathcal{R}$uf$\wedge$obs_Σ(u)$\neq$obs_Σ(u')
      $\Rightarrow$ $\exists$ t,t':T • {t,t'} $\subseteq$ $\mathcal{D}$uf $\Rightarrow$ uf(t)=u $\wedge$ uf(t')=u' $\wedge$ t$\neq$t'

The axioms express that the rail units of a unit function are indeed the "same" units. For any unit, its reset state is the empty set of paths. A reset unit has the same state space as that unit in any of its allowable states. Hence the closed, i.e., the empty state is always a member of the state space. For every timed unit, all its range units are the same, i.e., have the same state space, and if two of them are in different states then they are range units sampled at different times. $\mathcal{D}$ and $\mathcal{R}$ are not proper RSL functions: They yield the definition set, respectively the range, of any function. ∎

While time changes may change certain entity attributes others may remain the same. Example 5.3 illustrates this and indicates possible relations between time and space.

Example 5.3 *Dynamic Rail Nets*: From a rail net we can observe all its units. With any rail unit we can observe its spatial location: Assume, as a possibly refutable assertion, that no two units "occupy" overlapping "planes" of X, Y coordinates, unless their Z coordinates differ by a suitable amount.[1] For "neighbouring" units their "planes" of X, Y coordinates share a common "line". Between any two observations of a net, over time, the units with the same X, Y, Z coordinates have the same state space.

type
    X, Y, Z
    $DN = T \to N$
value
    obs_XYZs: $U \to (X \times Y \times Z)$-**set**
    obs_XYs: $U \to (X \times Y)$-**set**
    obs_Zs: $U \to Z$-**set**
    suitable: $Z \times Z \to$ **Bool**

axiom
    $\forall$ dn:DN,t:T • t $\in \mathcal{D}$dn •
        $\forall$ u,u':U • {u,u'}$\subseteq$obs_Us(dn(t))
            $\Rightarrow$ u=u' $\lor$ obs_XYs(u) $\cap$ obs_XYs(u') = {} $\lor$
                obs_XYs(u) $\cap$ obs_XYs(u') $\neq$ {} $\Rightarrow$
                    $\forall$ z,z':Z • z $\in$ obs_Zs(u) $\land$ z' $\in$ obs_Zs(u') $\Rightarrow$ suitable(z,z') $\land$
        $\forall$ t':T • t$\neq$t' $\Rightarrow$
            $\forall$ u,u':U • u $\in$ obs_Us(dn(t)) $\land$ u' $\in$ obs_Us(dn(t'))
                $\Rightarrow$ obs_XYs(u) = obs_XYs(u') $\Rightarrow$ obs_Ω(u) = obs_Ω(u')

This example also illustrates crucial issues of time/space.   ∎

Time and Dynamicity

In Vol. 3, Chap. 10 we focus on what we shall call static and dynamic attributes of entities. Example 5.3 illustrated one such kind of entity possessing, depending on the viewpoint (i.e., depending on the span of the scope), static and dynamic attributes. Time, as viewed in this section, is what gives rise to dynamicity: Dynamics is a temporal notion.

5.1.2 Time — General Issues

In the next sections we shall focus on various models of time, and we shall conclude with a simple view of the operations we shall assume when claiming that an abstract type models time. These sections are far from complete. They are necessary, but, as a general treatment of notions of time, they are

---

[1]That is, the height difference for two rail routes, one crossing the other by means of a bridge or tunnel.

not sufficient. We refer the interested reader to special monographs: [112,338, 405–411,434,508].

When you study and apply theories of, for example, *real-time, safety-critical, embedded systems*, then you will need a deeper seriousness about time than that presented here! A more serious treatment of time is presented in Chap. 15.

5.1.3 *"A-Series"* and *"B-Series"* Models of Time

Colloquially, in ordinary, everyday parlance, we think of time as a dense series of time points. We often illustrate time by a usually horizontal line with an arrow pointing towards the right. Sometimes that line arrowhead is labeled with either a *t* or the word *time*, or some such name. J.M.E. McTaggart (1908, [112,338,434]) discussed theories of time around two notions:

- **"A-series":** has terms like "past", "present" and "future".
- **"B-series":** has terms like "precede", "simultaneous" and "follow".

McTaggart argued that the B-series presupposes the A-series: If *t* precedes *t'* then there must be a "thing" *t''* at which *t* is past and *t'* is present. He argued that the A-series is incoherent: What was once 'future', becomes 'present' and then 'past'; and thus events 'will be events', 'are events' and 'were events', that is, will have all three properties.

5.1.4 A Continuum Theory of Time

The following is taken from Johan van Benthem [508]: Let P be a point structure (for example, a set). Think of time as a continuum; the following axioms characterise ordering ($<$, $=$, $>$) relations between (i.e., aspects of) time points. The axioms listed below are not thought of as an axiom system, that is, as a set of independent axioms all claimed to hold for the time concept, which we are encircling. Instead van Benthem offers the individual axioms as possible "blocks" from which we can then "build" our own time system — one that suits the application at hand, while also fitting our intuition.

Time is transitive: If $p<p'$ and $p'<p''$ then $p<p''$. Time may not loop, that is, is not reflexive: $p \not< p$. Linear time can be defined: Either one time comes before, or is equal to, or comes after another time. Time can be left-linear, i.e., linear "to the left" of a given time. One could designate a time axis as beginning at some time, that is, having no predecessor times. And one can designate a time axis as ending at some time, that is, having no successor times. General, past and future successors (predecessors, respectively successors in daily talk) can be defined. Time can be dense: Given any two times one can always find a time between them. Discrete time can be defined.

axiom

[TRANS: Transitivity] $\forall$ p,p',p'':P • p $<$ p' $<$ p'' $\Rightarrow$ p $<$ p''

[IRREF: Irreflexitivity] $\forall$ p:P • p $\not<$ p

[LIN: Linearity] $\forall$ p,p':P • (p=p' $\vee$ p<p' $\vee$ p>p')

[L–LIN: Left Linearity]
    $\forall$ p,p',p'':P • (p'<p $\wedge$ p''<p) $\Rightarrow$ (p'<p'' $\vee$ p'=p'' $\vee$ p''<p')

[BEG: Beginning] $\exists$ p:P • $\sim\exists$ p':P • p'<p

[END: Ending] $\exists$ p:P • $\sim\exists$ p':P • p<p'

[SUCC: Successor]
  [PAST: Predecessors] $\forall$ p:P,$\exists$ p':P • p'<p
  [FUTURE: Successor] $\forall$ p:P,$\exists$ p':P • p<p'

[DENS: Dense] $\forall$ p,p':P (p<p' $\Rightarrow$ $\exists$ p'':P • p<p''<p')

[DENS: Converse Dense] $\equiv$ [TRANS: Transitivity]
    $\forall$ p,p':P ($\exists$ p'':P • p<p''<p' $\Rightarrow$ p<p')

[DISC: Discrete]
    $\forall$ p,p':P • (p<p' $\Rightarrow$ $\exists$ p'':P • (p<p'' $\wedge$ $\sim\exists$ p''':P • (p<p'''<p''))) $\wedge$
    $\forall$ p,p':P • (p<p' $\Rightarrow$ $\exists$ p'':P • (p''<p' $\wedge$ $\sim\exists$ p''':P • (p''<p'''<p')))

A strict partial order, SPO, is a point structure satisfying TRANS and IRREF. TRANS, IRREF and SUCC imply infinite models. TRANS and SUCC may have finite, "looping time" models.

5.1.5 Temporal Events

We shall try elaborate a rather broad concept of events. Unfortunately, it is too broad to be useful. From that, too general, concept we can then, as it suits us, "narrow things down" to a more useful concept. First, in this section we introduce time events. In Sect. 5.2.4 we introduce a similarly broad concept of spatial events. Usually the concept of event is closely tied to the concept of time, but this will not be the only case here. The fact that time changes is considered a 'time change event'. The fact that time, while continuously changing, i.e., "progressing", reaches an a priori (perhaps, to some observers, arbitrarily) given time is considered a 'time passing event'. The fact that time, while continuously changing, i.e., "progressing", reaches an a priori (again, perhaps, to some observers, arbitrary) distance from a given time is considered a 'time elapse event'. One can thus consider any change in time an event, as well as define any number of 'time ξ' events.

5.1.6 Temporal Behaviour

Usually behaviour is understood to be a temporal notion: *Something changes, progresses over time.* Therefore, to single out a concept 'temporal behaviour' may be considered somewhat of an "overkill", i.e., we are juxtaposing two names for the same idea: 'temporal' and 'behaviour'. We shall do it anyway in our attempt to bring some unconventional thinking to bear on the classical, but rather abstract concepts of time, of space and of space/time. So, the behaviour of time is that it "flows"; that one can consider either continuous time or discrete time, as we shall see further on.

5.1.7 Representation of Time

We colloquially say: *The time is now five past eight pm.* — omitting the date. We shall generally think of a model of absolute time that includes "all there is to say":

type
    T, Date, Year, Month, Day, Hour, Minute, Second, ...
value
    obs_Date: T → Date
    obs_Year: T → Year
    obs_Month: T → Month
    obs_Day: T → Day
    obs_Hour: T → Hour
    obs_Minute: T → Minute
    obs_Second: T → Second

So we assume a time notion, T, such that from any such time we can observe the date, the year, the month, the day (in the month), the hour, the minute, the second, etc., of that time! But we do not, as of yet, prescribe a representation of such a time notion.

    But we shall also operate with a relative time, or time interval, ti:TI, concept: one for which we, at present, do not specify a representation, but one for which we say that there are some operations that involve times and time intervals. Subtracting one time from another yields a time interval. One can add a time interval to a time to get a time. One can divide two time intervals and get an integer fraction, i.e., a rounded natural number. For any two times there exists a time interval designating their difference. And for any time and any time interval there exists a time which is their sum. Observe that the arithmetic operators are overloaded: Here they do not apply to numbers or reals, but to times and time intervals.

type
    TI
value

elapsed_time: T × T → TI
−: T×T → TI
+: T×TI → T
/: TI×TI $\overset{\sim}{\to}$ **Nat**

axiom
∀ t,t′:T • t′>t ⇒ ∃ tδ:TI • tδ = t′−t
∀ t:T,tδ:TI • ∃ t′:T • t′>t ⇒ t+tδ = t′

Now a *TI year* does not mean an absolute, specific year, but *the number of years that have passed between two absolute (T) times.*

Example 5.4 *Timetable:* Typically an airline or a train (seasonal) timetable lists "times" modulo a week and grouped by days of the week, as from one absolute time to some other absolute time, the interval designating the season:

type
aT, P, Nm, mT
Day_of_week == monday | tuesday | wednesday
           | thursday | friday | saturday | sunday
TT = aT
    × (Nm $\overrightarrow{m}$ (Day_of_week-set × (P $\overrightarrow{m}$ (mT × mT))))
    × aT

where the first and the last aT's are absolute times, but the second and third times, mT, are the modulo times:

obs_Hour: mT → Hour
obs_Minute: mT → Minute

In words: TT lists, left-to-right: the date (aT) of the beginning of the season; for every name, nm:Nm, of a transport vehicle (train or flight or ...), the nonempty set of the days of the week it operates, and, for every name of a stop, p:P (station or airport), the arrival and departure hour and minute times; and, finally, the date, aT, of the ending of the season.   ∎

The notion of timetable illustrated above can be said to represent a discrete time notion, but, as we shall see later, denotes a continuous time behaviour.

5.1.8 Operations "on" Time

So we can compare times:

type
T
value
<, ≤, =, ≠, ≥, >: T × T ⇒ **Bool**

And we can add or subtract time intervals, time periods from absolute times, and subtract one absolute time from another in order to find the elapsed time, a time period:

type
    TI
value
    $+, -$: T × TI → T
    $-$: T × T → TI

5.2 Space

> Space: an eternal, infinite, isomorphic continuum
> (like air, only thinner)
> *Sir Isaac Newton*

5.2.1 Space — The Basics

Characterisation. Physically manifest entities occupy point set spaces. Different entities occupy disjoint point set spaces. We model, initially, point set spaces as locations. No location is an empty point set space, but empty point set spaces do exist! If two locations are different then they do not "overlap". If two locations are the same, i.e., are equal, then their intersection is "that same location".   ■

type
    L
value
    $\{\}=,\{\}\neq$: L → **Bool**
    $=,\neq$: L×L → **Bool**
    $\cup,\cap$: L×L → L
axiom
    $\forall\ \ell$:L • $\{\}\neq\ell$
    $\forall\ \ell,\ell'$:L •
        $\ell\neq\ell' \equiv \{\}=\ell\cap\ell' \wedge \ell=\ell' \equiv \ell\cap\ell'=\ell$

Note the prefix *is (not) equal to empty point set space.*

5.2.2 Location-Varying Entities

Physically manifest entities, E, may move in time, T. At no time can two ("different") such entities converge "infinitesimally close" to the same location, L.

type
    E, T, L
    $S' = T \to (E \xrightarrow{\sim} L)$
    $S = \{| \; s{:}S' \cdot \mathcal{CONTINUOUS}(s) \; |\}$
value
    $\mathcal{CONTINUOUS}$: $S \to$ **Bool**
axiom
    $\forall \; s{:}S \cdot \forall \; t,t'{:}T \cdot$
        $\{t,t'\} \subset \mathcal{D}s \Rightarrow \forall \; e,e'{:}E \cdot \{e,e'\} \subseteq \mathbf{dom} \; s(t) \wedge e \neq e' \Rightarrow (s(t))(e) \neq (s(t))(e')$

$\mathcal{CONTINUOUS}$ is not a definable RSL function. It is a metamathematical 'functional' designating whether its argument is a continuous function or not. For the particular system of time-located entities, continuity implies that at any two infinitesimally close time points an entity located at both times has moved at most infinitesimally, i.e., the two locations are infinitesimally close. At any two time points an entity located at both times is located at all time points between these two time points.

Example 5.5 *Documents, Originals and Copies:* Let us consider some concepts of documents. The concept of document itself is taken for granted. Each document can be uniquely identified. Some documents are originals. We do not say anything more than just: 'Some documents are originals'. Each original is made from some information at some time and at some location. No two documents, when disregarding their unique identification, are equal.[2] A document can be a ('direct') copy of some other document. From the unique identifier of a copy one can observe the unique identifier of the document from which the copy was made. From a copy one can observe the document from which it was copied. The "observed document" is itself not a document. From the unique identifier of a document one can observe the time and location of when and where the document was made or copied. No two documents can be made, or copied, at the same time and location.

type
    I, T, L, D, U, Δ
value
    obs_U: $(D|\Delta) \to U$
    obs_T: $(D|\Delta|U) \to T$
    obs_L: $(D|\Delta|U) \to L$
    is_Orig: $(D|\Delta) \to$ **Bool**
    is_Copy: $(D|\Delta) \to$ **Bool**

---

[2] This seemingly cryptic statements says: If I speak of two documents, then I mean two different documents. And then I mean that they are different, not by nature of having different unique names, but by being locatable in different physical locations. They may be stapled together, but they cannot physically "intersect" (i.e., "overlap").

make_D: I × T × L $\overset{\sim}{\to}$ D
copy_D: D × T × L $\overset{\sim}{\to}$ D
obs_Δ: D $\overset{\sim}{\to}$ Δ, equiv: D × Δ → **Bool**

axiom

$\forall$ i:I,t:T,ℓ:L,d:D •
  is_Orig(make_D(i,t,ℓ)) $\wedge$
  $\sim$is_Copy(make_D(i,t,ℓ)) $\wedge$
  $\sim$is_Orig(obs_Δ(copy_D(d,t,ℓ))) $\wedge$
  is_Copy(obs_Δ(copy_D(d,t,ℓ))) $\wedge$
  $\sim$is_Orig(copy_D(d,t,ℓ)) $\wedge$
  is_Copy(copy_D(d,t,ℓ)) $\wedge$
  is_Orig(obs_Δ(make_D(i,t,ℓ))) $\wedge$
  $\sim$is_Copy(obs_Δ(make_D(i,t,ℓ)))

$\forall$ u,u':U • u=u' $\equiv$ obs_T(u)=obs_T(u') $\wedge$ obs_L(u)=obs_L(u')
$\forall$ d,d':D • d=d' $\equiv$ obs_U(d)=obs_U(d') $\wedge$ obs_Δ(d)=obs_Δ(d'),
$\forall$ δ,δ':Δ •δ=δ' $\equiv$ obs_U(δ)=obs_U(δ'),
$\forall$ i:I,t:T,ℓ:L,d:D •
  obs_T(make_D(i,t,ℓ))=t$\wedge$obs_L(make_D(i,t,ℓ))=$\ell\wedge$
  obs_T(copy_D(d,t,ℓ))=t$\wedge$obs_L(copy_D(d,t,ℓ))=$\ell\wedge$
  obs_T(obs_U(make_D(i,t,ℓ)))=t$\wedge$obs_L(obs_U(make_D(i,t,ℓ)))=$\ell\wedge$
  obs_T(obs_U(copy_D(d,t,ℓ)))=t$\wedge$obs_L(obs_U(copy_D(d,t,ℓ)))=$\ell\wedge$
  obs_T(obs_Δ(make_D(i,t,ℓ)))=t$\wedge$obs_L(obs_Δ(make_D(i,t,ℓ)))=$\ell\wedge$
  obs_T(obs_Δ(copy_D(d,t,ℓ)))=t$\wedge$obs_L(obs_Δ(copy_D(d,t,ℓ)))=ℓ
$\forall$ d:D,δ:Δ •
  $\sim$is_Orig(d) $\wedge$ is_Copy(d) $\wedge$
  $\sim$is_Orig(δ) $\wedge$ is_Copy(δ) $\wedge$
  is_Orig(d) $\equiv$ is_Orig(obs_Δ(d)) $\wedge$
  is_Copy(d) $\equiv$ is_Copy(obs_Δ(d)) $\wedge$
  equiv(d,obs_Δ(d)) $\wedge$
  $\forall$ d':D • d$\neq$d' $\Rightarrow$ $\sim$equiv(d,obs_Δ(d'))

value

copy_D(d,t,l) **as** d' **pre**: obs_T(d) < t

We leave it to the reader to ponder over the above example!   ■

5.2.3 Locations and Dynamicity

Locations, as point sets, are here considered fixed, static quantities. That is, locations as a concept, are here considered independent of ("orthogonal" with respect to) time. Thus we work, if not otherwise mentioned, in a rather simpleminded Newtonian world, not in an Einsteinian world! Thus time and space are here, in this book, considered unrelated.

5.2.4 Space — General Issues

Point, Curve, Surface and Volume

We take, for granted, the concepts of: (i) point; (ii) curve (line); (iii) surface; (iv) volume; (v) points on (or off) a line, on (or away from) a surface, or inside (or outside) a volume; (vi) curves on a surface, including curves "crossing" ("intersecting") a surface, curves "touching tangentially" a surface, etc.; (vii) surface(s) of a volume; and (viii) 'cuts' through a volume defining "new" volumes and surfaces; etc. We shall anyway take a semiformal look at this space (spatial) notion. Consider Fig. 5.1.

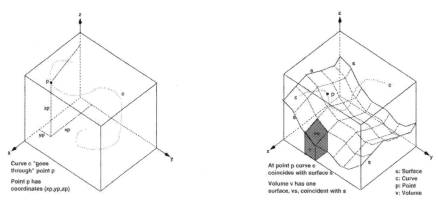

Fig. 5.1. Spatial concepts of axis, point, curve, surface, volume and coincidence

X, Y, X are an abstract concept of axes forming a notion of a rectilinear, orthogonal coordinate system. (These notions are here left further unexplained — i.e., we assume them known!)

Points are basic, further unexplained "atomic" notions, with which we shall, as a model, associate x, y, x coordinates in the X, Y, X coordinate system. A curve is a dense infinite set of points such that, with every "point on the curve", there is a notion of "left neighbours" and "right neighbours" ("taking limits"). A continuous curve has "neighbouring" points that "coincide in the limit"! A surface defines a special, dense, infinite set of (surface) points such that there is a notion of an infinite set of "neighbourhood" (surface) points. A volume (a definite spatial body, an entity) defines a special, dense, infinite set of points (within the body [entity]) such that there is a notion of an infinite set of "neighbourhood" (volume) points. The density of point sets can be defined.

Spatial "Events"

We can associate different notions of spatial events: If two points — otherwise considered different — coincide, i.e., have the same x, y, z coordinates, then that is called a "point/point coincidental event". If a point, p, and a curve, c, coincide, that is: there is a point p' on the curve and that "point coincides with" p, then that is called a "point/curve coincidental event". If a curve progresses, "continues" beyond a point, then that is called a 'curve continuation event'. If a curve changes direction, i.e., the tangent at a point and the curve after that point "deviate", then that is called a 'curve change event'. A "crossing" curve is a curve such that what might otherwise be considered two different points on the curve 'point/point coincides'. If a curve, c, and a surface, s, coincide at a point p (which lies both on the curve and on the surface), that is, there is a point p' on the curve that 'point coincides with' s, then that is called a "curve/space coincidental event". (A curve may have many curve/space "coincidental" events.) And so on for intersecting surfaces and volumes. Many more or less "artificial" event categories can easily be imagined.

We have brought in the above list of more or less "contrived" event classifications to alert the reader to the fact, or at least the possibility, that events can be associated with physical "changes". Before we allowed the following three kinds of time events: continuation of time, i.e., "next time"; or the reaching of a time point; or the the fact that a certain interval has elapsed. Now we seem to add other events, called "spatial events": continuation of curves (the "next points on a curve"), continuation of surfaces (the "immediately neighbouring points on a surface"), continuation of volumes (the "immediately neighbouring points of a volume"), "sharing" of points, etc. We must always be prepared to entertain that some notion is being designated an event (or a category of events).

Spatial "Behaviours"

If we consider the world from the position of a point, then a curve designates a behaviour: a trace — a sequence — of points, and an infinite one "to boot"! If we consider the world from the position of a curve, then a surface may designate a behaviour: a trace — a sequence — of curves, also infinite. If we consider the world from the position of a surface, then a finite (i.e., a closed) volume may designate a behaviour: a finite trace — a sequence — of one or more surfaces.

Again we have introduced a seeming "arbitrariness" — a "lofty generality" — in our implicit definition of behaviour. This is done deliberately, in order to introduce you later to some "narrower" definitions of a concept of 'behaviour'.

Representation of Spatial Bodies

We leave it to classical mathematics and engineering to deal with appropriate representations of spatial bodies (i.e., entities). Thus we assume two sorts of spaces: spherical and Cartesian, one sort of spatial bodies, and some observer functions:

type
    Space, Body
    X,Y,Z,R = **Real**
    Cartes = X×Y×Y
    Spherical = R × Lo × La
    Lo′=Rat, Lo = {| lo:Lo′ • 0≤lo<360 |}
    La′=Rat, La = {| la:La′ • 0≤la<90 |}
value
    obs_extent: Body → Space → Cartes
    obs_location: Body → Space → Spherical

where extent could be the smallest Cartesian volume that contains the body, and where the location is its spherical position is some planetary system such as Earth (Fig. 5.2).

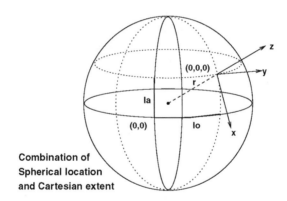

Fig. 5.2. An example spherical/Cartesian spatial system

Operations on Space

Given a spatial body one can identify its location, extent and volume; and one can identify its surface area, convexities, concavities, etc. Given a spatial body one can subdivide it into a finite set of two or more of bodies (i.e., entities — of which it is composed by "glueing"). Given two (or more) bodies one can find their possible intersection (i.e., overlap), surfaces they may share, and so on.

5.3 Space/Time

In this section we formalise some aspects of the above notion of space (in particular of entities [i.e., bodies]) together with a notion of time.

We now combine space and time. First we show an example.

5.3.1 A Guiding Example

Example 5.6 *Traffic:* Let P designate a ("continuum") set of positions (say of vehicles), T designate a ("continuum") set of times, and Nm designate a ("discrete") set of names (of the vehicles). Then, by continuous traffic, we understand a continuous function from time to functions (i.e., maps) from names to positions. By "sampled" traffic, we understand a discretised function (i.e., a map) from time to functions (i.e., maps) from names to positions.

type
  P, T, Nm
  cTF = T $\xrightarrow{\sim}$ (Nm $\overrightarrow{m}$ P)
  dTF = T $\overrightarrow{m}$ (Nm $\overrightarrow{m}$ P)
value
  wf_TF: (cTF|dTF) → **Bool**

P designates positions of named transport vehicles (flights or trains) Nm. cTF stands for continuous traffic, dTF stands for discrete traffic. (dtf:dTF relates to ctf:cTF iff at least for every time t in the definition set of dtf t is also in the definition set of ctf and "maps" onto identical maps from names of vehicles to (same) positions.) We say that dtf:dTF represents a "sampling", a 'discretisation' of ctf:cTF. ∎

5.3.2 Representation of Space/Time

The example illustrated a space/time phenomenon. Very typically we model such phenomena in either or both of the two ways shown above. In general,

type
  A
  cTP = T $\xrightarrow{\sim}$ A
  dTP = T $\overrightarrow{m}$ A

where A is any notion to which you may attach a concept of space. We usually choose partiality ($\xrightarrow{\sim}$) since we "only" assume the function ctf (in cTF) to be total in a nontrivial (i.e., in other than a single point) interval:

  ctTP = iT → A
  iT = {| t:T • begin$_t$ ≤ t ≤ end$_t$ |}

where the subtype comprehension predicate is informal jargon for: ... *and time lies in some closed interval from a definite begin to a definite end time.*

5.3.3 Blizard's Theory of Time-Space

We shall present an axiom system (Wayne D. Blizard, 1980, [57]) which relates abstracted entities to spatial points and time. Let $A, B, \ldots$ stand for entities, $p, q, \ldots$ for spatial points; and t, τ for times. 0 designates a first, a begin time. Let t' stand for the discrete time successor of time t. Let $N(p,q)$ express that p and q are spatial neighbours. Let $=$ be an overloaded equality operator applicable, pairwise to entities, spatial locations and times, respectively. A_p^t expresses that entity A is at location p at time t. We omit (obvious) typings of A, B, P, Q, and T. The suffix prime, $'$, designates the time successor function. Thus t' designates the next time after t.

$$
\begin{array}{lll}
(I) & \forall A \forall t \exists p \;:\; A_p^t & \\
(II) & (A_p^t \wedge A_q^t) \supset p = q & \\
(III) & (A_p^t \wedge B_p^t) \supset A = B & \\
(IV) & (A_p^t \wedge A_p^{t'}) \supset t = t' & \\
(V\ i) & \forall p,q \;:\; N(p,q) \supset p \neq q & \text{Irreflexivity} \\
(V\ ii) & \forall p,q \;:\; N(p,q) = N(q,p) & \text{Symmetry} \\
(V\ iii) & \forall p \exists q,r \;:\; N(p,q) \wedge N(p,r) \wedge q \neq r & \text{No isolated pts.} \\
(VI\ i) & \forall t \;:\; t \neq t' & \\
(VI\ ii) & \forall t \;:\; t' \neq 0 & \\
(VI\ iii) & \forall t \;:\; t \neq 0 \supset \exists \tau : t = \tau' & \\
(VI\ iv) & \forall t, \tau \;:\; \tau' = t' \supset \tau = t & \\
(VII) & A_p^t \wedge A_q^{t'} \supset N(p,q) & \\
(VIII) & A_p^t \wedge B_q^t \wedge N(p,q) \supset \sim (A_q^{t'} \wedge B_p^{t'}) &
\end{array}
$$

- (II–IV,VII, VIII): The axioms are universally 'closed', that is, we have omitted the usual $\forall A, B, p, q, t$s.
- (I): For every entity, A, and every time, t, there is a location, p, at which A is located at time t.
- (II): An entity cannot be in two locations at the same time.
- (III): Two distinct entities cannot be at the same location at the same time.
- (IV): Entities always move: An entity cannot be at the same location at different times. *This is more like a conjecture, and could be questioned.*
- (V): These three axioms define N.
- (V i): Same as $\forall p :\sim N(p,p)$. "Being a neighbour of", is the same as "being distinct from".
- (V ii): If p is a neighbour of q, then q is a neighbour of p.
- (V iii): Every location has at least two distinct neighbours.
- (VI): The next four axioms determine the time successor function $'$.
- (VI i): A time is always distinct from its successor: Time cannot rest. There are no time fix points.
- (VI ii): Any time successor is distinct from the begin time. Time 0 has no predecessor.
- (VI iii): Every nonbegin time has an immediate predecessor.

- (VI iv): The time successor function $'$ is a one-to-one (i.e., a bijection) function.
- (VII): The *continuous path axiom:* If entity A is at location p at time t, and it is at location q in the immediate next time t', then p and q are neighbours.
- (VIII): *No "switching":* If entities A and B occupy neighbouring locations at time t the it is not possible for A and B to have switched locations at the next time t'.

Discussion of the *Blizard* Model of Space/Time

Except for axiom (IV) the system applies to systems of entities that "sometimes" rest, i.e., do not move. These entities are spatial and occupy at least a point in space. If some entities "occupy more" space volume than others, then we may suitably "repair" the notion of the point space P (etc.), however, this is not shown here.

5.4 Discussion

We have, in this chapter, discussed some notions of time and space, and of their combination. In later chapters (Chaps. 12–15) we shall cover additional notions of time: *qualitative* as well as *quantitative*. And in Vol. 3, Chap. 10 we shall further cover time notions.

5.5 Bibliographical Notes

McTaggart's work is covered by [112, 338, 434], and Blizard's theory is found in [57]. The book by van Benthem is seminal: [508].

The considerations of time in this chapter find their final exposition in these volumes in Chap. 15. That chapter is focused solely on temporal logics, that is, logics that are capable of dealing with time events and durations. The, perhaps, most important contributor cum originator of temporal logics appears to be Arthur N. Prior. His work is covered by [218, 406–411].

5.6 Exercises

Exercise 5.1 *Supermarkets (II).* Reference is made to Exercise 4.2. Please read that exercise carefully. We assume here that you have also provided a solution to the questions asked.

Consider "the day of a supermarket" to be a suitably discretised function from supermarkets to supermarkets. Assume that the cash registers start their day empty (no cash is changed). And assume that no deliveries are made during open hours, i.e., the day, to the backup store.

Now write a well-formedness function over the "the day of a supermarket".

Exercise 5.2 *Manufacturing (II)*. Reference is made to Exercise 4.3. Please read that exercise carefully. We assume here that you have also provided a solution to the questions asked.

Now describe production, formally, as a discrete function from time (units) to states of stores, trucks and machines.

We assume that during daytime no deliveries are made to the supply store nor are any products sent away from the product store.

Formalise a well-formedness function which expresses the well-formedness of a production, i.e., the timewise progression from configurations to configurations.

Exercise 5.3 *Road Traffic*. The present exercise follows those of Exercise 2.3 and Exercise 4.1. You are well advised to first study those exercises and to attempt their solution.

Now consider road traffic as consisting of only one kind of vehicle, say four wheel automobiles (i.e., cars). A car is either parked, or it is standing still in traffic, or it is moving about in traffic. For a car to be in traffic means that it is not parked. We shall henceforth not consider parked cars! For a car to be in traffic (furthermore) means that it can move. A car will move if it can. For a car to move means that it is changing position along a street or in an intersection. A car can move if its next position is not occupied by another car. The next position of a car is a location, along a street or in an intersection, infinitesimally close to its present position.

Now assume an indefinite number of cars in traffic. Also consider that the road net has a number of entry and exit points at which cars may enter, or may leave the road net. These entry and exit points are like the roads "leading into or out of the city" as mentioned in Exercise 2.3. If a parked car ceases to be parked and starts moving, then it enters traffic. If a moving car ceases to be in traffic by parking, then it leaves traffic. At any moment only a finite number of cars may enter traffic, and at any moment only a finite number of cars may leave traffic.

1. Provide a definition of what a car position (i.e., car location on a street (segment) or in an intersection) is.
2. Provide a type definition of the concept of car, i.e., road traffic. Assume a time interval, from time t_{start} to time t_{end}, over which road traffic is defined.
3. Impose suitable constraints on road traffic.
4. Define a function which applies to any road traffic and which yields the first time, after t_{start}, at which a car accident occurs, i.e., when two cars collide, i.e., when their locations "overlap".

5. Define a function which applies to any road traffic and a time (point) and which yields the possibly empty map from cars — which are driving in the wrong direction of a one way street — and their positions along those street segments.

Exercise 5.4 *Air Traffic.* The present exercise follows those of Exercise 2.4 and Exercise 4.1. You are well advised to first study those exercises and to their solution.

Now consider air traffic as consisting of moving aircraft. That is, aircrafts on the ground are not moving! An aircraft can only start from an airport. It then enters air traffic by entering an air lane connected to that airport. Normally an aircraft then moves continuously along a route (i.e., within a sequence of air lanes), and normally an aircraft leaves air traffic when, or by, landing in an airport, i.e., by leaving an air lane connected to that airport. Abnormally an aircraft, or two, may leave air traffic by exploding in the air, for example, by collision.

1. Provide a definition of what an aircraft position, in the air, is.
2. Provide a type definition of the concept of air traffic. Assume a time interval, from time t_{start} to time t_{end}, over which air traffic is defined.
3. Impose suitable constraints on air traffic.
4. Define a function which applies to any air traffic and which yields the first time, after t_{start}, at which an aircraft collision occurs, i.e., when their locations "overlap".
5. Define another function which applies to any air traffic and which yields the first time, after t_{start}, at which a single aircraft explosion occurs, i.e., when the aircraft "suddenly" disappears from air traffic.

Exercise 5.5 *Ocean Traffic.* The present exercise follows those of Exercise 2.5 and Exercise 4.1. You are well advised to first study those exercises and to attempt their solution.

Now consider ocean traffic as consisting of moving ships. Ships sail from harbours to harbours. (Let us disregard ship movements within a harbour, from buoys to quays and/or container terminals, etc.) Please read the above exercise formulations, i.e., Exercises 5.3–5.4. From those make up your own informal description of the problem, and then formalise answers to those descriptions.

Exercise 5.6 *Documents: Masters, Copies, Versions.* We refer to Exercise 2.1.

Narrative, I: *First we consider an extension.* Documents, whether masters (i.e., originals) or copies, may be edited. Again it is observable whether a document is an edited version, v, as are also, in that case, the time and location of edit. Further, what has been changed by the editing can be observed. Let d be a document (i.e., in D), then we can postulate two functions, the edit and the undo functions: One takes d into v and one takes v back into d.

1. Now reformulate the formulas of Example 2.1.

Narrative, II: *Then we consider a concretisation of documents.* The documents, and hence master, copy and version (edited) documents are, in this exercise, to be considered structured. Assume, or suggest, some structure. Hint: It could, for example be (i) the structure of a book: chapters, sections, subsections, paragraphs with lines or formulas with lines. Or (ii) instead of using chapter, section and subsection terms one could use a fixed, finite number of names such as admininistrative, anamneses[3], tests, analyses, diagnostics, treatments, observations, and reconsiderations, with each of these having paragraphs with lines, or diagrams, or photos, or X-Rays, or ECGs, or MRSs, or CTRs, or other — as, in case (ii), would be typical of PMRs (patient medical records).

2. Now suggest a further reformulation, i.e., a refinement, of your previous formulas — including "narrowing" down, i.e., making a bit more concrete, the edit and the undo functions.
   Hint: it could, e.g., be observable where in a document an edit has taken place.

Exercise 5.7 *Document System.* We refer to Exercises 2.1 and 5.6.
Now assume a collection of documents and their behaviour over time.

1. Formalize a function type, cTLDs, from time to sets of spatially located documents.

Then assume the Blizard axiom system (Sect. 5.3.3), except its axiom (IV):

2. Reformulate the Wayne Blizard axioms in proper RSL.
3. Further define functions which apply to cTLDs (as well as other appropriate arguments) and which
   (a) inserts a master document (into some ctlds:cTLDs),
   (b) copies a document,
   (c) edits a document,
   (d) moves a document from one location to a "close-by" location, and
   (e) removes (e.g., "shreds") a document.
4. Argue, informally, that your function definitions maintain the invariant as defined by the (axiom (IV) exempted) Blizard axiom system.
5. Give an interpretation to the Blizard axiom (I).
6. Then formulate a discretised model of cTLDs, i.e., dTLDs.
7. Relate dTLDs to cTLDs. That is, express criteria for when a discretisation is a reasonable one.

Hints: (a) Assume a predicate close which applies to pairs of times or pairs of locations (in space) and yields truth when the pair of time points, respectively the pair of locations, are sufficiently close to one another. (b) Assume also a mathematical, i.e., a non-RSL, function $\mathcal{D}$ (and, if need be, another such function $\mathcal{R}$) which applies to arbitrary functions and yields their definition

---

[3]information that must be remembered

sets (respectively their image, i.e., range, sets). Finally, recall the notion of λ-functions (Vol. 1, Chap. 7). Let f be a function from time, T, to something, say $A \underset{m}{\rightarrow} B$. If from some time point, t_p, onwards we wish to express the function f' which is like f except that as from t_p the function f' maps an a, not into what was mapped in f but into b, then we express that as follows:

type
    T, A, B
    F = T → (A $\underset{m}{\rightarrow}$ B)
value
    change: F × T × A × B → F
    change(f,t_p,a,b) ≡ λ t:T • **if** t<t_p **then** f(t) **else** f(t) † [a↦b] **end**

Exercise 5.8 *Topological Space.* We wish to model such spatial concepts as *next to (close to, adjacent), overlapping (intersecting), within, separate from,* etc. Thus you are to model a concept of space:

- Assumptions:
    ⋆ There is a basic, further unexplained notion of spatial point.
    ⋆ A spatial location is a possibly finite, non-empty set of points.
    ⋆ Any spatial line, surface, or volume is a (most likely) infinite set of points.
    ⋆ There is a notion of distance.
    ⋆ Therefore for any two points one can observe their possibly zero distance.
    ⋆ There is a notion of circle, and a notion of sphere, hence notions of radius, diameter, segment of a circle and the angle it "spans".
- Questions:
    1. Define a notion of a straight line.
    2. Define a notion of a 'polyline', that is, a sequence of connected, but not "intersecting" straight lines (segments) such that these line segments are all in a plane.
    3. Define a notion of a polygon, that is, a polyline whose straight line (segments) do not intersect, and where the "first point" of a "first" line segment coincides with the "last point" of a "last" line segment.
    4. Assume that given a polygon one can observe the area that it spans.
    5. Now define a notion of spherical polygon: a figure analogous to a plane polygon that is formed on a sphere by arcs of great circles.

Part IV

LINGUISTICS

In this part we further develop, in four distinct chapters:

* the non-formalisable concepts of *pragmatics:* of use, of what we intend, of what social effect we wish to occur;
* the formalisable concepts of varieties of *semantics:* of what we mean according to varieties of viewpoints;
* the formalisable concepts of abstract and concrete *syntax:* of what we say and write; and
* the concept of *semiotics:* as "consisting" of the concepts of syntax, semantics and pragmatics.

But, contrary to popular tradition, we treat these three subjects in the order:

* first *pragmatics:* Chap. 6,
* then *semantics:* Chap. 7,
* then *syntax:* Chap. 8, and
* finally — summing up — *semiotics:* Chap. 9.

The four chapters can, however, be read in the reverse order — whereas the problems posed in the chapters should be tackled in the reverse order from Chap. 9 to Chap. 6.

On Exercises of Part IV

Most exercises of this part ask for solutions that contain both a property-oriented solution and a model-oriented solution — and along the lines of this part. Amongst the exercises of this part, and hence proposed below, there is a set which "slowly", i.e., stepwise, "unfolds", that is, designs a specific (first) programming language. We refer to Exercise 6.3 for the pragmatics, i.e., the motivation for, and justification and use of this language. Subsequent exercises then pose questions whose solutions eventually lead up to a design of this language. We thus pose these questions in the recommended order of:

- pragmatics: Exercises 6.3–6.5;
- semantic types and auxiliary semantic functions: Exercises 7.3–7.7;
- syntactic types and auxiliary syntactic functions, including well-formedness predicates: Exercises 8.7–8.8; and
- semantic (meaning) functions: Exercise 9.2.

Exercises 9.3–9.5 then asks for the "stepwise" development of the first language design (itemised above) via intermediate steps of increasingly more "versatile" languages to the language that we claim we are after!

6

Pragmatics

- The **prerequisite** for studying this chapter is that you are somewhat familiar with issues of syntax and semantics.
- The **aim** is to introduce the informal concept of pragmatics.
- The **objective** is to help make sure that you do not confuse the nonformalisable issues of pragmatics with the possibly formalisable issues of semantics, and to help make sure that you clearly remember to state modelling design decisions whether these were motivated by syntactic, semantic or pragmatic concerns.
- The **treatment** is discursive and informal.

6.1 Introduction

Characterisation. (I) *Pragmatics* is the study and practice of the factors that govern our choice of language in social interaction and the effects of our choice on others [84].

By pragmatics we thus understand issues of why we use a special construct, of why we constrain such a construct and of why we endow it with certain properties, and so on. ∎

Our "dogma" is this: We can formalise syntax and we can formalise semantics, but we cannot formalise pragmatics.

Our "dogma" is also this: Pragmatics is what we really are "aiming at", the real reason behind the use of a certain syntactical uttering, that is, the real reason for the use of a specific semantic metaphor. Pragmatics is what "links" (formal) uses of language to actions, to what is happening in a real world. Pragmatics thus has as its subject issues of choice of syntax and semantics. Thus it is metalinguistic wrt. these — and hence cannot possibly be expressed at the same level as these, and hence not — i.e., not without introducing rather complete confusion — in the same specification language.

Characterisation. (II) *Pragmatics* is the study of language in context, and the context-dependence of various aspects of linguistics interpretation.   ■

First, one and the same sentence can express different meanings or propositions from context to context, either because of ambiguity or due to indexicality,[1] or both. Examples of ambiguities are: *visiting doctors can be tedious*, or *the mouse tore up the street*. An indexical sentence can change in truth-value from context to context owing to the presence of an element whose reference, i.e., whose value changes. An example is: *it's time for that meeting now*.

We leave the metalinguistics of pragmatics here, but invite the reader to think about the epistemological issues involved.

6.2 Everyday Pragmatics

Everyday pragmatics may dictate more or less convolute, more or less transparent or opaque uses of syntax and semantics. Lack of precision leads to misunderstandings. Scope for different interpretations invariably implies that there will indeed be many — sometimes opposing, irreconcilable — interpretations.

When moving from everyday situations to software development we must tighten our grip, our mastery of the pragmatics to avoid opaqueness and misunderstandings.

6.3 "Formal" Pragmatics

By "formal" pragmatics we mean the kind of pragmatics considerations that we must consider when developing software, that is, when describing domains, prescribing requirements or specifying software designs.

Example 6.1 *Some Application Software Package Pragmatics:* Various classical examples of the pragmatics underlying different software packages are:

Budget Planning and Accounting Software: This software is acquired by customers in order to help them budget within means, keep track of committed and actual expenses, and thus be able *to assess the financial situation during a budget period.*

Order Processing and Tracing Software: This software is acquired by customers in order to improve the response to and tracing of the production and delivery status of orders, and thus *to improve their company's competitive status.*

---

[1] Merriam–Webster defines *indexicality*: varying in reference with the individual speaker (the indexical words *I, here, now*), associated with or identifying an individual speaker [483].

Software for Automobile Painting Robots: This software is acquired by customers with the triple aim of faster overall painting of series of cars, possibly in different colours, *to decrease worker accidents*, and to secure uniform and high quality paint jobs.

The *italic* phrase parts are examples of pragmatics.   ∎

When we design an end-user application program our design decisions are not themselves formalised, or perhaps not even formalisable. But their result is: the decision is recorded in the form of formal syntax and formal semantics.

When we design a programming language we choose to include certain value types and exclude others.

Example 6.2 *Programming Language Data Types and Expressions:* LISP [333] emphasises list structures and thus the manipulation of symbolic, typically logical, structures.

FORTRAN [13] emphasises arrays of floating point values, i.e., scientific and technical computations over one, two, three or more dimensional models of physical or engineering structures.

COBOL [11] emphasises records and business processing, i.e., the administrative handling of data, in particular text strings and formatted number values.   ∎

Example 6.3 *Variable Access:* We refer the reader to material given in Chap. 4: When, as implied by Examples 8.17, 8.19 and 7.5, we choose among any of the three environment and storage models (Example 7.5), then the choice was based on pragmatic considerations: "Either is as good as any other", in theory, but not, perhaps, in practice. And pragmatics is about practice, not theory.   ∎

6.4 Discussion

6.4.1 General

We have postulated that pragmatics is not formalisable, and that it is the most important aspect behind our designs. In fact, these are indeed postulates. They are statements made by us, and these statements are of philosophical nature. They hinge upon, they imply issues of, and they reflect issues of philosophies and theories of science and engineering.

It follows that there can be no formal resumé of issues of pragmatics — at least not based on the shallow treatment of this important subject as given here. We do, however, refer to an important mathematical investigation into this matter, made in:

- N. Nikitchenko: Towards Foundations of a General Theory of Transport Domains. Research Report 88, UNU/IIST, P.O.Box 3058, Macau (1996) [379].

• • •

But pragmatics, as a concept, is much broader than treated here. Our presentation has been rather utilitarian: We have singled out and focused only on the most trivial aspects of pragmatics. More general issues of pragmatics lie beyond what these volumes needs to cover. Some of those issues play a role in the concept of *agents*. Here the so-called *speech acts* performed between agents relate strongly to pragmatics. But further than this "teaser" we shall not go!

6.4.2 Principles and Techniques

Principles. A first principle of *pragmatics* is to "discover" what the pragmatics of a development problem is, that is, which parts cannot be formally explained, but must be documented.   ■

Principles. A second, derived principle of *pragmatics* states: When documenting a software development it is mandatory that we (i) start (i.e., prefix), (ii) annotate throughout (i.e., "infix"), and (iii) end (i.e., suffix) our informal and formal development documentation with necessarily informal expositions of the pragmatics underlying the documented development choices.   ■

In Vol. 3, Chap. 2 of this series, we introduce the notions of informative, descriptional and analytical documents (or document parts). The role of the informative parts is to be a placeholder for, i.e., to spur the careful documentation of, pragmatic concerns: those which really motivate software development.

Techniques. When "exposing" the *pragmatics*, or rather, when believing that a design decision is based on some pragmatics, it is important to analyse the pragmatics exposition for possible "pitfalls": It might be that the desired semantics is ambiguous or indexical.   ■

6.5 Bibliographical Note

Pragmatics relates strongly to philosophy of language and theory of signs. A wealth of books and journals cover the area. We refer only to a recent monograph by Mey: [342]. Pragmatics also relates to *speech act theory*. We refer here to two seminal works and a recent collection of papers [18,464,504].

6.6 Exercises

Exercise 6.1 *The Pragmatics of Implicit Goals. Background:* Most customers, i.e., buyers, of software, on one hand, express very specific functionalities that they expect the acquired (i.e., the developed) software to offer. On the other hand, they expect that use of such software will bring about changes in their life, or in the "life" of the company using the software. Examples are: (i) *Use of the accounting software will make it easier for me to keep track of my expenses and help ensure that I stay within budget.* (ii) *The software, when deployed, will help ensure our company's competitive edge wrt. our competitors.* (iii) *The software, when properly used, will help cut down on work-related accidents.*

Question: Can you list three further such implicit goals? And can you discuss whether these listings, (i–iii) above and your additional three, are of pragmatic nature, and why they might not be formalisable?

Exercise 6.2 *User-Friendliness and Pragmatics.* Try to find, from the literature, characterisations of the concept of *user-friendly software (systems)*. Discuss which aspects of those characterisations are of pragmatic nature.

• • •

The next exercises (Exercises 6.3–6.5) form a preamble for the subsequent design of STIL: a simply typed imperative language.

Future exercises relate to the design of STIL and are as follows:

- Exercise 7.3: a structured type concept
- Exercise 7.4: a structured value concept: types
- Exercise 7.5: a structured value concept: auxiliary functions
- Exercise 7.6: a structured location concept
- Exercise 7.7: a structured storage concept
- Exercise 8.7: syntax of STIL
- Exercise 8.8: syntactic well-formedness of STIL
- Exercise 9.2: semantic meaning functions for STIL

From STIL is designed three more, evolving languages: NaTaTIL, DiTIL and DaUTIL:

- Exercise 9.3: NaTaTIL: a named types and typed imperative language,
- Exercise 9.4: DiTIL: dimension typed imperative language,
- Exercise 9.5: DaUTIL: dimension and unit typed imperative language.

• • •

Exercise 6.3 *Type and Value System (Preamble for STIL). Background:* Normally programs, of a programming language, prescribe operations on data, i.e., on values. These values are such as Booleans, integers (i.e., "whole" numbers), floating point numbers, characters and structures — such as vectors and records — over these. Typically the programming language comes equipped (i.e., "built-in") with such basic operations as addition, subtraction, multiplication, and division (over numbers); conjunction, disjunction, and implication (over Booleans); and equality and non- or inequality (over pairs of numbers, or pairs of Booleans, or pairs of characters). And usually these operations do not extend, as built-in operations, to structures of data. The programmer has to write algorithms if such generalisations are needed. The operations on values are expressed by writing operator/operand expressions. But in all this there "lurks" the possibility that the programmer makes the mistakes of expressing the addition of two Booleans, of expressing the conjunction (the "and") between a Boolean and a number, etc.

Question: Explain, in words, how you would design a language of expressions which could be constrained in such a way as to prevent, at run-time, the addition of, for example, two Boolean values.

Exercise 6.4 *Scalar and Structured Values (Preamble for STIL).* *Background:* To variables one can express the assignation of values. To structured variables, such as vectors (of atomic type elements) or records (of atomic, i.e. scalar type field elements), one can prescribe the assignation either of scalar values to individual elements, respectively fields, or one could think of prescribing the assignation of "whole" vector, respectively "whole" record values to these variables. By a whole vector value we mean a value which stands for a vector value, i.e., which contains several, successive, vector element values, and similarly for whole record values.

Question: Discuss the pros and cons, the advantages and/or disadvantages of allowing only scalar values as being expressions, versus allowing also structured values to be expressions.

Exercise 6.5 *"Flat" vs. Structured Locations (Preamble for STIL).* *Background:* In certain programming languages, ALGOL 60 to wit, references passed say to procedure calls, could only be to scalar values. That is, if a reference was needed to elements of an array, they may have to be passed, array element by array element! In other programming languages, for example ALGOL 68 (or even PL/I), references could be passed to procedure invocation, of arbitrary "slices" of an array: a column, a row, or a submatrix (several but not all, but ordered, row elements of several, but not all, but ordered, column elements) of a matrix. (And similarly for arrays of arbitrary higher dimension.)

Question: Examine current programming languages with respect to their offering reference values, i.e., values that are references to (pointers to, locations of) structured values. Include such languages as SML [168, 359], C [263], C++ [492], C# [207, 346, 347, 401] and Java [8, 15, 146, 301, 465, 513] in your analysis.

Discuss the pragmatic reasons for thus allowing only flat or for allowing structured location values, i.e., values which refer to arbitrary, well-formed substructure of structured values.

7

Semantics

- The **prerequisites** for studying this chapter are that you are well-versed in Vol. 1's abstraction principles and techniques, and in Vol. 2, Chap. 3's treatment of denotational and computational semantics.
- The **aim** is to present a wider variety of kinds of semantics models than so far afforded.
- The **objective** is to bring the reader further along the road to choose pleasing and appropriate semantics modelling types — as well as to encourage the reader to more seriously study more specialised textbooks on mathematical semantics.
- The **treatment** is systematic and semiformal.

This chapter presents a variety of forms of semantics: denotational, macroexpansion, computational, attribute grammar, and, somewhat more lightly, axiomatic semantics. The chapter provides only a brief overview. Chapter 3 covered two of these main approaches to semantics: denotational and computation semantics. Chapters 16–19 cover several of these forms of semantics.

7.1 Introduction

Characterisation. *Semantics* is the study and knowledge (including specification) of meaning in language [84].

By *formal semantics* we understand a semantics, M, such that we can reason about properties of what the syntax describes.

type
    Syntax, Semantics
value
    M: Syntax $\rightarrow$ Semantics

The challenge of formal semantics is to describe precisely the syntactic and the semantics types as well as the meaning function which maps elements of the former into elements of the latter.   ▪

By *syntax* (as referred to above) we understand a set of abstract types (i.e., sorts) or concrete types of syntactic constructs (statements, expressions, clauses, commands, etc.). By *semantics* (as referred to above) we also understand a set of abstract (i.e., sorts) or concrete types of meanings.

If, for example, the syntax is of a notational system, i.e., a language (specification, programming or otherwise), then the meaning of the sentential forms, when denotationally expressed, are usually functions over certain types.

The structure of these types may have been given a syntax, and the meaning of these types are now that of the meaning of the language of description, not the language being described.

7.2 Concrete Semantics

Characterisation. By *concrete semantics* we understand an "everyday description" of meaning which is "heavily mixed up" with motivational, i.e., pragmatic, utilitarian and other "utterings", possibly including requirements to computing support for the "thing" that the syntax and semantics is "about".   ▪

7.3 "Abstract" Semantics

There are several forms of abstract semantics. They are not entirely distinct, that is, there are overlaps:

- denotational semantics
- macro-expansion semantics
- operational semantics
- attribute grammar semantics
- axiomatic semantics
- algebraic semantics

The variety given here is not always mathematically (i.e., metasemantically) justifiable. Sometimes it is historically determined (i.e., pragmatically given).

7.4 Preliminary Semantics Concepts

Before we more systematically cover some of the above-listed semantic forms we need to cover some common notions.

7.4.1 Syntactic and Semantic Types

By a *semantics elaborator* or an *interpreter* or an *evaluator*, we understand the main functions which apply to syntactic values and yield semantic values.

Characterisation. By a *syntactic type* we understand a set of (concrete or abstract) syntactic values. So, sooner or later, the specifier has to write down — has to construct, has to decide upon — an abstract, and later a concrete, syntax (respectively grammar) for the system or language in question:

type Syn

By Syn we shall in the following understand the syntactic types of interest. ∎

This chapter, however, is about what constitutes semantic types and on how to decide upon them.

Characterisation. By a *semantic type* we understand a set of (concrete or abstract) semantics values: meanings of syntactic values. So, sooner or later, the specifier has to write down — has to construct or to decide upon — abstract, and later concrete, semantic types for the system or language in question:

type Sem, Val

By Sem we shall in the following understand the semantic types of interest. By Val we shall mean some semantic type, colloquially thought of as values of expressions. ∎

In preparation for the next sections, we remind the reader of the notions of configurations, contexts and states, as introduced in Chap. 4.

7.4.2 Contexts

We refer to Sect. 4.4.1 for systematic coverage and a characterisation of the concept of context.

Characterisation. By the *context of a system*, or of the evaluation of a program, or of a specification in some programming, respectively some specification language, we usually understand an aggregation, a structuring, of those components whose values remain fixed, i.e., can be considered constant over some "sizable" ("macro") time interval, or over the sequence of many events or actions (operations), or over the evaluation of a sizable textual, so-called block part, of a program or of a specification. ∎

7.4.3 States

We refer to Sect. 4.4.1 for systematic coverage and a characterisation of the concept of state.

Characterisation. By the *state of a system*, or of the evaluation of a program, or of a specification in some programming, respectively some specification language, we usually understand an aggregation, a structuring, of those components whose values changeover time, or over the sequence of one or more events, or as the result of actions (operations), or over the evaluation of any textual part of a program or a specification — no matter how close in time or how many such events and actions there are.   ∎

7.4.4 Configurations

We refer to Sect. 4.4.1 for systematic coverage and a characterisation of the concept of context.

Characterisation. By a *configuration* we mean a pair of contexts and states that are appropriate for a consistent and complete elaboration of a system or a syntactic text.   ∎

7.4.5 Interpretation, Evaluation and Elaboration

For pragmatic reasons it is convenient to make the following distinctions.

Characterisation. By *interpretation* we, more narrowly, understand a process, a mathematical or a mechanical computation, which yields state results. So, sooner or later, the specifier has to write down — has to construct, has to decide upon — whether the semantics of the system or language in question calls for interpreter functions to be defined:

    value I: Syn $\rightarrow$ Context $\rightarrow$ State $\rightarrow$ State

Thus we shall typically interpret statements.   ∎

This chapter presents a number of principles and techniques for deciding upon the issue of interpreter functions and for their definition. We say that the meaning of the syntactic construct, usually what we would call a statement, solely represents a side-effect (on the state).

Characterisation. By *evaluation* we, more narrowly, understand a process, a mathematical or a mechanical computation, which does not yield state, but some other semantic value results. So, sooner or later, the specifier has to write down — has to construct, has to decide upon — whether the semantics of the system or language in question calls for evaluator functions to be defined:

value V: Syn $\rightarrow$ Context $\rightarrow$ State $\rightarrow$ Val

Thus we shall typically evaluate pure, no side-effect expressions.   ∎

This chapter presents a number of principles and techniques for deciding upon the issue of evaluator functions and for their definition. We say that the meaning of the syntactic construct, usually what we would call an expression, expresses no side-effect (on the state).

Characterisation. By *elaboration* we, more narrowly, understand a process, a mathematical or a mechanical computation, which yields both state and some other semantic value results. So, sooner or later, the specifier has to write down — has to construct, has to decide upon — whether the semantics of the system or language in question calls for elaborator functions to be defined:

value E: Syn $\rightarrow$ Context $\rightarrow$ State $\rightarrow$ State $\times$ Val

Thus we shall typically elaborate side-effect expressions or value-yielding statements.   ∎

This chapter presents a number of principles and techniques for deciding upon the issue of elaborator functions and for their definition. We say that the meaning of the syntactic construct, usually what we would call a clause (or state-changing expression), expresses both a side-effect (on the state) and a value result.

Summary: Collectively we refer to I, V, E as M (for Meaning). Let Σ stand for the state type. The three kinds of semantic functions can now be summarised:

- Interpretation: $I : \text{Syn} \rightarrow \text{Context} \rightarrow \Sigma \rightarrow \Sigma$
- Evaluation: $V : \text{Syn} \rightarrow \text{Context} \rightarrow \Sigma \rightarrow \text{VAL}$
- Elaboration: $E : \text{Syn} \rightarrow \text{Context} \rightarrow \Sigma \rightarrow \Sigma \times \text{VAL}$

7.5 Denotational Semantics

In Sect. 3.2 we covered the concept of denotational semantics, and we did so reasonably thoroughly. Suffice it here, therefore, to summarise.

Characterisation. By *denotational semantics* we understand a semantics which to syntactic constructs associate mathematical functions and whose formulation (i.e., composition) satisfies the homomorphism principle.   ∎

Next, we illustrate simple and composite generic examples of the denotational principle.

7.5.1 Simple Case

The meaning of a simple syntactic construct is a simple, explicitly presented mathematical function.

type Syn_a, A, B, Sem = A → B
value M: Syn_a → Sem

7.5.2 Composite Case

The meaning, M, of a composite construct is a (i.e., the homomorphic) function, F, of the meaning, M, of each of the immediate components of the composite construct.

type
   Syn_ac == atomic(a:Syn_a) | composite(c:Syn_c)
   Syn_c = Syn_ac × Syn_ac × ... × Syn_ac
value
   F: Sem × Sem × ... × Sem → Sem
   M: Syn_ac → Sem
   M(sy) ≡
      case sy **of**
         atomic(sy′) → M(sy′),
         composite(sy1,sy2,...,syn) → F(M(sy1),M(sy2),...,M(syn))
      end

Sometimes:

value
   F(se1,se2,...,sen) ≡ (M(sn))(...(M(s2)(M(s1)))...)

The above expresses the composition of functions.

A denotational semantics thus typically assigns to a program of a programming language a function from **input** arguments and (**begin** or **start**) states to output results and (**end** or **stop**) states. These **inputs** and **begin** states can be thought of as those presented during elaboration of the program, respectively those in which the elaboration **starts**.

type
   Program, Input, Output, State, ...
value
   M: Program → Input → State → State × Output

7.6 Macro-expansion Semantics

We classify macro-expansion semantics as an operational, that is, a computational semantics.

In Sect. 3.3 we covered the notion of computational semantics — a form of operational semantics. Here we shall cover another form of operational semantics: namely that of considering a semantics definition as prescribing some sort of rewriting. In Sect. 7.7 we review the computational semantics of Sect. 3.3.

7.6.1 Rewriting

We need to informally define some notions of rewriting a specification into another specification. In a specification we have a number of function definitions, typically of the form:

value
   f: A × B × ... × C → D × E × ... × F
   f(a,b,...,c) ≡ $\mathcal{E}$(a,b,...,c,f,g,...,h)
   g: X → Y, ...
   h: P → Q

Given a particular invocation of f, say $f(e_a, e_b, ..., e_c)$, we can now rewrite that "call" into something like: $\mathcal{E}(e_a, e_b, ..., e_c, f, g, ..., h)$. Here we must take into consideration the notions of free and bound variables, collision and confusion, substitution, α-renaming and β-reduction, for such subsidiary invocations as might be expressed by the fs, gs, ..., and hs in the function f definition body $\mathcal{E}(a, b, ..., c, f, g, ..., h)$. In other words, the invocation $f(e_a, e_b, ..., e_c)$ is rewritten into $\mathcal{E}(e_a, e_b, ..., e_c, f, g, ..., h)$, and again into ..., and so forth.

As the following short "symbol manipulation development" shows:

1. **let** f(x) = (... f ...) **in** f(a) **end**
2. **let** f = λ g.λx.(... g ...)(f) **in** f(a) **end**
3. **let** f = F(f) **in** f(a) **end where** F = λ g.λx.(... g ...)
4. **let** f = **YF in** f(a) **end**
5. **Law: YF** = F(**YF**)

one can eliminate named references to a recursively defined function by replacing the function name by its fix point. The operator **Y** is an example of such a fix point-taking operator. Any function f which satisfies the equation f=F(f) is said to be a fix point of F. **Y** "produces" one such fix point. There are many such fix points, but we refer the reader to more foundational language semantics texts for a proper treatment of this. Any of [93, 158, 432, 448, 499, 533] will do. We treated the notion of fix points in Vol. 1, Chap. 7, Sect. 7.8.

7.6.2 Macro-expansion

Characterisation. By a *macro-expansion semantics* we understand a semantics definition in which the meaning of some possibly recursively defined syntactical structure is expressed in terms of a possibly fix point-oriented rewriting of the semantic functions into expressions of the specification language void of any reference to semantic function definitions.

> **type**
>   Program, ..., **RSL_Text**
> **value**
>   M: Program $\to$ **RSL_Text**

Thus a macro-expansion semantics is like a compiling from syntactic values into RSL text.   ∎

Macro-expansion semantics is about substitution of "equals for equals", textwise. Let there be three semantic function definitions:

> $f(a) \equiv (\mathcal{F}_i(a)...g(\mathcal{G}_f(a))...\mathcal{F}_j(a))$
> $g(b) \equiv (\mathcal{G}_\ell(b)...h(\mathcal{H}_g(b))...\mathcal{G}_m(b))$
> $h(c) \equiv \mathcal{H}(c)$

Here the curly capital letter "labelled" expressions, $\mathcal{F}_i(a)$, $\mathcal{F}_j(a)$, $\mathcal{G}_f(a)$, $\mathcal{G}_\ell(a)$, $\mathcal{G}_m(a)$, $\mathcal{H}_g(b)$ and $\mathcal{H}(c)$, stand for arbitrary expressions with possible free variables a, b and c, respectively, and in which there are no references to any defined semantic functions like f, g and h.

    The function invocation:

> $f(e)$

macro-expands, $\leadsto$, stepwise:

> $\mathcal{F}_i(e)...g(\mathcal{G}_f(e))...\mathcal{F}_j(e)$
> $\leadsto \mathcal{F}_i(e)...(\mathcal{G}_\ell(\mathcal{G}_f(e))...h(\mathcal{H}_g(\mathcal{G}_f(e)))...\mathcal{G}_m(\mathcal{G}_f(e)))...\mathcal{F}_j(e)$
> $\leadsto \mathcal{F}_i(e)...(\mathcal{G}_\ell(\mathcal{G}_f(e))...\mathcal{H}(\mathcal{H}_g(\mathcal{G}_f(e)))...\mathcal{G}_m(\mathcal{G}_f(e)))...\mathcal{F}_j(e)$

We refer to the macro-expansion semantics example, Example 7.2.

    It is the ability to read any function definition as a macro-expansion definition that eventually allows us to "convert" programming language semantics definitions into compiling algorithm specifications, that is, definitions which specify which target language text a compiler should generate for any given source language text. For now we can read our semantics definitions as compiling from source languages to RSL text.

7.6.3 Inductive Rewritings

Two kinds of *semantic function recursion* are possible: Static and dynamic inductive semantics.

Static Inductive Semantics

Static inductive semantics derives from the recursive structure of the definition of the syntactic construct. Although a syntax description usually employs recursion to define the syntactic structures these latter are usually finite. Therefore the semantic function recursion will usually terminate due to finiteness of the argument. The *recursive descent* will finally "reach" atomic elements.

Example 7.1 *Maximal Depth:* Although hardly an example of a typical semantics, let us express the maximal depth of finite trees:

type
    Root, Branch, Leaf
    Tree == tree(root:Root subtrees(Branch $\overrightarrow{m}$ SubTree))
    SubTree == leaf(lf:Leaf) | Tree
value
    MaxDepth: Tree → **Nat**
    MaxDepth(tree(r,sts)) ≡ **max** md(tree(r,sts))
    md:Tree → **Nat-set**
    md(tree(r,sts)) ≡
        { n | n:**Nat**,st:SubTree • st ∈ **rng** sts ∧
        n = **case** st **of**: leaf(_) → 1, _ → 1+MaxDepth(st) **end** }

where **max** takes the largest number of a set of natural numbers.   ∎

Dynamic Inductive Semantics

The dynamic inductive semantics derives from the repeated computations designated by the syntactic constructs. Thus it does not refer to a possible recursive definition of a syntactic construct whose semantics is being defined, but to a recursive invocation of the semantic function.

Example 7.2 *While Loop:* A macro-expansion semantics of a while loop is a reasonable example at this stage:

type
    Expression, Variable
    Statement = Assign | While | Compound | ...
    Assign == mkAssign(v:Variable,e:Expression)
    While == mkWhile(e:Expression,s:Statement)
    Compound == mkComp(s1:Statement,s2:Statement)

    ENV = Variable $\overrightarrow{m}$ Location
    Σ = Location $\overrightarrow{m}$ Value

The above defines a "classical" fragment of an imperative language, syntactically with variables, assignments, while loops, compound statements and expressions; and semantically with environments, i.e., contexts (ENV) that bind scoped variables to their storage locations, and storages, i.e., states (Σ) that bind locations to values.

The following definition, although also "appearing" as a denotational semantics, is to be read as a macro-expansion semantics — this will be explained shortly:

value

  M: (Expression|Statement) $\rightarrow$ ENV $\rightarrow$ Σ $\rightarrow$ **RSL_text**
  M(mkAssign(v,e))(ρ)(σ) $\equiv$ σ † [ρ(v) $\mapsto$ M(e)(ρ)(σ)]

  M(mkWhile(e,s))(ρ)(σ) $\equiv$
    if M(e)(ρ)(σ) **then** M(mkComp(s,mkWhile(e,s)))(ρ)(σ) **else skip end**

  M(mkComp(s1,s2))(ρ)(σ) $\equiv$
    let σ' = M(s1)(ρ)(σ) **in** M(s2)(ρ)(σ') **end**

The macro-expansion semantics for the while statement thus amounts to the following identity:

  while e **do** s **end** $\equiv$ **if** e **then** (s;**while** e **do** s **end**) **else skip end**

And so on. The above macro-expansion semantics definition of M leads, after a few substitutions, to the following intermediate text:

  if M(e)(ρ)(σ)
    then
      let σ' = M(s)(ρ)(σ) **in**
      if M(e)(ρ)(σ')
        then
          let σ'' = M(s)(ρ)(σ') **in**
          if M(e)(ρ)(σ'')
            then let σ''' = M(s)(ρ)(σ'') **in** ... **end**
            else skip end end
        else skip end end
    else skip end

where the ellipses, ..., stand for an infinite unfolding of the M(mkWhile(e,s))(ρ)(σ) body.

If we also expand M as applied to the eventual assignment statements and to the finite expressions, then we end up with an infinite RSL text without any reference to, i.e., invocation of, M.

We can avoid that infinite expansion if we allow ourselves to instead either write the identities illustrated above and right below, or if we instead insert the fix point operator **Y**. That is, either:

while e do s end ≡ if e then (s;while e do s end) else skip end

or:

Yλw.λe.λs.if e then (s;w(e,s)) else skip end

The line above is an expression and can be inserted anywhere a **while** loop would otherwise appear.

7.6.4 Fix Point Evaluation

The fix point operator **Y**, as mentioned earlier (Sect. 7.6.1, and in Vol. 1, Chap. 7, Sect. 7.8), satisfies:

YF ≡ F(YF)
/* example */
F: λw.λe.λs.if e then (s;w(e,s)) else skip end

Y(λw.λe.λs.if e then (s;w(e,s)) else skip end)
≡
(λw.λe.λs.if e then (s;w(e,s)) else skip end)
    (Y(λw.λe.λs.if e then (s;w(e,s)) else skip end))
=
λe.λs.if e
    then (s;(Y(λw.λe.λs.if e then (s;w(e,s)) else skip end))(e,s))
    else skip end
= ...

And so on, ad infinitum!   ∎

7.7 Operational and Computational Semantics

In Sect. 3.3 we covered the concept of computational (i.e., operational) semantics, and done so reasonably thoroughly. Suffice it here, therefore, to summarise, but also to bring some additional variations on the theme of computational, cum operational semantics.

Characterisation. By *operational* or, which we will take as the same, *computational semantics*, we understand a meaning that is expressed in terms of the computation, that is, the "workings" of a possibly recursive machine which elaborates the meaning.   ∎

The operational semantics is thus often expressed in terms of a sequence of steps of transitions from one machine state to another. The machine state is itself oftentimes rather concretely presented.

An operational semantics thus typically assigns to a program of a programming language a sequence (a trace) of state-to-state transitions — where the state also contains the input and the output "media" on which input arguments and result values are placed.

type
    Program, Input, Output, ...
    State = Input $\times \Sigma \times$ Output
value
    M: Program $\rightarrow$ State$^\omega$

These inputs and begin states can be thought of as those presented during elaboration of the program, respectively those in which the elaboration starts.

7.7.1 Stack Semantics

We already covered the notion of stack semantics in Example 3.4 (Sect. 3.3.3).

Characterisation. By *operational stack semantics* we understand an operational semantics of a recursively defined syntax which is expressed without referring to a machine that can "recurse", i.e., a machine that is not allowed to recursively invoke the interpreter function. Recursion is resolved by suitable push and pop operations on one or more stacks.   ∎

7.7.2 Attribute Grammar Semantics

Characterisation. By an *attribute grammar semantics* we understand an operational semantics description which is *expressed* in terms of a state consisting of a (usually large) number of semantic category variables, one set for each syntactic category, and one instantiation of each such set for each syntactic category (i.e., nonterminal) labelled node in a parse tree of the language defined by the syntax.   ∎

More specifically, an attribute grammar can be *expressed* as a set of annotated syntactic concrete type (i.e., rule) definitions.

Each syntactic rule has (i) a left-hand side (lhs) syntactic category (nonterminal) name (c_i), (ii) a right-hand side possibly empty $(n = 0)$ list of syntactic category (i.e., nonterminal) names $(c_{i_1}, c_{i_2}, \ldots, c_{i_n})$ and syntactic constants (i.e., literals, omitted below),

$$<C_i> ::= <C_{i_1}> \ldots <C_{i_2}> \ldots \ldots <C_{i_n}>$$

and (iii) an unordered set of simple (f) assignments to a set of semantic category typed variables:

$$v_{t_{i_{c_a}}} := f(v_{t_{j_{c_b}}}, \ldots, v_{t_{k_{c_c}}})$$

(iv) The variables are associated with the lhs or the rhs cs: $a, b, \ldots, c = 0, 1, \ldots, n$.

We give two very simple examples. They both concern the evaluation of floating point numerals into real numbers. Thus we must establish a syntax for the numerals, a notion of parse trees and an abstract specification of the problem. From this we "derive" the sets of attributed variables and the sets of assignment statements to be associated with nodes of such trees.

Example 7.3 *Synthesised Evaluation:*

type
    D == nu|en|to|tr|fi|fe|se|sy|ot|ni
    P == p
    R = N × P × F
    N == s(d:D) | c(n:N,d:D)
    F == s(d:D) | c(d:D,f:F)
value
    fp: R → **Real**
    no: N → **Nat**
    fr: F → **Real**
    ci: D → **Nat**
    fp(n,,f) ≡ no(n) + fr(f)
    no(n) ≡ **case** n **of** s(d)→ci(d), c(n',d)→10∗no(n')+ci(d) **end**
    fr(f) ≡ **case** f **of** s(d)→ci(d)/10, c(d,f')→(ci(d)+fr(f'))/10 **end**
    ci(d) ≡ **case** d **of** nu→0,en→1,to→2,...,ni→9 **end**

variable
    vN **type Nat**, vF **type Real**, vD **type Nat**

A corresponding synthesised attribute grammar:

```
<D>   ::= 0           vD   := ci(0)
<D>   ::= 1           vD   := ci(1)
...
<D>   ::= 9           vD   := ci(9)
<R>   ::= <N> . <F>   vR   := vN + vF
<N>   ::= <D>         vN   := vD
<N>r  ::= <N>s <D>    vNr  := 10*vNs + vD
<F>   ::= <D>         vF   := vD/10
<F>r  ::= <D> <F>s    vFr  := (vFs + vD)/10
```

∎

The above attribute grammar "works", i.e., specifies evaluation, from the leaf nodes up, assignments are made at leaf nodes, and value computation proceeds from the leaf nodes towards the root node.

The next attribute grammar — shown after a conventional definition — "works", i.e., specifies evaluation, two ways: from the root node down, and from leaf nodes up. Assignments made at leaf nodes and value computation based on these proceed from the leaf nodes towards the root node. But assignments made at the root node propagate towards the leaves — where they merge with "opposite direction" evaluations.

Example 7.4 *Synthesised and Inherited Evaluation:*

type
    D == nu|en|to|tr|fi|fe|se|sy|ot|ni
    R = N × N
    N == s(d:D) | c(n:N,d:D)
value
    fp: R → **Real**, val: N → **Int** → **Nat**
    fp(n,f) ≡ val(n)(0) + val(f)(−1)
    val(n)(e) ≡
        case n **of**
            s(d) → ci(d)∗(10↑e),
            c(n′,d) → val(n′)(**if** e>0 **then** e+1 **else** e−1 **end**) + ci(d)∗(10↑e)
        end

f argument values "propagate" from the root towards leaves.

```
<D>  ::= d                  vD  := ci(d)
         d=0,1,...,9
<R>  ::= <N>n . <N>f        vR  := vNn + vNf,
                            eNn := +1, eNf := -1
<N>  ::= <D>                vN  := vD*(10**eN)
<N>r ::= <N>s <D>           vNr := vNs + vD
                            eNs := eNr + if eNr>0
                                   then -1 else +1 end
```

■

Some characterisations and comments are in order:

- **Synthesised attributes:** An assignment rule associated with a node c_0, and of the form:

$$v_{t_{i_{c_0}}} := f(v_{t_{j_{c_\alpha}}}, \ldots, v_{t_{k_{c_\omega}}}), \quad \alpha, \ldots, \omega \text{ some of } 1, \ldots, n$$

  that is, where a root attribute, i.e., a variable of type t_i is given a value that is a function f of the value of variables associated with immediate successor nodes $v_\alpha, \ldots, v_\omega$, defines v_{t_i} to be a *synthesised attribute*: That is, its value is computed "bottom up": from subtree attributes to the root attributes.

- **Inherited attributes:** An assignment rule associated with a node c_β (for β in $1, \ldots, n$), and of the form:

$$v_{t_{i_{c_\beta}}} := f(v_{t_{j_{c_0}}})$$

that is, where a subtree attribute, i.e., a variable of type t_i is given a value that is a function f of the value of a root attribute $v_{t_{j_{c_0}}}$, defines v_{t_i} to be an *inherited attribute*. Its value is computed "top up": from root attributes towards subtree attributes.

- **Composite attributes:** An assignment rule associated with a node c_β (for β in $1, \ldots, n$), and of the form:

$$v_{t_{i_{c_\beta}}} := f(v_{t_{j_{c_\alpha}}}, \ldots, v_{t_{k_{c_\omega}}}), \quad \alpha, \ldots, \omega \text{ some of } 0, \ldots, n$$

that is, where a subtree attribute, i.e., a variable of type t_i is given a value that is a function f of the value of both root attributes $v_{t_{j_{c_0}}}$ and immediate successor nodes $v_\alpha, \ldots, v_\omega$, defines v_{t_i} to be a *composite attribute*. Its value is computed "top down and bottom up": "across" subtree attributes towards subtree attributes. The notion of composite attributes is, strictly speaking, not necessary since one can express the same by a suitable introduction of additional attributes and both synthesised and inherited assignments.

- **Circular attributes:** The totality of parse tree node attribute assignments may, erroneously, define circular assignments, that is, assignments to an attribute which mutually depend on one another through the "path" of other assignments. We let Fig. 7.1 informally define what we mean by path, etc.

- **Theory:** The last anomaly points to the need for a proper theory of attribute grammars. Such a theory exists; see [128, 262, 270, 272, 304, 328, 376, 532, 541].

A Symbolic Attributed Parse Tree Example

Figure 7.1 shows a symbolic example of a fragment of a parse tree.

The parse tree is designated by the straight lines connecting the five fat bullets ($\bullet$). The rectangular boxes designate assignment statements. We have shown three at each node but mean to indicate an arbitrary number of these, hence the "two+...+one" rectangles. The ellipses, ..., between the "two" and the "one" indicate this "could be any finite number (even zero, one, two or just three)"! It is symbolic since we do not make the box assignments exactly precise. Dashed arrows designate sources of input values for the computation of target attribute values. The text at the bottom of the figure lists which variables are synthesised, inherited, composite and circular.

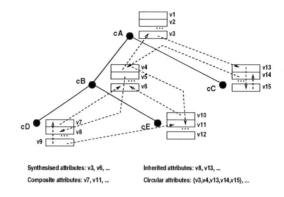

Synthesised attributes: v3, v6, ...   Inherited attributes: v8, v13, ...
Composite attributes: v7, v11, ...   Circular attributes: {v3,v4,v13,v14,v15}, ...

Fig. 7.1. A symbolic attributed parse tree example

7.8 Proof Rule Semantics

Characterisation. By an *axiomatic* or a *proof rule semantics* we understand a set of proof rules, one for each language clause.   ∎

We shall not exemplify the notion of proof rule semantics at this place in these volumes. Instead we will conclude the string of examples of storage models by presenting one where assignment is expressed as an axiom. See Example 7.5.
   The example presupposes material presented in subsequent chapters.

Example 7.5 *Axiomatic Specification of Storage: Assignment to Variables:*
   In Examples 8.17 and 8.19 we will illustrate (three) syntactical models of variable name, value, location and storage structures. In the present example we illustrate a model of assignment in the storage model of Example 8.17 of either scalar or composite values to similar locations.
   The structured storage value and location model we wish to build shall satisfy: *The contents of the i'th component of a (record or vector) structured location is the i'th component of the structured (corresponding record, respectively vector) value for that storage location.*

type
    VAL = ScaVAL | ComVAL
    ScaVAL == NumVAL(i:**Int**) | TruVAL(b:**Bool**)
    ComVAL == SeqVAL(xl:**Int***) | RecVAL(rv:(Nm $\overrightarrow{m}$ VAL))
    L
    LOC = ScaLOC | ComLOC
    ScaLOC == NumLOC(i:L) | TruLOC(b:L)
    ComLOC == SeqLOC(xl:LOC*) | RecLOC(rv:(Nm $\overrightarrow{m}$ LOC))
    ENV = V $\overrightarrow{m}$ LOC
    STG = LOC $\overrightarrow{m}$ VAL

It proves useful to define a number of auxiliary predicates and observer functions: SubLOCs: All (possibly nested) sublocations of a location.

value
    SubLOCs: LOC → LOC-set
    SubLOCs(l) ≡
      (**case** l **of**
          RecLOC(rm) → **rng** rm ∪ ∪ {SubLOCs(l′)|l′:LOC•l′ ∈ **rng** rm}
          SeqLOC(sl) → **elems** sl ∪ ∪ {SubLOCs(l′)|l′:LOC•l′ ∈ **elems** rm}
          _ → {} **end**) ∪ {l}

IndLOCs: independence of locations, that is, there are two common sublocations:

    IndLOCs: LOC × LOC → **Bool**
    IndLOCs(l,l′) ≡ SubLOCs(l) ∩ SubLOCs(l′) = {}

    isDense: A vector index set is dense:

    isDense: **Int-set** → **Bool**
    isDense(xs) ≡ xs = {**min** xs .. **max** xs}

Well-formedness of locations and values was already defined — except that we "glossed" over the independence of locations! We show only the wf_LOC case:

    wf_LOC: LOC → **Bool**
    wf_LOC(l) ≡
      case l **of**
          RecLOC(rm) → ∀ l′:LOC•l′ ∈ **rng** rm ⇒ wf_LOC(l′),
          SeqLOC(sl)
            → (isDense(**inds** sl)
               ∧ ∀ l′,l″:LOC•l′,l″isin **elems** sl ⇒
                   wf_LOC(l′) ∧ (l′≠l″ ⇒ IndLOCs(l′,l″)) ∧
                   x_type(l′)=x_type(l″))
          _ → **true end**

Well-formedness of storage:

    wf_STG: STG → **Bool**
    wf_STG(stg) ≡
      ∀ l:LOC•l ∈ **dom** stg ⇒
        wf_LOC(l) ∧ wf_VAL(stg(l))
        ∧ c_type(l) = c_type(stg(l))
        ∧ ∀ l′:LOC•l′ ∈ **dom** stg ∧ l∼−l′ ⇒ IndLOCs(l,l′)

Unfolding a well-formed structured storage into a storage also of all sublocations can be defined:

Unfold: STG → STG
Unfold(stg) ≡
   stg ∪
   merge { Unfold([l↦v]) | ∃ l':LOC •
            l' ∈ **dom** stg ⇒ l ∉ ScaLOC ∧
            case l' **of**
               RecLOC(rm) →
                  ∃ n:Nm•nm ∈ **dom** rm ⇒ (l=l'(n)) ∧ (v=(stg(l'))(n)),
               SeqLOC(sl) →
                  ∃ i:**Int**•i ∈ **elems** sl ⇒ (l=l'(i)) ∧ (v=(stg(l'))(i)) **end** }

merge: STG-**set** $\overset{\sim}{\to}$ STG
merge(stgs) ≡
   [l↦v | l:LOC,v:VAL•∃ stg:STG•stg ∈ stgs ∧ stg(l)=v]
   pre: ∀ s,s':STG•s,s' ∈ stgs⇒**dom** s' ∩ **dom** s={}

Finally, we are ready to bring in the three major storage functions. Please recall that a location passed to storage can be any sublocation:

Allocate "fresh", unused, independent storage:

Allocate: Kind → STG → STG × LOC
Allocate(k)(s) ≡
   let l:LOC • l∉ **dom** Unfold(s)∧wf_LOC(l)∧x_type(l)=m
   in s ∪ [l ↦ Undef(k)] **end**

We leave *Undef* undefined: It yields an arbitrary initial value of the right kind.

Take *Contents* of storage location:

Contents: LOC → STG $\overset{\sim}{\to}$ VAL
Contents(l)(s) ≡ (Unfold(s))(l)
   pre l ∈ **dom** Unfold(s)

Assign value to location in storage:

Assign: LOC × VAL → STG $\overset{\sim}{\to}$ STG
Assign(l,v)(s) **as** s'
   pre wf_LOC(l)∧wf_VAL(v) ∧
      l ∈ **dom** Unfold(s) ∧ x_type(l)=x_type(v)
   post wf_STG(s')∧
      let us=Unfold(s), us'=Unfold(s') **in**
      dom us = **dom** us' ∧ es'(l)=v ∧
      ∀ l':LOC•l' ∈ **dom** us ⇒ (IndLOCs(l,l') ⇒ us(l')=us'(l')) **end**

7.9 Discussion

7.9.1 General

Syntactical structures beg (i.e., "cry out for") a semantic explanation. Semantics is what we mean in a phenomenological sense. Semantics is expressed in terms of three things: the syntactical "things" to be explained, the semantical structures in terms of which to explain it, and the functions (or relations) mapping the former into the latter. Whereas syntax deals with inert structures, text strings or mathematical compounds, semantics is expressed in terms of functions or relations between such, that is, mappings from syntactical structures to semantics structures. The choice of technique for, or style of, semantical explication is based on pragmatic considerations.

7.9.2 Principles, Techniques and Tools

We summarise:

Principles. No syntax without a semantics, that is, semantics first, then syntactics.   ∎

Principles. Fit the form of semantics to the problem at hand.   ∎

Such forms are listed next:

Techniques. There are many forms and techniques involved when developing semantics: techniques related to denotational semantics, techniques related to computational semantics, techniques related to axiomatic semantics, etc.   ∎

Tools. There are many tools with which to express, i.e., to define syntax. RSL is restricted to not handling reflexive, i.e., recursively defined functional types, but is otherwise very useful. When faced with reflexive functional types then use an appropriate subset of RSL, one that syntactically is similar to the denotational semantics specification languages used in either of the books referred to in Sect. 7.10. Attribute grammars, as will also be illustrated in Sects. 16.9–16.10, are useful as a means for expressing steps toward automatable syntax checkers and code generators. When dealing with concurrency, e.g., parallel programming languages, you may have to use the "surrogate" structural operational semantics style of RSL introduced in Chap. 19. For other semantics situations use simple sorts and axioms.   ∎

7.10 Bibliographical Notes

There are many excellent textbooks on semantics. We list these explicitly:

[93]   J. de Bakker: *Control Flow Semantics* (The MIT Press, Cambridge, Mass., USA, 1995)

[158] C. Gunther: *Semantics of Programming Languages* (The MIT Press, Cambridge, Mass., USA, 1992)

[370] P.D. Mosses: *Action Semantics* (Cambridge University Press: Tracts in Theoretical Computer Science, 1992)

[432] J. Reynolds: *The Semantics of Programming Languages* (Cambridge University Press, 1999)

[448] D.A. Schmidt: *Denotational Semantics: a Methodology for Language Development* (Allyn & Bacon, 1986)

[499] R. Tennent: *The Semantics of Programming Languages* (Prentice Hall, 1997)

[533] G. Winskel: *The Formal Semantics of Programming Languages* (The MIT Press, 1993)

7.11 Exercises

Exercise 7.1 *Macro-expanding a λ-Calculus Semantics.* We refer to Vol.1, Sect. 20.2, where we presented and explained λ-expressions for a number of imperative language constructs:

```
───────────── λ-Expressions for Imperative Language Constructs ─────────────

1. Declarations: variable v:Type := expression

   type
       LOC, VAL
       ρ:ENV = V ⇸ LOC
       σ:STG = LOC ⇸ VAL
   value
       𝓘: RSL_Text ⥲ ENV ⥲ STATE ⥲ STATE

       𝓘[ variable v := e; txt ](ρ)(σ) ≡
           let loc:LOC • loc ∉ dom σ,
               val = 𝒱(e)(ρ)(σ) in
           let σ′ = σ ∪ [ loc ↦ val ] in
           𝓘[ txt ](ρ † [ v ↦ loc ])(σ′)
           end end

2. Assignments: v := expr

       𝓘[ v := e ](ρ)(σ) ≡ σ † [ ρ(v) ↦ 𝒱(e)(σ) ]
```

3. The **skip** statement:

$$\mathcal{I}[\textbf{skip}] \equiv \lambda\sigma{:}\Sigma \bullet \sigma$$

4. Statement sequences: stm_1;stm_2;...;stm_n

$$\mathcal{I}[s\_1;s\_2](\rho)(\sigma) \equiv \mathcal{I}(s\_2)(\mathcal{I}(s\_1)(\sigma))$$

5. Conditional statement: **if** expr **then** stm_c **else** stm_a **end**

$$\mathcal{I}[\textbf{if } e \textbf{ then } c\_s \textbf{ else } a\_s \textbf{ end}](\rho)(\sigma) \equiv$$
   let $b = \mathcal{V}[e](\rho)(\sigma)$ **in**
   if b **then** $\mathcal{I}[c\_s](\rho)(\sigma)$ **else** $\mathcal{I}[a\_s](\rho)(\sigma)$
   end end

6. Variable expressions: v

$$\mathcal{V}[v](\rho)(\sigma) \equiv \sigma(\rho(l))$$

Give a λ-calculus semantics to the following "program":

variable $v := e$; $v := e'$; **if** v **then** skip **else** $v := e''$ **end**; $v := e'''$

Exercise 7.2 *Macro-expanding a Tree-Depth Computation.* We refer to Example 7.1. Given a tree:

$\tau\colon \text{tree}(r,[\,b{\mapsto}\ell,b'{\mapsto}\text{tree}(r',[\,\beta{\mapsto}\text{tree}(\rho,[\,])\,])),b''{\mapsto}\text{tree}(r'',[\,])\,])$

use the definitions of Example 7.1 to macro-expand $\mathsf{MaxDepth}(\tau)$.

• • •

We continue the line of exercises which is centred around the design of a family of programming languages starting with STIL.

The STIL, NaTaTIL, DiTIL, and DUaLTIL series of language design exercises are: Exercises 6.3–6.5, 7.3–7.7, 8.7–8.8, 9.2–9.4, and 9.5.

• • •

Exercise 7.3 *A Structured Type Concept (STIL).* You are to formalise the below narrative:

1. A type is either a scalar type, or is a compound type.
2. A scalar type is either an **integer**, or is a **Boolean**, or is a **real**, or is a **character**.
3. A compound type is either a vector type or is a record type.

4. A vector type consists of vector lower and upper index bounds and a vector element type.
5. Vector lower and upper index bounds are pairs of integer numerals such that the first is smaller than the second.
6. A record type is a set of pairs where each pair consists of a record field identifier and a type — such that all record field identifiers of a record type are distinct.
7. A record field identifier is a simple identifier.

Exercise 7.4 *A Structured Value Concept: Types (STIL).* Isomorphic with the above type concept, you are to express, informally, as a narrative, and to formalise a value concept, i.e., to narrate and formalise value types.

Exercise 7.5 *A Structured Value Concept: Auxiliary Functions (STIL).* Some constraints are to be imposed on the structured values of Exercise 7.4:

1. A vector value must consist of at least two elements.
2. The element values of a vector value must all be of the same type.
3. The indexes of a vector value must form a dense set of integers: If i and j are indexes of a vector value, then for all integers k properly between i and j, k is also an index of the vector value.
4. A record value must consist of at least two fields, that is, each with their (distinct) field identifier.

Narrate and formalise the functions necessary to express the above.

Exercise 7.6 *A Structured Location Concept (STIL).* Isomorphic with the structured value concept of Exercise 7.5 you are to narrate and formalise a concept of structured locations and the auxiliary and well-formedness functions that go with the type definitions.

Exercise 7.7 *A Structured Storage Concept (STIL).* We now wish to design and document, i.e., narrate and formalise, a storage concept which allows for locations to be mapped into values of the same type, including, and this is the interesting bit, for structured locations to be mapped into structured values of the same type. Please do so! That is, narrate and formalise. Please consider the following issues: allocation of fresh, unused locations; assignment of values, also to sublocations; reading of values, also from sublocations; and freeing only of allocated locations.

8

Syntax

- The **prerequisite** for studying this chapter is that you are familiar with Vol. 1's abstract specification principles and techniques and the RSL type concept.
- The **aims** are to review the concept of grammars, notably BNF grammars, and their relation to the concept of abstract syntax, as found in, for example, RSL, to review and further cover the concept of abstract syntax, both as axiomatically specifiable, and as specifiable using, for example, the RSL abstract type concept, and to exemplify uses of the RSL concrete type concept in defining both syntactic and semantic structures, i.e., types.
- The **objective** is to ensure that you become a real software engineering professional, able to choose pleasing and appropriate type abstractions.
- The **treatment** is semiformal and systematic.

_____ Conventional View on Syntax _____

Syntax, is, in a sense, what we see (and hear). Syntax looks "smart" or it looks "ugly". A person's attention is captured by syntax. One often judges a technological gadget by its appearance, but one seldom asks: "What really is behind the syntax?"

_____ General View on Syntax _____

Syntax is more than "appearance". It is also structure: structure of meaning, structure of configurations, contexts, states and values — such as we have treated these concepts in previous chapters.

8.1 The Issues

8.1.1 Form and Content: Syntax and Semantics

Often, in ordinary, everyday talk, one speaks of *form and content*. By *form* is then meant: "What one sees". And by *content* one then means: "The significance, the meaning, of that which one sees".

Throughout these volumes we shall use types and type definitions to formalise *form* and we shall use function definitions and/or axioms to formalise *content*.

Usually syntax is taken to be a concept associated with sentential forms: "the syntax of a programming language", or "the grammar of English" [241–244]. The following delineation, as we usually find 'syntax' characterised, reflects this one-sidedness:

Characterisation. By *syntax* we understand (i) the ways in which words are arranged (cf. Greek: *syntaxis:* arrangement) to show meaning (cf. semantics) within and between sentences, and (ii) rules for forming *syntactically correct* sentences [84]. ■

Syntax is important. We need to communicate, between people, often via machines, and (thus also) between people and machines. We need to ensure that communication is effective, elegant and pleasing, and that what is written and said also covers what is meant — and, preferably, just that!

Characterisation. (I) By a *formal syntax* we understand a syntax such that we can also analyse sentential structures wrt. their possibly ambiguous composition. ■

But not only sentential structures have syntax. Meaning structures, i.e., semantical values also have syntax. Hence we expand on the above definition:

Characterisation. (II) By a *formal syntax* we understand (i) on one hand, the ways in which (i.1) either words are, or (i.2) information (i.e., data) is, arranged in order to show (i.1) meaning within and between sentences, (i.2) respectively relations between information parts. (ii) By *formal syntax* we, on the other hand, also understand rules for analysing *syntactically correct* (ii.1) sentences, respectively (ii.2) information (i.e., data) structures. ■

By the above distinction between (i) and (ii) we mean to express the following: (i) Any particular sentence (any one particular "piece" of information) has its own, specific, i.e., instantiated syntax. And (ii) there are, in general, rules for most likely infinite sets of 'particular sentences'. By the above distinction between (i-ii.1) and (i-ii.2) we mean to express the following: (i-ii.1) There is the syntax of sentences, usually uttered or written (hence syntactic) "things", and (i-ii.2) there are the syntax of information structures (i.e., semantic "things").

8.1.2 Structure and Contents of This Chapter

The present chapter is structured — and covers material — as follows. First, in Sect. 8.2 we delineate the two main occurrences of syntax: of grammatical sentence structures and of semantical information and data structures. In Sect. 8.3 we give the first presentation of abstract syntax, in the sense of John McCarthy's paper from 1962 [330]. In Sect. 8.5, we review the important area of conventional grammars and their dual role as generators of sentential structures, and as bases for constructing recognisers that parse sentential structures into parse trees. In Sect. 8.4 we review conventional BNF grammars and parse trees and their possible representation. The thread of this section is taken up from a previous section, i.e., Sect. 8.5. In Sect. 8.7 we revert to the concept of abstract syntaxes, but now as "embodied" in RSL. Finally, in Sect. 8.8 we indicate how abstract data types might be implemented in ordinary programming languages' rather more constrained concrete structures, notably using their conventional record types.

8.2 Sentential Versus Semantical Structures

—————————————— Syntax for Defining Syntax ——————————————

Rules of syntax can be and are used to describe classes of sentential structures as well as classes of meaning structures. We shall use the RSL type facility, both as concerns abstract types, i.e., property-oriented sorts, and as concerns concrete types, i.e., model-oriented type definitions, to state rules of syntax.

8.2.1 General

The syntax is sentential, i.e., of text-oriented structures, if we speak of the syntax of a language, including a specification or a programming language. The syntax is of semantic structures if we speak of a system of denotational or computational types.

Syntax of Sentential Structures

Characterisation. By *sentential structures* we mean sequences of characters such as you are reading right now, and such as those of formulas, expressions and statements of specification and programming languages.   ■

But the sentential structures could also be those of certain utterings, certain simple and composite terms of a domain-specific professional language such as the language of bank clerks, of air traffic controllers or of train dispatchers, etc.

Syntax of Semantical Structures

Characterisation. By *semantical structures* we mean atomic and composite configuration, context and state structures as well as the values that relate to (i.e., are parts of) these structures. ∎

The semantical structures are thus those of the data structures of RSL [130] and Java [8, 15, 146, 301, 465, 513] and other specification or programming languages, or of other mathematical systems: algebras, logics, etc. Semantical structures are also those of "real world" phenomena: the (context and state) structures of a financial service institution, or of air traffic or of a railway, etc.

8.2.2 Examples of Sentential Structures

Syntax is about form, not content, "appearance", not meaning. One can express the number seven in many different ways:

$$7, \text{seven}, \text{vii}, \text{uuuu}, 00111, 13$$

That is, we can express it as an Arabic-like numeral, as a name spelled out in letters, as a Roman numeral, as a sequence of seven "strokes", as a binary numeral or as a radix four numeral.

There may be many syntactic instances signifying the "same thing" (as here the number seven), but one may say that there is exactly one (instance of the) number (that we name) seven!

Example 8.1 *A Syntax for Sequences of Real Numerals:* A BNF-like[1] syntax, albeit in RSL, for real numerals, and for suitably bracketed sequences of real numerals is given next:

type
    RealNum = Sign × ISeq × Point × FSeq
    Sign == nosign | minus | plus
    Point == point
    ISeq == nil() | mkI(s:ISeq,d:Digit)
    FSeq == nil() | mkF(d:Digit,s:FSeq)
    Digit == zero | one | two | three | four | five | six | seven | eight | nine

    SeqRealNum = Left × RealNum × SRN × Right
    Left == left, Right == right
    SRN == void() | mkS(co:Co,rn:RealNum,sq:SRN)
    Co == comma

---

[1]By a BNF grammar we mean a Backus–Naur Form context-free syntax. The Glossary (Appendix B of Vol. 1) defines these and related terms.

A real numeral, one that we would normally write, for example:

$$12.40,$$

would, according to the above syntax, be represented by:

```
((nosign,
mkI(mkI(nil(),one),two)),
point,
mkF(one,mkF(two,nil()))))
```

A sequence of real numerals, one that we would normally write, for example:

$$< +1.2, -3.4 >$$

would, according to the above syntax, be represented by:

```
(left,
((plus,mkI(nil(),one)),point,mkF(two,nil())),
mkS(comma,
((minus,mkI(nil(),three)),point,mkF(four,nil())),void()),
right)
```

∎

Example 8.2 *A Syntax for Sequences of Reals:* The meaning of a real numeral is a real number, and the meaning of a syntactic juxtaposition of real numerals is here taken to be a mathematical sequence of the meanings of real numerals:

type
    RN = **Real**
    SR = RN*

Note the distinction: syntactic juxtapositions versus semantic sequences.   ∎

Modelling Simple Sentential Structures

On one hand, we have simple sentential structures such as identifiers and literals (such as numerals, truth value designators, etc.). On the other hand, we have their atomic meanings, viz.: denotations of identifiers, numbers, truth values, etc. The former may be elaborately structured, such as were real numerals; the latter were just atomic, semantic types.

Principles. When modelling *names of values that are atomic*, instead of modelling the syntax (i.e., the type) of these names, we suggest to represent such syntax directly by the type names of that which they denote.   ∎

Techniques. Thus, to spell the above principle out in clear, but fully generic examples, we have that:

- the syntax, i.e., the type for natural number numerals is **Nat**;
- the syntax, i.e., the type for integer number numerals is **Int**;
- the syntax, i.e., the type for truth value literals is **Bool**; and
- the syntax, i.e., the type for identifiers is some sort name, say Id, Nm, or other.

This simplifies matters.   ∎

There will still be a need for modelling literals in the form of enumerated types.

Example 8.3 *Syntax of Definite Sets of Literals:* We show some simple, rather obvious examples:

type
    Dice == one | two | three | four | five | six
    WeekDay == monday | tuesday | wednesday | thursday | friday
    Season == winter | spring | summer | fall
    ValveSetting == on | off
    JobStatus == not_scheduled | waiting | running | suspended

                                                                                         ∎

8.2.3 Examples of Semantical Structures

We give the syntax of three kinds of example of semantical structures: programming language data structures (and their types), operating system resource "state", and the state of a securities exchange, i.e., a stock exchange.

The reasons why we show these three examples are, they all illustrate concepts of semantical structures, they are widely different, i.e., come from "entirely" different domains, and they therefore suggest the width and depth of the concept of "semantical syntaxes".

Example 8.4 *Variant Record Structures of a Programming Language:* Let us assume the following kind of data structures of some (possibly hypothetical) programming language: integers, Booleans, characters, simple records, simple vectors and variant records. All but the last kind of data structure are called simple data structures. A simple record is a finite set of two or more uniquely named simple fields. A field name is a further unexplained quantity. A simple field is a simple data structure. A simple vector is a finite sequence of simple data structures. A variant record data structure is a finite set of two or more uniquely named variant or simple fields. A field is either a simple data structure, or is a conditional field. A conditional field is a pair: The first element of the pair is a simple enumerated value from a "small" set of such enumeration values. Let us refer to this enumeration set as $\{a, b, ..., c\}$. The second element is a simple data structure of a kind indicated by the first element enumeration value. If, for example, that first element is a, then the second element is a simple data structure of one kind. If, instead that first element is b, then the second element is a simple data structure of another kind, etcetera.

To formalise the above, we distinguish between kind of data structure and value of data structure. By 'kind' we mean the same, basically, as type. First, we define the types of data structures:

type

    Fn, Enum

    Nat2 = {| i:**Nat** • i$\geq$2 |}

    DST = SiDST | VaRT

    SiDST = IntT | BoolT | CharT | SiRT | SiVT

    IntT == integer

    BoolT == boolean

    ChaT == character

    SiRT == mkSiRT(rt:(Fn $\overrightarrow{m}$ SiDST))

    SiVT == mkSiVT(hi:Nat1,tp:SiDST)

    VaRT == mkVaRT(vt:(Enum $\overrightarrow{m}$ (Fn $\overrightarrow{m}$ SiDST)))

Then we define the values of data structures:

type

    DSV = SiDSV | VaRV

    SiDSV = IntV | BoolV | CharV | SiRV | SiVV

    IntV == mkIntV(i:**Int**)

    BoolV == mkBoolV(b:**Bool**)

    CharV == mkCharV(c:**Char**)

    SiRV == mkSiRV(rv:(Fn $\overrightarrow{m}$ SiDSV))

    SiVV == mkSiVV(hi:Nat1,vv:SiDSV*)

    VaRV == mkVaRV(e:Enum,rv:(Fn $\overrightarrow{m}$ SiDSV))

Type checking is now simple. Let a pair of a type and a value be postulated to match one another:

value

    type_check: DST × DSV → **Bool**

    type_check(t,v) ≡

      case (t,v) **of**

        (integer,mkIntV(i)) → **true**,

        (boolean,mkBoolV(b)) → **true**,

        (character,mkCharV(c)) → **true**,

        (mkSiRT(rt),mkSiRV(rv)) →

$$\textbf{dom } rt = \textbf{dom } rv \wedge$$
$$\forall \ f{:}Fn{\bullet}f \in \textbf{dom } rt \Rightarrow type\_check(rt(f),rv(f)),$$
$$(mkSiVT(hi,vt),mkSiVV(hi',vv)) \rightarrow$$
$$hi'{\le}hi \wedge \textbf{len } vv \le hi' \wedge$$
$$\forall \ v{:}SiDSV{\bullet}v \in \textbf{elems } vv \bullet type\_check(vt,vv),$$
$$(mkVaRT(vt),mkVaRV(e,rv)) \rightarrow$$
$$e \in \textbf{dom } vt \wedge type\_check(vt(e),rv).$$
$$\_ \rightarrow \textbf{false}$$
end

Example 8.5 *Directory Structures of an Operating System:* Let an operating system keep track of user resources: user directories (and their files), standard operating system facilities (compilers, database management systems, etc.), machine resources (storage by category, input/output units, etc.), and so on. Let, for each of the suitable categories of user, operating system and machine resources, there be a suitably, i.e., hierarchically (i.e., tree) structured subdirectory. Let the overall machine state "within" which the operating system operates be referred to as σ.

Here is a proposal:

$$\Sigma = SR \times STG \times ...$$
Uid, Cid, Mid
$$SR = UR \times OR \times MR$$
$$UR = Uid \ _{\overrightarrow{m}} \ U\_DIR$$
$$OR = Cid \ _{\overrightarrow{m}} \ O\_RES$$
$$MR = Mid \ _{\overrightarrow{m}} \ M\_RES$$
$$U\_DIR = (Fn \ _{\overrightarrow{m}} \ FILE) \times (Dn \ _{\overrightarrow{m}} \ U\_DIR)$$
$$FILE = \textbf{Text} \mid Exec \mid ...$$
$$Exec = \Sigma \ \overset{\sim}{\rightarrow} \ \Sigma$$
$$O\_RES = (Fn \ _{\overrightarrow{m}} \ FILE) \times (Dn \ _{\overrightarrow{m}} \ O\_RES)$$
$$M\_RES = ...$$

We leave it to the reader to decipher the above!

Example 8.6 *Context and State Structures of a Stock Exchange:* Let a securities instrument exchange, i.e., a stock exchange, at any one time, say during trading hours, be said to be in a state that reflects buy and sell offers. A buy (or a sell) offer refers to (i) the name of the buyer (seller), (ii) the name of a securities instrument (a stock, e.g., IBM), (iii) the quantity (i.e., the number of stocks) to be bought (respectively sold), (iv) the highest (respectively lowest) price beyond which it cannot be bought (sold), (v) the allowable lowest (highest) price beyond which it can (still) be sold (bought),

(vi) the time period, in terms of a pair of times (minute, hour, day, month, year), i.e., a time interval, during which the offer is (expected to be) valid. Let the stock exchange state also reflect the actually transacted buy and sell offers (i.e., of some past), as well as those buy and sell offers that might have been withdrawn from being offered.

type

    Sn, Nm, Hour, Min, Day, Month, Year

    SEC = OFFERS × ACTED × WTHDRWN

    OFFERS = BuyOffers × SellOffers

    BuyOffers,SellOffers = Sn $\overrightarrow{m}$ OFR

    OFR = Nm → (Intvl $\overrightarrow{m}$ (Quant × Low × High))

    Intvl = TimeDate × TimeDate

    TimeDate = Hour × Min × Day × Month × Year

    Quant = **Nat**

    Low, High = Price

    Price = **Nat**

    ACTED = Nm $\overrightarrow{m}$ (Sn $\overrightarrow{m}$ (TimeDate $\overrightarrow{m}$ Quant×Price×(Low×High)))

    WTHDRWN = TimeDate $\overrightarrow{m}$ (BuyOffers × SellOffers)

We leave it to the reader to decipher the above and to ponder about possible well-formedness constraints. Also, the above reflects just one of a possible variety of formalisations. Which to choose depends on which kind of operations one wishes to perform on a stock exchange: *place a buy offer, place a sell offer, effect a buy/sell transaction, withdraw an offer*, etc. ∎

8.3 The First Abstract Syntax, John McCarthy

In the present section we focus on abstract, implementation-unbiased syntaxes for sentential structures. The first abstract syntax proposal was put forward by John McCarthy in [330] where an *analytic abstract syntax* was given for arithmetic expressions — given in BNF in Example 8.8 — the latter in what McCarthy calls a *synthetic* manner. In an *analytic abstract syntax* we postulate, as sorts, a class of terms as a subset of all the "things" that can be analysed. And we associate a number of observer functions with these. We covered an axiomatisation of McCarthy's notion of Analytic and Synthetic Syntax in Vol. 1, Chap. 9, Sect. 9.6.5.

Example 8.7 *Property-Oriented Abstract Syntax of Expressions:* First we treat the notion of analytic grammar, then that of synthetic grammar.

8.3.1 Analytic Grammars: Observers and Selectors

For a "small" language of arithmetic expressions we focus just on constants, variables, and infix sum and product terms:

type
  A, Term
value
  is_term: A → **Bool**
  is_const: Term → **Bool**
  is_var: Term → **Bool**
  is_sum: Term → **Bool**
  is_prod: Term → **Bool**
  s_addend: Term → Term
  s_augend: Term → Term
  s_mplier: Term → Term
  s_mpcand: Term → Term
axiom
  ∀ t:Term •
    (is_const(t) ∧ ∼ (is_var(t) ∨ is_sum(t) ∨ is_prod(t))) ∧
    (is_var(t) ∧ ∼ (is_const(t) ∨ is_sum(t) ∨ is_prod(t))) ∧
    (is_sum(t) ∧ ∼ (is_const(t) ∨ is_var(t) ∨ is_prod(t))) ∧
    (is_prod(t) ∧ ∼ (isc_const(t) ∨ isv_ar(t) ∨ is_sum(t))),
  ∀ t:A • is_term(t) ≡
    (is_var(t) ∨ is_const(t) ∨ is_sum(t) ∨ is_prod(t)) ∧
    (is_sum(t) ≡ is_term(s_addend(t)) ∧ is_term(s_augend(t))) ∧
    (is_prod(t) ≡ is_term(s_mplier(t)) ∧ is_term(s_mpcand(t)))

A is a universe of "things": some are terms, some are not! The terms are restricted, in this example, to constants, variables, two argument sums and two argument products. How a sum is represented one way or another is immaterial to the above. Thus one could think of the following external, written representations:

$$a + b, +ab, (\text{PLUS } A \ B), 7^a \times 11^b.$$

8.3.2 Synthetic Grammars: Generators

A synthetic abstract syntax introduces generators of sort values, i.e., as here, of terms:

value
  mk_sum: Term × Term → Term
  mk_prod: Term × Term → Term
axiom

∀ u,v:Term •
    is_sum(mk_sum(u,v)) ∧ is_prod(mk_prod(u,v)) ∧
    s_addend(mk_sum(u,v)) ≡ u ∧ s_augend(mk_sum(u,v)) ≡ v ∧
    s_mplier(mk_prod(u,v)) ≡ u ∧ s_apcand(mk_prod(u,v)) ≡ v ∧
    is_sum(t) ⇒ mk_sum(s_addend(t),s_augend(t)) ≡ t ∧
    is_prod(t) ⇒ mk_prod(s_mplier(t),s_mpcand(t)) ≡ t

∎

McCarthy's notion of abstract syntax, both the analytic and the synthetic aspects, are found in most abstraction languages, thus are also in RSL.

8.4 BNF Grammars ≈ Concrete Syntax

In the present section we focus on concrete, implementation-biased syntaxes for sentential structures. Example 8.1 illustrated a BNF grammar-like usage of the RSL **type** definition facility. BNF stands for **Backus–Naur** Form — first widely publicised by the Algol 60 Report [24].

Section 8.5 will formalise the notions introduced in the present section.

Characterisation. By a BNF *grammar* we mean a context-free grammar — for which there are special prescriptions for designating nonterminals, and for designating sets of productions having the same left-hand side nonterminal symbol. Such a set is "condensed" into one rule, a BNF rule, whose left-hand side is the common nonterminal, and whose right-hand side is a list of alternatives separated by the alternative metasymbol: |. ∎

For natural languages we do not have precise means of specifying the exact set of their (syntactically) "correct" sentences, i.e., derivations. But for programming and for specification languages we do have means. In fact, a formal language is a language which has a precise way of delineating all and only its correct, i.e., allowable sentences. We use the term grammar to mean a concrete syntax whose structuring is intended to resemble the structuring of concrete representations.

8.4.1 BNF Grammars

Usually, the set of sentential (i.e., character string) forms that make up programs and specifications (logical formulas, mathematical expressions — such as in differential and integral calculi, etc.) are specified by a BNF (or a BNF-like) grammar. An example BNF grammar of simple arithmetic expressions is given in Example 8.8.

Example 8.8 *BNF Grammar of Simple Arithmetic Expressions:* We present a "classical" BNF grammar:

$$\langle E \rangle ::= \langle C \rangle \mid \langle V \rangle \mid \langle P \rangle \mid \langle I \rangle \mid (\langle E \rangle)$$
$$\langle C \rangle ::= \langle D \rangle \mid \langle D \rangle \langle C \rangle$$
$$\langle V \rangle ::= \langle A \rangle \mid \langle A \rangle \langle V \rangle$$
$$\langle P \rangle ::= - \langle E \rangle$$
$$\langle I \rangle ::= \langle E \rangle \, \langle O \rangle \, \langle E \rangle$$
$$\langle A \rangle ::= \langle L \rangle \mid \langle D \rangle$$
$$\langle L \rangle ::= a \mid b \mid ... \mid z \mid A \mid B \mid ... \mid Z$$
$$\langle D \rangle ::= 0 \mid 1 \mid ... \mid 9$$
$$\langle O \rangle ::= + \mid - \mid * \mid /$$

It is assumed that you are familiar with the form (i.e., syntax) of BNF grammars and their meaning. But just in case: Nonterminals ($\langle id \rangle$) denote sets of strings of terminals (i.e., the symbols not surrounded by pointed brackets). A terminal denotes the singleton set of strings consisting just of itself. Juxtaposition of terminals and nonterminals means concatenation of strings from respective denotations.

The concatenation of strings is thus the main operator.   ∎

8.4.2 BNF↔RSL Parse Trees Relations

We refer to Sect. 8.5.2, where we first treated the notion of parse trees. A syntax, whether — for example — given in the form of concrete (or even abstract) type definitions in RSL, or as a BNF grammar, defines a set of parse trees. Conventionally the language of BNF grammars corresponds to a subset of concrete type definitions of RSL:

- Terminals in BNF correspond to values of type **Char** or **Text** in RSL.
- Nonterminals in BNF correspond to type names in RSL.
- A BNF rule: $\langle Nt \rangle ::= Lhs$ corresponds to an RSL type equation Nt = Lhs.
- A set of BNF rules of the same right-hand side $\langle Nt \rangle$ but different left-hand sides: $Lhs_1, Lhs_2, \ldots, Lhs_n$, corresponds to an RSL type equation Nt = $Lhs_1 \mid Lhs_2 \mid \ldots \mid Lhs_n$.
- A BNF right-hand side expression of the Cartesian form $\langle Nt_1 \rangle \, \langle Nt_2 \rangle \ldots \langle Nt_n \rangle$ corresponds to the RSL type expression $Nt_1 \times Nt_2 \times \ldots \times Nt_n$.

Right-hand BNF sides with terminals usually have these terminals "abstracted away" (and "into" an appropriately chosen type name). Recursive sets of BNF rules either end up as recursive RSL type definitions or as RSL set, list or map type expressions.

Thus one BNF rule may end up in either of two RSL forms:

BNF: $\langle N \rangle ::= \langle A \rangle \, \langle B \rangle \, ... \, \langle C \rangle$
RSL: N = A × B × ... × C
RSL: N == mkN(a:A,b:B,...,c:C)

The parse tree notion, as seen from the BNF grammar point of view, is based on the Cartesian form rules, where (usually) $n = 2$ or more. The three rules defined just above leads to the parse trees shown in the upper part (and "across") in Figure 8.1.[2].

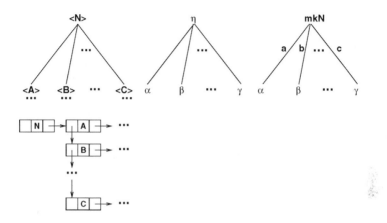

Fig. 8.1. One BNF parse tree + data structure (left), two RSL "parse" trees (right)

The RSL ("parse tree") forms are just illustrative, and are used sometimes for purely pragmatic, didactic or pedagogic reasons. One can devise a whole system of RSL parse trees for RSL values other than Cartesians. That is, for sets, lists, maps and functions. We shall, however, refrain!

The BNF parse tree notion is, however, "real" in that texts composed as per a BNF grammar can, and often must, be represented inside the computer in the form of some data structure. It is therefore convenient to call this data

---

[2]The three figures in the upper half of Fig. 8.1 depict what we will refer to as trees. As such they have roots and subtrees: leaves and proper trees. Roots and/or subtrees may be labelled. The slanted lines are said to designate branches and to "point to" subtrees. If a subtree label (is given and) is a terminal, then the subtree is said to be a leaf. Otherwise it is said to be a proper tree. If a branch is labeled then the label is said to designate a selector. If the root is labeled then that label is said to designate a constructor (cf. RSL terminology). If the tree is said to be a parse tree of a BNF grammar then the left-to-right ordering of subtrees reflects the same ordering of a terminal text obtained by a traversal of the tree traversing (i.e., visiting) left subtrees before right subtrees and then noting down only the leaves. The lower left boxes and arrow diagram are said to designate a data structure. It consists of records (the boxes) having pointer-valued fields (the arrows). The arrows that emanate from a part within the rectangular box and which are incident upon a rectangular box are pointers stored in pointer-valued fields of the records and which permit a linking (a traversal) to other records. The right pointing dangling arrows are said to designate, to link to, sub-subtrees not otherwise mentioned.

structure a parse tree. A possible form of such a parse tree is hinted at in Fig. 8.1's lower left corner.

8.5 Structure Generators and Recognisers

We must raise an important point about BNF grammars. For a certain class of BNF grammars one can, automatically, from the grammar, construct a finite state recogniser, i.e., a simple algorithm, which given a string of characters can decide, i.e., *recognise*, whether that string is in the language designated by the grammar, and, if so, can decide how that string was *generated* by that grammar. For another class of BNF grammars one can, automatically, from the grammar, construct a pushdown stack recogniser, i.e., an algorithm with a finite number of states and a stack, which given a string of characters can decide, i.e., *recognise*, whether that string is in the language designated by the grammar, and, if so, can decide how that string was *generated* by that grammar.

8.5.1 Context-Free Grammars and Languages

In this section we formalise what was informally covered in Sect. 8.4.

Definition. By a *context-free grammar*, CFG, we understand the following: a finite set, N, of what we shall call nonterminal symbols, i.e., names of syntactic categories; a finite set, T, of terminal symbols; a distinguished member, n_0 of N, the start symbol; and a finite set of productions of the form $n_i \to r$, i.e.:

$$n_i \to r, \quad n_i \in N, \quad r \in (N \mid T)^*$$

That is, each production (sometimes we call them rules) has a left-hand side nonterminal and a right-hand side sequence of zero, one or more nonterminals and terminals. For every nonterminal in the right-hand side of some production there is at least one (possibly) other production which has that nonterminal as its left-hand side.   ∎

Example 8.9 *A CFG Grammar:* We show a rather construed example:

    G = (N,T,P,R)
    N = {P,Q,R}
    T = {a,b,c,d}
    R = {P→aQc, Q→bQ, Q→(R), R→dR, R→ }

The last production, R→, also maps R into an empty string.   ∎

So the above defined and exemplified syntax of syntax! But what does it mean? That is, what is the meaning of a CFG? To this we turn next:

Definition. By a *context-free substitution* we understand the replacement of a nonterminal, n (in any string, sns', of terminals and nonterminals), with a string, r, of terminals and non-terminals, resulting in a string srs', and such that there exists a context-free grammar, G, for which $n \to r$ is a production. We write the substitution as: $sns' \to_G srs'$, said to be a substitution wrt. to grammar G. ∎

Definition. By a *context-free derivation*, we understand a sequence, s_1, s_2, ..., s_q, of strings, s_i, of terminal and nonterminals symbols such that there is a context-free grammar, G, for which, for all $1 \le i \le q-1$, we have that s_{i+1} represents a context-free substitution wrt. s_i, i.e.:

$$s_i \to_G s_{i+1}$$

and wrt. some production of that context-free grammar. We write the derivation as:

$$s_1 \to_G s_2 \to_G \ldots \to_G s_q.$$

And we abbreviate such a derivation by:

$$s_1 \to_G^* s_q,$$

the *closure* of a derivation. ∎

Definition. By a *context-free language*, CFL, we understand a possibly infinite set, ℓ_G, of finite length strings, s, of terminal symbols, such that there is a context-free grammar $G : (N, T, n, R)$ for which, for any (terminal) string, s, in ℓ_G, we have that $n \to^* s$, i.e.:

$$\ell_G = \{s \mid s : T^* \bullet n \to_G^* s\}$$

The above reads: The set of all those strings, s, which are terminal strings, and such that there is a derivation from the start symbol, n, to the string s. ∎

Example 8.10 *A CFG Derivation:* Based on Example 8.9:

P → aQc → abQc → ab(R)c → ab(dR)c → ab(ddR)c → ab(dd)c

The example is just that: an "abstract" example. ∎

Example 8.11 *A CFG Language:* From the example derivation of Example 8.10 we see that ab(dd)c is a sentence of CFL. Others are:

a()c, a()c, ab()c, a(d)c, ab(d)c, abb(d)c, a(dd)c, ab(dd)c, abb(dd)c,

etcetera. ∎

8.5.2 Parse Trees

Definition. We define the notion of a *production tree*. Let there be given a
CFG production $\ell \rightarrow r$, and let r be the symbol string $cc'c'' \ldots c'''$, where
each of the symbols $c, c', c'', \ldots$, and c''', is either a nonterminal or a terminal
symbol — any mixture — of some grammar G. Then $(\ell, (c, c', c'', \ldots, c'''))$ is
said to be a production tree. We can show production trees diagrammatically
(Fig. 8.2).   ∎

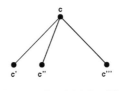

Production Tree: (c,(c',c'',....,c'''))

Fig. 8.2. A production tree

Definition. We define the notion of a *parse tree*. Let $G : (N, T, n, R)$ be a
context-free grammar. Let n_i be any nonterminal in N, and t_j be any terminal
in T, then n_i and t_j are parse trees with roots n_i and nothing else, respectively
of root t_j (equal to leaf t_j) and nothing else. Let $n_i \rightarrow c_{i_1} c_{i_2} \ldots c_{i_{m_i}}$, where c_{i_k}
(for all $i_1 \le k \le i_{m_i}$) is either a nonterminal or a terminal, be a production
in R, where $i_{m_i} \ge 0$, then $n_i(c_{i_1}, c_{i_2}, \ldots, c_{i_{m_i}})$ is a parse tree with root n_i.
Given the parse tree $n_i(c_{i_1}, c_{i_2}, \ldots, c_{i_{m_i}})$, let p_i and p_{i_j} be parse trees with
root symbol c_i or c_{i_j}, whether c_i and c_{i_j} is a nonterminal or a terminal, then
$(n_i, (p_{i_1}, p_{i_2}, \ldots, p_{i_{m_i}}))$, is a parse tree. See Fig. 8.3 for an example parse tree.
     If all "innermost" symbols $c_{i_{j \ldots k}}$ are terminals, then the parse tree is a
complete parse tree.   ∎

Recall that an empty production, $n_i \rightarrow$, gives rise to the parse tree $n_i()$. To
avoid confusion, one might wish to write this production as: $n_i \rightarrow \epsilon$.

Definition. We define the notion of a *frontier* of a parse tree. Let p_i :
$(n_i, (p_{i_1}, p_{i_2}, \ldots, p_{i_{m_i}}))$ be a parse tree. A frontier of a parse tree is a "reading" of the innermost symbols of p_i, as follows: If p_i is of the form $(n_i, ())$ then
the frontier of p_i, $\phi(p_i)$ is the null string (often written ϵ (so as to be able to
"see" it!)). If p_{i_j} of production p_i is of the form t, where t is a terminal or a
nonterminal symbol, then the frontier of p_{i_j}, $\phi(p_{i_j})$ is t. If p_{i_j} of production p_i
is of the form $p_{i_j} : (n_{i_j}, (p_{i_{j_1}}, p_{i_{j_2}}, \ldots, p_{i_{j_{m_i}}}))$, then the frontier of p_{i_j}, $\phi(p_{i_j})$
is $\phi(p_{i_{j_1}})\phi(p_{i_{j_2}}) \ldots \phi(p_{i_{j_{m_i}}})$.
     The frontier of (the original parse tree) p_i, $\phi(p_i)$ is thus:

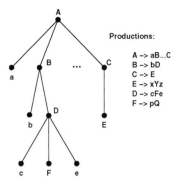

Fig. 8.3. A parse tree

$$\phi(p_{i_1})\phi(p_{i_2})\ldots\phi(p_{i_{m_i}}),$$

where the juxtaposition of the $\phi(p_{i_j})$'s amounts to the concatenation of strings of nonterminal and terminal symbols.   ∎

Example 8.12 *The Frontier of a Parse Tree:* We refer to Fig. 8.3. The frontier of that parse tree is $abcFe...E$.   ∎

8.5.3 Regular Expressions and Languages

Definition. By a *regular expression, r,* we understand an expression over an alphabet, $\mathcal{A}$, of terminal symbols, and over the operators $\cdot, ^*, |, (,)$, such that:

Basis clause: If $a, b, \ldots, c$ are in $\mathcal{A}$, then $a, b, \ldots$, and c are regular expressions.

Inductive clause: If r and r' are regular expressions, then $r \cdot r', r^*, r \mid r'$ and (r) are regular expressions.

Extremal clause: Only such expressions which can be formed from a finite number of applications of the basis and the inductive clauses are regular expressions.   ∎

Example 8.13 *Regular Expressions:* Let an alphabet, $\mathcal{A}$, of terminal symbols be that of a, b, c. A specific regular expression is a, another is $a \cdot a$, etc. Another specific regular expression is:

$$a^* \cdot ((a \cdot b)^* \mid (b \cdot c)^*)$$

And so forth.   ∎

Given a regular expression we can always, from it, extract the alphabet, $\mathcal{A}$, of terminal symbols.

The meaning of a regular expression, since a regular expression is "but a piece of syntax", is a regular language:

Definition. By a *regular language* we understand a possibly infinite set, ℓ_r, of finite sequences of symbols such that there is a regular expression r for which the following relation between sentences in ℓ_r and r can be established: If r is a, where $a \in \mathcal{A}$, then a is in ℓ_r. If r is $r' \cdot r''$, then for all s' in $\ell_{r'}$ and s'' in $\ell_{r''}$ we have that $s's''$ is in ℓ_r. If r is r'^*, then for all s' in $\ell_{r'}$ we have that $\epsilon, s', s's', s's'...s'$, etc., is in ℓ_r. Here ϵ is the null string of no symbols. If r is $r' \mid r''$, then for all s' in $\ell_{r'}$ and s'' in $\ell_{r''}$ we have that s' and s'' are in ℓ_r. If r is (r'), then for all s' in $\ell_{r'}$ we have that s' is in ℓ_r.   ∎

Example 8.14 *A Regular Language:* Let a regular expression be:

$$a^* \cdot ((a \cdot b)^* \mid (b \cdot c)^*)$$

Some sentences of the corresponding regular language are:

$$\epsilon, a, aa, aa \ldots a,$$

$$ab, abab, abab \ldots ab, bc, bcbc, bcbc \ldots bc$$

$$aab, aabab, aabab \ldots ab, abc, abcbc, abcbc \ldots bc$$

$$aaabab, aaabab, aaabab \ldots ab, aabc, aabcbc, aabcbc \ldots bc \ldots$$

∎

8.5.4 Language Recognisers

In Sects. 11.3–11.5 we shall touch upon the relationship between regular languages, respectively context-free grammars, on one hand, and "devices", on the other hand. We mean devices which, when provided with input in the form of sentences of some postulated regular or context-free language, can decide, i.e., recognise, whether the sentence is indeed a member of that language, and then provide one or more parse trees for that sentence. These "devices" are referred to as finite state automata, finite state machines and pushdown stack automata (resp. machines). It is indeed this ability to precisely specify which sentences are allowed, that is, can be generated, and to automatically construct a recogniser that makes regular expressions and context-free grammars interesting.

8.6 XML: Extensible Markup Language

Extensible Markup Language (XML) is a language for adorning linear texts with markers in a way that allows for easy parsing of the text into possibly meaningful units. XML is, as of 2006, a preferred such language for regulating the transfer of data over the Internet.

8.6.1 An Example

To relate to the topic of XML consider the following RSL type definition of programs in some small imperative programming language:

type
    Progr == mkProg(b:Block)
    Blk == mkBlk(vs:Var_Decls,ps:Proc_Defns,sl:Stmtlist)
    Var_Decls == nil_dcl | mkVDcls(v:Var,i:Expr,vs:Var_Decls)
    Pro_Defs == nil_proc | mkPDefs(pn:Pn,pl:Parlst,b:Blok,ps:Pro_Defs)
    Parlst == nil_parl | mkParL(fp:Id,pl:Parlist)
    Stmtlist == nil_stmt | mkStmtL(s:Stmt,sl:Stmtlist)
    Stmt = Block | Asgn | IfTE
    Asgn == mkAsgn(vr:Var,ex:Expr)
    IfTE == mkIfTE(be:Expr,cs:Stmt,**as**:Stmt)
    Expr = Var | Prefix | Infix
    Var == mkV(vn:Vn)
    Prefix == mkPre(po:POp,e:Expr)
    Infix == mkInf(le:Expr,io:IOp,re:Expr)
    POp == minus | not | ...
    IOp == add | subtract | multiply | divide | ...

Now consider the following concrete example program in the above language:

```
program
  begin
    variables
      v := e , v' := e' ;
    procedures
      p1(fp11,fp12,...,fp1n) = blk1 ,
      p2(fp21,fp22,...,fp2n) = blk2 ;
    v := e'' ;
    if be then cs else as fi ;
    begin
      variables  ...
      procedures ...
      ...
    end
  end
```

Abstractly the above program is a value in Progr which can be written as:

value
    p:Progr
axiom
    p = mkProg(
          mkBlk(

```
mkVDcls(v,e,
 mkVDcls(v′,e′,nil_dcl))
mkPDefs(p,pl,blk,
 mkPDefs(p′,pl′,blk′,nil_proc))
mkStmtL(mkAsgn(v,e″),
 mkStmtL(mkIfTE(be,cs,as),
  mkStmtL(mkBlk(vs,ps,sl)
 )))))
```

Here we have refrained from detailing "inner" clauses like: v, e, v′, e′, p, pl, blk, p′, pl′, blk′, e″, be, cs, as, vs, ps and sl. We are confident that the reader can complete the picture!

Now if we "balanced" (i.e., replaced) any opening parenthesis mkX('s with)unmkX's, then we get the following:

value
    xml_p:Progr
axiom
    xml_p = mkProg(
                mkBlk(
                  mkVDcls(v,e,
                   mkVDcls(v′,e′,nil_dcl)unmkVDcls)unmkVDcls
                  mkPDefs(p,pl,blk,
                   mkPDefs(p′,pl′,blk′,nil_proc)unmkPDefs)unmkPDefs
                  mkStmtL(mkAsgn(v,e″)unmkAsgn,
                  mkStmtL(mkIfTE(be,cs,as)unmkIfTE,
                    mkStmtL(mkBlk(vs,ps,sl)unmkBlk
)unmkStmtL)unmkStmtL)unmkStmtL)unmkBlk)unmkProg

8.6.2 Discussion

The above shows the essence of XML. The essence of XML is that any data — and here the data are the tokens of variables, operators, literals (for **procedure, block, =, :=, if, then, else, end,** etcetera), and the data are also the structure of the sentences into which they have been put — can be described as shown above. The mkX(and)unmkX "brackets" are like XML *tags*.

8.6.3 Historical Background

The tagging concept thus derives from the abstract syntax notion of McCarthy (1962 [330]) that we presented in Sect. 8.3.

McCarthy in a 1982 Stanford University report titled *Common Business Communication Language* [332] proposed — 20 years after his first publication on abstract syntax — a language for interbusiness intercomputer communication based on the ideas of an abstract syntax's is_A, s_A and mk_A functions

(Sect. 8.3). *Most of the ideas in that paper have been reinvented in connection with electronic commerce, specifically in connection with XML.*

8.6.4 The Current XML "Craze"

XML is (2006) a so-called "hot topic". It is strange that it had to take such a long time, 40 years, to reach this unscientific state of euphoria. Anyway, XML is nevertheless and obviously a good idea. XML, as should be obvious, can be used for describing not just sentential forms, but any kind of data structure. This will be made more clear in the next section (Sect. 8.6.5). And hence XML can be used when "moving" data from one computing platform to another, i.e., for the transfer of arbitrary files.

8.6.5 XML Expressions

Characterisation. An XML *expression* is a string over terminal symbols and over properly balanced opening and closing XML tags.   ∎

Characterisation. An XML *tag* is either an opening XML tag, which is written as <name>, where name is some identifier, or is a closing XML tag which is written as </name>, where name is some identifier.   ∎

Example 8.15 *From RSL Values to XML Expressions:* Let there be given the following RSL type definitions (of something otherwise irrelevant):

type
    A, B, C, D, E
    F = G | H | J | K
    G :: A-**set**
    H :: B × C × D
    J :: E*
    K :: A $\overrightarrow{m}$ B

Typical values of type F are:

value
    a,a',...,a'':A
    b,b':B, c:C, d:D,
    e,e':E
    g: mkG({a,a',a''}) : G
    h: mkH(b,c,d) : H
    j: mkJ(⟨e,e',e',e⟩) : J
    k: mkK([a↦b,a'↦b,a''↦b']) : K

Let sets be represented by lists, and let maps be represented by lists of pairs:

G′ :: A*
AB :: A × B
K′ :: AB*

Corresponding RSL values are:

value
  g′: mkG′(⟨a,a′,a″⟩) : G′
  k′: mkK′(⟨mkAB(a,b),mkAB(a′,b),mkAB(a″,b′)⟩) : K′

In proper XML the g′, h, j and k′ values could be represented as follows:

RSL:
  g′: mkG′(⟨a,a′,a″⟩)

XML:
  <G′>
      <A> a </A>
      <A> a′ </A>
      <A> a″ </A>
  </G′>

RSL:
  j: mkJ(⟨e,e′,e′,e⟩)
XML:
  <J>
      <E> e </E>
      <E> e″ </E>
      <E> e′ </E>
      <E> e </E>
  </J>

RSL:
  k′: mkK′(⟨(a,b),(a′,b),(a″,b′)⟩)
XML:
  <K′>
      <AB>
          <A> a </A>
          <B> b </B>
      </AB>
      <AB>
          <A> a′ </A>
          <B> b </B>
      </AB>

```
        <AB>
            <A> a″ </A>
            <B> b′ </B>
        </AB>
    </K′>
```

■

8.6.6 XML Schemas

Characterisation. An XML *schema* is a syntax which describes a language of strings over terminal symbols and over properly balanced opening and closing XML tags. ■

Example 8.16 *An XML Schema:* An XML schema corresponding to the XML expressions of Example 8.15 is:

<xs:schema>

  <xs: element name="A" type="sortA"/>
  <xs: element name="B" type="sortB"/>
  <xs: element name="C" type="sortC"/>
  <xs: element name="D" type="sortD"/>
  <xs: element name="E" type="sortE"/>

  <xs: simpleType name="sortA"> ... </xs: simpleType>
  <xs: simpleType name="sortB"> ... </xs: simpleType>
  <xs: simpleType name="sortC"> ... </xs: simpleType>
  <xs: simpleType name="sortD"> ... </xs: simpleType>
  <xs: simpleType name="sortE"> ... </xs: simpleType>

  <xs: element name="F" type="Ft"/>
  <xs: complextype name="Ft">
   <xs: choice>
    <xs: element name="G′" type="Gt"/>
    <xs: element name="H" type="Ht"/>
    <xs: element name="J" type="Jt"/>
    <xs: element name="K′" type="Kt"/>
   </xs: choice>
  </xs: complextype>

  <xs: element name="G′" type="Gt"/>
  <xs: complextype name="Gt">

```xml
    <xs: sequence maxOccurs="unbounded" minOccurs="0">
        <xs: element name="A" type="sortA"/>
    </xs: sequence>
</xs: complextype>


<xs: element name="H" type="Ht"/>
<xs: complextype name="Ht">
    <xs: sequence>
        <xs: element name="B" type="sortB"/>
        <xs: element name="C" type="sortC"/>
        <xs: element name="D" type="sortD"/>
    </xs: sequence>
</xs: complextype>


<xs: element name="J" type="Jt"/>
<xs: complextype name="J">
    <xs: sequence maxOccurs="unbounded" minOccurs="0">
        <xs: element name="E" type="sortE"/>
    </xs: sequence>
</xs: complextype>


<xs: element name="AB" type="ABt"/>
<xs: complextype name="ABt">
    <xs: sequence>
        <xs: element name="A" type="sortA"/>
        <xs: element name="B" type="sortB"/>
    </xs: sequence>
</xs: complextype>

<xs: element name="K'" type="Kt"/>
<xs: complextype name="K'">
    <xs: sequence maxOccurs="unbounded" minOccurs="0">
        <xs: element name="AB" type="ABt"/>
    </xs: sequence>
</xs: complextype>

</xs:schema>
```

We leave it to the reader to decipher the relationships between this and the previous example.   ∎

8.6.7 References

References are made to two books: [417] and [443]. [417] provides an easy-to-read introduction to XML. [443] provides a more technical treatment of XML. Otherwise we encourage the reader to "surf" the Internet looking for educational, instructional and training material on XML. References are finally made to a number a papers more or less relating to XML: [127, 261, 293, 450, 515].

8.7 Abstract Syntaxes

In the present section we focus on abstract, implementation-unbiased syntaxes for semantical structures.

Characterisation. By an *abstract syntax* we understand rules for mathematically characterising a structure in terms of its composition — whether property-oriented or model-oriented.   ▪

We speak of such mathematical, i.e. model-oriented, structures as sets, Cartesians, lists, maps, etc. A popular abstract form is that envisaged by a treelike hierarchy. And we thus speak of such logical (cum algebraic), i.e., property-oriented structures (that are characterised by their composition) — again — as "trees". Some examples may be useful.

8.7.1 Abstract Syntax of a Storage Model

Example 7.5 introduced an axiomatic specification of storage. That specification also illustrated uses of abstract syntax. Examples 8.17–8.19 illustrate further facets of abstract syntax and storage models.

Example 8.17 *Model-Oriented Formal Syntax of Storages:* We decompose the example presentation of storage into three parts: the values stored and their type, the structure of storage locations, and, finally, the combined storage as consisting of locations and values. We alternate between informal and formal presentations.

Values and Value Types

We assume knowledge of integer and Boolean values.

- *Informal:*
  - ⋆ Values are either scalar or are composite.
  - ⋆ There are two kinds of scalar values: integers and Booleans.
  - ⋆ There are two kinds of composite values: vectors and records.
  - ⋆ Vectors are definite length sequences of values of the same kind.

* ⋆ Records are (here) finite (Cartesian) collections of named values (of possibly, i.e., usually, different kinds).
* ⋆ An integer is of kind number.
* ⋆ A Boolean is of kind truth value.
* ⋆ A vector is of kind sequence of a specific length and of the kind of its element values.
* ⋆ A record is of kind Cartesian of a definite number of fields with their unique names and the kind of their values.
* Formal:

type
  VAL = ScaVAL | ComVAL
  ScaVAL = NumVAL | TruVAL
  NumVAL :: **Int**
  TruVAL :: **Bool**
  ComVAL = VecVAL | RecVAL
  VecVAL :: VAL*
  RecVAL :: Nm $\overrightarrow{m}$ VAL

  Kind == number | truth
       | mk_Seq(n:**Nat**,k:Kind)
       | mk_Car(r:(Nm $\overrightarrow{m}$ Kind))

Locations and Location Types

We continue the example just given. Before it was about values; now it is about their locations.

* Informal:
  * ⋆ Locations (of values, in some abstract notion of storage) are either scalar or composite.
  * ⋆ Scalar locations are either of kind number locations or truth value locations, and are further unspecified.
  * ⋆ Composite locations are either of kind vector locations or record locations.
  * ⋆ Vector locations associate vector element indexes (whose element values are contained in the overall vector locations) with locations (of the location kind of the contained element value).
  * ⋆ Record locations associate field names of the record with locations (of the location kind of the contained field value).
* Formal:

type
  LOC = ScaLOC | ComLOC

ScaLOC == numLOC | truLOC
ComLOC == SeqLOC | CarLOC
SeqLOC :: LOC*
CarLOC :: Nm $\overrightarrow{m}$ LOC

Storages

We now combine the value and the location definitions:

- *Informal:*
  - ⋆ Storages are functions from locations (of one kind) to values (of the same kind).
- *Formal:*

  type
     STG = LOC $\overrightarrow{m}$ VAL

Type Constraints

Implicit in the three model components of Example 8.17 are the type extraction and type-checking functions shown now in Example 8.18. We refer to the functions defined in Example 8.18 as *static semantics* functions.

Example 8.18 *Model-Oriented Type Checking of Abstract Storage:*

value
   x_type: (VAL|LOC) $\xrightarrow{\sim}$ Kind
   x_type(valo) ≡
     case valo **of**
       mk_Num(_) → number,
       mk_Tru(_) → truth,
       mk_VecVAL(vv) → mk_Seq(**len** vv,x_type(**hd** vv)),
       mk_CarVAL(cv) →
         mk_Car([n $\overrightarrow{m}$ x_type(cv(n)) |n:Nm • n ∈ **dom** cv]),
       numLOC → number,
       truLOC → truth,
       mk_VecLOC(vl) → mk_Seq(**len** vl,x_type(**hd** vl)),
       mk_CarVAL(cl) →
         mk_Car([n $\overrightarrow{m}$ x_type(cl(n)) |n:Nm • n ∈ **dom** cl])
     end
   pre: x_type(mk_VecVAL(vv)): ∀ v,v':VAL •
                v,v' ∈ **elems** vv ∧ v≠v' ⇒ x_type(v) = x_type(v'),

x_type(mk_VecLOC(vl)): etc. ...

Example 7.5 "digs" a bit deeper and secures independence of locations — not satisfied by the above!

We see how recursion in syntax definition conveniently, following the denotational principle, leads to recursion in function definition.

```
c_type: (VAL|LOC) → Bool
c_type(vls) ≡
  case vls of
    mk_VecVAL(vv) →
      ∀ v,v':VAL • v,v' ∈ elems vv ∧ v≠v' ⇒
        x_type(v) = x_type(v')
    mk_VecLOC(vl) →
      ∀ l,l':LOC • l,l' ∈ elems vl ∧ l≠l' ⇒
        x_type(l) = x_type(l')
    _ → true
  end
```

The above c_type function ("almost") expresses the **static semantics** of the "language" of values and locations. Example 7.5 additionally shows well-formedness of storages.   ∎

Independence of locations was introduced earlier in Example 7.5.

8.7.2 Abstract Syntaxes of Other Storage Models

Example 8.17 illustrated one syntactical model of storage. There are others. The one illustrated above models storages as found in such (past) programming languages as PL/I [12,29,33,36,110,111,312] and ALGOL 68 [31,61,511]. In Example 8.19 (next) we illustrate not only the storage models of other programming languages (such as ALGOL 60 [24] and Ada [54,103,222,223]), but we link these models (semantically) to the notion of environments. The models are all based on Bekič and Walk's work [37].

Example 8.19 *Models of Variables, Their Binding and Storage:*

Informal Exposition

In imperative languages variables are declared of simple or composite type, and assignments to either of these (entire) variables may occur, as implied, but not shown (since that is a semantic notion) in Example 8.17, or assignments may occur only to scalar parts. At the same time, variables may be 'passed by reference' to procedures — in whose bodies assignments may be specified as above — with procedure parameters either allowing "entire", i.e., full variable locations, or only scalar locations. Some languages may allow assignments only to scalar parts of composite variables but the passing of composite locations (as argument but not necessarily storable values). So we have basically three situations: (1) declaration and passing (as procedure arguments) of and assignment to scalar as well as composite location variables; (2) declaration and passing (as procedure arguments) of composite (etc.) location variables, but assignment only to scalar locations; and (3) declaration of composite (etc.) location variables, but passing of and assignments only to scalar locations. To keep track of, i.e., distinguish between these alternatives, we introduce a notion of environment. Environments bind explicitly declared variable or procedure parameter (i.e., argument) identifiers to locations. Storages then map either composite or (only) scalar locations to corresponding values.

Formal Exposition

type
   sV, kV
   $gV = sV \mid kV$
   $cV = kV \times (\mathbf{Nat}|Nm)^*$
   $V = sV \mid cV$
   $ENV\_1 = gV \xrightarrow{m} LOC$
   $ENV\_2 = gV \xrightarrow{m} LOC$
   $ENV\_3 = cV \xrightarrow{m} ScaLOC$
   $STG\_1 = LOC \xrightarrow{m} VAL$
   $STG\_2 = ScaLOC \xrightarrow{m} ScaVAL$
   $STG\_3 = ScaLOC \xrightarrow{m} ScaVAL$

Annotations: sV stands for further undefined scalar variable names. kV stands for names of ("entire") composite variables, also further undefined. gV thus stands for general variable names. cV stand for composite variable ground terms: the **Nat** and Nm lists designate indexes into compound variables — to either scalar or compound locations. ENV stands for environments. ENV_i and STG_i stand for respective models. Notice that ENV_1 and ENV_2 are similar, but that STG_1 and STG_2 are not! And so on.

   A model of assignment is a semantic model and hence is not illustrated here. ∎

We showed such a model of assignment in Example 7.5.

8.8 Converting RSL Types to BNF

```
_____ From Abstract RSL Types to Concrete BNF Types _____
```
Implementation of abstract data structures in terms of ordinary programming languages' concrete data structures need be indicated. When the abstract data structures are specified in terms of sets, lists and maps, then we need to give the reader a hint at possible structure- or record-oriented concrete data structures — the latter possibly with pointers. This is the aim, therefore, of this final section of this chapter on syntax.

The present section "ties" in with Sect. 8.6 on XML.

8.8.1 The Problem

The problem is that of being able to represent, using just Cartesians, any of the abstract data structures of sets, lists and maps. Why use Cartesians? Simply because that kind of data structure is provided by all current programming languages. Most, if any, of these, do not support sets, lists and maps of "variable size" (the "variable size" concept was defined in Vol. 1, Sect. 13.6).

8.8.2 A Possible Solution

We shall hint at a uniform set of solutions, basically along the same line for sets, lists and maps. That uniform solution defines a variable size data structure in terms of a recursively nested structure of Cartesians.

A *variable size data structure*, containing zero, one or more entities, such as sets, lists and maps either contains no entities, and then we represent it by a **nil** element or it contains one or more such entities and then we represent it by a Cartesian of the "one" such entity together with the rest, i.e., the "more minus one".

We now show generic type definitions of the "abstract" data structures of sets, lists and maps, followed by generic type definitions of the "concrete" data Cartesian structures. For each of the "pairs" of abstract and concrete data structures, we have to define functions converting between the abstract and the concrete data structures, i.e., injection functions (rather, relations), and vice versa, i.e., abstraction (or retrieval) functions. We also have to show that we can define concrete counterparts of the "built-in" operations on the abstract values.

type
$$sA_B = \text{B-set}, \quad \ell A_B = B^*, \quad mA_{BC} = B \overrightarrow{m} C$$

$$As_B == \text{nilBs} \mid \text{mk\_As}(b:kB, a:As_B)$$
$$A\ell_B == \text{nilB}\ell \mid \text{mk\_A}\ell(b:kB, a:A\ell_B)$$
$$Am_{BC} == \text{nilBCm} \mid \text{mk\_As}(b:kB, c:KC, a:Am_{BC})$$

value
    conv_sA_B_As$_B$: sA_B → As$_B$
    conv_ℓA_B_Aℓ_B: ℓA_B → Aℓ_B
    conv_mA_{BC}_Am$_{BC}$: mA_{BC} → Am$_{BC}$

    conv_sA_B_As$_B$(sa) ≡
      if sa={}
        then nilBs
        else
          let s ∪ {b} = sa **in**
          mk_As(b,conv_sA_B_As$_B$(s))
      end end

    ∈: B × sA_B → **Bool**
    ∪, ∩, \, /: sA_B × sA_B → sA_B
    ⊆, ⊂, =: sA_B × sA_B → **Bool**
    card: sA_B → **Nat**

    is_in: B × As$_B$ → **Bool**
    union, inter, remove, remain: As$_B$ × As$_B$ → As$_B$
    subseteq, subset, equal: As$_B$ × As$_B$ → **Bool**
    cardinality: As$_B$ → **Nat**

We leave it to the reader to complete the definition of the above, as well as stating the similar function signatures and definitions of the other data types. See Exercises 8.1–8.3.

8.9 Discussion of Informal and Formal Syntax

8.9.1 General

The point about informal and formal syntax is (also) this: When using formal syntax we commit ourselves to precise meanings of what the syntax itself denotes. Whereas, when we use informal syntax, we have to accept that it may not be fully clear what the scope of that informal syntax is.

    That is, there is a formal syntax, and its "meaning" is all the abstract or concrete structures generated by that syntax: Sentences or phrase trees for concrete syntaxes, i.e., for BNF grammars, and abstract, mathematical structures for abstract (RSL or other abstract) syntaxes. What the meanings of these sentences or phrase trees or abstract, mathematical structures are, we have yet to say.

Abstract (formal) syntax can be used to define sentential structures, such as we may concretely or abstractly communicate them between people or between man and machine. Or abstract (formal) syntax can be used to define mathematical structures, say internal to machines. In current practice, BNF is used to define concrete sentential forms and a programming languages' type definition facilities are used to define data structures. In RSL we use one mechanism to define either (i.e., both).

8.9.2 Principles, Techniques and Tools

We summarise:

Principles. Every structure that need be understood precisely need be given a precise syntax.   ■

Principles. Not just sentential structures, i.e., text strings, need be given syntax, also concrete or conceptual information (including data) structures. ■

Principles. Syntax must also be given to what appears as diagrammatic information from the software development field: GUIs, FlowCharts, UML Class Diagrams, Petri Nets, Message Sequence Charts, Live Sequence Charts, Statecharts, as well as from other universes of discourse: Civil engineering drawings, geodetic and cadastral charts, land maps, etc., mechanical engineering drawings, electrical engineering drawings, etc.   ■

Techniques. Depending on the problem at hand: If conceptual, trying to understand basic concepts, then abstraction is to be applied, if the problem is of final, implementational, nature, then concretisation is to be applied. Throughout express a suitable balance between expressiveness and capturing context-sensitive constraints. Thus choose also appropriate techniques for expressing well-formedness.   ■

Tools. There are many tools with which to express, i.e., to define syntax: The type expression and type definition constructs of RSL, those of BNF, those of XML, and those of "truly" abstract syntax: Sorts and axioms.   ■

8.10 Bibliographical Notes

Classical textbooks on compiler development cover some, but really not many BNF design techniques, but do cover implementation techniques: Design and coding of lexical scanners and error correcting syntax parsers [6, 21, 297].

We also refer to the useful Internet Web page [295] which informs on syntax handling tools (viz.: LEX, YACC and related or similar tools).

8.11 Exercises

Exercise 8.1 *Cartesian Sets.* We refer to Sect. 8.8.2. Please complete the definition of all the concrete versions of the $\in$, $\cup$, $\cap$, $\setminus$, $/$, $\subseteq$, $\subset$, $=$ and **card** functions, i.e., of is_in, union, inter, remove, subseteq, subset, equal, and cardinality functions.

Exercise 8.2 *Cartesian Lists.* We refer to Sect. 8.8.2. Please state the function signatures and the definitions of all the concrete versions of conv_ℓA_B_$A\ell_B$ and the basic list operations: **hd, tl,** $\hat{\ }$, $\cdot(\cdot)$, **elems, inds, len** and $=$, i.e., of head, tail, concatenate, index, elements, indices, length and equal.

Exercise 8.3 *Cartesian Maps.* We refer to Sect. 8.8.2. Please state the function signatures and the definitions of all the "concrete" versions of conv_mA_{BC}_Am_{BC} and the basic map operations: $\cup$, $\dagger$, $\cdot(\cdot)$, **dom, rng** and $=$, i.e., of union, override, apply, domain, range and equal.

Exercise 8.4 *RSL Type Expressions and Type Definitions.* This exercise is part of a series of three related exercises that continues in Exercises 8.5–8.6. Please read all three exercise texts carefully, as the solution to the present exercise depends on the ability to express solutions to the next two exercises reasonably elegantly. The problem to be solved in the present exercise is to suggest a suitable concrete RSL syntax for RSL type definitions. Here is, for your help, our simplified version of RSL type definitions, one that seems suitable for this series of exercises.

_____ Simplified RSL Type Expressions and Definitions _____

- An RSL type expression is:
  - ⋆ either an atomic type literal (**Bool, Int, Num, Real, Char, Text**)
  - ⋆ or a unit type literal (**Unit**)
  - ⋆ or a type name
  - ⋆ or a finite set type expression, which we take, for simplification, to just be a type name suffixed with the type constructor name **–set**
  - ⋆ or a Cartesian type expression, which we take, for simplification, to just be a finite sequence of two or more type names infixed with the type constructor name ×
  - ⋆ or a finite list type expression, which we take, for simplification, to just be a type name suffixed with the type constructor name *
  - ⋆ or a RSL type expression is a finite map type expression, which we take, for simplification, to just be a pair of type names infixed with the type constructor name $\overrightarrow{m}$
- In this exposition of simplified RSL type expressions and type definitions there are four kinds of RSL type definition:
  1. A sort definition
     - ⋆ which just consists of a type name;
  2. simple token alternatives

⋆   which have left-hand side type names,
⋆   and a right hand-side of one or more token names;
3. or a simple kind of type alternative:
⋆   which has a left-hand side type name,
⋆   and a right-hand side set of two or more type names;
4. or a record type constructor kind
⋆   which has a left-hand side type name,
⋆   and a right-hand side type expression.
• An RSL set of type definitions is now
⋆   a list of one or more type definitions
⋆   such that all sort and left-hand side names are distinct,
⋆   such that all token names are distinct, and distinct from type names,
⋆   and such that all uses of type names (in right-hand side type expressions) are defined, i.e., have a corresponding type definition of that left-hand side name.

Example:

type
[1]   A, B, C
[2]   D = alpha | beta | gamma | delta
[3]   E = P | Q | R
[4]   P :: A ₘ→ B
[4]   Q :: C-**set**
[4]   R :: **Bool**

Define a suitable set of RSL type definitions for the above form of simplified RSL type expressions and definitions.
    Define suitable well-formedness functions.

Exercise 8.5 *Abstract Syntax and Well-formedness for XML Schemas.* This exercise is part of a series of three related exercises, see Exercises 8.4 and 8.6. You are to find out, say from the Internet, how an XML schema is defined. We refer to [478]. Here is, in any case, our simplified version.

_____ Simplified XML Schemas _____

• A simplified XML schema consists of a set of pairs of distinctly named rules.
• Each pair has an element part and a simple or a complex type part.
• Each element part names a distinct type.
• A simple part identifies a further unexplained type.
• A complex part is either a choice rule or a sequence rule.
• A choice rule consists of a set of two or more element parts.
• A sequence rule consists of a list of one or more element parts.

Given the above, or your own version, propose an RSL type definition for XML schemas.

Define suitable well-formedness functions.

Please comment as to what might be missing from the simplified XML schemas as sketched above and the "real" XML Schemas as reported at [478].

Exercise 8.6 *Translation from Typed RSL Values to XML Values*. This exercise is part of a series of three related exercises: Exercises 8.4–8.6. You are to suggest a function, conv_RSL_to_XML, which takes values of type RSL type definitions and yields values of type XML Schema.

Exercise 8.7 *Syntax of STIL*. You are to present formal, concrete type definitions for STIL: Simply Typed Imperative Language whose design is covered in Exercises 7.3–7.7, 8.7–8.8, and 9.2. We help you by stating the syntax informally.

--- The Syntax ---

1. Programs are blocks.
2. Blocks consists of one or more variable declarations and a statement list.
3. A variable declaration consists of the name of the variable being declared, its type and an initialising expression.
   (a) Variable names are simple identifiers.
   (b) Identifiers are further unexplained atomic quantities.
   (c) Types are expressed by means of a ground term type expression.
   (d) A ground term type expression is either the literal of a scalar type, or is a ground term compound type expression.
   (e) The literal of a scalar type is either an **integer** literal, or is a **Boolean** literal, or is a **real** literal, or is a **character** literal.
   (f) A ground term compound type expression is either a ground term vector type expression or is a ground term record type expression.
   (g) A ground term vector type expression consists of a vector lower and upper index bounds expression and a ground term vector element type expression.
   (h) A vector lower and upper index bounds expression is either a pair of integer numerals such that the first is smaller than the second, or is an enumerated type expression, for example, *vector low: 1 high: 12 type type_expr*.
   (i) A ground term record type expression is a set of pairs where each pair consists of a record field identifier and a ground term type expression — such that all record field identifiers of a ground term record type expression are distinct and such that no two ground term record type expressions of a program share any record field identifiers, for example, *record: a integer, b boolean, c character end*
   (j) A record field identifier is a simple identifier.

(k) Some variable declarations are marked as input/output variables.
4. A statement list consists of a sequence of one or more statements.
5. A statement is either an assignment statement, or is a conditional, i.e., an if-then-else-end statement, or is a while loop, i.e., a while-do-end statement, or is a simple iteration, i.e., a for-in-do-end statement, or is a block, i.e., a begin-end statement.

   (a) An assignment statement consists of a pair: A (left-hand side) variable reference and a (right-hand side) which is an expression, for example, *var_ref := expression*.

   (b) A conditional, i.e., an if-then-else-end, statement consists of a test expression and two statement lists. Example: *if test_expr then cons_stmt_lst else alt_stmt_lst end*.

   (c) A while loop, i.e., a while-do-end, statement consists of a test expression and a statement list, for example, *while test_expr do stmt_lst end*.

   (d) A simple iteration, i.e., a for-in-do-end, statement consists of a step identifier, a step range expression and a statement list, for example, *for step_id in ⟨lb..ub⟩ do stmt_lst end*.

      i. A step identifier is a simple identifier.

      ii. A step range expression is a pair of integer lower and upper bound numerals (i.e., constants), i.e., akin to a vector lower and upper index bounds.

6. An expression is either a value, or is a variable reference expression, or is a prefix expression, or is an infix expression, or is a postfix expression, or is a conditional (mix-fix) expression, or is a vector expression, or is a record expression, or is a parenthesized expression.

   (a) A constant expression is either an integer numeral (12345), or is a real (or 'float') numeral (01234.56789), or is a Boolean literal (true, false), or is the mathematical constants: e (approx. 2.71828183...), or π (approx. 3.14159265...), or other.

   (b) A variable reference expression has two parts: A variable identifier and an optional index or field selector part.

      i. An index part has two subparts, first either an (integer-valued) expression or a step identifier, and then an optional index or field selector part.

      ii. A field selector part has two subparts, first a field identifier, and then an optional index or field selector part.

   (c) A prefix expression consists of two parts: a prefix operator and an operand expression.

      i. A prefix operator is either of the following (literals): either a Boolean operator: ¬ (Boolean negation), or one of the arithmetic operators: + (plus), − (minus), ↑ (ceil), ↓ (floor), sin (sine), cos (cosine), tan (tangent), cotan (cotangent), sinhy (hyperbolic sine), coshy (hyperbolic cosine), tanhy (hyperbolic tangent), cotanhy (hyperbolic cotangent), arcsin (arc sine), arccos (arc cosine), `arctan` (arc tangent), `arccotan` (arc cotangent), $\sqrt{\ }$ (square root), `log`$_{10}$ (logarithm radix 10), `log`$_2$ (logarithm radix 2), and possibly others.

    ii. An operand expression is an expression.

(d) An infix expression consists of three parts: a left operand expression, an infix operator and a right operand expression.

    i. Left and right operand expressions are expressions.

    ii. An infix operator is one of the following (literals): either a Boolean operator: $\wedge$ (and, Boolean conjunction), $\vee$ (or, Boolean disjunction), $\supset$ (implication, Boolean `if-then`), $=$ (equal), $\neq$ (not equal), or a character operator: $=$ (equal), $\neq$ (not equal), or an arithmetic operator: $+$ (add), $-$ (subtract), $/$ (divide), $\times$ (multiply), $=$ (equal), $\neq$ (not equal), $<$ (less than), $\not<$ (not less than), $>$ (larger than), $\not>$ (not larger than), $\leq$ (less than or equal), $\not\leq$ (not less than or equal, i.e., larger than), $\geq$ (greater than or equal), $\not\geq$ (not greater than or equal, i.e., less than), `modulo` (the modulo function), `gcd` (the greatest common divisor function), * (exponent), or other.

(e) A postfix expression consists of two parts: an operand expression, and a postfix operator.

    i. Operand expressions are expressions.

    ii. A postfix operator is one of the following (literals): ! (factorial), or other.

(f) A conditional (mixfix) expression has three parts: a test expression, a consequence expression, and an alternative expression — all being expressions.

7. A vector expression is a pair: a vector lower and upper index bounds, and a list of expressions (of the same type).

8. A record expression is a set of field-identifier marked expressions such that no two expressions are marked with the same field identifier.

(a) A field identifier-marked expression is a pair: a field identifier and an expression.

9. A test expression is an expression.

10. A parenthesised expression is an expression.

Exercise 8.8 *Syntactic Well-formedness of STIL.* The Syntactic Well-formedness Constraints: We first define, in an intertwined manner, the notion of the type of an expression, as well as the notion of type correctness of expressions.

—————— Syntactic Well-formedness ——————

1. The type of an expression which is a value is the type of that value.
2. Let variable identifier v be defined, in a block b, to be of type t.

3. Then in any expression of b in which v occurs the expression v is of type t.

4. Let v be a variable of type t vector whose elements have been defined to be of type t_e. Let i be a valid index into the defined vector type. Then $v[i]$ is a variable reference expression and is of type t_e.

5. Let v be a variable of type record t. Let f be a field identifier of record type t. Let the type expression associated with f in record type t be t_e. Then $v.f$ is a variable reference expression and is of type t_e.

6. Let v_r be a variable reference of type t.

7. Let t be a vector type with element type t_e and index range $\{i_1, i_2, \ldots, i_n\}$ (i.e., the set of consecutive integers from a lower bound i_{lo} to an upper bound i_{hi}), and let e be any integer valued expression whose value (which can only be determined at run-time) lies in the abovementioned index range, then $v_r[e]$ is a variable reference expression, and is of type t_e.

8. If t is a record type with field identifiers index set $\{f_1, f_2, \ldots, f_n\}$, and such that the type expression associated with field identifier f_i (where $i \in \{1 \ldots n\}$) is t_e, then $v_r \bullet f_i$ is a variable reference expression, and is of type t_e.

9. Let ωe be a syntactically well-formed prefix expression. (That is: Let the type of e be t.) If t is **Boolean**, then ω must be the operator $\neg$. Otherwise t must be either **integer** or **real**. If the operator in the latter case is either one of the arithmetic operators: sin, cos, tan, cotan, sinhy, coshy, tanhy, cotanhy, arcsin, arccos, arctan, arccotan, $\sqrt{\ }$, $\log_{10}$ or $\log_2$, then the type of the prefix expression is **real**. If t is **integer** and the operator is either one of $+, -$, then the type of the prefix expression is **integer**. If t is **real** and the operator is either one of $+, -$, then the type of the prefix expression is **real**. If t is **real** and the operator is either one of $\uparrow, \downarrow$, then the type of the prefix expression is **integer**. These are the only allowed type and operator combinations.

10. Let $e_l \omega e_r$ be a syntactically well-formed infix expression. That is: Let the types of e_l be t_l, and of e_r be t_r. Either t_l, t_r are both of type **character** and ω is either one of $=, \neq$. If so, type **Boolean** is the type of the infix expression. Or t_l, t_r are both of type **Boolean** in which case ω must be one of the operators $=, \neq, \wedge, \vee, \supset$. If so type **Boolean** is the type of the infix expression. Or t_l, t_r are of type **integer** and/or **real**. If so, the type of the infix expression is **Boolean** if the operator is one of $=, \neq, <, \nless, >, \ngtr, \leq, \nleq, \geq, \ngeq$. If the infix operator is one of $+, -, \times$ then the type of the infix expression is **integer** if both t_l, t_r are of type **integer**, else, including if $\omega = /$, the type of the infix expression is **real**.

11. Let $e\omega$ be a syntactically well-formed postfix or suffix expression. That is, let the type of e be t. We just assume ω to be the factorial operator !. Then t must be of type **integer**. The type of $e\omega$ is also **integer**.

12. Let e be a conditional expression: `if` e_t `then` e_c `else` e_a `end`. The type of e_t must be `Boolean`, and the types of e_c and e_a must be the same, say t. Then the type of e is t.

We define the notions of nesting, surrounding, scope and inheritance.

1. Let b be a block: `begin` var_dcls; stmt_lst `end`. The scope of any variable identifier, any record field identifier and any enumerated set identifier declared in var_dcls is the statement list stmt_lst.
2. If a block b' occurs in the statement list of another block b, then b' is said to be immediately nested within b, and b is said to be immediately surrounding b'. b' is in the scope of any identifier defined in b. Any identifier declared in b is inherited by b' — except if redeclared in b'.
3. Continuing the previous item: If b''s statement list contains blocks b'', then they are also nested within b, and b surrounds b'' — but no longer "immediately".
4. Let `for` step_id `in` $\langle lb..ub \rangle$ `do` stmt_lst `end` be any iteration statement. The scope of step_id is the statement list stmt_lst, including embedded (i.e., nested) blocks of stmt_lst.
5. Let id be an identifier declared in the var_dcls of a block b with statement list stmt_lst. If id occurs in some statement of stmt_lst which is not a block, then id is said to occur directly in b.
6. Continuing the item just above: If id occurs in some block statement b' of stmt_lst in which it is not redeclared, then id is said to occur indirectly, i.e., inherited, in b.
7. Continuing the two items just above: And id's nearest surrounding declaration is b — in both cases.

We finally list some of the remaining syntactic well-formedness constraints. Please formalise these.

1. Programs:
   (a) Programs are well-formed if their blocks are well-formed.
2. Declarations:
   (a) Let d be a declaration, for example, `variable` v `:=` value_expression `type` type_expr.
   (b) A declaration is well-formed if its type expression is well-formed and if its value expression is well-formed.
3. Statements:
   (a) Let b be a block: `begin` var_dcls; stmt_lst `end`. No two identifiers, whether variable identifiers, or record field identifiers mentioned in var_dcls must be the same. That is, if they occur at different textual positions in the text of var_dcls then they must be distinct.
   (b) The declaration of a variable, say v, of type, say t, establishes a contribution to the static context of the block b in which it occurs, and may do so for any inner block b' in which v is not redeclared.

(c) We call such a static context, when we speak of type checking, a dictionary. The dictionary inherited from outer blocks and modified by current block declarations is called the current dictionary for all statements in the statement list of the block.

(d) Any variable identifier of a statement must be declared either in the block of whose statement list s is part, or in some surrounding block. That is, must be found in the current dictionary.

(e) The type of a variable identifier is that prescribed in the current dictionary.

(f) Let **for** id **in** $\langle lb..ub \rangle$ **do** $stmt\_lst$ **end** be any iteration statement.

   i. The iteration "variable" id can only be used in variable reference expressions $v_r[id]$... of $stmt\_lst$ (and in its inner, i.e., nested, blocks).

   ii. Thus the occurrence of an iteration statement step "variable" id gives rise to a contribution to the current dictionary.

   iii. The new, the iteration statement ("current" or "local") dictionary associates id with the **integer** type.

   iv. You are invited, please, to think of id designating an index into a vector value.

9

Semiotics

- The **prerequisites** for studying this chapter are that you are familiar with the basic abstraction and modelling principles and techniques: property- and model-oriented specifications, respectively representation and operation abstractions in terms of sets, Cartesians, maps and functions. Understanding of Chap. 3 is also an advantage.
- The **aims** are to summarise and extend the concept of semiotics as consisting of the concepts of pragmatics, semantics and syntax, and to emphasise the utter importance of considering and of modelling the world semiotically: (i) adhering to pragmatics, (ii) focusing on achieving pleasing semantic types and functions, and (iii) based on pleasing abstract syntaxes.
- The **objective** is to free your mind so as to achieve a proper choice, emphasis and prioritisation of pragmatics, semantics and syntax in all phases of software development.
- The **treatment** is from systematic to formal.

9.1 Semiotics = Syntax ⊕ Semantics ⊕ Pragmatics

The *language* we use, whether informal or formal, whether our mother tongue, or a professional, i.e., occupational language, determines much of our intellectual thinking, as well as our material action. Mastery is therefore expected wrt. linguistic notions of language: (i) *syntax*, as formalisable rules of form, i.e., of syntactical systems for expressing such rules, of abstract ways of expressing this as well as concrete ways — where the latter corresponds to how we "utter" [or concretely model] sentences, respectively model conceptual [i.e., data] structures; (ii) *semantics*, as formalisable rules of meaning, i.e., of semantical systems for expressing meaning of sentences or of conceptual [data] structures; and (iii) *pragmatics*, as ("difficult to formalise") rules of use, i.e., of conventions as to why we utter certain things, why we "figure" or "picture" certain conceptual [data] structures. This mastery is needed, but the ability to express and to model "things", syntactically and semantically, while observing proper use, including effective communication (as also determined by pragmatic concerns) may be considered an art! Much can, however, be learned, and much confusion can be avoided, if we properly understand basic notions of *syntax*, *semantics* and *pragmatics*.

We have therefore investigated, and we shall further, in this chapter, treat various notions of syntax, various notions of semantics, and various notions of pragmatics, so that you can handle these concepts with ease. We have found — in the context of computing science and of software engineering — that the kind of understanding of these concepts (syntax, semantics, pragmatics) that we will put forward here, has been put to good use over the past 30 years and will undoubtedly come to good use for many more years. After all: computing is a rather mechanistic world and the *'theory of semiotics'* [73–75, 364, 365, 394–397, 553] as here promulgated, the *sum of syntax, semantics and pragmatics*, is a relevant one, one that seems to fit much in this world of computing. But not all!

Why is *"this thing"* about language, and therefore syntax, semantics and pragmatics, so important? It is important because *almost all we do, in software engineering is describing (is prescribing, is specifying):* is creating small, to medium, to indeed very large scale descriptions (etc.). So we communicate, first with one another, within and across stakeholder boundaries and communities, then with the computer. Our final descriptions are actually the basis for computations, i.e., for executions by computers. If these programs have to be utterly precise, syntactically as well as semantically, is it therefore any wonder that the prior communications — those among and between the software developers and the other stakeholders — must also be utterly precise? A mistake in the use of language, an imprecision, an unintended looseness or ambiguity made in early stages of development, in, for example, a domain description, may only be, and, as evidence shows, is only discovered long after the installation and first use of the software. No wonder we need to be utterly precise all the time!

9.2 Semiotics

Characterisation. By *semiotics* of a language, or a system of sentential or other structures, we understand a "sum" of the:

- *pragmatics*
- *semantics* and
- *syntax*

of that language or system.   ∎

What we mean by "sum" is the subject of this chapter. We have listed the components of semiotics in the direct order of their "importance". When we, being serious, utter something then there is a reason for doing so: the pragmatics. In what we utter there is a meaning: the semantics. How we utter it, depending on the language we use, is formed by grammatical rules: the syntax.

Normally, treatment of pragmatics, semantics and syntax is in the reverse order of their importance. The reason (metapragmatics as it were) for others doing so is partly historical, partly of convenience. First, the means for formalising syntax were discovered, then means for formalising semantics were discovered. Current technology seems not to provide a ready means for formalising pragmatics. Formal syntactical systems are simpler than formal semantical systems.

This chapter, although it is rather large, does not substitute for a proper text on semantics. We refer to such textbooks as [93, 158, 432, 448, 499, 533]. This chapter, however, treats the subject of programming language semantics from a point of view which we consider complementary to those views presented in the above-referenced literature. The treatment of those books lays a firm mathematical foundation for the semantics specification languages and deals with such issues as congruence between two different semantic definitions of the same languages, that is, the correctness of one wrt. the other.

9.3 Language Components

The following decomposition of language concepts and their explication is taken from [7]. The syntax-semantics-pragmatics sub-structuring is believed to be due to Morris [73–75, 364, 365, 553]. In fact, the term 'semiotics', as we use it, is really to be taken in its widest meaning [84].

Language concepts embody several constituent concepts. Some are important, others are not important to the subject of these volumes.

Characterisation. *Phonetics* is the study of and knowledge about how words are realised as sounds. In automatic speech recognition systems phonetics is a core issue.   ∎

Characterisation. *Morphology* is the study of and knowledge about how words are constructed from basic meaning units called morphemes. Again we shall not treat this subject further in these volumes.   ∎

Characterisation. *Semiotics* is the study of and knowledge about the structure of all 'sign systems'.   ∎

Conventional natural language as spoken by people is but one such system.[1]

---

[1]Examples of sign systems are sound (audio), sight (visual), touch (tactile), smell and taste and in all contexts: dance, film, politics, eating and clothing [84].

Characterisation. *Syntax* is the study of and knowledge about how words can be put together to form correct sentences and of how sentence words relate to one another.   ∎

This is, obviously, one of our central concerns: the correct syntactic use of specification, design and programming languages, and the design of effective such languages, and, as we shall see in Section 9.5, systems.

Characterisation. *Semantics* is the study of and knowledge about the meaning of words, sentences, and structures of sentences.   ∎

Semantics is perhaps the most crucial issue treated in these volumes.

Characterisation. *Pragmatics* is the study of and knowledge about the use of words, sentences and structures of sentences, and of how contexts affect the meanings of words, sentences, etc.   ∎

9.4 Linguistics

A number of concepts need be characterised:

Characterisation. *Linguistics* is the study of and knowledge about language.   ∎

Characterisation. *Natural linguistics* is the study of and knowledge about national, ethnic, cultural ancient and/or extinct languages.   ∎

Characterisation. *Computational linguistics* is the study of and knowledge about natural language processing by machine.   ∎

We shall not be concerned about this aspect!

Characterisation. *Language Comprehension:* In building computer systems for the support of man-made systems we build models of terms and fragments of sentences of the languages spoken by stakeholders in these systems.   ∎

Examples of man-made systems, i.e., domains, are: financial services, health care, transport, manufacturing, etc. Comprehension, effectively understanding what stakeholders of such domains utter, describe, etc., is of crucial concern.

Since natural languages are inherently informal and since "human frailty is endemic", we shall never come to completely mechanise natural languages. We shall forever have the greatest difficulties in ensuring that whatever world knowledge has been communicated by words and sentences has not been detrimentally misunderstood. The outlook may seem bleak. But we do know from successful uses of computers, in fact, from adequately functioning human enterprises and institutions, that "all is not lost". There is indeed a large body of knowledge, which, when adequately mastered, will help its users in achieving significant support in their work towards high-quality computing systems. Mastery of a great number of language concepts, many covered in this and the next chapters, has shown to assist greatly.

9.5 Languages and Systems

The problem tackled in this section is the following: Sometimes we refer to a structure[2] of composite phenomena as a system, sometimes as a language. What is the distinction? Is there any? In this section we basically equate an *intellectual concept* of *language* with a *formal, intellectual, physical world* phenomenon of system.

As we shall see, a language is a structure (i.e., a formal system) consisting of a *syntax*, a *semantics* and a *pragmatics*. Languages, in the conventional sense, are spoken and heard, and are written and read. They manifest themselves in the form of *sentences*, or as we shall see it, as *descriptions*, i.e., *designations*, *definitions* and *refutable assertions* collected in *specifications*, *designs* and *programs*.

A *real world*, *physical system* is, in this sense, perhaps not immediately conceivable as a language in the previous sense. A *system*, and since we emphasised its *real world*, *physical*, i.e., phenomenological,[3] nature, is perhaps more conventionally perceived by what can be seen through the eyes — when what is seen is *not* written texts — rather than heard through the ears or read as texts. We shall, however, in these volumes insist that the distinction between a formal system and a real world, physical system is merely a fiction, is merely psychologically and pragmatically motivated. We shall claim that since we have to *describe* these real world, physical systems they become linguistic. That since some, if not most, of these systems (viz.: railways, manufacturing, airports, fisheries industry, health care, etc.) contain sizable language components, they can also be understood as languages (or sets of languages), namely including those spoken by actors or stakeholders of these systems. And since we get to properly understand these real world, physical systems, through verbal and otherwise communicated (e.g., written) language-based discussion, they are languages. Some system components, such as a refraction

---

[2]By a structure we mean an aggregation of any number (incl. 0) of "things", that is, phenomena or concepts, in such a way that we can model them mathematically, for example, in terms of some functions, typically over Cartesians of numbers, sets, lists, maps and functions (over these), or logically in terms of a set of axioms. The term 'structure' is therefore basically the mathematical, or the logical structure of these mathematical (incl. logic) entities.

[3]By *phenomenology* is understood the study and knowledge about what can be perceived.

tower in a petrochemical plant, are describable, for example, in the form of the languages of differential equations and fuzzy control. Note the distinction between formal systems, on the one hand, and real systems or (real, human or formal, i.e., programming) languages, on the other hand. The former allow you to express models of the latter.

9.5.1 Professional Languages

We shall confine ourselves only to look at a small subset of languages: The languages of *domain-specific fields*, such as the those used by those people for whom we make software. These are, on one hand, the professional languages of, for example, the *financial service industry* (of *banking* people, of *insurance* people, of *stock exchange* staff and *stock brokers* and *traders*), of *railway* staff, of the *air transport* industry (of *airport*, *airline* and *air traffic control* staff) and, on the other hand, the *professional* language of *software* engineers: the *specification*, *design* and *programming languages*. We shall refer to the former group of languages as the *application domain-specific languages* and to the latter group as the *software engineering languages*. Together we refer to these languages as the *professional languages*.

Thus, in these volumes, we are not concerned with languages in general, that is, those used in everyday communication. We are only concerned with those (albeit natural language) subsets that relate to subjects that might be the target of *computing*.

The professional languages are characterised by a relatively precise use of terms. Certain verbs, nouns, adjectives and adverbs stand in relatively precise relations to the phenomena they designate — they are, so to speak, part of the jargon of the professional trade.

Example 9.1 *Professional Languages:* Some examples of professional language utterings are: (i) to *offer* a *block* of *stocks* for *sale*, (ii) to *dispatch* a *train according* to the *timetable* from one *station* to a *next (station)* along a specific *line*, (iii) to *plan* a *project* as a set of *actions* that *use* certain *resources* at certain *locations* and *according* to a certain *schedule*, (iv) to *abstractly model* the *domain* of a certain *application* and to *model* the *requirements* to support certain *operations* in that *domain*.   ∎

Examples 9.1(i–iii) are all application domain specific. Example 9.1(iv) is from software engineering.

The point we are now making is therefore this: with the techniques of these volumes, perhaps culminating with the description principles outlined in Vol. 3, Chaps. 5–7, we will be able to construct precise informal as well as formal descriptions of what these *terms* mean. As we shall see in this chapter, the *terms* are *syntax*, they are used in *pragmatically* determined (i.e., context conditioned) situations, and they have a *semantics*. It is our job, as software engineers, to make sure that we understand as precisely as is possible how these three aspects, *pragmatics*, *semantics* and *syntax*, relate to the *professional language terms*.

9.5.2 Metalanguages

We cannot describe a language in itself. That would lead to paradoxes and anomalies. Thus the language used in describing another language is called the metalanguage of the former. These volumes bring forth many metalanguages: *natural language*, in general; and *mathematics* and *logic* in particular; RSL, in general; and CSP, the Duration Calculi (DC) languages (Chap. 15) and other formal languages in particular.

   We will, however, not present the full formal syntax and semantics of these languages — other than generally expressing that there is a (set of) type(s) of syntactic values, a set of types of semantic values and denotations, cf. Sect. 3.2, and a set of semantic functions (M):[4]

type
   Syn, Sem
   DEN = Sem $\overset{\sim}{\to}$ Sem
value
   M: Syn $\to$ DEN

where the semantic functions assign denotations to each syntactic value. The design of a language is therefore based on properties of the domain within which it is going to be used. Hence it is also based on the pragmatics of the domain, the design of its semantic types ("what it is all about"), the design of its syntactic forms, and the definition of semantic functions. We refer to internal reports for the precise mathematical semantics of RSL [201,202,351–354].

9.5.3 Systems

We shall provide complementary answers to the question: "What is a system?": As physical and as linguistic "devices"!

A Physical System View

In the first, the conventional, "mechanistic" view — which, in the present formulation is due to Pim Borst, Hans Akkermans and Jan Top [60] — a system syntactically consists of a set of disjoint components, which are parts, where parts may have subparts which are parts, and where components have

---

[4]We have simplified and summarised the syntactic, semantic and denotation types considerably. First hints were given in Sect. 3.2. The present chapter will amply illustrate highly structured syntactic, semantic and denotational types.

terminals, with some or all terminals of one component being connected to terminals of other components by means of connectors. A connection is a sequence of terminals with "in-between" connectors.

A system semantically stands for the flow of "things" (energy, control, information, or other) across connections, with parts designating and hosting actions which consume and/or produce "things", and with disconnected, "dangling" terminals designating interfaces to a surrounding world.

Examples of Physical and Nonphysical Systems

It is time for examples.

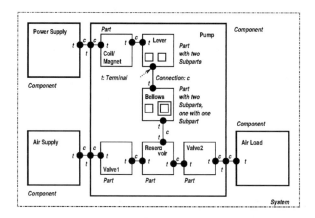

Fig. 9.1. An air pump, i.e., a physical mechanical system

Example 9.2 *System Illustrations:*
   Figure 9.1 illustrates the above for the case of a physical air pump system.
   Figure 9.2 might illustrate a rocket on a launch vehicle with six essential components: four wheels, a 'flatbed' and the rocket, which is assumed "flexibly" connected to the flatbed. Wheels are likewise connected to the flatbed.
   Figure 9.3, which is not a physical system, illustrates the related set of documents and also the set of related activities that are relevant to the development of a typed, parallel programming language. These are the language design, including syntax and (static and dynamic) semantics, the requirements (including their staged and stepwise development of semantics analysis requirements and requirements to generated code and to a runtime system for the support of multiple tasks), and the software design (a likewise staged and stepwise development of a multipass administrator and individual frontend and backend passes). Chapters 16–18 and Vol. 3, Chap. 27, Sect. 27.2 will illustrate what is behind a picture like that of Fig. 9.3.

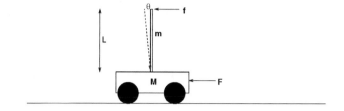

Fig. 9.2. An "inverted" pendulum

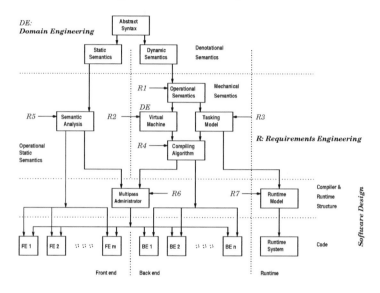

Fig. 9.3. A development graph for Ada compilers

Figure 9.4 illustrates a rail net system.

Figure 9.5 illustrates a software architecture as a system of $n + 2$ components (n clients (three shown, the rest indicated by ellipses (...)), a timetable-based reservation database and a staff) with (data communication) connections allowing the flow of control and information.

Figure 9.6 illustrates a program system structure as a system of $n + 8$ components. This latter figure relates to the former.

The last two figures are conceptual systems, not necessarily physical systems. The clients and the staff may be represented physically by terminals, but some of the client and staff software may reside, physically, i.e., storagewise, together with the timetable-based reservation database.   ∎

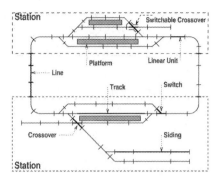

Fig. 9.4. A railway net

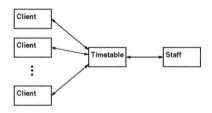

Fig. 9.5. A conceptual airline timetable system

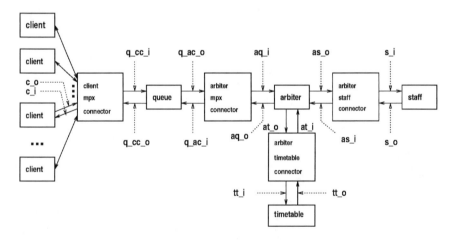

Fig. 9.6. The software components of an airline timetable system

A Linguistic Systems View

In the second, the linguistics view, a system determines one or more languages. For a given (professional) language, and referring to the "physical systems" view: The parts and components define certain nouns. Terminals define values. An "inside" of parts (and components) defines certain verbs. Dependent on whatever descriptive text may accompany a system diagram, one may define additional nouns, verbs, adjectives, adverbs, etc. Often a part is thought of as being a "carrier" of a behaviour, and several parts as a set of parallel behaviours. What the nouns, verbs, adjectives, adverbs, etc., may designate may be as follows: The things "residing" inside the parts and components may determine RSL-like types, classes, schemes and objects. That is, they may designate semantic notions and their structuring: Disjoint parts may correspond to a Cartesian type, and contained parts may correspond to a set, list or map type. Components typically correspond to a class or scheme definition. The parts and components may correspond to functions or processes. The terminals and connectors may determine any of a number of modelling choices: A set of two or more terminals connected together may correspond to a shared variable or object, in which case their connector corresponds to variable or object access from different functions (processes). Or a set of two or more terminals connected together may correspond to an input/output communication between two processes.

Example System Languages

Two examples of sentences of professional languages will be given.

Example 9.3 *An Air Pump System Language:* We refer back to Fig. 9.1 which illustrates an air pump system. The *air pump* consists of four components: a *power supply*, a *pump*, an *air supply* and an *air load*. The *pump* consists of six parts: a *coil/magnet*, a *lever*, a *bellows* arrangement, two *valves* (1 and 2) and an *air reservoir*. The *air supplies* are connected to respective *valves* by means of *air pump* to *air supply fittings*. The *power supply* is connected to the *coil/magnet*. The *lever* is connected to the *coil/magnet* and the *bellows* arrangement, which again is connected to the *air reservoir* — with the *air reservoir* again being connected to both *valves*.   ∎

For simplicity we focused here only on the assembly entities and their "topological" layout. We could have gone on to explain the inner workings of the parts and the transfer of energy (etc.) between the parts and components.

Example 9.4 *A File System Language:*
   A *file system* consists of four parts: A *sentinel*, a *file directory*, a set of disjoint *page directories* and a set of disjoint *pages* (Fig. 9.7). The *sentinel* and the *file directory* is kept in *storage*, while the *page directories* and *pages* are kept on *disks*. The *file directory* is a *linked list* of disjoint *records* with three *fields*: a *next record link*, a *file name* and a *storage to disk page directory address*. A first *record* is designated by the *sentinel*. A *page directory* is an *indexed table* whose entries *address distinct pages*. *Pages* are *contiguous sequences of bytes*.

We see that *storage* and *disk* are chosen as components, the *sentinel*, the *file directory* and the respective collections of *page directories*, and *pages* are proper immediate, i.e., direct parts. We also see that *records*, any one *page directory* and any one *page* are direct parts of these latter, and that the *fields* of *records* and *page directory table entries* again are direct parts of the previous parts. The *pointer*, *link* and *address fields* are terminals, and the *pointers* (themselves, i.e., the *pointer, link, address values*) are the connections.   ■

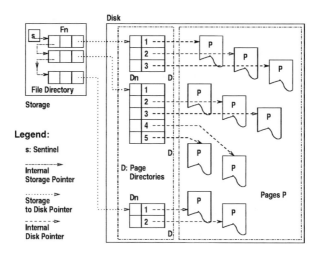

Fig. 9.7. A simple file system

Example 9.5 *A File System Formalisation, I:* We can formalise the system diagrams. We show first a simple, straightforward "solution" to the example of the software engineering of 'The File System'.

Earlier and later examples have and will illustrate models of physical, man-made systems.

type
    FS = STG × DSK
    STG = S × FD
    DSK = PDS × PGS
    S == nill() | ptr(l:LOC)
    FD = LOC ⇸ REC
    REC :: S × Fn × Dn
    PDS = Dn ⇸ TBL
    TBL = Entry*
    Entry == entry(pi:PgInfo,pn:Pn)

PGS = Pn $\overrightarrow{m}$ PAGE

The file system (fs:FS) consists of a storage (stg:STG) and a disk (disk:DSK). The storage contains (and we show only that) a sentinel (s:S) and a file directory (fd:FD). The disk (disk:DSK) consists of page directories (pds:PDS) and pages (pages:PGS). The sentinel is either nil, i.e., "contains" no storage location value, or contains a valid storage location value. The file directory (fd:FD) maps locations (LOC) to records (REC). A record has three fields: a (next) sentinel, a file name (fn:Fn) and a directory name (dn:Dn) which is like a disk address. The page directories map disk addresses (dn:Dn) to tables (tbl:TBL). A table is a list of entries (Entry), and an entry has two fields: a page information field (pi) and a page name (pn) field. The page names are treated like (other) disk addresses. The pages map a disk address to a page (page:PAGE). We omit expressing the usual constraints that ensure no "dangling" pointers: that sentinel storage location values are indeed proper storage locations of records, and that disk addresses point to appropriate page directories or pages.

value

    fstrec: STG $\xrightarrow{\sim}$ REC
    fstrec(s,fd) ≡ fd(l(s))
      pre ∃ loc:LOC • s=ptr(loc) ∧ l(s) ∈ **dom** fd

    nxtrec: S $\xrightarrow{\sim}$ STG $\xrightarrow{\sim}$ REC
    fstrec(s)(,fd) ≡ fd(l(s))
      pre ∃ loc:LOC • s=ptr(loc) ∧ l(s) ∈ **dom** fd

    pgdir: Dn → DSK $\xrightarrow{\sim}$ TBL
    pgdir(dn)(pds,) ≡ pds(dn) **pre** dn ∈ **dom** pds

    pg: Dn × **Nat** $\xrightarrow{\sim}$ DSK $\xrightarrow{\sim}$ PAGE
    pg(dn,i)(pds,pages) ≡ pages(pn((pds(dn))(i)))
      pre dn ∈ **dom** pds ∧ i ∈ **inds** pds(dn)
        ∧ pn((pds(dn))(i)) ∈ **dom** pages

The type definitions reflect the system part and component structure. The fstrec, nxtrec, pgdir and page function definitions reflect the system terminals and connectors.

    The types and functions are semantic models of syntactic software engineering professional language terms: *storage, disk, file directory, file names, pointers (links, chains, addresses), page directories, page directory, table, index, pages* and *page*, covering a view of information (noun), and *get first file directory entry, get next file directory entry, get page directory* and *get page*, covering a view of operations (verbs). ∎

Example 9.6 *A File System Formalisation, II:* The previous model (Example 9.5) expressed an abstract view, concentrating on the storage, disk, file directory, page directories, page directory, pages, and page data structures and on (some of) the basic, you may say primitive, functions that involve these data structures (fstrec, nxtrec, pgdir, and pg). The next model looks at the same issues but now "endowing and enriching" them with a process view.

type
    MSG == getpgdir(dn:Dn) | getpg(dn:Dn,i:**Nat**)
channel
    s_d : MSG | TBL | PAGE
value
    storage: STG → **out** s_d **in** s_d **Unit**
    storage(stg) ≡
        (... ; s_d!getpgdir(d) → s_d?tbl ; ... ; s_d!getpg(d,i) → s_d?page ;
        ... ; **let** stg' = ... **in** storage(stg') **end**)

    disk: DSK → **out** s_d **in** s_d **Unit**
    dsk(pds,pages) ≡
        s_d?getpgdir(dn) → s_d!pgdir(dn)(pds,) ; dsk(pds,pages)
        [] s_d?getpg(dn,i) → s_d!pg(dn,i)(pds,pages) ; dsk(pds,pages)
        [] ... → ... ; **let** disk = ... **in** dsk(disk) **end**

■

A Flowchart Language

The next example is quite extensive. It can be skipped in a first reading.

Example 9.7 *Flowcharts:*
    The domain of flowcharts includes that of sequential programs, usually presented in the linear form of lines of possibly structured statements. Some statements may contain or be **goto** statements. Labelled statements are then the target of such **goto**s. But the reader of a sequential program has to "link up", as it were, the **goto** source and targets. Flowcharts show these "link-ups" explicitly. So we need to make precise the syntax of sequential programs and their visual counterparts: that of flowcharts.
    The domain of flowcharts also includes their animation. In the domain we do not concretise exactly how the animation may take place: It may be your tracing, with some finger or pencil, the flow of control, or your placing a small token (a pebble or a coin) successively along the flowchart elements, or other.
    It is the purpose of a subsequent requirements to make precise exactly how we see a computer system providing the visualisation and animation. But first we must get the basic notions right: sequential programs, flowcharts, and the intrinsics of visualisation and animation.

We describe, informally and formally, the syntax of simple, unstructured flowcharts. We then describe a variant of an abstract interpretation, i.e., semantics of such flowcharts, namely a form of flowchart animation. Finally we describe structured flowcharts.

Informal Syntax of Simple Flowcharts

We give an example description of the syntax of simple flowcharts that is terse, i.e., is short and describes only the very essentials.

- A flowchart consists of a number of uniquely labelled boxes infixed by trees.
- There are four kinds of boxes:
  - ⋆ Circular "Begin" and circular "End" boxes, labelled with B's, respectively E's. Any one flowchart has exactly one B-box and one or more E-boxes.
  - ⋆ Rectangular "Statement" boxes, (externally) labelled with some distinct s, and internally filled out with some statement, S, — in a sequential programming language that we shall otherwise not detail. Each statement box has exactly one input and one output.
  - ⋆ Diamond-shaped "Predicate" boxes, (externally) labelled with some distinct p, and internally filled out with some predicate — in the otherwise not detailed sequential programming language. Each predicate box has exactly one input and two outputs: one affixed with **true**, the other with **false**.
- There is one kind of tree. The root of the tree is indicated by an arrow. The one or more leaves of the tree are left further unspecified. Each tree infixes two or more boxes: The arrow is incident upon a box, i.e., provides "its input". The leaves "provide box outputs".
- We say that a pair of boxes is connected if there is a tree one of whose leaves designates the first box of the pair and whose arrow designates the second box of the pair.
- A path of a flowchart is a pair of labels of connected boxes of the flowchart.
- A route of a flowchart is a sequence of labels such that an adjacent pair of the sequence is a path of the flow chart.
- A trace of a flowchart is a route whose first label is that of a begin box and whose last label is that of an end box.
- A cycle of a flowchart is a route whose first and last labels are the same.
- A well-formed flowchart is a flowchart such that for every box there is a trace of the flowchart that contains the label of that box.

That's all!

A Simple Flowchart

Figure 9.8 shows a simple flowchart according to the above description. There are seven trees, of which five are simple lines and two are binary trees. $S1, S2$, etc., stand for statements, and $P1, P2$ for predicates.

The notion of box labels is introduced solely to handle a number of technicalities such as for example well-formedness.

The syntax description was informal, but supported with an illustrative picture.

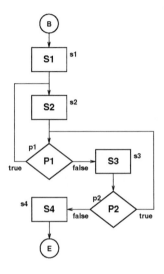

Fig. 9.8. A simple flowchart

Formal Syntax of Simple Flowcharts

We now give a formal syntax of simple flowcharts.

type
    L, S, P
    FC' = Box-set, FC = {| fc:FC' • wf_FC(fc) |}
    Box == mk_B(lbl:L,l:L)
        | mk_S(from:L-set,lbl:L,s:Stmt,to:L)
        | mk_P(from:L-set,lbl:L,p:Pred,tofalse:L,totrue:L)
        | mk_E(from:L-set,lbl:L)
value
    wf_FC(fc) ≡
        let lbls:L-set = { lbl(b) | b:Box • b ∈ fc } **in**

∃ ! beg:Box, ∃ e:L,l:L •
    beg ∈ fc ∧ beg=mk_B(e,l) ∧ ∀ b:Box • b ∈ fc ⇒
      case b **of**
        mk_B(,l) → l ∈ lbls,
        mk_S(ls,,,l) → ls ∪ {l} ⊆ lbls,
        mk_P(ls,,,fa,tr) → ls ∪ {fa,tr} ⊆ lbls,
        mk_E(ls,e) → ls ⊆ lbls **end**
∧ ... /* well-formedness wrt. traces */
end

Structured Flowcharts

The notion of simple flowcharts corresponds to sequential programs with labelled statements and conditional gotos. The flowchart of Figure 9.8 thus
corresponds to the following sequential program:

    b:
      s1: S1;
      s2: S2;
      p1: **if** P1 **then** goto s2 **end**;
      s3: S3;
      p2: **if** P2 **then** goto p1 **end**;
      s4: S4;
    e:

Structured statements are introduced in order to avoid "wild" **goto**s.

Therefore we now cover the notion of structured flowcharts. We do so by
first introducing the notion of structured statements. Recall that statements of
the flowcharts introduced above were designated by simple rectangular boxes.
Now we wish to restrict flowcharts to only contain such compositions of boxes
and trees such that any flowchart can be simply decomposed to a sequence of
subflowcharts where each has exactly one input box and one output box —
as we shall now see.

A structured statement has either of the forms informally expressed below:

skip
| var := expr
| stmt_1 ; stmt_2 ; ... ; stmt_n
| **if** expr **then** stmt **else** stmt **end**
| **while** expr **do** stmt **end**

To each of the structured statements there corresponds the "extended"
flowchart shown in Figure 9.9. The extension is that of providing shaded,
respectively black, begin and end boxes.

Composition of these extended flowcharts now proceeds as described:

- A structured flowchart is the composition of one or more extended flowcharts.
- Composition (";") of two extended flowcharts is the juxtaposition of these extended flowcharts such that the (black) end box of one "cancels" the (grey) begin box of the other — whereby the single arrow into a black box (i.e., circle) coincides with the single arrow out from a grey box (i.e., circle).
- Composition is associative:

$$c_1; (c_2; c_3) = (c_1; c_2); c_3 = c_1; c_2; c_3$$

- When no more compositions are needed the remaining grey box becomes a begin box and the remaining black box becomes an end box.

We leave it as an exercise to formalise structured flowcharts.

∎

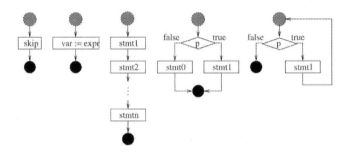

Fig. 9.9. Structured flowcharts

System Diagrams Versus Formal Specifications

Some comments may be in order. The terminals are now represented by the specific *guarded* and *unguarded input* or *output* RSL commands. The *connectors* are represented by the *channels*. The two *components* are represented by respective *processes*, and the various *parts* are represented by appropriate *data structures*.

Example 9.8 *An Air Pump System Formalisation:* We refer to Fig. 9.1. We can consider each of the boxes, i.e., each of the *parts*, a *process*, each of the connections a *channel*. We could structure their formalisation into one *scheme* for each of the three kinds of *components*, with one *class* for each *part*, and then instantiating one *power supply*, one *pump* and two *air supply* objects.

We will first summarise a process and channel structuring. ps_p, p_as, p_al stand for power supply to pump, pump to air supply, and pump to air load channels. These could be conceived of as externally observable. cm_l, l_b, b_r, r_v_1, r_v_2 stand for coil magnet to lever, lever to bellows, bellows to reservoir, and reservoir to the two valve channels. They could be conceived of as internally observable. air_pump is the overall system process. It is the parallel composition of four processes: power_supply, pump, air_supply and air_load.

channel
   ps_p, p_as, p_al
   cm_l, l_b, b_r, r_v_1, r_v_2
value
   air_pump: **Unit** → **Unit**
   air_pump() ≡ power_supply()‖pump()‖air_supply()‖air_load()

   power_supply: **Unit** → **in** ... **out** ps_p **Unit**
   pump: **Unit** → **in** ps_p **out** p_as_1, p_as_2 **Unit**
   coil_magnet: **Unit** → **in** ps_p **out** cm_l **Unit**
   lever: **Unit** → **in** sm_l **out** l_b **Unit**
   bellows: **Unit** → **in** l_b **out** b_r **Unit**

   power_supply() ≡ ...

   pump() ≡ coil_magnet()‖lever()‖bellows()‖reservoir()‖valves()
   coil_magnet() ≡ ...
   lever() ≡ ...
   bellows () ≡ ...

Before going on: You may think of these RSL/CSP-like process expressions as specifying a "simulator" for the air pump. It "is not the air pump itself", only a model. As such the model cannot actually perform the air "pumping". There is no power supply, there is no lever, there is no bellows arrangement, etc. The individual processes "fake" that, but can be used as a basis for implementing a "demo", that is, a software package which when deployed may "animate" the functions of the air pump.

value
   reservoir: **Unit** → **in** b_r **out** r_v_1, r_v_2 **Unit**
   reservoir() ≡ ...

   valves: **Unit** → **in** r_v_1, r_v_2 **out** p_as, p_al **Unit**
   valves() ≡ valve_1()‖valve_2()

   valve_1: **Unit** → **in** r_v_1 **out** p_as **Unit**

```
valve_1() ≡ ...

valve_2: Unit → in r_v_2 out p_al Unit
valve_2() ≡ ...

air_supply: Unit → in p_as Unit
air_supply() ≡ ...

air_load: Unit → in p_al Unit
air_load() ≡ ...
```

9.5.4 System Diagram Languages

We started with a systems view formulated in terms of conventional (to wit: mechanical) engineering diagrams. And we supplied "ourselves", being in software engineering, data structure diagrams. Thus there is a metalanguage of diagrams. We could not and cannot, not immediately that is, propose a semantics that would cover all such diagrams: mechanical as well as software engineering, civil engineering, etc. There is simply too big a "spread" in the denotations of boxes and arrows — as this chapter also shows. For both kinds of diagrams we instead provided specific semantics in terms of RSL specifications that were said to be specific to the specific diagram. Had we had a universal diagram language and its semantics, and if that semantics could be parameterised to the specific engineering field or subfield, as the case may be, then — perhaps — we could see our specific formalisations as "compilations" from the specific instances of the diagrams to the specific formalisations — given suitable actual arguments to be substituted for the formal parameters.

9.5.5 Discussion of System Concepts

We observe and summarise the following: The physical system notions of *parts, components, terminals* and *connectors* can be related to both classical engineering *system* concepts and to software *system* concepts. There are two complementary views of *systems*: The *physical* view and the *linguistic* view. The structure and contents of systems relate — via the ways in which the structure and contents are described — somehow to the formalisation of the system. The 'somehow' — how to achieve a pleasing, concise and (validly) relevant relation — is an art. But this series, in Vol. 3, Chaps. 5–7, presents many principles, techniques and tools that help achieve such relations: from the informal to the formal. We can schematically formalise the above. The meanings ($\mathcal{M}_\ell$) of syntactic structures of linguistic systems are usually mathematical

functions over semantic types. Whereas the meanings ($\mathcal{M}_\phi$) of syntactic structures of physical systems are usually processes. The latter are, of course, also
mathematical functions over semantic types, but their signatures differ:

type
    LingSyntax, PhysSyntax, SemType
    DEN_ℓ = SemType → SemType
    DEN_ϕ = **Unit** → **in** icl ... **out** ocl ... **Unit**
value
    $\mathcal{M}_\ell$: LingSyntax → DEN_ℓ
    $\mathcal{M}_\phi$: PhysSyntax → DEN_ϕ

A syntactic structure of a linguistic system is usually some text. A syntactic
structure of a physical system is usually the physically manifest mechanical
structure, but may be described by some diagram.

9.5.6 Systems as Languages

So we can claim that systems are languages. A system is "inhabited" by people, and, when "speaking" professionally about a system, they use terms that
designate system phenomena. So we should kindly advise the reader not to
make too much fuss about any difference: When an ISO standard deals with
"systems", it is actually characterising a limited kind of part/whole compositional and compositional, cohesive or not cohesive language properties. The
conclusion that we draw from all this is expressed in the principle and the
techniques given next.

Principles. *Physical Systems: Physical systems* are treated as linguistic systems.   ■

Techniques. *Physical Systems:* Models of *physical systems* therefore centres
around the identification and modelling of semantic and syntactic types and
of functions (including) processes over these.   ■

9.6 Discussion

It is time to summarise.

9.6.1 General

The point of showing the many figures of this chapter was to show you examples, primarily of informal syntax, and then, for some of the examples, and
derived from those syntax examples, of related semantics. The diagrams were
intended, by those who first drew them, to denote a whole class of artifacts.
The meaning of the diagrams, the possibility of redrawing them with slight
changes, and exactly which artifacts might "satisfy" respective diagrams was
informally explained by those proposing the diagrams.

9.6.2 Principles, Techniques and Tools

We enunciate only a principle. The techniques and tools of semiotics are as for respective parts: pragmatics, semantics and syntax.

Principles. Seek the *semiotics* of whatever "structure" of phenomena and concepts that you come across: Look for and discover syntactical structures; ask for, find and explore semantical structures; and inquire, all the time, about the pragmatics.   ∎

9.7 Charles Sanders Peirce

Of several founders of the field of semiotics, in particular the concept of signification, we single out Charles Sanders Peirce. The quoted paragraph is based on material from the *Free Online Dictionary* [118]:

> Charles Sanders Peirce (1839–1914) studied philosophy and chemistry at Harvard. Peirce's place as a founder of American pragmatism was secured by a pair of highly original essays that apply logical and scientific principles to philosophical method. In *The Fixation of Belief* (1877) he described how human beings converge upon a true opinion, each of us removing the irritation of doubt by forming beliefs from which successful habits of action may be derived. This theory was extended in *How to Make Our Ideas Clear* (1878) to the very meaning of concepts, which Peirce identified with the practical effects that would follow from our adoption of the concept. In his extensive logical studies, Peirce developed a theory of signification that anticipated many features of modern semiotics, emphasizing the rôle of the interpreting subject. To the traditional logic of deduction and induction, Peirce added explicit acknowledgment of abduction as a preliminary stage in productive human inquiry.

We recommend selected books on theories and philosophies of signs, pragmatics and semiotics: [394–397].

9.8 Bibliographical Notes

Several scholars, in addition to Peirce, have contributed to semiotics. Among these we single out Carnap [73–75], and Morris [364, 365]. Heinz Zemanek brought my attention to the works of Morris [553].

9.9 Exercises

Exercise 9.1 *Structured Flowcharts.* We refer to Example 9.7. Please complete that example by providing a syntax definition for structured flowcharts as described at the end of that example.

Exercise 9.2 *STIL: Semantic Meaning Functions.* This exercise completes Exercises 6.3–6.5 (pragmatics); 7.3–7.7 (semantics); and 8.7–8.8 (syntax). Please formalise the semantic functions of STIL.

Exercise 9.3 *NaTaTIL: Named Types and Typed Imperative Language:* This exercise is the second in a series of four exercises: (1) STIL: Exercises 6.3–6.5, 7.3–7.7, 8.7–8.8 and 9.2, (2) the present exercise (NaTaTIL), (3) DiTIL: Exercise 9.4, and (4) DaUTIL: Exercise 9.5.

Explication: NaTaTIL, as a programming language, represents a further development of the previous language STIL. The change in NaTaTIL with respect to STIL is only in the type "apparatus": Wherever in a STIL variable declaration a ground term type expression occurred a type name shall occur instead. And therefore we need the possibility of a new item in the block preamble. That is, where before only variable declarations occurred, now also a set of one or more type definitions shall occur:

1. By a set of one or more type definitions we understand a set of uniquely identified, i.e., type-named, type expressions.
2. By a type expression we mean either a scalar or a compound type expression.
3. A scalar type expression is the `boolean` type literal, or the `integer` type literal, or the `float` type literal, or the `character` type literal.
4. A compound type expression is a vector type expression or a record type expression.
5. A vector type expression consists of two parts: a (low integer to high integer numeral) index range part and a type name (for the vector element type).
6. A record type expression consists of a set of uniquely field-named (selector-named) type names. Two or more fields may have the same type name.
7. No type name is allowed to be recursively defined.

Questions: Please repeat all the developments of the previous exercise: That is modify the formalisations of the answers to Exercises 6.3–6.5, 7.3–7.7, 8.7–8.8 and Exercise 9.2.

Exercise 9.4 *DiTIL: Dimension Typed Imperative Language.* This exercise is the third in a series of four exercises: (1) STIL: Exercises 6.3–6.5, 7.3–7.7, 8.7–8.8 and Exercise 9.2, (2) NaTaTIL: Exercise 9.3, (3) the present exercise (DiTIL), and (4) DaUTIL: Exercise 9.5.

Explication: DiTIL, as a programming language, represents a further development of the previous language: NaTaTIL. The change in DiTIL with respect to NaTaTIL is as follows:

1. First we introduce a concept of dimension associated with scalar types.
   (a) By a dimension we mean either a base dimension or a derived dimension.
   (b) By a base dimension we mean one of the following: (1) A neutral dimension, (2) a length dimension, (3) a mass dimension, (4) a time dimension, (5) a current dimension, (6) a thermodynamic temperature dimension, (7) an amount of substance (8) and a luminous intensity dimension.
   (c) By a derived dimension we mean, for example, one of the following: (9) a time interval dimension, (10) A velocity dimension, (11) an acceleration dimension, (12) a resistance dimension, (13) a voltage dimension, (14) an area dimension, (15) a volume dimension.
   (d) These dimensions are either "measured" by integer or by floating point values.
   (e) There could be dimensions associated with Booleans, characters or text strings. We leave it to the reader to motivate such.
2. Then we observe that one can: (16) add lengths and get a length, (17) subtract lengths (or times) and get a length interval (respectively time interval) — not a length (time), (18) multiply lengths and get an area, multiply an area with a length and get a volume, (19) divide a length by a time and get a velocity.

The above causes us to suggest the following extensions to NaTaTIL:

1. Type expressions for scalars are further annotated with a dimension, but that dimension could be a neutral dimension — for example, concretely designated by [l] — as when one divides a value of dimension length by a value of dimension length;
2. and for every binary operator applicable to dimensioned (scalar) values we define what the resulting dimension will be (if applied to such values).

The DiTIL language shall be such that for every expression — whose value is a scalar — it is simply decidable which dimension it has. No inference (or unification) is to be invoked.

Let the phrase [dn] τ stand for a dimension type, like [Km] *float*. In general, we can characterise the relationship between scalar types, τ, and dimensions, d, with respect to the infix (i.e., binary, dyadic) operations, as follows:

axiom

$+,-$ $\forall$ d:Dn,τ:{integer,float} • [dn] τ × [dn] τ → [dn] τ

* $\forall$ dn',dn'':Dn,τ:{integer,float} • dn' τ × dn'' τ → [dn'dn''] τ

/ $\forall$ dn:Dn,τ:{integer,float} • dn τ × dn τ → [l] τ

/ $\forall$ dn',dn'':Dn,τ:{integer,float} • dn' τ × dn'' τ → [dn'/dn''] τ

etc., for other binary operations

For the unary operations:

axiom

exp, ln, sine, ... [l] → [l]

Questions: Please "repeat", basically, the definitions called for in Exercises 6.3–6.5, 7.3–7.7, 8.7–8.8 and 9.2–9.3. Focus, however, on the formulas that are different. That is: Do not "blindly repeat" everything. But show where the 'dimension' concept alters the previous definitions.

Exercise 9.5 *DUaLTIL: Dimension, Unit and Law Typed Imperative Language* This exercise is the last in a series of four exercises: (1) STIL: Exercises 6.3–6.5, 7.3–7.7, 8.7–8.8 and Exercise 9.2, (2) NaTaTIL: Exercise 9.3, (3) DiTIL: Exercise 9.4, and (4) the present exercise (DaUTIL).

Explication: DUaLTIL, as a programming language, represents a further development of the previous language DiTIL.

The change in DUaLTIL with respect to DiTIL is as follows: with every scalar type name we associate additionally a physical unit. For the length dimension we may associate the units of millimeter, centimeter, decimeter, meter, kilometer, etc. For the mass dimension we may associate the units of milligram, gram, hectogram, pound, kilogram, ton, etc. For the thermodynamic temperature dimension we may associate the units of either degree Kelvin, degrees Celsius (SI:[5] Celcius, centigrade), degrees Fahrenheit, or degrees Reamur. For the current dimension we may associate the unit Ampere (SI: ampere) or the unit milli-Ampere (mA). For the 'amount of substance' dimension we may associate the unit mole. For the luminous intensity dimension we may associate the unit candela.

We thus introduce yet another block preamble component: To every listed dimension we list a set of units of that dimension and their scale factors. For example:

- units:
  - ⋆ unit kilometer: km
  - ⋆ unit meter: m
  - ⋆ unit centimeter: cm
  - ⋆ unit millimeter: mm
  - ⋆ unit hour: h
  - ⋆ unit minute: min (not an SI unit)
  - ⋆ unit second: s
  - ⋆ ...
- variables:
  - ⋆ vkm1:km type float dim. length
  - ⋆ vkm2:km type float dim. length
  - ⋆ vm1:m type float dim. length
- ⋆ vm2:m type float dim. length
- ⋆ vcm:cm type float dim. length
- ⋆ vmm:mm type float dim. length
- ⋆ vhr:hr type integer dim. time
- ⋆ vmin:min type integer dim. time
- ⋆ vsec:sec type integer dim. time
- ⋆ ...
- dimensions and scales:
  - ⋆ dim.: length units:
    {1m=100cm=1000mm=0.001km}
  - ⋆ dim.: time units:
    {1h=60min=3600s}

The change is furthermore one of "adding" laws to our evolving language. The laws are of the following nature: If, for example, we decide to endow a variable

[5]SI stands for the international system of units [375].

with the type `velocity`, and we intend to assign to this variable only values that have arisen as the result of dividing a value of dimension `length` by a value of dimension `time`, then we ought say so:

dimension
    velocity : length/time
    acceleration : velocity/time
unit
    velocity : vel
    acceleration : acc
variables
    vvel : vel
    vacc : acc

So the `dimension` declaration is a place holder for expressing such laws.

Questions: Revise, appropriately, all type definitions, well-formedness conditions, semantics and auxiliary function definitions when now formalising DUaLTIL.

Exercise 9.6 *Description Logic and Ontology Languages. Background:* A number of researchers are, as of 2006, studying the largest decidable subsets of suitable mathematical logics for representing domain knowledge. One such "school" is called *Description Logic* [19,315]. One impetus to do so is the Internet, that is, because of the claim that "via the Internet" vast amounts of domain knowledge could be accessed if it was otherwise properly structured, using, for example, XML. If, in addition, that information was otherwise subject to logical constraints (also expressible using XML-like markers), then much such information could be queried semantically. We covered some aspects of XML in Sect. 8.6 and in Exercises 8.5–8.6.

A Description Logic: We give an example of a description logic (DL). The logic is concerned with expressing facts about classes and properties (of classes). To put it differently, to describe the structure of the entities, of a universe of discourse in terms of classes and properties. Classes are sets of resources, properties are relations over these. We can think of a "relation over these" as a set of pairs of resources, one from each of two classes, that might be the same. An ontology is now a set of axiomatic relationships between classes and properties. Thus we need expressions to designate classes.

The following class-forming operators over classes are often proposed:

Constructor	DL Syntax	Example
IntersectionOf	$C_1 \cap C_2 \cap \cdots C_n$	$Human \cap Male$
UnionOf	$C_1 \cup C_2 \cup \cdots C_n$	$Doctor \cup Lawyer$
ComplementOf	$\neg C$	$\neg Male$
OneOf	$\{x_1, x_2, \cdots, x_n\}$	$\{john, mary\}$

The following class-forming predicate operators are often proposed:

Constructor	DL Syntax	Example
ToClass	$\forall P.C$	$\forall$hasChild.Doctor
HasClass	$\exists P.C$	$\exists$hasChild.Lawyer
HasValue	$\exists P.\{x\}$	$\exists$citizenOf.$\{$USA$\}$

Further class-yielding operators are often proposed:

Constructor	DL Syntax	Example
MinCardQ	$\geq nP.C$	$\geq$ 2hasChild.Doctor
MaxCardQ	$\leq nP.C$	$\leq$ 1hasChild.Lawyer
CardQ	$= 1nP.C$	$=$ 1hasParent.Female

The meaning of these operators are as follows:

- **IntersectionOf**: Standard distributed set intersection, n-ary operator for $n \geq 2$
- **UnionOf**: Standard distributed set union, n-ary operator for $n \geq 2$
- **ComplementOf**: Standard set complement, binary operator
- **OneOf**: Standard set enumeration, n-ary operator for $n \geq 0$
- **ToClass**: The class of all those resources which are property P related to resources of type (i.e., of class) C
- **HasClass**: The class of all those resources which are property P related to at least one resource of type (i.e., of class) C
- **HasValue**: Shorthand for HasClass and OneOf

The next three operators are generalisations of the ToClass and HasClass operators.

- **MinCardQ**: The class $\leq nP.C$ is the class all of whose resources (instances) are related, via property P, to at least n different resources of class (type) C
- **MaxCardQ**: The class $\geq nP.C$ is the class all of whose resources (instances) are related, via property P, to at most n different resources of class (type) C
- **CardQ**: The class $= nP.C$ is the class all of whose resources (instances) are related, via property P, to exactly n different resources of class (type) C

Assume two built-in class expressions:

- **Thing**: The full class of all resources.
- **Nothing**: The empty, void class of no resources.

Questions: Define a suitable class and property definition and expression language, syntactically and semantically. That is, there must be facilities in the language for defining (i.e., naming) classes, for defining (i.e., naming) properties, and for expressions over these named classes and properties and the above operators.

Part V

FURTHER SPECIFICATION TECHNIQUES

We bring in two chapters on further specification techniques:

- Chapter 10, **Modularisation:** The specification technique of structuring (typically large) specifications into modules. Modules are textual units, themselves not necessarily "small" in (textual) "size". Modules come in various 'guises': in RSL they are called **schemes**, **classes**, and **objects**. In programming and in other specification languages they have other or similar names, including **module.** UML's notion of *Class Diagrams* is a module notion.

- Chapter 11, **Automata and Machines:** A classical discipline of computer science is that of *Automata and Formal Languages* [217]. The discovery, already in the 1940s, that the automata and machines discovered in connection with research studies of computability and in the engineering development of the first computers — that discovery — led to a flurry of research. That research "discovered" the close connection between (formal) languages, on one hand, and automata and machines, on the other hand. Automata and machines often offer a convenient, graphical, way of formally specifying a phenomenon. We will show the "conversion" between automata and machines, on one hand, and formal specifications or programs, on the other hand.

10

Modularisation

- The **prerequisite** for studying this chapter is that you have read and written large, formal specifications, which have — so far — not been modularised, i.e., expressed in terms of what will be known as schemes, classes, objects or modules.
- The **aims** are to introduce the concepts of modules and modularisation, to introduce the RSL mechanisms for expressing modules, and to introduce "older" and "newer" mechanisms for expressing modules, i.e., those of the concepts of entity relations (ER), frames, respectively the UML class diagrams [59, 237, 382, 440], and to relate the latter to the RSL **scheme, class** and **object** specification mechanisms.
- The **objective** is to enable the reader to structure large, abstract and formal specifications in terms of modules.
- The **treatment** is discursive, semiformal and systematic.

Example 10.22 and Sect. 10.3 is based on material first developed by Steffen Holmslykke [9, 10].

Little boxes on the hillside,
Little boxes made of ticky-tacky,
Little boxes, little boxes,
Little boxes, all the same.
There's a green one and a pink one —
And a blue one and a yellow one —
And they're all made out of ticky-tacky —
And they all look just the same.

And the people in the houses.
All go to the university,
And they all get put in boxes,
Little boxes, all the same.
And there's doctors and there's lawyers —
And business executives,
And they're all made out of ticky-tacky —
And they all look just the same.

And they all play on the golf-course,
And drink their Martini dry,
And they all have pretty children,
And the children go to school.
And the children go to summer camp —
And then to the university,
And they all get put in boxes —
And they all come out the same.

And the boys go into business,
And marry, and raise a family,
And they all get put in boxes,
Little boxes, all the same.
There's a green one and a pink one —
And a blue one and a yellow one —
And they're all made out of ticky-tacky —
And they all look just the same.

© Malvina Reynolds (1900–1978, USA)

We somehow like the above "poem", first sung by Pete Seeger in the 1960s, when we lived and worked near San Francisco from where Ms. Reynolds hailed. Although it must be said to represent a "radical cultural elite's" lack of human compassion and this elite's usual love for "abstract man" and disrespect for the specific ordinary man — who, in the eyes of God, is unique, and, lo and behold, indeed is unique — this 1960's "protest" song, in my mind, can be used to contrast with what this chapter is about: Namely putting parts of specifications in little boxes and they are all either, when in the same specification, different, or, when representing a series of steps of refinement, they are all the same!

10.1 Introduction

We have, notably in Vol. 1, Chap. 8, Sect. 8.5 (Specification Algebras) and in Vol. 1, Chap. 9, Sect. 9.6.5 (Property-Oriented Specifications), seen examples of what we shall in this chapter refer to as modules (abstract data types, classes, etc.).

Characterisation. By a *module* we shall understand a clearly delineated text which denotes either a single complex quantity, as does an object declaration in RSL, or a possibly empty, possibly infinite set of models of objects, as does a scheme declaration in RSL.   ∎

The RSL module concept is manifested in the use of one or more of the RSL *class* (**class ... end**), *object* (**object** identifier **class ... end**, etc.) and *scheme* (**scheme** identifier **class ... end**), etc., constructs.

Characterisation. By *modularisation* we shall understand the act of structuring a text using modules.   ∎

This chapter is more about principles and techniques for, i.e., the pragmatics of modularisation, than about the "nitty-gritty" syntactic and semantic details of specific languages' module constructs.

Characterisation. By a *specification* we shall, in RSL, understand a set of module declarations, i.e., of scheme and object declarations.   ∎

10.1.1 Some Examples

Let us show some nonmodule examples which then lead us on to a better understanding of the module concept:

Example 10.1 *Stacks — An Algebraic Model:* Assuming the Boolean data type, and assuming universal quantification wherever needed (!), we express a model in terms of sorts, function signatures and axioms.

type
  E, S
value
  empty: **Unit** → S
  is_empty: S → **Bool**
  push: E × S → S
  top: S $\overset{\sim}{\to}$ E
  pop: S $\overset{\sim}{\to}$ S
axiom
  is_empty(empty())
  top(empty())=**chaos**
  pop(empty())=**chaos**
  top(push(e,s))=e
  pop(push(e,s))=s
  ...

Where the ... indicates that, perhaps, we need some more axioms in order to properly dispense of the stack data type operations. ∎

Example 10.2 *Stacks — Model-Oriented Model:* We can express a model in terms of concrete types and explicit function definitions. Thus, if we gave a model for stacks, say as lists of elements, then we would get:

type
  E
  S = E*
value
  empty: **Unit** → S, empty() = ⟨⟩
  is_empty: S → **Bool**, is_empty(s) ≡ s=⟨⟩
  push: E × S → S, push(e,s) ≡ ⟨e⟩^s
  top: S $\overset{\sim}{\to}$ E, top(s) ≡ **if** s=⟨⟩ **then chaos else hd** s **end**
  pop: S $\overset{\sim}{\to}$ S, pop(s) ≡ **if** s=⟨⟩ **then chaos else tl** s **end**

∎

Example 10.3 *Hierarchical Directory:* In this example we only illustrate a model-oriented model. We leave it to the reader to decipher the formulas.

type
  Dn, En, E
  D = Dn $\overrightarrow{m}$ (D | (En $\overrightarrow{m}$ E))
value
  empty: **Unit** → D
  empty() ≡ [ ]

```
    is_empty: D → Bool
    is_empty(d) ≡ d=[ ]
```

type
```
    Ename == nil | mkEn(n:En)
```

value
```
    get: Dn* × Ename → D ⥲ (D | E)
    get(dnl,en)(d) ≡
        if dnl=⟨⟩
            then
                case en of
                    nil → d,
                    mkEn(n) → if n ∈ dom d then d(n) else chaos end
                end
            else
                if hd dnl ∈ dom d
                    then get(tl dnl,en)(d(hd dnl))
                    else chaos
                end
        end
```

type
```
    NmED == mkE(en:En,e:E) | mkD(dn:Dn,d:D)
```
value
```
    put: Dn* × NmED → D ⥲ D
    put(dnl,ned)(d) ≡
        case dnl of
            ⟨dn⟩ →
                if dn ∉ dom d
                    then chaos
                    else d † [ dn ↦ d(dn) †
                        case ned of
                            mkE(en,e) → [ en ↦ e ],
                            kmD(dn',d') → [ dn' ↦ d' ]
                        end ] end
            ⟨dn⟩^dnl' →
                if dn ∈ dom d
                    then put(dnl',ned)(d(dn))
                    else chaos
        end end
```

Example 10.4 *Graphs — An Algebraic Model:* We again leave it to the reader to decipher the formulas. Again sorts, observer functions, function signatures (with preconditions) and axioms.

type
  N, G
value
  obs_Ns: G → N-**set**
  obs_Es: G → (N×N)-**set**
  empty: **Unit** → G
  is_empty: G → **Bool**
  insert_node: N → G $\xrightarrow{\sim}$ G
    pre: insert_node(n)(g): n $\notin$ obs_Ns(g)

  delete_node: N → G $\xrightarrow{\sim}$ G
    pre: delete_node(n)(g): n $\in$ obs_Ns(g) $\wedge$
        $\sim$exist (n′,n″):N×N • (n′,n″) $\in$ obs_Es(g) $\wedge$ n=n′∨n=n″
  insert_edge: N×N → G $\xrightarrow{\sim}$ G
    pre: insert_edge(n,n′)(g): {n,n′}$\subseteq$obs_Ns(g) $\wedge$ (n,n′) $\notin$ obs_Es(g)
  delete_edge: N×N → G $\xrightarrow{\sim}$ G
    pre: delete_edge(n,n′)(g): (n,n′) $\in$ obs_Es(g)
axiom
  is_empty(empty()),
  obs_Ns(empty()) $\equiv$ {}
  obs_Ns(insert_node(n)(g)) $\equiv$ {n} $\cup$ obs_Ns(g)
  obs_Es(insert_edge(n,n′)(g)) $\equiv$ {(n,n′)} $\cup$ obs_Es(g)
  ...

Where the ... indicates that, perhaps, we need some more axioms in order to properly dispense of the graph data type operations.   ■

Example 10.5 *Graphs: A Model-Oriented Model:* We next give a rather simple model:

type
  N
  G = N $\xrightarrow[m]{}$ N-**set**
value
  empty: **Unit** → G
  is_empty: G → **Bool**
  insert_node: N → G $\xrightarrow{\sim}$ G
  delete_node: N → G $\xrightarrow{\sim}$ G
  insert_edge: N×N → G $\xrightarrow{\sim}$ G
  delete_edge: N×N → G $\xrightarrow{\sim}$ G

empty() = [ ]
is_empty(g) = g=[ ]

insert_node(n)(g) ≡
  if n ∈ **dom** g **then chaos else** g ∪ [n ↦ {}] **end**

delete_node(n)(g) ≡
  if n ∉ **dom** g **then chaos else** g\{n} **end**

insert_edge(n,n′)(g) ≡
  if {n,n′} ⊆ **dom** g ∧ n′ ∉ g(n)
    then g † [n ↦ g(n) ∪ {n′}] **else chaos end**

delete_edge(n,n′)(g) ≡
  if {n,n′} ⊆ **dom** g ∧ n′ ∈ g(n)
    then g † [n ↦ g(n)\{n′}] **else chaos end**

We could have chosen a model of graphs that represented these rather directly
as sets of pairs, and nothing else. Try it out yourself!   ∎

Review of Examples

We gave Examples 10.1–10.5 above so that we could make some remarks,
such that these observations would help us motivate and justify the notion of
modules.

On Module Delineation: Objects and Schemes

In our characterisation of what a module is, see Sect. 10.1, we "mandated"
that there be some clear delineation. None of the examples above provided for
that. An easy provision, such as we shall provide in RSL, is first "surrounding"
the *specification text* by the keywords **class** and **end**:

  class specification_text **end**

and then prefixing such a class expression in either of two ways:

  object name : **class** ... **end**
  scheme NAME = **class** ... **end**

A class expression (**class ... end**), as we shall see, denotes a set of models. An
object declaration (**object** name : **class ... end**) selects one such model and
binds it to the object name. A scheme declaration (**scheme** NAME = **class**
... end) gives the name NAME to the set of all the class expression models.

On Implementations

The property-oriented specifications gave no clue as how to implement, even using abstract mathematical quantities (sets, Cartesians, lists and maps). The model-oriented specifications gave some such clues. In particular, Example 10.3 presents a rather involved pair of function definitions. A further implementation of put and get (of Example 10.3) would, in order to be believable, most likely have to follow the involved structure of these function definitions.

It would therefore be nice to have a property-oriented specification of the hierarchical directory of Example 10.3 — then the developer who is charged with providing efficient implementations is helped. To have one, equally efficient implementation that covers a spectrum of "sizes" of directories, from maximum a few hundred entries within a few (say, five to six) levels of hierarchy, to millions of entries and depths of the order of hundreds, is not likely. Hence the provider of software that covers hierarchical directories can, depending on circumstances, replace one implementation with another.

Stepwise Development

In other words, we often find it desirable to develop software by first specifying its functionality abstractly, say by a property-oriented definition, and then, in steps of refinement, concretising the specification. For that purpose it is convenient, and helps focus our correctness reasoning, if what is being implemented can be clearly delineated, i.e., "boxed"!

Separation of Concerns

Developing specifications, whether descriptions of domains, prescriptions of requirements or definitions of software design, is hard. To keep track, in one's mind even on paper, i.e., amongst computerised documents, of all specification parts is a formidable task. It can be ameliorated, helped and better supported through separation of concerns: letting module specifications take care of separate abstract data types. That is, it can be supported through modularisation: through the judicious use of modules, of module interfaces and of genericity of module specifications. Still, it is not easy!

10.1.2 Preparatory Discussion

We discuss these next topics, in a leisurely manner, for the reader's "armchair reading". We do so before we move into somewhat detailed coverage of principles, techniques and tools for modularisation according to a number of specification paradigms: the *algebraic abstract data type* approach, the RAISE approach, the *frames* approach, the *entity/relations* (ER) approach, and the UML class diagram approach [59, 237, 382, 440].

Software Devices

Peter Lucas [307], we believe, was the first to enunciate the idea of "encapsulating" the types, variables, and functions (routines, etc.) that were specific to a specific data structure — like a stack, a queue, a tree, a graph, etcetera. He termed the name 'device', for such encapsulations. Devices usually are thought of as "mechanisms" that can be "plugged" in here, out there, and hence replaced. The idea of replacing one implementation of a device by another implementation of purportedly the same functions further justifies the device encapsulation concept.

In one context, say small graphs, one implementation provides efficiency (by, for example, having low storage overhead for the code and auxiliary data, i.e., variables). However, in another context, say graphs with millions of nodes and millions of edges, another implementation of, of course the same functions, provides a better efficiency than the former implementation.

Abstract Data Types ↦ Algebraic Semantics

It was not till some years later that the seminal paper by Barbara Liskov and Stephen Zilles on *Abstract Data Types* (ADTs) was published [302]. From then on, the so-called School of Algebraic Semantics (for specifying algebras of ADTs) "took off". In a flurry of papers, [68, 134, 138–140], (notably) Burstall, Goguen and Thatcher laid out the semantic foundations, in terms of initial algebra semantics, for the idea of ADTs. More generally, in [69,70,135,137] and [124, 136, 162] they, Jouannaud and Futatsugi, followed up by proposing the OBJ series of algebraic specification languages: OBJ-0-OBJ3. The most recent outgrowth of this line of research and development has been the two competing algebraic semantic specification languages Cafe-OBJ [123] and CASL [40,371].

The Frames Approach

We quote from Marvin Minsky [362]:

> "Here is the essence of the theory: when one encounters a new situation (or makes a substantial change in one's view of the present problem), one selects from memory a structure called a 'frame'. This is a remembered framework to be adapted to fit reality by changing details as necessary.
> We can think of a frame as a network of nodes and relations. The top levels of a frame are fixed and represent things that are always true about the supposed situation. The lower levels have many 'terminals' — slots that must be filled by specific instances or data.
> Much of the phenomenological power of the theory hinges on the inclusion of expectations and other kinds of presumptions. A 'frame's terminals are normally already filled with "default" assignments. Thus

a frame may contain a great many details whose supposition is not specifically warranted by the situation.

In this essay I draw no boundary between a theory of human thinking and a scheme for making an intelligent machine; no purpose would be served by separating them today, since neither domain has theories good enough to explain, or produce, enough mental capacity.

Are there general methods for constructing adequate frames? The answer is both yes and no! There are some often-useful strategies for adapting old frames to new purposes; but I should emphasize that humans certainly have no magical way to solve "all" hard problems! One must not fall into what Papert calls the superhuman-human fallacy and require a theory of human behavior to explain even things that people cannot really do!

More "logical" approaches will not work ...

In simple cases, one can get such systems to "perform", but as we approach reality, the obstacles become overwhelming. The problem of finding suitable axioms — the problem of "stating the facts" in terms of always-correct, logical assumptions — is very much harder than is generally believed."

Minsky's notion of 'frame' is often considered a precursor of object oriented programming.

The Entity-Relationship (ER) Approach

An entity represents a thing that can be identified. Usually a box is diagrammed to represent a classified set, A, of entities, that is an entity set — say a sharp-edged box. A box identifier, A, names the entity set. Entities of an entity set may have attributes (types $T_{A_1}, T_{A_2}, \ldots, T_{A_\alpha}$). They are usually shown with the entity set name "inside" the A box.

Entities can be related to each other. Relations are shown by lines between two or more boxes, $A, B, \ldots$. Usually lines connect just two boxes. One usually adorns the edge (say, between two boxes) by some form of m:n labelling: m near the edge and near one box, say A, and n near the edge and near the other box, say B. The labelling shall mean: The m:n relation over $A \times B$ binds up to m different occurences of A entities to up to n different occurences of B entities.

For different fixations of m and n we get various forms of general binary, or functional relations. As we shall see, entity-relationship diagrams (ER), can be said to be precursors to UML class diagrams.

So we shall not go further into ER theory. Any textbook on relational database design would be good to consult [129, 507], as would Peter Chen's paper on ER [79].

General Pragmatics of Modularisation

Modularisation is important for several reasons: Separation of concerns, discovery of basic concepts, validation and verification of developments, efficiency of tool support (i.e., document handling), etcetera.

General Semantics of Modularisation

"Small" modules (i.e., textually small, with few identifiers) capture "small" models. The models are an easy way to understand what is being specified. Small modules can better be ascertained as to whether they designate a single model, as do objects, or possibly a "large", or even an infinite set, as do underspecified abstract data types (i.e., modules).

General Syntax of Modularisation

Usually modules are simply and explicitly delineated by suitably suggestive keywords: a matching (i.e., balancing, as do parentheses) pair of **class** and **ends**, as in RSL, for classes. The named prefixing of a class expression, as **scheme** Scheme_Name = **class ... end**, for schemes that can be further extended, used as parameters in other scheme definitions, or used in object declarations.

> **scheme** A = **class ... end**
> **scheme** B = **extend** A **with class ... end**
> **scheme** C(a:B) = **class ... end**
> **object** d:C(B)

or as **object** Object_Name = **class ... end**

General Module Specification Method

But the real gist or crux of the matter is: "How does one, i.e., the software engineer, identify modules and compose specifications from modules?" This chapter shall try to cover some such principles, techniques and tools.

But let the reader be duly warned: It is not easy. That is, a decomposition of a specification into modules which is pleasing to some reader, may not be pleasing to another reader, and it is the writer who decides on the decomposition! So our advice, of this chapter, is not that clear-cut.

10.1.3 Structure of Chapter

First, we cover the RSL module and the RAISE modularisation concepts (Sect. 10.2). And then we cover the UML *class diagram* concept [59,237,382,440] (Sect. 10.3). We also show how to reformulate RSL specifications of types and type constraints using UML *class diagrams*, and suggest a model of UML *class diagram* syntax and semantics in RSL.

10.2 RSL Classes, Objects and Schemes

We now show, using RSL, how one can structure "large" specifications into "comfortable" parts. The key concepts of those parts are the RSL **class, object** and **scheme** concepts. The **class** concept is at the base of the two other.

10.2.1 Introducing the RSL "class" Concept

We need to motivate why we bundle declarations into **class**es.

Meaning of RSL Declarations — A Review

Each declaration of a **type**, a **value** (typically a function), **variable**, a **channel**, or an **axiom** stands for something. A **type** declaration, colloquially, such as we think about it when we write it down or read it, stands for a set of values. A function **value** declaration stands for a set of function values — a set because we may just give a signature, or because the function definition body is underspecified. A **variable** declaration, say with an initialising expression, stands for a set of variables, each with a specific initial value. A **channel** declaration stands for one channel. An **axiom** declaration typically constrains the values declared elsewhere.

First Motivation of the RSL "class" Concept: Focus

We saw, in the previous subsection, that a single declaration could have many denotations. And we saw, in Examples 10.1–10.5, of the previous section, that a "bundle", that is, a collection of declarations together defined a software device, an abstract data type, that is, a useful, separable concept. By bundling these declarations together by means of the delineating keywords **class ... end,** we may achieve a better structuring of large specifications, i.e., specifications defining many such concepts.

Second Motivation of the RSL "class" Concept: Semantic Algebras

Now, what is then the meaning of a construct like **class ... end** (where the ... is a set of declarations)? Well, we shall here take the meaning of a **class** clause to be a set of algebra mappings: one for each combination of values for each of the declarations. There can be many such algebras, or there can be zero. An algebra mapping maps identifiers of the declarations into a specific of the chosen values. Since the informal semantics of RSL is an important issue, let us give some contrasting examples:

Example 10.6 *A Small Set of Class Models:*

class type I:Int, value i:I, axiom i ∈ {1..7} end

The above class expression has seven models, expressed, not in RSL, but in "ordinary" mathematics. These models, which look a lot like RSL, are:

$$\{[i \mapsto 1], [i \mapsto 2], [i \mapsto 3], [i \mapsto 4], [i \mapsto 5], [i \mapsto 6], [i \mapsto 7]\}$$

▪

Example 10.7 *A Singleton Set of Class Models:* The simple class expression:

class type N:**Nat**, **variable** v:N := 7 **end**

yields the single model:
$$\{[v \mapsto 7]\}$$
That is, initialisation helps secure unique models. ▪

Example 10.8 *An Infinite Set of Class Models:* The simple class expression:

class value i:**Int end**

yields the infinite set of models:

$$\{[i \mapsto n] \mid n : \mathbf{Int}\}$$

That is, under-definedness usually results in many, sometimes an infinite set of models — and which one(s) were you thinking of when writing down the specification? ▪

Example 10.9 *An Empty Set of Class Models:* The simple class expression:

class value i:**Int**, **axiom** i<0 ∧ i>0 **end**

yields the empty set of models:
$$\{\}$$
That is, over-definedness sometimes results in no models. Make sure that your specification does indeed specify something! ▪

It is important to realise that the meaning of a model is also that all the identifiers of the definition set of the mapping of the model are *visible* "outside" the class expression.

Third Motivation of the RSL "class" Concept

Example 10.10 *Stack, I:* Let us take the example of a stack **class**:

class

```
type
    E, S = E*
variable
    stack:S := ⟨⟩
value
    is_empty: UNIT → read stack  Bool
    is_empty() ≡ stack=⟨⟩
    push: E → write stack  Unit
    push(e) ≡ stack := ⟨e⟩⌃stack
    top: Unit ⥲ E
    top() ≡ if is_empty() then chaos else hd stack end
    pop: Unit ⥲ Unit
    pop() ≡ stack := if is_empty() then chaos else tl stack end
end
```

■

Suppose we need to speak of a specific model of the class denoted by the above class expression. Now, the idea is to introduce objects:

Example 10.11 *Stack, II:*

```
object
    STACK:
        class
            type
                E, S = E*
            variable
                stack:S := ⟨⟩
            value
                is_empty: UNIT → read stack  Bool
                is_empty() ≡ stack=⟨⟩
                push: E → write stack  Unit
                push(e) ≡ stack := ⟨e⟩⌃stack
                top: Unit ⥲ E
                top() ≡ if is_empty() then chaos else hd stack end
                pop: Unit ⥲ Unit
                pop() ≡ stack := if is_empty() then chaos else tl stack end
        end
```

■

STACK denotes a specific choice of value assignments — in this case there really is only one model in the set anyway. When, in some text, we wish to express operations on stack we do so by *prefixing* operation names with STACK. For example, STACK.is_empty():

Example 10.12 *Stack, III:*

    ... STACK.push(e) ...
    ... **let** e = STACK.top() **in** ... **end** ...
    ... STACK.pop() ...

∎

Fourth Motivation of the RSL "class" Concept: Named Schemes

What are we to do when wishing several objects of the same class? Do we have to repeat the whole class expression again and again? No, we name the class expression, "making" it a scheme clause:

Example 10.13 *Stack IV:*

scheme
   STACKS =
     class
       type
         E, S = E*
       variable
         stack:S := ⟨⟩
       value
         is_empty: UNIT → **read** stack **Bool**
         is_empty() ≡ stack=⟨⟩

         push: E → **write** stack **Unit**
         push(e) ≡ stack := ⟨e⟩^stack
         ...
     end

Now declaration of several objects is easy and operations on these following the usual prefixing convention:

object
   S1 : STACKS, S2 : STACKS, ...

value
   ...
   ... **let** e = S1.top() **in** S2.push(e) **end** ...
   ...

∎

• • •

We are now ready to introduce the RSL class, scheme and object concepts more systematically.

10.2.2 The RSL "class" Concept

Let < declaration_1 > stand for a type, a value, a variable, a channel, or an axiom declaration. Then:

class
    < declaration_1 >
    < declaration_2 >
    ...
    < declaration_n >
end

is a class expression. It denotes a possibly empty, possible finite, possibly infinite set of models, each model being (like) an algebra: a set of values (i.e., models of types), a set of functions (over these values), etcetera (variables, channels). The axioms suitably constrain values, types, etc.

All identifiers of the declarations of a class expression are usually distinct. Two or more identical, i.e., overloaded identifiers need be identifiers of function values and need be distinguishable by their different signatures. Each identifier declared in the class expression is bound, in the model, to a specific value, a specific function, etc.

10.2.3 The RSL "object" Concept

We saw that an RSL class denotes a set of models. How do we designate just one of these models? The answer is: by designating an object. That is, the declaration: **object** <class_expression> designates one model, an arbitrary one selected from the set of models denoted by the <class_expression>. Since it may be cumbersome to list a whole <class_expression> every time we want to designate an object of that class, we name the <class_expression> and obtain a scheme. We shall show examples of object declarations later.

10.2.4 The RSL "scheme" Concept

There are several notions associated with schemes: naming, extension and hiding are the ones we shall treat now.

Simple Schemes

Let **class ... end** be some class expression. By a scheme we give a name to the set of models of that class expression:

scheme A = **class ... end**

Some examples are in order.

Example 10.14 *Stack Scheme:* We "schematise" Example 10.2:

scheme
    STACK =
        class
            type
                E
                S = E*
            value
                empty: **Unit** → S, empty() = ⟨⟩
                is_empty: S → **Bool**, is_empty(s) ≡ s=⟨⟩
                push: E × S → S, push(e,s) ≡ ⟨e⟩^s
                top: S ⤳ E, top(s) ≡ **if** s=⟨⟩ **then chaos else hd** s **end**
                pop: S ⤳ S, pop(s) ≡ **if** s=⟨⟩ **then chaos else tl** s **end**
        end

■

Example 10.15 *Graph Scheme:* We next "schematise" Example 10.4:

scheme
    GRAPH =
        class
            type N, G
            value
                obs_Ns: G → N-**set**
                obs_Es: G → (N×N)-**set**
                empty: **Unit** → G
                is_empty: G → **Bool**
                insert_node: N → G ⤳ G
                    pre: insert_node(n)(g): n ∉ obs_Ns(g)
                delete_node: N → G ⤳ G
                    pre: delete_node(n)(g): n ∈ obs_Ns(g) ∧
                            ~exist (n′,n″):N×N • (n′,n″) ∈ obs_Es(g) ∧ n=n′∨n=n″
                insert_edge: N×N → G ⤳ G
                    pre: insert_edge(n,n′)(g): {n,n′}⊆obs_Ns(g) ∧ (n,n′) ∉ obs_Es(g)
                delete_edge: N×N → G ⤳ G
                    pre: delete_edge(n,n′)(g): (n,n′) ∈ obs_Es(g)
            axiom
                is_empty(empty()),
                obs_Ns(empty()) ≡ {}
                obs_Ns(insert_node(n)(g)) ≡ {n} ∪ obs_Ns(g)
                obs_Es(insert_edge(n,n′)(g)) ≡ {(n,n′)} ∪ obs_Es(g) ...
        end

Where the ... indicates that, perhaps, we need some more axioms in order to properly dispense of the graph data type operations.   ■

Scheme Extensions

Often it may be useful to decompose a large "flat" specification, including a large class expression, into several smaller class expressions. Most, if not all, of the specifications we presented in Vol. 1 and so far in the present volume have been "flat" specifications. That is, they are without any class, object or scheme structuring.

Let in the following conceptual scheme clause:

scheme A =
  class
    < declaration$_{1_1}$ >
    < declaration$_{1_2}$ >
    ...
    < declaration$_{1_{n_1}}$ >

    < declaration$_{2_1}$ >
    < declaration$_{2_2}$ >
    ...
    < declaration$_{2_{n_2}}$ >

    < declaration$_{3_1}$ >
    < declaration$_{3_2}$ >
    ...
    < declaration$_{3_{n_3}}$ >
  end

If declarations <declaration$_{j_{k'}}$> only depend on declarations <declaration$_{i_{k''}}$> for i strictly smaller than j, for j equal to 2 or 3, then the above scheme can be decomposed into the following sequence of scheme extensions:

scheme A =
  class
    < declaration$_{1_1}$ >
    < declaration$_{1_2}$ >
    ...
    < declaration$_{1_{n_1}}$ >
  end

scheme B =
  extend A **with**
  class
    < declaration$_{2_1}$ >
    < declaration$_{2_2}$ >
    ...
    < declaration$_{2_{n_2}}$ >
  end

scheme D =
  extend B **with**
  class
    < declaration$_{3_1}$ >
    < declaration$_{3_2}$ >
    ...
    < declaration$_{3_{n_3}}$ >
  end

Example 10.16 *Scheme Extensions:* From Example 10.1 we had:

scheme
  STACK =
    class
      type
        E, S
      value
        empty: **Unit** → S
        is_empty: S → **Bool**
        push: E × S → S
        top: S $\xrightarrow{\sim}$ E

        pop: S $\xrightarrow{\sim}$ S
      axiom
        is_empty(empty())
        top(empty())=**chaos**
        pop(empty())=**chaos**
        top(push(e,s))=e
        pop(push(e,s))=s
        ...
      end

This scheme can be decomposed into three "successive" schemes:

scheme
  STACK$_\text{types}$ = **class type** E, S **end**

scheme
  STACK$_\text{signatures}$ =
    extend STACK$_\text{types}$ **with**
      class
        value
          empty: **Unit** → S
          is_empty: S → **Bool**
          push: E × S → S
          top: S $\xrightarrow{\sim}$ E
          pop: S $\xrightarrow{\sim}$ S
      end

scheme
  STACK$_\text{axioms}$ =
    extend STACK$_\text{signatures}$ **with**
      class
        axiom
          is_empty(empty())
          top(empty())=**chaos**
          pop(empty())=**chaos**
          top(push(e,s))=e
          pop(push(e,s))=s
          ...
      end

where the ... indicates that, perhaps, we need some more axioms in order properly to dispense of the stack data type operations.   ∎

Hiding

By "hiding" we mean to only "filter" some of the quantities, i.e., names (i.e., identifiers), away from being "visible" outside a scheme definition. But why? Well, let us examine two scheme definitions. Examples 10.17 and 10.18, without, respectively with, hiding clauses.

Example 10.17 *An Example in Need of Hiding:*

scheme AlgS =
class
  type E, S
  value
    empty: **Unit** → S
    is_empty: S → **Bool**
    push: E × S → S
    top: S $\xrightarrow{\sim}$ E
    pop: S $\xrightarrow{\sim}$ S
  axiom
    is_empty(empty())
    top(empty())=**chaos**
    pop(empty())=**chaos**
    top(push(e,s))=e

```
        pop(push(e,s))=s ...
end


scheme ModS =
class
    type E, S = E*
    variable stack:S := ⟨⟩
    value
        is_empty: Unit → read stack  Bool
        is_empty() ≡ stack=⟨⟩

        push: E → write stack  Unit
        push(e) ≡ stack := ⟨e⟩^stack

        top: Unit ⇸ E
        top() ≡ if is_empty() then chaos else hd stack end

        pop: Unit ⇸ Unit
        pop() ≡ stack := if is_empty() then chaos else tl stack end
end
```

In the algebraic specification we basically had to introduce the empty and the is_empty operations only implicitly "used" in the model-oriented specification. Also, outside the model-oriented scheme definition there really is no need to know how stacks, s:S, are implemented, nor to know the variable stack. So thus arises the idea of *hiding* what need not be knowable, that is, visible "outside" respective scheme definitions. Let us therefore repeat the scheme definitions, now with proper hiding clauses (**hide ... in class ... end**).

Example 10.18 *Example 10.17, but with hiding:*

```
scheme AlgS =
    hide empty, is_empty in
    class
        type
            E, S
        value
            empty: Unit → S
            is_empty: S → Bool
            push: E × S → S
            top: S ⇸ E
            pop: S ⇸ S
```

```
    axiom
        is_empty(empty())
        top(empty())=chaos
        pop(empty())=chaos
        top(push(e,s))=e
        pop(push(e,s))=s
        ...
end


scheme ModS =
    hide stack, S in
    class
        type E, S = E*
        variable stack:S := ⟨⟩
        value
            is_empty: Unit → read stack  Bool
            is_empty() ≡ stack=⟨⟩
            push: E → write stack  Unit
            push(e) ≡ stack := ⟨e⟩^stack
            top: Unit →̃ E
            top() ≡ if is_empty() then chaos else hd stack end
            pop: Unit →̃ Unit
            pop() ≡
                stack := if is_empty() then chaos else tl stack end
    end
```

Thus the basic hide clause syntactically is:

hide id_1, id_2, ..., id_n **in class** ... **end**

where the identifiers id_j are those of some of the declarations in the class expression.

Please recall that all identifiers declared in a class expression are visible outside that class expression. The hiding "takes place" at the level of the scheme definition.

Etcetera

In the next section we treat a very important scheme concept: That of parameterisation. There are other scheme concepts. We shall not cover them all here. That is, this book is not a reference manual to RSL. We leave that to [130].[1] The concepts that we shall not cover are those of module nesting and renaming.

10.2.5 RSL "scheme" Parameterisation

Motivation: Why and How Scheme Parameters?

We motivate the pragmatic need for parameterised schemes through a commented example.

Example 10.19 *Motivation for Parameterised Schemes: Arbitrary Stack Elements:* Let us consider the stack example of earlier. Now "imperialised" (i.e., made imperative), "classified", (partially) "hidden" and "schematised":

```
scheme STACK(E:class type Struct ... end) =
    hide S,s in
    class
        type
            S = E.Struct*
        variable s:S := ⟨⟩
        value
            push: E.Struct → write s  Unit
            push(e) ≡ s:=⟨e⟩^s
            top: Unit →̃ read s  E.Struct
            top() ≡ if s=⟨⟩ then chaos else hd s end
            pop: Unit →̃ Unit,
            pop() ≡ s:=if s=⟨⟩ then chaos else tl s end
    end
```

Nothing has been said about stack elements. What are they? Well, as it appears, it seems they are defined by the STACK scheme. But is that really convenient? Probably not! Since the visible operations need provide (stack) element arguments, it might be useful to have the stack concept, i.e., the type that E is, be defined "elsewhere" and then "imported" into the STACK scheme. In this way we can "instantiate" the STACK scheme to different kinds of elements: graphs and directories. ∎

The above example leads us to the next example.

Example 10.20 *Parameterised Graph and Directory Schemes:* In this example we "rewrite" the directory and graph definitions of Examples 10.3 and 10.5 in scheme and class form. For these schemes (and classes) we make sure,

---

[1] This book is out of print, but it is hoped that soon a revised edition will appear on the open Internet.

in this example, that the type name of the "things" to be put on (inspected on, and popped from) the stack, is the same type name as for its elements, namely Struct:

scheme DIRECTORY =
  class
    type
      Dn, En, E
      Struct = Dn $\overrightarrow{m}$ (Struct | (En $\overrightarrow{m}$ E))
      Ename == nil | mkEn(n:En)
    value
      get: Dn* × Ename → Struct $\xrightarrow{\sim}$ (Struct | E)
      get(dnl,en)(d) ≡ ...
    type
      NmED == mkE(en:En,e:E) | mkD(dn:Dn,d:Struct)
    value
      put: Dn* × NmED → Struct $\xrightarrow{\sim}$ Struct
      put(dnl,ned)(d) ≡ ...
  end

scheme GRAPH =
  class
    type
      E
      Struct = E $\overrightarrow{m}$ E-**set**
    value
      insert_node: E → Struct $\xrightarrow{\sim}$ Struct
      delete_node: E → Struct $\xrightarrow{\sim}$ Struct
      insert_edge: E×E → Struct $\xrightarrow{\sim}$ Struct
      delete_edge: E×E → Struct $\xrightarrow{\sim}$ Struct

      insert_node(n)(g) ≡ ...
      delete_node(n)(g) ≡ ...
      insert_edge(n,n')(g) ≡ ...
      delete_edge(n,n')(g) ≡ ...
  end

Now we can instantiate the abstract stack data type in at least two ways:

  ... STACK(GRAPH) ... STACK(DIRECTORY) ...

Such instantiations could be done in connection with object creations:

  object graph_stack : STACK(GRAPH)
  object directory_stack : STACK(DIRECTORY)

```
... graph_stack.push(g) ...
... let g = graph_stack.top() in ... end ...
... graph_stack.pop() ...


... director_stack.push(d) ...
... let d = director_stack.top() in ... end ...
... director_stack.pop() ...
```

∎

The Syntax and Semantics of Parameterised Schemes

The general syntax of scheme declarations looks like:

scheme
    < scheme_definition$_1$ >
    < scheme_definition$_2$ >
    ...
    < scheme_definition$_m$ >

The general syntax of scheme definitions without and with parameters look, respectively, like:

id$_s$ = class_expression
id$_p$(id$_1$:class_expression$_1$, ... , id$_n$:class_expression$_n$) = class_expression

for $n \geq 1$. If oid$_1$, ... , oid$_n$ are object identifiers, then the parameterised scheme id$_p$ may be *instantiated* in a *scheme instantiation* as follows:

id$_p$(oid$_1$, ... , oid$_n$)

The scheme instantiation is thus used when instantiating objects.

We shall leave out many technical details concerning proper matching of argument objects to parameter class expressions. This book is not a reference manual for RSL. For that consult a proper RSL reference manual such as the definitive [130]. These books propagate proper, generally applicable abstract and modelling principles and techniques. If we begin on the road to detailing "nitty-gritty" syntactic issues of this or that specification language, then we can easily lose sight of that.

It is high time for a realistic, large example!

10.2.6 A "Large-Scale" Example

The first part of Example 10.21 presents an "old" double-example, given as Examples 2.5 and 2.6 in Sect. 2.3. Example 10.21 shall serve as a motivating (and reminding) background for the main example, i.e., Example 10.22.

The Contrasting Background Example

Example 10.21 *A Railway Net Specification: No Schemes:*

Narrative

We introduce the phenomena of railway nets, lines, stations, tracks, (rail) units, and connectors.

1. A railway net consists of one or more lines and two or more stations.
2. A railway net consists of rail units.
3. A line is a linear sequence of one or more linear rail units.
4. The rail units of a line must be rail units of the railway net of the line.
5. A station is a set of one or more rail units.
6. The rail units of a station must be rail units of the railway net of the station.
7. No two distinct lines and/or stations of a railway net share rail units.
8. A station consists of one or more tracks.
9. A track is a linear sequence of one or more linear rail units.
10. No two distinct tracks share rail units.
11. The rail units of a track must be rail units of the station (of that track).
12. A rail unit is either a linear, or is a switch, or a is simple crossover, or is a switchable crossover, etc., rail unit.
13. A rail unit has one or more connectors.
14. A linear rail unit has two distinct connectors; a switch rail unit has three distinct connectors; crossover rail units have four distinct connectors (whether simple or switchable), and so on.
15. For every connector there are at most two rail units which have that connector in common.
16. Every line of a railway net is connected to exactly two distinct stations of that railway net.
17. A linear sequence of (linear) rail units is a noncyclic sequence of linear units such that neighbouring units share connectors.

Formalisation

type
    N, L, S, Tr, U, C
value
1.   obs_Ls: N → L-set,
1.   obs_Ss: N → S-set
2.   obs_Us: N → U-set,
3.   obs_Us: L → U-set
5.   obs_Us: S → U-set,

8. obs_Trs: S → Tr-**set**
12. is_Linear: U → **Bool**,
12. is_Switch: U → **Bool**
12. is_Simple_Crossover: U → **Bool**,
12. is_Switchable_Crossover: U → **Bool**
13. obs_Cs: U → C-**set**

17. lin_seq: U-**set** → **Bool**
  lin_seq(us) ≡
   ∀ u:U • u ∈ us ⇒ is_Linear(u) ∧
    ∃ q:U* • **len** q = **card** us ∧ **elems** q = us ∧
     ∀ i:**Nat** • {i,i+1} ⊆ **inds** q ⇒ ∃ c:C •
      obs_Cs(q(i)) ∩ obs_Cs(q(i+1)) = {c} ∧
     len q > 1 ⇒ obs_Cs(q(i)) ∩ obs_Cs(q(**len** q)) = {}

Some formal axioms are now given; but not all!

axiom
1. ∀ n:N • **card** obs_Ls(n) ≥ 1,
1. ∀ n:N • **card** obs_Ss(n) ≥ 2,
3. l:L • lin_seq(l)
4. ∀ n:N, l:L • l ∈ obs_Ls(n) ⇒ obs_Us(l) ⊆ obs_Us(n)
5. ∀ n:N, s:S • s ∈ obs_Ss(n) ⇒ **card** obs_Us(s) ≥ 1
6. ∀ s:S • obs_Us(s) ⊆ obs_Us(n)
7. ∀ n:N,l,l':L•{l,l'}⊆obs_Ls(n)∧l≠l'⇒obs_Us(l)∩ obs_Us(l')={}
7. ∀ n:N,l:L,s:S•l ∈ obs_Ls(n)∧s ∈ obs_Ss(n)⇒obs_Us(l)∩ obs_Us(s)={}
7. ∀ n:N,s,s':S•{s,s'}⊆obs_Ss(n)∧s≠s'⇒obs_Us(s)∩ obs_Us(s')={}
8. ∀ s:S • **card** obs_Trs(s) ≥ 1

9. ∀ n:N, s:S, t:T • s ∈ obs_Ss(n) ∧ t ∈ obs_Trs(s) ⇒ lin_seq(t)
10. ∀ n:N, s:S, t,t':T •
  s ∈ obs_Ss(n) ∧ {t,t'} ⊆ obs_Trs(s) ∧ t≠t'
   ⇒ obs_Us(t) ∩ obs_Us(t') = {}
15. ∀ n:N • ∀ c:C •
  c ∈ ∪ { obs_Cs(u) | u:U • u ∈ obs_Us(n) }
   ⇒ **card**{ u | u:U • u ∈ obs_Us(n) ∧ c ∈ obs_Cs(u) } ≤ 2
16. ∀ n:N,l:L • l ∈ obs_Ls(n) ⇒
  ∃ s,s':S • {s,s'} ⊆ obs_Ss(n) ∧ s≠s' ⇒
   let sus = obs_Us(s), sus' = obs_Us(s'), lus = obs_Us(l) **in**
   ∃ u:U • u ∈ sus, u':U • u' ∈ sus', u'',u''':U • {u'',u'''} ⊆ lus •
   let scs = obs_Cs(u), scs' = obs_Cs(u'),
    lcs = obs_Cs(u''), lcs' = obs_Cs(u''') **in**
   ∃ ! c,c':C • c ≠ c' ∧ scs ∩ lcs = {c} ∧ scs' ∩ lcs' = {c'}
  end end

More axioms need be formulated to fully constrain the sorts.   ∎

The Schematised Example

The presentation of Example 10.21 was what we in Chap. 2 called hierarchical, from "largest" parts towards increasingly "smaller" (i.e., physically smaller) parts. In the reworking of Example 10.21 we shall "turn things around": presenting the schemes in order from what we may consider the physically "smallest" phenomena towards the "largest" such. There is a lesson to be seen here: Namely that, when composing specifications (i.e., collections of scheme declarations) one may be well served in both developing and in presenting them "compositionally", i.e., (colloquially speaking) "bottom-up"!

Example 10.22 *A Railway Net Specification: Parameterised Schemes:* To each sort in Example 10.21 we associate a scheme.

scheme Connectors = **class type** C **end**

scheme Units(connectors : Connectors) =
class
   type U
    value
       12 is_Linear: U→**Bool**,
       12 is_Switch: U→**Bool**,
       12 is_SimpleCrossover: U→**Bool**,
       12 is_SwitchableCrossover: U→**Bool**,
       13 obs_Cs: U→connectors.C-**set**,
       17 lin_seq: U-**set**→**Bool**
       lin_seq(us) ≡
          (∀ u:U•u ∈ us ⇒ is_Linear(u)∧
           (∃ q:U*•**len** q = **card** us∧**elems** q=us∧
            (∀ i:**Nat**•{i,i+1}⊆**inds** q ⇒
             (∃ c:connectors.C•
               obs_Cs(q(i)) ∩ obs_Cs(q(i+1))={c}∧
               len q>1 ⇒ obs_Cs(q(i)) ∩ obs_Cs(q(**len** q))={}))))
end

We could single out each of the mentioned four disjoint kinds of units, U, representing them as schemes. We show it only for the linear case:

scheme Linear(connectors : Connectors) =
extend Units(connectors) **with**
class
   type LU = U
    axiom

      ∀ u:LU•is__Linear(u)∧~is_Switch(u)
          ∧~is_SimpleCrossover(u)∧~is_SwitchableCrossover(u),
    ∀ u:LU: **card** obs_Cs(u)=2
end

We go on:

scheme Sequence(connectors: Connectors,units: Units(connectors)) =
class
  type Seq
  value obs_Us: Seq→units.U-**set**
  axiom ∀ s: Seq•units.lin_seq(obs_Us(s))
end

scheme Lines(connectors: Connectors,units: Units(connectors)) =
extend Sequence(connectors,units) **with**
class
  type L
  value
  obs_Seq: L→Seq,
  obs_Us: L→units.U-**set**
  obs_Us(l) ≡ obs_Us(obs_Seq(l))
end

scheme Tracks(connectors: Connectors,units: Units(connectors)) =
extend Sequence(connectors,units) **with**
class
  type Tr
  value
  obs_Seq: Tr→Seq,
  obs_Us: Tr→units.U-**set**
  obs_Us(t) ≡ obs_Us(obs_Seq(t))
end

scheme Stations(
  connectors: Connectors,
  units: Units(connectors),
  tracks: Tracks(connectors,units)) =
class
  type S
  value
  5 obs_Us: S→units.U-**set**,
  8 obs_Trs: S→tracks.Tr-**set**

axiom
  5 ∀ s:S•**card** obs_Us(s)≥1,
  8 ∀ s:S•**card** obs_Trs(s)≥1,
  7 ∀ s,s′:S•s≠s′ ⇒ obs_Us(s) ∩ obs_Us(s′)={}
end

scheme Nets(
  connectors: Connectors,
  units: Units(connectors),
  lines: Lines(connectors,units),
  tracks: Tracks(connectors,units),
  stations: Stations(connectors,units,tracks)) =
class
  type N
  value
  1 obs_Ls: N→lines.L-**set**,
  1 obs_Ss: N→stations.S-**set**,
  2 obs_Us: N→units.U-**set**
  axiom
  1 ∀ n:N•**card** obs_Ls(n)≥1,
  1 ∀ n:N•**card** obs_Ss(n)≥2,
  4 ∀ n:N,l:lines.L•l ∈ obs_Ls(n)⇒lines.obs_Us(l)⊆obs_Us(n),
  6 ∀ n:N,s:stations.S•s ∈ obs_Ss(n)⇒stations.obs_Us(s)⊆obs_Us(n),
  7 ∀ n:N,l:lines.L,s:stations.S•l ∈ obs_Ls(n)∧s ∈ obs_Ss(n)⇒
                     lines.obs_Us(l) ∩ stations.obs_Us(s)={}
  end

We leave it to the reader to check that the previous and the present formalisations "cover the same ground".   ■

10.2.7 Definitions: Class, Scheme and Object

Characterisation. By an RSL *class* we mean, basically, a set of algebras; each algebra being a set of distinctly named entities: types and values, including functions and behaviours; and variables and channels.   ■

Characterisation. By a RSL *scheme* we mean a named class.   ■

Characterisation. By a RSL *object* we mean a specific algebra.   ■

10.3 UML and RSL

———————————— Note ————————————

This section was written by Steffen Holmslykke and edited by Dines Bjørner.

The Unified Modeling Language, UML, is roughly a diagrammatic approach to object-oriented modelling. UML has been widely used in industry as an aid in the software development process, this is probably due to the wide use of diagrams. A quality that diagrams provide is that they, for some, seem easy to comprehend and are therefore a supplement to a structured description.

We refer to [59,237,382,440] for literature on UML. The Object Management Group, OMG [382], is an industry association which tends to the interests of UML users.

10.3.1 Overview of UML Diagrams

Some of the more basic and classic diagrams of UML include: *use case diagrams*, *sequence/collaboration diagrams*, *statechart diagrams* (or just statecharts), and UML class diagrams.

Use Case Diagrams

Use case diagrams give an overview of the use cases (behaviours) and the actors (including humans) who or which can perform them. A use case is a requirement that the system must fulfill. This kind of diagram is used in the requirements stage of the software development process and is a supplement to textual (informal or formal) language (Fig. 10.1).

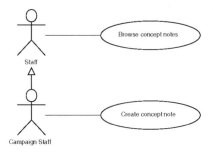

Fig. 10.1. Use case diagram with two use cases

Figure 10.1 shows two use cases: *browse concept notes* and *create concept notes*. The figure is modified from [39].

We shall not cover use case diagrams in these volumes. The use case diagrams of UML correspond to domain descriptions and requirements prescriptions where we model users (agents, actors) by processes that communicate with the "things" shown as ovals in the use case diagrams, where these things are also modelled as processes. So there is nothing in use case diagrams that is not already to be modelled as behaviours according to the principles and techniques of these volumes.

Sequence/Collaboration Diagrams

Sequence/collaboration diagrams are used in order to describe interaction between objects. Sequence diagrams and collaboration diagrams are isomorphic, that is, the syntax of the diagrams is different but the semantics are the same. Sequence diagrams have a strong resemblance to message sequence charts.

We shall cover sequence/collaboration diagrams, under the name of message sequence charts and live sequences charts, extensively in Chap. 13.

Statechart Diagrams

Statechart diagrams are intended to model the internal state of an object and its transition from one state to another. We shall cover statecharts extensively in Chap. 14.

10.3.2 Class Diagrams

Class diagrams describe the static structure of a system, i.e., all the possible states which the entire system can be in at any given time. Class diagrams can be used both to describe a system at an abstract level focusing on relations, and later at an implementation level focusing on the specification of states. Figure 10.2 shows a class diagram for a stack such as described in RSL schemes in earlier examples: from Example 10.10 to Example 10.19.

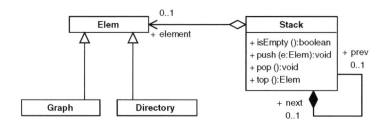

Fig. 10.2. UML Class diagram of a stack

UML "Standardisation"

UML is under continuing development both in adding new diagrams to the existing collection and in refining existing diagrams. This is coordinated by the Object Management Group (OMG) [382].

• • •

Class diagrams are the subject of the rest of this section.

10.3.3 Class Diagrams

A class diagram is a set of boxes and lines. Lines connect boxes, and a box either represents a class or an object construct. The lines connecting the boxes denote relationships of which there exist several kinds. In this section the association and the generalisation will be mentioned — leaving out the dependency relation and its derivatives.[2]

Classes

A class, syntactically speaking — i.e., a box — has three compartments: A name compartment, a compartment for attributes and a compartment for operations. Each class is uniquely named and represents a set of models, much like the **scheme** construct in RSL.

An attribute corresponds to a variable declaration in RSL, and has a type and a binding. It is the set of attributes which constitute the state of the models which the class represents.

A class diagram operation definition is equivalent to the signature of a value function declaration in RSL. A method in UML is an operation (a function) in RSL. The function (method) definition body can, however, not be given in class diagrams. The function can be specified, in UML, external to the box, using the English language or any language that is relevant.

Unit_Measure
− length **Real**
+ GetLengthInMeters () : **Real**
+ GetLengthInMeters () : **Real**

Fig. 10.3. A UML class with one private variable and two public operations

The following RSL specification gives an "equivalent" description to the one presented by the UML class diagram in Fig. 10.3. It should be noticed that

---

[2]One argument for doing so is that the semantics of dependency is unclear and its use mainly (and rarely) applies only when other relationships of class diagrams do not suffice.

the visibility concept in UML denoted by the signs "+" for Public and "−" for Private in the class is also to some extent available in RSL through the *hide* construct.

scheme Unit_Measure =
   hide length,conv_to_meters,conv_to_yards **in**
   class
      variable length : **Real**
      value
         getLengthInMeters : **Unit** → **read** length **Real**
         getLengthInMeters() ≡ conv_to_meters(length)
         getLengthInYards : **Unit** → **read** length **Real**
         getLengthInMeters() ≡ conv_to_yards(length)
         conv_to_meters: **Real** → **Real**
         conv_to_yards: **Real** → **Real**
   end

object SomeUnit : Unit_Measure

Objects are often used to depict complex situations of a system. This is useful when generic descriptions with only classes are becoming hard to grasp.

Association

Syntactically an association is a line between two or more classes, possibly decorated with several ornaments at the ends and around the centre of the line. An association semantically denotes the set of relationships (links) that can exist between the instances of the classes which it connects. So-called multiplicities can be added at the ends of the association denoting a constraint on the number of participating instances in the relationship, thus also reducing the valid relationships.

The line connecting *Station* and *Line* classes in Figure 10.4 is an ordinary association. That is, instances of the two classes may communicate with (or "call") each other. The multiplicities mean that an instance of the *Line* class must be connected to two instances of the *Station* class, and an instance of the *Station* class must be connected to one or more instances of the *Line* class.

The lines connecting the classes in Fig. 10.5 are also association relationships, however, the filled diamonds at the *Net* class denote that they are composite associations. This is a whole-part relationship which is an extension of the ordinary association — meaning that the *Net* class is partly defined by the three classes *Unit*, *Line* and *Station*. It also makes the whole, which in this case is the *Net* class, "responsible" for the parts, that is, instantiating the parts and establishing the links between them.

The line connecting the *Sequence* class with the *Linear* class in Fig. 10.6 is a shareable aggregation relationship denoted by the hollow diamond, and

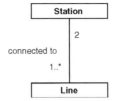

Fig. 10.4. Ordinary association with multiplicities at both ends

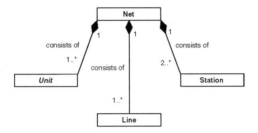

Fig. 10.5. Composite aggregate

is also an association relationship. The relationship has the same semantics as composite aggregation apart from the "responsibility" for the parts.

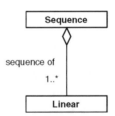

Fig. 10.6. Shareable aggregate

Links

A link is a relationship between objects. It is an instance of an association. The objects which it connects must thus be instances of the participating classes of the association. So the link represents one of the relationships in the set that the association holds. Consequently, the link must satisfy the constraints added to the association through multiplicity. An association is thus a prerequisite for a link to exist.

Generalisations

Generalisations introduce a taxonomic structure between classes. The generalisation is a relationship between two classes which are designated as child and parent. The nonprivate attributes and operations of the parent class are inherited by the child class in addition to the association relationships in which the parent participates.

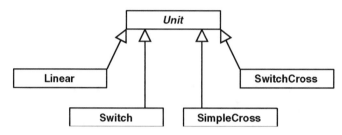

Fig. 10.7. Generalisation of U class: parent for remaining classes

The *extend* construct in RSL is the counterpart corresponding to the generalisation relationship. A simple example follows:

scheme Linear $=$ **extend U with class end**

10.3.4 Example: Railway Nets

The UML class diagram presented in this section is based on the informal and formal descriptions of railway nets from Examples 10.21 and 10.22. It is therefore particularly interesting to compare the latter — which is a modularized formal version — with the UML class diagram in Fig. 10.8 since it gives a hint of the strengths and weaknesses of the two specification languages (one, RSL, is formal, while the other, UML class diagrams, is informal).

    Note: Where, in the RSL specifications we used and use U for the sort of rail units, we shall, in the UML diagrams, use Unit, not to be confused with RSL's **Unit** literal (as the meaning of ()). In the class diagram of Fig. 10.8 the model is divided into several smaller pieces which describe smaller parts. In this case the classes represent the phenomena introduced in the informal description. These are basically the same which were used in Sect. 10.2.6 except for the (rail) *Unit* class, which instead uses generalisation to partially describe each of the specialised rail units.

    Items 1, 2, and 8 of Example 10.21 describe a *consist of* relationship between two phenomena. The latter item describes that a station consists of

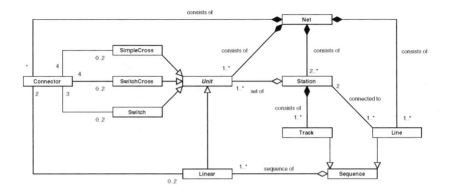

Fig. 10.8. UML class diagram of railway nets

one or more tracks. This fits with the whole-part relationship that composition provides in the class diagram. Here the station is the whole, and it is not complete unless it has tracks, and the tracks cannot exist without a station. For example, item 8 is depicted in the class diagram as a solid line between the *Station* and *Track* classes, where the first is marked with a filled diamond at the end of the line indicating that it is the *whole*.

Items 3, 9, and 5 of Example 10.21 use respectively a *sequence of* and *set of* to describe a relationship. This is again a whole-part relationship, however this time the parts are already part of the net. So to be able to maintain a reference to an existing part a shareable aggregation is used as a relation. For example, item 3 of Example 10.21 is depicted in the class diagram as a solid line between the *Station* and the *Unit* classes, where the first is marked with a hollow diamond at the end of the line indicating that it is the *whole*.

In item 12 in the formalisation of Example 10.21 a unit is described as being either a *Linear, Switch, SimpleCross* or *SwitchCross* which in the class diagram is substituted by a generalisation relationship where the *Unit* is an abstract class (its class name is written in italics) so it cannot be instantiated. Both the informal description in item 12 of Example 10.21 and the corresponding way it is modelled in the class diagram suggest that another axiom should be added. In the formal model four Boolean functions are used to determine the type of a given unit. Here an axiom could be added which ensures that a unit only can be of one type. This is achieved in the class diagram since an object can only instantiate one class. The axiom could be as follows:

$\forall\ u : U \bullet$ is_Linear(u) $\Rightarrow$
   $\sim$ (is_Switch(u) $\vee$ is_SwitchableCrossover(u) $\vee$ is_SimpleCrossover(u))

Additional axioms should be added for each of the three other possible situations.

The two items 13 and 14 of Example 10.21 are overlapping, where the latter contains more information. The latter explicitly describes the number of connectors which a given unit must have, while the former just states that a unit has at least one connector attached. If the latter is fulfilled then so is the former, which makes it superfluous in this model. This was noticed while drawing the associations between the *Unit* class and its specialisations. Here item 14 would in the class diagram amount to an association between each of the specialised classes of *Unit* to the *Connector* class which is shown in the class diagrams. Item 13 would be an association between the abstract *Unit* class to the *Connector* class. If this were to be added then it would mean that each of the specialisations also would have this relation due to inheritance through generalisation, which is not intended.

It is not possible to show items 4, 6, 7, 10, 11, 15, 16 and 17 of Example 10.21 in a class diagram, since they describe constraints on instances of a static structure. For example, item 4 is used and redisplayed for convenience: "The rail units of a line must be rail units of the railway net of the line". To be able to express this requirement we must be able to identify a particular unit and, if it is part of a line, then it must also be part of the net. This could be achieved by using the Object Constraint Language [382, Sect. 6]. We will not do so here.

There is some similarity between the two classes *Track* and *Line* since they both represent a sequence of linear rail units. They are, however, still different since a *Line* connects two stations and a *Track* only exists within a station. The common features of the two can be generalised into a class *Sequence*, which represents a sequence of linear rail units, and then the two classes *Line* and *Track* can be specialisations of that class respectively specifying their restrictions.

10.3.5 Comparison of UML and RSL OO Constructs

Phenomena described in informal domain descriptions or in informal requirements prescriptions are, in RSL specifications, usually represented by sorts. Besides a few observer functions these sorts are further unspecified. In class diagrams they are represented by classes, and these, as for RSL schemes, can be instantiated as objects (respectively RSL objects).

Initially we usually choose an applicative style for RSL specifications. There is perhaps a closer relationship between schemes and classes if an imperative modelling style had been used since the object in RSL would then contain an explicit state based on variables. It is, however, a typical approach — when using the RAISE Method — to start with an applicative specification and later refine it to an imperative specification, one which is more implementation oriented. Hence we could argue that it is too early to determine the (assignable variable) states by which the phenomena could be modelled. This approach has also been used for class diagrams since none of the classes have any attributes or operations. (This is also the reason for not showing compartments in the diagrams above.)

Links (which in UML are instances of associations) are (in terms of UML) used to express the communication of messages, that is, to designate the invocation of methods at the target UML object. The associations/links used in class diagrams in RSL can perhaps best be compared with qualification, that is, declarations from other objects including types, variables, functions, etc. With the use of qualification it also becomes possible, in RSL, to access the encapsulation of other objects and to invoke functions.

The generalisation relationship in UML and the **extend** construct in RSL are similar since they both take respectively a class and a scheme and add more information. A specialised class, in UML, can add attributes or operations to the ones already present from the generalised class. This is also possible with the **extend** construct in RSL.

10.3.6 References

Although RSL has modules it may be claimed, by some, not to be a "true object-oriented language". This does not, however, mean that it is impossible to express object-oriented models in RSL. The reason that RSL may be said to not be directly object-oriented is that it does not support references — in particular with regard to objects.

As an example we use the three schemes *Connectors*, *Units*, and *Lines* from Example 10.22. The headers of the mentioned schemes are replicated below for convenience. The first scheme has no parameters since it does not use any sorts or functions from outside its own scheme. The *Unit* scheme needs to know of the *Connectors* scheme since it uses its sort.

> **scheme** Connectors = **class end**,
> **scheme** Units(connectors : Connectors) = **class end**

The *Lines* scheme only needs information from the *Units* scheme and not from the *Connectors* scheme. However, to be able to instantiate the *Units* scheme an object instantiated from the *Connectors* scheme must be provided.

It is not possible to pass an already instantiated object of units as the only parameter to the *Lines* scheme or, formulated in another way, it is not possible to pass an object by reference. This is a major difference between RSL and object-oriented modelling. Thus it is necessary to give an object of type *Connectors* as a parameter although it is not used by the *Lines* scheme.

> **scheme** Lines(
>   connectors : Connectors,
>   units : Units(connectors)) = **class** ... **end**

10.3.7 Class Diagram Limitations

As mentioned earlier, class diagrams do not provide "compartment" space for all the information given in the informal description of railway nets, particularly information that refers to the unique identity of an instance. Here it is necessary to use UML's Object Constraint Language, OCL [526, 527], or resort, as we do, to RSL's predicate calculus. It is possible to express some (trivial) information in UML class diagrams which in RSL models is described using axioms. There are constraints on numbers such as the minimum number of stations in a net: Here one may use multiplicities.

10.4 Discussion

Several diverse issues need to be discussed. Our discussion, below, is not exhaustive. More discussion will follow at the ends of other chapters and in other volumes of this series of three textbooks on software engineering. We lump a discussion of selected issues into one part, and then conclude with a 'principles, techniques and tools' part.

10.4.1 Modularity Issues

We have selected just five issues for closer examination.

Modular Specification and Programming

The concept of modularity appears in many guises in the many different specification and programming languages claiming to provide some form of modularity constructs. In this chapter we showed two extreme kinds of modularity: that of RSL, provided for in textual form, and that of UML, provided for in diagrammatic form. There are other formal specification languages also providing modularity: B [2] and event-B [4], CAFEOBJ [96, 123], CASL [40, 369, 371] and Z [210, 230, 479, 480, 542, 543].

Stability of Modularity Concepts

In the mind of the current author the last word on modularity has yet to find its way into a proper formal specification language, respectively into a proper programming language. We have covered the modularity concept in these volumes. But we have done it less deeply than many a reader might have expected. We are happy with that. More final treatments are needed. Some fascinating ones are already available — reflecting, in our mind, crucial bases which still have to find their way into commercially supported programming languages. The most exciting is that of Abadi and Cardelli [1].

Whither Object-Oriented (OO) "Programming"?

Object-oriented (OO) programming is but one of many useful programming styles, but it is not the only one. Other programming styles focus on functions (SML [168], and so on). Since languages like Java [8, 15, 146, 301, 465, 513] and C# [207], for all their virtues, rather heavily represent the OO school, their way of offering concurrent, i.e., parallel programming is "heavy-handed". It is complicated and "expensive", therefore *programmers might be led to believe that concurrency is complicated and expensive* [510], whereas it might not be so! Indeed, it is not so. We refer to the delightful [510] for a view of programming that plays down the singular importance of OO.

Schema, Object and Module Calculi

So an essence of this chapter and of our coverage is that it is, in our mind, too early to decide on which singular set of modularity concepts, whether those of UML, those of RSL, respectively those of C#, or other, to use.

How to know what to ask for when choosing specification and programming languages? This question will not be answered here. To ask it properly the reader must have studied all volumes of this series of textbooks in software engineering.

Become familiar with, for example, the two modularity concepts of this chapter and those of Java [8,15,146,301,465,513], Eiffel [344,345] or C# [207, 346,347,401]. And then, in future projects find out what is then available, in some formal specification language or other (B, eventB, ..., RSL, Z) and in some programming language. Then settle for what you consider the most appropriate in which to abstract your ideas, respectively to finally program their concretisation.

Formalisations of UML's Class Concept

We should also, in this closing section, not forget to mention attempts to formalise the UML class (diagram) concept. One is given by the author of Sect. 10.3, Steffen Holmslykke [9, 10]; a previous, also in RSL, is given by Ana Funes and Chris George [122]. A thorough, more theoretical treatment of many UML concepts is given in Martin Große-Rhode's book [153].

10.4.2 Principles, Techniques and Tools

We summarise:

Principles. The principle of *modularity* is that it is indeed possible to *divide and conquer*. ∎

Techniques. We have shown, basically, two sets of *modularisation* techniques: First we showed the RSL techniques of identifying classes, naming classes (thus defining schemes), and declaring objects, being instances of classes, i.e., one model out of the set denoted by a class. We also showed the UML techniques of boxes and relationships, the latter of various kinds: associations, links, generalisations, etc.   ■

Tools. Thus we have shown two tools for *modularisation:* the RSL *class, object* and *scheme* constructs; and the UML class diagram constructs.   ■

10.5 Bibliographical Notes

The literature on modularisation is vast. The first object-oriented programming concepts, together with a language for expressing them, were those of Simula'67 [41,85,87,88]. See also the Internet Web page [472]. David Lorge Parnas has written persuasively about many issues of modularisation. We mention a few works [388–391] — where the last reference is to a collection of a sizable part of Parnas's rich production. SmallTalk is another fascinating object oriented programming language. It has, as of 2004, its own home page: [476]. See also [141,142,544].

We refrain here from referencing the vast literature on UML.

10.6 Exercises

Exercise 10.1 *Scheme Constructions.* You are to select and solve one or more exercises, preferably one from each of the 6 groups of exercises listed below and to convert their formalisation into a set of two or more scheme definitions:

1. Exercises 2.1 and 5.7: *Documents*
2. Exercise 2.2: *Part Assemblies*
3. Networks. Common to the next three exercises is that of a previous exercise, Exercise 4.1. Select one of either of:
   (a) Exercises 2.3 and 5.3: *City Road Nets — Streets and Intersections*
   (b) Exercises 2.4 and 5.4: *Air Traffic Route Nets: Air Lanes and Airports*
   (c) Exercises 2.5 and 5.5: *Shipping Nets: Lanes and Harbours*
4. Exercise 2.6: *Robots*
5. Languages. Select one of either of:
   (a) Exercise 3.3: *Denotational Semantics: A Simple Bank*
   (b) Exercise 3.4: *Denotational Semantics: A Simple Banking Script Language*
   (c) Exercise 3.5: *Denotational (Continuation) Semantics: Language with Storable Label Values*

    (d) Exercise 3.6: *Denotational (Continuation) Semantics: A Proper Coroutine Programming Language*

6. Systems. Select one of either of:

    (a) Exercises 4.2 and 5.1: *Supermarkets*

    (b) Exercises 4.3 and 5.2: *Manufacturing*

11

Automata and Machines

- The **prerequisite** for studying this chapter is that you are well familiarised with Chap. 4's coverage of Configurations: context and States.
- The **aims** are to introduce the related concepts of finite state, infinite state, and pushdown stack automata and machines, and to show the usefulness of finite state and pushdown stack automata and machines in — mostly — concrete, operational (i.e., computational) specifications.
- The **objective** is to help make sure that the reader can freely choose and usefully apply, when appropriate, the modelling principles and techniques of finite state and pushdown stack automata and machines — as well as to encourage the reader to more seriously study more specialised textbooks on automata and formal languages.
- The **treatment** is informal, but systematic.

States
A state is a summary of past behaviour. We may speak of a usually very large — and as we shall call it — actual state space. And we may model this actual state space in terms of abstracted model states. Often the actual state space of past behaviours can be summarised in a small number of discrete model states. A kind of equivalence relation over the actual state space can be imposed. When this is possible, the principles and techniques of the present chapter apply.

In this chapter we will survey a way of representing and hence "talking about" a certain class of states concept — a way that is different, in style but not in essence, from the way we have so far, above, treated the state concept. First we will define the general notions of *discrete state automata* and *discrete state machines*. These are "gadgets", or systems, sometimes also called "devices" (i) that possess either a finite or an infinite set of ("internal") states, (ii) that 'accept', i.e., read, in any one state, (iii) any *input* from an environment, and of a finite or infinite type, called an *alphabet* of inputs. Upon (iv) reading such an input they undergo a state *transition* to a (possibly same) *next state*,

(v) while, possibly, yielding an *output* to an environment, and again of a finite or infinite type, called an *alphabet* of outputs. Then we shall specialise this notion to the two by two subclasses of finite and pushdown stack automata and machines — usually abbreviated by: FSAs, FSMs, PDAs and PDMs.

11.1 Discrete State Automata

Recall that the valves of the liquid container tank in Example 4.3 are said to be in either of two (mutually exclusive) states: open or closed. As a pair they can thus be in any of four states. What "drives" them from state to state? In this case it is the set and close valve operations. These operations sometimes change the state, and sometimes not! In the formalisation of the valve states in the imperative process model we used assignable variables. Their value range was finite and small, to wit: open or closed! When the value range of certain variables is finite and small, say two or three, then we can model the state of the "things" — which leads us to the variable model — instead in terms of finite *state diagrams*.

Example 11.1 *A Liquid Container System, III: Finite State Valve Automaton:* With each valve we can thus associate a two-state *state diagram*, or, as we shall call it, a finite state automaton (left side of Fig. 11.1). We can also combine the two automata into one that has four states. Figure 11.1 shows the state transition effects in response to valve open and close actions (open_k and close_k). ∎

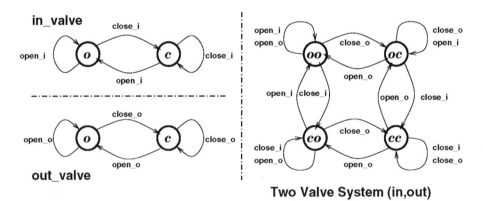

Legend:
o open, c closed, oo both open, cc both closed, oc in_valve open out_valve closed, co – vice versa
close_k: close valve k, open_k: open valve k – for k in {i,o}, i: in, o: out

Fig. 11.1. The valve system: separate valves versus combined

We explain Fig. 11.1: The left side shows two state diagrams: The upper for the in valve; the lower for the out valve. Each of these state diagrams consists of two states and four transitions. States and transitions are labelled: states with state identifiers, and transitions with automaton input. The right side of Fig. 11.1 shows a four-state automaton. It is the product of the two automata shown on the left. State labels are pairs of abbreviations of the state labels of the left-hand-side diagrams. Transition labels are sets of possible automaton inputs. A transition, labelled i, from state s to state s' (where s may be s'), expresses that the automaton, when in state s and accepting input i, transits to state s'. At any one time the automata can be in exactly one state. How the inputs are presented and how the state changes are effected are not described, either by the diagram of Fig. 11.1 or by the formalisation given next. What is described is that in certain states certain inputs are acceptable, and when accepted will lead to a state change.

Definition. By a *deterministic state automaton* we formally understand a three grouping:

type
SA$'$ = I-**infset** × S-**infset** × $((I{\times}S) \xrightarrow{\sim} S)$
SA = $\{|(\alpha,\sigma,\phi){:}SA'{\bullet}\forall(i,s){:}(I{\times}S){\bullet}(i,s) \in \textbf{dom } \phi{\Rightarrow}i \in \alpha {\wedge} s \in \sigma {\wedge} \phi(i,s) \in \sigma|\}$

There is an input alphabet, α, a set of states, σ, and an input and state to next state transition function, ϕ. Any or all of the three automaton components (alphabet, states and transition function) may be finite or infinite. The deterministic nature of the automata stems from there being at most one transition defined for every input and state pair.   ∎

Had there been two or more such next state transitions for any given input and state pair then the automaton would have been nondeterministic.

Definition. By a *nondeterministic state automaton* we formally understand a three grouping:

type
SA$'$ = I-**infset** × S-**infset** × $((I{\times}S) \xrightarrow{\sim} $ S-**infset**$)$
SA = $\{|(\alpha,\sigma,\phi){:}SA'{\bullet}\forall(i,s){:}(I{\times}S){\bullet}(i,s) \in \textbf{dom } \phi{\Rightarrow}i \in \alpha {\wedge} s \in \sigma {\wedge} \phi(i,s) \subseteq \sigma|\}$

Possibly the same inputs and the same states. The difference between the deterministic and the nondeterministic finite state automata is that the state transitions of the deterministic automata are deterministic, that is, to one next state, whereas the state transitions of the nondeterministic automata are nondeterministic, that is, to any one of several next states. This is reflected in the two transition functions: $(I{\times}S) \xrightarrow{\sim} S$ versus $(I{\times}S) \xrightarrow{\sim} $ S-**infset**.   ∎

11.1.1 Intuition

The intuition behind a deterministic state automaton is as follows: The automaton is in some state. Upon receiving, and we do not tell how, an input, the automaton undergoes a transition to a possibly other state. Thus the automaton is a discrete, conceptual device. It either remains in states when no next input is presented (and hence is stable), or it "moves" to a next state when an input is presented — where this next state may be the same state as the automaton was in before the input was presented. We do not explain, at present, what we mean by "input is presented". You may think of it as the automaton deciding, now and then, to input a symbol, i.e., to read from an input stream of symbols.

11.1.2 Motivation

We motivate, partly, the existence of (finite) state automata by presenting some derived examples.

Example 11.2 *"Concrete" Finite State Automata: Intuition:* To help your intuition, let us present some familiar examples of automata. (i) The automaton that models the state of a four-door automobile with a (say, rear entry) luggage compartment. Any of the five mechanisms, the four doors and the one lid of the trunk, may be in an open or a closed "state". Hence the combined automaton may be in one of $2^5 (= 32)$ states. State transitions may allow only for the single closing or the single opening of a door or the lid, or may allow for multiple, simultaneous both openings and closings of these. A closed [an open] door (lid) cannot undergo a "local state" transition "being closed" ["being opened"]. (ii) Next, we present an automaton that is based on the previous example, (i), but where no distinction is made as to which of the four doors is open or closed. That is, there are two contributions: All or some doors open, and all doors closed. Join to that the state of the compartment lid and one gets a total of four states. (iii) Finally, we present an automaton that is based on the previous example, (ii), but where no distinction is made as to whether it is a door or a trunk lid that is open, or closed. Thus we have just two states. Exercises 11.1 and 11.2 are based on the above example, and ask you to draw appropriate finite state automata diagrams.   ∎

11.1.3 Pragmatics

We are fine with intuition, but why do we model certain phenomena and certain concepts as (finite) state automata? Again, we answer that question by discussing Example 11.2.

Example 11.3 *"Concrete" Finite State Automata: Pragmatics:* Let us focus on case (ii) of Example 11.2. The four states could be labelled: $S_{dc}^{\ell c}$, all doors and the lid closed; $S_{dc}^{\ell o}$, all doors closed and the lid open; $S_{do}^{\ell c}$, some or all doors open and the lid closed; and $S_{do}^{\ell o}$, some or all doors open and the lid open. Now, why might we wish to make those four distinctions? An answer might be that we wish to make the performance of certain driver operations contingent upon the state. For example: In $S_{dc}^{\ell c}$ the ignition key can be engaged, but headlamps cannot be turned off. In $S_{dc}^{\ell o}$ the ignition key cannot be engaged but the compartment light can be turned on (and off). In $S_{do}^{\ell c}$ the ignition key cannot be engaged but headlamps can be turned on (and off). In $S_{do}^{\ell o}$ only headlamps can be turned on (and off). This is just a very tiny sample of possibilities.   ∎

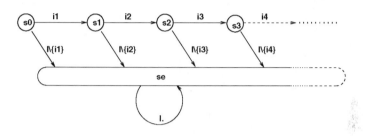

Fig. 11.2. An infinite state automaton

Example 11.4 *An "Abstract, Informal" State Automaton:* Figure 11.2 illustrates an infinite state automaton. State transition arrows labelled i have i designating inputs. State transition arrows labelled I\\{ij}, where ij designates an input, stand for the possibly infinite set of labels ik for ik being an input, except ij. An, albeit, construed class of examples of such automata as just hinted at could be those which go from nonerror state to nonerror state when input an increasing series of numbers adhering to some predicate: *next_prime, next_Fibonacci number, next_factorial*, etc. At present, please do not ask for the "usefulness" of such an automaton!   ∎

We explain Fig. 11.2: The dashed and dotted right hand-side is intended to show that the state machine is infinite, and, in this case, that its state structure "continues" as indicated in the left part of the figure. By state structure we, in this case, mean: The upper part sequence of input symbol transitions (labelled i_1, i_2, i_3, i_4) and next states (s_0, s_1, s_2, s_3) continues with $i_5, \ldots, i_{n-1}, i_n, \ldots$, respectively $s_4, \ldots, s_n, s_{n+1}, \ldots$, "ad infinitum", and the lower part ("error") state diversion s_e (with their ingoing, labelled transitions), is intended to also be the next state for the "ad infinitum" extension. How the infiniteness, shown very informally in the otherwise formal state diagram, is representable, say inside a computer, is not indicated. In the two-dimensional figure it is shown by the informal use of ellipses ($\ldots$), dashed lines, etc.

We will now show how one might be able to formally represent an infinite state automaton.

Example 11.5 *An "Abstract, Formal" State Automaton:* We continue Example 11.4 above. The problem we tackle is that of choosing the sequence of inputs. We arbitrarily — so as to be able to represent infiniteness as a closed, finite size expression — choose to let the sequence of acceptable inputs be the sequence of (say) Fibonacci numbers:

$$F(0) = 1, F(1) = 1, F(n) = F(n-1) + F(n-2), n \geq 1$$

We could have chosen any other sequence for which some functional expression, as above, can be established. Now the formal representation of the infinite state automaton follows the definition of state automata:

$\alpha = $ **Nat**, $\sigma = \{$ s(i) • i:**Nat** $\}$,
$\phi = [$ (F(i),s(i)) $\mapsto$ s(i+1),(j_i,s(i)) $\mapsto$ s_e|i,j_i:**Nat•**j_i$\neq$F(i)$]$

Even this definition is informal, i.e., it falls outside the formal syntax of RSL, but it is mathematically precise. By s(i) is understood, not necessarily a function s applied to a natural number i, but basically just an ith state symbol such that no two such state symbols (s(i),s(k) for i$\neq$k) are the same.[1] By j_i is understood a natural number other than the ith Fibonacci number. The use of the suffix i in j_i here is an informal but sufficiently precise usage. By s_e is understood a state symbol different from any s(i).   ■

11.2 Discrete State Machines

State automata can be extended into state machines. State automata have input and states. State machines have input, states and output.

Definition. By a *deterministic state machine* we formally understand a four grouping:

type
    SM$'$ = I-**infset** × S-**infset** × O-**infset** × ((I×S) $\xrightarrow{\sim}$ (S×O))
    SM = $\{|(\alpha,\sigma,\psi,\omega):SM'$ •
            $\forall$ (i,s):(I×S) • (i,s) $\in$ **dom** $\psi \Rightarrow$
               i $\in \alpha \wedge$ s $\in \sigma \wedge$**let** (s$'$,o)=ψ(i,s) **in** s$' \in \sigma \wedge$o $\in \omega$ **end**$|\}$

where α, σ and ϕ are as for state automata, and ω is an output alphabet (Fig. 11.3). We will defer further explanation of the rôle of the output alphabet and its appearance in ψ.   ■

Example 11.6 *An "Abstract" State Machine:* Figure 11.3 illustrates an (i.e., some arbitrarily chosen) infinite state machine. State transition arrows labelled 'i.o' have i designating inputs and o outputs. State transition arrows labelled I\{ij}.o' where

---

[1]You could, of course think of s being such a state-generating function. It would then be a bijection: no two s(i) and s(k) for i$\neq$k generating the same symbol!

i j designates an input and o' an output, stand for the possibly infinite set of labels
i k.o' for i k being any input, except i j, and o' some output. State transition arrows
labelled l.o' stand for the possibly infinite set of labels i.o' for i being any input, and
o' some output.   ■

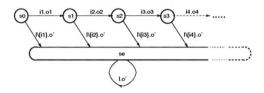

Fig. 11.3. An infinite state machine

We explain Fig. 11.3: We refer to Figure 11.2 for the basic explanation
of this state diagram. The new concept in machines, different from that of
automata, is that of a specialised output. A state transition label i.o between
states s and s' shall mean: Upon input i in state s the state machine transits
to next state s' while yielding the output o. Neither the formalisation nor the
graphic representation tells us anything about how this output is presented
to an outside world: Only that it is.

11.3 Finite State Automata

On the basis of Example 11.1 we now generalise: Finite state diagrams — like
that of Figure 11.1 — are sometimes called finite state automata, and sometimes finite state machines. Figure 11.1 is called a finite state automaton. It
is concretely characterised by a two-dimensional layout of a finite number of
states, drawn here as "fat" state name-labelled circles, and directed, labelled
edges (i.e., arrows) between these states. In the finite state automaton definition below we shall abstract (i.e., formalise) this concrete representation —
making the drawing into a mathematical structure.

We can "arrow and box" conceive of a machine, more generally of a system,
as a box with input and output (Fig. 11.4).

We explain Fig. 11.4: It is just a very simple abstraction. It really "carries" only symbolic, iconic meaning: The box is intended to designate an
arbitrarily complex or simple system: Here any kind of finite state automaton. The input arrow is intended to show that this system 'accepts' (i.e.,
reads) input. The "sketchy", incomplete state machine "inside" the box is
intended to show two things: That inputs lead to next states and that the
system focus is on the state behaviour. The output arrow is finally intended
to show that the current state of the system can always be observed from
an outside.

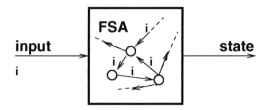

Fig. 11.4. An abstract machine [system]

You can disregard the fragment automaton shown inside the box in Figure 11.4. It is there only to relate back to state diagrams like Figure 11.1: The i's on arrows are the input i's provided to the machine [i.e., to the system]. The *state* output only means that one can observe, from outside the "box", which state "its" state machine (the finite state automaton) is in.

11.3.1 Regular Expression Language Recognisers

Usually finite state automata are seen as acceptors, or recognisers, of sentences of regular expression languages. We will define the concept of regular expressions shortly. For now, let us show an example.

Example 11.7 *A finite state recognising automaton:* The example starts with showing an *initial and final state* finite state automaton (Fig. 11.5). The automaton accepts, for example, the following sequence of symbols: Initially either an a or a b, then either a c followed by any number, including zero, es, and then another c, or a d followed by any number, including zero, fs, and then another d — with all of this "terminated" by either an a or a b. The above informal sentences are "modelled" by what is known as a *regular expression* shown at the bottom of Fig. 11.5. As explained, we show some of the acceptable transitions, but not all of the unacceptable transitions. The latter are thought of as being suitably labelled and going to an error or reject state which is not shown, but, as is the case for the also not shown transitions, the error state and error transitions can easily be added to the diagram. ∎

We explain Fig. 11.5: In the initial state 0 the automaton of Figure 11.5 accepts either a or b. All other inputs are rejected, i.e., not shown. Hence this leads to an error state, also not shown! We have shown the transitions from state 0 to state 1 as two separate arcs. They could have been "collapsed" into one whose label would then be the set of acceptable inputs (in state 0): a,b — as a list of symbols separated by commas. The choice of showing one or more arcs is just a stylistic choice! Accepting a or b leads to next state 1. In state 1 either c or d will be accepted. All other input will be rejected — and is hence not shown, again for simplicity. (As before, their input would lead to a transition to an error state.) Input c leads to next state 2. Input d

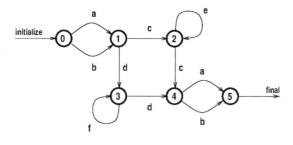

$$R = (\,a\mid b\,)(\,c\,e^*\,c\mid d\,f^*d\,)(\,a\mid b\,)$$

Fig. 11.5. Finite state recogniser automaton

leads to next state 3. In states 2 and 3, any number of inputs e, respectively f will be accepted — leading to the same state 2, respectively 3. Also in states 2 and 3, inputs c, respectively d, will be accepted (all inputs other than e,c, respectively f,d will be rejected, etc.), and lead to same next state 4. Finally, in state 4 either a or b will be accepted and lead to final state 5.

Example 11.7 shows that finite state automata can be used to model devices that recognise certain input sequences while rejecting others. Rejection takes place when a transition to an error state takes place. The languages of acceptable sequences are called regular languages, and an acceptable sequence is called a sentence of a regular expression (language).

11.3.2 Regular Expressions

In Sect. 8.5.3 we covered the notion of regular expressions. For the sake of continuity, we present here another version of our explanation of this concept.

Definition. By a *regular expression* we understand the following:

- There is an *alphabet*, A.
- Letters a, b, ..., c (etc., of the alphabet A) are *regular expressions*.
- If R and R' are regular expressions, then so are:

$$RR', R^*, R \mid R', (R)$$

The meaning of regular expressions $a, RR', R^*, R \mid R'$ and (R) are:

- Regular expression a stands for the set $\{\langle a \rangle\}$
- Regular expression RR' stands for the set

$$\{r \widehat{\ } r' \mid r : R \wedge r' : R'\}$$

where $\widehat{\ }$ denotes concatenation of strings.

- Regular expression R^* stands for the set

$$\{\epsilon, r, r\,\widehat{\ }\,r', r\,\widehat{\ }\,r'\,\widehat{\ }\,r'', r\,\widehat{\ }\,r'\,\widehat{\ }\ldots\widehat{\ }\,r'', r\,\widehat{\ }\,r'\,\widehat{\ }\ldots \mid r, r', r'' : R\}$$

where ... informally designate an arbitrary, including infinite number of repetitions of string (i.e., sentence) concatenations, and where ϵ designates the empty (the null, the void) string[2].

- Regular expression $R \mid R'$ stands for the set

$$\{r \mid r : R \ \lor \ r : R'\}$$

- Regular expression (R) stands for the set

$$\{r \mid r : R\}$$

that is: Parentheses are used for grouping and for disambiguation.

So regular expressions denote regular languages: specific strings, i.e., sentences, of symbols of an alphabet.   ∎

Definition. By a *regular language* we understand the denotation of a regular expression.   ∎

11.3.3 Formal Languages and Automata

So we have identified a class of languages called the regular languages. They can be defined by a regular expression. We postulate, i.e., we claim, but do not show:

Theorem 11.1. *Regular Language Recognition: To every regular expression there corresponds a finite state automaton that accepts exactly the sentences in the language of the regular expression.*   ∎

Theorem 11.2. *Regular Language Generation: To every finite state automaton there corresponds a regular expression exactly whose sentences are accepted by that automaton.*   ∎

We refer to appropriate textbooks (e.g., [6, 200, 217, 444]) on *automata and formal languages* for proper treatment of the concepts of finite state automata and regular languages, including algorithms for constructing regular expressions from finite state automata and finite state automata from regular expressions.

---

[2]The empty string ϵ juxtaposed (concatenated: $\widehat{\ }$) to any string s yields that string: $s\,\widehat{\ }\,\epsilon = s = \epsilon\,\widehat{\ }\,s$.

11.3.4 Automaton Completion

In, for example, the *finite state recogniser automaton* of Fig. 11.5 only acceptable transitions were shown, but a "completion" was described in the explanation of Fig. 11.5. We show, in Fig. 11.6, the result of such a completion: Now all states have (emanating) transitions which together "label" the full automaton alphabet.

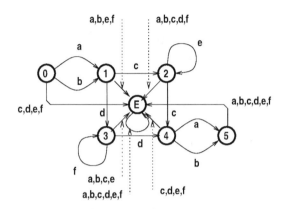

Regular epression : (a|b)(ce*c|df*d)(a|b)

Fig. 11.6. Complete finite state recogniser automaton

11.3.5 Nondeterministic Automata

So far we have assumed deterministic automata, and we will continue to do so, and to consider also only deterministic machines. A deterministic (finite state) automaton (dFSA) is one for which there is at most one transition leading out from any state for any input. So, a nondeterministic (finite state) automaton (nFSA) is one for which there may be more than one transition leading out from any state for any input. Figure 11.7 shows an example nFSA.

It can be shown that:

Theorem 11.3. *Nondeterministic FSA ≡ Deterministic FSA. The recognising power of nFSA is exactly the same as that of dFSA. In other words: To every nFSA there corresponds a dFSA with the same 'behaviour'.*   ∎

We refer to classical texts [6, 200, 217, 444] for more on nondeterministic automata.

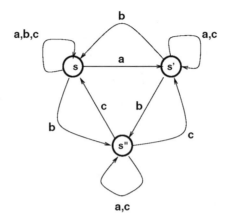

Fig. 11.7. Nondeterministic finite state automaton

11.3.6 Minimal State Finite Automata

Figure 11.8 shows two finite state (regular language recognising) automata.

Definition. Minimal State Finite Automaton: An FSA is said to be minimal if there is no other FSA which recognises the same language but with fewer (number of) states.   ∎

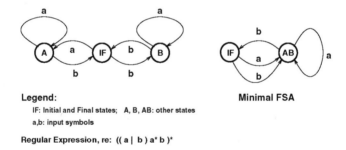

Legend:
IF: Initial and Final states;   A, B, AB: other states
a,b: input symbols

Regular Expression, re: ((a | b) a* b)*

Fig. 11.8. Two FSAs for the same regular language

The automaton to the left in Fig. 11.8 is not a minimal state automaton for the language denoted by the regular expression, re, shown in the Fig. 11.8. The one to the right is minimal wrt. the re shown in the figure.

Theorem 11.4. *Minimalisation of FSAs: There is an algorithm for constructing a minimal state finite state automaton from a given finite state automaton.*   ∎

We refer to [6, 200, 217, 444] for more on minimalisation.

11.3.7 Finite State Automata Formalisation, I

We state:

Definition. Deterministic Finite State Automaton: Formally speaking, a deterministic finite state automaton, FSA, is a five grouping:

type
$$S_i = S = S_o$$
$$\text{FSA}' = \text{I-set} \times \text{S-set} \times S_i\text{-set} \times S_o\text{-set} \times F$$
$$F = (\text{I}\times\text{S}) \xrightarrow{\;m\;} S$$
$$\text{FSA} = \{| \text{ fsa:FSA}' \bullet \text{wf\_FSA(fsa) } |\}$$
value
$$\text{wf\_FSA}(\alpha,\sigma,i\sigma s,o\sigma s,\phi) \equiv$$
$$\alpha\neq\{\} \wedge \sigma\neq\{\} \wedge i\sigma s\neq\{\} \wedge i\sigma s\subseteq\sigma \wedge o\sigma s\neq\{\} \wedge o\sigma s\subseteq\sigma \wedge$$
$$\forall (i,s):(\text{I}\times\text{S}) \bullet (i,s) \in \textbf{dom } \phi \Rightarrow i \in \alpha \wedge s \in \sigma \wedge \phi(i,s) \in \sigma$$

Here we have that α:I-set is a finite set of further unspecified tokens, the input alphabet; S is a finite set of further unspecified tokens; $i\sigma$:S_i are the initial states; $o\sigma$:S_o are the final states; and $\phi : F$ is a finite map which represents an (input,present_state) to next_state transition function. The (completed) finite state automata, as defined, are said to be deterministic. For every state there is one next state defined for every input. ∎

11.3.8 Finite State Automata Realisation, I

The pragmatics of *the initial state set* is that the automaton is started in one of its initial states. Usually the set is a singleton set of just one state, *the initial state*. The pragmatics of *the final state set* is that the automaton is expected to reach, sooner or later, one of its final states. Usually the set is a singleton set of just one state, *the final state*. Once a sentence delivers the automaton, from an initial state, into a final state, the sentence is said to have been *recognised*, i.e., to have been *accepted*. The definition is loose: It allows incomplete, but not nondeterministic automata.

Example 11.8 *A Finite State Automaton: The State Transition Function:* We continue Example 11.7. We seek the representation of the automaton of Figure 11.5 The representation is:

$$\text{fsa: } (\{a,b,c,d,e\},\{0,1,2,3,4,5\},\{0\},\{5\},\phi)$$
$$\phi = [\,(0,a)\mapsto 1,$$
$$(0,b)\mapsto 1,$$
$$(1,c)\mapsto 2,$$
$$(1,d)\mapsto 3,$$
$$(2,e)\mapsto 2,$$
$$(2,c)\mapsto 4,$$

$$(3,f) \mapsto 3,$$
$$(3,d) \mapsto 4,$$
$$(4,a) \mapsto 5,$$
$$(4,b) \mapsto 5]$$

Its regular expression was shown at the bottom of Figure 11.5.   ∎

11.3.9 Finite State Automaton Formalisation, II

We can pseudo-formalise the notions of automaton input, state transition, input acceptance and rejection. Let il be a sentence (i.e., a string in some alphabet), fsa some finite state automaton, s_i some (supposedly initial) state, s_e an error state — possibly completing the fsa, and bl a list of outputs from the fsa when started in state s_i with input il.

value

    fsa:FSA, sentence:I^ω

    start: $\mathrm{FSA} \to \mathrm{S} \xrightarrow{\sim} \mathrm{I}^\omega \xrightarrow{\sim} \mathbf{Bool}^\omega$

    start$(\alpha,\sigma,i\sigma s,o\sigma s,\phi)(s_i)(il) \equiv$

        let s_e:S • $s_e \notin \sigma$ **in**

        if $s_i \notin i\sigma s$ **then chaos**

            else run$(\alpha,\sigma,i\sigma s,o\sigma s,\phi)(s_e)(il)(s_i)(\langle\rangle)$

        end end

    run: $\mathrm{FSA} \xrightarrow{\sim} \mathrm{S} \to \mathrm{I}^\omega \to \mathrm{S} \xrightarrow{\sim} \mathbf{Bool}^\omega \xrightarrow{\sim} \mathbf{Bool}^\omega$

    run(fsa)$(s_e)(il)(s)(bl) \equiv$

        if il$=\langle\rangle$ **then** bl **else**

            let $(\alpha,\sigma,i\sigma s,o\sigma s,\phi) = $ fsa, i = **hd** il **in**

            if i $\notin \alpha$ **then chaos**

                else

                    if (i,s) **dom** ϕ

                        then

                            let $s' = \phi$(i,s) **in**

                            run(fsa)(s_e)(**tl** il)$(s')(\langle s' \in o\sigma s\rangle\hat{\ }bl)$ **end**

                        else

                            run(fsa)(s_e)(**tl** il)$(s_e)(\langle$**false**$\rangle\hat{\ }bl)$

        end end end end

The functions start and run are not proper RSL functions for infinite input — since they would then never terminate (hence the prefix "pseudo").

    If the fsa is not complete, then a supposed error state, s_e, generated by the start function, and its use in the run function can "mimic" completion. If a supposed initial state, s_i, is not an initial state of the fsa then **chaos** ensues. If a next state, s', is in $o\sigma s$ then the sentence so far input has been accepted. We decided to let the output response bl be reversed wrt. the sentence input.

In this way all we need to look at is the head of a possibly indefinitely long output to see whether the sentence received so far has been accepted.

11.3.10 Finite State Automata Realisation, II

In general, we can represent an automaton in row/column tabular form, cF: the number of rows to equal the number of (completed) states, and the number of columns to equal the number of symbols in the input alphabet. The table entries to contain next states. Thus we may encode states and alphabet symbols as natural numbers:

type
$\quad$ cSs′,cIs′:**Nat-set**
$\quad$ cSs = {| css:cSs′ • css = {**min** css ... **max** css} |}
$\quad$ cIs = {| cis:cIs′ • cis = {**min** cis ... **max** cis} |}

$\quad$ cF′ = (**Nat**^{m})^n, cF = {| cf:cF′ • wf_cF(cf) |}
value
$\quad$ wf_cF: cF′ → **Bool**
$\quad$ wf_cF(cf) ≡
$\quad\quad$ ∀ i,j:**Nat** • i,j ∈ **elems** cf ⇒
$\quad\quad\quad$ **len** cf(i)=**len** cf(j)∧∀ k:**Nat**•k ∈ **elems** cf(i)⇒(cf(i))(k)∈ **elems** cf

The notation (**Nat**^{m})^n is not proper RSL. The type expression (**Nat**^{m})^n denotes the n-fold Cartesians of m-fold Cartesians of natural numbers, i.e., the encoded states. We leave it as an exercise to the reader to reformulate the start and run functions (but consult Sect. 4.8.3). See Exercise 11.3.

11.3.11 Finite State Automata — A Summary

We have introduced core concepts of finite state automata: their structure, their recognising power, notions of determinism and nondeterminism, notions of minimality and ideas on realisation. It remains to summarise principles and techniques for introducing and using finite state automata.

Principles. The principle of *finite state automata* expresses when and where to consider modelling a phenomenon or a concept as a finite state automaton. The principle applies when a phenomenon or a concept (the thing) satisfies the following three criteria: (a) the thing can be thought of as consisting of one or more subthings (components, parts), each of which can be thought of as taking on values, i.e., having (sub-state space) attributes that vary over a finite set of discrete, enumerable tokens (cf., Vol. 1, Chap. 10, Sect. 10.3), (b) where the "whole thing" can then be thought of as taking on a state space (of not necessarily all) of the combinations of the subthing attribute values, and (c) where the resulting states can be associated with the possibility or nonpossibility of certain events and actions occurring: That is, they are acceptable or are being generated.   ∎

Examples 11.2 and 11.3 illustrated applicability of the above criteria. (a) The doors formed one subsystem, the compartment lid another (Example 11.2). (b) And their composition into one state space made sense (Example 11.2), (c) especially when, as illustrated in Example 11.3, seen in the light of permissible operator actions.

Techniques. There are three parts to the formalisation of *finite state automata:* (1) first, identification of possible state spaces; (2) then their "thinning" ("pruning") to just the "right" number; and (3) finally, the full representation of the automation as a two-dimensional diagram followed by its "embedding" as a value in the **FSA** type is postulated. As for (2): In determining the number of states to be modelled the deciding factor is whether the resulting state space provides adequate *discrimination.* Either it is sufficient (not too few states) or it is redundant (too many states) to make deterministic (i.e., unambiguous) decisions as to admissibility of events and actions.   ∎

Examples 11.2 and 11.3 also illustrated applicability of the sufficiency and redundancy of state spaces: Cases (i) and (iii) provided too many, respectively too few, states, whereas case (ii) provided the right number and kind of states when compared with the desired driver operations (events and actions).

11.4 Finite State Machines

We refer to the definition of state machines given in Sect. 11.2. In this section we will motivate the concept of finite state machines through two examples. Example 11.9 shows the specification of the controller for a variant of the liquid tank example discussed in Examples 4.3 and 4.5. Example 11.10 shows the specification of a parser: a device which accepts sentences in a regular language specified by some grammar — a set of numbered rules — and which yields grammar rule numbers as their derivations[3] are being recognised.

11.4.1 Finite State Machine Controllers

We will now illustrate the use of finite state machines as a means of specifying controllers for reactive systems.[4] The example of this section does not even touch upon the proper techniques for designing controllers for safety-critical

---

[3] A derivation from a rule, Ri, of a grammar, G (of rules R1, R2, . . . , Rn), is a sentence of the language defined by G starting with rule Ri.

[4] We are not going to present definitive material on how to properly specify such controllers! The reactive, embedded systems in question are usually also highly prone to faults in the physical equipment they control, and may thus be safety critical.

systems. We refer to hints made and references given to proper literature in
Vol. 3, Chap. 27, Sect. 27.7. The example is illustrative. It is meant to motivate
the concept of finite state machines. It is not meant to give specific controller
design techniques.

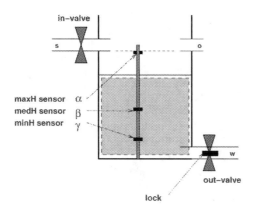

Fig. 11.9. A liquid container sensor/actuator system

Example 11.9 *A Liquid Container System (IV): Control:* In Example 4.3
we illustrated a notion of states of a physical system. In Example 4.5 we
illustrated a notion of *system development* through *domain modelling, requirements specification* and *software design.* In this example we will look at
the notion of *system development* from another viewpoint— with respect to
a system essentially similar to that of Examples 4.3–4.5. Thus we shall exemplify the *system development* notions of *domain, requirements,* and *design.*
We shall, as part of the *system development* (rather than just *software development*) notion exemplify the addition of (further) nonsoftware components
to the liquid container system: A *lock,* and some *sensors* and *actuators,* are
joined to the physical system in order to facilitate certain control requirements. In Vol. 3, Chap. 25 we shall review the concept of *systems engineering*
— in contrast to the more narrow concept of software engineering that these
volumes primarily cover.

Compare Fig. 11.9 to Fig. 4.1. Basically the two systems that are designated by these diagrams have very much in common.

Changes to the liquid tank system (as compared to Example 4.3) are: A
controller can (actuator) lock and unlock the out valve. A locked out valve
is closed and cannot be opened. When unlocked, anyone can (actuator) open
and close the out valve. A controller will be "sent" one of up to six inputs
(from appropriate sensors) when the height of liquid in the tank reaches one
of three positions: a maximal height, Hi, "from above" (sic!) or "from below"

(dHi, uHi), a medium height, Me, "from above" or "from below" (dMe, uMe), and a minimum height, Lo, "from above" or (even) "from below" (dLo, uLo).

We assume that the reader understands the colloquial terms "reaches", "from above", "from below" and "sent an input". We make no assumptions about any specific relationship between s, the inflow capacity through the in valve (actuator) and the outflow capacity, w, through the out valve. We also assume that the controller system can be started in any state and that the liquid content may evaporate or be replenished, say through precipitation, or the like.

An example of a possible control *requirements specification* is: The liquid tank contents must be fully replenished as soon as they reach the Low metering point (i.e.: the in valve must be open[ed]). During initial parts of this replenishment no one must withdraw liquid from the tank (i.e., the out valve must be closed). The in and out valves are otherwise allowed to be open at the same times. The controller may be started in any of the states of the in and out valves: opened/closed and locked/unlocked (with unlocked out valve being either opened or closed.) The controller must anticipate that liquid may disappear (e.g., evaporate) from or seep into the tank irrespective of the states of the valves. The designer is allowed to interpret the requirements initial part as is seen fit. The designer may, for example, make use, or may not make use, of the Medium [liquid height] sensing position. The controller is not to send open commands to an already open in valve, or to send unlock commands to an already unlocked out valve.

A *design specification* for a finite state machine showing a controller that satisfies these requirements is shown in Figure 11.10.

We now comment on the finite state controller *design* of Figure 11.10. The *design* is one of several possible solutions to the (loose) *requirements*. That is, the *design* reflects a number of *design decisions* that were taken by the designer as a result of the *requirements* not being complete. That is, not formulated in such a way as to answer all questions that a designer might wish to pose. More specifically, the *design* specifies: Whenever the liquid content falls below the minimum height, Lo, lock the out valve, and open — if not already so — the in valve. Whenever the liquid content falls below a medium height, Me, open — if not already so — the in valve. Whenever the liquid content goes above a medium height, Me, unlock — if not already so — the out valve. Whenever the liquid content attempts to rise above Hi, the maximum height, unlock — if not already so — the out valve, and close the in valve, and so on. Thus we leave it to the reader to decipher the meaning of all the state transitions. Please observe that there might be transitions which would only be encountered in a system that is started in a state (of the valves) and with certain (seemingly abnormal) liquid contents.   ∎

We have seen an example of a finite state machine primarily designed to cope with, i.e., control a system in, a number of normal as well as seemingly

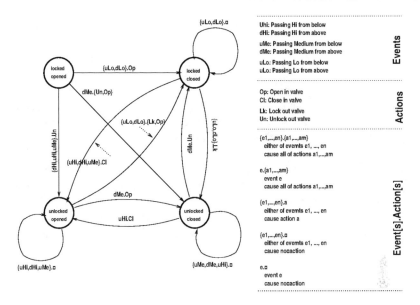

Fig. 11.10. A liquid container controller

abnormal states. We will now show an example of a more straightforward use of finite state machines, as so-called parsers.

11.4.2 Finite State Machine Parsers

A parser is the same as a syntax analyser. By a syntax we shall here mean an ordinary BNF grammar.[5] There is given a grammar, in the form of a set of distinctly numbered rules. Each rule left-hand side names a nonterminal which, through the full grammar, denotes a language: a set of sentences. A parser for the grammar (wrt. some identified nonterminal root) inputs strings in the alphabet of the grammar and issues (outputs) rule numbers if and whenever part of an otherwise acceptable input string is a sentence in the language of the left-hand side of the numbered rule. As is shown in the literature [6, 200, 217, 444], finite state machines can parse regular languages. We will show an example.

Example 11.10 *A Finite State Parser:* There is given a BNF grammar which defines a language of numerals. That BNF grammar is known to generate (to denote) a regular language. Without presenting the algorithms, either for deciding upon regularity, or for constructing the finite state (machine) parser we present that parser (Fig. 11.11).

---

[5]We assume that the reader is familiar with the notion of BNF grammars — and otherwise refer to Sects. 8.4–8.5.

We comment on the parser: The finite state parser requires what is known as a "stop" character. It is here chosen as the blank (_). It helps the parser to decide when a complete input has been received. We say that the grammar is LR(1): can left-to-right parse its input with a look-ahead (Left to Right) of one. Rule 0. is — separately from the other rules — introduced to provide for that "stop", and for separating the "stop" concern from the definition of the language, $\mathcal{L}_N$, of numerals. The states **s, i, p, r** and **f** stand for the start, integer, (fraction) point, rational numeral, respectively final states. The next state label pairs $\{i_j, \ldots, i_k\}$. $< r_p; \ldots; r_q >$ express: any of the inputs i_ℓ (for ℓ from j to k) result in the output sequence $r_p; \ldots; r_q$ of BNF rule identifiers (here numerals). Empty outputs are allowed. The error output designates an error message. An error state and its transitions complete the machine. Notice that we have not provided for input (next state) transitions beyond the final and the error states. The machine is supposed to have served its purpose when it reaches either of these states and can be taken out of service, i.e., can be freed!   ∎

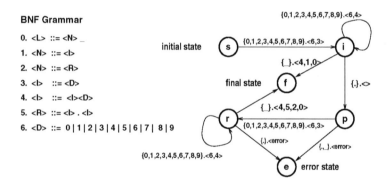

BNF Grammar

0. <L> ::= <N> _

1. <N> ::= <I>

2. <N> ::= <R>

3. <I> ::= <D>

4. <I> ::= <I><D>

5. <R> ::= <I> . <I>

6. <D> ::= 0 | 1 | 2 | 3 | 4 | 5 | 6 | 7 | 8 | 9

Fig. 11.11. A BNF grammar and its finite state parser

11.4.3 Finite State Machine Formalisation

We express:

Definition. By a *finite state machine* we generally understand a seven grouping:

type
    I, S, O
    $FSM' = I\text{-set} \times S\text{-set} \times S \times S \times S \times O\text{-set} \times F$
    $F = (I \times S) \xrightarrow{\sim} (S \times O^*)$

FSM = {| fsm:FSM′ • wf_FSM(fsm) |}
value
  wf_FSM: FSM′ → **Bool**
  wf_FSM(α,σ,i_s,f_s,e_s,o_s,ψ) ≡
    {i_s,f_s,e_s}$\subseteq\sigma\wedge\forall$ (i,s):(I×S) • (i,s) ∈ **dom** ψ
      ⇒ i ∈ i_s$\wedge$s ∈ $\sigma\wedge$**let** (s′,ol)=ψ(i,s) **in** s′ ∈ $\sigma\wedge$**elems** ol$\subseteq$o_s **end**

Notation: α is an input alphabet, σ is a state set, i_s is an initial state,[6] f_s
is a final state,[7] e_s is an error state,[8] o_s is an action set, and ψ is an "input
and current state to next state transition and action output function". A
finite state machine is also, sometimes, called a finite state transducer. Given
a prefix, pil, of any input il, an fsm delivers, when started in an appropriate
state, a transduction, that is, a prefix output, pol.   ∎

11.4.4 Finite State Machine Realisation

Generally we can associate actions with machine outputs. And we can generalise the finite state automaton functions start and run to machines. Let us
assume an action context and state configuration type Γ, and let action designators o:O denote functions that transform configurations into configurations:

type
  S, I, Γ
  O = $\Gamma \to \Gamma$
value
  run: FSM $\overset{\sim}{\to}$ S $\overset{\sim}{\to}$ I* $\overset{\sim}{\to}$ Γ $\overset{\sim}{\to}$ Γ
  run(α,σ,i_s,f_s,e_s,o_s,ψ)(s)(il)γ ≡
    if il=$\langle\rangle$
      then γ
      else
        let i = **hd** il **in let** (s′,ol) = ψ(i,s) **in**
        run(α,σ,i_s,f_s,e_s,o_s,ψ)(s′)(**tl** il)(M(ol)γ) **end end end**
    pre s ∈ σ ∧ **elems** il ⊆ α ∧ ...

  M: O* → Γ → Γ
  M(ol)γ ≡ **if** ol=$\langle\rangle$ **then** γ **else** M(**tl** ol)(M(**hd** ol)γ) **end**

  M: O → Γ → Γ
  M(o)γ ≡ o(γ)

---

[6]In this definition we specify just one initial state. The reader is encouraged to
reflect on a set of initial states.

[7]In this definition we specify just one final state. The reader is encouraged to
reflect on a set of final states.

[8]Usually there is no need for more than exactly one error state. But the reader
is encouraged to reflect on the possibility of discriminating among error states.

Dispensing with the semantic (i.e., the meaning) function M, we can replace the output list of action descriptions with a list of indices into branches of a **case** construct:

type

    $O = \{1..n\}$

    $FSM' = \text{I-set} \times \text{S-set} \times S \times S \times S \times \text{O-set} \times \Psi,$

    $\Psi == \text{mk}\_\Psi(f\text{:}F,t\text{:}(O \overrightarrow{m} \text{ "RSL-Text"})),$

    $F = (I \times S) \overrightarrow{m} (S \times O), \text{etc.}$

The use of double quotes ("...") is metalinguistic. The idea, as shown below, is that the semantic M function (for meaning) above is replaced by a macro-substitution M function (also M). Recall, from definition of Ψ, that t in M below selects the map in Ψ which when applied to indices yields action text to be interpreted. This is a rather informal explication.

value

    run: FSM $\overset{\sim}{\to}$ S $\overset{\sim}{\to}$ I* $\overset{\sim}{\to}$ Γ $\overset{\sim}{\to}$ Γ

    $\text{run}(\alpha,\sigma,\text{i\_s,f\_s,e\_s,o\_s},\psi)(s)(il)(\gamma) \equiv$

        if il$=\langle\rangle$

            then γ

            else

                let i = **hd** il **in let** $(s',o) = (f(\psi))(i,s)$ **in**

                let $\gamma' = {}''M(\text{'psi}){}''(o)(\gamma)$ **in**

                $\text{run}(\alpha,\sigma,\text{i\_s,f\_s,e\_s,o\_s},\psi)(s')(\textbf{tl}\ il)(\gamma')$ **end end end end**

        pre s $\in \sigma \wedge$ **elems** il $\subseteq \alpha \wedge$ ...

The next function mimics a microprogrammed hardware computer:

    M: $\Psi \to$ **Nat** $\to \Gamma \to \Gamma$

    $M(\psi)(o)(\gamma) \equiv$

        (**case** o **of**:

            $1 \to \mathcal{M}((t(\psi))(1)),$

            $2 \to \mathcal{M}((t(\psi))(2)),$

            ... ,

            $n \to \mathcal{M}((t(\psi))(n))$

        end)(γ)

        pre o $\in \{1..n\} \wedge$ **dom** $t(\psi) = \{1..n\}$

    $\mathcal{M}({}''\text{RSL-Text}{}'') \equiv$ ...

n is the maximum number of different output symbols. Each output symbol corresponds to an action as prescribed by some RSL expression RSL-Expr(i).

11.4.5 Finite State Machines — A Summary

We have introduced core concepts of finite state machines: their structure, their transducing power and ideas on realisation. Issues such as determinism and minimality carry over from the concept of finite state automata. It remains to summarise principles and techniques for introducing and using finite state machines.

Principles. The principle of *finite state machines* is based on the principle of finite state automata (Sect. 11.3.11). If criteria (a–c) of the principle of finite state automata apply and if, in addition, the event phenomenon or an event concept of a transition into a next state is associated with an action being performed by the system being (hence) understood as a finite state machine, then one may well choose such an abstraction. ∎

Techniques. The run and M functions together with the techniques for modelling finite state automata apply when modelling *finite state machines*. ∎

11.5 Pushdown Stack Devices

> Next, we move from finite states to infinite states. That is, we move from finite state controllers to finite state controllers plus an infinite stack whose (stacked) items encode "return" states. That is the topic of this section.

11.5.1 Pushdown Stack Automata and Machines

We have exemplified the use of pushdown stack machines in the section on computational semantics (Sect. 3.3). Pushdown stack devices (whether just automata or machines) are indispensable in practical compiler technology (as well as in many other forms of software technology), and their theory has been thoroughly studied [6, 200, 217, 444]. We shall not, in these volumes, cover this theory other than through recalling a few theorems. In this brief introduction to pushdown stack devices (such as automata and machines) we shall, however, attempt to motivate their existence — their pragmatics and hence aid the reader in deploying such devices whenever appropriate, and in studying *automata and formal languages* seriously. In the introduction to this section on automata and machines we briefly touched upon the notion of infinite state automata and machines. Pushdown stacks is one proper subclass of infinite state devices. Basically, they consist of a finite state device connected to a potentially infinite depth stack.

One way of explaining these pushdown stack devices is as follows: A finite state device can handle regular languages. If a language consists of recursively nested "almost" regular sentences — where the beginning ("[", "(", "{", "⟨") and ending (")", "}", ")", respectively "]") of recursion, in the sentences, is marked with nonregular language input symbols ("[,]", etc.) — then the finite state device that recognises the regular sublanguage can be extended with transitions corresponding to the recursion markers ("[,]", etc.) where the output actions consist in stacking (pushing), respectively unstacking (popping), state symbols corresponding to the bracketing symbols, and where the next state transitions are to the initial state for the parser of the specific language "between" the bracketing symbols, respectively to the popped state (Fig. 11.12).

Example 11.11 *A Conceptual Pushdown Stack Device:* The language L, defined in Fig. 11.12, is a "toy" language that is, just about "smallest" wrt. recursion. Notice that upon input of "]", the device resumes (dotted ... transition) in either state i or state p depending on the top stack state symbol. We have not bothered to show error input transitions and an error state. ∎

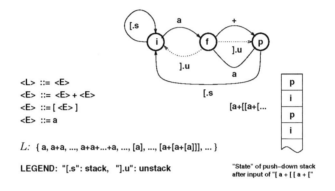

<L> ::= <E>
<E> ::= <E> + <E>
<E> ::= [<E>]
<E> ::= a

L: { a, a+a, ..., a+a+...+a, ..., [a], ..., [a+[a+[a]]], ... }

LEGEND: "[.s": stack, "].u": unstack

"State" of push-down stack after input of "[a + [[a + ["

Fig. 11.12. A "toy" language and pushdown stack device

We have motivated the existence of pushdown stack devices in one way: by referring to the handling (e.g., recognition) of sentences of a recursive — properly "nested" — language. We could exemplify the use of finite state controlled stack devices without first introducing (properly defining, etc.) a proper language. That is, we could exemplify them without first conceiving of the problem as that of handling (recognising or parsing) such a language.

Example 11.12 *A "Last In/First Out" System:* An example could be the "last in, first out" (LIFO) handling of processes by an operating system for a monoprocessor. Processes present themselves to the operating system through interrupts (√). The process π_e being served at the moment of interrupt is stacked. The new (the interrupting) process π_i is served. When a served process has to wait for a monoprocessor resource it replaces the top stacked process, which is then served (i.e., unstacked). When a served process terminates it is removed from the system and the top stacked process is then served (i.e., unstacked). See Fig. 11.13. Notice that an interrupt can only occur when a process is running. We leave it to the reader to formalise the language of "inputs" that correspond to the above, "casual" specification. ∎

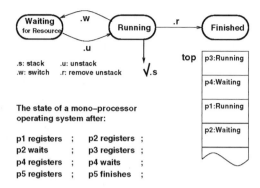

Fig. 11.13. A monoprocessor operating system LIFO job stack

11.5.2 Formalisation of Pushdown Stack Machines

We shall only define a concept of pushdown stack machines — leaving it to the reader to define a concept of pushdown stack automata, should that be needed! We cover the case only of finite state controls for these stack devices.

Definition. A *finite state pushdown stack machine* is a seven grouping:

type
    I, S, O, M
    PDM′ = I-set × S-set × O-set × S × S × Ψ × Φ
    PDM = {| pda:PDA′ • wf_PDA(pda) |}
    Ψ = Symbol*
    Symbol == I | S | O | M
    Φ = (In × S × Sy) $\overrightarrow{m}$ (S × PP × Ou)
    In == nil | input(i:I)
    Sy == null | Symbol
    PP == void | push(sy:Symbol) | pop
    Ou == nix | output(o:O)
value
    wf_PDM: PDM′ → **Bool**
    wf_PDM(α,σ,ω,i_s,f_s,ψ,ϕ) ≡
        {i_s,f_s} ⊆ σ ∧
        ∀ (input(i),s,y):(In×S×Sy) • (input(i),s,y) ∈ **dom** ϕ ⇒
            i ∈ α ∧ s ∈ σ ∧ y ∈ {I,S,O,M,null} ∧
        ∀ (i,s,y):(In×S×Sy) • (i,s,y) ∈ **dom** ϕ ⇒
            let (s′,,o) = ϕ(i,s,y) **in** s′ ∈ σ ∧
            case o **of** output(o) → o ∈ ω,_→**true end end**

The nil, null and nix "markers" are not input, are not stack-top symbols, are not output symbols, and void is not a symbol to be pushed onto the stack. Instead, when encountered in a next state transition they designate that the current input, or the current stack-top is ignored, or that no output symbol is issued, respectively that no symbol is pushed onto the stack. Appropriate well-formedness conditions express (for example) that a next state transition either accepts an input (i.e., input is different from nil), or accepts the stack-top symbol (i.e., the Sy component is different from null), or both. You may assume that an accepted input or stack-top symbol is consumed (i.e., removed). Many more "formal" things may be said about pushdown machines — but we leave that to appropriate textbooks.   ■

We leave it to the reader, as Exercise 11.4, to formalise the behaviour of a pushdown stack machine — along the lines of the run function for finite state machines (cf. Sect. 11.4.4).

Definition. We also leave it to the reader, as Exercise 11.5, to define and formalise, as above, the concept of a *pushdown stack automaton* — achieving the same kind of similarity between pushdown stack automata (Sects. 11.3.7 and 11.3.9) and pushdown stack machines (Sect. 11.4.3) as there exists between finite state automata and finite state machines.   ■

The idea is, of course, and as hinted at in Sect. 8.5, that pushdown stack automata recognise context-free languages as now recalled:

Definition. By a *context-free grammar* we understand a BNF grammar.   ■

BNF grammars were introduced in Sect. 8.4.

Definition. By a *context-free language* we understand the denotation of a context-free grammar.   ■

We refer to Sect. 8.5 for the story on context-free grammars, context-free languages and the pushdown stack automata that recognise whether a sentence (a string of terminal symbols) is a member of a context-free language as denoted by a context-free grammar.

11.5.3 Pushdown Stack Device Summary

We summarise this very brief survey of pushdown stack devices by stating a principle and referring to modelling techniques.

Principles. The principle of *pushdown stack devices* builds on the principle of finite state automata and machines (Sects. 11.3.11 and 11.4.5), cf. selection criteria (a–c) and (d), respectively. If these criteria (either just (a–c) or all: (a–d)) apply, and if (e) in addition the phenomenon or concept being analysed exhibits, or can be understood as possessing, some form of recursion, i.e., of properly embedded ("nested") instances of the same phenomenon or concept, or similar phenomena or concepts, then one may well choose abstraction in the form of a pushdown stack device: as an automaton if criterion (d) does not apply, as a machine otherwise.   ■

Techniques. The techniques for modelling *pushdown stack devices* extend those of modelling finite state automata and machines (Sects. 11.3.11 and 11.4.5). The extension amounts to the modelling of recursion. Many examples already shown have illustrated such modelling. We refer to Examples 3.4 and 3.5. ■

11.6 Bibliographical Notes: Automata and Machines

The first paper on automata (and neural nets) was that of McCulloch and Pitts [335] (1943). The next papers on automata — in the context of computers — seem to have been those of Arthur W. Burks and Hao Wang [65,66] (1957), Stephen Kleene [265] (1956), Marvin Minsky [360] (1956), and Michael O. Rabin and Dana Scott [413] (1959).

The following information (relating to the above references) is from H.V. McIntosh [336]:

> Automata theory itself has an ancient history, if one thinks of automata as mechanisms capable of performing intricate movements; but if the actual apparatus is discarded in favor of the activity itself, such a theory more properly begins with the neurophysiological abstractions of McCulloch and Pitts. Their refinement into the theory of regular expressions by Kleene constitutes one of several viewpoints, which have gone on to include semigroups (or monoids) of mappings of a set into itself, or even the theory of grammars.

A decisive textbook on the theoretical foundations of automata and formal languages was, and is John E. Hopcroft and Jeffrey D. Ullman's [217] (1979).

In our treatment we have covered the so-called Mealy Machines. In contrast a Moore Machine is a machine whose output depends only on the state, whereas a Mealy Machine [548] is a machine whose output depends on the input and the state.

11.7 Exercises

Exercise 11.1 *Automobile Door and Lid State Automata.* Please draw the varieties of two-dimensional figures of finite state automata that model the three cases (i–iii) outlined in Example 11.2 (and the singular only or multiple openings and closings of doors and the lid) of an automobile.

Once you have drawn the finite state automata, answer the following question: Which is its contribution to the context of the automobile and which is its contribution to the state of the automobile?

Exercise 11.2 *Automobile States.* We refer to Example 11.2 and to Exercise 11.1. In addition to the open or closed state of doors and the trunk lid of an automobile, you are to come up with three or four other examples of physical components of the automobile whose state value may affect the "drivability" of the car. You are then to draw a two-dimensional figure of the finite state automaton resulting from these considerations. For simplicity adopt case (iii) of Example 11.2 as a starting point.

   Once you have drawn the finite state automata, answer the following question: Which is its contribution to the contexts of an automobile and which is its contribution to the state of an automobile?

Exercise 11.3 *Finite State Automaton Realisation.* We refer to Sects. 11.3.9 and 11.3.10. You are to redefine, for the formal model of Sect. 11.3.10, the start and run functions, as per Sect. 11.3.9.

Exercise 11.4 *Pushdown Stack Machine Behaviour.* We refer to Sect. 11.5.2's formalisation of pushdown stack machines, and to Sect. 11.4.4's formalisation of the behaviour of finite state machines. Please formalise a function that describes the behaviour of pushdown stack machines.

Exercise 11.5 *Pushdown Stack Automata.* We refer to Sect. 11.5.2's formalisation of pushdown stack machines and to Sects. 11.3.7, 11.3.9 and 11.4.3's formalisation of finite state automaton and machines. Please formalise a definition of pushdown stack automata.

Part VI

CONCURRENCY AND TEMPORALITY

- In this part we shall cover material that allows us to model both *qualitative* and *quantitative* aspects of concurrency and temporality.
- The terms concurrency, temporality, qualitative, and quantitative will be briefly explained here:
  - ⋆ By concurrency we mean the occurrence of two or more behaviours (i.e., processes) at the same time, or, in other words, concurrently.
  - ⋆ By temporality we mean to characterise something with respect to time, or emphasising the timewise, or absolute, or relative time behaviour of a phenomenon.
  - ⋆ By qualitative aspects of concurrency and temporality we mean to emphasise when two or more behaviours (i.e., processes) synchronise, or exchange messages (i.e., communicate), or when one event occurs before, or after, or at the same time as some other event, or that a behaviour (i.e., a process) is deadlocked (unable to perform any action), or live (i.e., ready to perform a next action).
  - ⋆ By quantitative aspects of concurrency and temporality we mean to emphasise some absolute time of, or time interval between, the occurrence of some events.
- Our coverage occurs in chapters named rather differently than how we normally name chapters. Whereas we elsewhere in these volumes name chapters after the methodological *principles* and *techniques* they cover, we shall, in this part, name three chapters after the *tools* they cover: Petri nets, message and live sequence charts, and statecharts.

12

Petri Nets

Christian Krog Madsen is chief author of this chapter [317].

- The **prerequisites** for studying this chapter are that you have an all-round awareness of abstract specification (principles and techniques) and that you have a more specific awareness of parallel programming, for example, using CSP — as illustrated in Vol. 1, Chap. 21 of this series of textbooks — and that you have wondered if there are other mechanisms than, say, RSL/CSP, for modelling concurrency.
- The **aims** are to introduce three kinds of Petri net languages: condition events, place transitions, and coloured Petri nets, to show varieties of examples illustrating these specification mechanisms, and to relate Petri nets to RSL: To define, more precisely, when a Petri net specification can be expressed as an RSL specification — and vice versa!
- The **objective** is to enable the reader to expand on the kind of phenomena and concepts that can be formally modelled, now also, or specifically, by Petri nets, alone, or in conjunction with, for example, RSL — as well as to encourage the reader to more seriously study more specialised textbooks on Petri nets.
- The **treatment** is from systematic to semi-formal.

The field of Petri nets is fascinating. They were first conceived in the very early 1960s [400] as a means for understanding, through modelling, issues of concurrency, notably in physics. Petri nets have become a standard technique and tool in software engineering.

12.1 The Issues

In this chapter we review several variants of Petri nets, ranging from the basic condition event nets to coloured Petri nets. Each of the discussed types of Petri nets is modelled formally in RSL. Petri nets were first described by Carl Adam Petri in his doctoral thesis [400] in 1962.

Petri nets are composed from graphical symbols designating states (usually shown as circles: ○), transitions (usually shown as rectangles: []), and arrows (shown as arrows: →), linking states to transitions and transitions to states: ○→[]→○. Depending on the type of Petri net, states may be called places or conditions, while transitions are also referred to as events. We refer to Fig. 12.1 for a "picture" of these basic building blocks.

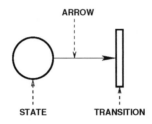

Fig. 12.1. Petri net symbols

The description of condition event nets and place transition nets is based on Reisig [420]. The description of coloured Petri nets is based on Jensen [238].

In what follows we shall avail ourselves of a somewhat imprecise use of language. This is done for reasons for readability. When some abstract entity has a graphical representation we shall use the name of the abstract entity to also denote its graphical representation. For example, in a Petri net a state is usually represented graphically as a circle, while a transition is represented by a rectangle. Suppose an arrow extends from the perimeter of the circle to the border of the rectangle. Then, we shall say that the arrow links the state to the transition. Really, what we should say is that the arrow links the graphical representation of the state to the graphical representation of the transition.

Three kinds of Petri nets will be covered in Sects. 12.2–12.4.

12.2 Condition Event Nets (CENs)

This section is structured as follows: First, in Sect. 12.2.1, we informally explain the syntax and semantics of condition event nets (CENs). Then, in Sect. 12.2.2 we present some small, typical examples. In Sect. 12.2.3 we develop a model of the syntax and semantics of CENs, in RSL.

12.2.1 Description

Condition event nets (CEN) are the most basic type of Petri nets. A CEN consists of *conditions* (states), *events* (transitions) and links (arrows) from conditions to events and from events to conditions. Syntactically conditions are represented as circles, while events are represented as oblong, i.e., "thin", rectangles.

An event may have a set of *preconditions,* which are conditions — that is, may be predicated by the holding of some conditions. Similarly, an event may have a set of *postconditions,* which are also conditions — that is, may be predicated by the holding of some conditions. A precondition of an event is represented graphically by an arrow emanating from the precondition and ending at the event. Similarly, a postcondition is represented by an arrow emanating from the event and ending at the postcondition.

A condition may be *marked* with a *token.* Graphically this is represented by drawing a disc, •, inside the condition. A *marking* of a CEN is an assignment of tokens to some of the conditions in the CEN. A condition that is marked with a token is said to be *fulfilled.* Conversely, a condition that is not marked is said to be *unfulfilled.* If all the preconditions of an event are fulfilled and all the postconditions of the event are unfulfilled, the event is said to be *activated* (*enabled*).[1] An event that is activated may *occur.* If an event occurs, all its preconditions become unfulfilled and all its postconditions become fulfilled. Figure 12.2 illustrates the occurrence of an event.

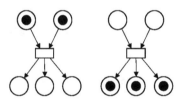

Fig. 12.2. CEN event occurrence with markings before and after the occurrence

12.2.2 Small CEN Examples

The first three examples of this subsection are all edited from Reisig's delightful *Elements of Distributed Algorithms: Modelling and Analysis with Petri Nets* [421].

Example 12.1 *Producer-Consumer System, A One Element Buffer:* We refer to Fig. 12.3. The producer is shown as the leftmost five symbols: the leftmost transition, the two leftmost states and the two leftmost arrows. The consumer is shown as the rightmost five symbols: the rightmost transition, the two

---

[1] This form of enablement amounts to the Petri net being contact-free. One can also define a Petri net theory based on events that do not rely on the postcondition being fulfilled.

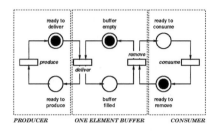

Fig. 12.3. A producer-consumer Petri net — Example 12.1

rightmost states and the two rightmost arrows. The interface between the producer and the consumer represents a one-element buffer. It is shown as the centre two states, two transitions and eight arrows!

One scenario of behaviour could be: The producer-consumer system is in a "total" state where the producer is ready to produce data, where the one-element buffer is empty, and where the consumer is ready to remove data. See the leftmost Petri net of Fig. 12.4.

A next "total" state is therefore one in which the producer makes a state transition, that is, actually produces. See the leftmost Petri net of Fig. 12.4.

Now the deliver transition is enabled, and a next total state sees one transition and two state changes: The produced "something" is delivered, the producer changes from being ready to deliver to being ready to produce and the buffer is no longer empty.

We leave it to the reader to show a next firing.   ∎

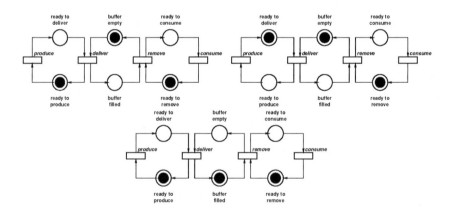

Fig. 12.4. A sequence of two firings (three "total" states) — Example 12.1

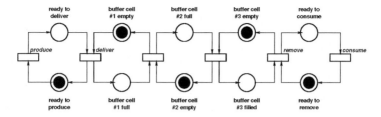

Fig. 12.5. Three element sequential producer-consumer buffer — Example 12.2

Example 12.2 *Producer-Consumer, Three Element Sequential Buffer System:* To make a sequential queue, i.e., a first-in, first-out buffer, we replicate the one-element buffer three times (Fig. 12.5).

We leave it to the reader to "experiment" with initial states and "try out" some firing sequences. ∎

Example 12.3 *A Producer-Consumer, Parallel (Heap) Buffer System:* In this example, the producer, when ready to deliver, may choose either of the two buffer cells, if both are empty. In that case, the choice is nondeterministic. If one is filled, the producer will choose the other (deterministically). If both are filled, and one of these buffer cells gets emptied before the other, then the producer will choose that which gets first emptied. The buffer is no longer sequential, i.e., a queue, but is a heap (of capacity two). One buffer cell may be filled before, but emptied after the other buffer cell. ∎

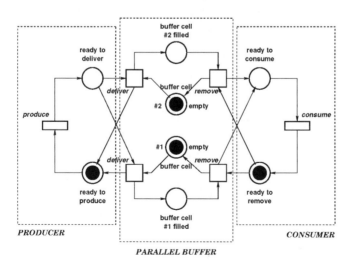

Fig. 12.6. Nondeterministic parallel buffer producer-consumer — Example 12.3

The next example is a "classic". Many have tried their hand at expressing, in one notation or another, the problem of the "Dining Philosophers", a problem posed by Dijkstra [102]. See Reisig's delightful *Elements of Distributed Algorithms: Modelling and Analysis with Petri Nets* [421] for a thorough treatment of various Petri net solutions to the "Dining Philosophers" problem.

Example 12.4 *Dining Philosophers:* Figure 12.7 illustrates a CEN with a marking. The net represents a simplified model of the classical Dining Philosophers problem. The problem is set, say, in a monastery where five philosophers spend their life engaged in thinking. Their thinking is only interrupted when they have to eat. The monastery has a circular dining table with a place for each of the philosophers. At the centre of the table is a bowl with an endless supply of spaghetti. On the table there is a plate for each place and a fork between each pair of adjacent plates. To eat, a philosopher must use the two forks adjacent to his plate. The problem is then to devise a strategy that will allow the philosophers to eat without risking starvation.

In the CEN there are only four philosophers, each of which is represented by two conditions, labelled Pxt and Pxe, where x is the number of the philosopher. When Pxt is marked, philosopher x is thinking. When Pxe is marked, philosopher x is eating. The final four conditions, Fx, represent the four forks. When Fx is marked, fork x is free.

In order for philosopher x to begin eating, he must currently be thinking, and the two adjacent forks must be free. This is represented by an event with preconditions Pxt, Fx and $F(x + 1 \bmod 4)$. While philosopher x is eating he cannot be thinking, and the two adjacent forks are not free. This is represented by letting the postcondition of the event be Pxe.

When philosopher x stops eating, he places the two forks on the table and begins thinking. This is represented by an event with precondition Pxe and postconditions Pxt, Fx and $F(x + 1 \bmod 4)$.   ∎

12.2.3 An RSL Model of Condition Event Nets

Definition. By a *condition event Petri net* we shall understand a structure as formalised in this section.   ∎

Syntax of CENs and a Static Semantics

We first formalise a syntax and then a static semantics for CENs.

type
    CEN = {| c : CEN' • wf_CEN(c) |}
    CEN' = Cond-**set** × Event-**set** × PreCond × PostCond × Marking
    Cond
    Event

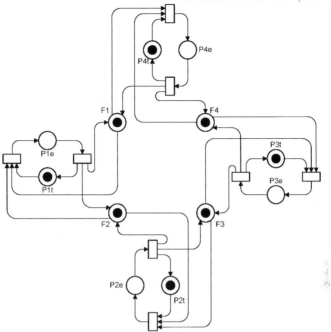

Fig. 12.7. Four dining philosophers condition event net — Example 12.4

PreCond = Event $\vec{m}$ Cond-**set**
PostCond = Event $\vec{m}$ Cond-**set**
Marking = Cond $\vec{m}$ Mark
Mark == empty | token
value
    wf_CEN : CEN' → **Bool**
    wf_CEN(cs,es,precs,postcs,mark) ≡
[1] **dom** precs = es ∧
[2] **dom** postcs = es ∧
[3] cs = ⋃ {**rng** precs ∪ **rng** postcs}∧
[4] (∀ e:Event • e ∈ es ⇒ precs(e) ∪ postcs(e)≠{}) ∧
[5] **dom** mark = cs

Annotations

- A condition event Petri net (CEN) consists of a set of conditions, a set of events, preconditions, postconditions and a marking.

- Only well-formed CENs will be considered.

- Conditions and events are further unspecified entities.

- Preconditions are mappings from events to sets of conditions.

- Postconditions are mappings from events to sets of conditions.

- A marking is an assignment of marks to conditions.

- A mark is either empty or a token.

- A CEN is well-formed if:

  1–2 The set of events is identical to the definition sets of the maps of pre- and postconditions, and

3 every condition is a pre- or postcondition of some event, and

4 every event has at least one pre- or postcondition, and

5 the marking includes all conditions.

∎

A Dynamic Semantics

Next, we describe the dynamic aspects of CENs, namely what it means for a condition to be *fulfilled* or *unfulfilled* and what it means for an event to be *activated* and to *occur*.

value

    fulfilled : Cond × CEN $\overset{\sim}{\to}$ **Bool**
    fulfilled(cond,(cs,es,precs,postcs,mark)) ≡ mark(cond)=token
    pre cond ∈ cs

    unfulfilled : Cond × CEN $\overset{\sim}{\to}$ **Bool**
    unfulfilled(cond,(cs,es,precs,postcs,mark)) ≡ mark(cond)=empty
    pre cond ∈ cs

    activated : Event × CEN $\overset{\sim}{\to}$ **Bool**
    activated(evt,cen) ≡
      let (cs,es,precs,postcs,mark) = cen **in**
        (∀ c : Cond • c ∈ precs(evt) ⇒ fulfilled(c,cen)) ∧
        (∀ c : Cond • c ∈ postcs(evt) ⇒ unfulfilled(c,cen))
      end
    pre let (cs,es,precs,postcs,mark) = cen **in** evt ∈ es **end**

    occur : Event × CEN $\overset{\sim}{\to}$ CEN
    occur(evt,cen) ≡
      let (cs,es,precs,postcs,mark) = cen **in**
        (cs,es,precs,postcs,
        mark † [c ↦ empty | c : Cond • c ∈ precs(evt)] †
        [c ↦ token | c : Cond • c ∈ postcs(evt)])
      end
    pre activated(evt,cen)

Annotations

- A condition is fulfilled in a CEN if the marking assigns a token to that condition.

- A condition is unfulfilled if the marking assigns empty to that condition.

- An event is activated if all its preconditions are fulfilled and all its postconditions are unfulfilled.
- The occurrence of an activated event gives a new CEN where all

preconditions of the event are unfulfilled and all postconditions of the event are fulfilled.   ∎

12.3 Place Transition Nets (PTNs)

This section is structured as follows: First, in Sect. 12.3.1, we explain, informally, the syntax and semantics of place transition nets (PTNs). Then, in Sect. 12.3.2 we present some small, typical examples. In Sect. 12.3.3 we develop a model of the syntax and semantics of PTNs, in RSL. Section 12.3.4 brings in further examples.

12.3.1 Description

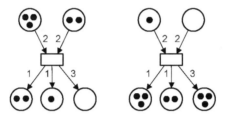

Fig. 12.8. Transition in a place transition net, markings before and after occurrence

We start by showing a place transition net, then we explain place transition nets more systematically. A simple extension to the condition event nets is to allow a marking to assign more than one token to a condition. The extended nets are known as place transition nets (PTNs). Conditions are now called *places*, and events are called *transitions*. In a PTN the places are labelled with a positive integer called the *capacity*. This indicates the maximum number of tokens that may be assigned to that place. The capacity may be omitted, which is interpreted as unlimited capacity. Additionally, arrows are labelled with a positive integer called the *weight*. If an arrow from a place, P, to a transition, T, is labelled with x, this signifies that for T to be activated, there must be at least x tokens at P, and when T occurs, x tokens will be removed from P. If an arrow from a transition, T, to a place, P, is labelled with x, this signifies that for T to be activated, x added to the number of tokens at P must be at most equal to the capacity of P, and if T occurs, x tokens will be added to the marking of P. If an arrow is not labelled it is to be understood as an implicit labelling with 1. Figure 12.8 shows the occurrence of a transition in a PTN.

12.3.2 Small PTN Examples

The two examples of this section are edited from Reisig's two books: *A Primer in Petri Net Design* [420] and *Petri Nets: An Introduction* [419].

Example 12.5 *System of Two Producers, a Capacity 10 Buffer, and Three Consumers:* The PTN of Fig. 12.9 shows a system that can be understood as a two-producer, three-consumer and an intermediate maximum 10 production unit buffer system. Compare the present PTN with the CEN of Example 12.2. In the present system the capacity limit removes the need for the place (i.e., state) distinction between empty and filled buffers.   ∎

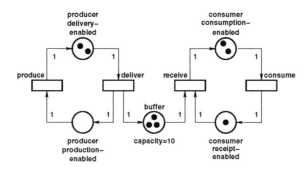

Fig. 12.9. Two producer, buffer capacity 10 and three consumer system

Example 12.6 *Critical Resource Sharing:* Figure 12.10 shows an example PTN modelling four processes that access a common critical resource. One process writes to the resource, while the other three processes read from the resource. To ensure data integrity, mutual exclusion must be enforced between the writing process and the reading processes. The protocol for mutual exclusion requires a reading process to claim a key before it may read, while the writing process is required to claim three keys before it may write. A process that cannot get the required number of keys must wait until more keys become available. The place *Keys* holds a token for each key that is unused. When a process finishes reading or writing it returns the claimed keys to the place *Keys* and proceeds to do some processing that does not access the critical resource.   ∎

12.3.3 An RSL Model of Place Transition Nets

Definition. By a *place transition Petri net* we shall understand a structure as formalised in this section.   ∎

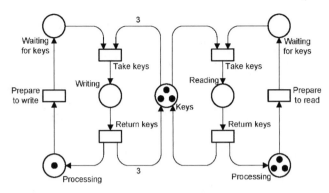

Fig. 12.10. Critical resource sharing

Syntax of PTNs and a Static Semantics

We first formalise a syntax and then a static semantics for PTNs (with finite capacity places).

type

    PTN = {| ptn:PTN′ • wf_PTN(ptn) |}
    PTN′ = (Place $\underset{m}{\rightarrow}$ **Nat**) × Trans-**set** × Preset × Postset × Marking
    Place
    Trans
    Preset = Trans $\underset{m}{\rightarrow}$ (Place × **Nat**)-**set**
    Postset = Trans $\underset{m}{\rightarrow}$ (Place × **Nat**)-**set**
    Marking = Place $\underset{m}{\rightarrow}$ **Nat**

value

    wf_PTN : PTN′ → **Bool**
    wf_PTN(ps, ts, pres, posts, mark) ≡
[1] **dom** pres = ts ∧
[2] **dom** posts = ts ∧
[3] {p | p:Place •
        ∃ pns: (Place×**Nat**)-**set**, n:**Nat** •
          (p,n) ∈ pns∧pns ∈ **rng** pres ∪ **rng** posts} = **dom** ps ∧
[4] (∀ t:Trans • t ∈ ts ⇒ pres(t) ∪ posts(t) ≠ {}) ∧
[5] (∀ t:Trans •
        ∼(∃ n1, n2 : **Nat**, p : Place •
          n1 ≠ n2 ∧ p ∈ **dom** ps ∧
          ({(p,n1), (p,n2)} ⊆ pres(t) ∨
          {(p,n1), (p,n2)} ⊆ posts(t)))) ∧
[6] **dom** mark = **dom** ps ∧
[7] (∀ p:Place • p ∈ **dom** ps ⇒ mark(p)≤ps(p))

Annotations

- A place transition net consists of a set of places with associated capacities, a set of transitions, a preset, a postset and a marking.
- Only well-formed PTNs will be considered.
- Places and transitions are further unspecified entities.
- Presets are a mapping from transitions to sets of pairs of places and weights.
- Postsets are a mapping from transitions to sets of pairs of places and weights.
- A marking is a mapping of places to marks.
- A mark is a nonnegative integer.
- A PTN is well-formed if:

1-2 every transition in the set of transitions is included in the domain of the maps of presets and postsets, and

3 every place is in the pre- or postset of some transition, and

4 every transition has a non-empty preset or postset, and

5 no transition can have a preset or postset that includes the same place more than once with different weights, and

6 the marking covers all places, and

7 for every place the number of tokens assigned to it in the marking must be at most equal to the capacity of the place.

∎

A Dynamic Semantics

We formalise the dynamic aspects of PTN, namely what it means for a transition to be *activated* and for a transition to *occur*.

value

    activated: Trans×PTN $\xrightarrow{\sim}$ **Bool**

    activated(t,ptn) ≡

        let (ps,ts,pres,posts,mark) = ptn **in**

            ($\forall$ p:Place,n:**Nat** • (p,n) ∈ pres(t) $\Rightarrow$ mark(p)≥n) $\wedge$

            ($\forall$ p:Place,n:**Nat** • (p,n) ∈ posts(t) $\Rightarrow$ mark(p)+n≤ps(p))

        end

        pre let (ps,ts,pres,posts,mark) = ptn **in** t ∈ ts **end**

    occur: Trans×PTN $\xrightarrow{\sim}$ PTN

    occur(t,ptn) ≡

        let (ps,ts,pres,posts,mark) = ptn **in**

            (ps,ts,pres,posts,

                mark †

                [p $\mapsto$ mark(p)−n | p:Place,n:**Nat** • (p,n) ∈ pres(t)] †

                [p $\mapsto$ mark(p)+n | p:Place,n:**Nat** • (p,n) ∈ posts(t)])

        end

        pre activated(t,ptn)

Note, unlike for CENs, there is no notion of a place being fulfilled or unfulfilled.

Annotations

- A transition is activated:
  - ⋆ if for every place in its preset there are at least as many tokens as the weight of the corresponding arrow, and
  - ⋆ if for every place in its postset the number of tokens at that place added to the weight of the corresponding arrow is at most equal to the capacity of the place.

- The occurrence of an activated transition produces a new marking
  - ⋆ in which the number of tokens at each of the places in the preset is reduced by the weight of the corresponding arrow, and
  - ⋆ in which the number of tokens at each of the places in the postset is increased by the weight of the corresponding arrow.

  ∎

Example 12.7 *PTN for Two-Producer/Three-Consumer System:* We refer to Example 12.5. We illustrate, in this example, the RSL value of type PTN corresponding to the Two-Producer, Three-Consumer example Petri net in Fig. 12.9.

scheme TwoProducerThreeConsumer =
extend PlaceTransitionNet **with**
class
    value
        pd, pp, b, cr, cc : Place,
        produce, deliver, receive, consume : Trans,
        ptn : PTN = ([pd $\mapsto$ 2, pp $\mapsto$ 2, b $\mapsto$ 10, cr $\mapsto$ 3, cc $\mapsto$ 3],
                  {produce, deliver, receive, consume},
                  [produce $\mapsto$ { (pp, 1) },
                    deliver $\mapsto$ { (pd, 1) },
                    receive $\mapsto$ { (b, 1), (cr, 1) },
                    consume $\mapsto$ { (cc, 1) }],
                  [produce $\mapsto$ { (pd, 1) },
                    deliver $\mapsto$ { (pp, 1), (b, 1) },
                    receive $\mapsto$ { (cc, 1) },
                    consume $\mapsto$ { (cr, 1) }],
                  [pd $\mapsto$ 2, pp $\mapsto$ 0, b $\mapsto$ 3, cc $\mapsto$ 2, cr $\mapsto$ 1]) **end**

Here we first define the five places, *pd* represents *producer delivery-enabled*, *pp* represents *producer production-enabled*, *b* represents *buffer*, *cr* represents *consumer receipt-enabled* and, finally, *cc* represents *consumer consumption-enabled*. Next, we define the four transitions using the names from the Petri net. Finally, we can define the value *ptn* representing the Petri net in Fig. 12.9. Notice that we define the capacity of the places *pd* and *pp* to two even though they do not have a capacity in the figure. This capacity is chosen such that it never becomes a constraint, since the initial marking limits the number of tokens in *pd* and *pp* to two. Similarly, the two places *cr* and *cc* have a capacity of three.   ∎

12.3.4 Railway Domain Petri Net Examples

────────────────────── Acknowledgement ──────────────────────

Martin Pěnička, Czech Technical University, Prague, kindly provided the example of this subsection from his PhD Thesis [398].

We now bring in an example that can be linked to the railway net examples of either Chap. 2 (Examples 2.5–2.9) or Chap. 10 (Example 10.22).

Example 12.8 *Railway System Petri Nets:* The example is large — so we dispense of shading. We will present a shaded paragraph to signal the end of this example.   ∎

Route Descriptions

The subjects of this example are interlocking: the setting up of proper routes from station approach ("line departure") signals to platform tracks, and from these to the lines connecting to other stations. We shall therefore focus on constructing, for all such "interesting" routes of a station, a Petri net that models a proper interlocking control scheme.

Routes are described in terms of units, switches and signals. In Sect. 2.3.3 informal statements 22 and 23 (and like-numbered formula) defined routes and open routes. Routes are sequences of pairs of units and paths, such that the path of a unit/path pair is a possible path of some state of the unit, and such that "neighbouring" connectors are identical. There can be many such routes in a station. We are interested only in routes which start at an approach signal and end either at the track or on the line. In the example station of Fig. 12.11 there are 16 such routes.

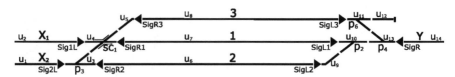

Fig. 12.11. Example station

Interlocking Tables

Depending on the local or national traditions, there are rules and regulations which stipulate how signals and switches are to be set (and reset) in order to facilitate the safe movement of trains within a station. One can formalise such rules (see, for example, [264]). From a mechanisation of such a formalisation and from the specific topology of a station layout, for example that abstracted in Fig. 12.11, one can then construct an interlocking table, such as the one given in Table 12.1. In that table S and T stand for straight and turn (position of switch), and R and G for red and green (colour of signal).

Each row in an interlocking table corresponds to a proper route. The table expresses for each interesting route the requirements for switches (points and switchable crossovers) and the requirements for signal states. The table also lists all units which compose the route. If there are no requirements on the setting of switch or signal, it is marked with dash (–). We do not show how to formally construct such a table, but we refer to [164, 165, 264, 471].

Table 12.1. Interlocking table for example station (by S_i is meant Sig_i)

Requirements → Routes ↓	sc_1	p_2	p_3	p_4	p_6	S_{1L}	S_{2L}	S_{L1}	S_{L2}	S_{L3}	S_R	S_{R1}	S_{R2}	S_{R3}	Units
	Switches					Signals									Units
1. $S_{1L}-1$	S	-	S	-	-	G	-	-	-	-	-	R	-	R	$u_{2,2,4,7}$
2. $S_{1L}-3$	T	-	S	-	-	G	-	-	-	-	-	R	-	R	$u_{2,2,5,8}$
3. $S_{2L}-1$	T	-	T	-	-	R	G	-	-	-	-	R	R	R	$u_{1,3,4,7}$
4. $S_{2L}-2$	-	-	S	-	-	-	G	-	-	-	-	-	R	-	$u_{1,3,6}$
5. $S_{2L}-3$	S	-	T	-	-	R	G	-	-	-	-	R	R	R	$u_{1,3,4,5,8}$
6. $S_{L1}-Y$	-	S	-	S	S	-	-	G	R	R	R	-	-	-	$u_{10,13,14}$
7. $S_{L2}-Y$	-	T	-	S	S	-	-	R	G	R	R	-	-	-	$u_{9,10,13,14}$
8. $S_{L3}-Y$	-	-	-	T	T	-	-	R	R	G	R	-	-	-	$u_{11,13,14}$
9. S_R-1	-	S	-	S	S	-	-	R	R	R	G	-	-	-	$u_{13,10,7}$
10. S_R-2	-	T	-	S	S	-	-	R	R	R	G	-	-	-	$u_{13,10,9,6}$
11. S_R-3	-	-	-	T	T	-	-	R	R	R	G	-	-	-	$u_{13,10,11,8}$
12. $S_{R1}-x_1$	S	-	S	-	-	R	-	-	-	-	-	G	-	R	$u_{4,2}$
13. $S_{R1}-x_2$	T	-	T	-	-	R	R	-	-	-	-	G	R	R	$u_{4,3,1}$
14. $S_{R2}-x_2$	-	-	S	-	-	-	R	-	-	-	-	-	G	-	$u_{3,1}$
15. $S_{R3}-x_1$	T	-	S	-	-	R	-	-	-	-	-	R	-	G	$u_{5,4,2}$
16. $S_{R3}-x_2$	S	-	T	-	-	R	R	-	-	-	-	R	R	G	$u_{5,4,3,1}$

We can now start to build up Petri nets for a partial railway net from four subparts: Petri net for a unit, for a switch (i.e., point or switchable crossover), for a signal, and for a route. Please observe that all units have a basic Petri net. Additionally, switches have additional basic Petri nets — as we shall soon see. And, finally, although routes are basically sequences of units, routes also have their separate basic Petri nets. The full Petri net for a route is then a composition of all its unit, all its switch, and all its signal Petri nets — where the composition is implied by the interlocking table.

Petri Net for Units

A unit can be in either of two basic states. It is either free (a new route can be opened through the unit) or it is blocked, i.e., there is an already opened route through the unit.

The Petri net for units is shown in Fig. 12.12a. Two places represent the two states: free and blocked. The initial marking consists of a token at the free place.

One can notice that the Petri net for a unit in Fig. 12.12a will interminably circulate ("oscillate"). But this is not the final Petri net for a route. It is just one component. Later on, extra arcs will be added that will prevent "oscillations".

Petri Net for Switches

A switch can be either a point or switchable crossover. A typical switch has two states: straight (S) and turn (T). A switch may be required to be set in a certain state in two ways: as a direct part of a route, or because it must be set for side protection (to avoid trains touching each other). In both cases, if there is an open route through switches, these switches must never change their states.

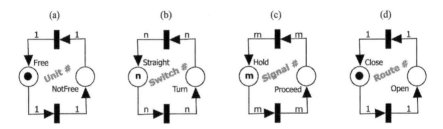

Fig. 12.12. Petri nets for (a) units, (b) switches, (c) signals, and (d) routes

Thus the Petri net for a switch has two places representing the two mentioned states: straight and turn.

The initial marking consists of n tokens at the straight place, where n is the total number of routes which require settings of that switch. This number can be found from the interlocking table (here Table 12.1) as a count of required setting in the switch column. For the example station in Fig. 12.11, one finds that for switchable crossover $sc1$, n is 8; for point $p2$, n is 4 (that is, 4 routes require settings of switch $p2$); etc. The switch can change state if and only if all n tokens are available. Later, when the whole Petri net will be constructed, we shall see that open routes through the switch cause the decrease of switch token numbers. This will help ensure that the switch can only change its state when no route — that requires the actual state — is active. But the switch can still be part of several routes, as long as these routes require the switch to be in the same state. These requirements are captured by the Petri net in Fig. 12.12b.

Petri Net for Signals

A signal has two states: hold and proceed[2]. The Petri net for a signal has two places representing the two settings hold and proceed.

The initial marking consists of m tokens at the 'Hold' place, where m is the number of routes which require setting of that signal. With Table 12.1, for the example station in Fig. 12.11, one finds that for for signal Sig_{1L}, m is 8, for signal Sig_{2L}, n is 6, etc. The signal can only change setting if all m tokens are available. This will ensure that the signal can only change its state when no route that requires the actual state is active, but the signal can still be part of several routes, as long as these routes require the signal to be in the same state. These requirements are captured by the Petri net in Fig. 12.12c.

Petri Net for Routes

From text item 23 (Example 2.5, and formula 23 (Example 2.6)) of Sect. 2.3.3 you can find that routes can be open or closed. A route can be open only when all its requirements on switch settings, signal settings and units occupancies are fulfilled.

The Petri net for a route also has two places representing the two states: Open and Closed. The initial marking consists of one token at the 'Closed' place. The basic Petri net for a route is shown in Figure 12.12d. This corresponds to the route that has no requirements on switches, signals or units.

Construction of Petri Net for Interlocking Tables

We will now indicate how to construct a Petri net, for the interlocking table of a station, from the four components already described (unit, switch, signal and route). The Petri net will be made by adding extra pairs of arcs for each requirement between these components. The example station of Fig. 12.11 will be composed by these components: 16 Petri nets for routes, 14 Petri nets for units, 5 Petri nets for switches and 9 Petri nets for signals. The station shown has these numbers.

---

[2]This is a simplistic view — a real signal is able to indicate the speed with which it may be passed.

Routes and Units

A route can be open when all units that the route is composed of are free (not occupied by trains or blocked by another route in the station). To satisfy this requirement, a pair of arcs needs to be added between each route Petri net and all unit Petri nets that make up the route (Fig. 12.13A).

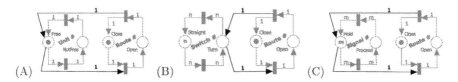

Fig. 12.13. Arc additions for route (A) units, (B) switches and (C) signals

Routes and Switches

For each switch requirement it must be ensured that the switch cannot change state while the route through that switch is open. To satisfy this requirement, a pair of arcs has to be added between each route Petri net and all switch Petri nets of that route. The particular insertion of arcs depends on the required state of the switch (as given in the interlocking table). This insertion is captured in the Petri net of Fig. 12.13B. Note that it is assumed that the route requires the switch to be set to the 'Turn' state. The case for 'Straight' follows accordingly.

Routes and Signals

The signal can be in the 'Proceed' state if and only if the route that starts at the signal is open. How to add a pair of arcs for a signal is illustrated in Fig. 12.13C. This is clearly the precondition for opening the route, which is the same as the precondition for adding switches.

Summary

The full Petri net for the example railway station and interlocking table thus contains 16 Petri nets for routes, 14 Petri nets for units, 5 Petri nets for switches, and 9 Petri nets for signals. The interlocking table then dictates very many of the arcs to be inserted — so many that readable diagrams become impossible. Clearly then, this is a case for tools. These tools can create the complete control program, based on Petri nets, for a station, and can check for liveness, deadlock, etc.

This is the end of Example 12.8.   ∎

Where the railway net examples of either Chap. 2 (Examples 2.5–2.9) or
Chap. 10 (Example 10.22) expressed basic domain properties of static and
dynamic rail nets, Example 12.8 (above) expresses basic requirements properties of what a monitoring and control (computing) system must do.

   We have thus, in an engineering way, shown how to relate formal textual, in
this case RSL descriptions, to likewise formal, but now diagrammatic prescriptions. A formal, scientifically well-founded relationship between the Petri net
prescription and the RSL description requires more research before it can be
soundly presented. This kind of research, of "integrating formal techniques",
is currently a rich field of study.[3]

12.4 Coloured Petri Nets (CPNs)

This section is structured as follows: First, in Sect. 12.4.1 we explain, informally, the syntax and semantics of coloured Petri nets (CPNs). Then, in
Sect. 12.4.2 we present some typical examples. In Sect. 12.4.3 we develop a
model of the syntax and semantics of CPNs, in RSL. In Sect. 12.4.4 we consider
timed CPNs.

12.4.1 Description

In the Petri net variants described above, tokens are indistinguishable, i.e.,
there is no way to tell one token apart from another. In this section we discuss
coloured Petri nets (CPNs), which are an extension of PTNs: A type-value
system for tokens is now introduced. The term coloured refers to the fact that
tokens are now distinguishable in that they have a *value,* called their *colour,*
which is of a particular type, called their *colour set.* A colour set may define
both simple and composite values. In a CPN each place has an associated
colour set specifying the colour set of tokens at that place. The marking of
a place is a *multiset*[4] over the colour set of the place. A transition may have
a sequence of *guard* expressions which evaluate to a Boolean value. Arrows
from places to transitions and from transitions to places are called *arcs*. Arcs
are inscribed with expressions that evaluate to a multiset over the colour set
associated with the place from which they emanate or terminate.

---

[3]— under the name: IFM: Integrating Formal Methods

[4]A multiset is an unordered collection of values, in which the same value may
appear more than once. Multisets are also known as bags. The notation $1`a+2`b+4`c$
denotes a multiset containing one a value, two b values and four c values. If the
number and reverse prime symbol are omitted, it is interpreted as a single value,
e.g., $a + 2`b$ is equivalent to $1`a + 2`b$.

Expressions may contain *variables*. A variable is typed with a colour set and may be bound to any value in that colour set. A *binding* is an assignment of colours to variables. A *binding element* is a pair (t, b) of a transition, t, and a binding, b, where b assigns a colour to each variable that appears in an arc expression of an arc emanating from or terminating at t. For a given binding a transition is *enabled* if the conjunction of its guard expressions evaluates to true, and for each arc terminating at the transition the multiset value of the arc expression may be removed from the place at which the arc emanates. A transition that is enabled under a given binding may *occur*. In that case tokens are removed from its input places and tokens are added to its output places. The colours of the tokens are determined by the value of the corresponding arc expressions.

Complex CPNs may be simplified by splitting them into several smaller nets organised in a hierarchy. The simple nets are called *pages*. A page may have several *instances* that differ only in that each has its own marking, which is independent of the markings of the other instances of the page.

A transition in a net may be elaborated as a page, such that the page specifies the detailed behaviour of the transition. In this case the transition is labelled with the letters *HS*. It is important to realise that a hierarchical net can always be converted to a nonhierarchical net specifying the same behaviour. Therefore, allowing hierarchical nets does not add to the expressibility of CPNs, but it may improve readability.

The definition of CPNs does not mandate a particular language for declarations. The most often used language for specifying colours, colour sets, functions and expressions is known as CPN ML. This language is an extension of Standard ML [359]. Here, we briefly list the additional facilities and assume the reader is familiar with Standard ML. Consult [341] for a thorough reference to CPN ML.

Table 12.2 lists the facilities available in CPN ML for declaring colour sets. A range of built-in operators are available for the simple colour sets derived from *bool*, *int*, *real* and *string*. These operators include logical operators for *bool*, arithmetic operators for *int* and *real*, standard trigonometric, logarithmic and exponential functions for *real* and concatenation, substring and conversion functions for *string*. Multisets play an important role in CPNs, so CPN ML has operators for constructing, manipulating and comparing multisets over colour sets. Multisets are constructed using the back-quote operator (`) and the multiset union operator (+). The value *empty* denotes the empty multiset.

CPN ML supports typed variables, which are local to a transition. Reference variables with global-, page- or instance-level scope are also supported.

Table 12.2. CPN ML colour set declarations

CPN ML Colour Set Declaration	RSL Equivalent
Simple Colour Sets	
color A = unit	type A = Unit
color B = bool	type B = Bool
color C = int	type C = Int
color D = real	type D = Real
color E = string	type E = Text
color F = unit with e	type F == e
color G = bool with (no, yes)	type G == no | yes †
color H = int with 10..40	type H = $\{\| i : \mathbf{Int} \bullet i \in \{ 10..40 \} \|\}$
color I = real with 0.5..1.5	type I = $\{\| r : \mathbf{Real} \bullet r \geq 0.5 \wedge r \leq 1.5 \|\}$
color J = string with "a".."z"	type J = $\{\|t:\mathbf{Text}\bullet\forall i:\mathbf{Nat}\bullet i\in\mathbf{inds}\,t\Rightarrow t(i)\geq'a'\wedge t(i)\leq'z'\|\}$
color K = string with "a".."z" and 2..4	type K = $\{\|t:\mathbf{Text}\bullet\mathbf{len}\,t\in\{2..4\}\wedge\forall i:\mathbf{Nat}\bullet i\in\mathbf{inds}\,t\Rightarrow t(i)\geq'a'\wedge t(i)\leq'z'\|\}$
color L = with red | green | blue | yellow	type L == red | green | blue | yellow
color M = index list with 2..6	type M == list2 | list3 | list4 | list5 | list6 ★
Compound Colour Sets	
color N = product A * B * C	type N = $A \times B \times C$
color O = record a:A * b:B * c:C	type O :: a : A b : B c : C
color P = list A	type P = A*
color Q = list A with 2..5	type Q = $\{\| a : A^* \bullet \mathbf{len}\,a \geq 2 \wedge \mathbf{len}\,a \leq 5 \|\}$
color R = union a + b:B + c:C	type R1 = a, R2 == b(B), R3 === c(C), R = R1 | R2 | R3
color S = subset C by Even	type S = $\{\| c : C \bullet even(c) \|\}$
color T = subset C with [1, 2, 4, 8, 16]	type T = $\{\| c : C \bullet c \in \{1, 2, 4, 8, 16\} \|\}$

†: The only effect of this colour set is to rename *false* to *no* and *true* to *yes*. Standard ML Boolean operators such as *not, andalso* and *orelse* may be applied to *no* and *yes* just as to *false* and *true*.

★: There is no proper RSL equivalent for this colour set. A value definition is probably the closest match: **type** M1 == list2 \| list3 \| list4 \| list5 \| list6 **value** M = [2 ↦ list2, 3 ↦ list3, 4 ↦ list4, 5 ↦ list5, 6 ↦ list6]

12.4.2 A CPN Example

Example 12.9 *Dining Philosophers Revisited: CPN:* We illustrate CPN by revisiting the Dining Philosophers example (Example 12.4). This time we have five dining philosophers. The CPN diagram is shown in Fig. 12.14. Because of the expressibility of CPN we need only three places compared with the 12 conditions in the CEN model. Before, we had a condition for each fork. Now, there is only one place which can be marked with a colour to indicate which of the forks are free. Similarly, the two conditions for each philosopher in the first example are translated into two shared places which are marked with a colour to indicate which philosophers are eating and which are thinking. The function $S(x)$ is introduced to provide the mapping from a philosopher to the forks he uses.   ∎

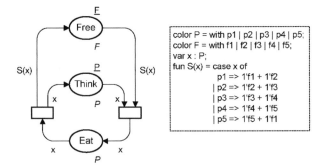

Fig. 12.14. Coloured Petri net: dining philosophers

Comment on Fig. 12.14:

The underlined characters $\underline{F}$ and $\underline{P}$ designate initial markings. $\underline{P}$ means that place Think is initially marked with all values of its colour set, i.e., $\{p_1, p_2, p_3, p_4, p_5\}$. Correspondingly for Free.

12.4.3 An RSL Model of Coloured Petri Nets

Definition. By a *coloured Petri net* we shall understand a structure as formalised in this section.   ∎

Syntax of CPNs and a Static Semantics

We first formalise a syntax and then a static semantics for CPNs.

The net inscriptions (i.e., colour set declarations, colour definitions, arc expressions and transition guards) are abstracted as sorts to avoid having to define the full syntax of CPN ML or some other inscription language.

——————— Syntax and a Static Semantics ———————

```
1     type
2        CPN = {| cpn:CPN' • wf_CPN(cpn) |}
3        CPN' = ColDcls × Guard × Preset × Postset × Marking
4        Ω = Σ-infset
5        Σ
6        ColDcls = Place ⇸ Ω
7        Guard = Trans ⇸ Pred*
8        Place
9        Trans
10       Preset = Trans ⇸ ((Place × Exp) ⇸ Nat)
11       Postset = Trans ⇸ ((Place × Exp) ⇸ Nat)
12       Marking = Place ⇸ (Σ ⇸ Nat)
13       Binding = Var ⇸ (Σ ⇸ Nat)
14       Var
15       Exp
16       Pred


17    value
18       wf_CPN: CPN' → Bool
19       wf_CPN(cf,g,pres,posts,mark) ≡
20          dom pres = dom g ∧
21          dom posts = dom g ∧
22          {p|p:Place •
23             ∃ e:Exp,t:Trans •
24                (p,e) ∈ dom pres(t) ∪ dom posts(t)} = dom cf ∧
25          (∀ t:Trans•dom pres(t)≠{}∧dom posts(t)≠{}) ∧
26          dom mark = dom cf ∧
27          (∀ p:Place•
28             p ∈ dom cf ⇒
29                (∀ c:Σ • c ∈ dom mark(p) ⇒ typeof(c) = cf(p))) ∧
30          (∀ t:Trans •
31             t ∈ dom pres ∪ dom posts ⇒
32                (∀ p:Place,e:Exp •
33                   (p,e) ∈ dom pres(t) ∪ dom posts(t)
34                      ⇒ typeof(e) = cf(p)))
35          (∀ t:Trans, p:Place, e,e':Exp •
36             ({(p,e),(p,e')}⊆pres(t)∨
37             {(p,e),(p,e')}⊆posts(t) ⇒ e=e'))
```

38	eval : Exp×Binding $\overset{\sim}{\to}$ $\Sigma \overset{}{\underset{m}{\to}}$ **Nat**
39	evalP : Pred×Binding $\overset{\sim}{\to}$ **Bool**
40	evalPl : Pred*×Binding $\overset{\sim}{\to}$ **Bool**
41	evalPl(pl,b) $\equiv$ evalP(**hd** pl,b) $\wedge$ evalPl(**tl** pl,b)
42	**pre dom** b = obs_var(pl)
43	typeof: (Exp$|\Sigma$) $\to$ Ω
44	typm: ($\Sigma \overset{}{\underset{m}{\to}}$ **Nat**) $\to$ **Bool**
45	typm(ms) $\equiv$ $\forall$ c,c':Σ•{c, c'}$\subseteq$**dom** ms $\Rightarrow$ typeof(c)=typeof(c')
46	typeof: ($\Sigma \overset{}{\underset{m}{\to}}$ **Nat**) $\overset{\sim}{\to}$ Σ
47	typeof(ms) $\equiv$ **let** c:Σ•c $\in$ **dom** ms **in** typeof(c) **end**
48	**pre** typm(ms)
49	obs_var: (Exp$|$Pred) $\to$ Var-**set**
50	obs_var: Pred* $\to$ Var-**set**
51	obs_var(pl) $\equiv$ $\bigcup$\{obs_var(p)$|$p:Pred•p $\in$ **elems** pl\}

Annotations

- (2-3) A CPN consists of a colouring declaration, a set of guards, presets, postsets and a marking.
- (4) A colour set (Ω) is a possibly infinite set of colours.
- (5) A colour (Σ) is a further undefined entity.
- (6) The colouring declaration maps places to colour sets.
- (7) For each transition there is a guard, which is a possibly empty sequence of predicates.
- (8–9) Places and transitions are further undefined entities.
- (10) Each transition has a preset, which is a multiset of pairs of places and expressions.
- (11) Each transition has a postset, which is a multiset of pairs of places and expressions.
- (12) A marking assigns a multiset of colours to each place.
- (13) A binding maps variables to multisets of colours.

- (14–16) Variables, expressions and predicates are further undefined entities.
- (17–19) A CPN is well-formed, if, among other trivial things:
  - ★ (20) the set of transitions which have a preset is identical to the set of transitions which have a guard, and
  - ★ (21) the set of transitions which have a postset is identical to the set of transitions which have a guard, and
  - ★ (22–25) the set of places which are in the preset or postset of some transition is identical to the set of those places which are associated with a colour set, and
  - ★ (26) no transition has an empty preset or postset, and
  - ★ (27) every place which is associated with a colour set also has a marking, and

★ (28–30) the marking of every place consists of a multiset over the colour set associated with the place,

★ (31–34) for every transition every arc emanating from or terminating at the transition is inscribed with an expression, which has a colour set equal to the colour set associated with the place of the arc, and

★ (35–37) two (or more) "parallel" arrows collapse into one single arrow.

• (38) There is a function which evaluates an expression under a given binding to a multiset over some colour set.

• (39) There is a function which evaluates a predicate under a given binding to a Boolean value.

• (40–42) A predicate list is evaluated as the conjunction of the values of the member predicates.

• (43) It is possible to observe the colour set (type) of an expression and from a colour.

• (44–45) A multiset of colours has matching types if any two colours in the multiset have the same type.

• (46–47) It is possible to observe the colour set from a multiset of colours if the multiset has matching types.

• (49–51) The variables of an expression, predicate or predicate list can be observed.   ∎

                                        ∎

Dynamic Semantics of Coloured Petri Nets

Auxiliary Semantic Functions

Before we turn to the dynamic aspects of CPNs, we specify four operations on multisets over colour sets: *union, distributed union, difference* and *subset*.

─────── Auxiliary Semantic Functions ───────

value
  ms_union: $(\Sigma \xrightarrow{m} \mathbf{Nat}) \times (\Sigma \xrightarrow{m} \mathbf{Nat}) \to (\Sigma \xrightarrow{m} \mathbf{Nat})$
  ms_union(msa,msb) $\equiv$
    msa**dom** msb $\cup$ msb**dom** msa $\cup$
    $[\,\mathrm{c} \mapsto \mathrm{msa(c)} + \mathrm{msb(c)} \mid \mathrm{c}{:}\Sigma \bullet \mathrm{c} \in \mathbf{dom}\ \mathrm{msa} \cap \mathbf{dom}\ \mathrm{msb}\,]$

  ms_dunion: $(\Sigma \xrightarrow{m} \mathbf{Nat})$-**set** $\to (\Sigma \xrightarrow{m} \mathbf{Nat})$
  ms_dunion(mss) $\equiv$
    if mss $= \{\}$ **then** $[\,]$
    else
      let ms$:(\Sigma \xrightarrow{m} \mathbf{Nat}) \bullet$ ms $\in$ mss **in**
        ms_union(ms, ms_dunion(mss\\{ms}))
      end
    end

  ms_diff : $(\Sigma \xrightarrow{m} \mathbf{Nat}) \times (\Sigma \xrightarrow{m} \mathbf{Nat}) \to (\Sigma \xrightarrow{m} \mathbf{Nat})$
  ms_diff(msr,msa) $\equiv$
    msa \\ **dom** msr $\cup$

$[c \mapsto \textbf{if} \ \mathrm{msa}(c) - \mathrm{msr}(c) \geq 0 \ \textbf{then} \ \mathrm{msa}(c) - \mathrm{msr}(c) \ \textbf{else} \ 0 \ \textbf{end} \ |$
$c{:}\Sigma{\cdot}c \in \textbf{dom} \ \mathrm{msr} \cap \textbf{dom} \ \mathrm{msa} \,]$

$\mathrm{ms\_subset}: (\Sigma \underset{\widetilde{m}}{\rightarrow} \textbf{Nat}) \times (\Sigma \underset{\widetilde{m}}{\rightarrow} \textbf{Nat}) \rightarrow \textbf{Bool}$
$\mathrm{ms\_subset}(\mathrm{msr},\mathrm{msa}) \equiv$
$\quad \forall \ c{:}\Sigma{\cdot}c \in \textbf{dom} \ \mathrm{msr} \Rightarrow c \in \textbf{dom} \ \mathrm{msa} \wedge \mathrm{msa}(c) \geq \mathrm{msr}(c)$

Annotations

- The union of two multisets is obtained as the union of those elements which are in only one of the multisets with the sum of those elements which are in both multisets.
- The distributed union of a set of multisets is defined recursively as the union of one member of the set with the distributed union of the rest of the set. The distributed union of the empty set is the empty multiset.

- The difference between two multisets is obtained by removing the elements of the first multiset from the second multiset. If the second multiset does not contain as many elements as should be removed, all elements are removed.
- A multiset is a subset of another multiset, if and only if for every element in the first multiset, the second multiset contains at least as many instances of that element as the first multiset. ∎

Transition Functions for Coloured Petri Nets

With the above specification of multisets of colours we are now ready to specify what it means for a transition to be *enabled* and to *occur* in a CPN.

─────────────── Transition Functions ───────────────

value
    enabled : Trans × Binding × CPN $\overset{\sim}{\rightarrow}$ **Bool**
    enabled(t, b, cpn) $\equiv$
        let (cf, gu, pres, posts, mark) = cpn **in**
           evalPl(gu(t), b) $\wedge$
           ($\forall$ p : Place •
               let ms={eval(e, b)|e:Exp•(p,e) $\in$ **dom** pres(t)}
               in ms_subset(ms_dunion(ms), mark(p))
               end)
      end
    pre let (cf, gu, pres, posts, mark) = cpn **in**
      t $\in$ **dom** gu $\wedge$
      dom b = obs_var(gu(t)) $\cup$ variables(t)(cpn) **end**

    variables: Trans $\rightarrow$ CPN $\rightarrow$ Var-set

variables(t)(_,_,pres,posts,_) ≡
  ⋃{obs_var(e)|e:Exp • ∃ p:Place • (p,e)∈ pres(t) ∪ posts(t)}

occur : Trans × Binding × CPN $\overset{\sim}{\to}$ CPN
occur(t, b, cpn) ≡
  let (cf, gu, pres, posts, mark) = cpn **in**
    (cf, gu, pres, posts,
    mark †
    [p ↦
      let ms={eval(e,b)|e:Exp•(p,e) ∈ **dom** pres(t)}
      in ms_diff(ms_dunion(ms),mark(p))
      end | p:Place•∃ e:Exp•(p,e) ∈ **dom** pres(t)] †
    [p ↦
      let ms={eval(e,b)|e:Exp•(p,e) ∈ **dom** posts(t)}
      in ms_union(ms_dunion(ms), mark(p))
      end | p:Place•∃ e:Exp•(p,e) ∈ **dom** posts(t)])
  end
  pre let (cf, gu, pres, posts, mark) = cpn **in**
    t ∈ **dom** gu ∧
    dom b = obs_var(gu(t)) ∪ variables(t)(cpn)
    ∧ enabled(t, b, cpn) **end**

Annotations

- A transition is enabled under a given binding if its guard condition evaluates to true, and for every input place the value of the corresponding arc expression is a subset of the marking of the place.

- When an enabled transition occurs, tokens are removed from its input places and tokens are added to its output places, as determined by the value of the arc expressions under the given binding. ∎

12.4.4 Timed Coloured Petri Nets

In the above description of CPNs we have neglected temporal aspects in CPNs. The CPN model of time is based on a global discrete or continuous clock. Discrete or continuous durations may be attached to transitions and arc expressions of arcs from transitions to places. Tokens may be labelled with a time-stamp indicating the earliest time the token may be removed from a place.

To indicate that tokens of a particular colour set should have timestamps, the keyword **timed** is appended to the declaration of the colour set: **color** A = **product int** * **string timed**; A *timed multi-set* is a multi-set with time-stamps: 2` (2,″monday″)@[5,16]+3` (3,″tuesday″)@[14,20,21].

Durations of transitions are specified as $@+x$ indicating that tokens added to the output places should be time-stamped with the time of the global clock plus x, where x is an integer or real value. Durations may also be specified on output arcs by appending $@+x$ to the arc expressions.

In a timed CPN a transition may occur if it is both *enabled* and *ready*, i.e., guards are fulfilled, the required tokens are available, and the time-stamps of the tokens to be removed are less than or equal to the current model time.

The execution of a timed CPN proceeds by executing all transitions that are enabled and ready. Whenever no further transitions are ready to be executed, the global clock is advanced to the next time at which one or more transitions are enabled and ready.

The model of CPNs given above could be refined to include a global clock, timestamps and durations, but we will not give such a model here.

12.5 CEN Example: Work Flow System

Example 12.10 *Flow Systems and Petri Nets:* This entire section (i.e., Sect. 12.5) is really one large example. Hence it is registered in this short, shaded paragraph, but otherwise set in ordinary text, figures and formulas! ∎

In this section we shall analyse manufacturing production projects (i.e., their planning and execution) from the point of view of what goes on in the "real world". That is, our investigation is one of examining mostly the application domain, and only secondarily the requirements to possible software support.

12.5.1 Project Planning

Project Plans

We make a distinction between project plans and projects. A project plan describes, generically, in which order, i.e., by what flow of control, the activities of a project must be carried out. (Whether they will be carried out in this way is immaterial to the problem we have decided to tackle.) A project is one of perhaps several ways in which a set of project plan-prescribed activities are indeed carried out. The project plan thus describes flow of control: in which orders activities are sequenced, etc. From a syntactic point of view, a project plan consists of nodes and directed edges. From a semantic point of view nodes denote activities, and edges denote transfer of control, i.e., flow of control. From a syntactic point of view, some edges are incident upon nodes from an "outside"; some edges emanate from nodes to an "outside"; and remaining edges connect nodes. Thus, to summarise, nodes prescribe actions (a_i), and edges prescribe two things: the conveyance of resources of a specific kind (k_j), and the flow of control from a set of activities to a next set of activities.

Figure 12.15 shows an example project plan that prescribes five activities. By a_i we here mean both the distinct labels of the nodes as well as further attributes of these nodes. By k_j we mean some description of the kinds of "things" that flow from a node, or an outside, to a next node, or the outside. These things can be materials when the project is about manufacturing, or documents when the project is about software development, or completion and status (measurement, test) reports when the project is that of a major (preventive maintenance) overhaul of an aircraft.

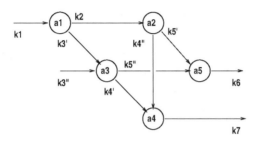

Fig. 12.15. A project plan

type
    An, Ad, K
    PP′ :: s_i:(An $\xrightarrow{m}$ K)
        × s_g:(An $\xrightarrow{m}$ Ad × (An $\xrightarrow{m}$ K))
        × s_o:(An $\xrightarrow{m}$ K)
    PP = {| pp:PP′ • wf_PP(pp) |}
value
    mk_PP(
        [a1 ↦ k1, a3 ↦ k3″],   /∗ s_i ∗/
        [a1 ↦ (ad1,[a2 ↦ k2, a3 ↦ k3′]),   /∗ s_g ∗/
         a2 ↦ (ad2,[a4 ↦ k4″, a5 ↦ k5′]),
         a3 ↦ (ad3,[a4 ↦ k4′, a5 ↦ k5″]),
         a4 ↦ (ad4,[ ]),
         a5 ↦ (ad5,[ ])],
        [a4 ↦ k7,a5 ↦ k6])   /∗ s_o ∗/

The s_i part models which nodes are initial, i.e., input nodes and which kinds of resources flow into these nodes. The s_o part models which nodes are final, i.e., output nodes and which kinds of resources flow out from these nodes. The s_g part models the graph structure of the project plan: an acyclic — something not mentioned above — graph. A project might consist of several unrelated activities. But each activity has some inputs and some outputs, whether internally or externally. All project activities are distinctly designated (named, An). All input and all output activities (i.e., nodes) are nodes of the project plan graph with no other inputs, respectively outputs, than those defined by the the s_i and the s_o parts. Ad and K denote activity and resource descriptions (i.e., types and definitions).

The expression value mk_PP(...) is that of the project plan of Figure 12.15. PP is a subtype of PP'. Well-formedness of pp:PP expresses that the "i/o" graph formed by the triple of the set of all external input nodes, the graph of nodes mapping to sets of successor nodes and the set of all external output nodes is a well-formed i/o graph.

A well-formed i/o graph has (i) all external input and (ii) output nodes are nodes of the graph (i.e., in the definition set of this graph). In addition, (iii) no external input node has any predecessor nodes in the graph, (iv) no external output nodes has any successor nodes in the graph, and the graph itself is well-defined and acyclic.

The well-definedness of a graph is that all nodes that can be reached, in one step, from a node (of the definition set **dom** g) are defined in that set, and that no node can reach itself in one or more steps. The graph mapping g defines what a step is: If a is a node defined in the graph, then g(a) is the set of nodes that can be reached in one step from a.

wf_PP: PP' → **Bool**
wf_PP(xim,im,xom) ≡
   wf_IOGraph(**dom** xim,
        [a ↦ nas |
            a:An,nas:An-**set**•a ∈ **dom** im ∧
            let (,nxt) = im(a) **in** nas = **dom** nxt **end**],
        dom xom)

wf_IOGraph: An-**set** × (An $\xrightarrow{m}$ An-**set**) × An-**set**
wf_IOGraph(ias,g,oas) ≡
(i,ii) ias ⊆ **dom** g ∧ oas ⊆ **dom** g ∧
(iii)   ∀ a:An • a ∈ ias ⇒
        ~∃ a':An • a' ∈ **dom** g ∧ a ∉ g(a')
(iv)   ∀ a:An • a ∈ oas ⇒ g(a)={} ∧
(v)   wf_Graph(g)

wf_Graph: (An $\xrightarrow{m}$ An-**set**) → **Bool**
wf_Graph(g) ≡ DefNodes(g) ∧ aCyclic(g)

DefNodes: (An $\xrightarrow{m}$ An-**set**) → **Bool**
DefNodes(g) ≡ **dom** g = ∪ **rng** g

aCyclic: (An $\xrightarrow{m}$ An-**set**) → **Bool**
aCyclic(g) ≡ ∀ a:An • a ∈ **dom** g ⇒ a ∉ Nodes(a,g)

Nodes: An×(An $\overrightarrow{m}$ An-set) $\overset{\sim}{\rightarrow}$ An-set
Nodes(a,g) ≡
  let as = g(a)∪{a′ | a′,a″:An•a″ ∈ as∧a′isin g(a″)} **in** as **end**
  pre a ∈ **dom** g

The function Nodes recursively gather the nodes, as, that can be reached from the node a in graph g in one or more steps. The recursion is well-founded: It starts with the set of successor nodes of a in g (which might be empty, and recursion stops), and goes on to gather successor nodes of those nodes already gathered in as. When no more nodes can be gathered — figuratively speaking, when a next recursion yields only nodes already in as — recursion stops. That is, a minimum fixed point has been computed. So we here assumed a minimum fixed point semantics of such recursive equations as defining as.[5]

Project Plan Construction

We distinguish between two kinds of project plan information: the structure of the input/output graph and its content. The structure has to do solely with nodes and edges and the labelling of nodes. The content has to do solely with attributes (descriptions) to be attached to nodes and edges. The below items cover both.

  Project plans can be initialised: A project plan name is all that is provided. The project plan (i.e., the input/output graph) is initialised to empty. Activity descriptions (i.e., nodes and their attributes) can be inserted, [re]defined and deleted. Flow of control (i.e., edges and their attributes) can be inserted, [re]prescribed and removed. These project plan editions can be thought of as describing domain properties or prescribing requirements. In any case project plans are programmable active dynamic components.

type
  PPn
  PPS = PPn $\overrightarrow{m}$ PP
  Cmd == mk_initPP(ppn:PPn)
    | mk_newAct(an:An,ad:Ad) | mk_oldAct(an:An,ad:Ad) | ...
    | mk_newCtl(en:En,k:K) | mk_oldCtl(en:En,k:K) | ...
value
  Int_Cmd: Cmd → PPS $\overset{\sim}{\rightarrow}$ PPS

PPS models a project plan repository (a file cabinet full of plans, as in the domain description, or a database of such, as in a requirements prescription). Cmd models our scribblings when, with paper and pencil we draw and annotate project plans, as in the domain, or a set of update commands that

---

[5]Please note, however, that RSL does not have a minimum fixed point, but an all fixed point semantics.

can be issued against such a database, as in requirements. The semantic function expresses that the project planning system (PPS) is a dynamic active programmable one.

The node attributes, ad:Ad, may contain a rich variety of components, structured in some schematic way or another. We list some example of ad:Ad attributes.

- A description of the operation to be performed at the node, i.e., the action, together with its type (also called signature): from which predecessor nodes does it receive input values to the operation, of which type and in which quantities.
- Which kind of other, the production resources, may be needed in order to carry out the operation: people (how many and with which skill qualifications), equipment (machinery, etc.).
- A further example: what is the expected duration of the operation (τ time units $\pm\delta$ time units, where $\delta \ll \tau$).
- What might be an earliest start time of the operation (say relative to project start time), and a latest such start time, and what might be the earliest, respectively latest finish time (etc.).
- What is the (expected and/or actual) cost per time unit, or total cost of carrying out the operation.
- A final example: which are the reporting requirements: Must notification of readiness to commence (for example, arrival of all input) be given and to whom, notification of progress (or just recording thereof) and completion of activity, notification of unexpected events, including failures.
- And so on.

12.5.2 Project Activities

The following two sections present an analysis of the intended semantics of project plans.

Project Flow of Control: "Waves" and Traces

Project plans are "programs" that denote projects. Activities take time. Once an activity has finished, it "flows" [49, 143–145] the produced resources (materials, products) to an outside or provides these as input to next activities, thereby passing flow of control toward those next activities. An activity can, at the earliest, be commenced, i.e., initiated, once flow of control resides on all input edges. This is a clear restriction of the kind of meaning we attach to project plans. If we wished to let two syntactically sequenced nodes stand for possibly overlapped, or overlappable activities, then we would advise another kind of graph, with perhaps more than one kind of node and one kind of edge. But we would basically describe those other graphs as we describe the present proposal: informally and formally. Once initiated flow of control passes from the incident edges to the activity. A project plan may thus give rise to flow of control residing across many edges or in many nodes such that no two edges or nodes of a flow of control are on a path between any two activities or edges, and such that the flow of control captures all paths from any in-edge to any out-edge.

We define a few technical terms: *Priming:* When a node activity has completed it places the results of this activity (simultaneously) on each emanating edge, thereby priming all the edges. *Firing:* A node activity can be fired, i.e., starts at the earliest when all edges incident upon it are primed. Whether it actually fires is subject to a nondeterministic choice. For the time being we assume that that choice is internal to the node. Later we can refer to that choice externally, that is, to a project monitoring and control system.

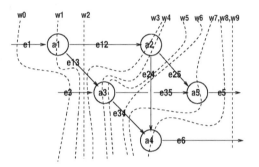

Fig. 12.16. A project trace: $w_0 - w_9$

Figure 12.16 shows an example "execution" of a project plan. Each dashed curve, a "wave", w_t, stands for a point in time. At time $t = 5$ (w_5) the project activities reside at node a_3 and on edges from a_2 to a_4 and a_2 to a_5. The transition from time $t = 5$ to $t = 6$ results in no activities in any node. In transiting from (sometime after) time $t = 6$ to (possibly sometime before) time $t = 7$ an input takes place of "things" to node a_5 from nodes a_2 and a_3 (and the two corresponding edges are preempted; a firing or transition has taken place). Execution around this point in time could have seen a transition that also fired node a_4 (simultaneously with that of node a_5). Thus there are many traces for any one graph. For the graph of Fig. 12.17 we have four example traces as shown in Fig. 12.18.

We have not shown, but could show, several successive waves covering the same set of edges and nodes. We explain this as follows: Since activities in a node take time that would be fine wrt. just the nodes. Since flow of control transitions, in general, depend on the availability, i.e., also the nonavailability, of production resources that actually carry out the activities of a node, projects will, in general, have to be prepared for what appears to be "waiting" time along edges.

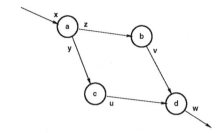

Fig. 12.17. Production plan

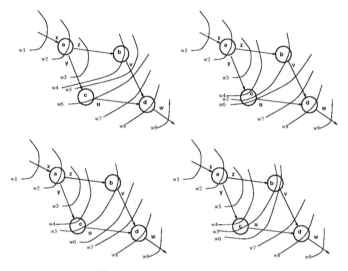

Fig. 12.18. Production traces

Theoretically speaking an edge does not, in and by itself, incur time consumption, but since firing a node can only take place when all edges incident upon it are primed, it may so appear as if time is "consumed" by an edge.

Let En stand for edge names (i.e., names of possible locus of one flow of control), made up in either of three ways from relevant activity names: input, infix (graph internal) and output. We use the following abbreviations: FoC, flow of control; PT, project trace and PPD, project plan denotation.

type
      En == mk_i(i:An) | mk_g(fn:An,tn:An) | mk_o(o:An)
      FoC = (An|En)-**set**
      PT = FoC*
      PPD = PT-**set**

Figure 12.16 shows the following project trace:

⟨{e1,e3},{a1,e3},{e12,e13,e3},{a2,e13,e3},{a2,a3},{e24,e25,a3},
{e24,e25,e34,e35},{e24,a5,e34},{a4,e5},{e5,e6}⟩

Many other project traces are possible. We chose not to show any repetitions of successive waves (project execution states). We leave to the reader to pencil a few alternatives onto Fig. 12.16.

Project Plan "Execution"

Given a project plan we can analyse it, and we can set it in motion! We will here only show the latter. We elaborate on the above: Given a project planning system, i.e., a collection of named project plans, and given a project plan name, we can initiate a project. For the time being we omit supplying the initial resources required to satisfy flow of control material needs. What this means will be explained later, but it essentially means that we can start the project, but no initial nodes will have anything to do, and will not fire since no input material is being provided. We model a project as a set of processes, one activity process for each node, an in-edge (input flow of control) process for each complete set of edges into a node, and an out-edge (output flow of control) process for each complete set of edges from a node of a project plan. Each in-edge process gathers input from a number of predecessor activities. Once all have been gathered, the sum total of input (material, documents, or other) is delivered to 'its' node process. (By *'its' node process* we mean the node [activity process] of the triple: in-edge, node and out-edge processes.) Each initial node in-edge gathers its sole input from an outside activity node which is not defined, i.e., which is not part of the project plan as we have so far defined it. Each node process accepts such input from its in-edge process, processes the input, and delivers the result to its out-edge process. Each out-edge process accepts input from 'its' activity process and then distributes it to a number of successor activity nodes' in-edge processes.

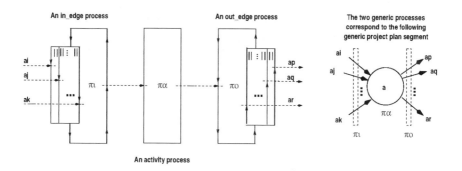

Fig. 12.19. Generic flows of control and activities

Figure 12.19 shows what was implicit in the narrative above: that flows of control and activities can be modelled by generic processes. We show only the interior edge processes and related activities.

For the project plan of Fig. 12.15, also shown to the left in Fig. 12.20, we get the configuration of in- and out-edge processes and of activity processes as shown to the right in Fig. 12.20.

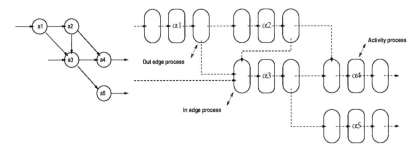

| Abstract Project Plan | In–edge, Activity and Out–edge Process Diagram |

Fig. 12.20. An instantiated process diagram

For each activity process there are two channels: one from its in-edge process and another to its out-edge process. For each distinct (node-to-node) edge in the project plan (graph) there is a distinct channel from an out-edge process to an in-edge process.

Tables **CM**, modelled as a maps, record some unique allocation of channels by indexes into collections of channels. No two recordings of channel indexes are the same, i.e., all (channels) are distinct. Tables **CM** record resource origins: "such-and-such" nodes deliver "such-and-such" resources. Functions O model activity input/output functions: Activities take resources and deliver resources (having machined them, or assembled and/or disassembled them, having augmented them, or otherwise). From the rm:RM's the activity is able to see the identity of the source activities which provide it with input. Similarly, the result resources are marked (or labelled) as to where they should be sent.

type
    Ca, Ce, R
    CM′ :: xim:(An $\overrightarrow{m}$ Ce) /* in-edge in channel index */
        im:(An $\overrightarrow{m}$ ((Ca×Ca) × (An $\overrightarrow{m}$ Ce)))
        xom:(An $\overrightarrow{m}$ Ce) /* out-edge out channel index */
    CM = {| cm:CM′ • wf_CM(cm) |}
    RM = An $\overrightarrow{m}$ R
    O = RM → RM
value

obs_K: R → K

To edges correspond a set of edge channels and their indexes, Ce; to nodes correspond a set of node (input and output) channels and their indexes. Edge channels carry (i.e., communicate) value pairs (i.e., values): the identity a:An of the source node of its other component, the resource value r:R of kind (type and quantity) k:K. Node input and output channels carry aggregations (here modelled as maps) of such pairings, rm:RM.

Looked at in isolation, channel index maps, cm:CM, must satisfy the index uniqueness criterion and otherwise be well-structured as (i.e., wrt.) an input/output graph — since it must fit, "hand-in-glove", with a project plan input/output graph.

value
    wf_CM: CM' → **Bool**
    wf_CM(xim,im,xom) ≡
        wf_IOGraph(**dom** xim,
            [a ↦ nas | a:An,nas:An-**set** • a ∈ **dom** im ∧
                    let (_,nxt) = im(a) **in** nas = **dom** nxt **end**],
                dom xom) ∧
    let cs = ⋃ { {c,c',cr,cd,co} ∪ **rng** nxt
            | a:An,c,c':Ca,nxt:(A $\overrightarrow{m}$ C) •
                    a ∈ **dom** im ∧ ((c,c'),nxt) = im(a) } **in**
    card cs = 2 ∗ **card dom** im + noe(xim,im,xom) **end**

    noe: CM' → **Nat**
    noe(xim,im,xom) ≡
        card (**dom** xim ∪ **dom** xom)
        + { **card as**
            | a:An • a ∈ **dom** im ∧
                let (,acm) = im(a) **in as** = **dom** acm **end** }
        /∗ + is a distributive sum operator ∗/

The number of distinct channel indexes is calculable as follows: There will be two channels per node and one per edge. Among the edges we also have the external input and output edges.

So we collect in cs a set of all the nonexternal channels and compare its cardinality to the what it should be based on the number of nodes and edges. If the values are equal, then all channel indexes are distinct.

Please refer to Fig. 12.21. Given a node label (a:An) and given an appropriate cm:CM one can identify, Cxi, the in-edge process input channel index for a, with a designating an input node; Cie, the internal out-edge process to internal in-edge process channel for for a, with a designating an internal node with successor node a'; and Cxo, the out-edge process output channel index for a, with a designating an output node. Cai and Cao yields activity a input, respectively output, channels.

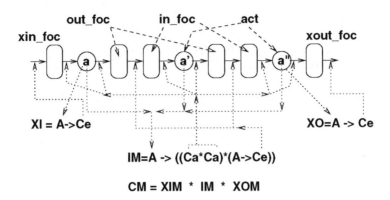

Fig. 12.21. A channel allocation

channel ke[i:Ce] (An × K), ka[i:Ca] RM

value
    /* external input flow of control in-edge channel */
    Cxi: An → CM → Ce, Cxi(a)(xim,,) ≡ xim(a)

    /* flow of control infix-edge channel */
    Cie: An×An → CM → Ce
    Cie(a,a')(,im,) ≡ **let** (,imm) = im(a) **in let** ce = iim(a) **in** ce **end end**

    /* activity in channel */
    Cai: An → CM → Ca, Cai(a)(,im,) ≡ **let** ((ci,,),) = im(a) **in** ci **end**

    /* activity out channel */
    Cao: An → CM → Ca, Cao(a)(,im,) ≡ **let** ((,co,),) = im(a) **in** co **end**

    /* external output flow of control out channel */
    Cxo: An → CM → Ce, Cxo(a)(,,xom) ≡ xom(a)

Note: The specification of **in** and **out** channels in the xin_foc, in_foc, act, out_foc and xout_foc signatures is not proper RSL [130]. Instead we use an ad hoc "shorthand" as follows:

- In the function (i.e., process) signature we not only give the type of function (i.e., process) parameters, but also the generic name of the parameter, viz.: a:An, sas:An-**set**, etc.
- Then we use this parameter name to calculate the specific index of the **in** and **out** channels defined elsewhere in the signature.

The above "improvisation" can be properly expressed in RSL by suitable use of parameterised schemes and object arrays.

Any input edge flow of control process of an activity a maintains a variable, initialised to "empty", in which is collected the output from predecessor activities, designated by the set of names of these (pas), i.e., from predecessor output edge flow of control processes. Once all predecessor activity results have been collected the accumulated result is provided as input to the activity.

Technically this is modelled in terms of parallel comprehension.

in_foc: pas:An-**set**×a:An×CM
      → **in** {ke[Cie(a′,a)(cm)]|a′:**as**} **out** ka[Cai(a)(cm)] **Unit**
in_foc(pas,a) ≡
  (**variable** rm:RM := [ ];
  ‖ {**let** r=ke[Cie(a′,a)(cm)]? **in**
      rm:=rm ∪ [a′↦r] **end**|a′:An•a′ ∈ pas};
  ka[Cai(a)(cm)]!rm)

Any output edge flow of control process parallel distributes to all its successor activities, designated by the set of names of these (sas), the result of ('its') activity a operation.

out_foc: a:An×sas:An-**set**×CM
      → **in** ka[Cao(a)(cm)] **out** {ke[Cie(a,a′)(cm)]|a′:sas} **Unit**
out_foc(a,sas) ≡
  let rm = ka[Cao(a)(cm)]? **in**
  ‖ {**let** r=rm(a′) **in**
      ke[Cie(a′,a)(cm)]!r **end**|a′:An•a′ ∈ sas} **end**

Any activity process collects input from its in-edge process, applies the activity operation, o:O, to the input, and outputs the operation result to its out-edge process.

act: o:O×a:An×CM → **in** ka[Cai(a)(cm)] **out** ka[Cao(a)(cm)] **Unit**
act(o,a,**as**) ≡ ka[Cao(a)(cm)]!o(ka[Cai(a)(cm)]?)

External input and output edge processes are special:

value
  xin_foc: An → CM → **Unit**
  xin_foc(a)(cm) ≡ c[Cai(a)(cm)]!c[Cxi(a)]?

  xout_foc: An → CM → **Unit**
  xout_foc(a)(cm) ≡ c[Cxi(a)(cm)]!c[Cao(a)(cm)]?

12.5.3 Project Generation

Plans are to be carried out. The denotation of a plan, which is a syntactic entity, is a possibly infinite set of projects, i.e., a possibly infinite set of traces.

Traces are semantic entities. In this section we shall see how we "convert" from a plan to its denotation.

The denotation is embodied in the behaviour of a set of processes, i.e., of their communication along edge and node channels. So we need "convert" a project plan, pp:PP to an RSL expression. We shall first state the pp:PP to RSL "conversion", in Section 12.5.3. Then, in Section 12.5.3, an abstract algorithm for assigning channel indexes to node and edge processes.

Process Generation

Project processes are multidimensional graphs.

Given a project plan, pp:PP, we can express a comprehension of the project (process) of all the processes. That is, a project plan, pp:PP, can be considered a program, i.e., "a piece of syntax", in the form of a data structure. Given the informal and formal expression of the semantics of each node and its input/output edges, a translation is required from the data structure, pp:PP, into RSL text. We do not express the translation in the form of a compiling algorithm from pp:PP into abstract RSL text, but in the form of the concrete text. You may thus consider project as being an interpreter: It takes the project plan data structure (i.e., syntax) and expresses the interpretation in the form of a comprehended RSL process expression.

gCM(xi,g,xo) generates a pair of channels for each node in g, and one channel for each internal (infix) and each external (in or out) edge and structures these into a cm:CM.

value
    cm:CM ≡ gCM(pp),

    project: PP → **Unit**
    project(xi,g,xo) ≡
        || {xin_foc(a)(cm)
            | a:An • a ∈ **dom** xi}
        || (||{in_foc(pas,a)(cm)
            | a:An•a ∈ **dom** g ∧
                pas={a'|a':A•a' ∈ **dom** g ∧
                    let (,m)=g(a') **in** a ∈ **dom** m **end**}})
        || (||{act(o,a)(cm)
            | a:An•aisin **dom** g ∧
                    let (o',)=g(a) **in** o=o' **end**})
        || (||{out_foc(a,sas)(cm)
            | a:An•a ∈ **dom** g ∧
                    let (,m)=g(a) **in** sas=**dom** m **end**})
        || (||{xout_foc(a)(cm)
            | a:An•a ∈ **dom** xo})

The above generates, based on a project plan, a set of in and out flow of control edge and activity processes, and starts these.

Channel Allocation

The channel index generator function is now defined.

Let us first recall the syntax of project plans pp:PP and the structure of the cm:CM channel allocations:

type
    A, K
    PP′ :: (An $\overrightarrow{m}$ K)
        × (An $\overrightarrow{m}$ Ad × (An $\overrightarrow{m}$ K))
        × (An $\overrightarrow{m}$ K)
    PP = {| pp:PP′ • wf_PP(pp) |}
    Ce, Ca
    CM′ :: xim:(An $\overrightarrow{m}$ Ce) /* in-edge in channel index */
        im:(An $\overrightarrow{m}$ ((Ca×Ca) × (An $\overrightarrow{m}$ Ce)))
        xom:(An $\overrightarrow{m}$ Ce) /* out-edge out channel index */
    CM = {| cm:CM′ • wf_CM(cm) |}

Ce and Ca are index sets. Each index indexes a channel in an appropriate object array of channels.

object
    channel ke[i:Ce]:(An×R), ka[i:Ca]:RM

From a pp:PP a "link_load_and_go-time" channel index generator process gen generates an appropriate cm:CM. gCM "traverses" the pp:PP data structure. For each distinct node and each distinct edge gCM invokes appropriate gCs, five times, respectively once, by accepting input from them via "compile-time" channels cke, cka.

object
    channel cke:Ce, cka:Ca, chs:{**stop**}

value
    gen: PP → CM **Unit**, gen() ≡ gCM(pp) || gCa() || gCe()

    gcm: PP → **in** cke,cka **out** chs CM **Unit**
    gCM(i,g,o) ≡
      let cm =
        ([a ↦ cke? | a:An • a ∈ **dom** i],
         [a ↦ ((cka?,cka?),
              (**let** (,m) = g(a) **in**
               [a′ ↦ cke? | a′:An • a′ ∈ **dom** m] **end**)

```
                | a:An • a ∈ dom g)],
          [a ↦ cke? | a:An • a ∈ dom o]) in
     (chs!stop||chs!stop);
     cm end
```

The generation of channel indexes is left to two gCν processes, one for $\nu = a$, and one for $\nu = e$. As long as the gCM process requests generation of indexes it does so. As soon as the gCM process signals that all necessary indexes have been generated they stop. We show just the generic such process. The reader is asked to edit the below process into five similar processes each with their syntactic value (e or a) for ν.

```
gC𝜈: Unit → out ck𝜈 in ck𝜈 Unit
gC𝜈() ≡
    variable cs𝜈:C𝜈-set := {}; loop:Bool := true;
    (while loop do
        let c𝜈:C𝜈•c𝜈 ∉ cs𝜈 in
        cs𝜈:=cs𝜈 ∪{c𝜈};
        ck𝜈!c𝜈 end
    end)
    ⌷
    (chs?; loop := false)
```

12.6 CPN and RSL Examples: Superscalar Processor

In this section we present two models of the MIPS R10000 superscalar processor [549]. One model is specified as a CPN, while the other is specified in RSL. The aim here is to compare the two styles of models rather than to give a complete model. The CPN model is closely based on a model by Burns et al. [67].

12.6.1 Description

The description of this section is common to Examples 12.11 and 12.12.

The R10000 is a 64-bit RISC microprocessor implementing the MIPS 4 instruction set. The processor fetches and decodes four instructions per cycle and employs branch prediction. The processor has five fully pipelined execution units: one load/store unit, two 64-bit integer ALUs, one 64-bit IEEE 754-1985 floating point adder and one 64-bit floating point multiplier. The entire pipeline has seven stages. The R10000 has 33 64-bit logical integer registers and 32 64-bit logical floating point registers.

Instructions are issued and executed out of order which may lead to data hazards. Data hazards arise when two instructions reference the same register.

If these instructions are executed out of order, the meaning of the program may be altered. To avoid data hazards the processor analyses dependencies among instructions and stalls instructions when there is a read-after-write (RAW), write-after-read (WAR) or write-after-write (WAW) dependency.

When a conditional jump instruction is encountered, the processor attempts to predict the direction of the jump before the condition is evaluated. The prediction algorithm simply assumes the branch will go in the same direction as it did the last time it was evaluated. If it has not been evaluated before, it is assumed that no branch occurs.

Subsequent instructions are fetched from the predicted direction and executed speculatively. When the value of the condition is later evaluated, it is checked whether the branch prediction was correct. If the prediction was incorrect, instructions following the jump are cleared from the pipeline and new instructions are fetched from the other direction of the jump. Data evaluated by instructions following a predicted branch is only written back to registers when the prediction has been confirmed. The R10000 may execute speculatively with up to four unconfirmed branches at a time.

The MIPS instruction set uses three operand instructions, i.e., all arithmetic instructions take three arguments: two source registers and one destination register. The integer ALUs have a dual-stage pipeline, so they can operate on two instructions at a time. The floating point units have a four-stage pipeline. The address unit has a three-stage pipeline.

12.6.2 Coloured Petri Net Model

Example 12.11 *Super Scalar Processor; Petri Net:* The example is large, six pages, so we leave it unshaded. We end it with a shaded paragraph. ∎

Figure 12.22 shows the CPN model of the R10000 microprocessor. The accompanying colour set declarations and function definitions are given below. We consider a model with five types of instructions: INT for integer operations to be handled by one of the two ALUs, FPADD for floating point addition, FPMULT for floating point multiplication, LS for load/store operations handled by the load/store unit and BRA for conditional jump.

The model only represents the control part of the processor. Thus we cannot from the model infer the value of a given register at a particular place in the execution. Since the behaviour of jumps depends on values evaluated in the registers, we need some way to decide which instruction should be executed after a conditional jump. We choose to let this be a nondeterministic choice with an equal probablility of branching and continuing.

The model is divided into six phases: instruction fetch, decoding, issue, execution, writeback and retire.

In the fetch phase, instructions are loaded from memory (represented by the place *In*) one at a time. With each instruction loaded the program counter

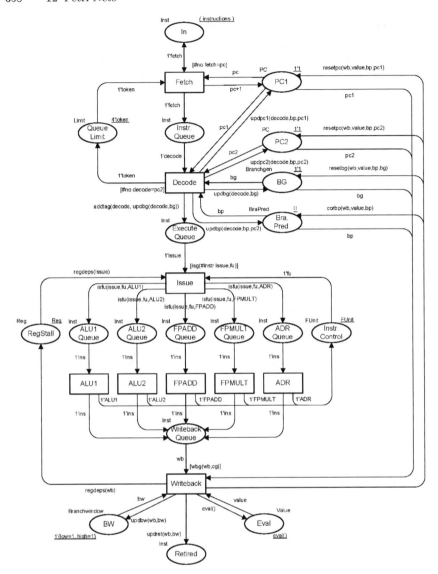

Fig. 12.22. Simplified CPN model of the superscalar microprocessor MIPS R10000

(*PC1*) is incremented by one. Instructions are buffered in the instruction queue (*Instr. Queue*) which may hold up to four instructions (this limit is enforced using the place *Queue Limit*).

In the decode phase, the instructions are labelled with a branch generation number. The branch generation number is incremented each time a conditional jump instruction is decoded and is used to ensure that instructions which depend on unconfirmed branch predictions are not written back to registers before the predictions have been confirmed. The program counter *PC2* is used to ensure instructions are decoded in order. The place *BP* holds a branch prediction table, which records the direction of each of the previously evaluated branches. If a branch instruction is decoded, the program counters are updated to the address the branch is predicted to go to.

In the issue phase, instructions are issued to one of the five execution units. Instructions are only issued if they have no conflicting register dependencies with any of the currently executing instructions and if the required execution unit is available. Instructions may be issued out of order when some instructions are stalled.

In the execution phase, instructions are evaluated simultaneously in the five execution units and the results are stored temporarily.

In the writeback phase, the place *BW* records the window for confirmed branch predictions. The lower bound is used to discard instructions that have been evaluated under an erroneous prediction, while the upper bound is used to stall instructions that depend on unconfirmed predictions. When jump instructions pass the writeback phase, the branch prediction table is updated to reflect the actual direction taken by the jump. If the branch prediction is confirmed, the upper bound of the branch window is incremented. If the prediction is found to be erroneous, the lower and upper bound of the branch window are increased to the current branch generation plus one. This ensures that instructions depending on the erroneous prediction will be discarded once they reach the writeback phase. Also, the program counters are changed to the actual target address of the jump. The place *Eval* is used to simulate the evaluation of conditions by randomly producing either the value true or false.

color

Line	= int ;
PC	= int ;
Branchgen	= int ;
Branchwindow	= **record** low : int * high : int ;
Value	= bool;
InstType	= **with** INT | ADD | MULT | LS | BRA;
Inst	= **record**
	no : Line *
	instr : InstType *
	sou1 : Reg *
	sou2 : Reg *
	tar : RegLine *
	branchgen : Branchgen;
IReg	= **index** ireg **with** 1..33;
FReg	= **index** freg **with** 1..32;
Reg	= **union** ir : IReg + fr : FReg;
RegLine	= **union** reg : Reg + line : Line;
BraPredElem	= **record**
	no : Line *
	jmp : Line;

```
BraPred       = list BraPredElem;
FUnit         = with ALU1 | ALU2 | FPADD | FPMULT | ADR;
Limit         = with token;
```

The colour set definitions are fairly straightforward. Line numbers (i.e., addresses), program counters and branch generations are all integers. The branch window is a record with an upper and a lower bound. The instruction type is one of the five options. An instruction is characterised by a line number, an instruction type, two source and one target register and a branch generation. For load/store and branch instructions, the two source registers are not used. The branch generation is not initially specified, but is added in the decode phase. There are 33 integer registers and 32 floating point registers, each identified by an indexed identifier (e.g., ireg(10) or freq(32)). A register may be either an integer register or a floating point register. For load/store and branch instructions, the target field contains an address rather than a register, hence the colour set *RegLine*. The branch prediction table is a list of records with the line number of the branch instruction and the line number of the instruction most recently jumped to.

```
(* lookup : Line * BraPred → Line *)
lookup(no, bp) =
   if bp=[] then 0 else
   if #no (hd bp) =no then #jmp (hd bp) else lookup(no, tl bp)


(* modbp : Inst * Line * BraPred → BraPred *)
modbp(inst, a, bp) = if #instr inst=BRA then
                        if bp=[] then [{no=#no inst, jmp=a}] else
                           if #no (hd bp)=#no inst
                           then {no=#no inst, jmp=a} :: (tl bp)
                           else (hd bp) :: modbp(inst, a, tl bp)
                     else bp


(* evaljmp : Inst * bool → Line *)
evaljmp(inst, tr) = if tr then #line (#tar inst) else (#no inst)+1


(* updpc1 : Inst * BraPred * PC → PC *)
updpc1(inst, bp, pc1) = if #instr inst=BRA then
                           let val a =lookup(#no inst, bp) in
                              if a<>0 then a else pc1+1
                           end
                        else pc1


(* updpc2 : Inst * BraPred * PC → PC *)
updpc2(inst, bp, pc2) = if #instr inst=BRA then
                           let val a =lookup(#no inst, bp) in
                              if a<>0 then a else pc2+1
                           end
                        else pc2+1
```

```
(* updbg : Inst * Branchgen → Branchgen *)
updbg(inst, bg) = if #instr inst=BRA then bg+1 else bg

(* updbp : Inst * BraPred * Line → BraPred *)
updbp(inst, bp, pc) = if lookup(#no inst, bp) =0
                          then modbp(inst, pc+1, bp)
                          else bp

(* addtag : Inst * BraStack → Inst *)
addtag(inst, bg) = { no=#no inst,
                      instr =#instr inst,
                      sou1=#sou1 inst,
                      sou2=#sou2 inst,
                      tar=#tar inst,
                      branchgen=bg }

(* isg  : InstType * FUnit → bool *)
isg (instt , fu) = case instt of
                  BRA    ⇒ fu=ALU1 orelse fu=ALU2
                | LS     ⇒ fu=ADR
                | MULT   ⇒ fu=FPMULT
                | ADD    ⇒ fu=FPADD
                | INT    ⇒ fu=ALU1 orelse fu=ALU2

(* regdeps : Inst → Reg *)
regdeps(inst) =
  case #instr inst of
      BRA     ⇒ empty
    | LS      ⇒ #reg (#tar inst)
    | MULT    ⇒ 1'(#sou1 inst) +1'(#sou2 inst) +1'(#reg (#tar inst))
    | ADD     ⇒ 1'(#sou1 inst) +1'(#sou2 inst) +1'(#reg (#tar inst))
    | INT     ⇒ 1'(#sou1 inst) +1'(#sou2 inst) +1'(#reg (#tar inst))

(* isfu  : Inst * FUnit * FUnit → Inst *)
isfu (inst , fu, fud) = if fu=fud then inst else empty

(* wbg : Inst * Branchgen → bool *)
wbg(inst, bw) =(#instr inst=BRA andalso #branchgen inst≤(#high bw)+1)
              orelse #branchgen inst≤#high bw

(* eval : unit → bool *)
eval () = Random.rnd() <0.5

(* resetpc : Inst * Value * BraPred * PC → PC *)
resetpc(inst , value, bp, pc) =
        if #instr inst=BRA then
            let jt =evaljmp(inst,value) in
                if jt=lookup(#no inst, bp) then pc else jt
            end
```

```
        else
            pc
```

(* corbp : Inst * Value * BraPred → BraPred *)
corbp(inst, value, bp) = if value then modbp(inst, #line (#tar inst), bp)
                          else modbp(inst, (#no inst)+1)

(* updret : Inst * Branchwindow → Inst *)
updret(inst, bw) = if #branchgen inst<#low bw then empty else inst

(* bpOK : Inst * Value * BraPred → bool *)
bpOK(inst, value, bp) = if value then #line (#tar inst)=lookup(#no inst, bp)
                         else (#no inst)+1=lookup(#no inst, bp)

(* updbw : Inst * Branchwindow * Branchgen * Value * BraPred
                                          → Branchwindow *)
updbw(inst, bw, bg, value, bp) =
        if #instr inst=BRA then
            if bpOK(inst, value, bp) then
                { low=#low bw, high=#branchgen inst }
            else
                { low=bg+1, high=bg+1 }
        else bw

(* resetbg : Inst * Value * BraPred * Branchgen → Branchgen *)
resetbg(inst, value, bp, bg) =
        if #instr inst=BRA then
            if bpOK(inst, value, bp) then
                bg
            else
                bg+1
        else bg
```

This paragraph marks the end of Example 12.11.

### 12.6.3 RSL Model: Superscalar Processor

**Example 12.12** *An RSL Model of the Superscalar Processor:* We now present an RSL model corresponding to the CPN model. Again the example is large, eight pages, so we leave it unshaded. We end it with a shaded paragraph. ∎

First, types corresponding to the colour sets of the CPN model are defined. The translation from CPN ML to RSL is straightforward. The map type in RSL is used to simplify the type for the branch prediction table. The last four types in the RSL model are needed for communication along channels or to return composite values from functions.

**scheme** SuperscalarProcessorTypes =
```

class
  type
    Line = **Int**,
    PC = **Int**,
    Branchgen = **Int**,
    Branchwindow :: low : **Int**   high : **Int**,
    InstType == INT | ADD | MULT | LS | BRA,
    Inst ==
      mk_Inst(
        no : Line,
        instr : InstType,
        sou1 : Reg,
        sou2 : Reg,
        tar : RegLine,
        branchgen : Branchgen $\leftrightarrow$ recon_bg),
    Reg' == IReg(**Nat**) | FReg(**Nat**),
    Reg =
      {| r : Reg' •
        case r **of**
          IReg(n) $\rightarrow$ n $\in$ {1 .. 33},
          FReg(n) $\rightarrow$ n $\in$ {1 .. 32}
        end |},
    RegLine = Reg | Line,
    BraPred = Line $\xrightarrow{m}$ Line,
    FUnit == ALU1 | ALU2 | FPADD | FPMULT | ADR,
    Limit = **Nat**,
    BGCom == RequestBG | UpdateBG(Branchgen),
    BPCom == RequestBP | UpdateBP(BraPred),
    InstReadyIs == Some(**Nat**, Reg-**set**, FUnit) | None,
    InstReadyWb == Some(**Nat**) | None
  end

Annotations

- Program line numbers, program counters and branch generations are integers.
- A branch window has a lower and upper bound, both integers.
- There are five types of instructions: integer instructions, floating point addition, floating point multiplication, load/store and conditional branch.
- An instruction is characterised by a line number, an instruction type, two source registers and one destination register, and a branch generation.
- A register is one of 33 integer registers or 32 floating point registers.
- The branch prediction table maps branch instruction line numbers to the line they most recently caused a jump to.
- There are five functional units: two ALUs, one floating point adder, one floating point multiplier and one address unit.

- *Limit* is used to limit the number of instructions in the instruction queue to four.
- *BGCom* describes the syntax for requesting and updating the current branch generation in the decode phase.
- *BPCom* describes the similar syntax for requesting and updating the branch prediction table.
- *InstReadyIs* and *InstReadyWb* are returned by functions indicating whether instructions are ready in the issue and writeback phases, respectively.   ∎

In moving from the CPN model to the RSL model we use the following principle: transitions become processes and places become parameters for processes. The principle is motivated by the observation that places are really buffers for values needed for computations, i.e., transitions. We aim to join places and transitions to form processes in such a way that we achieve a minimum of interprocess communication.

Figure 12.23 illustrates the processes and channels in the RSL model. Processes are represented as boxes and channels as arrows. The arrow head indicates the direction of communication. All channels are used for one-way communication only.

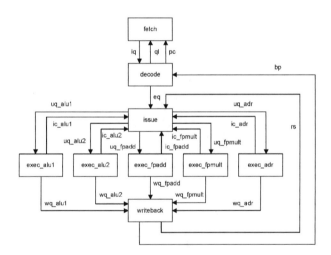

Fig. 12.23. RSL channels and processes

context: SuperscalarProcessorTypes

scheme SuperscalarProcessor =
  extend SuperscalarProcessorTypes **with**
  class
    channel
      iq,eq,uq_alu1,uq_alu2,uq_fpadd,uq_fpmult,uq_adr,wq,rq : Inst,

ql : **Unit**,
rs : Reg-**set**,
pc1, pc2 : PC,
ic : FUnit,
wb_bp : BraPred,
bp_wb : BPCom,
wb_bg : Branchgen,
bg_wb : BGCom

value

1   system : (Line $\xrightarrow{m}$ Inst) → **in any out any Unit**
        system(prg) ≡
            fetch(prg, 4, 1)
            ∥
            decode(⟨⟩, [ ], 1, 1)
            ∥
            issue(
                ⟨⟩, {r | r : Reg},
                [ALU1↦2,ALU2↦2,FPADD↦4,FPMULT↦4,ADR↦3])
            ∥
            execute()
            ∥
            writeback(⟨⟩, mk_Branchwindow(1, 1))
            ∥
            retire(⟨⟩)

2   fetch : (Line $\xrightarrow{m}$ Inst) × Limit × PC → **in** ql, pc1 **out** iq **Unit**
        fetch(prg, l, pc1) ≡
            if pc1 ∉ **dom** prg **then chaos**
            else
                (**if** l > 0 **then** iq!prg(pc1) ; fetch(prg, l − 1, pc1 + 1) **end**)
                ⌷
                (ql? ; fetch(prg, l + 1, pc1))
                ⌷
                (**let** pc1′ = pc1? **in** fetch(prg, l, pc1′) **end**)
            end

3   decode :
            Inst* × BraPred × PC × Branchgen →
                in iq, bp_wb, bg_wb **out** ql, pc1, eq, wb_bp, wb_bg **Unit**
        decode(il, bp, pc2, bg) ≡
            if no(**hd** il) ≠ pc2 **then** decode(**tl** il, bp, pc2, bg)
            else
                (**let** i = iq? **in** decode(il ⌢ ⟨i⟩, bp, pc2, bg) **end**)
                ⌷

```
(case bp_wb? of
    RequestBP → wb_bp!bp ; decode(il, bp, pc2, bg),
    UpdateBP(bp′) → decode(il, bp′, pc2, bg)
 end)
[]
(case bg_wb? of
    RequestBG → wb_bg!bg ; decode(il, bp, pc2, bg),
    UpdateBG(bg′) → decode(il, bp, pc2, bg′)
 end)
[]
(let i = hd il in
    if instr(i) = BRA
    then
        eq!recon_bg(bg + 1, i) ;
        ql!() ;
        if pc2 ∈ dom bp
        then pc1!bp(pc2);decode(tl il,bp,bp(pc2),bg+1)
        else decode(tl il,bp†[pc2↦pc2+1],pc2+1,bg+1)
        end
    else eq!recon_bg(bg,i);ql!();decode(tl il,bp,pc2+1,bg)
    end
 end)
end
```

4   issue : Inst*×Reg-set×(FUnit ↛ Nat) → in eq,rs,ic
         out uq_alu1,uq_alu2,uq_fpadd,uq_fpmult,uq_adr Unit

```
issue(il, regs, units) ≡
    (let i = eq? in issue(il ⌢ ⟨i⟩, regs, units) end)
    []
    (let r = rs? in issue(il, regs ∪ r, units) end)
    []
    (let u = ic? in issue(il, regs, units † [u ↦ units(u) + 1]) end)
    []
    (case findready_is(1, il, regs, units) of
        None → issue(il, regs, units),
        Some(n, re, fu) →
            (case fu of
                ALU1 → uq_alu1!il(n),
                ALU2 → uq_alu2!il(n),
                FPADD → uq_fpadd!il(n),
                FPMULT → uq_fpmult!il(n),
                ADR → uq_adr!il(n)
            end) ;
            issue(remove(n,il),regs\ re,units†[fu↦units(fu)−1])
    end)
```

5   execute : **Unit** → **in any out any Unit**
        execute() ≡
            exec_alu1(⟨⟩)
            ‖
            exec_alu2(⟨⟩)
            ‖
            exec_fpadd(⟨⟩)
            ‖
            exec_fpmult(⟨⟩)
            ‖
            exec_adr(⟨⟩)

6   exec_alu1 : Inst* → **in** uq_alu1 **out** wq, ic **Unit**
        exec_alu1(il) ≡
            (**let** i = uq_alu1? **in** exec_alu1(il ⌢ ⟨i⟩) **end**)
            ⏐̸
            (wq!**hd** il ; ic!ALU1 ; exec_alu1(**tl** il))

7   writeback :
        Inst* × Branchwindow →
            in wq,wb_bp,wb_bg **out** bp_wb,bg_wb,rq,pc1,pc2 **Unit**
        writeback(il, bw) ≡
            (**let** i = wq? **in** writeback(il ⌢ ⟨i⟩, bw) **end**)
            ⏐̸
            (**case** findready_wb(1, il, bw) **of**
                None → writeback(il, bw),
                Some(n) →
                    let i = il(n), valu = random() **in**
                        if branchgen(i) < low(bw)
                        then writeback(remove(n, il), bw)
                        else
                            if instr(i) = BRA
                            then /∗ Branch instruction ∗/
                                bp_wb!RequestBP ;
                                let bp = wb_bp?, target = evaljmp(i, valu) **in**
                                    if target = bp(no(i))
                                    then /∗ Branch prediction correct ∗/
                                        rq!i ;
                                        writeback(
                                            remove(n, il),
                                            mk_Branchwindow(
                                                low(bw),
                                                if high(bw) > branchgen(i)
                                                then high(bw)

```
                               else branchgen(i)
                             end))
               else  /* Branch prediction incorrect */
                  rq!i ;
                  pc1!target ;
                  pc2!target ;
                  bp_wb!UpdateBP(bp†[no(i)↦target]);
                  let bg = wb_bg? in
                     bg_wb!UpdateBG(bg + 1) ;
                     writeback(remove(n,il),
                        mk_Branchwindow(bg+1,bg+1))
                  end
               end
            end
         else  /* Nonbranch instruction */
            rq!i ; writeback(remove(n, il), bw)
         end
      end
   end
end),
```

8   retire : Inst* → **in** rq **Unit**
        retire(il) ≡ retire(il ⌢ ⟨rq?⟩)

9   findready_is :
            Int × Inst* × Reg-set × (FUnit ⇸ **Nat**) → InstReadyIs
        findready_is(j, il, rs, fu) ≡
        if il = ⟨⟩ **then** None
        else
           let i = **hd** il **in**
              case instr(i) **of**
                 INT →
                    avail(j,il,
                       {sou1(i),sou2(i),RegLine_to_Reg(tar(i))},
                       ⟨ALU1, ALU2⟩,rs,fu),
                 ADD →
                    avail(j,il,
                       {sou1(i),sou2(i),RegLine_to_Reg(tar(i))},
                       ⟨FPADD⟩,rs,fu),
                 MULT →
                    avail(j,il,
                       {sou1(i),sou2(i),RegLine_to_Reg(tar(i))},
                       ⟨FPMULT⟩,rs,fu),
                 LS →
                    avail(j,il,{RegLine_to_Reg(tar(i))},⟨ADR⟩,rs,fu),
```
```

```
                BRA →
                    avail(j, il, {}, ⟨ALU1, ALU2⟩, rs, fu)
            end
        end
    end
```

10   avail : $\text{Int} \times \text{Inst}^* \times \text{Reg-set} \times \text{FUnit}^* \times \text{Reg-set} \times (\text{FUnit} \xrightarrow{m} \text{Nat}) \rightarrow$
InstReadyIs

```
    avail(j, il, regreq, fureq, rs, fu) ≡
        if fureq = ⟨⟩
        then
            findready_is(j + 1, tl il, rs, fu)
        else
            if regreq ⊆ rs ∧ fu(hd fureq) > 0
            then Some(j, regreq, hd fureq)
            else avail(j, il, regreq, tl fureq, rs, fu)
            end
        end
```

11   findready_wb : $\text{Int} \times \text{Inst}^* \times \text{Branchwindow} \rightarrow \text{InstReadyWb}$

```
    findready_wb(j, il, bw) ≡
        if il = ⟨⟩ then None
        else
            if branchgen(hd il)≤high(bw) ∨
                (instr(hd il)= BRA∧branchgen(hd il)≤high(bw)+1)
            then Some(j) else findready_wb(j + 1, il, bw)
            end
        end
```

12   evaljmp : $\text{Inst} \times \text{Bool} \rightarrow \text{Line}$

```
    evaljmp(i, t) ≡
        if t then RegLine_to_Line(tar(i)) else no(i) + 1 end
```

13   remove : $\text{Nat} \times \text{Inst}^* \rightarrow \text{Inst}^*$

```
    remove(n, il) ≡
        if il = ⟨⟩ then ⟨⟩ else
        if n = 1
            then tl il else ⟨hd il⟩ ⌃ remove(n − 1, tl il) end
        end
```

14   random : $\text{Unit} \rightarrow \text{Bool}$
    end

Annotations

- (1) The effect of running the system with a program *prg* is the parallel composition of the six phases.
- (2) The parameters of the fetch process are the program, the number of free places in the instruction queue and the program counter. The process will either send the next instruction to the instruction queue, provided it has a free place, or receive notification that a place has been freed in the instruction queue, or receive a request to change the program counter.
- (3) The parameters of the *decode* process are the list of instructions in the instruction queue, the branch prediction table, the second program counter and the branch generation counter. *decode* will either receive an instruction from *fetch*, or receive a request to send or update the branch prediction table, or receive a request to send or update the branch generation, or decode an instruction. If a branch instruction is decoded, the branch generation is incremented and the program counters set to the predicted direction of the jump, otherwise the instruction is labeled with the current branch generation and the program counter is incremented.
- (4) The parameters of *issue* are the instructions in the execute queue, the set of unblocked registers and the free functional units. The *issue* process will either receive an instruction from *decode*, or receive notification of a register being freed, or receive notification of a functional unit being freed, or find an instruction that is ready to be issued and send it to the appropriate functional unit.
- (5) The execute process is simply the parallel composition of the five functional units. The *exec_alu1* process will either receive an instruction from *issue*, or execute an instruction, pass it to *writeback* and signal that the unit is free.
- (6) The processes for the remaining functional units are entirely analogous and are omitted.
- (7) The parameters for *writeback* are the instructions in the writeback queue and the branch window. *writeback* will either input an instruction from the execute phase, or find an instruction whose result is ready to be written back. Instructions labeled with branch generations below the lower bound of the branch window are discarded. For branch instructions, the actual target is evaluated. If the branch prediction was correct, the branch window is updated and the instruction passed to *retire*. If the branch prediction was incorrect, the program counters are set to the correct target, the branch prediction table, the branch generation and the branch window are updated.
- (8) The *retire* process records all instructions that have been fully executed.
- (9) *findready_is* finds an instruction that may be issued, or signals that no such instruction is available. An instruction can be issued when there are no data hazards or structural hazards. A data hazard arises when two instructions require the same register. A structural hazard arises when two instructions require the same functional unit.

- (10) *avail* checks whether a given instruction may be issued.
- (11) *findready_wb* finds an instruction whose result is ready to be written back, or signals that no such instruction exists.
- (12) *evaljmp* evaluates the actual target of a branch instruction.
- (13) *remove* removes the nth instruction in the instruction list.
- (14) *random* produces a random value simulating the nondeterminism of branching.

■

This paragraph marks the end of Example 12.12.

12.7 Discussion

The two models of the superscalar processor presented above describe the same behaviour using two very different notations.

Of the two models, it seems to be easiest to get an initial understanding of the CPN model. This is because the graphical notation supports a layering of understanding. One layer is the structure of the diagram viewed as a directed graph combined with the labels of places and transitions. At this layer an initial intuitive understanding of the parts of the system and the main data flow is built. The next layer adds the colour set of places to get an idea of the possible values at that place. The last layer of understanding adds arc inscriptions to get the full picture. This is essentially a top-down progression of understanding.

It is more difficult to get an initial understanding of the RSL model. This is because all the aspects of the model are mixed in the equations. This means that the layered way of understanding is not feasible. Instead, the way to understand the specification is to study each function in isolation and then build up the full picture by composition. This is essentially a bottom-up progression of understanding.

Even though the two models are in essence the same, there are some subtle differences, since the Petri net semantics is a true concurrency semantics, where two events (i.e., occurrences) may take place simultaneously. The RSL semantics, on the other hand, is an interleaved semantics, where two concurrent events are interleaved, i.e. they may occur in arbitrary order, but not simultaneously. This difference is mostly a theoretical problem.

Unlike most other graphical notations, coloured Petri nets have a well-established formal semantics and there are several tools available for verification of Petri net models. Therefore, coloured Petri nets might not be an obvious candidate for integration with a formal specification language, such as RSL. However, one could imagine replacing CPN ML with a subset of RSL as the language for inscriptions to give greater expressivity.

372 12 Petri Nets

12.8 Bibliographical Notes

The — by now — classical literature on Petri Nets is made up from the following one report [400] and seven books [238, 399, 419–421] — [238] is a three volume book on Coloured Petri Nets. The field ('Petri Nets') is very much "alive and kicking" — as is witnessed by a vast, ever growing literature and regular conferences. Cf. the following URLs [239]:

- www.daimi.au.dk/PetriNets/:
  Welcome to the Petri Net World
- www.informatik.hu-berlin.de/top/pnml/about.html:
  Petri Net XML Markup Language.
- petri-net.sourceforge.net/:
  Platform Independent Petri Net Editor (PIPE).
- pdv.cs.tu-berlin.de/~azi/petri.html:
  What Is a Petri Net?
- www.informatik.uni-hamburg.de/TGI/pnbib/:
  The Petri Nets Bibliography
- www.informatik.uni-hamburg.de/TGI/pnbib/newsletter.html:
  Petri Net Newsletter.

12.9 Exercises

Exercise 12.1 *PTN for a Reader/Writer System.* Consider a system where five processes access a common resource. Two of the processes write to the common resource, and the three other processes read from the resource. Devise a PTN model of this system, such that the following requirements are met:

- A reader can read if no writers are currently writing.
- A writer can write if no readers are currently reading and no writers are currently writing.
- A process that cannot read or write must wait until it can do so.

Exercise 12.2 *PTN for a Fair Reader/Writer System.* A simple solution to Exercise 12.1 has the problem that if readers continually arrive to read, a writer may have to wait indefinitely. This situation is called starvation. Modify the solution to Exercise 12.1 so that starvation can not occur, i.e. any process which attempts to access the common resource will eventually be granted access to the resource. Use the following strategy:

- If a reader arrives when there are writers waiting, the reader must wait until one writer has written.
- If a writer arrives when there are readers waiting, the writer must wait until all the readers have read.

Exercise 12.3 *CPN for a Fair Reader/Writer System:* Solve Exercise 12.2 using a coloured Petri net instead.

Exercise 12.4 *Petri Nets for Railway Nets:* Study the following papers: [161, 276, 277]. Suggest comparative, complementing Petri net models of railway phenomena based on CENs, PTNs and CPNs.

13

Message and Live Sequence Charts

Christian Krog Madsen is chief author of this chapter [316,317].

- The **prerequisite** for studying this chapter is that you have an all-round awareness of abstract specification (principles and techniques).
- The **aims** are to introduce the concepts of message sequence charts and of live sequence charts, and to relate these sequence charts to RSL/CSP.
- The **objective** is to enable the reader to expand the kind of phenomena and concepts that can be formally modelled using message sequence charts and live sequence charts — or, we suggest, live sequence charts in conjunction with, for example, RSL.
- The **treatment** ranges from systematic to formal.

Live sequence charts (LSC) is a graphical language introduced by Damm and Harel [89] for specifying interactions between components in a system. It is an extension of the language of message sequence charts (MSC). MSCs are frequently used in the specification of telecommunication systems and are closely related to the sequence diagrams of UML [59, 237, 382, 440]. Both the graphical and textual syntax of MSCs are standardised by the ITU in Recommendation Z.120 [227–229]. The standard gives an algebraic semantics of MSCs. LSC extends MSC by promoting conditions to first-class elements and providing notations for specifying mandatory and optional behaviour.

Reader's Guide

The description material on basic (and on high-level) MSCs in Sects. 13.1.2–13.1.3 and on LSC in Sect. 13.2.1 is intended as quick tutorials as well as for quick reference. Sect. 13.3, on the important computer science topic of *process algebra*, and Sect. 13.4, on an algebraic semantics of LSCs, are both rather involved and may seem a bit detached from the context. The reader is encouraged to refer to the example in Sect. 13.2.2 for an understanding of LSCs, and to its continuation in Sect. 13.4.3 to see how the algebraic semantics of a chart is derived using the material of Sect. 13.3.

13.1 Message Sequence Charts

13.1.1 The Issues

In this section we describe message sequence charts (MSCs). They are a graphical notation for specifying sequences of messages exchanged between behaviours.[1] We describe the components of MSCs and then provide a formalisation of the syntax in RSL. We follow the syntax requirements defined by Reniers [422, 423]. Finally, we give a trace semantics of MSCs.

Message sequence charts were first standardised by the CCITT (now ITU-T) as Recommendation Z.120 in 1992 [227]. The standard was later revised and extended in 1996 [228] and in 1999 [229]. The original standard specified the components of an MSC. The 1996 standard also specified how several MSCs (called *basic* MSCs) can be combined to form an MSC document, in which the relation between the basic MSCs is defined by a *high-level* MSC (HMSC). The most recent standard provides additional facilities for specifying the data that is passed in messages and also allows in-line expressions.

13.1.2 Basic MSCs (BMSCs)

Informal Presentation

A basic MSC (BMSC) consists of a collection of instances. An instance is an abstract entity on which events can be specified. Events are message inputs, message outputs, actions, conditions, timers, process control events and coregions. An instance is denoted by a hollow box with a vertical line extending from the bottom. The vertical line represents a time axis, where time runs from top to bottom. Each instance thus has its own time axis, and time may progress differently on two axes. Events specified on an instance are totally ordered in time. Events execute instantaneously and two events cannot take place at the same time. Events on different instances are partially ordered, since the only requirement is that message input by one instance must be preceded by the corresponding message output in another instance.

Actions are events that are local to an instance. Actions are represented by a box on the timeline with an action label inside. Actions are used to specify some computation that changes the internal state of the instance.

A *message output* represents the sending of a message to another instance or the environment.

A *message input* represents the reception of a message from another instance or the environment. For each message output to another instance there must be a matching message input.

---

[1] An alternative way of phrasing *sequences of messages exchanged between behaviours* is *events shared between two behaviours* where these events may involve the communication of information.

A *message exchange* consists of a message output and a message input. A message exchange is represented as an arrow from the timeline of the sending instance to the timeline of the receiving instance. In case of messages exchanged with the environment, the side of the diagram can be considered to be the timeline of the environment. Each arrow is labelled with a message identifier. Message exchange is asynchronous, i.e., message input is not necessarily simultaneous with message output.

Example 13.1 Figure 13.1 shows an MSC with two instances, A and B. Instance A sends the message m_1 to instance B followed by message m_2 sent to the environment. B then performs some action, a, and sends the message m_3 to A. ∎

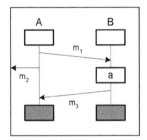

Fig. 13.1. Message and action events

Example 13.2 Figure 13.2 shows two situations that violate the partial order induced by message exchange. Thus it is an invalid MSC. Because events are totally ordered on an instance timeline, the reception of message m_1 precedes the sending of m_1. This conflicts with the requirement that message input be preceded by message output.

The exchange of messages m_2 and m_3 illustrates another situation that violates the partial order, as shown by the following informal argument. Let the partial order be denoted $\leq$ and let the input and output of message m be denoted by $in(m)$ and $out(m)$, respectively. Using the total ordering on events on an instance timeline we have:

$$in(m_3) \leq out(m_2)$$
$$in(m_2) \leq out(m_3)$$

Using the partial ordering on message events we have

$$out(m_2) \leq in(m_2)$$

Now, by transitivity of $\leq$, $in(m_3) \leq out(m_3)$, thus violating the partial ordering on message events. ∎

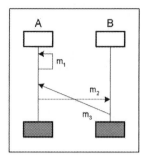

Fig. 13.2. Illegal message exchanges

Conditions describe a state that is common to a subset of instances in an MSC. Conditions in MSCs have no semantic importance and merely serve as documentation. (As we shall later see, they do have meaning in LSCs.) Conditions are represented as hexagons extending across the timelines of the instances for which the condition applies. The condition text is placed inside the hexagon.

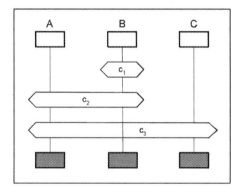

Fig. 13.3. Conditions

Example 13.3 Figure 13.3 illustrates conditions. Condition c_1 is local to instance B. Condition c_2 is a shared condition on instances A and B. Condition c_3 is a shared condition on instances A and C. Note that the timeline of B is passed through the hexagon for condition c_3 to indicate that B does not share condition c_3. ∎

There are three *timer* events: *timer set, timer reset* and *timeout*. Timers are local to an instance. The setting of a timer is represented by an hourglass symbol placed next to the instance timeline and labelled with a timer identifier. Timer reset is represented by a cross (×) linked by a horizontal line to the timeline. Timer timeout is represented by an arrow from the hourglass symbol to the timeline. Every timer reset and timeout event must be preceded by the corresponding timer set event. There is no notion of quantitative time in MSC, so timer events are purely symbolic. Extensions of MSC with time have been studied in [38, 280, 296].

Example 13.4 Figure 13.4 shows the syntax for timer events. On instance A, the timer T is set and subsequently timeout occurs. On instance B, the timer T' is set and subsequently reset. ∎

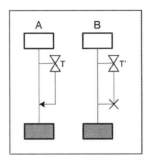

Fig. 13.4. Timer events

An instance may create a new instance, which is called *process creation*. An instance may also cause itself to terminate. This is called *process termination*. Process creation is represented by a dashed arrow from the timeline of the creating instance to a new instance symbol with associated timeline. Process termination is represented by a cross as the last symbol on the timeline of the instance that terminates.

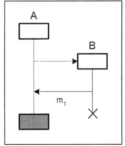

Fig. 13.5. Process creation and termination

Example 13.5 Figure 13.5 shows the creation of instance B by instance A and the subsequent termination of B. ∎

Coregions are parts of the timeline of an instance where the usual requirement of total ordering is lifted. Coregions are represented by replacing part of the fully drawn timeline with a dashed line. Within a coregion only message exchange events may be specified and these events may happen in any order, regardless of the sequence in which they are specified. Message exchanges between two instances may be ordered in one instance and unordered in the other instance.

Example 13.6 Figure 13.6 illustrates a coregion in instance B. Because of the coregion, there is no ordering on the input of messages m_1 and m_2 in instance B, so they may occur in any order.   ∎

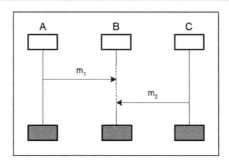

Fig. 13.6. Coregion

In order to increase the readability of complex MSCs, the standard specifies a form of hierarchical decomposition of complex diagrams into a collection of simpler diagrams. This is known as *instance decomposition*. For each decomposed instance there is a sub-MSC, which is itself an MSC. The single instance that is decomposed is represented by more than one instance in the sub-MSC. The behaviour observable by the environment of the sub-MSC should be equivalent to the observable behaviour of the decomposed instance.

Example 13.7 In Fig. 13.7 instance B is decomposed into two instances, B_1 and B_2 in the sub-MSC. The message events in which B participates are represented as message exchanges with the environment in the sub-MSC. The message m_{int} exchanged between B_1 and B_2 is internal to the decomposed instance, and is thus not visible in the main MSC.   ∎

An Example BMSC

Example 13.8 *A Basic Message Sequence Chart:* Figure 13.8 shows an example BMSC that displays most of the event types discussed above. The chart contains three instances, A, B and C. Five events are specified on instance A: message output of a message labelled *Msg1* to instance B, a local action *Act1*, a condition *Cond1* shared with B, message output of *Msg4* and message input of *Msg5*. Seven events are specified on instance B: input of message *Msg1* from A, a process creation event creating instance C, two message exchanges with C, a condition shared with A, and a coregion with two

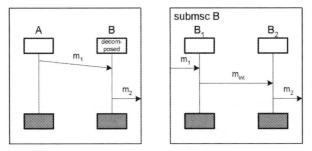

Fig. 13.7. Instance decomposition

message exchanges with A. Note that B may either receive *Msg4* and then send *Msg5*, or may send *Msg5* and then receive *Msg4*. Instance C has six events: its creation by B, the setting of a timer, two message exchanges with B, timer timeout and subsequent process termination. ∎

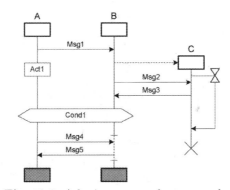

Fig. 13.8. A basic message chart example

An RSL Model of BMSC Syntax

We first formalise basic message sequence charts. We defer the discussion of well-formedness conditions to Section 13.1.6.

Definition. By a *basic message sequence chart* we shall understand a structure as formalised in this section and in Sect. 13.1.8. ∎

.

scheme BasicMessageSequenceChart =
   class
     type
       BMSC′ = BMSC_Name×InstanceSpec*×Body*,
       InstanceSpec = Inst_Name×Kind,
       Kind = Type×Kind_Name,
       Type == System|Block|Process|Service|None,
       Body = Instance|Note,
       Instance == mk_Inst(instn:Inst_Name,kind:Kind,evtl:Event*),
       Note == mk_Note(t:**Text**),
       Event =
         ActionEvent|MessageEvent|ConditionEvent|TimerEvent|
         ProcessEvent|CoregionEvent,
       ActionEvent == mk_Action(actname:Act_Name),
       MessageEvent ==
         mk_Input(inpid:MsgID,inpar:Par_Name*,inaddr:Address)|
         mk_Output(outid:MsgID,outpar:Par_Name*,outaddr:Address),
       ConditionEvent == mk_Condition(conname:Con_Name,share:Share),
       TimerEvent ==
         mk_Set(setname:TimerId,dur:Duration)|
         mk_Reset(resetname:TimerId)|
         mk_Timeout(toname:TimerId),
       ProcessEvent == mk_Create(name:Inst_Name,par:Par_Name*)|mk_Stop,
       CoregionEvent == mk_Concurrent(mess:MessageEvent*),
       MsgID ==
         mk_MsgN(mn:Msg_Name,parn:Par_Name*)|
         mk_MsgID(mid:Msg_Name,min:MsgInst_Name,parid:Par_Name*),
       Address == mk_Env|mk_InstName(name:Inst_Name),
       Share == mk_None|mk_All|mk_Shared(instl:Inst_Name*),
       TimerId ==
         mk_Tn(nametn:Timer_Name)|
         mk_Tid(nametid:Timer_Name,tin:TimerInst_Name),
       Duration == mk_None|mk_Name(name:Dur_Name),
       BMSC_Name,
       Inst_Name,
       Kind_Name,
       Act_Name,
       Par_Name,
       Con_Name,
       Timer_Name,
       TimerInst_Name,
       Dur_Name,
       Msg_Name,
       MsgInst_Name
   end

Annotations

- A BMSC has a name, a sequence of instance specifications and a sequence of body elements.
- An instance specification has an instance name and an instance kind.
- An instance kind has a type and a name.
- The type of an instance is either missing or is one of system, block, process or service.
- A body element is either an instance or a note.
- An instance has an instance name, an instance kind and a sequence of events.
- A note is a textual description or comment.
- An event is an action, message, condition, timer, process or is a coregion event.
- An action event has a name.
- A message event is either a message input or a message output. A message input is characterised by a message identifier, a possibly empty sequence of input parameters and an address identifying the sender. A message output has a message identifier, a possibly empty sequence of output parameters and an address identifying the recipient.
- A condition event has a name and an identification of the instances that share the condition.
- A timer event is the setting of a timer, the resetting of a timer or a timeout. All are characterised by a timer identifier, and, additionally, timer setting may specify a duration.
- A process event is either a process creation or a process termination. A process creation gives a name and a sequence of parameters to the new process.
- A coregion event contains a sequence of message events.
- An address is either the environment or the name of an instance.
- A condition may be local to an instance shared by all instances or shared by a subset of instances.
- A timer identifier is either a timer name, or a timer name and a timer instance name.
- A (timer-specified) duration is either unspecified or has a name.
- Names are further unspecified entities.   ▪

13.1.3 High-Level MSCs (HMSCs)

An Informal Presentation

We now extend the above definition of BMSCs to allow several BMSCs to form an MSC document. To provide the link between BMSCs the high-level message sequence chart (HMSC) is defined.

A HMSC consists of a number of nodes, each representing a BMSC, connected with arrows. One node is the start node and several nodes may be end nodes. Arrows denote vertical composition of the BMSCs they connect, i.e., the events of the origin BMSC occur first, followed by the events of the destination BMSC. Nodes may have arrows to several other nodes, indicating alternatives. In that case the origin BMSC is composed vertically with one of the alternative destination BMSCs. The graph of nodes and arrows may have loops, indicating iteration.

Nodes are represented by circles or rounded rectangles labelled with the name of the BMSC it denotes. Start nodes are indicated by an upside-down triangle (∇) with an arrow pointing to the node. End nodes are indicated by a triangle (Δ) pointed to by an arrow from the node. *Connectors* may be introduced to improve legibility. When connectors are used, each node may have at most one incoming arrow and one outgoing arrow. Connectors then serve as junctions for arrows, where one incoming arrow may split into several outgoing arrows or vice versa. Connectors are represented as small circles. The annotations of the formal model of the syntax of HMSCs provide more specific details, see below.

An Example HMSC

Example 13.9 *A High-Level Message Chart:* Figures 13.9–13.10 show a simple HMSC with three BMSCs. The chart models a client-server system, where a server offers some service, which the client can access. The start node of the HMSC is the BMSC *Init* in which the client logs on to the server and the server responds with a confirmation. Then one or more cycles of the BMSC *Transfer* follow, in which the client requests a resource and the server responds by returning that resource. Finally, the client logs off and the server closes the connection.   ■

Fig. 13.9. HMSC example, part 1 of 2

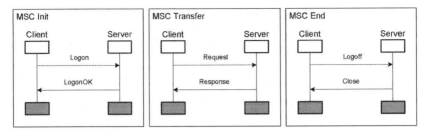

Fig. 13.10. HMSC example, part 2 of 2

13.1.4 An RSL Model of HMSC Syntax

Definition. By a *high-level message sequence chart* we shall understand a structure as formalised in this section, in Sects. 13.1.6 and 13.1.8 and as a solution to Exercise 13.3.   ∎

The formalisation of HMSCs is simple, given the formalisation of BMSCs.

context: BasicMessageSequenceChart

scheme HighLevelMessageSequenceChart =
   extend BasicMessageSequenceChart **with**
   class
     type
       HMSC′ = (BMSC_Name $\overrightarrow{m}$ BMSC)
           × (BMSC_Name $\overrightarrow{m}$ BMSC_Name-set)
           × BMSC_Name
           × BMSC_Name-set
   end

Annotations

- A high-level message sequence chart is composed of a mapping of BMSC names to BMSCs,
- a set of outgoing arrows for each BMSC,
- a start node
- and a possibly empty set of end nodes.   ∎

13.1.5 MSCs Are HMSCs

Definition. By a *message sequence chart* we shall understand a high-level message sequence chart.   ∎

13.1.6 Syntactic Well-formedness of MSCs

Now that we have defined the full syntax of MSCs we are ready to specify the requirements for a chart to be well-formed. First, we specify conditions for a BMSC to be well-formed. These conditions were derived by Reniers [423].

context: HighLevelMessageSequenceChart
scheme WellformedBMSC =
extend HighLevelMessageSequenceChart **with**
class
  type BMSC = {| b:BMSC′•wf_BMSC(b) |}

  value
  wf_BMSC:BMSC′ → **Bool**
  wf_BMSC(n,s,b) ≡
    let
    inst=instances(n,s,b),
    instnames={instn(i)|i:Instance•i ∈ **elems** inst}
    in
    /* 1 */
    (∀ j,k:**Nat**•
        j ≠ k∧{j,k}⊆**inds** inst⇒
            inst(j) ≠ inst(k)∧instn(inst(j)) ≠ instn(inst(k)))∧
    /* 2 */
    (s ≠ ⟨⟩⇒
        (∀ i:Instance•
            (i ∈ **elems** inst) ≡ ((instn(i),kind(i)) ∈ **elems** s)))∧
    /* 3 */
    ({name(a)|
      a:Address•
        ∃ i:Instance,inpid:MsgID,pl:Par_Name*•
          i ∈ **elems** inst∧a ≠ mk_Env∧
          mk_Input(inpid,pl,a) ∈ **elems** inputEvts(i)} ∪
      {name(a)|
      a:Address•
        ∃ i:Instance,inpid:MsgID,pl:Par_Name*•
          i ∈ **elems** inst∧a ≠ mk_Env∧
          mk_Input(inpid,pl,a) ∈ **elems** outputEvts(i)}⊆instnames)∧
    /* 4 */
    (∀ i:Instance•
        i ∈ **elems** inst⇒
          (∀ evt,evt′:MessageEvent•
              (evt ∈ inputEvts(i)∧evt′ ∈ inputEvts(i)∧
                inpid(evt)=inpid(evt′)∧inaddr(evt)=inaddr(evt′)⇒
                  evt=evt′)∧
              (evt ∈ outputEvts(i)∧evt′ ∈ outputEvts(i)∧
                outid(evt)=outid(evt′)∧outaddr(evt)=outaddr(evt′)⇒
                  evt=evt′)))∧
    /* 5 */

($\forall$ i:Instance•
    i $\in$ **elems** inst$\Rightarrow$
        ($\forall$ mi:MsgID,pl:Par_Name*,inaddr:Address•
            mk_Input(mi,pl,inaddr) $\in$ inputEvts(i)$\wedge$inaddr $\neq$ mk_Env$\Rightarrow$
                mk_Output(mi,pl,mk_InstName(instn(i))) $\in$
                    outputEvts(lookup(name(inaddr),b)))$\wedge$
        ($\forall$ mi:MsgID,pl:Par_Name*,outaddr:Address•
            mk_Output(mi,pl,outaddr) $\in$ outputEvts(i)$\wedge$
            outaddr $\neq$ mk_Env$\Rightarrow$
                mk_Input(mi,pl,mk_InstName(instn(i))) $\in$
                    inputEvts(lookup(name(outaddr),b))))$\wedge$
/* 6 */
$\sim$is_cyclic(
    {ss|
        ss:S$\times$S,sss:(S$\times$S)-**set**•
            ss $\in$ sss$\wedge$
            sss $\in$
                {po_inst(i,el,{}) $\cup$ po_comm(i,el)|
                i:Inst_Name,k:Kind,el:Event*•
                    mk_Inst(i,k,el) $\in$ inst}})$\wedge$
/* 7 */
($\forall$ i:Instance•
    i $\in$ **elems** inst$\Rightarrow$
        ($\forall$ c:ConditionEvent•
            c $\in$ evtl(i)$\Rightarrow$
                case share(c) **of**
                    mk_Shared(il) $\rightarrow$
                        ($\forall$ i:Inst_Name•
                            i $\in$ il$\Rightarrow$
                              ($\exists$ k:Kind,el:Event*•
                                mk_Inst(i,k,el) $\in$ b)),
                _ $\rightarrow$ **true**
                end))$\wedge$
/* 8 */
($\forall$ i:Instance•
    i $\in$ inst$\Rightarrow$
        ($\forall$ cn:Con_Name,sh:Share•
            mk_Condition(cn,sh) $\in$ evtl(i)$\Rightarrow$
            case sh **of**
                mk_None $\rightarrow$ **true**,
                mk_All $\rightarrow$
                    ($\forall$ i$'$:Instance•
                      i$'$ $\in$ inst$\Rightarrow$
                        len $\langle$c|c **in** evtl(i)•c=mk_Condition(cn,sh)$\rangle$=
                          len $\langle$c|c **in** evtl(i$'$)•
                            c=mk_Condition(cn,mk_All)$\rangle$),
                mk_Shared(il) $\rightarrow$
                    ($\forall$ i$'$:Instance•
                      i$'$ $\in$ inst$\wedge$instn(i$'$) $\in$ **elems** il$\Rightarrow$

$$\textbf{len}\ \langle c|c\ \textbf{in}\ \text{evtl}(i)\bullet c=\text{mk\_Condition}(cn,sh)\rangle=$$
$$\textbf{len}\ \langle c|c\ \textbf{in}\ \text{evtl}(i')\bullet$$
$$\exists\ il':\text{Inst\_Name}^*\bullet$$
$$c=\text{mk\_Condition}(cn,\text{mk\_Shared}(il'))\wedge$$
$$\textbf{elems}\ il'=$$
$$(\textbf{elems}\ il\setminus\{\text{instn}(i')\})\cup$$
$$\{\text{instn}(i)\}))$$
$$\qquad\qquad\textbf{end}))\wedge$$

/* 9 */
$(\forall\ i:\text{Instance}\bullet$
$\quad i\in\text{inst}\Rightarrow$
$\qquad(\forall\ n:\text{Inst\_Name},p:\text{Par\_Name}^*\bullet$
$\qquad\quad \text{mk\_Create}(n,p)\in\text{evtl}(i)\Rightarrow$
$\qquad\qquad n\in\text{instnames}\wedge n\neq\text{instn}(i)))\wedge$

/* 10 */
$(\textbf{let}$

$\quad\text{pcl}=$
$\qquad\langle\langle\text{name}(\text{Event\_to\_ProcessEvent}(pc))|$
$\qquad\qquad pc\ \textbf{in}\ \text{evtl}(\text{Body\_to\_Instance}(i))\bullet$
$\qquad\qquad\quad \exists\ n:\text{Inst\_Name},p:\text{Par\_Name}^*\bullet$
$\qquad\qquad\qquad pc=\text{mk\_Create}(n,p)\rangle|i\ \textbf{in}\ b\bullet i\in\text{inst}\rangle$

$\quad\textbf{in}$
$\qquad(\forall\ l:\text{Inst\_Name}^*\bullet l\in\textbf{elems}\ \text{pcl}\Rightarrow\textbf{len}\ l=\textbf{card elems}\ l)\wedge$
$\qquad(\forall\ j,j':\textbf{Nat}\bullet$
$\qquad\quad \{j,j'\}\subseteq\textbf{inds}\ \text{pcl}\wedge j\neq j'\Rightarrow$
$\qquad\qquad \textbf{elems}\ \text{pcl}(j)\cap\textbf{elems}\ \text{pcl}(j')=\{\})$
$\quad\textbf{end})$
$\textbf{end},$

$\text{instances}:\text{BMSC}\rightarrow\text{Instance}^*$
$\text{instances}(n,s,b)\equiv$
$\quad\langle\text{Body\_to\_Instance}(i)|i\ \textbf{in}\ b\bullet(\forall\ t:\textbf{Text}\bullet i\neq\text{mk\_Note}(t))\rangle,$

$\text{inputEvts}:\text{Instance}\rightarrow\text{MessageEvent}^*$
$\text{inputEvts}(i)\equiv$
$\quad\langle\text{Event\_to\_MessageEvent}(e)|$
$\qquad e\ \textbf{in}\ \text{evtl}(i)\bullet$
$\qquad\quad (\exists\ \text{inpid}:\text{MsgID},\text{inpar}:\text{Par\_Name}^*,\text{inaddr}:\text{Address}\bullet$
$\qquad\qquad e=\text{mk\_Input}(\text{inpid},\text{inpar},\text{inaddr}))\rangle,$

$\text{outputEvts}:\text{Instance}\rightarrow\text{MessageEvent}^*$
$\text{outputEvts}(i)\equiv$
$\quad\langle\text{Event\_to\_MessageEvent}(e)|$
$\qquad e\ \textbf{in}\ \text{evtl}(i)\bullet$
$\qquad\quad (\exists\ \text{outid}:\text{MsgID},\text{outpar}:\text{Par\_Name}^*,\text{outaddr}:\text{Address}\bullet$
$\qquad\qquad e=\text{mk\_Input}(\text{outid},\text{outpar},\text{outaddr}))\rangle,$

$\text{lookup}:\text{Inst\_Name}\times\text{Body}^*\xrightarrow{\sim}\text{Instance}$
$\text{lookup}(i,bl)\equiv$

```
      case hd bl of
          mk_Inst(i′,_,_) →
              if i=i′ then Body_to_Instance(hd bl) else lookup(i,tl bl) end,
              → lookup(i,tl bl)
      end
  pre (∃ k:Kind,el:Event*•mk_Inst(i,k,el) ∈ bl)
```

type
    Dir == In|Out,S=Dir×(Inst_Name×Inst_Name×MsgID)

value
    po_inst:Inst_Name×Event*×S-**set** → (S×S)-**set**
    po_inst(i,el,prev) ≡
        if el=⟨⟩ **then** {}
        else
            case hd el **of**
                mk_Input(mi,p,ia) →
                    {(n,(In,(i,name(ia),mi)))|n:S•n ∈ prev} ∪
                    po_inst(i,**tl** el,{((In,(i,name(ia),mi))}),
                mk_Output(mi,p,oa) →
                    {(n,(Out,(i,name(oa),mi)))|n:S•n ∈ prev} ∪
                    po_inst(i,**tl** el,{((Out,(i,name(oa),mi))}),
                mk_Concurrent(mel) →
                    {(n,(In,(i,ia,mi)))|
                      n:S,ia:Inst_Name,mi:MsgID,p:Par_Name*•
                          n ∈ prev∧mk_Input(mi,p,mk_InstName(ia)) ∈ mel} ∪
                    {(n,(Out,(i,oa,mi)))|
                      n:S,oa:Inst_Name,mi:MsgID,p:Par_Name*•
                          n ∈ prev∧mk_Output(mi,p,mk_InstName(oa)) ∈ mel} ∪
                    po_inst(
                        i,**tl** el,
                        {(In,(i,ia,mi))|
                        ia:Inst_Name,mi:MsgID,p:Par_Name*•
                            mk_Input(mi,p,mk_InstName(ia)) ∈ mel} ∪
                        {(Out,(i,oa,mi))|
                        oa:Inst_Name,mi:MsgID,p:Par_Name*•
                            mk_Output(mi,p,mk_InstName(oa)) ∈ mel}),
                _ → po_inst(i,**tl** el,prev)
            end
        end,

    po_comm:Inst_Name×Event* → (S×S)-**set**
    po_comm(i,el) ≡
        if el=⟨⟩ **then** {}
        else
            case hd el **of**
                mk_Output(mi,p,oa) →
                    {((Out,(i,name(oa),mi)),(In,(name(oa),i,mi)))} ∪
                    po_comm(i,**tl** el),
```
```

$$\_ \rightarrow \text{po\_comm}(i,\textbf{tl } el)$$
          end
        end,

is_cyclic:$(S \times S)$-**set** $\rightarrow$ **Bool**
is_cyclic(sss) $\equiv$
    ($\exists$ s:S*•
        ($\forall$ i:**Nat**•i>0$\wedge$i $<$ **len** s$\Rightarrow$(s(i),s(i+1)) $\in$ sss)$\wedge$
        s(1)=s(**len** s))
end

Annotations

- A BMSC is well-formed if each of the following conditions hold:
    1. In a BMSC instances are uniquely named.
    2. If an interface is specified for a BMSC, then for each instance in the interface there must be an instance with the same name and kind in the body of the chart and vice versa.
    3. Every input and output event must reference instances which are declared in the body of the chart.
    4. On an instance there may be at most one message input with a given message identifier and address. On an instance there may be at most one message output with a given message identifier and address.
    5. For each message output to an instance, there must be a corresponding message input specified on that instance. For each message input from an instance, there must be a corresponding message output specified on that instance.
    6. A message output may not be causally dependent on its corresponding message input, directly or via other messages. This property is verified by constructing a partial order on communication events and checking that the directed graph obtained from this partial order does not contain cycles. A message event precedes all message events that follow it in an instance specification, and every message input is preceded by its corresponding message output.
    7. Only declared instances may be referenced in the shared instance list of a condition.
    8. A shared condition must appear equally many times in the instances sharing it.
    9. Only declared instances may be referenced in a process creation.
    10. There must not be more than one process creation event with a given instance name.
- A timeout or reset event can only occur after a corresponding timer set event, and a stop event must be the last on the time line. ∎

Now, we specify conditions for a HMSC to be well-formed.

context: WellformedBMSC

scheme WellformedHMSC =
  extend WellformedBMSC **with**
  class
    type HMSC = {| h : HMSC′ • wf_HMSC(h) |}

    value
      wf_HMSC : HMSC′ → **Bool**
      wf_HMSC(b, a, s, e) ≡
        /∗ 1 ∗/
        dom a = **dom** b ∧
        /∗ 2 ∗/
        (∀ bmscs : BMSC_Name-**set** • bmscs ∈ **rng** a ⇒ bmscs ⊆ **dom** a) ∧
        /∗ 3 ∗/
        s ∈ **dom** b ∧
        /∗ 4 ∗/
        e ⊆ **dom** b
  end

Annotations

- A HMSC is well-formed, if each of the following conditions hold:
- The set of arrows must emanate from BMSCs that are in the mapping of BMSC names to BMSCs.
- The set of arrows must terminate at BMSCs that are in the mapping of BMSC names to BMSCs.
- The start node must be in the mapping of BMSC names to BMSCs.
- The end nodes must be in the mapping of BMSC names to BMSCs. ∎

13.1.7 An Example: IEEE 802.11 Wireless Network

Example 13.10 *An IEEE 802.11 Wireless Network:* We bring in a large example, this time without shading. ∎

Description

We illustrate the use of MSCs by modelling the possible exchanges of frames between an access point and a station in an IEEE 802.11 wireless network [224].

We assume the wireless network is operating under the Distributed Coordination Function and that no frames are lost due to transmission errors or collisions. Also, we omit some frame subtypes used for power save functions, etc.

A station is any device that conforms to the physical layer and medium access control layer specifications in the IEEE 802.11 standard. An access point is a station that additionally routes frames between the wireless network and some other network (usually a wired LAN). IEEE 802.11 uses the carrier sense multiple access/collision avoidance (CSMA/CA) technology for accessing the medium. The HMSC is shown in Fig. 13.11 and the referenced BMSCs in Fig. 13.12.

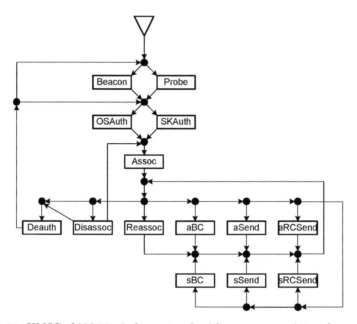

Fig. 13.11. HMSC of 802.11 wireless network with one access point and one station.

Initially, the station has no contact with the access point. It discovers the access point by scanning the available channels. Scanning may be either passive, in which case it waits for a beacon frame from the access point, or it may be active, in which case it emits probe frames. If an access point receives a probe frame it will respond with a probe response frame giving information (timing, SSID, etc.) necessary for joining the network. Once the station has contact with a network, it must be authenticated. In an 802.11 network there are two authentication methods: *open system* and *shared key*. In the former, any station requesting authentication may become authenticated. More specifically, the station will send an authentication request and the access point will respond with an authentication response. In the latter, only stations with knowledge of a shared secret key may become authenticated. In this case the authentication protocol consists of four messages.

First, the station sends an authentication request. The access point replies with a challenge message containing a nonce value. The station encrypts the nonce value using the shared secret key and returns it in an authentication response frame. Then the access point decrypts the received encrypted nonce

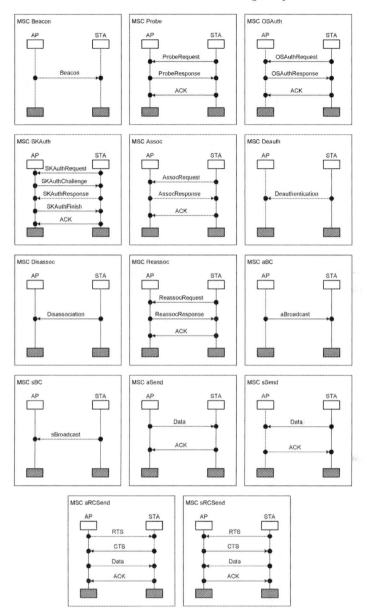

Fig. 13.12. BMSCs referenced in Fig. 13.11

and compares it with the original nonce. If they match the station is considered authenticated. The outcome of the comparison is sent to the station, confirming either that it is authenticated or that authentication failed.

The next step is for the station to become associated with the access point. Several 802.11 networks, each with their own acces point, may be joined to form an extended logical network, within which stations may move freely. Association is a means of recording which access point in such an extended network a given station is currently able to communicate with. Each station may be associated with only one access point at a time, while an access point may be associated with zero, one or more stations. An association is established by the station sending an association request frame to the access point it wishes to associate with. The access point replies with an association response frame.

An RSL Model of the IEEE 802.11 Example

Example 13.11 *An RSL Model of the IEEE 802.11 Example:* We now show an RSL model that conveys the same information as the MSC model, namely the sequence of messages that may be passed in the given 802.11 wireless network. We model the two entities as two concurrent processes which exchange messages by communicating on two channels. We do not take advantage of the features of RSL to describe the contents of the messages or how they are formed.

Text and formulas are not framed.   ∎

First, we define the types of frames. In IEEE 802.11 there are three overall types of frames: data, management and control frames. Each type of frame has several subtypes.

```
scheme IEEE80211 =
  class
    type
      Frame = ManFrame | CtrFrame | DataFrame,
      ManFrame ==
        Beacon |
        ProbeRequest |
        ProbeResponse |
        OSAuthRequest |
        OSAuthResponse |
        SKAuthRequest |
        SKAuthChallenge |
        SKAuthResponse |
        SKAuthFinish |
        AssocRequest |
        AssocResponse |
        Deauthentication |
        Disassociation |
        ReassocRequest |
        ReassocResponse,
```

CtrFrame == ACK | CTS | RTS,
DataFrame == Data | Broadcast

    channel s_a : Frame, a_s : Frame
end

Annotations

- A *frame* is a *management, control,* or *data* frame.
- A *management* frame has one of 15 subtypes.
- A *control* frame has subtype *acknowledgement, clear-to-send,* or *request-to-send.*
- A *data* frame is a unicast *data* frame or a *broadcast* frame.
- There is a pair of channels between the access point and the stations.   ∎

Now we describe the behaviour of the access point in terms of the communications in which it will participate. Note that received messages only serve to advance the communication, while the contents and type of message received is ignored. Also note that in situations where the access point may do one of several things we abstract this choice as a nondeterministic internal choice. The specification is not robust in the sense that the access point does not check that the messages received from the station are of the correct type and subtype.

context: IEEE80211

scheme IEEE80211_ap =
    extend IEEE80211 **with**
    class
      value
        AP : **Unit** → **in** s_a **out** a_s **Unit**
        AP() ≡ (a_beacon() ⫿ a_probe()),

        a_beacon : **Unit** → **in** s_a **out** a_s **Unit**
        a_beacon() ≡ a_s!Beacon ; (a_osauth() ⊓ a_skauth()),

        a_probe : **Unit** → **in** s_a **out** a_s **Unit**
        a_probe() ≡
          let proberequest = s_a? **in skip end** ;
          a_s!ProbeResponse ;
          let ack = s_a? **in skip end** ;
          (a_osauth() ⊓ a_skauth()),

        a_osauth : **Unit** → **in** s_a **out** a_s **Unit**
        a_osauth() ≡
          let osauthrequest = s_a? **in skip end** ;

a_s!OSAuthResponse ;
let ack = s_a? **in skip end** ;
a_assoc(),

a_skauth : **Unit** → **in** s_a **out** a_s **Unit**
a_skauth() ≡
   let skauthrequest = s_a? **in skip end** ;
   a_s!SKAuthChallenge ;
   let skauthresponse = s_a? **in skip end** ;
   a_s!SKAuthFinish ;
   let ack = s_a? **in skip end** ;
   a_assoc(),

a_assoc : **Unit** → **in** s_a **out** a_s **Unit**
a_assoc() ≡
   let assocrequest = s_a? **in skip end** ;
   a_s!AssocResponse ;
   let ack = s_a? **in skip end** ;
   a_op(),

a_op : **Unit** → **in** s_a **out** a_s **Unit**
a_op() ≡
   a_deauth()
   ⏸
   a_disassoc()
   ⏸
   a_reassoc()
   ⏸
   a_abc()
   ⏸
   a_asend()
   ⏸
   a_arcsend()
   ⏸
   a_sbc()
   ⏸
   a_ssend()
   ⏸
   a_srcsend(),

a_deauth : **Unit** → **in** s_a **out** a_s **Unit**
a_deauth() ≡
   let deauthentication = s_a? **in skip end** ;
   (a_osauth() ⌈⌉ (a_skauth() ⌈⌉ AP())),

a_disassoc : **Unit** → **in** s_a **out** a_s **Unit**
a_disassoc() ≡
   let disassociation = s_a? **in skip end** ;
   (a_deauth() [] a_assoc()),

a_reassoc : **Unit** → **in** s_a **out** a_s **Unit**
a_reassoc() ≡
   let reassocrequest = s_a? **in skip end** ;
   a_s!ReassocResponse ;
   let ack = s_a? **in skip end** ;
   a_op(),

a_sbc : **Unit** → **in** s_a **out** a_s **Unit**
a_sbc() ≡ **let** broadcast = s_a? **in skip end** ; a_op(),

a_ssend : **Unit** → **in** s_a **out** a_s **Unit**
a_ssend() ≡ **let** data = s_a? **in skip end** ; a_s!ACK ; a_op(),

a_srcsend : **Unit** → **in** s_a **out** a_s **Unit**
a_srcsend() ≡
   let rts = s_a? **in skip end** ;
   a_s!CTS ;
   let data = s_a? **in skip end** ;
   a_s!ACK ;
   a_op(),

a_abc : **Unit** → **in** s_a **out** a_s **Unit**
a_abc() ≡ a_s!Broadcast ; a_op(),

a_asend : **Unit** → **in** s_a **out** a_s **Unit**
a_asend() ≡ a_s!Data ; **let** ack = s_a? **in skip end** ; a_op(),

a_arcsend : **Unit** → **in** s_a **out** a_s **Unit**
a_arcsend() ≡
   a_s!RTS ;
   let cts = s_a? **in skip end** ;
   a_s!Data ;
   let ack = s_a? **in skip end** ;
   a_op()

end

We now give the corresponding behaviour of the station. This is essentially the inverse of that of the access point. Again, choices are abstracted as internal nondeterminism.

context: IEEE80211_ap

scheme IEEE80211_sta =
    extend IEEE80211_ap **with**
    class
      value
          STA : **Unit** → **in** a_s **out** s_a **Unit**
          STA() ≡ (s_beacon() ⫿ s_probe()),

          s_beacon : **Unit** → **in** a_s **out** s_a **Unit**
          s_beacon() ≡
            let beacon = a_s? **in skip end** ;
            (s_osauth() ⫿ s_akauth()),

          s_probe : **Unit** → **in** a_s **out** s_a **Unit**
          s_probe() ≡
            s_a!ProbeRequest ;
            let proberesponse = a_s? **in skip end** ;
            s_a!ACK ;
            (s_osauth() ⫿ s_akauth()),

          s_osauth : **Unit** → **in** a_s **out** s_a **Unit**
          s_osauth() ≡
            s_a!OSAuthRequest ;
            let osauthresponse = a_s? **in skip end** ;
            s_a!ACK ;
            s_assoc(),

          s_akauth : **Unit** → **in** a_s **out** s_a **Unit**
          s_akauth() ≡
            s_a!SKAuthRequest ;
            let skauthchallenge = a_s? **in skip end** ;
            s_a!SKAuthResponse ;
            let skauthfinish = a_s? **in skip end** ;
            s_a!ACK ;
            s_assoc(),

          s_assoc : **Unit** → **in** a_s **out** s_a **Unit**
          s_assoc() ≡
            s_a!AssocRequest ;
            let assocresponse = a_s? **in skip end** ;
            s_a!ACK ;
            s_op(),

          s_op : **Unit** → **in** a_s **out** s_a **Unit**
          s_op() ≡

s_deauth()
⊓
s_disassoc()
⊓
s_reassoc()
⊓
s_abc()
⊓
s_asend()
⊓
s_arcsend()
⊓
s_abc()
⊓
s_asend()
⊓
s_arcsend(),

s_deauth : **Unit** → **in** a_s **out** s_a **Unit**
s_deauth() ≡
    s_a!Deauthentication ; ((s_osauth() [] s_akauth()) ⊓ STA()),

s_disassoc : **Unit** → **in** a_s **out** s_a **Unit**
s_disassoc() ≡ s_a!Disassociation ; (s_deauth() [] s_assoc()),

s_reassoc : **Unit** → **in** a_s **out** s_a **Unit**
s_reassoc() ≡
    s_a!ReassocRequest ;
    let reassocresponse = a_s? **in skip end** ;
    s_a!ACK ;
    s_op(),

s_sbc : **Unit** → **in** a_s **out** s_a **Unit**
s_sbc() ≡ s_a!Broadcast ; s_op(),

s_ssend : **Unit** → **in** a_s **out** s_a **Unit**
s_ssend() ≡ s_a!Data ; **let** ack = a_s? **in skip end** ; s_op(),

s_srcsend : **Unit** → **in** a_s **out** s_a **Unit**
s_srcsend() ≡
    s_a!RTS ;
    let cts = a_s? **in skip end** ;
    s_a!Data ;
    let ack = a_s? **in skip end** ;
    s_op(),

s_abc : **Unit** → **in** a_s **out** s_a **Unit**
s_abc() ≡ **let** broadcast = a_s? **in skip end** ; s_op(),

s_asend : **Unit** → **in** a_s **out** s_a **Unit**
s_asend() ≡ **let** data = a_s? **in skip end** ; s_a!ACK ; s_op(),

s_arcsend : **Unit** → **in** a_s **out** s_a **Unit**
s_arcsend() ≡
   let rts = a_s? **in skip end** ;
   s_a!CTS ;
   let data = a_s? **in skip end** ;
   s_a!ACK ;
   s_op()
end

This example has hopefully demonstrated the power of MSCs as a specification method. Clearly, the MSC specification is much more compact than the corresponding RSL specification, and it is also much more readable. The power of RSL, however, becomes apparent if one wants to add an additional layer of detail, for example, by adding parameters to the messages and explaining how parameters from incoming messages are related to the parameters of outgoing messages. While MSCs are good at specifying one aspect (namely sequences of events) of a system, RSL is expressive enough to specify many aspects.

13.1.8 Semantics of Basic Message Sequence Charts

We now give a semantics of BMSCs by defining an RSL function, S, that yields the possible traces of a given BMSC. A trace is a causally ordered sequence of events. Note that the semantics is in general nondeterministic, in the sense that a given BMSC may have many legal sequences of events.

scheme BMSC_Semantics =
  extend WellformedBMSC **with**
  class
    value
      S : BMSC → (Event*)-**set**
      S(bmsc) ≡
        {el|el:Event*•el ∈ interleave(bmsc)∧isValid(el,{})}

      interleave : BMSC → (Event*)-**set**
      interleave(bmsc) ≡
        interleave(⟨evtl(inst)|inst **in** instances(bmsc)⟩,⟨⟩)

      interleave : (Event*)* × (Event*)* → (Event*)-**set**

interleave(evtll, evtll′) ≡
  if evtll = ⟨⟩
a   **then** {}
    else
      let head = **hd** evtll **in**
      (**let** rest = interleave(⟨**tl** head⟩⌢**tl** evtll⌢evtll′,⟨⟩) **in**
b   {⟨**hd** head⟩⌢r|r:Event*•r ∈ rest} **end**)
c   ∪ interleave(**tl** evtll,⟨head⟩⌢evtll′)
      end
  end

isValid : Event* × Msg_Name-**set** → **Bool**
isValid(evtl, mnms) ≡
  case hd evtl **of**
    mk_Output(mnm,pars,adr) →
      isValid(**tl** evtl,mnms ∪{mnm}),
    mk_Input(mnm,pars,adr) →
      id ∈ ids ∧ isValid(**tl** evtl,mnms\{mnm})
  end
end

Annotations

- The semantics of a BMSC, S(bmsc), is a set of lists of events, where each list is an interleaving of the events of each of the instances in the BMSC, and the set contains only those lists that are valid.
- The interleaving of a BMSC is an interleaving of the event lists of its instances.
  (a) The interleaving of an empty list of events is the empty set.
  (b) The interleaving of a non-empty list of event lists is obtained by selecting the head element of the head of the list and adding that element as the first element of all interleavings of the remaining event-lists,
  (c) and forming the union with the set of interleavings obtained from the rest of the list.
- An event list is valid if every input event causally follows its corresponding output event in the list.   ∎

13.1.9 Semantics of High-Level Message Sequence Charts

We leave it as Exercise 13.3 for the reader to combine the above into functions which give a semantics of HMSCs.

13.2 Live Sequence Charts: Informal Presentation

13.2.1 Live Sequence Chart Syntax

In this section we informally describe the components of live sequence charts (LSC). We return to the question of a formal semantics of a subset of LSCs in Sect. 13.4.

Graphical Syntax of Live Sequence Charts

LSCs were proposed by Damm and Harel [89] as an extension of MSCs. They identified a number of shortcomings and weaknesses of the MSC standard and proposed a range of new concepts and notation to overcome these problems.

One of the major problems with the semantics of MSCs is that it is not clear whether an MSC describes all behaviours of a system or just a set of possible behaviours. Typically, the latter view would be used in early stages of development, while the former would apply in later stages when the behaviour is more fixed. Another problem noted by Damm and Harel is the inability of MSCs to specify liveness, i.e., MSCs have no constructions for enforcing progress. Damm and Harel also view the lack of semantics for conditions to be a problem.

Universal and Existential Charts

The most prominent feature of LSCs is the introduction of a distinction between optional and mandatory behaviour. This applies to several elements in charts. A distinction is introduced between *universal* charts and *existential* charts.

Universal charts specify behaviour that must be satisfied by every possible run of a system. This may be compared to universal quantification over the runs of the system. On the other hand, existential charts specify behaviour that must be satisfied by at least one run of the system. This is like existential quantification over the runs of the system. The typical application of existential charts would be in the early stages of the development process, particularly in domain modelling. An existential chart specifies a scenario that may be used to describe characteristic behaviours of the domain.

Universal charts would typically be used later in the development process, particularly in requirements engineering and in requirements documents. Universal charts are designated by a fully drawn box around the chart, while existential charts are designated by a dashed box.

Example 13.12 Figure 13.13 shows a universal LSC with two instances, A and B. The behaviour specified by this chart must (i.e., shall) be satisfied by every run of the system.

Figure 13.13 shows an existential LSC. This represents a scenario that at least one run of the system must satisfy.

The four messages of Fig. 13.13 are discussed in Example 13.14 below. ∎

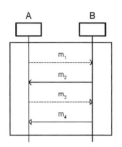

Fig. 13.13. Universal LSC

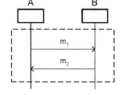

Fig. 13.14. Existential LSC

Precharts

LSC introduces the notion of a *prechart* to restrict the applicability of a chart. The prechart is like a precondition that when satisfied activates the main chart. A given system need only satisfy a universal chart whenever it satisfies the prechart. An empty prechart is satisfied by any system. A prechart can be considered as the expression in an IF statement where the body of the THEN part is the universal chart. The prechart is denoted by a dashed hexagon containing zero, one or more events.

Example 13.13 Figure 13.15 shows a universal LSC with a prechart consisting of the single message *activate*. In this case, the behaviour specified in the body of the chart only applies to those runs of the system where the message *activate* is sent from instance A to instance B. ∎

"Hot" and "Cold" Messages

LSC allow messages to be "hot" or "cold". A hot message is mandatory, i.e., if it is sent then it must be received eventually. This is denoted by a fully drawn arrow. For a cold message reception is not required, i.e., it may be "lost". This is denoted by a dashed arrow.

Synchronous and Asynchronous Messages

Also, a message may be specified as either synchronous or asynchronous. Synchronous messages are denoted by an open arrowhead $\gg$, while asynchronous messages are denoted by a closed arrowhead $\twoheadrightarrow$.

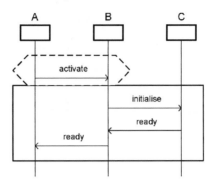

Fig. 13.15. Prechart

Example 13.14 Figure 13.13 illustrates the four kinds of messages: hot and cold, synchronous and asynchronous. Message m_1 is cold and synchronous. Message m_2 is hot and synchronous. Message m_3 is cold and asynchronous. Finally, message m_4 is hot and asynchronous. ∎

Conditions

In LSC conditions are promoted to first-class events. The difference is that conditions now have an influence on the execution of a chart, while in MSC they were merely comments. Again, a distinction is made between a hot (mandatory) condition, which, if evaluated to false, causes nonsuccessful termination of the chart, and a cold condition (optional) which, if evaluated to false, causes successful termination of the chart. A hot condition is like an invariant which must be satisfied.

By combining a prechart with a universal chart containing just a single hot condition that always evaluates to false, it is possible to specify forbidden scenarios, since the scenario expressed in the prechart will then always cause nonsuccessful termination. A shared condition forces synchronisation among the sharing instances, i.e., the condition will not be evaluated before all instances have reached it and no instance will progress beyond the condition until it has been evaluated.

Example 13.15 Figure 13.16 illustrates two conditions. The first is hot, while the second is cold. If the hot condition evaluates to false, the chart is aborted, indicating an erroneous situation. If the second condition evaluates to false, the current (sub)chart is exited successfully. ∎

Subcharts

Iteration and conditional execution are obtained by means of *subcharts*. Subcharts are LSCs that are specified for a subset of the instances of the containing

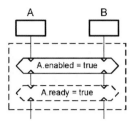

Fig. 13.16. Conditions

LSC and possibly additional new instances. Iteration is denoted by annotating the top-left corner of the chart with an integer constant for limited iteration or an asterisk for unlimited iteration. A subchart is exited successfully either when a limited iteration has executed the specified number of times, or when a cold condition evaluates to false.

By combining subcharts with cold conditions, WHILE and DO–WHILE loops may be created. Additionally, a special form of subchart with two parts is used to create an IF–THEN–ELSE construct. The first part of the subchart has a cold condition as the first event. If the condition evaluates to true, the first part of the subchart is executed. If the condition evaluates to false, the second part of the subchart is executed.

Example 13.16 Figure 13.17 illustrates limited iteration. Instance A will send the message m_1 60 times to instance B.   ▪

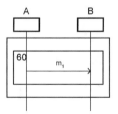

Fig. 13.17. Limited iteration

Example 13.17 Figure 13.18 illustrates unlimited iteration with a stop condition, essentially like a DO–WHILE loop. The message m_1 will be sent repeatedly until the condition becomes false. Once that happens, the subchart is exited.   ▪

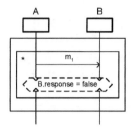

Fig. 13.18. DO–WHILE loop

Example 13.18 Figure 13.19 is similar to the previous situation, except that the condition is now checked before the first message is sent, thus mimicking a WHILE loop. ∎

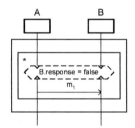

Fig. 13.19. WHILE loop

Example 13.19 Figure 13.20 is like Fig. 13.19 except that there is no iteration. Thus, the message m_1 will be sent once if the condition evaluates to true, and it will not be sent if the condition evaluates to false. Therefore, this construction is like an IF–THEN construct. ∎

Example 13.20 In Fig. 13.21 the special construction for IF–THEN–ELSE is illustrated. The two subcharts represent the THEN and ELSE branches. If the condition evaluates to true, the first subchart is executed, otherwise the second subchart is executed. In either case, the subchart not chosen is skipped entirely. ∎

Locations

The distinction between hot and cold is also applied to the timeline of an instance. Any point where an event is specified on the timeline is called a

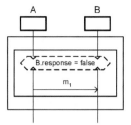

Fig. 13.20. IF–THEN conditional

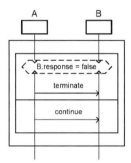

Fig. 13.21. IF–THEN–ELSE conditional

location. A location may be hot indicating that the corresponding event must eventually take place, or cold indicating that event might never occur. A hot location is represented by the time line being fully drawn, while a cold location is represented by a dashed time line. The timeline may alternate between being fully drawn and dashed.

The addition of cold locations conflicts with the representation of coregions inherited from MSCs. For this reason, the syntax for a coregion is modified to be a dashed line positioned next to the part of the time line that the coregion spans.

Example 13.21 Figure 13.22 illustrates the syntax for optional progress. The timeline is fully drawn at the location where the message m_1 is sent and received, indicating that these events must eventually take place. This guarantees liveness. At the location where the message m_2 is sent and received, the time line is dashed, indicating that neither instance is required to progress to the sending or receiving of m_2. If an instance does not progress beyond a location l, then no event on the time line of that instance following l will take place. Thus, in this case, if m_2 is never sent, m_3 will never be sent. ∎

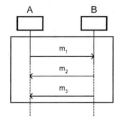

Fig. 13.22. Optional progress

13.2.2 A Live Sequence Chart Example, I

Example 13.22 *A Live Sequence Chart, Part I:* We conclude this section with an example. This example is concluded by Example 13.23 in Sect. 13.4.3. We omit shading. ∎

Figure 13.23 shows an example LSC with three instances. The first step is to convert the graphical syntax into the textual syntax. The result is shown below.

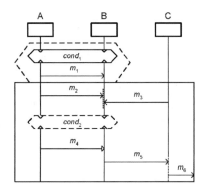

Fig. 13.23. Example live sequence chart

```
lsc Example;
    instance A
        prechart
            hot hotcondition(cond₁) ;
            hot out m₁ to B async ;
        end prechart body hot out m₂ to B async ;
            hot coldcondition(cond₂) ;
            hot out m₄ to B sync ;
        end body
```

```
    end instance
    instance B
        prechart
            hot hotcondition(cond₁) ;
            hot in m₁ from A async ;
        end prechart
        body
            hot concurrent
                in m₂ from A async ;
                in m₃ from C async ;
            end concurrent ;
            hot coldcondition(cond₂) ;
            hot in m₄ from A sync ;
            hot out m₅ to C async ;
        end body
    end instance
    instance C
        body
            hot out m₃ to B async ;
            cold in m₅ from B async ;
            cold out m₆ to env async ;
        end body
    end instance
end lsc
```

13.3 Process Algebra

The ITU standard Z.120 for MSCs includes a formal algebraic semantics based on the process algebra PA_ϵ introduced by Baeten and Weijland [27]. In this section we first briefly review the definition of PA_ϵ following [326] and [26], and then present an extension of that algebra (named PAc_ϵ), which will be used for defining the semantics of a subset of LSCs in Section 13.4.2 and for expressing communication behaviours of RSL specifications in Sect. 13.5.2.

The material in this section cannot be considered to belong to the field of software engineering. Rather, it belongs to the field of computer science. The reader whose interest is mainly focused on the application of MSCs and LSCs to actual engineering problems may skip the rest of this chapter. Those who wish to gain a deeper understanding of the relations between sequence charts and RSL are encouraged to read on.

The material that follows only scratches the surface of the topic of process algebras. The theoretical foundations for the process algebras presented here are given in [317].

13.3.1 The Process Algebra PA_ϵ

The algebraic theory of PA_ϵ is given as an equational specification $(\Sigma_{PA_\epsilon}, E_{PA_\epsilon})$, consisting of the signature, Σ_{PA_ϵ}, and a set of equations, E_{PA_ϵ}. We first define the signature and equations and then give the intuition behind the definitions.

Signature

The one-sorted signature, Σ_{PA_ϵ}, consists of

1. two special constants δ and ϵ
2. a set of unspecified constants A, for which $\{\delta, \epsilon\} \cap A = \emptyset$
3. the unary operator $\sqrt{}$
4. the binary operators $+$, $\cdot$, $\parallel$ and $\parallel\!\!\!\!\underline{}$

The unspecified set A is a parameter of the theory. Thus, applications of the theory require the theory to be instantiated with a specific set A. When the theory is applied to MSCs, the set A consists of identifiers for the atomic events of the chart.

For convenience and following tradition, we will apply the binary operators in infix notation, i.e., instead of $+(x, y)$ we will write $x + y$. To reduce the need for parentheses, operator precedences are introduced. The $\cdot$ operator binds strongest, the $+$ operator binds weakest.

Let V be a set of variables. Then terms over the signature Σ_{PA_ϵ} with variables from V, denoted $T(\Sigma_{PA_\epsilon}, V)$, are given by the inductive definition

1. $v \in V$ is a term.
2. $a \in A$ is a term.
3. δ is a term.
4. ϵ is a term.
5. If t is a term, then $\sqrt{}(t)$ is a term.
6. If t_1 and t_2 are terms, then $t_1 \, op \, t_2$ is a term, for $op \in \{+, \cdot, \parallel, \parallel\!\!\!\!\underline{}\}$.

A term is called *closed* if it contains no variables. The set of closed terms over Σ_{PA_ϵ} is denoted $T(\Sigma_{PA_\epsilon})$.

Equations

The equations of PA_ϵ are of the form $t_1 = t_2$, where $t_1, t_2 \in T(\Sigma_{PA_\epsilon}, V)$. For $a \in A$ and $x, y, z \in V$ the equations, E_{PA_ϵ}, are given in Table 13.1.

The special constant δ is called *deadlock*. It denotes the process that has stopped executing actions and can never resume. The special constant ϵ is called the *empty process*. It denotes the process that terminates successfully without executing any actions. The elements of the set A are called *atomic actions*. These represent processes that cannot be decomposed into smaller parts. As mentioned above, the set A is given a concrete definition when

Table 13.1. Equations of PA_ϵ

$$x + y = y + x \tag{A1}$$
$$(x + y) + z = x + (y + z) \tag{A2}$$
$$x + x = x \tag{A3}$$
$$(x + y) \cdot z = x \cdot z + y \cdot z \tag{A4}$$
$$(x \cdot y) \cdot z = x \cdot (y \cdot z) \tag{A5}$$
$$x + \delta = x \tag{A6}$$
$$\delta \cdot x = \delta \tag{A7}$$
$$x \cdot \epsilon = x \tag{A8}$$
$$\epsilon \cdot x = x \tag{A9}$$

$$x \parallel y = x \mathbin{\lfloor \! \lfloor} y + y \mathbin{\lfloor \! \lfloor} x + \sqrt{}(x) \cdot \sqrt{}(y) \tag{F1}$$
$$\epsilon \mathbin{\lfloor \! \lfloor} x = \delta \tag{F2}$$
$$\delta \mathbin{\lfloor \! \lfloor} x = \delta \tag{F3}$$
$$a \cdot x \mathbin{\lfloor \! \lfloor} y = a \cdot (x \parallel y) \tag{F4}$$
$$(x + y) \mathbin{\lfloor \! \lfloor} z = x \mathbin{\lfloor \! \lfloor} z + y \mathbin{\lfloor \! \lfloor} z \tag{F5}$$

$$\sqrt{}(\epsilon) = \epsilon \tag{T1}$$
$$\sqrt{}(\delta) = \delta \tag{T2}$$
$$\sqrt{}(a \cdot x) = \delta \tag{T3}$$
$$\sqrt{}(x + y) = \sqrt{}(x) + \sqrt{}(y) \tag{T4}$$

the theory is applied. For example, in defining the semantics of MSCs, the set A will contain the symbols that identify the events in the chart, such as $in(a, b, m1)$ identifying the event of instance b receiving message $m1$ from instance a.

The binary operators $+$ and $\cdot$ are called *alternative* and *sequential composition*, respectively. The alternative composition of processes x and y is the process that behaves as either x or y, but not both. The sequential composition of processes x and y is the process that first behaves as x until it reaches a terminated state and then behaves as y.

The binary operator $\parallel$ is called the *free merge*. The free merge of processes x and y is the process that executes an interleaving of the actions of x and y. The unary *termination operator* $\sqrt{}$ indicates whether the process it is applied to may terminate immediately. The termination operator is an auxiliary operator needed to define the free merge. The binary operator $\mathbin{\lfloor \! \lfloor}$ is called the *left merge* and denotes the process that executes the first atomic action of the left operand followed by the interleaving of the remainder of the left operand with the right operand. Like the termination operator, the left merge operator is an auxiliary operator needed to define free merge.

To see why the termination operator is necessary, consider Eq. F1. What happens in the free merge is that all possible sequences of atomic actions from the two operands are generated. When both operands become the empty process, we want the free merge to be the empty process as well, i.e., we want the equation $\epsilon \parallel \epsilon = \epsilon$ to hold. Because of Eq. F2, the two first alternatives in F1 become deadlock. However, the last alternative becomes the empty process, because of Eq. T1. Thus, with Eq. A6 we get the desired result. It is possible to give a simpler definition of the free merge without using the empty process or the termination operator, see [26], but for our purposes we need the empty process.

Derivability

We now define what it means for a term to be derivable from an equational specification. First, the two auxiliary notions of a substitution and a context are introduced.

Definition 13.1. A substitution $\sigma : V \to T(\Sigma, V)$ replaces variables with terms over Σ. The extension of σ to terms over Σ, denoted $\bar{\sigma} : T(\Sigma, V) \to T(\Sigma, V)$, is given by

1. $\bar{\sigma}(\delta) = \delta$
2. $\bar{\sigma}(\epsilon) = \epsilon$
3. $\bar{\sigma}(a) = a$ for $a \in A$
4. $\bar{\sigma}(v) = \sigma(v)$ for $v \in V$
5. $\bar{\sigma}(\surd(x)) = \surd(\bar{\sigma}(x))$
6. $\bar{\sigma}(x \; op \; y) = \bar{\sigma}(x) \; op \; \bar{\sigma}(y)$ for $op \in \{+, \cdot, \parallel, \lfloor\!\lfloor\}$

A substitution that replaces all variables with variable-free terms, i.e., closed terms, is called *closed*.   ∎

Definition 13.2. A Σ context is a term $C \in T(\Sigma, V \cup \{\Box\})$, containing exactly one occurrence of the distinguished variable $\Box$. The context is written $C[\;]$ to suggest that C should be considered as a term with a hole in it. Substitution of a term $t \in T(\Sigma, V)$ in $C[\;]$ gives the term $C[\Box \mapsto t]$, written $C[t]$.   ∎

Definition 13.3. Let (Σ, E) be an equational specification and let t, s and u be arbitrary terms over Σ. The derivability relation, $\vdash$, is then given by the following inductive definition.

$$s = t \in E \quad \Rightarrow \quad (\Sigma, E) \vdash s = t$$
$$(\Sigma, E) \vdash t = t$$
$$(\Sigma, E) \vdash s = t \quad \Rightarrow \quad (\Sigma, E) \vdash t = s$$
$$(\Sigma, E) \vdash s = t \quad \wedge \quad (\Sigma, E) \vdash t = u \quad \Rightarrow \quad (\Sigma, E) \vdash s = u$$
$$(\Sigma, E) \vdash s = t \quad \Rightarrow \quad (\Sigma, E) \vdash \bar{\sigma}(s) = \bar{\sigma}(t) \quad \textit{for any substitution } \sigma$$
$$(\Sigma, E) \vdash s = t \quad \Rightarrow \quad (\Sigma, E) \vdash C[s] = C[t] \quad \textit{for any context } C[-]$$

If $(\Sigma, E) \vdash s = t$, abbreviated $E \vdash s = t$, then the equation $s = t$ is said to be derivable from the equational specification (Σ, E).   ∎

Reduction to Basic Terms

We now venture deeper into the theory of process algebra and term rewriting systems. The goal is to show that there exists a model of the equational specification for PA_ϵ and that the equations E_{PA_ϵ} form a complete axiomatisation, i.e., that whenever two terms are equal in the model, then they are provably equal using the equations.

The first step is to show that any PA_ϵ term can be reduced to an equivalent so-called basic term consisting of only atomic actions, δ, ϵ, $+$ and $\cdot$. This result makes subsequent proofs easier, because we need only consider these simpler terms.

Definition 13.4. δ and ϵ are basic terms. An atomic action $a \in A$ is a *basic term*. If $a \in A$ and t is a basic term, then $a \cdot t$ is a basic term. If t and s are basic terms, then $t + s$ is a basic term.   ∎

The next step is to show that any PA_ϵ term can be reduced to a basic term. To do this, a term rewriting system is defined.

Definition 13.5. A *term rewriting system* is a pair (Σ, R) of a signature, Σ, and a set, R, of rewriting rules. A rewriting rule is of the form $s \rightarrow t$, where $s, t \in T(\Sigma, V)$ are open terms over Σ, such that s is not a variable and $vars(t) \subseteq vars(s)$, where $vars(t)$ denotes the set of variables in the term t.

The one-step reduction relation, $\rightarrow$, is the smallest relation containing the rules, R, that is closed under substitutions and contexts.   ∎

Definition 13.6. A term s is in *normal form* if there does not exist a term t, such that $s \rightarrow t$. A term s is called *strongly normalising* if there exist no infinite sequences of rewritings starting with s:

$$s \rightarrow s_1 \rightarrow s_2 \rightarrow \ldots$$

A term reduction system is called strongly normalising if every term in the system is strongly normalising.   ∎

Table 13.2. Term rewriting system for PA_ϵ

$$x + x \to x \tag{RA3}$$
$$(x + y) \cdot z \to x \cdot z + y \cdot z \tag{RA4}$$
$$(x \cdot y) \cdot z \to x \cdot (y \cdot z) \tag{RA5}$$
$$x + \delta \to x \tag{RA6}$$
$$\delta \cdot x \to \delta \tag{RA7}$$
$$x \cdot \epsilon \to x \tag{RA8}$$
$$\epsilon \cdot x \to x \tag{RA9}$$

$$x \parallel y \to x \lfloor\!\lfloor y + y \rfloor\!\rfloor x + \sqrt(x) \cdot \sqrt(y) \tag{RF1}$$
$$\epsilon \lfloor\!\lfloor x \to \delta \tag{RF2}$$
$$\delta \lfloor\!\lfloor x \to \delta \tag{RF3}$$
$$a \cdot x \lfloor\!\lfloor y \to a \cdot (x \parallel y) \tag{RF4}$$
$$a \lfloor\!\lfloor x \to a \cdot x \tag{RF4'}$$
$$(x + y) \lfloor\!\lfloor z \to x \lfloor\!\lfloor z + y \lfloor\!\lfloor z \tag{RF5}$$

$$\sqrt(\epsilon) \to \epsilon \tag{RT1}$$
$$\sqrt(\delta) \to \delta \tag{RT2}$$
$$\sqrt(a \cdot x) \to \delta \tag{RT3}$$
$$\sqrt(x + y) \to \sqrt(x) + \sqrt(y) \tag{RT4}$$

The term rewriting system for PA_ϵ is shown in Table 13.2. Essentially, a term rewriting system is a collection of equations, that can be applied only one way. Compared with the equations of PA_ϵ in Table 13.1, there are no rewrite rules corresponding to A1 and A2, because these equations have no clear direction. Also, having a rule for A1 would render the rewrite system non-terminating.

A common method for proving normalisation of a term rewriting system is to define a partial ordering on the operators and constants of the signature Σ, and then extend this ordering to terms over Σ. There are several ways to define this extension. For our purposes, the so-called lexicographical variant of the recursive path ordering will suffice. The main reference for the following material is [26]. Other references are [27, 95, 251, 267].

Definition 13.7. Let $s, t \in T(\Sigma, V)$. We write $s >_{lpo} t$ if $s \to^+ t$, where $\to^+$ is the transitive closure of the reduction relation $\to$ defined by the rules RPO1-5 and LPO in Table 13.3. ∎

Table 13.3. Reduction rules

___ Reduction rules for lexicographical variant of recursive partial ordering ___

- RPO1. Mark head symbol ($k \geq 0$):
  $H(t_1, \ldots, t_k) \to H^*(t_1, \ldots, t_k)$
- RPO2. Make copies under smaller head symbol ($H > G$, $k \geq 0$):
  $H^*(t_1, \ldots, t_k) \to G(H^*(t_1, \ldots, t_k), \ldots, H^*(t_1, \ldots, t_k))$
- RPO3. Select argument ($k \geq 1$, $1 \leq i \leq k$):
  $H^*(t_1, \ldots, t_k) \to t_i$
- RPO4. Push $*$ down ($k \geq 1$, $l \geq 0$):
  $H^*(t_1, \ldots, G(s_1, \ldots, s_l), \ldots, t_k) \to H(t_1, \ldots, G^*(s_1, \ldots, s_l), \ldots, t_k)$
- RPO5. Handling contexts:
  $s \to t \quad \Rightarrow \quad H(\ldots, s, \ldots) \to H(\ldots, t, \ldots)$
- LPO. Reduce ith argument ($k \geq 1$, $1 \leq i \leq k$, $l \geq 0$,
  H has lexicographical status wrt. the ith argument):
  Let $t \equiv H^*(t_1, \ldots, t_{i-1}, G(s_1, \ldots, s_l), t_{i+1}, \ldots, t_k)$
  then $t \to H(t, \ldots, t, G^*(s_1, \ldots, s_l), t, \ldots, t)$

Theorem 13.8. *Strong Normalisation (I)* (Kamin and Lévy [259]). *Let (Σ, R) be a term rewriting system with finitely many rewrite rules and let $>$ be a well-founded partial ordering on Σ. If $s >_{lpo} t$ for each rewriting rule $s \to t \in R$, then the term rewriting system (Σ, R) is strongly normalising.* ∎

Proof. See [259]. ∎

The intuition behind Theorem 13.8 is that if $x >_{lpo} y$, then y is a less complicated term than x, where we consider basic terms to be the simplest and general terms to be the most complicated. Thus, if all the rules can only make terms less complicated, we are bound to eventually reach a term that can not be simplified.

Lemma 13.9. *Strong Normalisation (II)* The term rewriting system for PA_ϵ in Table 13.2 is strongly normalizing. ∎

Proof. According to Theorem 13.8, it is sufficient to define a partial ordering on Σ_{PA_ϵ} and show that each rewriting rule satisfies the extension of the ordering to $T(\Sigma)$. We use the partial order $\| > \| > \sqrt{} > \cdot > + > \epsilon > \delta$. $\cdot$ has lexicographical status with regard to the first argument. Below, we illustrate the derivation for rewrite rules RA4 and RA5. The remaining derivations are given in [316].

$$(x + y) \cdot z \;>_{lpo}\; (x + y) \cdot^* z \qquad\qquad \text{RPO1}$$
$$>_{lpo}\; (x + y) \cdot^* z + (x + y) \cdot^* z \qquad\qquad \text{RPO2}$$
$$>_{lpo}\; (x +^* y) \cdot z + (x +^* y) \cdot z \qquad\qquad \text{RPO4, RPO5}$$
$$>_{lpo}\; x \cdot z + y \cdot z \qquad\qquad \text{RPO3, RPO5}$$

$$(x \cdot y) \cdot z \;>_{lpo}\; (x \cdot y) \cdot^* z \hspace{5cm} \text{RPO1}$$
$$>_{lpo}\; (x \cdot^* y) \cdot ((x \cdot y) \cdot^* z) \hspace{3cm} \text{LPO}$$
$$>_{lpo}\; x \cdot ((x \cdot^* y) \cdot z) \hspace{2.5cm} \text{RPO3, RPO5, RPO5}$$
$$>_{lpo}\; x \cdot (y \cdot z) \hspace{4cm} \text{RPO3, RPO5}$$

Thus, the term rewriting system for PA_ϵ is strongly normalising.   ∎

We are now ready to prove that every PA_ϵ term has an equivalent basic term.

Theorem 13.10. For every PA_ϵ term, s, there is a corresponding basic term, t, such that $PA_\epsilon \vdash s = t$.   ∎

Proof. By the *strong normalisation (II)* theorem the term rewriting system for PA_ϵ is strongly normalizing. Thus, for every term t, there is a finite sequence of rewritings

$$t \to t_1 \to t_2 \to \cdots \to s$$

where s is in normal form.

We use a proof by contradiction to show that s cannot contain $\|$, $\lfloor\!\lfloor$ or $\sqrt{}$. Assume, therefore, that s is in normal form and that $s = C[x \| y]$. But then the rewriting RF1 can be used, thus contradicting that s is in normal form. Now assume that s is in normal form and that $s = C[x \lfloor\!\lfloor y]$. Then there are three cases

- $x = u \lfloor\!\lfloor w$: in this case we can use the argument recursively to show that u or one of its sub-terms can be reduced by a rewrite rule. This line of reasoning is valid since we deal with finite terms.
- $x = \sqrt{}(u)$: in this case either x can be rewritten using one of RT1-4, or we can apply the whole argument to u to show that some sub-term of u can be rewritten.
- in all other cases one of the four rewrite rules RF2-4 may be applied to s, thus forming a contradiction.

Finally, we can use the same argument as above to show that if $s = C[\sqrt{}(x)]$ then either we can use one of the rewriting rules RT1-4 on s directly, or some sub-term of x can be reduced using a rewrite rule.

Thus, in all cases we have a contradiction and the theorem follows.   ∎

13.3.2 Semantics of PA_ϵ

We now proceed to define a semantics for PA_ϵ. See Table 13.4.

We use a structural operational semantics in the style of Plotkin [402]. Based on the semantics, we define a behavioural equivalence on PA_ϵ terms, called bisimulation equivalence. We then show that the quotient algebra of PA_ϵ terms under bisimulation equivalence is a model of the equational specification

PA_ϵ, which implies soundness of the equations. Finally, we prove completeness of the equations.

A Plotkin-style operational semantics is defined using a set of derivation rules. For our purpose, the premises and conclusion of a derivation rule are formulas of either the form

$$x \xrightarrow{a} x'$$

or of the form

$$x \downarrow$$

Informally, the former formula means that process x can evolve into process x' by performing action a. The latter formula means that process x can terminate immediately and successfully.

A formula ϕ is provable from a set of deduction rules, if there is a rule

$$\frac{\varphi_1 \quad \varphi_2 \quad \cdots \quad \varphi_n}{\varphi}$$

such that there exists a substitution $\sigma : V \to T(\Sigma, V)$ satisfying $\sigma(\varphi) = \phi$ and if $\sigma(\varphi_i)$ is provable from the deduction rules for $i = 1, 2, \ldots, n$.

The deduction rules of the operational semantics for PA_ϵ are shown in Table 13.4. An empty premise is designated by a $\Box$ above the line.

Table 13.4. Structural operational semantics of PA_ϵ

$$\frac{\Box}{a \xrightarrow{a} \epsilon} \quad \text{Act}$$

$$\frac{x \xrightarrow{a} x'}{x + y \xrightarrow{a} x'} \quad \text{Cho1}$$

$$\frac{y \xrightarrow{a} y'}{x + y \xrightarrow{a} y'} \quad \text{Cho2}$$

$$\frac{x \xrightarrow{a} x'}{x \cdot y \xrightarrow{a} x' \cdot y} \quad \text{Seq1}$$

$$\frac{x \downarrow \quad y \xrightarrow{a} y'}{x \cdot y \xrightarrow{a} y'} \quad \text{Seq2}$$

$$\frac{x \xrightarrow{a} x'}{x \parallel y \xrightarrow{a} x' \parallel y} \quad \text{Par1}$$

$$\frac{y \xrightarrow{a} y'}{x \parallel y \xrightarrow{a} x \parallel y'} \quad \text{Par2}$$

$$\frac{x \xrightarrow{a} x'}{x \lfloor\!\lfloor y \xrightarrow{a} x' \parallel y} \quad \text{Lme}$$

$$\frac{\Box}{\epsilon \downarrow} \quad \text{EpT}$$

$$\frac{x \downarrow}{x + y \downarrow} \quad \text{ChoT1}$$

$$\frac{y \downarrow}{x + y \downarrow} \quad \text{ChoT2}$$

$$\frac{x \downarrow \quad y \downarrow}{x \cdot y \downarrow} \quad \text{SeqT}$$

$$\frac{x \downarrow \quad y \downarrow}{x \parallel y \downarrow} \quad \text{ParT}$$

$$\frac{x \downarrow \quad y \downarrow \quad x \xrightarrow{a} x'}{x \lfloor\!\lfloor y \downarrow} \quad \text{LmeT}$$

$$\frac{x \downarrow}{\sqrt{(x)} \downarrow} \quad \text{TerT}$$

We seek a means of identifying terms that behave "in the same way". This form of behavioural equivalence is captured in the notion of *bisimulation*. Here, we use the strong formulation of bisimulation, due to Park [387].

Definition 13.11. *Strong bisimulation equivalence* $\sim \subseteq T(\Sigma) \times T(\Sigma)$, is the largest symmetric relation, such that for all $x, y \in T(\Sigma)$, if $x \sim y$, then the following conditions hold

1. $\forall x' \in T(\Sigma) : x \xrightarrow{a} x' \Rightarrow \exists y' \in T(\Sigma) : y \xrightarrow{a} y' \wedge x' \sim y'$
2. $x \downarrow \Leftrightarrow y \downarrow$

Two terms, x and y, are called *bisimilar*, if there exists a bisimulation relation, $\sim$, such that $x \sim y$. ∎

It follows from the definition that the bisimulation relation is an equivalence relation, since it is reflexive, symmetric and transitive.

The next step is to show that the bisimulation relation is a congruence. Having established this result, it is easy to show that the deduction system in Table 13.4 is a model of the equational specification PA_ϵ. This is the same as saying that the equations for PA_ϵ are sound.

Definition 13.12. *(Congruence)* Let R be an equivalence relation on $T(\Sigma)$. R is called a congruence if for all n-ary function symbols $f \in \Sigma$

$$x_1 R y_1 \wedge \ldots \wedge x_n R y_n \quad \Rightarrow \quad f(x_1, \ldots, x_n) R f(y_1, \ldots, y_n)$$

where $x_1, \ldots, x_n, y_1, \ldots, y_n \in T(\Sigma)$. ∎

Definition 13.13. *(Baeten and Verhoef [25])* Let $T = (\Sigma, D)$ be a term deduction system and let $D = D(T_p, T_r)$, where T_p are the rules for the predicate (here $\downarrow$) and T_r are the rules for the relation (here $\xrightarrow{a}$). Let I and J be index sets of arbitrary cardinality, let $t_i, s_j, t \in T(\Sigma, V)$ for all $i \in I$ and $j \in J$, let $P_j, P \in T_p$ be predicate symbols for all $j \in J$, and let $R_i, R \in T_r$ be relation symbols for all $i \in I$. A deduction rule $d \in D$ is in *path formal* if it has one of the following four forms

$$\frac{\{P_j s_j \mid j \in J\} \cup \{t_i R_i y_i \mid i \in I\}}{f(x_1, \ldots, x_n) R t}$$

with $f \in \Sigma$ an n-ary function symbol, $X = \{x_1, \ldots, x_n\}, Y = \{y_i \mid i \in I\}$, and $X \cup Y \subseteq V$ a set of distinct variables;

$$\frac{\{P_j s_j \mid j \in J\} \cup \{t_i R_i y_i \mid i \in I\}}{x R t}$$

with $X = \{x\}, Y = \{y_i \mid i \in I\}$, and $X \cup Y \subseteq V$ a set of distinct variables;

$$\frac{\{P_j s_j \mid j \in J\} \cup \{t_i R_i y_i \mid i \in I\}}{P f(x_1, \ldots, x_n)}$$

with $f \in \Sigma$ and n-ary function symbol, $X = \{x_1, \ldots, x_n\}, Y = \{y_i \mid i \in I\}$, and $X \cup Y \subseteq V$ a set of distinct variables or

$$\frac{\{P_j s_j \mid j \in J\} \cup \{t_i R_i y_i \mid i \in I\}}{P x}$$

with $X = \{x\}, Y = \{y_i \mid i \in I\}$, and $X \cup Y \subseteq V$ a set of distinct variables.

A term deduction system is said to be in *path* format if all its deduction rules are in *path* format. ∎

Theorem 13.14. *(Baeten and Verhoef [25], Fokkink [117])* Let $T = (\Sigma, D)$ be a term deduction system. If T is in *path* format, then strong bisimulation equivalence is a congruence for all function symbols in Σ. ∎

Proof. See [25]. ∎

Lemma 13.15. Let T_{PA_ϵ} be the term deduction system defined in Table 13.4. Bisimulation equivalence is a congruence on the set of closed PA_ϵ terms. ∎

Proof. We show that the deduction rules EpT and Cho1 are in path format. Writing $\downarrow$ in non-fix notation, deduction rule EpT can be rewritten to

$$\frac{\{\,\}}{\downarrow(\epsilon)}$$

which is in the third form in Definition 13.13. Similarly, Cho1 can be rewritten to

$$\frac{\{x \xrightarrow{a} x'\}}{x + y \xrightarrow{a} x'}$$

which is in the first form.

It is easily verified that the remaining deduction rules are also in *path* format, so the lemma follows from Theorem 13.14. ∎

Having established that bisimulation equivalence is a congruence, we can construct the term quotient algebra $T(\Sigma_{PA_\epsilon})/\sim$. The reason we want to construct the quotient algebra is that it is an initial algebra, which is characterised by being the smallest algebra that captures the properties of the specification.

Recall that given an algebra A with signature Σ, the quotient algebra under the congruence $\equiv$, written $A/\equiv$ is defined as

- The carrier set of $A/\equiv$ consists of the equivalence classes of the carrier set of A under the equivalence relation $\equiv$, i.e., $|A/\equiv| = \{\ [x]_\equiv \mid x \in |A|\ \}$, where $[x]_\equiv = \{\ y \mid y \in |A| \wedge x \equiv y\ \}$.
- For each n-ary function symbol f_A in A, there is a corresponding n-ary function symbol $f_{A/\equiv}$ in $A/\equiv$, defined by

$$f_{A/\equiv}([x_1]_\equiv, \ldots, [x_n]_\equiv) = [f_A(x_1, \ldots, x_n)]_\equiv$$

Theorem 13.16. The set of closed PA_ϵ terms modulo bisimulation equivalence, notation $T(\Sigma_{PA_\epsilon})/\sim$, is a model of PA_ϵ.   ∎

Proof. Recall that a Σ-algebra, A, is a model of an equational specification (Σ, E), if $A \models E$, i.e., if every equation derivable from E holds in A. Because bisimulation equivalence on PA_ϵ terms is a congruence by Lemma 13.15, it is sufficient to separately verify the soundness of each axiom in E_{PA_ϵ}, i.e., to show if $PA_\epsilon \vdash x = y$, then $x \sim y$.

We illustrate the procedure by verifying equation A1. We have to show that there exists a bisimulation equivalence $\sim_*$ such that $x + y \sim_* y + x$. Let $\sim_*$ be defined as $\{\, (x+y, y+x) \mid x, y \in T(\Sigma_{PA_\epsilon}) \,\} \cup \{\, (x, x) \mid x \in T(\Sigma_{PA_\epsilon}) \}$. Clearly, $\sim_*$ is symmetric. We now check the first bisimulation condition. $x + y$ can evolve only by following one of the two deduction rules Cho1 and Cho2. Suppose $x \xrightarrow{a} x'$, then $x + y \xrightarrow{a} x'$, but then we also have $y + x \xrightarrow{a} x'$. By definition $x' \sim_* x'$, so the condition is satisfied in this case. The symmetric case $y \xrightarrow{a} y'$ follows from the same argument. Next, the second bisimulation condition must be checked. Suppose $x \downarrow$, then by ChoT1 $x + y \downarrow$. But in that case by ChoT2 $y + x \downarrow$. Again the symmetric case $y \downarrow$ follows immediately.

The above procedure can be applied to the remaining equations to show that equal terms are bisimilar. Thus, the theorem follows.   ∎

Finally, we show that PA_ϵ is a complete axiomatisation of the set of closed terms modulo bisimulation equivalence, i.e., whenever $x \sim y$, then $PA_\epsilon \vdash x = y$.

Theorem 13.17. The axiom system PA_ϵ is a complete axiomatisation of the set of closed terms modulo bisimulation equivalence.   ∎

Proof. Due to Theorems 13.16 and 13.10 it suffices to prove the theorem for basic terms. The proof for basic terms is given in [26].   ∎

13.3.3 The Process Algebra PAc_ϵ

The process algebra PA_ϵ introduced in the previous section is sufficiently expressive to define the semantics of MSCs. However, the extension to LSCs calls for the introduction of an additional operator.

In this subsection we introduce the extended process algebra, called PAc_ϵ, for process algebra with conditional behaviour. PAc_ϵ is a conservative extension of PA_ϵ, meaning that the theory of PA_ϵ also holds in PAc_ϵ. We give an axiom system and a model of PAc_ϵ, and show that the axiom system is sound and complete. Our task now is considerably easier, since most of the results for PA_ϵ can be directly transferred to PAc_ϵ.

The signature of PAc_ϵ, Σ_{PAc_ϵ}, consists of

1. two special constants δ and ϵ

Table 13.5. Additional equations of PAc_ϵ

$$\epsilon \triangleright x = x \qquad \text{C1}$$
$$\delta \triangleright x = \epsilon \qquad \text{C2}$$
$$x + y \triangleright z = (x \triangleright z) + (y \triangleright z) \qquad \text{C3}$$
$$a \cdot x \triangleright y = a \cdot (x \triangleright y) + \bar{a}, \quad \text{where } \bar{a} \in A \setminus \{a\} \qquad \text{C4}$$

2. a set of unspecified constants A, for which $\{\delta, \epsilon\} \cap A = \emptyset$
3. the unary operator $\sqrt{}$
4. the binary operators $+$, $\cdot$, $\|$, $\|\!\|$ and $\triangleright$

The binary operator $\triangleright$ is the *conditional behaviour* operator. The conditional behaviour of processes x and y is the process that either terminates successfully or executes x followed by y. The other operators and constants have the same meaning as they do in PA_ϵ.

Table 13.5 lists the additional equations E_{PAc_ϵ} for $a \in A$ and $x, y, z \in V$.

Table 13.6. Additional term rewriting rules for PAc_ϵ

$$\epsilon \triangleright x \rightarrow x \qquad \text{RC1}$$
$$\delta \triangleright x \rightarrow \epsilon \qquad \text{RC2}$$
$$x + y \triangleright z \rightarrow x \triangleright z + y \triangleright z \qquad \text{RC3}$$
$$a \cdot x \triangleright y \rightarrow a \cdot (x \triangleright y) + \bar{a} \qquad \text{RC4}$$
$$a \triangleright y \rightarrow a \cdot y + \bar{a} \qquad \text{RC4'}$$

Theorem 13.18. The term rewriting system for PAc_ϵ in Table 13.6 is strongly normalizing. ∎

Proof. The proof is based on the proof of theorem 13.9. We add the conditional operator to the partial ordering: $\triangleright > \|\!\| > \| > \sqrt{} > \cdot > + > \epsilon > \delta$. We now show that the additional rewrite rules for PAc_ϵ satisfy the extension of the partial ordering to terms.

$$\epsilon \triangleright x >_{lpo} \epsilon \triangleright^* x \qquad \text{RPO1}$$
$$>_{lpo} \epsilon \qquad \text{RPO3}$$

$$\delta \triangleright x \;>_{lpo}\; \delta \triangleright^* x \qquad\qquad \text{RPO1}$$
$$>_{lpo}\; \epsilon \qquad\qquad \text{RPO2}$$

$$x + y \triangleright z \;>_{lpo}\; x + y \triangleright^* z \qquad\qquad\qquad \text{RPO1}$$
$$>_{lpo}\; (x + y \triangleright^* z) + (x + y \triangleright^* z) \qquad\qquad \text{RPO2}$$
$$>_{lpo}\; (x +^* y \triangleright z) + (x +^* y \triangleright z) \qquad \text{RPO4, RPO5}$$
$$>_{lpo}\; (x \triangleright z) + (y \triangleright z) \qquad\qquad \text{RPO4, RPO5}$$

$$a \cdot x \triangleright y \;>_{lpo}\; a \cdot x \triangleright^* y \qquad\qquad\qquad \text{RPO1}$$
$$>_{lpo}\; (a \cdot x \triangleright^* y) + (a \cdot x \triangleright^* y) \qquad\qquad \text{RPO2}$$
$$>_{lpo}\; (a \cdot x \triangleright^* y) + \bar{a} \qquad\qquad \text{RPO2, RPO5}$$
$$>_{lpo}\; (a \cdot x \triangleright^* y) \cdot (a \cdot x \triangleright^* y) + \bar{a} \qquad\qquad \text{RPO2}$$
$$>_{lpo}\; (a \cdot^* x) \cdot (x \triangleright y) + \bar{a} \qquad \text{RPO1, RPO3, RPO5}$$
$$>_{lpo}\; a \cdot (x \triangleright y) + \bar{a} \qquad\qquad \text{RPO1, RPO3}$$

$$a \triangleright y \;>_{lpo}\; a \triangleright^* y \qquad\qquad\qquad \text{RPO1}$$
$$>_{lpo}\; (a \triangleright^* y) + (a \triangleright^* y) \qquad\qquad \text{RPO2}$$
$$>_{lpo}\; (a \triangleright^* y) + \bar{a} \qquad\qquad \text{RPO2, RPO5}$$
$$>_{lpo}\; (a \triangleright^* y) \cdot (a \triangleright^* y) + \bar{a} \qquad\qquad \text{RPO1, RPO3}$$
$$>_{lpo}\; a \cdot y + \bar{a} \qquad\qquad \text{RPO3, RPO5}$$

Thus, the rewrite system for PAc_ϵ is strongly normalizing. ∎

In Theorem 13.10 we showed that every PA_ϵ term has an equivalent basic term. With the definition of a basic term from Definition 13.4, we have the similar result for PAc_ϵ.

Theorem 13.19. For every PAc_ϵ term, s, there is a corresponding basic term, t, such that $PA_\epsilon \vdash s = t$. ∎

Proof. We have already shown that the subset of PAc_ϵ that corresponds to PA_ϵ can be reduced to basic terms. Thus, we only need to show that terms with the conditional operator can be reduced to basic terms.

Because the term rewriting system for PAc_ϵ is strongly normalizing by Theorem 13.18, then for every term t, there exists a finite sequence of rewritings

$$t \rightarrow t_1 \rightarrow t_2 \rightarrow \cdots \rightarrow s$$

where s is in normal form.

We use a proof by contradiction to show that s cannot contain $\triangleright$. Assume therefore, that s is in normal form and that $s = C[x \triangleright y]$.

If $x = C[u \triangleright w]$ then the argument can be applied recursively to show that $u \triangleright w$ or one of u's sub-terms can be reduced, thus contradicting that s is in normal form. Otherwise, there are five possibilities

- $x = \epsilon$: then s can be reduced by RC1.
- $x = \delta$: then s can be reduced by RC2.
- $x = u + w$: then s can be reduced by RC4.
- $x = a \cdot x'$: then s can be reduced by RC5.
- $x = a$: then s can be reduced by RC5'.

All cases contradict that s is in normal form. Thus, every PAc_ϵ term can be reduced to an equivalent basic term.   ∎

13.3.4 Semantics for PAc_ϵ

The additional semantical rules for PAc_ϵ are shown in Table 13.7.

Table 13.7. Extra semantic rules for PAc_ϵ

$$\frac{x \xrightarrow{a} x'}{x \triangleright y \xrightarrow{\bar{a}} \epsilon} \qquad \text{Con1}$$

$$\frac{x \xrightarrow{a} x'}{x \triangleright y \xrightarrow{a} x' \triangleright y} \qquad \text{Con2}$$

$$\frac{x \xrightarrow{a} x'}{\epsilon \triangleright x \xrightarrow{a} x'} \qquad \text{Con3}$$

$$\frac{x \downarrow \quad y \downarrow}{x \triangleright y \downarrow} \qquad \text{ConT1}$$

$$\frac{x \not\downarrow}{x \triangleright y \downarrow} \qquad \text{ConT2}$$

In order to prove that bisimulation is a congruence on the set of closed PAc_ϵ terms we need to introduce a generalisation of the *path* format used in the previous section. The generalisation is known as *panth* format for "predicates and *ntyft/ntyxt* hybrid format". It generalises the *path* format by allowing negative premises in the deduction rules. It is also a generalisation of the *ntyft/ntyxt* of Groote [154], which in turn along with the *path* format is a generalisation of the *tyft/tyxt* format of Groote and Vaandrager [155]. The names of these formats are derived from the format of the premises and conclusion of the deduction rules, see Verhoef [514] for an explanation.

The reference for the following material is Verhoef [514].

Definition 13.20. *(Verhoef [514])* Let $T = (\Sigma, D)$ be a term deduction system and let $D = D(T_p, T_r)$, where T_p is the set of predicate symbols and T_r is the set of relation symbols. Let I, J, K and L be index sets of arbitrary cardinality, let $s_j, t_i, u_l, v_k, t \in T(\Sigma, V)$ for all $i \in I$, $j \in J$, $k \in K$ and $l \in L$, and let $P_j, P \in T_p$ be predicate symbols for all $j \in J$, and let $R_i, R \in T_r$ be relation symbols for all $i \in I$. A deduction rule $d \in D$ is in *panth format* if it has one of the following four forms

$$\frac{\{P_j s_j \mid j \in J\} \cup \{t_i R_i y_i \mid i \in I\} \cup \{\neg P_l u_l \mid l \in L\} \cup \{v_k \neg R_k \mid k \in K\}}{f(x_1, \ldots, x_n) R t}$$

with $f \in \Sigma$ an n-ary function symbol, $X = \{x_1, \ldots, x_n\}, Y = \{y_i \mid i \in I\}$, and $X \cup Y \subseteq V$ a set of distinct variables;

$$\frac{\{P_j s_j \mid j \in J\} \cup \{t_i R_i y_i \mid i \in I\} \cup \{\neg P_l u_l \mid l \in L\} \cup \{v_k \neg R_k \mid k \in K\}}{x R t}$$

with $X = \{x\}, Y = \{y_i \mid i \in I\}$, and $X \cup Y \subseteq V$ a set of distinct variables;

$$\frac{\{P_j s_j \mid j \in J\} \cup \{t_i R_i y_i \mid i \in I\} \cup \{\neg P_l u_l \mid l \in L\} \cup \{v_k \neg R_k \mid k \in K\}}{P f(x_1, \ldots, x_n)}$$

with $f \in \Sigma$ and n-ary function symbol, $X = \{x_1, \ldots, x_n\}, Y = \{y_i \mid i \in I\}$, and $X \cup Y \subseteq V$ a set of distinct variables or

$$\frac{\{P_j s_j \mid j \in J\} \cup \{t_i R_i y_i \mid i \in I\} \cup \{\neg P_l u_l \mid l \in L\} \cup \{v_k \neg R_k \mid k \in K\}}{P x}$$

with $X = \{x\}, Y = \{y_i \mid i \in I\}$, and $X \cup Y \subseteq V$ a set of distinct variables.

A term deduction system is said to be in *panth* format if all its deduction rules are in *panth* format.   ∎

Before we can introduce the congruence theorem for the *panth* format we need to define some additional notions.

Definition 13.21. Let $T = (\Sigma, D)$ be a term deduction system. The formula dependency graph G of T is a labelled directed graph with the positive formulas of D as nodes. Let $PF(H)$ denote the set of all positive formulas in H and let $NF(H)$ denote all the negative formulas in H, then for all deduction rules $H/C \in D$ and for all closed substitutions σ we have the following edges in G:

- for all $h \in PF(H)$ there is an edge $\sigma(h) \xrightarrow{p} \sigma(C)$;
- for all $s \neg R \in NF(H)$ there is for all $t \in T(\Sigma)$ an edge $\sigma(sRt) \xrightarrow{n} \sigma(C)$;
- for all $\neg Ps \in NF(H)$ there is an edge $\sigma(Ps) \xrightarrow{n} \sigma(C)$.

An edge labelled with a p is called positive and an edge labelled with an n is called negative. A set of edges is called positive if all its elements are positive and negative if the edges are all negative.   ∎

Definition 13.22. A term deduction system is stratifiable if there is no node in its formula dependency graph that is the start of a backward chain of edges containing an infinite negative subset.   ∎

Definition 13.23. Let $T = (\Sigma, D)$ be a term deduction system and let F be a set of formulas. The variable dependency graph of F is a directed graph with the variables occurring in F as its nodes. The edge $x \to y$ is an edge of the variable dependency graph if and only if there is a positive relation $tRs \in F$ with $x \in vars(t)$ and $y \in vars(s)$.

The set F is called well-founded if any backward chain of edges in its variable dependency graph is finite. A deduction rule is called well-founded if its set of premises is so. A term deduction system is called well-founded if all its deduction rules are well-founded.   ∎

We are now ready to formulate the main result of Verhoef [514].

Theorem 13.24. *(Verhoef [514]).* Let $T = (\Sigma, D)$ be a well-founded stratifiable term deduction system in *panth* format, then strong bisimulation is a congruence for all function symbols in Σ.   ∎

Proof. See [514].   ∎

Lemma 13.25. Let $T = (\Sigma_{PAc_\epsilon}, D)$ be the term deduction system in Table 13.7, then strong bisimulation is a congruence on the set of closed PAc_ϵ terms.   ∎

Proof. The proof relies on Theorem 13.24.

First, we must check that the term deduction system is well-founded. No variable occurs more than once in the set of premises for any of the deduction rules, so it is clear that there are no cycles in the variable dependency graph. Hence, the term deduction system is well-founded.

Next, we must show that the term deduction system is stratifiable. We use proof by contradiction. Assume the term deduction is not stratifiable. Then, there is some backward chain of edges in the formula dependency graph that contains an infinite negative subset of edges. The only negative edge in the graph is the one that stems from ConT2. Thus, there must be a cycle containing the edge $\sigma(x \downarrow) \xrightarrow{n} \sigma(x \triangleright y \downarrow)$. This cycle must also contain at least one edge originating at the node $\sigma(x \triangleright y \downarrow)$ and terminating at some node, Z, see Figure 13.24.

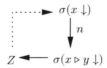

Fig. 13.24. Illustration for proof of congruence

By the definition of the formula dependency graph, the edge $\sigma(x \triangleright y \downarrow) \to Z$ can only be in the graph because there is a deduction rule with $x \triangleright y \downarrow$ as one of its premises. However, there is no such rule, and we have a contradiction. Therefore, the term deduction system is stratifiable.

Finally, we must verify that each of the deduction rules is in *panth* format. Since any rule that is in *path* format is also in *panth* format, we only need to check the additional rules for PAc_ϵ, since the remaining rules were shown to be in *path* format in the proof for Lemma 13.15. The rule Con1 can be trivially rewritten to

$$\frac{\{x \xrightarrow{a} x'\}}{x \rhd y \xrightarrow{\bar{a}} \epsilon}$$

which is in the first *panth* form. The rule ConT2 can similarly be rewritten to

$$\frac{\{\neg \downarrow (x)\}}{\downarrow (x \rhd y)}$$

which is in the third *panth* form. The remaining three rules are easily shown to also be in *panth* format.

Thus, all the conditions of Theorem 13.24 are satisfied and the result follows.   ∎

Theorem 13.26. The set of closed PAc_ϵ terms modulo bisimulation equivalence, notation $T(\Sigma_{PAc_\epsilon})/\sim$, is a model of PAc_ϵ.   ∎

Proof. Recalling the proof for Theorem 13.16 we have to show that for each of the equations in E_{PAc_ϵ}, $PAc_\epsilon \vdash x = y$ implies the existence of a bisimulation, $\sim$, such that $x \sim y$.

We give the proof for axiom C4. Let $\sim_*$ be defined by $\{ (a \cdot x \rhd y, a \cdot (x \rhd y) + \bar{a}) \mid x, y \in T(\Sigma_{PAc_\epsilon}), a \in A \} \cup \{ (x,y) \mid x, y \in T(\Sigma_{PAc_\epsilon}) \}$. Clearly, $\sim_*$ is symmetric. We first check the termination condition. By ConT1 $a \cdot x \rhd y \downarrow$, since $a \cdot x \not\downarrow$. Similarly, $a \cdot (x \rhd y) + \bar{a} \downarrow$, since $\bar{a} \not\downarrow$ (and actually also $a \cdot (x \rhd y) \not\downarrow$). Thus, the termination condition for bisimulation equivalence is satisfied.

Now, we check the first bisimulation condition. There are two ways $a \cdot x \rhd y$ can evolve:

- $a \cdot x \rhd y \xrightarrow{\bar{a}} \epsilon$: then we get $a \cdot (x \rhd y) + \bar{a} \xrightarrow{\bar{a}} \epsilon$ and since $\epsilon \sim_* \epsilon$ by definition, the bisimulation condition is satisfied in this case.
- $a \cdot x \rhd y \xrightarrow{a} x \rhd y$: similarly, $a \cdot (x \rhd y) + \bar{a} \xrightarrow{a} x \rhd y$ and again $x \rhd y \sim_* x \rhd y$, so the bisimulation condition is satisfied.

The symmetric case for evolutions of $a \cdot (x \rhd y) + \bar{a}$ is entirely analogous.

The remaining axioms can be checked with the same technique.   ∎

We now come to the final result showing that the axiom system for PAc_ϵ is both sound and complete.

Theorem 13.27. The axiom system PAc_ϵ is a complete axiomatisation of the set of closed PAc_ϵ terms modulo bisimulation equivalence.   ∎

Proof. Due to Theorems 13.26 and 13.19 it suffices to prove the theorem for basic terms. The proof for basic terms is given in [26].   ∎

13.4 Algebraic Semantics of Live Sequence Charts

In this section a subset of LSCs is given an algebraic semantics using the process algebra PAc_ϵ from the previous section (Sect. 13.3). The presentation here is adapted from the description of the semantics of MSC given by Mauw and Reniers [326].

13.4.1 Textual Syntax of Live Sequence Charts

We give a textual syntax for LSC. The textual syntax is used to define the semantics in the next section. The textual syntax is presented as an extended BNF (EBNF) grammar below. The nonterminals *lscid, msgid* and *inst name* are further unspecified identifiers. The nonterminal *cond* represents a further unspecified conditional expression.

Table 13.8. EBNF grammar for textual syntax of LSCs

$\langle chart \rangle$ ::= **lsc** <lscid> ; <inst def list> **end lsc**

$\langle inst\ def\ list \rangle$ ::= <inst def> <inst def list> | <>

$\langle inst\ def \rangle$ ::= **instance** <inst name> <prechart> <body> **end instance**

$\langle prechart \rangle$ ::= **prechart** <location> **end prechart**

$\langle body \rangle$ ::= **body** <location> **end body**

$\langle location \rangle$ ::= **hot** <event> ; <location> | **cold** <event> ; <location> | <>

$\langle event \rangle$ ::= <input> | <output> | <condition> | <coregion>

$\langle input \rangle$ ::= **in** <msgid> **from** <address> <mode>

$\langle output \rangle$ ::= **out** <msgid > **to** <address> <mode>

$\langle condition \rangle$ ::= **hot condition** <cond> | **cold condition** <cond>

$\langle coregion \rangle$ ::= **concurrent** <coeventlist> **end concurrent**

$\langle coeventlist \rangle$ ::= <input> <coeventlist> | <output> <coeventlist> | <>

$\langle address \rangle$ ::= <inst name> | **env**

$\langle mode \rangle$ ::= **sync** | **async**

We do not explain the mapping from an LSC to the textual syntax further as this is straightforward. Example 13.22 in Sect. 13.2.2 illustrates the mapping.

13.4.2 Semantics of Live Sequence Charts

In order to define the semantics of the subset of LSC, we instantiate the process algebra PAc_ϵ by specifying the set of atomic actions. We assume a set, A_o, of atomic actions representing asynchronous (*out*) and synchronous (*outs*) message output

$$A_o = \{out(i,j,m) \mid i,j \in \mathcal{L}(\langle inst\ name\rangle), m \in \mathcal{L}(\langle msgid\rangle)\} \cup$$
$$\{outs(i,j,m) \mid i,j \in \mathcal{L}(\langle inst\ name\rangle), m \in \mathcal{L}(\langle msgid\rangle)\}$$

Similarly, we assume a set, A_i, of atomic actions representing asynchronous (*in*) and synchronous (*ins*) message input

$$A_i = \{in(i,j,m) \mid i,j \in \mathcal{L}(\langle inst\ name\rangle), m \in \mathcal{L}(\langle msgid\rangle)\} \cup$$
$$\{ins(i,j,m) \mid i,j \in \mathcal{L}(\langle inst\ name\rangle), m \in \mathcal{L}(\langle msgid\rangle)\}$$

Conditions are also viewed as actions, so there is a set of atomic actions representing hot conditions

$$A_{hc} = \{hotcond(c) \mid c \in \mathcal{L}(\langle cond\rangle)\ \}$$

and a set of atomic actions representing cold conditions

$$A_{cc} = \{coldcond(c) \mid c \in \mathcal{L}(\langle cond\rangle)\ \}$$

The set of atomic actions, A, of the instantiated process algebra is then

$$A = A_o \cup A_i \cup A_{hc} \cup A_{cc}$$

The process algebra PAc_ϵ defined above does not place any constraints on the order of atomic events. In expressing the semantics of LSC the constraint that message input must follow the corresponding message output has to be expressed. To do this, the state operator $\lambda_{M,C}$ is introduced. It is an instance of the general state operator [27].

For $M \subseteq \mathcal{L}(\langle msgid\rangle)$, $x,y \in V$, $a \in A$, $i,j \in \mathcal{L}(\langle inst\ name\rangle)$ and $m \in \mathcal{L}(\langle msgid\rangle)$, the state operator is defined by the equations in Table 13.9. The subscript M records the message identifiers of messages that have been output, but not yet input. The subscript C records the message identifiers of those synchronous messages that have been output, but not yet input. If C is nonempty and the next event is not the corresponding input event, deadlock occurs. This ensures that no other events can come between the output and input of a synchronous message. The instantiated process algebra with $\lambda_{M,C}$ will be referred to as PA_{LSC} in the following.

The semantics of LSCs will be defined by semantic functions over the syntactical categories of the textual syntax of LSCs. If $\langle cat\rangle$ denotes a syntactical category (nonterminal) in the ENBF grammar, then $\mathcal{L}(\langle cat\rangle)$ denotes the language of text strings derivable from that syntactical category. The notation $\mathcal{P}X$ denotes the power set of the set X.

Table 13.9. Definition of state operator $\lambda_{M,C}$

$\lambda_{M,C}(\epsilon) = \epsilon$	if $M = \emptyset$
$\lambda_{M,C}(\epsilon) = \delta$	if $M \neq \emptyset$
$\lambda_{M,C}(\delta) = \delta$	
$\lambda_{M,C}(a \cdot x) = \delta$	if $a \notin A_o \cup A_i$ and $C \neq \emptyset$
$\lambda_{M,C}(a \cdot x) = a \cdot \lambda_{M,\emptyset}(x)$	if $a \notin A_o \cup A_i$ and $C = \emptyset$
$\lambda_{M,C}(out(i, env, m) \cdot x) = \delta$	if $C \neq \emptyset$
$\lambda_{M,C}(out(i, env, m) \cdot x) = out(i, env, m) \cdot \lambda_{M,\emptyset}(x)$	if $C = \emptyset$
$\lambda_{M,C}(out(i, j, m) \cdot x) = \delta$	if $m \in M$ or $C \neq \emptyset$
$\lambda_{M,C}(out(i, j, m) \cdot x) = out(i, j, m) \cdot \lambda_{M \cup \{m\},\emptyset}(x)$	if $m \notin M$ and $C = \emptyset$
$\lambda_{M,C}(outs(i, env, m) \cdot x) = \delta$	if $C \neq \emptyset$
$\lambda_{M,C}(outs(i, env, m) \cdot x) = outs(i, env, m) \cdot \lambda_{M,\emptyset}(x)$	if $C = \emptyset$
$\lambda_{M,C}(outs(i, j, m) \cdot x) = \delta$	if $m \in M$ or $C \neq \emptyset$
$\lambda_{M,C}(outs(i, j, m) \cdot x) = outs(i, j, m) \cdot \lambda_{M \cup \{m\},\{m\}}(x)$	if $m \notin M$ and $C \neq \emptyset$
$\lambda_{M,C}(in(env, j, m) \cdot x) = \delta$	if $C \neq \emptyset$
$\lambda_{M,C}(in(env, j, m) \cdot x) = in(env, j, m) \cdot \lambda_{M,\emptyset}(x)$	if $C = \emptyset$
$\lambda_{M,C}(in(i, j, m) \cdot x) = in(i, j, m) \cdot \lambda_{M \setminus \{m\},\emptyset}(x)$	if $m \in M$ and $C = \emptyset$
$\lambda_{M,C}(in(i, j, m) \cdot x) = \delta$	if $m \notin M$ or $C \neq \emptyset$
$\lambda_{M,C}(ins(env, j, m) \cdot x) = \delta$	if $C \neq \emptyset$
$\lambda_{M,C}(ins(env, j, m) \cdot x) = ins(env, j, m) \cdot \lambda_{M,\emptyset}(x)$	if $C = \emptyset$
$\lambda_{M,C}(ins(i, j, m) \cdot x) = ins(i, j, m) \cdot \lambda_{M \setminus \{m\},\emptyset}(x)$	if $m \in M$ and $C = \{m\}$
$\lambda_{M,C}(ins(i, j, m) \cdot x) = \delta$	if $m \notin M$ or $C \neq \{m\}$
$\lambda_{M,C}(x + y) = \lambda_{M,C}(x) + \lambda_{M,C}(y)$	
$\lambda_{M,C}(x \triangleright y) = \lambda_M(x) \triangleright \lambda_M(y)$	

The semantic function for LSCs,

$$S_{LSC}[\![\cdot]\!] : \mathcal{L}(\langle chart \rangle) \to T(\Sigma_{PA_{LSC}}),$$

is defined by

$$S_{LSC}[\![ch]\!] = \lambda_{\emptyset,\emptyset}\left(\left(\|_{i \in Inst_c(ch)}\ S_{instpc}[\![i]\!]\right) \triangleright \left(\|_{i \in Inst_c(ch)}\ S_{instbody}[\![i]\!]\right)\right)$$

where $Inst_c : \mathcal{L}(\langle chart \rangle) \to \mathcal{P}(\mathcal{L}(\langle inst\ def \rangle))$ is the set of instance definitions in the chart. It is defined by

$$Inst_c(\mathbf{lsc}\ \langle lscid \rangle\ ;\ \langle inst\ def\ list \rangle\ \mathbf{endlsc}) = Inst_{idl}(\langle inst\ def\ list \rangle)$$

where in turn $Inst_{idl} : \mathcal{L}(\langle inst\ def\ list \rangle) \to \mathcal{P}(\mathcal{L}(\langle inst\ def \rangle))$ is defined by

$$Inst_{idl}(\langle\rangle) = \emptyset$$

$$Inst_{idl}(\langle inst\ def \rangle\ \langle inst\ def\ list \rangle) = \{\langle inst\ def \rangle\} \cup Inst_{idl}(\langle inst\ def\ list \rangle)$$

The semantic function for instance precharts,

$$S_{instpc}[\![\cdot]\!] : \mathcal{L}(\langle inst\ def \rangle) \to T(\Sigma_{PA_{LSC}}),$$

is defined by

$$S_{instpc}[\![\mathbf{instance}\ \langle inst\ name \rangle\ \langle prechart \rangle\ \langle body \rangle\ \mathbf{endinstance}]\!] =$$
$$S_{pre-chart}^{\langle inst\ name \rangle}[\![\langle prechart \rangle]\!]$$

The semantic function for instance bodies,

$$S_{instbody}[\![\ \cdot\ ]\!] : \mathcal{L}(\langle inst\ def \rangle) \rightarrow T(\Sigma_{PA_{LSC}}),$$

is defined by

$$S_{instbody}[\![\mathbf{instance}\ \langle inst\ name \rangle\ \langle prechart \rangle\ \langle body \rangle\ \mathbf{endinstance}]\!] =$$
$$S_{body}^{\langle inst\ name \rangle}[\![\langle body \rangle]\!]$$

For $iid \in \mathcal{L}(\langle inst\ name \rangle)$ the semantic function for precharts,

$$S_{body}^{iid}[\![\ \cdot\ ]\!] : \mathcal{L}(\langle prechart \rangle) \rightarrow T(\Sigma_{PA_{LSC}}),$$

is defined by

$$S_{prechart}^{iid}[\![\mathbf{prechart}\ \langle location \rangle\ \mathbf{endprechart}]\!] = S_{location}^{iid}[\![\langle location \rangle]\!]$$

For $iid \in \mathcal{L}(\langle inst\ name \rangle)$ the semantic function for instance bodies,

$$S_{body}^{iid}[\![\ \cdot\ ]\!] : \mathcal{L}(\langle body \rangle) \rightarrow T(\Sigma_{PA_{LSC}}),$$

is defined by

$$S_{body}^{iid}[\![\mathbf{body}\ \langle location \rangle\ \mathbf{endbody}]\!] = S_{location}^{iid}[\![\langle location \rangle]\!]$$

For $iid \in \mathcal{L}(\langle inst\ name \rangle)$ the semantic function for event lists,

$$S_{location}^{iid}[\![\ \cdot\ ]\!] : \mathcal{L}(\langle location \rangle) \rightarrow T(\Sigma_{PA_{LSC}}),$$

is defined by:

$$S_{location}^{iid}[\![\langle\rangle]\!] = \epsilon$$
$$S_{location}^{iid}[\![\mathbf{hot}\ \langle event \rangle\ ;\ \langle location \rangle]\!] = S_{event}^{iid}[\![\langle event \rangle]\!] \cdot S_{location}^{iid}[\![\langle location \rangle]\!]$$
$$S_{location}^{iid}[\![\mathbf{cold}\ \langle event \rangle\ ;\ \langle location \rangle]\!] = \epsilon + \left(S_{event}^{iid}[\![\langle event \rangle]\!] \cdot S_{location}^{iid}[\![\langle location \rangle]\!] \right)$$

For $iid \in \mathcal{L}(\langle inst\ name \rangle)$ the semantic function for events,

$$S_{event}^{iid}[\![\ \cdot\ ]\!] : \mathcal{L}(\langle event \rangle) \rightarrow T(\Sigma_{PA_{LSC}}),$$

is defined by:

$$S_{event}^{iid}[\![\textbf{out}\ \langle msgid\rangle\ \textbf{to}\ \langle address\rangle\ \textbf{async}]\!] = out(iid, \langle address\rangle, \langle msgid\rangle)$$

$$S_{event}^{iid}[\![\textbf{out}\ \langle msgid\rangle\ \textbf{to}\ \langle address\rangle\ \textbf{sync}]\!] = outs(iid, \langle address\rangle, \langle msgid\rangle)$$

$$S_{event}^{iid}[\![\textbf{in}\ \langle msgid\rangle\ \textbf{from}\ \langle address\rangle\ \textbf{async}]\!] = in(\langle address\rangle, iid, \langle msgid\rangle)$$

$$S_{event}^{iid}[\![\textbf{in}\ \langle msgid\rangle\ \textbf{from}\ \langle address\rangle\ \textbf{sync}]\!] = ins(\langle address\rangle, iid, \langle msgid\rangle)$$

$$S_{event}^{iid}[\![\textbf{hotcondition}\ \langle cond\rangle\,]\!] = hotcond(\langle cond\rangle)$$

$$S_{event}^{iid}[\![\textbf{coldcondition}\ \langle cond\rangle\,]\!] = coldcond(\langle cond\rangle)$$

$$S_{event}^{iid}[\![\textbf{concurrent}\ \langle coeventlist\rangle\ \textbf{endconcurrent}]\!]$$
$$= \|_{e\in CoEvents(\langle coeventlist\rangle)}\ S_{event}^{iid}[\![e]\!]$$

where $CoEvents : \mathcal{L}(\langle eventlist\rangle) \to \mathcal{P}(\mathcal{L}(\langle event\rangle))$ is defined by:

$$CoEvents(\langle\rangle) = \emptyset$$
$$CoEvents(\langle event\rangle\ \langle eventlist\rangle) = \{\langle event\rangle\} \cup CoEvents(\langle eventlist\rangle)$$

13.4.3 The Live Sequence Chart Example, II

Example 13.23 *The Live Sequence Chart, Part II:* We end this section with an example that concludes Example 13.22 of Sect. 13.2.2. The example illustrates the process of deriving a PA_{LSC} term from the LSC diagram of Sect. 13.2.2. We derive the PA_{LSC} term from the textual syntax by using the semantic function for LSCs. Let the chart be denoted by ch, then the semantics of ch is given by the PA_{LSC} term below.

$$S_{LSC}[\![ch]\!] =$$
$$\lambda_{\emptyset,\emptyset}((hotcond(cond_1) \cdot out(A, B, m_1) \ \|$$
$$\quad hotcond(cond_1) \cdot in(A, B, m_1))$$
$$\quad \rhd$$
$$\quad (out(A, B, m_2) \cdot coldcond(cond_2) \cdot outs(A, B, m_4)$$
$$\quad \|$$
$$\quad (in(A, B, m_2)\ \|\ in(C, A, m_3)) \cdot coldcond(cond_2)\ \cdot$$
$$\quad ins(A, B, m_4) \cdot out(B, C, m_3)$$
$$\quad \|$$
$$\quad out(C, B, m_3) \cdot (\epsilon + in(B, C, m_5) \cdot (\epsilon + out(C, env, m_6)))))$$

13.5 Relating Message Charts to RSL

In this section, as well as in Sect. 14.7, we briefly review a number of ways of integrating different specification notations. We then define a subset of RSL and give an operational semantics based on the semantics for Timed RSL as defined by George and Xia [132] (see Sect. 15.4). We extend the semantic rules with behaviour annotations capturing the communication behaviour of the RSL expression. Utilizing these behaviours, we define three satisfaction relations: one relating a universal LSC to an RSL specification, one relating an existential LSC to an RSL specification and, in Sect. 14.7, one relating a statechart to an RSL specification.

13.5.1 Types of Integration

Haxthausen [203] identifies three approaches to integrating different specification techniques:

- the *unifying, wide-spectrum* approach
- the *family* approach
- the *linking* approach

The wide-spectrum approach provides a complete semantical integration of the techniques. This was the approach adopted in the development of RSL. The advantage of this approach is that the same language is used throughout the development process. The disadvantage is that this approach results in a complicated semantics.

The idea in the family approach is to define a reasonably expressive base language and then integrate other techniques by defining extension languages. The semantics of the extension languages are required to be consistent with the semantics of the base language. This approach is used in the CoFI [371] project, for which the base language is called CASL [40]. The advantage of the family approach is that the semantics is "only as complicated as it needs to be", in the sense that for a particular project, one uses the smallest language in the family that has the required facilities.

In the previous two approaches a new semantics that subsumes the semantics of the individual techniques is developed. In contrast, in the linking approach the individual semantics are preserved, and the integration instead takes the form of a formal relation between the individual semantics. This approach is particularly suited for specification techniques that are fundamentally different.

There is also a fourth approach to integration, namely what we call the combination approach. In this approach one notation is embedded in the other to extend its expressiveness. An example is the coloured Petri nets, which are the result of the combination of classical Petri nets with an ML-like language [238, 275] used for inscriptions on arcs and type definitions. Other examples are the combinations of statecharts with CASL and statecharts with Z mentioned in the introduction.

We believe that of the four approaches described, the linking approach is most suited for our purpose. By using this approach we do not have to "massage" the familiar semantics of the individual techniques into a new framework. Additionally, all the tools (proof system, syntax checkers, code generators) developed for RSL are immediately available in the integrated method.

In the rest of this chapter we therefore present how to link LSCs with RSL. In the next chapter we will explain how to link statecharts with RSL.

13.5.2 An RSL Subset

Syntax

The subset of RSL defined below is almost the same as the subset defined by George and Xia [132] for Timed RSL. We omit the **wait** construct and use the standard input and output operators from RSL rather than the corresponding operators in timed RSL (TRSL, [132]). Also, we exclude the special notation for recursive functions. For use in establishing the relation to LSCs and statecharts, we annotate the input and output operators with a message identifier. Similarly, the parallel and interlocking operators are annotated with two process identifiers.

We assume familiarity with RSL and therefore skip an informal description of the operators and constructs of the RSL subset.

The syntactic categories are

- expressions denoted by E
- variables denoted by x
- identifiers denoted by id
- channels denoted by c
- reals denoted by r
- types denoted by τ
- value definitions denoted by V
- message identifiers denoted by $msgid$
- process identifiers denoted by n

The grammar of the subset of RSL is given below.

$$V ::= id : \tau \mid id : \tau, V$$

$$
\begin{aligned}
E ::= &\; () \mid \textbf{true} \mid \textbf{false} \mid r \mid id \mid x \mid \textbf{skip} \mid \textbf{stop} \mid \textbf{chaos} \\
&\mid x := E \mid \textbf{if } E \textbf{ then } E \textbf{ else } E \mid \textbf{let } id = E \textbf{ in } E \mid c?_{msgid} \mid c!_{msgid}E \\
&\mid E \sqcap E \mid E \; [] \; E \mid E \;_{n}\|_{n} E \mid E \;_{n}\|\!|_{n} E \mid E \; ; \; E \\
&\mid \lambda\, id : \tau \bullet E \mid E \; E
\end{aligned}
$$

When in the following we refer to an RSL expression, we mean an expression within the subset of RSL defined here.

Operational Semantics with Communication Behaviour

Before presenting the rules of the operational semantics a number of definitions are needed. A store s is a finite map from variables (x) to values (v): $s = [x \mapsto v, \ldots]$. An environment ρ is a finite map from identifiers (id) to values (v) : $\rho = [id \mapsto v, \ldots]$. A closure is a pair consisting of a lambda expression $(\lambda\, id : \tau \bullet E)$ and an environment (ρ): $[\lambda\, id : \tau \bullet E, \rho]$.

Compared to George and Xia [132], we modify the notion of a configuration to a triple $< E, s, n >$, where E is an expression, s is a store and n is a process identifier. Moreover, we augment configurations of the form α *op* s *op* β for *op* $=\|$, $\|$ to include three process identifiers, i.e., α *op* (s, n, n_1, n_2) *op* β, where n_1 is the identifier of the process represented by the configuration α, while n_2 is the identifier of the process represented by β.

Inspired by Haxthausen and Xia [204], the rules of the operational semantics are extended to include communication behaviour in the form of a PA_{LSC} term. The transition relation has the form

$$\rho \vdash \alpha_{\text{with } \phi} \xrightarrow{e} \alpha'_{\text{with } \phi'}$$

where ρ is the environment, α and α' are configurations, ϕ and ϕ' are behaviours and e is an event. The intuition is that the configuration α with the behaviour ϕ can evolve to the configuration α' with behaviour ϕ' by performing the event e.

There are two types of events, silent events and communication events. The silent event, ϵ, denotes an internal change that is not externally visible. Communication events are either input events of the form $c?_{msgid}$ or output events of the form $c!_{msgid} E$. The symbol $\diamond$ is used to denote any event, i.e., a situation where the transition is the same for a silent event and for a communication event.

The only operational rules that change the communication behaviour are the rules for input, output, communication across a parallel or interlocking combinator and merging of two parallel processes. In all other rules, the communication behaviour is preserved.

The process identifier, n, stored in a configuration is used to name processes in PA_{LSC} events. This information is needed to identify the sender and recipient in message input and message output events in the behaviours.

The rules for the parallel and interlocking combinators apply the function *merge* that merges the stores on either side of a parallel composition. It is defined in RSL notation by:

value
$$\text{merge}(s,s',s'') \equiv s'\dagger[\,x\mapsto s''(x) \mid x \in \textbf{dom}(s'')\cap \textbf{dom}(s)\cdot s(x)\neq s''(x)\,]$$

In the rules below we use a notation of the form:

$$\frac{C}{\rho \vdash C_2}$$
$$C_3$$

as a shorthand for the two rules:

$$\frac{C}{\rho \vdash C_2}$$

and:

$$\frac{C}{\rho \vdash C_3}.$$

Also, for rules without premises, i.e., axioms, we write the symbol $\square$ above the line.

Tables 13.10–13.23 each contain one rule. They are:

Table 13.10. Basic expressions

$$\frac{\square}{\rho \vdash\ <\mathbf{skip}, s, n>_{\mathbf{with}\ \phi} \xrightarrow{\epsilon} <(), s, n>_{\mathbf{with}\ \phi}}$$

$$\frac{\square}{\rho \vdash\ <\mathbf{chaos}, s, n>_{\mathbf{with}\ \phi} \xrightarrow{\epsilon} <\mathbf{chaos}, s, n>_{\mathbf{with}\ \phi}}$$

Table 13.11. Configuration fork

$$\frac{\square}{\rho \vdash\ <E_1\ op\ E_2, s, n>_{\mathbf{with}\ \phi} \xrightarrow{\epsilon} <E_1, s, n>_{\mathbf{with}\ \phi}\ op\ <E_2, s, n>_{\mathbf{with}\ \phi}}$$

where $op \in \{\lceil\rceil, \lceil\rfloor\}$

Table 13.12. Look up

$$\frac{\square}{\rho \dagger [id \mapsto v] \ \vdash \ < id, s, n >_{\textbf{with } \phi} \ \xrightarrow{\epsilon} \ < v, s, n >_{\textbf{with } \phi}}$$

$$\frac{\square}{\rho \ \vdash \ < id, s \dagger [id \mapsto v], n >_{\textbf{with } \phi} \ \xrightarrow{\epsilon} \ < v, s \dagger [id \mapsto v], n >_{\textbf{with } \phi}}$$

Table 13.13. Sequencing

$$\frac{\square}{\rho \ \vdash \ < E_1; E_2, s, n >_{\textbf{with } \phi} \ \xrightarrow{\epsilon} \ (< E_1, s, n >; E_2)_{\textbf{with } \phi}}$$

$$\frac{\rho \ \vdash \ \alpha_{\textbf{with } \phi} \ \xrightarrow{\diamond} \ \alpha'_{\textbf{with } \phi'}}{\rho \ \vdash \ (\alpha; E)_{\textbf{with } \phi} \ \xrightarrow{\diamond} \ (\alpha'; E)_{\textbf{with } \phi'}}$$

$$\frac{\square}{\rho \ \vdash \ (< v, s, n >; E)_{\textbf{with } \phi} \ \xrightarrow{\epsilon} \ < E, s, n >_{\textbf{with } \phi}}$$

Table 13.14. Assignment

$$\frac{\square}{\rho \ \vdash \ < x := E, s, n >_{\textbf{with } \phi} \ \xrightarrow{\epsilon} \ (x := < E, s, n >)_{\textbf{with } \phi}}$$

$$\frac{\rho \ \vdash \ \alpha_{\textbf{with } \phi} \ \xrightarrow{\diamond} \ \alpha'_{\textbf{with } \phi'}}{\rho \ \vdash \ (x := \alpha)_{\textbf{with } \phi} \ \xrightarrow{\diamond} \ (x := \alpha')_{\textbf{with } \phi'}}$$

$$\frac{\square}{\rho \ \vdash \ < v, s, n >_{\textbf{with } \phi} \ \xrightarrow{\epsilon} \ < (), s \dagger [x \mapsto v], n >_{\textbf{with } \phi}}$$

13.5.3 Relating Live Sequence Charts to RSL

Syntactical Restrictions

There are a number of problematic issues with conditions in LSCs. For that reason we choose to omit hot and cold conditions when relating an RSL specification to an LSC. This is done by removing all condition events from the PA_{LSC} term prior to checking satisfaction.

Table 13.15. Input

$$\frac{\square}{\rho \ \vdash \ < c?_{msgid}, s, n >_{\textbf{with}} \ \phi \ \xrightarrow{c?_{msgid}v} \ < v, s, n >_{\textbf{with}} \ \phi \ \cdot \ ins(env,n,msgid)}$$

Table 13.16. Output

$$\frac{\square}{\rho \ \vdash \ < c!_{msgid}E, s, n >_{\textbf{with}} \ \phi \ \xrightarrow{\epsilon} \ (c!_{msgid} < E, s, n >)_{\textbf{with}} \ \phi}$$

$$\frac{\rho \ \vdash \ \alpha_{\textbf{with}} \ \phi \ \xrightarrow{\diamond} \ \alpha'_{\textbf{with}} \ \phi'}{\rho \ \vdash \ (c!_{msgid}\alpha)_{\textbf{with}} \ \phi \ \xrightarrow{\diamond} \ (c!_{msgid}\alpha')_{\textbf{with}} \ \phi'}$$

$$\frac{\square}{\rho \ \vdash \ (c!_{msgid} < v, s, n >)_{\textbf{with}} \ \phi \ \xrightarrow{c!_{msgid}v} \ < (), s, n >_{\textbf{with}} \ \phi \ \cdot \ outs(n,env,msgid)}$$

Table 13.17. Internal choice

$$\frac{\square}{\rho \ \vdash \ (\alpha \sqcap \beta)_{\textbf{with}} \ \phi \ \xrightarrow{\epsilon} \ \alpha_{\textbf{with}} \ \phi}$$
$$\xrightarrow{\epsilon} \ \beta_{\textbf{with}} \ \phi$$

Since RSL only supports synchronous communication on channels, we restrict the relation to cover synchronous messages only. More specifically, if an LSC contains asynchronous messages, no RSL specification can satisfy it.

Satisfaction Relation

Before we can define what it means for an RSL expression to satisfy an LSC, we introduce some auxiliary notions. In most cases we do not want an LSC to constrain all parts of an RSL specification. Typically, we only want to constrain the sequence of a limited number of messages. For this reason we label each LSC with the set of events it constrains. We allow this set to contain events that are not mentioned in the chart. For an LSC ch this set is denoted $\mathcal{C}_{ch}$.

Below we need an event extraction function that yields the set of those event identifiers that occur in the PA_{LSC} term for an LSC. The event extraction function, $events : T(\Sigma_{PA_{C_e}}) \rightarrow \mathcal{P}Event$, is defined as

Table 13.18. External choice

$$
\frac{\rho \vdash \alpha_{\mathbf{with}\ \phi} \xrightarrow{a} \alpha'_{\mathbf{with}\ \phi'}}{\begin{array}{l} \rho \vdash \alpha_{\mathbf{with}\ \phi} [\!] \beta_{\mathbf{with}\ \varphi} \xrightarrow{a} \alpha'_{\mathbf{with}\ \phi'} \\ \beta_{\mathbf{with}\ \varphi} [\!] \alpha_{\mathbf{with}\ \phi} \xrightarrow{a} \alpha'_{\mathbf{with}\ \phi'} \end{array}}
$$

$$
\frac{\rho \vdash \alpha_{\mathbf{with}\ \phi} \xrightarrow{\epsilon} \alpha'_{\mathbf{with}\ \phi'}}{\begin{array}{l} \rho \vdash \alpha_{\mathbf{with}\ \phi} [\!] \beta_{\mathbf{with}\ \varphi} \xrightarrow{\epsilon} \alpha'_{\mathbf{with}\ \phi'} [\!] \beta_{\mathbf{with}\ \varphi} \\ \beta_{\mathbf{with}\ \varphi} [\!] \alpha_{\mathbf{with}\ \phi} \xrightarrow{\epsilon} \beta_{\mathbf{with}\ \varphi} [\!] \alpha'_{\mathbf{with}\ \phi'} \end{array}}
$$

$$
\frac{\square}{\begin{array}{l} \rho \vdash\ <v,s,n>_{\mathbf{with}\ \phi} [\!] \alpha_{\mathbf{with}\ \phi'} \xrightarrow{\epsilon} <v,s,n>_{\mathbf{with}\ \phi} \\ \alpha_{\mathbf{with}\ \phi'} [\!]\ <v,s,n>_{\mathbf{with}\ \phi} \xrightarrow{\epsilon}\ <v,s,n>_{\mathbf{with}\ \phi} \end{array}}
$$

$$
events(\epsilon) = \emptyset
$$
$$
events(in(n_1, n_2, m)) = \{m\}
$$
$$
events(out(n_1, n_2, m)) = \{m\}
$$
$$
events(ins(n_1, n_2, m)) = \{m\}
$$
$$
events(outs(n_1, n_2, m)) = \{m\}
$$
$$
events(hotcondition(cond)) = \emptyset
$$
$$
events(coldcondition(cond)) = \emptyset
$$
$$
events(X \cdot Y) = events(X) \cup events(Y)
$$
$$
events(X + Y) = events(X) \cup events(Y)
$$
$$
events(X \parallel Y) = events(X) \cup events(Y)
$$
$$
events(X \triangleright Y) = events(X) \cup events(Y)
$$
$$
remcond(\epsilon) = \epsilon
$$

As explained above, we do not check LSC conditions when making the relation to RSL. The function removing conditions, $remcond : T(\Sigma_{PAc_\epsilon}) \to T(\Sigma_{PAc_\epsilon})$, is defined as:

$$
remcond(in(n_1, n_2, m)) = in(n_1, n_2, m)
$$
$$
remcond(out(n_1, n_2, m)) = out(n_1, n_2, m)
$$
$$
remcond(ins(n_1, n_2, m)) = in(n_1, n_2, m)
$$
$$
remcond(outs(n_1, n_2, m)) = out(n_1, n_2, m)
$$

Table 13.19. Parallel combinator

$$\square$$

$$\rho \vdash\; < E_1 \;_{n_1}\|_{n_2}\; E_2, s, n >_{\mathbf{with}\ \phi} \xrightarrow{\epsilon} < E_1, s, n_1 >_{\mathbf{with}\ \phi} \| (s, n, n_1, n_2) \| < E_1, s, n_2 >_{\mathbf{with}\ \phi}$$

$$\rho \vdash \alpha_{\mathbf{with}\ \phi} \xrightarrow{c!_{msgid}v} \alpha'_{\mathbf{with}\ \phi'} \qquad \rho \vdash \beta_{\mathbf{with}\ \varphi} \xrightarrow{c?_{msgid}v} \beta'_{\mathbf{with}\ \varphi'}$$

$$\rho \vdash \alpha_{\mathbf{with}\ \phi} \| (s, n, n_1, n_2) \| \beta_{\mathbf{with}\ \varphi} \xrightarrow{\epsilon} \alpha'_{\mathbf{with}\ \phi\ \cdot\ out(n_1, n_2, id)} \| (s, n, n_1, n_2)$$

$$\| \beta'_{\mathbf{with}\ \varphi\ \cdot\ in(n_1, n_2, msgid)}$$

$$\beta_{\mathbf{with}\ \varphi} \| (s, n, n_1, n_2) \| \alpha_{\mathbf{with}\ \phi} \xrightarrow{\epsilon} \beta'_{\mathbf{with}\ \varphi\ \cdot\ in(n_2, n_1, id)} \| (s, n, n_1, n_2)$$

$$\| \alpha'_{\mathbf{with}\ \phi\ \cdot\ out(n_2, n_1, msgid)}$$

$$\rho \vdash \alpha_{\mathbf{with}\ \phi} \xrightarrow{\diamond} \alpha'_{\mathbf{with}\ \phi'}$$

$$\rho \vdash \alpha_{\mathbf{with}\ \phi} \| (s, n, n_1, n_2) \| \beta_{\mathbf{with}\ \varphi} \xrightarrow{\diamond} \alpha'_{\mathbf{with}\ \phi'} \| (s, n, n_1, n_2) \| \beta_{\mathbf{with}\ \varphi}$$

$$\beta_{\mathbf{with}\ \varphi} \| (s, n, n_1, n_2) \| \alpha_{\mathbf{with}\ \phi} \xrightarrow{\diamond} \beta_{\mathbf{with}\ \varphi} \| (s, n, n_1, n_2) \| \alpha'_{\mathbf{with}\ \phi'}$$

$$\square$$

$$\rho \vdash \alpha_{\mathbf{with}\ \phi} \| (s, n, n_1, n_2) \| < v, s', n_2 >_{\mathbf{with}\ \varphi} \xrightarrow{\epsilon} \alpha_{\mathbf{with}\ \phi} \| (s, n, n_1, n_2) \| s'_{\mathbf{with}\ \varphi}$$

$$< v, s', n_2 >_{\mathbf{with}\ \varphi} \| (s, n, n_1, n_2) \| \alpha_{\mathbf{with}\ \phi} \xrightarrow{\epsilon} s'_{\mathbf{with}\ \varphi} \| (s, n, n_1, n_2) \| \alpha_{\mathbf{with}\ \phi}$$

$$\rho \vdash \alpha_{\mathbf{with}\ \phi} \xrightarrow{\diamond} \alpha'_{\mathbf{with}\ \phi'}$$

$$\rho \vdash \alpha_{\mathbf{with}\ \phi} \| (s, n, n_1, n_2) \| s'_{\mathbf{with}\ \varphi} \xrightarrow{\diamond} \alpha'_{\mathbf{with}\ \phi'} \| (s, n, n_1, n_2) \| s'_{\mathbf{with}\ \varphi}$$

$$s'_{\mathbf{with}\ \varphi} \| (s, n, n_1, n_2) \| \alpha_{\mathbf{with}\ \phi} \xrightarrow{\diamond} s'_{\mathbf{with}\ \varphi} \| (s, n, n_1, n_2) \| \alpha'_{\mathbf{with}\ \phi'}$$

$$\square$$

$$\rho \vdash\; < v, s'', n_1 >_{\mathbf{with}\ \phi} \| (s, n, n_1, n_2) \| s'_{\mathbf{with}\ \varphi} \xrightarrow{\epsilon} < v, merge(s, s', s''), n >_{\mathbf{with}\ \phi\|\varphi}$$

$$s'_{\mathbf{with}\ \varphi} \| (s, n, n_1, n_2) \| < v, s'', n_1 >_{\mathbf{with}\ \phi} \xrightarrow{\epsilon} < v, merge(s, s', s''), n >_{\mathbf{with}\ \phi\|\varphi}$$

$$remcond(hotcondition(cond)) = \epsilon$$
$$remcond(coldcondition(cond)) = \epsilon$$
$$remcond(X \cdot Y) = remcond(X) \cdot remcond(Y)$$
$$remcond(X + Y) = remcond(X) + remcond(Y)$$
$$remcond(X \| Y) = remcond(X) \| remcond(Y)$$
$$remcond(X \triangleright Y) = remcond(X) \triangleright remcond(Y)$$

Definition. A PA_{LSC} term, x, can *simulate* a PAc_ϵ term, y, notation $x \succeq y$, if

$$y \downarrow \Rightarrow x \downarrow\ \wedge\ \forall y' : y \xrightarrow{a} y' \Rightarrow \exists x' : x \xrightarrow{a} x' \wedge x' \succeq y'$$

■

Table 13.20. Interlocking combinator

$$\square$$

$$\rho \vdash\; < E_1 \;_{n_1}\|_{n_2} E_2, s, n >_{\textbf{with } \phi} \;\xrightarrow{\epsilon}\; < E_1, s, n_1 >_{\textbf{with } \phi} \;\|\; (s, n, n_1, n_2)$$
$$\|\; < E_1, s, n_2 >_{\textbf{with } \phi}$$

$$\rho \vdash\; \alpha_{\textbf{with } \phi} \xrightarrow{c!msgid\, v} \alpha'_{\textbf{with } \phi'} \qquad \rho \vdash\; \beta_{\textbf{with } \varphi} \xrightarrow{c?msgid\, v} \beta'_{\textbf{with } \varphi'}$$

$$\rho \vdash\; \alpha_{\textbf{with } \phi} \;\|\; (s, n, n_1, n_2) \;\|\; \beta_{\textbf{with } \varphi} \;\xrightarrow{\epsilon}\; \alpha'_{\textbf{with } \phi\,\cdot\,out(n_1, n_2, id)} \;\|\; (s, n, n_1, n_2)$$
$$\|\; \beta'_{\textbf{with } \varphi\,\cdot\,in(n_1, n_2, msgid)}$$

$$\beta_{\textbf{with } \varphi} \;\|\; (s, n, n_1, n_2) \;\|\; \alpha_{\textbf{with } \phi} \;\xrightarrow{\epsilon}\; \beta'_{\textbf{with } \varphi\,\cdot\,in(n_2, n_1, id)} \;\|\; (s, n, n_1, n_2)$$
$$\|\; \alpha'_{\textbf{with } \phi\,\cdot\,out(n_2, n_1, msgid)}$$

$$\rho \vdash\; \alpha_{\textbf{with } \phi} \;\xrightarrow{\epsilon}\; \alpha'_{\textbf{with } \phi'}$$

$$\rho \vdash\; \alpha_{\textbf{with } \phi} \;\|\; (s, n, n_1, n_2) \;\|\; \beta_{\textbf{with } \varphi} \;\xrightarrow{\epsilon}\; \alpha'_{\textbf{with } \phi'} \;\|\; (s, n, n_1, n_2) \;\|\; \beta_{\textbf{with } \varphi}$$

$$\beta_{\textbf{with } \varphi} \;\|\; (s, n, n_1, n_2) \;\|\; \alpha_{\textbf{with } \phi} \;\xrightarrow{\epsilon}\; \beta_{\textbf{with } \varphi} \;\|\; (s, n, n_1, n_2) \;\|\; \alpha'_{\textbf{with } \phi'}$$

$$\square$$

$$\rho \vdash\; \alpha_{\textbf{with } \phi} \;\|\; (s, n, n_1, n_2) \;\|\; < v, s', n_2 >_{\textbf{with } \varphi} \;\xrightarrow{\epsilon}\; \alpha_{\textbf{with } \phi} \;\|\; (s, n, n_1, n_2) \;\|\; s'_{\textbf{with } \varphi}$$

$$< v, s', n_2 >_{\textbf{with } \varphi} \;\|\; (s, n, n_1, n_2) \;\|\; \alpha_{\textbf{with } \phi} \;\xrightarrow{\epsilon}\; s'_{\textbf{with } \varphi} \;\|\; (s, n, n_1, n_2) \;\|\; \alpha_{\textbf{with } \phi}$$

$$\rho \vdash\; \alpha_{\textbf{with } \phi} \;\xrightarrow{\diamond}\; \alpha'_{\textbf{with } \phi'}$$

$$\rho \vdash\; \alpha_{\textbf{with } \phi} \;\|\; (s, n, n_1, n_2) \;\|\; s'_{\textbf{with } \varphi} \;\xrightarrow{\diamond}\; \alpha'_{\textbf{with } \phi'} \;\|\; (s, n, n_1, n_2) \;\|\; s'_{\textbf{with } \varphi}$$

$$s'_{\textbf{with } \varphi} \;\|\; (s, n, n_1, n_2) \;\|\; \alpha_{\textbf{with } \phi} \;\xrightarrow{\diamond}\; s'_{\textbf{with } \varphi} \;\|\; (s, n, n_1, n_2) \;\|\; \alpha'_{\textbf{with } \phi'}$$

$$\square$$

$$\rho \vdash\; < v, s'', n_1 >_{\textbf{with } \phi} \;\|\; (s, n, n_1, n_2) \;\|\; s'_{\textbf{with } \varphi} \;\xrightarrow{\epsilon}\; < v, merge(s, s', s''), n >_{\textbf{with } \phi\|\varphi}$$

$$s'_{\textbf{with } \varphi} \;\|\; (s, n, n_1, n_2) \;\|\; < v, s'', n_1 >_{\textbf{with } \phi} \;\xrightarrow{\epsilon}\; < v, merge(s, s', s''), n >_{\textbf{with } \phi\|\varphi}$$

Definition. A PA_{LSC} formula *cbh* is called a *communication behaviour* of an RSL expression E wrt. an initial store s_0, if and only if there exists a configuration α, such that

$$[\,] \vdash\; < E, s_0, n >_{\textbf{with } \epsilon} \quad (\xrightarrow{\diamond})^* \quad \alpha_{\textbf{with } cbh}$$

where $(\xrightarrow{\diamond})^*$ denotes the transitive closure of the transition relation. If α is of the form $< v, s, n >$, where v is a value literal or a lambda expression, *cbh* is called a *terminated behaviour*. ∎

We are now ready to define the satisfaction relations for universal and existential LSCs.

Table 13.21. Function

$$\frac{\square}{\rho \ \vdash \ < E_1 \ E_2, s, n >_{\textbf{with } \phi} \ \xrightarrow{\epsilon} \ (< E_1, s, n > E_2)_{\textbf{with } \phi}}$$

$$\frac{\rho \ \vdash \ \alpha_{\textbf{with } \phi} \ \xrightarrow{\diamond} \ \alpha'_{\textbf{with } \phi'}}{\rho \ \vdash \ (\alpha \ E)_{\textbf{with } \phi} \ \xrightarrow{\diamond} \ (\alpha' \ E)_{\textbf{with } \phi'}}$$

$$\frac{\square}{\rho \ \vdash \ < \lambda \, id : \tau \bullet E, s, n >_{\textbf{with } \phi} \ \xrightarrow{\epsilon} \ < [\![\lambda \, id : \tau \bullet E, \rho]\!], s, n >_{\textbf{with } \phi}}$$

$$\frac{\square}{\rho \ \vdash \ (< [\![\lambda \, id : \tau \bullet E_1, \rho_1]\!], s, n > \ E_2)_{\textbf{with } \phi} \ \xrightarrow{\epsilon} \ ([\![\lambda \, id : \tau \bullet E_1, \rho_1]\!] < E_2, s, n >)_{\textbf{with } \phi}}$$

$$\frac{\rho \ \vdash \ \alpha_{\textbf{with } \phi} \ \xrightarrow{\diamond} \ \alpha'_{\textbf{with } \phi'}}{\rho \ \vdash \ ([\![\lambda \, id : \tau \bullet E, \rho_1]\!] \ \alpha)_{\textbf{with } \phi} \ \xrightarrow{\diamond} \ ([\![\lambda \, id : \tau \bullet E, \rho_1]\!] \ \alpha')_{\textbf{with } \phi'}}$$

$$\frac{\square}{\rho \ \vdash \ ([\![\lambda \, id : \tau \bullet E, \rho_1]\!] \ < v, s, n >)_{\textbf{with } \phi} \ \xrightarrow{\diamond} \ ([\![\lambda \, id : \tau \bullet E, \rho_1]\!] \ v)_{\textbf{with } \phi}}$$

$$\frac{\rho_1 \ \dagger \ [id \mapsto v] \ \vdash \ \alpha_{\textbf{with } \phi} \ \xrightarrow{\diamond} \ \alpha'_{\textbf{with } \phi'}}{\rho \ \vdash \ ([\![\lambda \, id : \tau \bullet \alpha, \rho_1]\!] \ v)_{\textbf{with } \phi} \ \xrightarrow{\diamond} \ ([\![\lambda \, id : \tau \bullet \alpha', \rho_1]\!] \ v)_{\textbf{with } \phi'}}$$

$$\frac{\rho_1 \ \dagger \ [id \mapsto v] \ \vdash \ \alpha_{\textbf{with } \phi} \ \xrightarrow{\diamond} \ < v', s, n >_{\textbf{with } \phi'}}{\rho \ \vdash \ ([\![\lambda \, id : \tau \bullet \alpha, \rho_1]\!] \ v)_{\textbf{with } \phi} \ \xrightarrow{\diamond} \ < v', s, n >_{\textbf{with } \phi'}}$$

Definition. (Satisfaction for universal LSC) An RSL expression E *satisfies* a universal LSC, ch, if for any initial store, s_0, for any terminated behaviour, cbh, of E there exists a PA_{LSC} term ϕ_{prefix} and a PA_{LSC} term ϕ_{suffix}, such that

$$events(\phi_{\text{prefix}}) \cap C_{ch} = \emptyset$$
$$events(\phi_{\text{suffix}}) \cap C_{ch} = \emptyset$$

and

$$\phi_{\text{prefix}} \cdot remcond(S_{LSC}[\![ch]\!]) \cdot \phi_{\text{suffix}} \succeq cbh$$

■

Definition. (Satisfaction for existential LSC) An RSL expression E *satisfies* an existential LSC, ch, if for any initial store, s_0, there exists a terminated behaviour, cbh, of E, a PA_{LSC} term ϕ_{prefix} and a PA_{LSC} term ϕ_{suffix}, such that

Table 13.22. Let expression

$$\frac{\square}{\rho \vdash\; <\mathbf{let}\; id = E_1 \;\mathbf{in}\; E_2, s, n >_{\mathbf{with}\; \phi} \xrightarrow{\epsilon} (\mathbf{let}\; id =< E_1, s, > \mathbf{in}\; E_2)_{\mathbf{with}\; \phi}}$$

$$\frac{\rho \vdash \alpha_{\mathbf{with}\; \phi} \xrightarrow{\Diamond} \alpha'_{\mathbf{with}\; \phi'}}{\rho \vdash (\mathbf{let}\; id = \alpha \;\mathbf{in}\; E)_{\mathbf{with}\; \phi} \xrightarrow{\Diamond} (\mathbf{let}\; id = \alpha' \;\mathbf{in}\; E)_{\mathbf{with}\; \phi'}}$$

$$\frac{\square}{\rho \vdash (\mathbf{let}\; id =< v, s, n > \;\mathbf{in}\; E)_{\mathbf{with}\; \phi} \xrightarrow{\epsilon} < E[v/id], s, n >_{\mathbf{with}\; \phi}}$$

Table 13.23. If expression

$$\frac{\square}{\rho \vdash\; <\mathbf{if}\; E \;\mathbf{then}\; E_1 \;\mathbf{else}\; E_2, s, n >_{\mathbf{with}\; \phi} \xrightarrow{\epsilon} (\mathbf{if}\; < E, s, n > \;\mathbf{then}\; E_1 \;\mathbf{else}\; E_2)_{\mathbf{with}\; \phi}}$$

$$\frac{\rho \vdash \alpha_{\mathbf{with}\; \phi} \xrightarrow{\Diamond} \alpha'_{\mathbf{with}\; \phi'}}{\rho \vdash (\mathbf{if}\; \alpha \;\mathbf{then}\; E_1 \;\mathbf{else}\; E_2)_{\mathbf{with}\; \phi} \xrightarrow{\Diamond} (\mathbf{if}\; \alpha' \;\mathbf{then}\; E_1 \;\mathbf{else}\; E_2)_{\mathbf{with}\; \phi'}}$$

$$\frac{\square}{\rho \vdash (\mathbf{if}\; < \mathbf{true}, s, n > \;\mathbf{then}\; E_1 \;\mathbf{else}\; E_2)_{\mathbf{with}\; \phi} \xrightarrow{\epsilon} < E_1, s, n >_{\mathbf{with}\; \phi}}$$

$$\frac{\square}{\rho \vdash (\mathbf{if}\; < \mathbf{false}, s, n > \;\mathbf{then}\; E_1 \;\mathbf{else}\; E_2)_{\mathbf{with}\; \phi} \xrightarrow{\epsilon} < E_2, s, n >_{\mathbf{with}\; \phi}}$$

$$events(\phi_{\mathrm{prefix}}) \cap \mathcal{C}_{ch} = \emptyset$$
$$events(\phi_{\mathrm{suffix}}) \cap \mathcal{C}_{ch} = \emptyset$$

and

$$\phi_{\mathrm{prefix}} \cdot remcond(S_{LSC}[\![ch]\!]) \cdot \phi_{\mathrm{suffix}} \succeq cbh$$

■

13.5.4 Checking Satisfaction

The satisfaction criteria defined in Definition 13.5.3 require checking that all behaviours of the RSL expression can be simulated by the semantics of the corresponding chart. In some situations the RSL expressions may have infinitely many behaviours, so in that case, this simple form of checking is not possible.

13.5.5 Tool Support

Actually checking an RSL specification against a behavioural specification in the form of LSCs can be very tedious. For that reason, the methods defined above are of limited applicability without tool support. Tools should be developed to extract the semantic terms from LSCs and RSL specifications and for checking the satisfaction relations. It would also be convenient to have a way of translating an LSC into a skeleton RSL specification. An automatic conversion would force the software engineer to use one particular style.

13.6 Communicating Transaction Processes (CTP)

> Section 13.6 is the joint work of Yang Shaofa and Dines Bjørner. Yang provided the Dining Philosophers example, Sect. 13.6.3, and the formalisation, Sect. 13.6.4.

We refer to the published paper [439]. CTPs are formed by a relatively simple and elegant composition of Petri net places and sets of message sequence charts.

13.6.1 Intuition

CTPs are motivated by considering first a Petri net such as the one depicted in the upper half of Fig. 13.25. The conditions (or places) are labelled $S_{P_{1_1}}, S_{P_{1_2}}, S_{P_{1_3}}, S_{P_{2_1}}, S_{P_{2_2}}, S_{P_{3_1}}$ and $S_{P_{3_2}}$. The events (or transitions) are labelled T_1, T_2 and T_3. Our labelling of places reflects a pragmatic desire to group three of these $(S_{P_{1_1}}, S_{P_{1_2}}, S_{P_{1_3}})$ into what we may then call control states of a process P_1, two of these $(S_{P_{2_1}}, S_{P_{2_2}})$ into control states of process P_2 and the remaining two $(S_{P_{2_1}}, S_{P_{2_2}})$ into control states of process P_3.

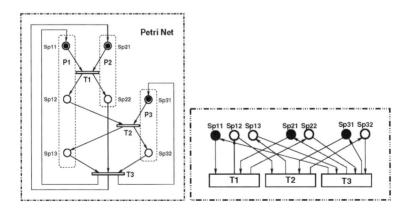

Fig. 13.25. Left: a Petri net. Right: a concrete CTP diagram

Secondly we consider each event as a message sequence chart. T_1 has two instances corresponding to processes P_1 and P_2. For that (and the below implied) message sequence chart(s) messages are being specified for communication between these instances and internal actions are being specified for execution. The firing of event T_1 shall thus correspond to the execution of this message sequence chart. T_2 has two instances corresponding to processes P_2 and P_3 and T_3 has three instances corresponding to processes P_1, P_2 and P_3.

As for condition event Petri nets, tokens are placed in exactly one of the control states for each process. Enabling and firing take place as for condition event Petri nets. Transfer of tokens from input places to output places shall take place in two steps. First when invoking the transition message sequence chart where tokens are removed from enabling input places, and then when all instances of the invoked message sequence chart have been completed (where tokens are placed at designated output places).

Thirdly we consider each event as a set of one or more message sequence charts with all message sequence charts of any given event involving the same processes. In doing so, we refine each event into a transaction schema. There is now the question as to which of the message sequence charts is to be selected. That question is clarified by the fourth step motivating CTPs.

Fourthly we predicate the selection of which message sequence charts are to be selected once a transaction schema is fired by equipping each of the message sequence charts with a guard, that is, a proposition. Associated with each process there is a set of local variables that can be, and usually are updated by the internal actions of the instances. The propositions are the conjunctions of one proposition for each of the instances, i.e., processes. A message sequence chart of a transaction schema is enabled if its guard evaluates to true. If two or more message sequence charts are enabled one is nondeterministically (internal choice) selected. A transaction schema is enabled if its input places are marked and at least one of the message sequence charts in this transaction schema is enabled. If a transaction schema has no message sequence charts enabled, then we will not enter this transaction schema.

We are now ready to introduce CTPs properly.

13.6.2 Narration of CTPs

CTP Diagrams

Consider Fig. 13.26. It is a generalisation of the right part of Fig. 13.25 which itself is just a reformatting of the left part of Fig. 13.25.

A CTP diagram consists of **an indexed set of sets of process (control) states,** an indexed set of transaction schemas, an indexed set of sets of process variables, and a "wiring" connecting control states via transaction schemas to control states. (The wiring of Fig. 13.26 is shown by pairs of opposite directed arrows.)

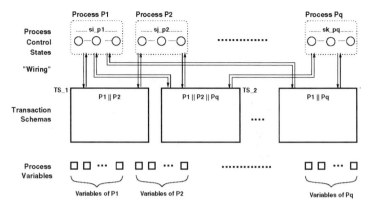

Fig. 13.26. A schematic CTP diagram

CTP Processes

Figure 13.26 suggests a notion of processes, here named p_1, p_2, ..., p_q (in Fig. 13.26 $P1$, $P2$, ..., Pq). It also suggests a number of transaction schemas, here named TS_1, TS_2, ..., TS_s. The figure then suggests that the processes have the following control states:

- $p_1 : \{s_{p_1}^1, s_{p_1}^2, \ldots, s_{p_1}^{m_1}\}$ in Fig. 13.26: si_p1,
- $p_2 : \{s_{p_2}^1, s_{p_2}^2, \ldots, s_{p_2}^{m_2}\}$ in Fig. 13.26: sj_p2,
- ...
- $p_q : \{s_{p_q}^1, s_{p_q}^2, \ldots, s_{p_q}^{m_q}\}$ in Fig. 13.26: sk_pq.

The schematic CTP diagram indicates some transaction schema input states for process p_i:

- $\{s_{p_i}^1, s_{p_i}^2, \ldots, s_{p_i}^{m_i}\}$,

by an arrow from the p_i control states to TS_j and some transaction schema output states for process p_i by an arrow from TS_j (back) to the p_i control states. These two sets are usually the same.

- The set of all allowable, i.e., specified state to next state transitions can be specified as a set of triples, each triple being of the form:
  - ⋆ (s, ts_n, s') for process p_i: $(s_{p_i}, ts_n, s'_{p_i})$

where ts_n names a transaction schema and where s and s' belong to a process.

- If ts_n supports processes p_i, p_j, ..., p_k, then there will be triples:
  - ⋆ $(s_{p_i}, ts_n, s'_{p_i}), (s_{p_j}, ts_n, s'_{p_j}), \ldots, (s_{p_k}, ts_n, s'_{p_k})$

Figure 13.27 hints at such transition triples.

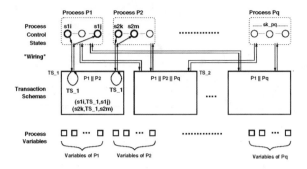

Fig. 13.27. State to next state transitions shown for TS_1 only

CTP Transaction Schemas

Figure 13.28 indicates that a transaction schema consists of one or more transaction charts.

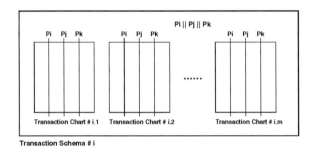

Fig. 13.28. Transaction charts of a transaction schema

Each transaction schema, TS_i, thus contains one or more transaction charts: Ch_i^j (for suitable i's and j's).[2] Each transaction chart contains one simple message sequence chart. Instances (i.e., vertical lines) of the message sequence charts are labelled by distinct process names. All transaction charts of a transaction schema contain message sequence charts whose instances are labelled by the same set of process names.

CTP Transaction Charts

To each transaction chart there is associated a process name indexed set, G_n^j, of propositions for TS_n transaction chart Ch_n^j. See Fig. 13.29.

---

[2]In Fig. 13.28 Ch_i^j is represented by Transaction Chart # i.j.

Simple CTP Message Sequence Charts

Each instance of each simple message sequence chart of each transaction chart of each transaction schema may contain zero, one or more internal actions,

- $a_i^{j_k}$,

and input/output events:

- $(p_i \leftarrow p_j)?v_i^\nu$

(input value offered on channel from process p_j to process p_i and assigned to process p_i's variable v_i^ν), respectively,

- $(p_i \rightarrow p_j)!e_i^k$

(output value of expression e_i^k over variables of process p_i from process p_i to process p_j). The variables of respective processes are shown as square boxes in Fig. 13.26.

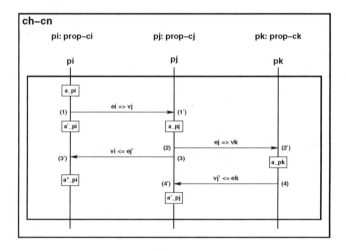

Fig. 13.29. A transaction chart with a simple message sequence chart

Figure 13.29 shows a transaction chart with a simple message sequence chart which prescribes the interaction among three processes, p_i, p_j and p_k. Instance p_i shows the following sequence of events:

- $\langle a_{pi}$, $(p_i \rightarrow p_j)!e_i$, a'_{pi} , $(p_i \leftarrow p_j)?v_i$, $a''_{pi}\rangle$

The output/input messages (ℓ, ℓ') [or (ℓ', ℓ)], shown as labelled arrows: $\stackrel{e \Rightarrow v}{\longrightarrow}$ or $\stackrel{v \Leftarrow e}{\longleftarrow}$ correspond to the pairs of (output,input) events in respective processes.

$(1 \stackrel{ei \Rightarrow vj}{\longrightarrow} 1')$: the pair of $((p_i \rightarrow p_j)!e_i, (p_j \leftarrow p_i)?v_j)$,

$(2 \xrightarrow{ej \Rightarrow vk} 2')$: the pair of $((p_j \rightarrow p_k)!e_j, (p_k \leftarrow p_j)?v_k)$,

$(3' \xleftarrow{vi \Leftarrow ej'} 3)$: the pair of $((p_j \rightarrow p_i)!e'_j, (p_i \leftarrow p_j)?v_i)$,

$(4' \xleftarrow{vj' \Leftarrow ek} 4)$: the pair of $((p_k \rightarrow p_j)!e_k, (p_j \leftarrow p_k)?v'_j)$.

Enabled CTP Transaction Charts

If the transaction schema is labelled with process names $\{p_i, p_j, p_k\}$ then one transition from control states of each of processes p_i, p_j and p_k leads into each transaction chart of that transaction schema. In order for a transaction chart (of a transaction schema) to be enabled the following two conditions must be fulfilled:

- One each of the input control states of processes p_i, p_j and p_k must be marked. That is, one each of $s^1_{p_i}, s^2_{p_i}, \ldots, s^{m_1}_{p_i}$, and $s^1_{p_j}, s^2_{p_j}, \ldots, s^{m_1}_{p_j}$, and $s^1_{p_k}, s^2_{p_k}, \ldots, s^{m_1}_{p_k}$, must be marked. More precisely, all the control state preconditions of the transaction schema to which this chart belongs are fulfilled.
- The indexed set of propositions for the transaction chart must all evaluate to true.

In the example of the transaction chart of Fig. 13.29 the indexed set of propositions are the three propositions *prop-ci*, *prop-cj* and *prop-ck*. Each proposition for any process p_i of any transaction chart may contain variables, if so they must only be variables of that process.

Enabled Versus Invoked Schemas and Charts

A distinction is being made between being enabled and being invoked. An invoked schema or chart must be enabled. Enablement means that the conditions for invocation are satisfied. Invocation means that an actual interpretation (i.e., execution) takes place with all attendant state changes possibly occurring.

Details of Invocation and Execution

We elaborate a bit further on the interpretation of a CTP program (i.e., diagram). Initially control rests in the process initial control states. No transaction schema is invoked.

Now zero, one or more transaction schemas may be enabled. For a transaction schema to be enabled the following must hold. One or more of the transaction charts of this transaction schema must be enabled. That is, their guards must hold. That is evaluate to true in the initial state of the process variables. One or more enabled transaction schema may now be invoked provided that no two of them share processes. Invoking an enabled transaction schema means the following: One of its enabled transaction charts will be non-deterministically selected. To thus invoke an enabled and selected transaction chart means that the marking (i.e., the tokens) of the enabling process control states will be removed and "converted" into an instance ("program point") pointer for each of the process instances of the enabled and selected transaction chart, and those pointers are initially set to zero (0), i.e., the beginning, the "entry", of the transaction chart instances.

The preceding paragraph outlines a step (in this case a zeroth step) of CTP program interpretation (i.e., execution).

Now an interpretation of the instances of the enabled and selected transaction chart takes place. Here we refer to the description of the semantics of BMSCs (basic MSCs) earlier in this chapter. A step is made up from either interpreting an internal action (which usually will update process control variables and hence atomic propositions), or interpreting an output event, or interpreting an input event. The instance program pointers are advanced one position for each such interpretation. When all instance program pointers of a specific transaction chart (of a specific transaction schema) reach their respective last positions, then the transaction chart and its transaction schema are disabled and the designated output control states are marked.

At the same time as a step related to one particular enabled and invoked transaction schema and a transaction chart within it is being performed similar steps may be performed, concurrently, at or within other enabled and invoked transaction schemas and transaction charts within them. So, as an illustration, as one step of interpretation occurs properly within a transaction chart of one transaction schema, another such step of interpretation may occur properly within a transaction chart of another transaction schema, and yet a third transaction chart may be enabled, selected, invoked, and so on.

CTP Transitions

The semantics of CTP calls for transitions from input control states via enabled transaction schemas to (output) control states. Figure 13.27 hinted at such transitions.

An invoked transaction chart will then result in the appropriate input states no longer being marked, in the execution of the simple message sequence chart, from top to bottom, in the updating of process variables (as the result of execution of each of the instances of the simple message sequence chart), and, once message sequence chart execution terminates, in the marking of one appropriate output state for each of the processes labelling that transaction chart.

Which of the output states, for processes p_i, p_j and p_k, that is,

- which of $s_{p_i}'^1, s_{p_i}'^2, \ldots, s_{p_i}'^{m_i}$, and
- which of $s_{p_j}'^1, s_{p_j}'^2, \ldots, s_{p_j}'^{m_j}$, and
- which of $s_{p_k}'^1, s_{p_k}'^2, \ldots, s_{p_k}'^{m_k}$

are selected is determined by which of the

- $(s_{p_i}^\alpha, ts_n, s_{p_i}^\beta)$

transition rules had their

- $s_{p_i}^\alpha$

part apply in the invocation of transaction schema ts_n to which this chart belongs.

For technical reasons no two otherwise distinct transition rules $(s_{p_i}^\gamma, ts_n, s_{p_i}^\delta)$ and $(s_{p_i}^\phi, ts_n, s_{p_i}^\psi)$ can have identical first pairs, i.e., $\gamma \neq \phi$, and cannot have identical last pairs, i.e. $\delta \neq \psi$. Thus we assume that each transaction schema ts_n, has exactly one input and one output control state for each process.

The process control states are like places (conditions), and the transaction schemas are like transitions in a condition event Petri net.

Firing (i.e., invocation) means that one or more enabled transaction schemas (that do not share processes) are selected, that is, one or more transaction schemas for which the guards of one or more transaction charts evaluate to true (i.e., is enabled) — and that within each such selected transaction schema one such (enabled) transaction chart is selected (invoked). The invoked transaction charts are then "executed", as would a normal message sequence chart. Once any such message sequence chart execution has completed, the transition completes by marking the designated output control states. Since several transaction schemas may be enabled in this way one or more are chosen nondeterministically. And since within each transaction schema several transaction charts may be enabled one is chosen nondeterministically.

13.6.3 A Dining Philosophers Example

Before we formalise the diagrammatic language of CTPs we bring in an example.

Example 13.24 *Dining Philosophers:* This whole section is one example, but we omit shading.   ∎

We model the classical dining philosophers problem using CTP. For simplicity, we consider the setting of just two philosophers. As illustrated in Fig. 13.30, two philosophers $P1$ and $P2$ are seated on opposite sides of a round table and two forks $F1$ and $F2$ are placed between $P1$ and $P2$.

A plate of spaghetti is placed at the centre of the dining table. A philosopher alternates between eating and thinking. To eat the spaghetti, a philosopher must try to grab (the) two forks (here $F1$ and $F2$). And when a philosopher finishes eating, he puts down both forks. The problem is to devise a strategy of using the forks such that the philosophers do not suffer starvation.

The CTP program for the dining philosophers problem is shown in Fig. 13.31.

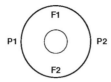

Fig. 13.30. Two dining philosophers table with forks

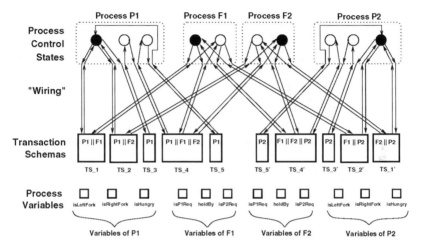

Fig. 13.31. Two dining philosophers CTP program

There are four processes $P1$, $P2$, $F1$ and $F2$ corresponding to the two philosophers and the two forks. In transaction schema TS_1, $P1$ tries to grab its left fork $F1$. In TS_2, $P1$ tries to grab its right fork $F2$. TS_3 represents the behaviour where $P1$ is eating (after getting hold of both forks $F1$ and $F2$). TS_4 represents the behaviour where $P1$ puts down both forks (after finishing eating). Finally, TS_5 models the behaviour where $P1$ is thinking. Analogously, transaction schemas TS_1', TS_2', TS_3', TS_4', TS_5' represent the behaviours where $P2$ tries to grab its left fork $F2$, $P2$ tries to grab its right fork $F1$, $P2$ is eating, $P2$ puts down both forks, and $P2$ is thinking.

The initial control states of each process are shown by darkened places.

The process $P1$ has three variables, isLeftFork, isRightFork and isHungry, all of which are of type **Bool**. These three variables indicate whether $P1$ holds its left fork, whether $P1$ holds its right fork, respectively whether $P1$ is hungry. Initially, $P1$ holds neither fork and is hungry. The variables of $P2$ are set up similarly to $P1$.

The process $F1$ has three variables isP1Req, heldBy and isP2Req. The variable isP1Req (respectively isP2Req) is of type **Bool** and records whether there is a request from $P1$ (respectively $P2$) to hold $F1$. The variable heldBy is an enumerated type variable that takes one of the three values mkNil (meaning that $F1$ is held by neither philosopher), mkP1 (meaning that $F1$ is held by $P1$) and mkP2 (meaning that $F1$ is held by $P2$). The variables of $F2$ are set up similarly to $F1$.

In Fig. 13.32 we show the transaction charts of TS_1.

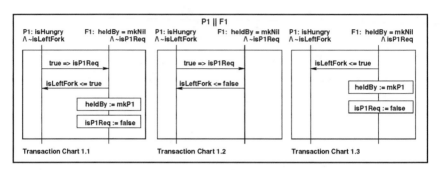

Fig. 13.32. Transaction schema TS_1

There are three transaction charts 1.1, 1.2, 1.3. Chart 1.1 models the scenario that $F1$ grants a fresh "grab" request by $P1$, while chart 1.2 models that $F1$ rejects a fresh "grab" request by $P1$ (but remembers this request). The chart 1.3 models that $F1$ grants a previously recorded request from $P1$. Obviously, the transaction charts of TS_2 are similar to those of TS_1 and thus we omit the details of TS_2.

Transaction schema TS_3 is shown in Fig. 13.33.

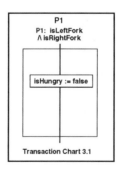

Fig. 13.33. Transaction schema TS_3

Since it only involves $P1$, we would have only internal actions of $P1$. In particular, the activity of eating is modelled by setting isHungry to false.

The transaction schema TS_4 is shown in Fig. 13.34.

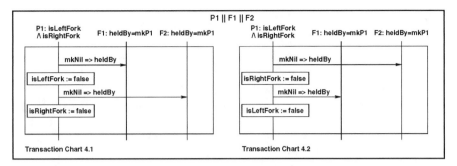

Fig. 13.34. Transaction schema TS_4

There are two charts corresponding to whether $P1$ first puts down its left fork or its right fork.

Similarly to TS_3, the transaction schema TS_5 (shown in Fig. 13.35) models the activity of thinking by setting isHungry to true! Process $F1$ (and also $F2$) alternates between communicating with $P1$ and $P2$. Initially $F1$ is ready to communicate with $P1$ and $F2$ is ready to communicate with $P2$.

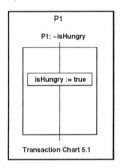

Fig. 13.35. Transaction schema TS_5

We omit the details of TS_1', TS_2', TS_3', TS_4', TS_5' as they are analogous to $TS\_1, TS\_2, TS\_3, TS\_4, TS\_5$.

End of Example 13.24.   ∎

13.6.4 Formalisation of CTPs

The Syntactic and Some Semantic Types

type
    P, T, S, Var, Typ, VAL, Chtn, Exp, AP, Act

Annotation:

P, T, S, Var, Typ, VAL, Chtn, Exp, AP, Act: Process names, transaction schema names, process control states (i.e., names), variable identifiers, type designators (for example `integer`, `Boolean` and so on), semantic values (for example **Int, Bool** and so on), chart names, expressions (further undefined, but are usually variables, prefix expressions and infix expressions over usual integer operators and Boolean connectives), atomic propositions (i.e., Boolean valued expressions over variables) and internal actions (assignments, conditional actions, etc.).   ∎[3]

type
   Prog′ = PDecls × TDecls × Wiring × Init
   Prog = {| prog:Prog′• wf_Prog(prog) |}

Annotation:

Prog: A CTP program consists of well-formed combinations of process variable and transaction schema declarations, of wiring and the definition of an initialisation (of process control states and variable values).   ∎

type
   PDecls = P $\overrightarrow{m}$ VarDecl
   TDecls = T $\overrightarrow{m}$ (Chtn $\overrightarrow{m}$ (Gd × Cht))

Annotation:

PDecls, VarDecl: For each process there is a set of variables of specified type.
TDecls: For each transaction schema name, T, there is a set of uniquely named, Chtn, transaction charts, with each chart consisting of a guard, Gd, and the chart proper Cht.   ∎

type
   Wiring = T $\overrightarrow{m}$ (P $\overrightarrow{m}$ S × S)
   Init = P $\overrightarrow{m}$ (S × VarInit)
   VarDecl = Var $\overrightarrow{m}$ Typ

Annotation:

Wiring: For each transaction schema and for each process (that applies to this schema) there is a pair of respectively input and output control states.
Init, VarInit: With each process a control state, S, is associated an initialisation, respectively the current values of all variables of this process.   ∎

type
   Gd = P $\overrightarrow{m}$ Prop
   Prop == mkTrue | mkAP(ap:AP) | mkNot(pr:Prop)
          | mkAnd(pr:Prop,pr′:Prop) | mkOr(pr:Prop,pr′:Prop)

---

[3] ∎ means: end of annotation.

Annotation:

Gd, Prop: A transaction chart guard associates
- to each of the processes associated with that chart
- a proposition which is
- either the value true,
- or is an atomic proposition,
- or a negated,
- or a conjunctive
- or a disjunctive

proposition.   ∎

type

    Cht = (P $\overrightarrow{m}$ Ev*) × SendRecv

    Ev == mkSe(p:P,e:Exp) | mkRe(p:P,v:Var) | mkAct(act:Act)

    SendRecv = (P × Pos) $\overrightarrow{m}$ (P × Pos)

    Pos = **Nat**

    Σ = Var $\overrightarrow{m}$ VAL

    VarInit = Σ

Annotation:

Cht, Ev*, SendRecv: A transaction chart maps each of its associated processes
into an instance — which is an event list — and a mapping, SendRecv,
that relates output and input events in respective process instances.

Ev: An event is either a send event (sending to p the value of expression e), or
a receive event (receiving a value from p and storing it in v); or an event
is an internal action.

Pos: A position is an index into an event list.   ∎

Auxiliary Syntactic and Semantic Function Signatures

value

    typeof: Exp → VarDecl → Typ

    wf_AP: AP → VarDecl → **Bool**

    wf_Exp: Exp → VarDecl → **Bool**

    wf_Act: Act → VarDecl → **Bool**

Annotation:

typeof: Extracts from an expression, given a set of variable declarations, the
type of the value of the expression, if well-formed.

wf_AP: Examines whether an atomic proposition is well-formed.

wf_Exp: Examines whether an expression is well-formed.

wf_Act: Examines whether an internal action text is well-formed.   ∎

value
    eval_AP: AP → Σ → **Bool**
    eval_Exp: Exp → Σ → VAL
    int_Act: Act → Σ → Σ

Annotation:

eval_AP: Evaluates an atomic proposition.
eval_Exp: Evaluates an expression.
int_Act: Interprets an internal action, possibly leading to changes in the values of variables.   ∎

Auxiliary Function Signatures and Definitions

value
    participants: T → Prog′ → P-set
    participants(t)(prog) ≡ **let** (_,_,wiring,_)= prog **in dom** wiring(t) **end**

    instances : Cht → P-set
    instances(cht) ≡ **let** (pevs,_) = cht **in dom** pevs **end**

Annotation:

participants: Extracts the set of process (names) participating in a transaction schema
instances: Extracts the set of instances of a chart.   ∎

value
    xtr_APs: Prop → AP-set
    xtr_APs(pr) ≡ **case** pr **of** mkTrue → {}, mkAP(ap) → {ap}, ... **end**

    eval_Prop: Prop → Σ → **Bool**
    eval_Prop(pr)(σ) ≡
        case pr **of** mkTrue → **true**, mkAP(ap) → eval_AP(ap)(σ), ... **end**

Annotation:

xtr_APs: Extracts, from a proposition, the set of atomic propositions occurring in a proposition.
eval_Prop: Evaluates a proposition.   ∎

Well-formedness of CTP

value
    wf_Prog : Prog′ → **Bool**
    wf_Prog(prog) ≡
        All_Wired(prog) ∧ All_Initialized(prog) ∧
        wf_Gds_and_Chts(prog) ∧ wf_Wiring(prog) ∧ wf_Init(prog)

Annotation:

wf_Prog: Conjunction of five constraints.   ∎

value
    All_Wired: Prog$'$ → **Bool**
    All_Wired(_,tdecls,wiring,_) ≡ **dom** tdecls = **dom** wiring

    All_Initialized: Prog$'$ → **Bool**
    All_Initialized(pdecls,_,_,init) ≡ **dom** pdecls = **dom** init

Annotation:

All_Wired: All transaction schemas are wired.
All_Initialized: Each process is initialized. (The initialization of a process includes not only the variables but also an initial control state.)   ∎

value
    wf_Gds_and_Chts: Prog$'$ → **Bool**
    wf_Gds_and_Chts(prog) ≡
        let (pdecls,tdecls,_,_) = prog **in**
        ∀ t:T•t ∈ **dom** tdecls ⇒
            let (gd,cht) = tdecls(t)(chtn) **in**
            dom gd = instances(cht) = participants(t)(prog) ∧
            wf_Gd(gd)(pdecls) ∧ wf_Cht(cht)(pdecls)
        end end

    wf_Gd: Gd → PDecls → **Bool**
    wf_Gd(gd)(pdecls) ≡
        ∀ p:P•p ∈ **dom** gd ⇒ ∀ ap:AP • ap ∈ xtr_APs(gd(p))
           ⇒ wf_AP(ap)(pdecls(p))

Annotation:

wf_Gds_and_Chts: The guards and charts are well-formed.
wf_Gd: Examines whether a guard is well-formed.   ∎

value
    wf_Cht: Cht → PDecls → **Bool**
    /* see later */

    wf_Wiring: Prog$'$ → **Bool**
    wf_Wiring(prog) ≡
        let (pdecls,_,wiring,_) = prog **in**
           ∀ t:T•t ∈ **dom** wiring ⇒
           participants(t)(prog)⊆**dom** pdecls
        end

Annotation:

wf_Wiring: The wiring is well-formed.   ■

value
wf_Init: Prog$'$ → **Bool**
wf_Init(prog) ≡
    let (pdecls,_,_,init) = prog **in**
    ∀ p:P•p ∈ **dom** init ⇒
      let (s,varinit) = init(p) **in**
      (∃ t:T,s$'$:S • (s,s$'$)=wiring(t)(p)) ∧ wf_VarInit(varinit)(vardecl(p))
    end end

Annotation:

wf_Init: The initialisation is well-formed (the initialisation includes both initial control states and initial values of variables).   ■

value
    wf_VarInit: VarInit → VarDecl → **Bool**
    wf_VarInit(varinit)(vardecl) ≡
      dom vardecl = **dom** varinit ∧
      ∀ var:Var•var ∈ **dom** vardecl ⇒
        typeof_VAL(varinit(var))=vardecl(var)

    typeof_VAL: VAL → Typ

Annotation:

wf_VarInit: All variables are initialised to values of the declared type.
typeof_VAL: Similar to typeof.   ■

Well-formedness of Charts

value
    wf_Cht: Cht → PDecls → **Bool**
    wf_Cht(cht)(pdecls) ≡ wf_Evs(cht)(pdecls) ∧ wf_SendRecv(cht)(pdecls)

Annotation:

wf_Cht: All events are well-formed and so are all send-receive pairs.   ■

value
    wf_Evs: Cht → PDecls → **Bool**
    wf_Evs(pevs,_)(pdecls) ≡
      ∀ p:P,ev:Ev•
        p ∈ **dom** pevs ∧ ev ∈ **elems** pevs(p) ⇒
          case ev **of**

$\text{mkSe}(q,\text{exp}) \rightarrow q \in \textbf{dom } \text{pevs} \backslash \{p\} \wedge \text{wf\_Exp(exp)(pdecls(p))},$
$\text{mkRe}(q,\text{var}) \rightarrow q \in \textbf{dom } \text{pevs} \backslash \{p\} \wedge \text{is\_decl(var)(pdecls(p))},$
$\text{mkAct(act)} \rightarrow \text{wf\_Act(act)(pdecls(p))}$
end

Annotation:

wf_Evs: All events are well-formed (with respect to source/target processes, expressions, etc.)
- Sends and receives are between different instances, that is, processes.
- Corresponding expressions are well-formed and corresponding variables are declared.
- Internal actions are well-formed. ∎

value
　is_decl: Var → VarDecl → **Bool**
　is_decl(var)(vardecl) ≡ var ∈ **dom** vardecl

　wf_SendRecv: Cht → PDecls → **Bool**
　wf_SendRecv(cht)(pdecls) ≡
　　Well_Matched(cht)(pdecls) ∧ All_Matched(cht) ∧ ~is_cyclic(cht)

Annotation:

is_decl: Examines whether the variable is properly declared.
wf_SendRecv: The send-receive matching relation is well-formed. ∎

value
　is_cyclic: Cht → **Bool**
　is_cyclic(cht) ≡ ... /∗ straightforward ∗/

Annotation:

is_cyclic: The transitive closure of the send-receive and instancewise message ordering relation contains cycles. (The specification of this predicate is clear from item /∗6∗/ (Page 387) of Sect. 13.1.6 "Syntactic Well-formedness of MSCs".) ∎

value
　Well_Matched: Cht → PDecls → **Bool**
　Well_Matched(pevs,sendrecv)(pdecls) ≡
　　card dom sendrecv = **card rng** sendrecv ∧
　　∀ (p,i),(q,j):P×Pos • sendrecv((p,i))=(q,j) ⇒
　　　∃ exp:Exp,var:Var•
　　　　pevs(p)(i) = (q,exp) ∧
　　　　pevs(q)(j) = (p,var) ∧
　　　　typeof(exp)(pdecls(p)) = pdecls(q)(var)

Annotation:

Well_Matched: The matching is proper.   ∎

value
   All_Matched: Cht → **Bool**
   All_Matched(pevs,sendrecv) ≡
      dom sendrecv = {(p,i)|(p,i):P×Pos • is_Send_Ev(pevs(p)(i))}

Annotation:

All_Matched: All send/receive events are matched.   ∎

value
   is_Send_Ev: Ev → **Bool**
   is_Send_Ev(ev) ≡ **case** ev **of** mkSe(_,_) → **true**, _ → **false end**

Annotation:

is_Send_Ev: Examines whether an event is a send event.   ∎

Dynamic Semantics, Types

Semantic Types

type
   PΨ = P $\overrightarrow{m}$ Ψ
   Ψ = Π × Σ × Θ

Annotation:

PΨ : The current "stage" of a CTP program is given by associating with each
   process, a stage, Ψ.

Ψ: The process stage consists of a triple: the current program point, Π, the
   current values of all its variables, Σ, and the (evaluated) values of expressions of executed output (send) events, Θ.   ∎

type
   Π == mkS(s:S) | mkT(t:T,chtn:Chtn,i:Pos)
   Θ = Pos $\overrightarrow{m}$ VAL
   Pos = **Nat**

Annotation:

Π : The program pointer (of a process) either designates a process control
   state mkS(s:S) or a position i:Pos within a transaction chart chtn:Chtn of
   a transaction schema t:T; i=0 indicates that the process has just entered
   the chart.

Θ: The output value queue (of executed output events) is a map from positions, Pos, of output events to values VAL.

Pos: Position of events (input/output events and internal actions).   ∎

type
$$P\Delta = P \underset{m}{\overrightarrow{\rightarrow}} \Delta$$

Annotation:

$P\Delta$: For each (invoked) process P we record its stepwise progress Δ.   ∎

type
$$\Delta = T \times Chtn \times \Phi$$
$$\Phi == mkEnter \mid mkEv(i:Pos) \mid mkExit$$

Annotation:

Δ : The stepwise progress within a transaction chart, Chtn, of a transaction schema, T, is recorded by a quantity Φ.

Φ : Either the process, at an instance, is at the point of entering, mkEnter, or leaving, mkExit, or is at some event position, mkEv(i:Pos).   ∎

Well-formedness

value
  wf_PΔ: P$\Delta \to$ Prog $\to$ **Bool**
  wf_PΔ(pδ)(prog) $\equiv$
    let (pdecls,_,_,_) = prog **in**
    dom p$\delta \subseteq$ **dom** pdecls $\wedge$
    $\forall$ p:P•p $\in$ **dom** $\delta \Rightarrow$ wf_Δ(p)(pδ)(prog)
    end

Annotation:

wf_PΔ :
  • The invoked processes must first have been declared.
  • And for each such process its progress must be well-formed.   ∎

value
  wf_Δ: P $\to$ P$\Delta \to$ Prog $\to$ **Bool**
  wf_Δ(p)(pδ)(prog) $\equiv$
    let (pdecls,tdecls,_,_) = prog, (t,chtn,ϕ) = pδ(p) **in**
    t $\in$ **dom** tdecls $\wedge$ chtn $\in$ **dom** tdecls(t) $\wedge$ p $\in$ participants(t)(prog) $\wedge$
    case ϕ **of**
      mkEv(i)
        $\to$ **let** (pevs,_) = tdecls(t)(chtn) **in** i $\in$ **inds** pevs(p) **end**
      _ $\to$ $\forall$ q:P•q $\in$ participants(t)(prog) $\Rightarrow$ pδ(q) = pδ(p)
    end end

Annotation:

wf_Δ : For the invoked process
- the designated transaction schema and transaction chart (of that schema) must be declared, and the designated process (name) must be an instance of that chart.
- In addition the program point (ppt) must be well-formed:
  - ⋆ if an event index it must be into the process instance, otherwise
  - ⋆ all processes of that transaction chart must be in the same (either entry or exit) state. ∎

Dynamic Semantics, Functions

Auxiliary Functions

value
> xtr_preS: Prog → T → P → S
> xtr_preS(_,_,wiring,_)(t)(p) ≡
>   **let** (s,_) = wiring(t)(p) **in** s **end**
>   **pre** t ∈ **dom** wiring ∧ p ∈ **dom** wiring(t)

Annotation:

xtr_preS : Extract from a transaction schema, the precondition (a control state) corresponding to a process. ∎

value
> xtr_postS: Prog → T → P → S
> xtr_postS(_,_,wiring,_)(t)(p) ≡
>   **let** (_,s) = wiring(t)(p) **in** s **end**
>   **pre** t ∈ **dom** wiring ∧ p ∈ **dom** wiring(t)

Annotation:

xtr_postS : Given a
- program, a transaction schema (name) and a process (name)
- yield the output control state (from the wiring). ∎

value
> xtr_Ev: Prog → (T × Chtn × P × Pos) → Ev
> xtr_Ev(_,tdecls,_,_)(t,chtn,p,i) ≡
>   **let** (_,(pevs,_)) = tdecls(t)(chtn) **in** pevs(p)(i) **end**
>   **pre** t ∈ **dom** tdecls ∧ chtn ∈ **dom** tdecls(t) ∧
>   **let** (_,(pevs,_)) = tdecls(t)(chtn) **in**
>   p ∈ **dom** pevs ∧ i ∈ **inds** pevs(p) **end**

Annotation:

xtr_Ev : Given
- a program,
- a transaction schema name (within that program),
- the name of a chart (within that schema),
- a process (name) and
- a position (within the designated chart),

yield the designated event.   ∎

value

    xtr_Prop: Prog → (T × Chtn) → P → Prop
    xtr_Prop(_,tdecls,_,_)(t,chtn)(p) ≡
        let (gd,_) = tdecls(t)(chtn) **in** gd(p) **end**
        pre t ∈ **dom** tdecls ∧ chtn ∈ **dom** tdecls(t) ∧
            let (_,cht) = tdecls(t)(chtn) **in** p ∈ instances(cht) **end**

Annotation:

xtr_Prop :
- Given
  - ⋆ a program,
  - ⋆ a transaction schema name (within that program),
  - ⋆ the name of a chart (within that schema), and
  - ⋆ a process (name)
- yield the designated proposition.   ∎

value

    last_Pos: Prog → (T × Chtn) → P → Pos
    last_Pos(_,tdecls,_,_)(t,chtn)(p) ≡
        let (_,(pevs,_)) = tdecls(t)(chtn) **in** len pevs(p) **end**
        pre t ∈ **dom** tdecls ∧ chtn ∈ **dom** tdecls(t)∧
            let (_,cht) = tdecls(t)(chtn) **in** p ∈ instances(cht) **end**

Annotation:

last_Pos :
- Given
  - ⋆ a program,
  - ⋆ a transaction schema (name, within that program),
  - ⋆ a chart (name, within that schema), and
  - ⋆ a process (name, within that chart)
- yield the position of the last event of the designated process instance.∎

value

    xtr_Send: Prog → (T × Chtn) → (P × Pos) → (P × Pos)
    xtr_Send(_,tdecls,_,_)(t,chtn)(p,i) **as** (q,j)
        pre t ∈ **dom** tdecls ∧ chtn ∈ **dom** tdecls(t) ∧
            let (_,(pevs,_))=tdecls(t)(chtn) **in**

p ∈ **dom** pevs ∧ i ∈ **inds** pevs(p) **end**
post let (_,(_,sendrecv))=tdecls(t)(chtn) **in**
sendrecv((q,j)) = (p,i) **end**

Annotation:

xtr_Send : Extract the matching send event, given a receiving event.
- The transaction schema and chart names must be declared and the event position be appropriate.
- The matching send event (q,j) is then found from the send-receive mapping. ∎

Initialization

value
    init_PΨ: Prog → PΨ
    init_PΨ(prog) ≡
        let (_,_,_,init) = prog **in**
        [p↦convert_Ψ(init(p))|p:P•p ∈ **dom** init] **end**

    convert_Ψ: (S × VarInit) → Ψ
    convert_Ψ(s,varinit) ≡ (mkS(s),varinit,[ ])

Annotation:

init_PΨ : To initialise a program is to create the collection of all process initial states.
convert_Ψ : Mark the initial control state, use the initial control variable values and set the initial queues of values of expression of send events to empty. ∎

Enabling

value
    is_enabled: PΔ → (Prog × PΨ) → **Bool**
    is_enabled(pδ)(prog,pψ) ≡
        ∀ p:P•p ∈ **dom** pδ ⇒ **let** (t,chtn,ϕ) = pδ(p) **in**
        case ϕ **of**
            mkEnter → is_enabled_Enter_Chtn(t,chtn)(prog,pψ),
            mkExit → is_enabled_Exit_Chtn(t,chtn)(prog,pψ),
            mkEv(i) → is_enabled_Ev(t,chtn,p,i)(prog,pψ)
        end end
        pre wf_PΔ(pδ)(prog)

Annotation:

is_enabled : A program step, pδ, is enabled at the current stage of the program, if every process step corresponding to processes in the domain of this program step is enabled. ∎

value

    is_enabled_Enter_Chtn: (T × Chtn) → (Prog × PΨ) → **Bool**

    is_enabled_Enter_Chtn(t,chtn)(prog,pψ) ≡

      ∀ p:P•p ∈ participants(t)(prog) ⇒

        let s = xtr_preS(prog)(t)(p),

            pr = xtr_Prop(prog)(t,chtn)(p),

            (π,σ,_) = pψ(p) **in**

      (π=mkS(s)) ∧ eval_Prop(pr)(σ) **end**

Annotation:

is_enabled_Enter_Chtn : A chart of a transaction schema can be entered if for every process participating in this transaction schema, its current control state is the precondition of this transaction schema, and the proposition associated with this process in the guard associated with this chart evaluates to true with respect to the current values of variables. ■

value

    is_enabled_Exit_Chtn: (T × Chtn) → (Prog × PΨ) → **Bool**

    is_enabled_Exit_Chtn(t,chtn)(prog,pψ) ≡

      ∀ p:P•p ∈ participants(t)(prog) ⇒

        let (mkT(t,chtn,i),σ,_)=pψ(p) **in** i=last_Pos(prog)(t,chtn)(p) **end**

Annotation:

is_enabled_Exit_Chtn : A chart of a transaction schema can be exited if for every process participating in this transaction schema, it has executed all its events in this chart. ■

value

    is_enabled_Ev: (T × Chtn × P × Pos) → (Prog × PΨ) → **Bool**

    is_enabled_Ev(t,chtn,p,i)(prog,pψ) ≡

      let (mkT(t,chtn,i′),_,_) = pψ(p) **in** i′=i−1 ∧

      case xtr_Ev(prog)(t,chtn,p,i) **of**

        mkRe(q,_) →

          let (q,j) = xtr_Send(prog)(t,chtn)(p,i) **in**

          let (mkT(t,chtn,j′),_,_) = pψ(q) **in** j ≤ j′ **end end**

        _ → **true**

      end end

Annotation:

is_enabled_Ev : An event at a position of a process in a chart of a transaction schema is enabled, if this process has come to the previous position, and in case this event is a receive event, the matching send event has been executed. ■

Firing

value
   fire: (Prog × PΨ) → PΔ → (Prog × PΨ)
   fire(prog,pψ)(pδ) **as** (prog,pψ')
     pre is_enabled(pδ)(prog,pψ)
     post pψ'=pψ†[p↦upd_Ψ(prog,pψ)(pδ)(p)|p ∈ **dom** pδ]

Annotation:

fire : Firing an enabled program step updates the current stage of every process.   ■

value
   upd_Ψ: (Prog × PΨ) → PΔ → P → Ψ
   upd_Ψ(prog,pψ)(pδ)(p) ≡
     let (π,σ,θ) = pψ(p), (t,chtn,φ) = pδ(p) **in**
       case φ **of**
         mkEnter → (mkT(t,chtn,0),σ,[ ])
         mkEv(i) →
           let σ' = upd_Σ(prog,σ)(p)(t,chtn,i),
               θ' = upd_Θ(prog,θ)(p)(t,chtn,i) **in**
           (mkT(t,chtn,i),σ',θ') **end**
         mkExit → **let** s = xtr_postS(prog)(t)(p) **in** (mkS(s),σ,[ ]) **end**
     end end
   pre ...

Annotation:

upd_Ψ : Upon firing an enabled program step, the current stage of a process should be updated as follows.
- If this process enters a chart of a transaction schema, then this process goes to position zero of this chart (in this transaction schema), retains the current values of variables and initializes an empty map of positions to values of expressions of send events.
- If this process executes an event at a position of a chart of a transaction schema, then this process goes to this position and updates the current values of variables and the map of positions to values of expressions of send events.
- If this process exits a chart of a transaction schema, then this process goes to the postcondition associated with this process of this transaction schema, retains the current values of variables and empties the map of positions to values of expressions of send events.   ■

value
   upd_Σ: (Prog × PΨ) → P → (T × Chtn × Pos) → Σ
   upd_Σ(prog,pψ)(p)(t,chtn,i) ≡

let (_,σ,_) = pψ(p), ev = xtr_Ev(prog)(t,chtn,p,i) **in**
case ev **of**
   mkSe(q,exp) → σ,
   mkRe(q,var) →
     let (_,_,θ) = pψ(q),
     (q,j) = xtr_Send(prog)(t,chtn)(p,i) **in** σ † [var ↦ θ(j)] **end**,
   mkAct(act) → int_Act(act)(σ)
end end
pre ...

Annotation:

upd_Σ : Upon execution of an event, the current values of variables should be updated as follows.
- Executing a send event does not change the value of any variable.
- Executing a receive event amounts to assigning the value of the expression of the matching send event to the variable associated with this receive event, and leaving the values of all other variables untouched.
- Executing an internal action amounts to evaluating it with respect to the current values of variables, possibly leading to changes in the values of variables. ∎

value
   upd_Θ: (Prog × PΨ) → P → (T × Chtn × Pos) → Θ
   upd_Θ(prog,pψ)(p)(t,chtn,i) ≡
     let (_,σ,θ) = pψ(p) **in**
     case ev **of** mkSe(q,exp) → θ ∪ [i ↦ eval_Exp(exp)(σ)],
                           _ → θ **end end**
   pre ...

Annotation:

upd_Θ : Upon execution of an event, the map of positions to values of expression of send events is updated as follows. Executing a send event amounts to adding to this map the value of the expression of this send event associated with its position. Executing a receive event or an internal action does not touch this map. ∎

13.7 Discussion

13.7.1 General

We have covered two notions of sequence charts (SCs): Message SCs (MSCs) and Live SCs (LSCs).

MSCs arose in connection with the design of software for telephone switching and data communication systems in the 1970s. MSC, as a language, was then known as the System Description Language (SDL). Work on SDL and MSC took place mainly under the auspices of the International Telecommunication Union, ITU. We refer to various URLs related to ITU, SDL and MSC [226].

MSCs, most likely due to the influence of Ivar Jacobson, one of the three technologists who did the principal design of UML[4] [59, 237, 382, 440], became one of the many diagrammatic facets of UML.

LSCs took off from MSC. On one hand, David Harel and his colleagues (notably Werner Damm), have spearheaded LSC research and development, notably through the *Come, Let's Play — Scenario-Based Programming Using LSCs and the Play-Engine* [195]. On the other hand, it seems that, so far, the mostly software oriented computer science community has been at work on studying LSCs. The author happily confesses: The *Play-Engine* is a fascinating concept.

We have also presented some material on theoretical foundations of MSCs and LSCs. The material presented in Sects. 13.3–13.5 represents one direction of research in the field of integrated formal methods. It is included to illustrate that certain techniques have advantages for certain applications in software engineering, and that choosing one technique (e.g., diagrams) does not preclude also using other techniques (e.g., formal specification in RSL). Indeed, in complex software engineering projects, several techniques will be needed to specify all the relevant aspects of a system. To ensure consistency between the different parts of the system specified using different techniques, relations among these techniques must be established. The relation between LSCs and RSL presented above and the corresponding relation between statecharts and RSL — presented in the next chapter (Sect. 14.7) — are two such examples.

13.7.2 Principles, Techniques and Tools

This chapter has basically covered a tool: The sequence charts (MSCs and LCSs). As such we can hardly speak of 'A Principle of Sequence Charts' — such as we could for most other chapters' title subjects. So we shall rearrange things a bit in this section on "Principles, Techniques and Tools".

Principles. *Choosing Sequence Charts:* Sequence charts, as a modelling device, can be chosen when the phenomenon to be abstracted and modelled exhibits concurrent and interacting behaviours, where the interaction "patterns" are of main interest, and then usually when there is a definite, "small" number of behaviours, typically less than a couple of dozen.   ∎

---

[4]Ivar Jacobson was with Ericsson in the later 1970s and early 1980s when SDL was first designed, and played a decisive role in that effort.

Which kind of sequence chart, whether MSCs or LSCs are chosen, is then a matter of sophistication, whether MSCs will do, or whether the more elaborate properties of LSCs are needed. Please contrast the above principle with that of *Choosing Statecharts* Sect. 14.8.2.

Techniques. *Creating Sequence Charts:* The basic parts of sequence charts are the instances, corresponding to behaviours (i.e., processes), and the inputs/outputs, corresponding to events (in the CSP jargon). All else are adornments.   ∎

Tools. *Sequence Charts:* We refer to [226] for reference to MSC tools. The main, and overwhelmingly sophisticated, LSC tool is that of the *Play-Engine* [195]. A number of research investigation and exploratory tools are provided by Sun and Dong [493] for model-checking LSCs via translation to CSP and then using the FDR2 tool [442]. Others are provided by Wang, Roychoudhury, Yap and Choudhary [525] for symbolically executing LSCs using translation to constraint logic programming. There are many more.   ∎

13.8 Bibliographical Notes

The basic references to MSCs are the three consecutive recommendations from the International Telecommunication Union, labelled Z.120 [227–229] (1992, 1996 and 1999). Syntax recommendations for MSCs are given in Reniers [423]. Extensions of MSCs with time have been studied in [38, 280, 296].

The basic reference to LSCs is Damm and Harel's paper [89]. The main text on LSCs is now the book [195]. A delightful presentation of MSCs and LSCs is Harel and Thiagarajan [199]. The literature on Live Sequence Charts is emerging. A sample is: [58, 64, 89, 187, 191, 278, 493, 525]. In [191] Harel, Kugler and Pnueli put forward further proposals for time in LSC, i.e., the "rich version" of LSC. Report [493] shows relations between the language of LSCs and CSP, and reports on translations of LSCs into CSP for purposes of using CSP's model checker FDR2 http://www.fsel.com/fdr2_manual.html [442]. [525] shows how LSCs can be "symbolically executed" using constraint logic programming. Christian Krog Madsen [316, 317] analyses both MSCs, HMSCs and LSCs, establishes proper semantics for these and relates LSCs to RSL. UML contains various rudiments of MSCs [59, 237, 382, 440].

Recent work by Roychoudhury and Thiagarajan merges ideas of Petri nets and MSCs. The result is called *communicating transaction processes* (CTP) [439] — and was treated in Sect. 13.6.

A flurry of recent publications explore various uses of live sequence charts in software engineering and in biology! They are all authored or coauthored by D. Harel. Some recurrent coauthors are I.R. Cohen, S. Efroni, N. Kam, H. Kugler, R. Marelly and A. Pnueli [106–108, 115, 116, 133, 176–180, 182–184, 186, 188–192, 194, 196, 253–258, 279, 325].

13.9 Exercises

Exercise 13.1 *Automatic Teller Machine.* Automatic teller machines (ATM) usually services credit and cash cards of a consortium of financial institutions (Diners, Mastercard, Visa, etc., as well as Citibank (New York, NY, USA), HSBC (Hong Kong and Shanghai Bank Corporation, London, UK), etc.). So you may think of four sets of "players": You, the card holders, the ATMs, the consortia, and the specific financial institutions of the consortia. A particular ATM is bound to a specific set of card types, one consortium, and a specific set of financial institutions. An ATM usually offers a number of services: cash withdrawal, cash deposit, cash transfer, inquiry about account status, etc. An example protocol for the opening of a card transaction using an ATM is as follows: user inserts card into the ATM; the ATM requests card password from the user; the user keys password into the ATM; the ATM requests verification from the consortium; the consortium requests verification from the financial institution of the card; the financial institution either OKs or does not OK the transaction and so informs the consortium; the consortium passes the verification response back to the ATM; and the ATM passes it back to the user. If response was OK, the user may continue.

Exercise 13.1.1: Develop an appropriate MSC for a quadruplet of *User, ATM, Consortium* and *Financial Institution* instances.

Exercise 13.1.2: Develop a possible MSC, following a successful, i.e., OK'ed verification opening, for a cash withdrawal transaction.

Exercise 13.1.3: Develop a possible MSC, following a successful, i.e., OK'ed verification opening, for a cash transfer transaction.

You are to fill in all relevant details left out above and to take into account that the user makes mistakes.

Exercise 13.2 *Two-Phase Commit Protocol.* In many forms of distributed systems, the need arises for a group of parties to reach an agreement to perform some action. Each party has the option of vetoing the action, in which case all the other parties must not perform the action. Another possibility is that one or more parties fail before either committing or vetoing the action. In that case, the action must also be aborted by all parties.

One application of this protocol is to implement distributed transactions. In this case, the parties must agree whether to commit or roll back the transaction, such that it is either performed by all parties or by none.

The protocol to be formalised is centralised, since a single distinguished party acts as the coordinator. The remaining parties are slaves (*A* and *B*).

The informal description (given below) derives from [147] and is based on [469]. Based on this informal description you are to solve the following problems.

Exercises 13.2.1–5: Formalise interactions between the environment, the coordinator and the slaves in terms of live sequence charts.

Exercise 13.2.6: Formalise the internal behaviour of the coordinator in terms of a finite state machine.

Exercise 13.2.7: Formalise all of the above in RSL.

The informal description of our version of the two-phase commit protocol goes as follows, one description part per live sequence chart:

1. *Protocol initiation:* To start the whole thing it is assumed that an environment requests the coordinator to set up requests to all slaves (here just two). Once that *assumption* (modelled in terms of a prechart) is satisfied, the coordinator in any order sends requests to all (i.e., both) slaves.

2. *Commit:* When all (both) slaves commit to the requests (by sending such messages to the coordinator) the coordinator informs the slaves that the protocol has been successfully opened (by sending appropriate messages to the slaves).

3. *Abort by slave A:* If slave A cannot participate in the protocol (i.e., send an abort message), but slave B can (i.e., commits), then the coordinator has to inform slave B of the abort.

4. *Abort by slave B:* Vice versa: If slave B cannot the protocol (i.e., aborts), but slave A can (i.e., commits), then the coordinator has to inform slave A of the abort.

5. *Abort by both slaves:* If all (i.e., both) slaves cannot participate in the protocol (i.e., abort), then the coordinator has to inform all slaves of the abort.

It is suggested that the *assumption*, the *when* and the *if*'s of the above five cases be modelled by precharts.

6. *Internal behaviour of coordinator:*

Coordination evolves around a finite state machine. In each state the coordinator expects input (i.e., messages) from either (initially) the environment, or, subsequently, from the slaves. In response to an input the coordinator sends outputs that amount to messages being sent to some or all slaves.

In an initial state the coordinator will expect the environment, i.e., a user to request some action to be performed as a distributed transaction. Once the coordinator receives such a request it is passed on to, i.e., transmitted to the slaves. The coordinator now waits for responses from the slaves. The coordinator can only receive one response at a time. Either a commit from some slave or an abort from some slave. The coordinator, upon receiving one commit or one abort enters respective states in order to be able to receive, distinguish and properly react to subsequent responses from remaining slaves. If all slaves responds with commit, the transaction is committed. If at least one slave responds with abort, the whole transaction is aborted.

7. *An RSL Model:*

You are to model the protocol in RSL. More specifically, to define a number of processes for the system, for example, the coordinator and the two slaves. The system process is suggested to be just the parallel composition of the coordinator process and the two slave processes.

The coordinator process will wait to be invoked by inputting a request from the user. The requested action is transmitted to the two slaves. Next, the coordinator will input the responses from slave A and B, in some order. If both choose to commit, they are informed that agreement has been reached to commit. A function *commit-action* can be postulated to abstract the actual action to be performed. If either slave responds with abort, the other slave is informed that the transaction is aborted and the coordinator performs the necessary clean-up, abstracted, for example, by a function *abort-action*.

The slave processes are entirely analogous. They first wait for a request to be received from the coordinator. Upon receipt, they decide – internal nondeterminism choice – to commit or abort. In the latter case, they tell the coordinator to abort and perform the necessary clean-up, abstracted by *abort-action*. In the former case, they tell the coordinator to commit and await the response. Based on the coordinator's response, they either commit or abort the transaction. The nondeterministic choice is an abstraction of the process used to decide whether to commit or abort.

Exercise 13.3 *Semantics of HMSCs.* We refer to the syntax and well-formedness of BMSCs (Sects. 13.1.2 and 13.1.6), the semantics of BMSCs (Sect. 13.1.8), the syntax and well-formedness of HMSCs (Sects. 13.1.4 and 13.1.6).

Please define the semantics of HMSCs based on the formalisation given in the above referenced sections.

Exercise 13.4 *Remote Procedure Calls/Remote Method Invocation and Broker Design Pattern.*

Procedure calls are a fundamental notion in most imperative computer languages. A procedure call occurs when the calling procedure requests the execution of the behaviour of the body of the called procedure. Typically, the called procedure returns some value once (and if) its execution terminates. A prerequisite for procedure calls is that the caller and callee are contained in the same executable or in shared libraries, which are linked in at runtime. The extended notion of *remote procedure calls (RPC)* does away with this limitation by allowing the caller and callee procedures to be contained in different executables, processes and even on different computers. In the context of Java, RPC is called *remote method invocation (RMI)*. The basic principle of "remoting" is to replace the callee with a proxy procedure, which exposes the same interface as the callee. Instead of performing the action the callee would, the proxy encodes the parameters it is passed, sends them to another proxy, which decodes the parameters and calls the real callee. Figure 13.36 illustrates the setup, where the caller is named the *Client*, while the callee is named the *Server*. The *ClientProxy* appears to the Client as the Server would (i.e., it has the same interface). The *ServerProxy* appears to the Server as the Client would.

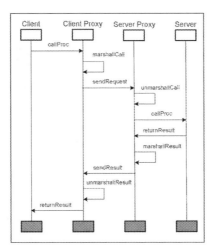

Fig. 13.36. A remote procedure call protocol

The purpose of the two *Proxy* objects is to hide the details of the transmission of the call parameters and return value over some medium, which could be a network connection (for processes distributed on separate computers) or shared memory (for inter-process communication within the same computer). The operation of encoding a call including its parameters is traditionally called *marshalling*. The inverse operation of decoding a call with parameters is traditionally called *unmarshalling*.

Exercise 13.4.1: Formulate an RSL specification of a simple RPC mechanism for a procedure (function) that takes two integers as arguments and returns their sum. Create a type to represent the marshalled format of the arguments.

A downside with RPC is that once the program is written, the Client is locked to the Server. Suppose now that a more efficient implementation of the addition function is written (call it Server′). To make Client call Server′ instead of Server, Client must be modified. Thus this system works best in a static environment, where both Client and Server are developed at the same time. It can not easily adapt to a dynamic environment. One mechanism to introduce dynamic binding of the Client and Server is captured in the so-called *Broker Design Pattern* [71], which is central to CORBA [381] and Java Jini (Jini extensible remote invocation (Jini ERI)) [494] technology. The idea is to introduce a broker, which maintains a list of available services in a distributed system. In the broker architecture, the ServerProxy will register itself as a service with the broker and provide some form of identification of what the service does. When the ClientProxy is called, it will query the broker to find the location of a service that performs the action it needs. The broker will return some form of address or pointer to the ServerProxy. At this point, the rest of the protocol behaves like the RPC protocol. Hence, once the broker has pointed the ClientProxy to the service, it no longer participates in the communication.

Typically a service is identified by a text string, so the ClientProxy will ask for a service called Addition.

Exercise 13.4.2: Extend the MSC in Fig. 13.36 to include the broker.
Exercise 13.4.3: Extend the previous RSL specification to include the broker.

The interested reader may like to compare the above description to the building blocks of Web services such as XML [417,443,478,546], SOAP [516], WSDL [517] and UDDI [506].

Exercise 13.5 *Generalised Dining Philosophers.* We refer to Sect. 13.6.3. The example of that section showed a two-dining philosophers CTP program. Please show a CTP program solution for five dining philosophers

14

Statecharts

Christian Krog Madsen is chief author of this chapter [316, 317].

- The **prerequisites** for studying this chapter are that you have an all-round awareness of abstract specification (principles and techniques) and that you have a more specific awareness of parallel programming, for example, using CSP — as illustrated in Vol. 1 of this series of textbooks — and you have wondered about, or desired, other mechanisms than, say, RSL/CSP for modelling concurrency.
- The **aims** are to introduce the concept, principles and techniques of using statecharts, to show varieties of examples illustrating uses of Statecharts, and to relate Statecharts to RSL/CSP: To define, more precisely, when a statechart specification can be expressed as an RSL/CSP specification — and vice versa!
- The **objective** is to enable the reader to expand the kind of phenomena and concepts that can be formally modelled by, or in conjunction (complementary) with, for example, RSL using statecharts.
- The **treatment** is systematic and semiformal.

Statecharts are ascribed to David Harel [174, 175, 185, 193, 197]. Others have contributed, notably Amir Pnueli [404]. Besides very professional tool support, in the form of STATEMATE [197, 198], the diagrammatic Statechart language has achieved some prominence by being coopted into UML [59, 237, 382, 440].

14.1 Introduction

In this section we describe statecharts [174, 175]. As a language, Statecharts provides a graphical notation tailored for specifying the *control flow* of *reactive systems*, i.e., event-driven systems which react to internal and external stimuli. Many electronic devices, such as digital clocks, radios, kitchen appliances, smoke alarms, motion sensors, etc., are reactive systems. Computer programs, such as word processors and Internet browsers, that require some form of input from the user during execution are other examples of reactive systems. An "opposite" to reactive systems are transformational systems. They perform some computation and terminate once the result has been evaluated. On closer examination, a reactive system actually encompasses several transformational systems, since whenever an event triggers a transition, the resulting change of state may be expressed as a function from states to states, i.e., a transformation on the state. There are several well-established methods for specifying transformational systems, for example, a direct definition of a function relating input values to output values, or indirectly through postconditions stating properties of the output values, assuming the inputs satisfy some pre-conditions.

Statecharts extends conventional state machines and state diagrams. It does so by providing a notation for hierarchical states and ways of specifying concurrency and communication. The addition of hierarchy is intended to prevent exponential increases in the number of states required to model complex systems. A variant of Harel's Statechart language has been included in the UML suite of diagram types [59, 237, 382, 440].

14.2 A Narrative Description of Statecharts

Like state machines and state diagrams, statecharts are centred around *states* and *transitions*. The behaviour of the system in response to internal and external stimuli depends on the state(s) it is currently in, called the *active state(s)*. A transition describes a change of active state. A transition is *triggered* by an *event* or action and may set off other actions. Statecharts are represented graphically as so-called *higraphs* [175], utilizing area inclusion rather than the more conventional tree or graph structure for representing hierarchy. States are represented as rounded rectangles (for simplicity called boxes in the following). A state, s_c, that is fully contained within another state, s_p, is called a *substate* of s_p.

States may be decomposed into substates using either AND or XOR decomposition. *AND decomposition* captures the property that when a system is in a given state, it must also be in all substates of that state. Conversely, *XOR decomposition* captures the property that when a system is in a given state, it must be in exactly one of the substates of that state. XOR decomposition is represented by having several substates. AND decomposition is represented by subdividing the box of the containing state with a dashed line and placing concurrent substates on either side of the line.

Transitions are represented as *arrows* from states to states. An arrow is labelled with an identifier for the event that triggers the transition and, optionally, a *condition* enclosed in parentheses. In an extension of the original Statechart language, Pnueli and Shalev [404] allowed *negative events* to trigger transitions. A negative event is interpreted as the absence of the event itself. The unary logical negation operator, ¬, is used to *negate events*. Typically, a transition will be triggered by both positive and negative events, i.e., it will only occur if all the positive events are offered by the environment, while none of the negative events are offered.

When a transition occurs, control is transferred from the *origin state* to the *destination state*. If the origin of a transition is a state with substates, control is relinquished by all substates. If the destination of a transition is a state that is AND decomposed into substates, control is assumed by all substates. If the destination is XOR decomposed, control is assumed by the *default substate*. Default states are indicated by a small filled circle with an arrow pointing to the box of the default substate. A default state functions like an *initial state* in a state machine.

Example 14.1 Figure 14.1 shows a statechart with four states, A, B, C and D. State A is XOR decomposed into B and C, with B being the default state. The statechart responds to three different events, a, b and c. When the system is in state D it may go to state C upon receiving event c, or it may go to state A upon receiving event a. Since A is XOR decomposed, activating state A leads to activating state B as well, since B is the default substate for A. If state A is active and event b occurs, the system will transition to state D, regardless of which substate of A is active.   ∎

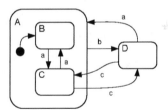

Fig. 14.1. Statechart with XOR decomposition

Example 14.2 Figure 14.2 shows a statechart with AND decomposition. The statechart responds to three events, a, b, and c. When the system is in state G and receives event a, states C and E will be activated concurrently. If either a substate of A or a substate of B is active, the occurrence of event c will cause G to become the active state.   ∎

The introduction of the concepts of *AND* and *XOR states* is the key to avoiding the exponential blow-up in the number of states as the system being modelled becomes increasingly complex. However, any statechart including either form of decomposition may be transformed into an equivalent (in a sense to

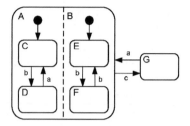

Fig. 14.2. Statechart with AND decomposition

be defined precisely later) statechart without hierarchical states. The procedure to eliminate an XOR state is to extend every incoming transition to the
default substate and for every outgoing transition add an outgoing transition
with the same event trigger and action and target state to every substate. An
AND decomposed state may be eliminated by forming new states for every
possible combination of concurrent substates.

Example 14.3 Figure 14.3(L) illustrates the unwinding of the statechart with
XOR decomposition in Fig. 14.1 into a nonhierarchical statechart. In this
case the unwound statechart is not more complicated than the original, since
it has one less state but one more transition. In general, an unwound AND
decomposed statechart will have at most the same number of states as the
original and at least the same number of transitions as the original.

Similarly Fig. 14.3(R) illustrates the unwinding of the Statechart with AND
decomposition in Fig. 14.2 into a nonhierarchical statechart. In this case the
resulting Statechart is considerably more complicated that the original. There
are only 5 states compared to 6 in the original, but there are 13 transitions
compared to 6 in the original.   ∎

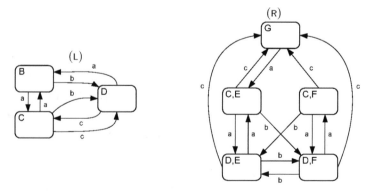

Fig. 14.3. Unwinding of XOR (L) and AND (R) into a simple statechart

Statechart supports the modelling concepts of *abstraction* and *refinement*. Abstraction is the process of extracting common properties from a model. Refinement is the process of adding additional details to a model. In the setting of statecharts both concepts rely on hierarchical decomposition.

Abstraction is supported by moving the common properties (i.e., transitions with the same event trigger and same destination state) of a set of states to a new state that has the original states as substates. Refinement is supported by adding new substates and internal transitions to an existing state.

Example 14.4 (Example is taken from [174].) Figure 14.4 illustrates the process of abstraction for statecharts. In the statechart on the left, the transition on event *b* from states *B* and *C* is a common property of these two states. By introducing a new superstate, these two transitions can be replaced by one common transition, as shown in the statechart on the right.

Figure 14.5 shows the process of refinement. In the intermediate step in the middle, the state *D* is refined to show additional details of its internal structure. However, now the two transitions from *A* to *D* become underspecified, since it is not clear which of *B* and *C* should become active after one of the transitions has occurred. In the statechart on the right, the transitions have been extended to remove the underspecification. Alternatively, either *B* or *C* could have been defined as the default substate of *D*.   ∎

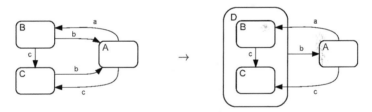

Fig. 14.4. Abstraction

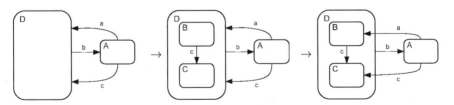

Fig. 14.5. Refinement

A special kind of transition causes control to be transferred to the substate(s) that most recently had control instead of the default substate. This *history-*

dependent type of transition may be related only to the immediate substates, or recursively to substates, substates of substates, and so on.

In cases where no history is available, i.e., the first time control is transferred to a state, the default substates are used. History-dependent transitions are represented by letting the arrow of the transition point to a symbol composed of an 'H' inside a circle. If the transition depends on the recursive history, the H symbol is decorated with an asterisk.

In some situations, it is convenient to be able to forget the past history. For this purpose, a distinguished action, $clh(S)$, that resets the history of a state S and all substates of S is introduced. Once the history has been reset, the next time a history-dependent transition occurs, the default state and not the most recently visited state will become the active state.

Example 14.5 Figure 14.6 illustrates a Statechart with history dependent transitions. The first time a state is activated by a history transition, there is no history, so the default substate becomes the active state. Thus, in this case, the first time B is activated, F becomes active.

Suppose now that E is the active state and that event a occurs, so A becomes the new active state. If event a occurs now, D becomes the active state, since only the first level of the activation history is used. C was the most recently activated substate of B, so the default substate of C, namely D, is activated. If, on the other hand, event b occurs, E becomes the active state, since in this case the entire history is used. Finally, if B is active and event d occurs, all history is cleared for B, so the next history transition will cause the default substate to be activated.   ∎

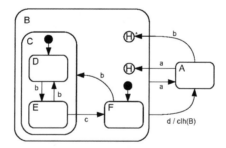

Fig. 14.6. Statechart with history and recursive history

The events that trigger transitions are typically the result of *external stimuli*, but may also be generated by timeouts when control has been in a given state for a predetermined period of time. We do not consider such timeouts here.

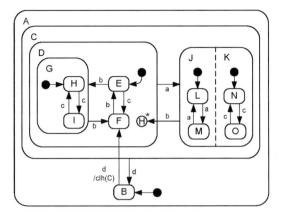

Fig. 14.7. Example statechart

Example 14.6 Figure 14.7 shows an example statechart modelling a reactive system that receives four kinds of stimuli from the environment (essentially like four buttons).

Each kind of stimulus generates a unique event, called a, b, c and d. The system is represented by state A. Initially, the system is in state B. When an event d occurs, control is transferred to state F. A b event will now transfer control to state E. An additional b event will transfer control to state G and H, which is the default substate of G, while a c event will transfer control back to state F. When the system is in any of the substates of G, a b event will cause control to be transferred to F.

When the system is in any substate of D, an a event will transfer control to both J and K. Similarly, when another b event occurs, control is relinquished by both J and K and all their substates. Control is then transferred to the most recently visited states in D down to the lowest level, i.e., the states from which control was relinquished when the last a event occurred.

The label "/clh(C)" on the transition from B to C is an action that indicates that when this transition occurs, the history of C and its substates is deleted all the way down to the lowest level. Thus, the next time the transition from J/K to D occurs, the default state will be entered.

∎

14.3 An RSL Model of the Syntax of Statecharts

Definition. By a *statechart* we shall understand a structure such as informally described in Sect. 14.2, a structure whose syntax is given in this section and a structure whose semantics is given in Sects. 14.5 and 14.6.   ∎

The syntactic description of the Statechart language, as given in Sect. 14.2, is formalised in RSL.

scheme Statechart =
  class
    type
      Statechart = {| sc : Statechart$'$ • wf_Statechart(sc) |},
      Statechart$'$ = StateId × StateHier × Trans × History,
      StateHier = StateId $\overrightarrow{m}$ StateDef,
      StateDef == mk_XOR(OptSId, StateId-**set**) | mk_AND(StateId-**set**),
      OptSId == mk_None | mk_Id(StateId),
      Trans = StateId $\overrightarrow{m}$ Tr-**set**,
      Tr ::
        stid : StateId
        typ : Type
        evt : Event
        cond : Condition
        act : Action,
      Type == mk_History | mk_HistoryRec | mk_Direct,
      Event = **Text**,
      Condition,
      Action,
      History = StateId $\overrightarrow{m}$ StateId,
      StateId

    value
      wf_Statechart : Statechart$'$ → **Bool**
      wf_Statechart(sid, shi, tr, hi) ≡
        /* 1 */
        sid ∈ **dom** shi ∧
        /* 2 */
        dom tr ⊆ **dom** shi ∧
        /* 3 */
        dom hi ⊆ **dom** shi ∧
        /* 4 */
        (∀ s : StateId •
          s ∈ **dom** shi ⇒
            case shi(s) **of**
              mk_XOR(_,ss) → ss ⊆ **dom** shi,
              mk_AND(ss) → ss ⊆ **dom** shi
            end) ∧
        /* 5 */
        (∀ s : StateId •
          s ∈ **dom** shi ⇒
            case shi(s) **of**

$$\text{mk\_XOR(os, ss)} \rightarrow$$
$$\quad \textbf{case os of}$$
$$\quad\quad \text{mk\_None} \rightarrow \textbf{true},$$
$$\quad\quad \text{mk\_Id(sid')} \rightarrow \text{sid'} \in \text{ss}$$
$$\quad \textbf{end},$$
$$\quad \text{mk\_AND(ss)} \rightarrow \textbf{true}$$
$$\textbf{end}) \wedge$$

/* 6 */

$$(\forall \text{ s : StateId} \bullet$$
$$\quad \text{s} \in \textbf{dom} \text{ shi} \Rightarrow$$
$$\quad\quad \textbf{case} \text{ shi(s)} \textbf{ of}$$
$$\quad\quad\quad \text{mk\_XOR(os, ss)} \rightarrow$$
$$\quad\quad\quad\quad \text{ss} \neq \{\} \Rightarrow$$
$$\quad\quad\quad\quad\quad (\exists \text{ s' : StateId, t : Tr} \bullet$$
$$\quad\quad\quad\quad\quad\quad \text{s'} \in \textbf{dom} \text{ tr} \wedge \text{t} \in \text{tr(s')} \wedge \text{stid(t)} = \text{s}) \Rightarrow$$
$$\quad\quad\quad\quad\quad \text{has\_default(s, shi)},$$
$$\quad\quad\quad \text{mk\_AND(ss)} \rightarrow$$
$$\quad\quad\quad\quad \text{ss} \neq \{\} \Rightarrow$$
$$\quad\quad\quad\quad\quad (\exists \text{ s' : StateId, t : Tr} \bullet$$
$$\quad\quad\quad\quad\quad\quad \text{s'} \in \textbf{dom} \text{ tr} \wedge \text{t} \in \text{tr(s')} \wedge \text{stid(t)} = \text{s}) \Rightarrow$$
$$\quad\quad\quad\quad\quad \text{has\_default(s, shi)}$$
$$\quad\quad \textbf{end}),$$

has_default : StateId × StateHier $\rightarrow$ **Bool**
has_default(sid, shi) $\equiv$
$\quad$ **case** shi(sid) **of**
$\quad\quad$ mk_XOR(os, ss) $\rightarrow$
$\quad\quad\quad$ ss = {} $\vee$
$\quad\quad\quad$ **case** os **of**
$\quad\quad\quad\quad$ mk_None $\rightarrow$ **false**,
$\quad\quad\quad\quad$ mk_Id(sid') $\rightarrow$ has_default(sid', shi)
$\quad\quad\quad$ **end**,
$\quad\quad$ mk_AND(ss) $\rightarrow$
$\quad\quad\quad$ ss = {} $\vee$ ($\forall$ s : StateId $\bullet$ s $\in$ ss $\Rightarrow$ has_default(s, shi))
$\quad$ **end**
end

Annotations

- A statechart consists of an initial state identifier, a state hierarchy, a set of transitions and a history.
- A state hierarchy maps state identifiers to state definitions.
- A state definition is either an exclusive-or state or a both-and state. An exclusive-or state has an optional default substate identifier and a set of identifiers of substates. A both-and state has a set of identifiers of substates. A substate is a state.

- From a state identifier the set of transitions emanating from that state can be found.
- A transition is composed of destination stated identifier, a type, a triggering event, a condition and an action.
- A transition may either cause a transfer of control to the most recently visited state at the top level, or a recursive transfer of control to the most recently visited state all the way down to the lowest level, or a direct transfer of control to the destination state.
- An event is a textual label identifying an exterior interaction.
- Conditions, actions and state identifiers are further undefined entities.
- The history is a mapping from state identifiers to substate identifiers.
- A statechart is well-formed if
  - ⋆ the initial state is in the state hierarchy, and
  - ⋆ the states from which transitions emanate are in the state hierarchy, and
  - ⋆ the states with a history are in the state hierarchy, and
  - ⋆ all substates are in the state hierarchy, and
  - ⋆ when an exclusive-or state has a default substate, then that substate is in the state hierarchy, and
  - ⋆ if a transition terminates at a composite state, then that state has a default substate.
- A state has a default state if it has no substates, or if it is an exclusive-or state and it has a default substate which in turn has a default state, or if it is a both-and state and all its substates have a default state.   ∎

The stdi function in case /* 6 */ is a selector function defined by the type equation for Tr.

14.4 Examples

We give a number of examples. The first two are by Martin Pěnička.

14.4.1 Railway Line Automatic Blocking

———————————— Author: Martin Pěnička ————————————
This example was provided by Martin Pěnička, the Faculty of Transportation, Czech Technical University, Prague.

Example 14.7 *Railway Line Automatic Blocking*: The example is large — so we present it without shading.   ∎

The problem with high train speeds and low coefficients of friction between train wheels and tracks is that the drivers cannot stop their trains within sighting distance of another train or within sighting distance of a signal. This is the reason why automatic signalling is used on some lines. If there are junctions or turnouts then semiautomatic signalling is required.

In this example we first narrate the principle of automatic line signalling. Then we give formal descriptions using statecharts.

Narrative

Lines are usually divided into segments $l = \langle s_1, s_2, ..., s_{i-1}, s_i, s_{i+1}, ..., s_n \rangle$ (Fig. 14.8). Line l connects exactly two stations, staA and staB. A line can be in one of three possible states: OpenAB, OpenBA and Close. These states and their possible transition are described in detail in Sect. 14.4.2 on line direction agreement systems (LDAS).

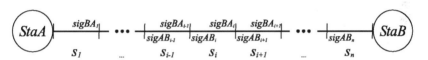

Fig. 14.8. Automatic line signalling

Each segment can be in two states: segFree and segOccupied. Segment s_i is in segFree when no train is detected in the segment. Segment s_i is in segOccupied when a train is detected in the segment.

General Line Segment

For each inner segment s_i, where $i = \langle 2, ..., n-1 \rangle$, there are two signals $sigAB_i$ and $sigBA_i$ (one in each direction of travel). With each signal we associate four possible states: sigOnRed, sigOnYellow, sigOnGreen and sigOff (Fig. 14.9).
Signal $sigAB_i$ is in

sigOnRed	state, when line l is in OpenAB state and segment s_i is in segOccupied state;
sigOnGreen	state, when line l is in OpenAB state and both segment s_i and s_{i+1} are in segFree state;
sigOnYellow	state, when line l is in OpenAB state, and segment s_i is in segFree and segment s_{i+1} is in segOccupied state,
sigOff	state, when line l is in OpenBA or Closed state.

Signal $sigBA_i$ is in

sigOnRed   state, when line l is in OpenBA state,
and segment s_i is in segOccupied state;

sigOnGreen state, when line l is in OpenBA state,
and both segment s_i and s_{i-1} are in segFree state;

sigOnYellow state, when line l is in OpenBA state,
and segment s_i is in segFree,
and segment s_{i-1} is in segOccupied state;

sigOff   state, when line l is in OpenAB,
or Closed state.

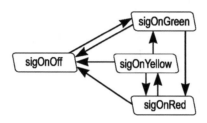

Fig. 14.9. Signal state machine — possible transitions

Each segment has two signals, and each signal can be in four states. Therefore we have a potential number of 16 states, but possible combinations are:

$sigAB_i$	$sigBA_i$
sigOnRed	sigOff
sigOnYellow	sigOff
sigOnGreen	sigOff
sigOff	sigOff
sigOff	sigOnRed
sigOff	sigOnYellow
sigOff	sigOnGreen

First Line Segment

For segment s_1 there is only one signal $sigBA_1$. And for segment s_n there is only one signal $sigAB_n$ (Fig. 14.8). The signals in the opposite directions ($sigAB_1$ and $sigBA_n$) are controlled manually or by interlocking in the stations.

Statecharts

In this section, we show how description of automatic line signalling can be expressed using statecharts.

General Model

See Fig. 14.10.

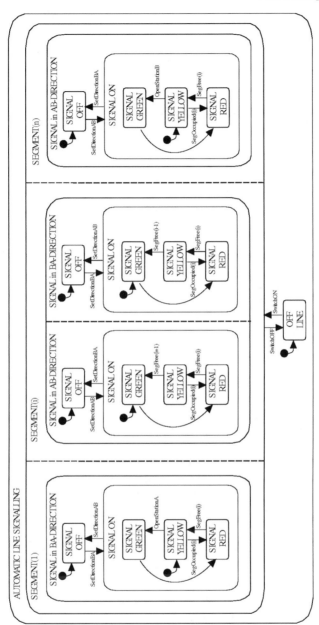

Fig. 14.10. Statecharts of automatic line signalling

Special Cases

- First segment of a line: Fig. 14.11 left part.

- Last segment of a line: Fig. 14.11 right part.
- General line segment: Fig. 14.12 left part.
- Line with one segment: no line signals.
- Line with two segments: Fig. 14.12 right part.

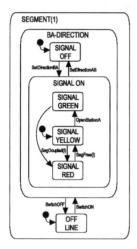 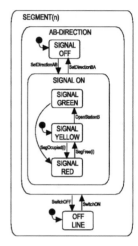

Fig. 14.11. First and last line segment

14.4.2 Railway Line Direction Agreement System

———————— Author: Martin Pěnička ————————

This example was also provided by Martin Pěnička, the Faculty of Transportation, Czech Technical University, Prague.

Example 14.8 *Railway Line Direction Agreement System:* The example is large — so we present it without shading.   ∎

In this example we first narrate the principle of the line direction agreement device. Then we give formal description examples using statecharts and live sequence charts.

Each line connects exactly two stations. At any point in time, the line can be open in at most one direction. This is a safety requirement to protect head-on train crashes on the line. In the old days, a line specific sheet of paper (or a baton) was used, and only the station that had the sheet (or the baton) could send trains to the line. The sheet (or the baton) was sent by trains between stations. Later on, the sheet of paper was replaced by abstract

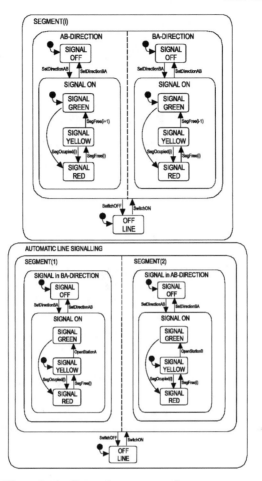

Fig. 14.12. General segment and two segments

tokens with electronically produced transitions (electric token block or radio electronic token block).

Narrative

The line direction agreement system (LDAS) is a device that is responsible for fail-safe communication (token transition) and train direction control on the line between two stations.

Consider a line l that connects two stations: stationA and stationB. The line can be in one of three basic states: OpenAB (trains are allowed to travel from stationA to stationB), OpenBA (trains are allowed to travel from stationB to stationA) and Close (trains are not allowed to travel in either direction).

In each station there is one operator, who is responsible for sending trains to the line. Agreement on train direction between two such stations is then made by sending messages between the stations and the LDAS (Fig. 14.13).

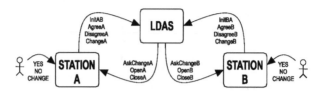

Fig. 14.13. Communication with LDAS

The line direction agreement device therefore comprises three parts: LDAS, STATION A and STATION B.

In both stations, the operator has three buttons: YES, NO and CHANGE. From STATION A to LDAS there are four types of commands which can be sent: ChangeA, AgreeA, DisagreeA and InitAB. From STATION B to LDAS there are also four types of commands: ChangeB, AgreeB, DisagreeB and InitBA. LDAS can send any of three different commands to STATION A: OpenA, CloseA or AskChangeA, or three different commands to STATION B: OpenB, CloseB or AskChangeB.

The behaviour of the system in response to internal and external stimuli depends on the state(s) it is currently in. Therefore, for graphical representation of internal behaviour we introduce statecharts. The line direction agreement problem can be described by three statecharts and eight live sequence charts.

Internal Behaviour of LDAS (Statechart)

The first statechart that represents internal behaviour of the LDAS is shown in Fig. 14.14. The LDAS can be any one of several states during its operation. The three basic states that correspond with directions of the trains on the line are OPEN AB, OPEN BA and CLOSE. These basic states have several substates. All possible transmissions between these states are shown as arrows with a label in Fig. 14.14.

The initialisation process starts in a default state of the system. The default state is when the line is closed for both directions of train travel. The state is called the DEAD state. Two other states, INIT AB and INIT BA, can be reached from the state by receiving InitAB or InitBA.

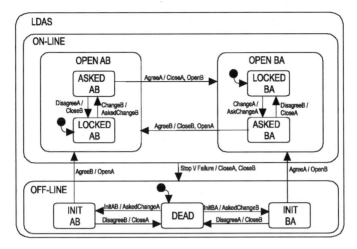

Fig. 14.14. LDAS statechart

Internal Behaviour of Station A (Statechart)

The statechart that represents the internal behaviour of **STATION A** is shown
in Fig. 14.15 (left). It is composed of four states: **LINE CLOSED**, **ASKED OPEN**,
ASKED CLOSE and **LINE OPEN**.

The **LINE CLOSED** state is the default state of the station component. In
Statecharts, default states are indicated by an arrow with a filled black dot
at the end.

When station manager presses the **CHANGE** button, a `ChangeA` command is
sent to **LDAS** and the state is changed to **ASKED OPEN**. An answer `CloseA`
changes the state back to **LINE CLOSED**, and an answer `OpenA` changes the
state to **LINE OPEN**. When the **STATION A** component is in **LINE OPEN** state
and **LDAS** sends `AskChangeA` command, a reply from the station manager is
expected.

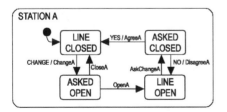 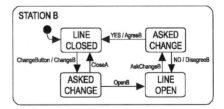

Fig. 14.15. Station A (left) and B (right) statecharts

Internal Behaviour of Station B (Statechart)

The statechart that represents the internal behaviour of **STATION B** is shown in Fig. 14.15 (right).

External Behaviour (Live Sequence Chart)

In this section we show all possible communication scenarios — there are nine such — as live sequence charts. See Figs. 14.16–14.19.

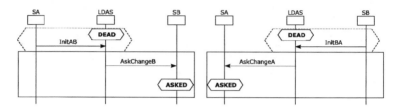

Fig. 14.16. Initialisations to AB and BA directions

The first pair of scenarios in Fig. 14.16 expresses the initialisations of the device. LDAS sends AskChange to one of the stations when two preconditions are fulfilled. These preconditions are: LDAS is switched off, and one of the stations has sent an initialisation command. A reply from the station manager is expected. The reply can be either YES or NO.

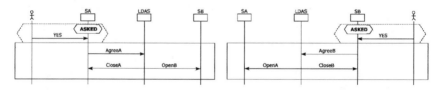

Fig. 14.17. Change direction approvals

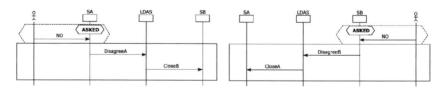

Fig. 14.18. Change direction disapprovals

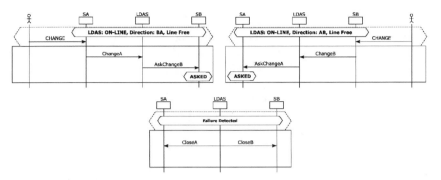

Fig. 14.19. Change direction requests and failure detection

14.4.3 Wireless Rain Gauge

Example 14.9 *Wireless Rain Gauge:* In this section we present a model of a wireless rain gauge. ∎

Description

The rain gauge has two units: a container that collects and measures rain drops and a base station that displays the measurements. The container is mounted outdoors, while the base station is placed indoors. The two units communicate via a radio signal. The base station is shown in Figure 14.20.

Fig. 14.20. OBH wireless rain gauge base station

The base station records the daily precipitation and keeps a history of the precipitation for each of the previous nine days. Also, it records the accumulated precipitation from a given start date. The base station also includes a digital clock.

The base station has three displays and four buttons that are used to set up the station and switch between its modes. Additionally, the station has a *reset* button for restarting the station. The top display initially shows the current time and accumulated precipitation. If the button *mode/set* is pressed, the date is displayed, and if the button *since* is pressed, the start date of the accumulated precipitation measurement is displayed. The middle display indicates whether the base station receives a signal from the container. The button *search* is used to initiate a scan for a signal. The bottom display shows the daily precipitation, and with repeated presses of button *history* the daily precipitation for each of the previous nine days.

Statechart Model

Figure 14.21 shows the statechart for the rain gauge. In the initial state there are no batteries in the rain gauge. When batteries are inserted the three displays become operational. This is modelled by AND decomposition giving three concurrent states.

The date/time (top) display has four overall modes: time, date, start date of cumulative measuring and setup. Setup mode is entered by pressing and holding button *mode/set* for two seconds. If the button is released (indicated by the symbol m/̂s in the chart) before 2 seconds have elapsed, the date is displayed.

The signal (middle) display has three modes: either there is no signal, or a scanning is in progress, or there is a correct signal. A new scan may be initiated by pressing *search.*

The rain (bottom) display has two modes: normal operation showing precipitation for the current day, or history mode, where total precipitation for one of the last nine days is shown.

RSL Model

We translate the above statechart into RSL by creating a process for each state that has no sub-states. The process then responds to the events that cause transitions from the corresponding state. Special attention must be awarded to the AND composition. Whenever a transition causes several concurrent states to assume control, the translation in RSL starts multiple concurrent processes in parallel. Whenever several concurrent states lose control, the translation in RSL causes all but one of the concurrent processes to terminate. The single remaining process calls the process corresponding to the next state.

Timeouts are modelled as an external event. Note that the timeout durations specified in the Statechart are lost in this translation to RSL. If this quantitative temporal information is to be preserved, the extension of RSL with the Duration Calculus, called Timed RSL (TRSL [132]), may be used.

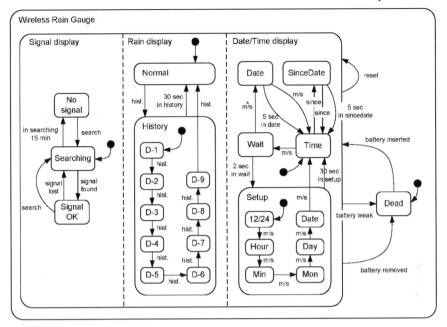

Fig. 14.21. Statechart for wireless rain gauge

```
scheme RainGauge =
  class
    type
      Event ==
        BattIns |
        BattWeak |
        BattRem |
        SigFound |
        SigLost |
        ModeSet |
        ModeSetRel |
        History |
        Since |
        Search |
        Reset |
        Timeout

    channel evt : Event

    value
      Dead : Unit → in evt Unit
      Dead() ≡
        case evt? of
          BattIns
```

```
          → Searching()
          || Normal()
          || Time(),
        _ → Dead()
      end,

  SinceDate : Unit → in evt Unit
  SinceDate() ≡
    case evt? of
      Timeout → Time(),
      Since → Time(),
      Reset → Time(),
      BattRem → skip,
      BattWeak → skip,
      _ → SinceDate()
    end,

  Date : Unit → in evt Unit
  Date() ≡
    case evt? of
      Timeout → Time(),
      ModeSet → Time(),
      Reset → Time(),
      BattRem → skip,
```

BattWeak → **skip**,
  _ → Date()
end,

Wait : **Unit** → **in** evt **Unit**
Wait() ≡
  case evt? **of**
    Timeout → S_1224(),
    ModeSetRel → Date(),
    Reset → Time(),
    BattRem → **skip**,
    BattWeak → **skip**,
    _ → Wait()
  end,

Time : **Unit** → **in** evt **Unit**
Time() ≡
  case evt? **of**
    ModeSet → Wait(),
    Since → SinceDate(),
    Reset → Time(),
    BattRem → **skip**,
    BattWeak → **skip**,
    _ → Time()
  end,

S_1224 : **Unit** → **in** evt **Unit**
S_1224() ≡
  case evt? **of**
    Timeout → Time(),
    ModeSet → S_Hour(),
    Reset → Time(),
    BattRem → **skip**,
    BattWeak → **skip**,
    _ → S_1224()
  end,

S_Hour : **Unit** → **in** evt **Unit**
S_Hour() ≡
  case evt? **of**
    Timeout → Time(),
    ModeSet → S_Min(),
    Reset → Time(),
    BattRem → **skip**,
    BattWeak → **skip**,
    _ → S_Hour()
  end,

S_Min : **Unit** → **in** evt **Unit**

S_Min() ≡
  case evt? **of**
    Timeout → Time(),
    ModeSet → S_Mon(),
    Reset → Time(),
    BattRem → **skip**,
    BattWeak → **skip**,
    _ → S_Min()
  end,

S_Mon : **Unit** → **in** evt **Unit**
S_Mon() ≡
  case evt? **of**
    Timeout → Time(),
    ModeSet → S_Day(),
    Reset → Time(),
    BattRem → **skip**,
    BattWeak → **skip**,
    _ → S_Mon()
  end,

S_Day : **Unit** → **in** evt **Unit**
S_Day() ≡
  case evt? **of**
    Timeout → Time(),
    ModeSet → S_Date(),
    Reset → Time(),
    BattRem → **skip**,
    BattWeak → **skip**,
    _ → S_Day()
  end,

S_Date : **Unit** → **in** evt **Unit**
S_Date() ≡
  case evt? **of**
    Timeout → Time(),
    ModeSet → Time(),
    Reset → Time(),
    BattRem → **skip**,
    BattWeak → **skip**,
    _ → S_Date()
  end,

Normal : **Unit** → **in** evt **Unit**
Normal() ≡
  case evt? **of**
    History → H_D1(),
    Reset → Normal(),
    BattRem → Dead(),

```
    BattWeak → Dead(),
    _ → Normal()
end,

H_D1 : Unit → in evt Unit
H_D1() ≡
  case evt? of
    Timeout → Normal(),
    History → H_D2(),
    Reset → Normal(),
    BattRem → Dead(),
    BattWeak → Dead(),
    _ → H_D1()
  end,

H_D2 : Unit → in evt Unit
H_D2() ≡
  case evt? of
    Timeout → Normal(),
    History → H_D3(),
    Reset → Normal(),
    BattRem → Dead(),
    BattWeak → Dead(),
    _ → H_D2()
  end,

H_D3 : Unit → in evt Unit
H_D3() ≡
  case evt? of
    Timeout → Normal(),
    History → H_D4(),
    Reset → Normal(),
    BattRem → Dead(),
    BattWeak → Dead(),
    _ → H_D3()
  end,

H_D4 : Unit → in evt Unit
H_D4() ≡
  case evt? of
    Timeout → Normal(),
    History → H_D5(),
    Reset → Normal(),
    BattRem → Dead(),
    BattWeak → Dead(),
    _ → H_D4()
  end,

H_D5 : Unit → in evt Unit
```

```
H_D5() ≡
  case evt? of
    Timeout → Normal(),
    History → H_D6(),
    Reset → Normal(),
    BattRem → Dead(),
    BattWeak → Dead(),
    _ → H_D5()
  end,

H_D6 : Unit → in evt Unit
H_D6() ≡
  case evt? of
    Timeout → Normal(),
    History → H_D7(),
    Reset → Normal(),
    BattRem → Dead(),
    BattWeak → Dead(),
    _ → H_D6()
  end,

H_D7 : Unit → in evt Unit
H_D7() ≡
  case evt? of
    Timeout → Normal(),
    History → H_D8(),
    Reset → Normal(),
    BattRem → Dead(),
    BattWeak → Dead(),
    _ → H_D7()
  end,

H_D8 : Unit → in evt Unit
H_D8() ≡
  case evt? of
    Timeout → Normal(),
    History → H_D9(),
    Reset → Normal(),
    BattRem → Dead(),
    BattWeak → Dead(),
    _ → H_D8()
  end,

H_D9 : Unit → in evt Unit
H_D9() ≡
  case evt? of
    Timeout → Normal(),
    History → Normal(),
    Reset → Normal(),
```

```
        BattRem → Dead(),                    Timeout → NoSignal(),
        BattWeak → Dead(),                   SigFound → SignalOK(),
        _ → H_D9()                           Reset → Searching(),
    end,                                     BattRem → skip,
                                             BattWeak → skip,
NoSignal : Unit → in evt Unit               _ → Searching()
NoSignal() ≡                             end,
    case evt? of
        Search → Searching(),         SignalOK : Unit → in evt Unit
        Reset → Searching(),          SignalOK() ≡
        BattRem → skip,                   case evt? of
        BattWeak → skip,                      Search → Searching(),
        _ → NoSignal()                        SigLost → Searching(),
    end,                                      BattRem → skip,
                                              BattWeak → skip,
Searching : Unit → in evt Unit                _ → SignalOK()
Searching() ≡                           end
    case evt? of              end
```

This example vividly demonstrates the compactness of the Statechart notation. The diagram fits on half a page, while the corresponding RSL specification takes up three pages double column. The statechart is certainly the easiest of the two models to gain an initial understanding of. The advantage of the RSL specification is that the expressivity of RSL allows the RSL model to be augmented to give a full specification of the system.

Another issue is the ease with which one may go from a specification to an implementation. The step from a statechart to an implementation language is not obvious. As it stands, the RSL specification is closer to an implementation language, and the step may be made smaller by one or more steps of refinement of the model.

14.5 A Process Algebra for Statecharts

In this section we shall present a process algebra that may be used to give a semantics for the Statechart language. In the next section we link this process algebra to statecharts. Both of these sections contain advanced material that really belongs to the field of computer science rather than software engineering. The reader primarily interested in the applications of statecharts may skip these two sections.

It has proven difficult to provide a semantics for Statecharts This difficulty arises partly because of the property that an external event may trigger a transition that produces an event that in turn triggers a transition, etc. Thus one event may start a chain reaction of internal events. Furthermore, if a statechart is in a given state, it is also in all states enclosing the first state. Therefore, the global state or configuration of a statechart consists of a variable number of states. An internal transition is called a microstep, while the whole chain reaction caused by an external event is called a macrostep.

There are three desirable properties for a semantics for statecharts: the *synchrony hypothesis, compositionality* and *causality*. The *synchrony hypothesis* states that for any set of input events, the reaction of a statechart must be *maximal* in the sense that the chain reaction of microsteps should continue until no further microstep is possible. This is sometimes referred to as the *maximal progress assumption*. Also, the chain reaction must terminate before the next external event enters the system. The *compositionality* property ensures that the behaviour of a system composed from subsystems is defined in terms of the observable behaviour of the subsystems. Thus the internal details of the sub-systems need not be known. The *causality* property ensures that for every event, there is a chain of events that lead to that event. Thus, no event can occur spontaneously. This property only applies to internal events, since external events — when viewed from the Statechart — will occur spontaneously.

14.5.1 SPL: The Statechart Process Language

The process algebraic semantics for Statecharts is presented by Lüttgen, van der Beeck and Cleaveland [314]. It is defined using the *process algebra* named Statechart*s Process Language (SPL)*, which is inspired by the *Timed Process Language* of Hennessy and Regan [209].

The SPL process algebra is defined as a labelled transition system with two types of transitions: *action transitions* and *clock transitions*. Action transitions correspond to events in Statecharts. Clock transitions represent progression of time. The previously discussed microsteps of a Statechart correspond to action transitions, while clock transitions signal the beginning and end of a macrostep composed of a sequence of microsteps.

Let Λ be a countable set of events, and let $\sigma \notin \Lambda$ be a distinguished event called a *clock event*. *Input actions* are defined as $\langle E, N \rangle$, where $E, N \subseteq \Lambda$. The special case of $\langle \emptyset, \emptyset \rangle$ is called an *unobservable* or *internal* event, designated by $\bullet$ (bullet). *Output actions* E are defined as subsets of Λ.

The syntax of SPL is given by the BNF grammar:

$$P ::= \mathbf{0} \mid X \mid \langle E, N \rangle.P \mid [E]\sigma(P) \mid P + P \mid P \triangleright P \mid P \triangleright_\sigma P \mid P \parallel P \mid P \setminus L$$

where X is a *process variable* that stands for a process term, and L is a *restriction set*, i.e., a set of action identifiers that are hidden from the environment of $X \setminus L$. $\mathbf{0}$ is the empty process, i.e., the process which does not perform any actions. $\langle E, N \rangle.P$ is the *prefix operator* applied to the process P. It represents the instantaneous input of the input action $\langle E, N \rangle$, which can only occur if all the events in E are offered by the environment, and none of the events in N are offered by the environment. The *signal operator* $[E]\sigma(P)$ signals the output of output action E to the environment of process P. The output action is cleared by the next clock transition. The *disabling operator* applied to processes P and Q, written $P \triangleright Q$, is the process that either behaves as Q permanently disabling P, or behaves as $P \triangleright_\sigma Q$. The *enabling operator* applied to processes P and Q, written $P \triangleright_\sigma Q$, behaves as P disabling Q until the next clock transition. In combination, the disabling and enabling operators serve to define the behaviour when there are enabled transitions on several layers of a hierarchical state.

14.5.2 Semantics of SPL

The semantics of SPL is a Plotkin-style operational semantics [402] in the form of a labelled transition system. The labelled transition system is defined as $\langle \mathcal{S}, E, \rightarrow, S \rangle$, where $\mathcal{S}$ is the set of states, $E = A \cup \{\sigma\}$ is the set of actions, including the special clock action, σ, $\rightarrow \in \mathcal{S} \times E \times \mathcal{S}$ is the transition relation, and S is the start state. Following tradition, $P \xrightarrow[N]{E} P'$ will be used as an abbreviation for $(P, \langle E, N \rangle, P') \in \rightarrow$, and $P \xrightarrow{\sigma} P'$ as an abbreviation for $(P, \sigma, P') \in \rightarrow$. The meaning of $P \xrightarrow[N]{E} P'$ is that process P can evolve to a process P' whenever the environment of P outputs all the actions in E and none of the actions in N.

Before the transition deduction system can be defined, the *initial output action set* must be defined. The initial output action set, notation $\bar{\mathbb{I}}(P)$ for $P \in \mathcal{S}$, is defined by the equations in Table 14.1. Intuitively, $\bar{\mathbb{I}}(P)$ is the set of actions that process P is immediately ready to output.

Table 14.1. Initial output action sets

$\bar{\mathbb{I}}([E]\sigma(P)) = E$	$\bar{\mathbb{I}}(X) = \bar{\mathbb{I}}(P)$, if $X \overset{def}{=} P$
$\bar{\mathbb{I}}(P + Q) = \bar{\mathbb{I}}(P) \cup \bar{\mathbb{I}}(Q)$	$\bar{\mathbb{I}}(P \setminus L) = \bar{\mathbb{I}}(P) \setminus L$
$\bar{\mathbb{I}}(P \parallel Q) = \bar{\mathbb{I}}(P) \cup \bar{\mathbb{I}}(Q)$	$\bar{\mathbb{I}}(P \triangleright_\sigma Q) = \bar{\mathbb{I}}(P)$
$\bar{\mathbb{I}}(P \triangleright Q) = \bar{\mathbb{I}}(P) \cup \bar{\mathbb{I}}(Q)$	

The *term deduction system* for *action transitions* is presented in Table 14.2. The *term deduction system* for *clock transitions* is presented in Table 14.3.

14.5.3 Equivalence for SPL Terms

We can now define a *behavioural equivalence* on SPL terms. As we did previously for PA_ϵ, we choose the *strong bisimulation equivalence*.

Table 14.2. Action transitions

$$\frac{\square}{\langle E, N\rangle.P \xrightarrow[N]{E} P} \qquad \text{Act}$$

$$\frac{P \xrightarrow[N]{E} P'}{X \xrightarrow[N]{E} P'} \text{ if } X \stackrel{def}{=} P \qquad \text{Rec}$$

$$\frac{P \xrightarrow[N]{E} P'}{P \triangleright_\sigma Q \xrightarrow[N]{E} P' \triangleright_\sigma Q} \qquad \text{En}$$

$$\frac{P \xrightarrow[N]{E} P'}{P \triangleright Q \xrightarrow[N]{E} P' \triangleright_\sigma Q} \qquad \text{Dis1}$$

$$\frac{P \xrightarrow[N]{E} P'}{P + Q \xrightarrow[N]{E} P'} \qquad \text{Sum1}$$

$$\frac{Q \xrightarrow[N]{E} Q'}{P + Q \xrightarrow[N]{E} Q'} \qquad \text{Sum2}$$

$$\frac{Q \xrightarrow[N]{E} Q'}{P \triangleright Q \xrightarrow[N]{E} Q'} \qquad \text{Dis2}$$

$$\frac{P \xrightarrow[N]{E} P'}{P \parallel Q \xrightarrow[N]{E \setminus \bar{\mathbb{I}}(Q)} P' \parallel Q} \text{ if } N \cap \bar{\mathbb{I}}(Q) = \emptyset \qquad \text{Par1}$$

$$\frac{Q \xrightarrow[N]{E} Q'}{P \parallel Q \xrightarrow[N]{E \setminus \bar{\mathbb{I}}(P)} P \parallel Q'} \text{ if } N \cap \bar{\mathbb{I}}(P) = \emptyset \qquad \text{Par2}$$

$$\frac{P \xrightarrow[N]{E} P'}{P \setminus L \xrightarrow[N \setminus L]{E} P' \setminus L} \text{ if } E \cap L = \emptyset \qquad \text{Par1}$$

Definition 14.1. Bisimulation[1] equivalence, $\sim \subseteq \mathcal{S} \times \mathcal{S}$, is the largest symmetric relation such that whenever $P \sim Q$, then the following conditions hold:

---

[1] In theoretical computer science a bisimulation is an equivalence relation between state transition systems, associating systems which behave in the same way in the

Table 14.3. Clock transitions

$$\frac{\square}{0 \xrightarrow{\sigma} 0} \qquad\qquad \text{tNil}$$

$$\frac{\square}{\langle E, N \rangle.P \xrightarrow{\sigma} \langle E, N \rangle.P} \; \text{if } \langle E, N \rangle \neq \bullet \qquad \text{tAct}$$

$$\frac{P \xrightarrow{\sigma} P', Q \xrightarrow{\sigma} Q'}{P \parallel Q \xrightarrow{\sigma} P' \parallel Q'} \; \text{if } \bullet \notin I(P \parallel Q) \qquad \text{tPar}$$

$$\frac{P \xrightarrow{\sigma} P', Q \xrightarrow{\sigma} Q'}{P \triangleright Q \xrightarrow{\sigma} P' \triangleright Q'} \qquad \text{tDis}$$

$$\frac{P \xrightarrow{\sigma} P'}{P \setminus L \xrightarrow{\sigma} P' \setminus L} \; \text{if } \bullet \notin I(P \setminus L) \qquad \text{tRes}$$

$$\frac{\square}{[E]\sigma(P) \xrightarrow{\sigma} P} \qquad \text{tOut}$$

$$\frac{P \xrightarrow{\sigma} P', Q \xrightarrow{\sigma} Q'}{P + Q \xrightarrow{\sigma} P' + Q'} \qquad \text{tSum}$$

$$\frac{P \xrightarrow{\sigma} P'}{P \triangleright_\sigma Q \xrightarrow{\sigma} P' \triangleright Q} \qquad \text{tEn}$$

$$\frac{P \xrightarrow{\sigma} P'}{X \xrightarrow{\sigma} P'} \; \text{if } X \overset{def}{=} P \qquad \text{tRec}$$

1. $\bar{\mathbb{I}}(P) \subseteq \bar{\mathbb{I}}(Q)$
2. If $P \xrightarrow[N]{E} P'$, then $\exists Q' \in \mathcal{S} : Q \xrightarrow[N]{E} Q' \wedge Q \sim Q'$.   ∎

Note that compared to the bisimulation relations defined for the process algebras PA_ϵ and PAc_ϵ in Sect. 13.3.2 we have the extra requirement that bisimilar processes have the same initial output sets. This requirement ensures that bisimilar processes have the same observable behaviour in terms of both input and output actions.

---

sense that one system simulates the other and vice versa. Intuitively two systems are bisimilar if they match each other's moves. In this sense, each of the systems cannot be distinguished from the other by an observer [530].

14.6 Semantics of Statecharts

14.6.1 An SPL Semantics for Statecharts

We have now presented the tools for expressing the semantics of Statechart. The next step is to define the correspondence between a statechart and an SPL term. First, we place some restrictions on the composition of statecharts by defining a textual syntax, in the form of Statechart terms. Then we define a semantic function that maps Statechart terms to SPL terms.

We need some additional notation. Let $\mathcal{N}$ be a countable set of names for statechart states, $\mathcal{T}$ be a countable set of names for statechart transitions and Π a countable set of Statechart events. Every event $e \in \Pi$ has a negated event $\neg e$. By definition, $\neg \neg e = e$. If $E \subseteq \Pi \cup \{\neg e \mid e \in \Pi\}$ then $\neg E$ is an abbreviation for $\{\neg e \mid e \in E\}$.

Now, Statechart terms are introduced. In order for a statechart to be expressible as a Statechart term, it must have exactly one top-level state and it must have no history or interlevel transitions, i.e., transitions that cross the boundary of its containing state. History transitions are disallowed because they make the semantics much more complicated. Interlevel transitions are disallowed because they preclude compositionality in both the syntax and semantics. Note, however, that a statechart with interlevel transitions can always be transformed into an equivalent statechart without interlevel transitions.

1. Basic state: If $n \in \mathcal{N}$, then $s = [n]$ is a Statechart term.
2. XOR state: If $n \in \mathcal{N}$, $s_1, \ldots, s_k$ are Statechart terms for $k > 0$, $T \subseteq \mathcal{T} \times \{1, \ldots, k\} \times \mathcal{P}(\Pi \cup \neg \Pi) \times \mathcal{P}(\Pi) \times \{1, \ldots, k\}$, and $1 \leq l \leq k$, then $s = [n : (s_1, \ldots, s_k), l, T]$ is a Statechart term. Here, $s_1, \ldots, s_k$ are the sub-states of s, l is the index of the currently active state and T is the set of transitions between the substates of s. The default state is defined to be s_1. A transition $\langle t, n_1, E, A, n_2 \rangle$ with name t links state s_{n_1} to state s_{n_2}, is triggered by the events in E and produces the actions in A.
3. AND state: If $n \in \mathcal{N}$, and $s_1, \ldots, s_k$ are Statechart terms for $k > 0$, then $s = [n : (s_1, \ldots, s_k)]$ is a Statechart term.

A Statechart term is considered well-formed if:

- the set of names for states is disjoint from the set of names for transitions, i.e., $\mathcal{N} \cap \mathcal{T} = \emptyset$;
- no transition produces an event that contradicts its trigger, i.e., for every transition $\langle t, n_1, E, A, n_2 \rangle$, $E \cap \neg A = \emptyset$;
- no transition produces an event that is in its trigger, i.e., for every transition $\langle t, n_1, E, A, n_2 \rangle$, $E \cap A = \emptyset$.

The set of well-formed Statechart terms is denoted SC.

The function *root* yields the name of the state it is applied to. The function *out* yields the name of the destination state of the transition it is applied to.

Now, the embedding is defined. We give the definition first and then explain it below. The process algebra SPL is instantiated with the set of events $\Lambda = \Pi \cup \neg \Pi$ and the set of process variables $\mathcal{V} = \{\hat{n} \mid n \in \mathcal{N}\}$. Let $\Sigma\, Q$ be the distributed nondeterministic choice between the elements of the set Q, with $\Sigma\{\ \} = \mathbf{0}$. Then the embedding function $S_{StC}[\![\,\cdot\,]\!] : SC \to T_{\Sigma_{SPL}}$ is defined as:

1. If $s = [n]$, then $S_{StC}[\![s]\!] = \mathbf{0}$.
2. If $s = [n : (s_1,\ldots,s_n), l, T]$, then if $n_l = root(s_l)$, $S_{StC}[\![s]\!] = \hat{n}_l$, where for $1 \le i \le n$, $\hat{n}_i = S_{StC}[\![s_i]\!] \triangleright \Sigma\{\{t\}\} \mid t \in T \wedge root(out(t)) = n_i\}$ along with the equations produced by $S_{StC}[\![s_1]\!],\ldots,S_{StC}[\![s_n]\!]$. The translation $\{t\}\}$ of a transition t is defined below.
3. If $s = [n : (s_1,\ldots,s_n)]$, then $S_{StC}[\![s]\!] = S_{StC}[\![s_1]\!] \parallel \cdots \parallel S_{StC}[\![s_n]\!]$, along with the equations produced by $S_{StC}[\![s_1]\!],\ldots,S_{StC}[\![s_n]\!]$.

The translation of a transition $t = \langle t, i, E, A, j \rangle$ is defined as

$$\{t\}\} = \langle E', N' \rangle.[A \cup (E \cap \neg \Pi)]\sigma(\hat{n}_j),$$

where $E' = E \cap \Pi$ is the set of positive events in E, and $N' = \neg(E \cap \neg \Pi) \cup \neg A$ is the set of negated negative events in E combined with the negated events in A.

The definition of the embedding requires an explanation. First, the semantics of a statechart is expressed as a set of equations rather than a single process term. This allows for recursion. The semantics of a basic state is the inactive process $\mathbf{0}$, since a basic state will not take part in any transitions. The semantics of an AND state is just the parallel composition of the semantics of its substates. The semantics of an XOR state is more involved. First observe that an XOR state may either stay in the currently active substate, or a transition t may occur, making $out(t)$ the new active substate. This behaviour is modelled by the disabling operator. In the former case the XOR state behaves like the currently active substate, disabling all transitions until the next clock event. In the latter case, the transition becomes an input prefix handling the triggering events in E, and an output signalling handling the actions in A. For the transition to occur, all the positive events in E and none of the negative events in E must be offered by the environment. This explains E' and partly N'. We include $\neg A$ in N' to ensure *global consistency*, meaning that no subsequent transition which requires the absence of the events in A fires in the same macrostep. The global consistency requirement also explains why the output includes the negative events in E, since the process is not allowed to produce an event which contradicts its trigger.

14.6.2 Statechart Example

In this section the process of deriving an SPL expression from a statechart is illustrated. The example statechart is shown in Fig. 14.22. In this case, the statechart is already in a form suitable for conversion to a Statechart term.

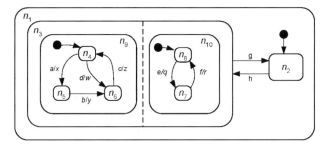

Fig. 14.22. Example statechart

If this were not the case, the statechart would first have to be modified to remove interlevel transitions and to have exactly one top-level state.

The corresponding Statechart term s_1 is listed in Table 14.4, along with terms for each of the substates of state n_1. The translation of the Statechart terms into SPL is straightforward. The result is listed in Table 14.5.

$s_1 = [n_1 : (s_2, s_3); 1; \{\langle t_1, 3, \{g\}, \emptyset, 2\rangle, \langle t_2, 2, \{h\}, \emptyset, 3\rangle\}]$

$s_2 = [n_2]$

$s_3 = [n_3 : (s_9, s_1 0)]$

$s_4 = [n_4]$

$s_5 = [n_5]$

$s_6 = [n_6]$

$s_7 = [n_7]$

$s_8 = [n_8]$

$s_9 = [n_9 : (s_4, s_5, s_6); 4; \{\langle t_3, 4, \{a\}, \{x\}, 5\rangle, \langle t_4, 6, \{b\}, \{y\}, 5\rangle, \langle 5, s_4, \{c\}, \{z\}, 6\rangle,$
$\qquad \langle t_6, 4, \{d\}, \{w\}, 6\rangle\}]$

$s_{10} = [n_{10} : (s_7, s_8); s_7; \{\langle t_6, 8, \{e\}, \{q\}, 7\rangle, \langle t_7, 7, \{f\}, \{r\}, 8\rangle\}]$

Table 14.4. Statechart and substate terms

14.7 Relating Statecharts to RSL

We continue the subject of relating diagrammatic notations to RSL that we started in Sect. 13.5.

$$[\![s_1]\!] = \hat{n}_2$$
$$\hat{n}_2 = [\![s_2]\!] \triangleright \langle\{h\}, \emptyset\rangle.[\emptyset]\sigma(\hat{n}_3)$$
$$\hat{n}_3 = [\![s_3]\!] \triangleright \langle\{g\}, \emptyset\rangle.[\emptyset]\sigma(\hat{n}_2)$$
$$[\![s_2]\!] = \mathbf{0}$$
$$[\![s_3]\!] = [\![s_9]\!] \parallel [\![s_10]\!]$$
$$[\![s_4]\!] = \mathbf{0}$$
$$[\![s_5]\!] = \mathbf{0}$$
$$[\![s_6]\!] = \mathbf{0}$$
$$[\![s_7]\!] = \mathbf{0}$$
$$[\![s_8]\!] = \mathbf{0}$$
$$[\![s_9]\!] = \hat{n}_4$$
$$\hat{n}_4 = [\![s_4]\!] \triangleright \langle\{a\}, \{\neg x\}\rangle.[\{x\}]\sigma(\hat{n}_5) + \langle\{d\}, \{\neg w\}\rangle.[\{w\}]\sigma(\hat{n}_6)$$
$$\hat{n}_5 = [\![s_5]\!] \triangleright \langle\{b\}, \{\neg y\}\rangle.[\{y\}]\sigma(\hat{n}_6)$$
$$\hat{n}_6 = [\![s_6]\!] \triangleright \langle\{c\}, \{\neg z\}\rangle.[\{z\}]\sigma(\hat{n}_7)$$
$$[\![s_{10}]\!] = \hat{n}_8$$
$$\hat{n}_8 = [\![s_8]\!] \triangleright \langle\{e\}, \{\neg q\}\rangle.[\{q\}]\sigma(\hat{n}_7)$$
$$\hat{n}_7 = [\![s_7]\!] \triangleright \langle\{f\}, \{\neg r\}\rangle.[\{r\}]\sigma(\hat{n}_8)$$

Table 14.5. Translation of statechart terms into SPL

14.7.1 Syntactical Restrictions

In statecharts negative events, i.e., the absence of events, can be part of the trigger of a transition. In RSL there is no way of checking whether a message is available on a channel without actually performing an input. Thus, the absence of an event cannot be detected. We therefore restrict the relation between Statechart and RSL to cover only triggers with all positive events. Specifically, if a statechart contains a negative event in a trigger, no RSL specification can satisfy it.

14.7.2 Satisfaction Relation

Similar to the approach for live sequence charts, we now want a method of extracting from an RSL specification its communication behaviour in the form of an SPL term. We do this in two steps: first we extract the communication behaviour as a PA_{LSC} term using the procedure defined for LSCs and then apply a function translating a PA_{LSC} expression into an SPL expression.

Definition 14.2. Let *translate* : $PA_{LSC} \to SPL$ be the function defined by

$translate(\epsilon) = \mathbf{0}$

$translate(in(s,r,m)) \cdot X) = \mathbf{0} \triangleright \langle\{m\},\emptyset\rangle.[\emptyset]\sigma(translate(X))$

$translate(ins(s,r,m)) \cdot X) = \mathbf{0} \triangleright \langle\{m\},\emptyset\rangle.[\emptyset]\sigma(translate(X))$

$translate(out(s,r,m)) \cdot X) = [\{m\}]\sigma(translate(X))$

$translate(outs(s,r,m)) \cdot X) = [\{m\}]\sigma(translate(X))$

$translate(X \parallel Y) = translate(X) \parallel translate(Y)$

$translate(X + Y) = translate(X) + translate(Y)$

∎

The result of the *translate* function may not be in a convenient form, so we define an additional function, *normalise*, that simplifies an SPL term.

Definition 14.3. Let $normalise : SPL \rightarrow SPL$ be the function defined by

$normalise(\mathbf{0}) = \mathbf{0}$

$normalise(\mathbf{0} \triangleright \langle m,\emptyset\rangle.(X)) = (\mathbf{0} \triangleright \langle m,\emptyset\rangle.normalise(X))$

$normalise([m]\sigma(X)) = \begin{cases} [m]\sigma(normalise(X)) & \text{if } X \neq [n]\sigma(Y) \text{ for every } n \text{ and } Y \\ normalise([m \cup n]\sigma(Y)) & \text{if } X = [n]\sigma(Y) \text{ for some } n \text{ and } Y \end{cases}$

$normalise(X \parallel Y) = normalise(X) \parallel normalise(Y)$

$normalise(X + Y) = normalise(X) + normalise(Y)$

∎

We can now define the satisfaction relation for a statechart. Unlike for LSCs we do not allow prefixes and suffixes, since the single statechart is supposed to provide the full specification of the communication behaviour of the object.

Definition 14.4. (Satisfaction for statechart) An RSL expression E *satisfies* a statechart, ch, if for any initial store, s_0, for any terminated behaviour, cbh, of E

$$S_{StC}[\![ch]\!] \succeq normalise(translate(cbh))$$

∎

14.7.3 Checking Satisfaction

The satisfaction criteria given in Definition 14.2 require checking that all behaviours of the RSL expression can be simulated by the semantics of the corresponding chart. In some situations the RSL expressions may have infinitely many behaviours, so in that case this simple form of checking is not possible.

Another problem arises when processes are recursive, as is often the case for statecharts. In this case, it is not enough to simply perform the transitions to check satisfaction. If the processes eventually terminate, an inductive proof on the number of recursions may be used to prove satisfaction. If the processes are nonterminating there is no base case, so induction cannot be used. In this case the more powerful principle of coinduction may be used.

14.7.4 Tool Support

Actually checking an RSL specification against a behavioral specification in the form of statecharts can be very tedious. For that reason, the methods defined above are of limited applicability without tool support. Tools should be developed to extract the semantic terms from diagrams and RSL specifications and for checking the satisfaction relations. It would also be convenient to have a way of translating a statechart into a skeleton RSL specification. An automatic conversion would force the software engineer to use one particular style.

14.8 Discussion

14.8.1 General

We have covered the concept of statecharts. An important property of statecharts, as of Petri nets and of the sequence charts, is its reliance and focus on visualisation [174,175]. Over the years since statecharts were first put forward (around 1987), the semantics of the Statechart language has been studied and changed, both by the originators and by other researchers. So it is in keeping with this dynamic state of Statechart semantics that we also present ours!

The material presented in the latter part of this chapter, i.e., Sects. 14.5–14.7, like that of the latter part of the previous chapter, represents one direction of research in the field of integrated formal methods. So we repeat the words of Sect. 13.7.1: The later parts of the present chapter are included in order to illustrate that certain techniques have advantages for certain applications in software engineering, and that choosing one technique (e.g., diagrams) does not preclude also using other techniques (e.g., formal specification in RSL). Indeed, in complex software engineering projects, several techniques will be needed to specify all the relevant aspects of a system. To ensure consistency between the different parts of the system specified using different techniques, relations among these techniques must be established. The relation between Statechart and RSL presented in Sect. 14.7, and the corresponding relation between LSC and RSL, presented in the previous chapter, are two such examples.

14.8.2 Principles, Techniques and Tools

This chapter has basically covered a tool: the Statechart language. As such we can hardly speak of 'a principle of statecharts' — such as we could for most other chapters' title subjects. So we shall rearrange things a bit in this section.

Principles. *Choosing Statecharts:* Statecharts, as a modelling device, can be chosen when the phenomenon to be abstracted and modelled exhibits concurrent and interacting behaviours, where the internal state "machinery" of each behaviour is of main interest, and usually when there is a definite, "small" number of behaviours, typically less than a couple of dozen.   ∎

Please contrast the above principle with that of Choosing Sequence Charts, Sect. 13.7.2. Note the distinction between *interaction "patterns"* in the former and *internal state "machinery"* as here.

Techniques. The main techniques for constructing *statecharts* have been covered in Sects. 14.1, 14.2, and 14.4. Some techniques focus just on the construction of the statechart. Other techniques combine statecharts with sequence charts. And yet other techniques combine these with RSL.   ∎

Tools. The main *statechart* tool is that of STATEMATE. It is provided commercially by the firm of i-Logix (www.ilogix.com).   ∎

14.9 Bibliographical Notes

The Statechart literature has been mentioned at various points in this chapter. A series of introductions and semantics have been presented by David Harel et al. [174,175,185,193,197]. Others have contributed, notably Amir Pnueli [404]. Professional tool support in the form of STATEMATE is covered in [197,198].

The process algebraic semantics for Statechart covered in this chapter is presented by Lüttgen, van der Beeck and Cleaveland [314]. It is defined using the *process algebra* named Statecharts *Process Language (SPL)*, which is inspired by the *Timed Process Language* of Hennessy and Regan [209].

Christian Krog Madsen, in his pre-MSc and his MSc thesis work [316,317] analysed Statecharts, and reformulated the above process algebraic semantic models and related a semantics of Statechart to RSL.

Various forms of statecharts are found in UML [59,237,382,440].

14.10 Exercises

Exercise 14.1 *An Automated Train System.*
     The following exercise is based on [185,188]. Consider Fig. 14.23. To the left is shown an abstraction of the simple topology of a cyclic railway net with six train terminals. Exactly two lines connect adjacent terminals, and terminals are connected to exactly two (other) terminals. Each pair of lines between adjacent terminals allows train traffic in opposite directions (as indicated by track arrows). Trains consists of single cars. Trains thus travel in clockwise and counterclockwise directions along the lines and may stop at terminals.

Within each terminal there are four tracks. All tracks can be reached from each of the two input lines. Both of the two output lines can be reached from all tracks. (This is, for example, secured by the shown topology of rail units: simple switch units, crossover switch units, crossover units and linear units. But the reader can ignore this detail.)

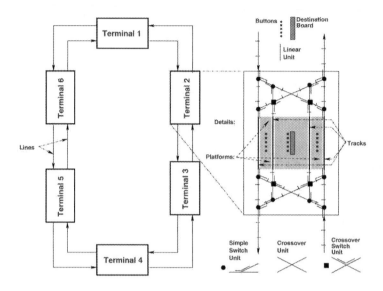

Fig. 14.23. An automated train system: net and terminal

A sequence of connected rail units between a line (into or out of a terminal) and a track (of that terminal) is called a route: an entry, respectively an exit route. A sequence of connected rail units is called a path. (Routes are special paths.)

Each track can hold one train. Several trains are available to transport passengers between terminals.

The system that we are to model, besides the lines, tracks and trains, also contains for each terminal a destination board, and also for each terminal a set of (as shown in Fig. 14.23, three) panels of buttons. Each panel provides a pushbutton for each destination terminal, i.e., five buttons.

Each train[2] is equipped with an engine and a cruise control, the latter for controlling the train speed. The cruise control can be off or engaged or disengaged. A train in movement is to maintain maximum speed as long as it never comes within 80 meters of any other train (on a path). A stopped train will continue its travel only if the shortest distance to any other train (on a

---

[2]We do not show trains in Fig. 14.23 — but encourage the reader to sketch possible distributions of trains.

path) is at least 100 meters. A train also has a destination board (with six buttons). The train destination board is otherwise as for terminals.

A control centre receives (i.e., monitors), processes and sends (i.e., controls) data from and to the components indicated above and as implied below.

There possible *scenarios*, or, as they are called in UML [59, 237, 382, 440], *use cases* — stated as requirements — are:

Train approaching terminal: When a train is 100 meters from a terminal, the system shall (i) allocate it a track, shall (ii) allocate it an entry route (which connects from the line of the train to the allocated track) and shall (iii) set the relevant rail unit simple crossover switches from the incoming line along the entry route. If the train is to pass through the terminal without stopping, the system shall also (iv) allocate it an exit route. If allocations are not completed within the train being 80 meters from the terminal, the system shall (v) delay the train until all is ready.

Train departing terminal: A train departs the terminal (vi) after being parked at a track (i.e., along a platform) for 90 seconds. The automated train system shall (vii) set the relevant rail unit simple crossover switches to the outgoing line along the exit route, shall (viii) engage the train engine and shall (ix) turn off the destination indicators on the terminal destination board. The train can then depart (x) unless it is within 100 meters of another (moving) train; if so, the system delays departure.

Passenger in terminal: A passenger in a terminal wishes to travel to some destination terminal (other than the terminal at which the passenger is located). If there is no available train in the terminal destined for that terminal the passenger shall (xi) push the desired destination button (on a relevant panel) and shall wait until an appropriate train arrives. If the terminal contains an idle train, the system shall (xii) allocate it to that destination. If not, the system shall (xiii) send in a train from some other terminal. The system shall (xiv) indicate that a train is available by turning on a flashing sign on the destination board.

The problems to be solved are indicated as follows:

1. Analyse the above text. Sharpen it if believed imprecise. State assumptions not explicitly stated, but needed for answering below questions.
2. Identify all relevant events.
3. Draw suitable finite state machines, if felt useful in the prescription of requirements to the automated train system.
4. Draw suitable UML (object) class diagrams, if felt useful in the prescription of requirements to the automated train system.
5. Draw appropriate statecharts for trains, arrival, departure, and so on.
6. Compare your solution to that of [185].

You may wish to augment and/or contrast your solutions, or that of [185], to solutions of either or both of the following questions:

7. Draw appropriate message or live sequence charts for relevant aspects of the automated train system.
8. Reformulate the whole set of requirements in terms of:
   (a) An applicative specification program expressed in RSL.
   (b) An imperative specification program expressed in RSL.
   (c) A concurrent specification program expressed in RSL, i.e., in CSP/RSL.

Exercise 14.2 *A Shooting Game.* The following exercise is based on material placed on the Internet by Matthew Carey [72]. It illustrates the reverse concept of unwinding. Unwinding a statechart was exemplified in Example 14.3. In this exercise we present a finite state machine and ask you to wind it into a statechart.

Consider Fig. 14.24. The finite state machine represents the behaviour of a simple opponent in a computer game. State transitions are labelled by event names.

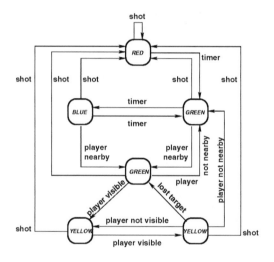

Fig. 14.24. Shooting game

You can either read the text now following or, after carefully having studied Figs. 14.24 and 14.25, go straight to the formulation of the exercise at the end, just before the start of the next exercise. That is, the following *italicised text* pragmatically motivates the finite state machine of Fig. 14.24, but brings no material that is relevant to the construction of a proper statechart!

The player is called H (for human) and the computer game is referred to as G (for game). The computer game G has four basic behaviours: stationary BLUE, *random* GREEN, *hunting* YELLOW, *and fleeing* RED.

G starts in stationary BLUE. *In stationary* BLUE *G waits for an event to occur. Either of the events* TIMER *going off, H approaching (*PLAYER NEARBY*),*

or being SHOT. Suppose that the TIMER goes off while $\mathcal{G}$ waits in stationary BLUE. This causes a transition to random GREEN. $\mathcal{G}$ will start to move
aimlessly about. This state prevents the world going into stasis when $\mathcal{H}$ is
not around. At any one time most of $\mathcal{G}$'s fellows (so it is assumed) just stand
there, but occasionally somebody will move to a new location. Relevant events
for this state, i.e., random GREEN, are similar to stationary BLUE. The only
difference is a separate timer setting. A $\mathcal{H}$ approaches. $\mathcal{G}$ is informed that
PLAYER $\mathcal{H}$ is NEARBY. $\mathcal{G}$ then moves to a different random GREEN state. Behaviour is same as before but different events become relevant. $\mathcal{G}$ will now
respond to observing SEEING PLAYER $\mathcal{H}$ (PLAYER VISIBLE), $\mathcal{H}$ LEAVING the
area (PLAYER NOT VISIBLE), and $\mathcal{H}$ being SHOT. If player $\mathcal{H}$ leaves (PLAYER
NOT VISIBLE) then $\mathcal{G}$ changes back to previous state. If $\mathcal{G}$ spots player $\mathcal{H}$
(PLAYER VISIBLE) then $\mathcal{G}$ will change to hunting YELLOW, trying to home in
on PLAYER $\mathcal{H}$. While hunting $\mathcal{G}$ may lose sight of the target (LOST TARGET).
$\mathcal{G}$ will then move back to most recent random GREEN. Etcetera, etcetera. We
leave it to the reader to further analyse and verbalise Fig. 14.24.

There are, however, some aspects with the finite state machine diagram of
Fig. 14.24 that are less than desirable. As the reader may discover, there are
several duplicate event transitions, for example, many shot events. This is a
relatively simple behaviour.

The idea therefore is to replace the finite state machine description of
this game by a statechart description in which, approximately the states of
the finite state machine of Fig. 14.24 are aggregated into superstates of the
desired statechart as hinted at in Fig. 14.25.

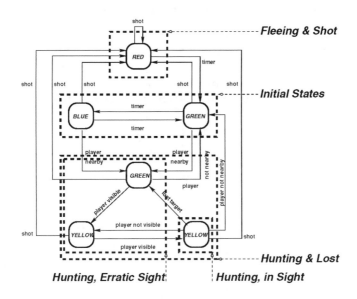

Fig. 14.25. Shooting game

Exercise 14.2.1 Shooting game statechart: In the statechart to be drawn by the reader there will be three superstates: The fleeing RED, the initial *Blue & Green* and the hunting *Green & Yellow*. The latter has two substates, etc. You are to redraw Fig. 14.25 into a proper statechart with indications of default states, etcetera. Instead of the 17 state transitions of the finite state machine of Fig. 14.25 one can come down to nine state transitions, one for *shot* (in contrast to six), three for *timer* and one each for all of the rest.

Exercise 14.3 *A Digital Watch.* This exercise derives from [174, 175]. We have changed the informal specification of the digital watch since there seem to be some inconsistencies and a certain kind of incompleteness amongst and in those papers. Harel's seminal papers also illustrates stepwise, albeit informal, but convincing development.

The digital watch has a (i) display, (ii) five external buttons (α, β, γ, δ, ω), a (iii) chime, an (iv) alarm, a (v) stopwatch, a (vi) a light illuminator, and a (vii) weak-battery indicator.

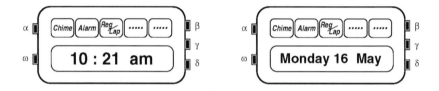

Fig. 14.26. A digital watch showing time or date

The display (i) can show the time (hour, minutes and seconds) or the date (weekday, day of month and month). The chime (iii) can be turned on or off, i.e., be enabled or disabled, beeping on the hour if enabled. The alarm (iv) can likewise be enabled or disabled. The alarm beeps for 2 minutes when the time in the alarm setting is reached — unless any one of the buttons is pressed earlier. The stopwatch (v) has two display modes: regular and lap.

External events (ii) α, β, γ, δ and ω signify the pressing of respective buttons. Event 2^m (not shown in Fig. 14.26, since it cannot be shown!) signifies that two minutes have elapsed since the last time any button was pressed.

The digital watch states:

The watch embodies the following states: *time, alarm, chime, stopwatch, date, time/date update* and *alarm update,* with *time* being the default state. A cycle of pressings of button α leads from state *time* through states *alarm, chime,* and *stopwatch* back to state *time.* The *date* state can be entered and left by pressing button δ. When in the *date* state the display shows the date. The *time/date update* state is thus reached by pressing button γ. It can be left from any of its substates by a pressing button β. The *alarm update* state is likewise reached by pressing button γ. It can be left from any of its substates by a pressing button β. If the user of the digital watch lingers on in the *alarm*, *date*, *time/date update* or *alarm update* states for more then 2 minutes, then an automatic time-out occurs, and the watch returns to the *time* state.

Exercise 14.3.1: A statechart for the digital watch states: Construct a statechart for the digital watch as described up to this point.

The time/date update state:

The watch display *time/date update* occurs as the result of the cyclic settings of buttons γ and ω as follows. From the initial *time/date update* state *sec* one can reach the *min*, *hour*, *day of week*, *day of month*, and *month* substate by successive pressings of button γ while button ω is not pressed. In any of the states *sec*, *min*, *hour*, *day of week*, *day of month*, and *month* holding button ω pressed continuously while repeatedly pressing button γ (one or more times) will advance the corresponding time or date counter.

Exercise 14.3.2: A Statechart for the update state: Construct a statechart for the *time update* state as described up to this point.

The alarm update state:

The *alarm update* occurs as the result of the cyclic settings of button γ. From the initial *alarm update* substate *min* one can reach the *min* and *hour* substates, and one can update the corresponding setting by repeated pressings of the γ and ω buttons as explained for the *time/date update* state. When in the *alarm date* state the display shows the alarm setting. If the user of the digital watch lingers on in the *alarm date* state for more then 2 minutes, then an automatic time-out occurs, and the watch returns to the *time* state.

Exercise 14.3.3: Construct a statechart for the *alarm update* state as described up to this point.

The stopwatch state:

The *stop watch* state has two substates: *zero* and *display/run*, the first being the default state. The *display/run* state consists of two (orthogonal) states: *display* and *run*. The *display* state has two substates: *regular* and *lap*. The *run* state likewise has two substates: *on* and *off*. In the *regular* state the digital watch display shows the ordinary time, while in the *lap* state it shows the lap time. In the *on* state the stopwatch is running. And in the *off* state it is stopped. Pressing button β from the *zero* to the *display/run* state causes it to make a transition to both (orthogonal) states: *display* and *run*, and to their substates *regular* and *on*, respectively. Repeatedly pressing button β while the digital watch is in the *run* causes it to stop and start alternatively. If button

δ is pressed in substate *regular* while state *run* is in substate *off* then the digital watch leaves the *display/run* state and returns to the *zero* state, else (state *run* in substate *on*) a transition is made to substate *lap*. Repeatedly pressing button δ (state *run* in substate *on*) causes the display to switch to *lap* and back to *regular*.

Exercise 14.3.4: Construct a statechart for the *stop watch* state as described up to this point.

High-level description of the digital watch:

We now assume that repeated pressing of the α button will lead the digital watch into substates of the states as they were previously left, i.e., we assume history dependence.

Exercise 14.3.5: Combine the above statecharts, and add initialisations and history to the individual statecharts. Then construct an overall statechart for the digital watch.

15

Quantitative Models of Time

- The **prerequisite** for studying this chapter is that you are well familiarised with abstract modelling, but have wondered how to model temporal issues such as explicit timing and explicit time durations.
- The **aims** are to introduce the modal logics of temporal logic (TL), linear temporal logic (LTL), interval temporal logic (ITL), the duration calculus (DC), `Timed RSL` (TRSL), and to relate TRSL to the duration calculus.
- The **objective** is to finally, with earlier chapters' coverage also of Petri nets, live sequence charts and statecharts, put the reader on a very strong, professional footing as concerns modelling concurrency and timing.
- The **treatment** ranges from systematic to formal.

Chapters 12–14 covered methods: principles, techniques and tools for expressing *qualitative* aspects of systems such as concurrency, synchronisation between behaviours and events. We now cover methods for expressing such *quantitative* aspects of concurrent systems as timing within and between behaviours.

15.1 The Issues

We first identify a spectrum of from "soft" to "hard" temporalities, through some informally worded texts. On that background we can introduce the term real-time, and hence distinguish between soft and hard real-time issues. From an example of trying to formalise these in RSL, we then set the course for this chapter.

15.1.1 Soft Temporalities

First we present some examples of soft real-time statements:

- You have often wished, we assume, that "your salary never goes down, say between your ages of 25 to 65".

- Taking into account other factors, you may additionally wish that "your salary goes up".
- Taking also into account that your job is a seasonal one, we may need to refine the above into "between un-employments your salary does not go down".

The issue now is: How do we formalise those statements?

15.1.2 Hard Temporalities

The above statements may not have convinced you about the importance of what this chapter has to offer. So let's try some other examples:

- "The alarm clock must sound exactly at 6 am unless someone has turned it off sometime between 5 am and 6 am the same morning".
- "The gas valve must be open for exactly 20 seconds every 60 seconds".
- "The sum total of time periods — during which the gas valve is open and there is no flame consuming the gas — must not exceed one twentieth of the time the gas valve is open".
- "The time between pressing an elevator call button on any floor and the arrival of the cage and the opening of the cage door at that floor must not exceed a given time $t_{arrival}$".

This chapter presents some tools, i.e., languages, and some principles and techniques for expressing and analysing such, as we shall call them, *temporal* matters.

15.1.3 Soft and Hard Real-Time

The informally worded temporalities of Sect. 15.1.1 can be said to involve time in a very "soft" way: No explicit times (e.g., 15:45:00), deadlines (e.g., "9 February 2006") or time intervals (e.g., "within 2 hours") were expressed. The informally worded temporalities of Sect. 15.1.2, in contrast, can be said to involve time in a "hard" way: Explicit times were mentioned.

For pragmatic reasons, we refer to the former examples, the former invocations of temporality, as being representative of soft real-time, whereas we say that the latter invocations are typical of hard real-time.

Please do not confuse the issue of soft versus hard real-time. It is as much hard real-time if we say that something must happen two years and five seconds from tomorrow at noon!

15.1.4 Examples — "Ye Olde Way"!

To paraphrase the point we try express the soft temporalities in an ordinary RSL way, in which we use an explicit model of time.

Example 15.1 *Soft Real-Time Models Expressed in "Ordinary" RSL Logic:*
Let us assume a salary data base SDB which at any time records your salary.
In the conventional way of modelling time in RSL we assume that SDB maps
time into Salary:

type
  Time, Sal
  SDB = Time $\overrightarrow{m}$ Sal
value
  hi: (Sal×Sal)|(Time×Time) → **Bool**
  eq: (Sal×Sal)|(Time×Time) → **Bool**
  lo: (Sal×Sal)|(Time×Time) → **Bool**
axiom
  ∀ σ:SDB,t,t':Time • {t,t'}⊆**dom**σ∧hi(t',t)⇒∼lo(σ(t'),σ(t))
  ∀ t,t':Time •
    (hi(t',t)≡∼(eq(t',t)∨lo(t',t))) ∧
    (lo(t',t)≡∼(eq(t',t)∨hi(t',t))) ∧
    (eq(t',t)≡∼(lo(t',t)∨hi(t',t))) ... /∗ same for Sal ∗/

∎

Example 15.2 *Hard Real-Time Models Expressed in "Ordinary" RSL:* To
express hard real-time using just RSL we must assume a demon, a process
which represents the clock:

type
  Time = **Real**
value
  time: **Unit** → Time
  time() **as** t
axiom
  time() ≠ time()

The axiom is informal: It states that no two invocations of the time function
yield the same value. But this is not enough. We need to express that "immediately consecutive" invocations of the time function yield "adjacent" time
points. Time provides a linear model of real-time.

variable
  t1,t2 : Time
axiom
  □ (t1 := time();
    t2 := time();
    t2 − t1 = /∗ infinitesimally small time interval: ITime∗/ ∧
    t2 > t1 ∧ ∼∃ t:Time• t1 < t < t2)

ITime provides a linear model of intervals of real-time.[1] The □ operator is here the standard RSL modal operator over states: Let P be a predicate involving globally declared variables. Then $\Box P$ asserts that P holds in any state of these variables. But even this is not enough; much more is needed.   ■

At any rate, with the above extensions we really do have a "hard (even soft) time" in expressing the hard real-time problems! So we give up, and turn to the duration calculus to provide appropriate means. We shall, in Sect. 15.4, take up the above attempt.

15.1.5 Structure of This Chapter

In Sect. 15.2 we first briefly cover notions of intervals and some simple interval modal operators, indicating a logic of intervals, before we briefly survey classical temporal logic. In Sect. 15.3, the main part of this chapter, we then cover the duration calculus. We do so by first showing examples before we build up a proper, albeit basically informal, presentation of the duration calculus. Some larger, strongly related examples end our treatment of the duration calculus. They span from domain descriptions via requirements prescriptions to the specification of software design decisions. In Sect. 15.4 we extend RSL with timing, i.e., we introduce explicit temporal constructs thus making RSL into TRSL. Finally, in Sect. 15.5 we extend TRSL with features of the duration calculus.

15.2 Temporal Logic

We quote from [126]:

> "The term temporal logic has been broadly used to cover all approaches to the representation of temporal information within a logical framework, and also more narrowly to refer specifically to the modal-logic type of approach introduced around 1960 by Arthur Prior under the name of tense logic and subsequently developed further by logicians and computer scientists."

> "Applications of temporal logic include its use as a formalism for clarifying philosophical issues about time, as a framework within which to define the semantics of temporal expressions in natural language, as a language for encoding temporal knowledge in artificial intelligence, and as a tool for handling the temporal aspects of the execution of computer programs."

---

[1] Of course, we really do not need to make a distinction between Time and ITime. The former tries to model a real-time since time immemorial, i.e., the creation of the universe. If we always work with a time axis that "started recently", i.e., a relative one, then we can "collapse" Time and ITime into just Time.

15.2.1 The Issues

The basic issue is simple: to be able to speak of temporal phenomena without having to explicitly mention time. That goes for vague, or soft notions of time: what we could call soft real-time, that something happens at a time, or during a time interval, but with no "fixing" of absolute times nor time intervals. It also, of course, goes for precise, or hard notions of time: What we could call hard real-time, that something happens at a very definitive point in time, or during a time interval of a very specific length, and thus with "fixing" of absolute times or time intervals.

Definition. By a *temporal logic* we shall understand a formal logic, for example, a propositional logic or a predicate calculus which is extended with one or more logical connectives that allow one to express time without explicitly having to quantify over times.   ∎

In this chapter we shall see a variety of systems of such connectives. These systems are referred to as *temporal logic, linear temporal logic, interval temporal logic* and the *duration calculi*.

15.2.2 A Philosophical Linguistics Background

According to [126], Arthur Prior [409–411] developed a *tense logic* along the lines presented below:

- *Pp*: "It has at some time been the case that p held"
- *Fp*: "It will at some time be the case that p holds"
- *Hp*: "It has always been the case that p held"
- *Gp*: "It will always be the case that p holds"

P and F are known as the weak tense operators, while H and G are known as the strong tense operators. The two pairs are generally regarded as interdefinable by way of the equivalences:

$$Pp \equiv \sim H(\sim p)$$
$$Fp \equiv \sim G(\sim p)$$

On the basis of these intended meanings, Prior used the operators to build formulas expressing various philosophical theses about time, which might be taken as axioms of a formal system if so desired. Some examples of such formulas, with Prior's own glosses (from [410]), are:

$Gp \Rightarrow Fp$:
   What will always be, will be.

$G(p{\Rightarrow}q){\Rightarrow}(Gp{\Rightarrow}Gq)$
>   If p will always imply q, then if p will always be the case, so will q.

$Fp{\Rightarrow}FFp$
>   If it will be the case that p, it will be (in between) that it will be.

$\sim Fp{\Rightarrow}F\sim Fp$
>   If it will never be that p then it will be that it will never be that p.

A special temporal logic is the minimal tense logic Kt. It is generated by the four axioms:

$p{\Rightarrow}HFp$
>   What is, has always been going to be.

$p{\Rightarrow}GPp$
>   What is, will always have been.

$H(p{\Rightarrow}q){\Rightarrow}(Hp{\Rightarrow}Hq)$
>   Whatever always follows from what always has been, always has been.

$G(p{\Rightarrow}q){\Rightarrow}(Gp{\Rightarrow}Gq)$
>   Whatever always follows from what always will be, always will be.

We will end our philosophy-based tense (i.e., temporal) logic discourse here, to take up a line more akin to how temporal logics are usually presented in software engineering. We strongly encourage the reader to, for example, read the Web page: `http://plato.stanford.edu/entries/prior/` [126].

15.2.3 Interval Temporal Logic, ITL

Although of broader importance than just for the classical temporal logic, we will now bring in some general notions of time intervals and time-interval-related properties. Thus this section amounts to a very brief introduction to a variant of an interval temporal logic [105, 372, 373].

   To paraphrase that we are working with a real-time concept, we use the type name Time:[2]

type
   Time $=$ **Real**

We assume, for simplicity, Time to be linear in the sense of Sect. 5.1.4.

---

[2] We remind the reader that we are using a relative time interval, cf., Footnote 1.

Intervals and Subintervals: $[c, d] \sqsubseteq [b, e]$

By an interval we here mean an interval of time. By a subinterval we mean an interval embedded within another interval: Let b and e denote times, i.e., be **Reals**. Allow e to "move" toward ∞. Let $b \leq e$. Then $[b, e]$ denotes an interval. If $b = e$ then $[b, e]$ denotes a point (interval) of length 0. Let c and d denote times such that $b \leq c < d \leq e$, then the interval $[c, d]$ is a subinterval of $[b, e]$, written $[c, d] \sqsubseteq [b, e]$.

Length of an Interval: $\lceil \cdot \rceil$

Let $[b, e]$ designate an interval. Assume $b < e$. That is, the interval is not a point. Let ϕ be a predicate (over a state, i.e., over some state variables), such that ϕ holds exactly in the interval $[b, e]$. Then we say that $\lceil \phi \rceil$ designates the length of time when ϕ holds, and that that length is exactly $e - b$.

In general $\lceil \phi \rceil$ designates a length of time:

$$\lceil \cdot \rceil : (\text{State} \rightarrow \textbf{Bool}) \rightarrow \textbf{ITime}$$

Where **ITime** stand for time intervals over real numbers. That is: Not a **Time**, but a time interval, i.e., the difference between two real **Times**. We shall later 'interpret' **States** in the formula above as functions from **Time** to **Bool**.

Example 15.3 *Some Standard Subintervals:*

- The time period of a weekday is a subinterval of the week, and its length is exactly 24 hours, or 1,440 minutes, or 86,400 seconds, or ... 86.4 billion microseconds, etc.
- The next hour is a subinterval of the future, and its length is exactly 60 minutes, etc.
- The previous hour was a subinterval of the past, and its length was exactly 60 minutes, etc.
- The present hour is a subinterval of my life, and its length is exactly 60 minutes, etc.

∎

The "Sometime" Modality: $\Diamond$

We often wish to express that some property, ϕ, holds of a phenomenon in some (possibly point) subinterval $[c, d], c \leq d$ of an interval $[b, e], b < e$. For that we use the 'sometime' modality, i.e., operator, $\Diamond$:

$$\Diamond \phi$$

We read $\Diamond \phi$ as: It will *sometime*, from now on, but not necessarily just now, into a future, which, for our consideration starts now, at time b and stretching until time e, be the case that ϕ holds.

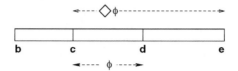

Fig. 15.1. Visualisation of the $\Diamond$ modality

Graphically we can show a meaning of $\Diamond\phi$ (Fig. 15.1).

Example 15.4 $\Diamond$: *Some Current Possibilities:*

- $\Diamond$ *Emergency services will show up.*
- $\Diamond$ *Lunch will arrive.*

■

The "'Always" Modality: $\Box$

Given $\Diamond$, we can define the 'always' modality, $\Box$:

$$\Box\phi \equiv \neg\Diamond\neg\phi$$

We thus read the above as: It will *always*, from now, and necessarily from just now, into a future, which, for our consideration starts now, at time b and stretching until time e, be the case that ϕ holds. Here we have to make allowance for e going to infinity, ∞.

Example 15.5 *Platitudes and Truisms:*

- $\Box$ *The sun rises every day.*
- $\Box$ *The grass is greener on the other side.*

■

The Right Neighbourhood Expanding Modalities: $\Diamond_r, \Box_r$

An interval $[b,e]$ satisfies $\Diamond_r\phi$ iff a *right neighbourhood* $([e,c], c \geq e)$ of the interval satisfies ϕ.

Graphically we can show a meaning of $\Diamond_r\phi$ (Fig. 15.2).
We read $\Diamond_r\phi$ as follows: We are considering the usual time span: $[b,e]$. The expression $\Diamond_r\phi$ is to be thought of as being expressed, at a time sometime within that interval. $\Diamond_r\phi$ then expresses that right after expiration of that interval, i.e., as from time e and for some time (i.e., up till c), ϕ will hold. $\Diamond_r$ "provides access" to the immediate future.

We can define $\Box_r$: $\Box_r\phi \equiv \neg\Diamond_r\neg\phi$. That is, $\Box_r\phi$ iff any right (i.e., immediate or very next future) neighbourhood of the ending point e of the

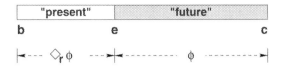

Fig. 15.2. Visualisation of the $\Diamond_r$ modality

interval $[b, e]$ satisfies ϕ. We read $\Box_r\phi$ as follows: We are considering the usual time span: $[b, e]$. The expression $\Box_r\phi$ is to be thought of as being expressed, at a time sometime within that interval. $\Box_r\phi$ then expresses that right after expiration of that interval, i.e., as from time e and for any time (into the future), ϕ will hold.

Example 15.6 *Future Hopes, Political Claims:*

- $\Diamond_r$ *Peace in our time.*
- $\Box_r$ *It will get better and better.*

∎

The Left Neighbourhood Expanding Modalities: $\Diamond_\ell, \Box_\ell$

An interval $[b, e]$ satisfies $\Diamond_\ell\phi$ iff a *left neighbourhood* $([a, b], a \leq)$ of the interval satisfies ϕ.

Graphically we can show a meaning of $\Diamond_\ell\phi$ (Fig. 15.3). $\Diamond_\ell$ "provides access" to "the immediate past".

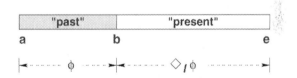

Fig. 15.3. Visualisation of the $\Diamond_\ell$ Modality

We read $\Diamond_\ell\phi$ as follows: We are considering the usual time span: $[b, e]$. The expression $\Diamond_\ell\phi$ is to be thought of as being expressed, at a time sometime within that interval. $\Diamond_\ell\phi$ then expresses that just before commencement of that interval, i.e., as from time a and for some time (i.e., up till b), ϕ will hold.

We can define $\Box_\ell$: $\Box_\ell\phi \equiv \neg\Diamond_\ell\neg\phi$. $\Box_\ell\phi$ iff any left (i.e., immediate past) neighbourhood of the begin point b of the interval $[b, e]$ satisfies ϕ. We read $\Box_\ell\phi$ as follows: We are still considering the usual time span: $[b, e]$. The expression $\Box_\ell\phi$ is to be thought of as being expressed, at a time sometime within that interval. $\Box_\ell\phi$ then expresses that for all times, a, stretching "infinitely" back into a past, and up to b, ϕ will hold.

Example 15.7 *"Rewriting History":*

- $\Diamond_\ell$ *It was better under the previous regime.*
- $\Box_\ell$ *The past was always better.*

The "Chop" Modality: ; ($\frown$)

We often wish to express that some property, ϕ, holds of a phenomenon in some initial subinterval of an interval $[b, e]$, and then that another property, ψ, holds of a phenomenon in the remaining subinterval of an interval. For that we use the "chop" modality, i.e., operator, ;:

$$\phi \; ; \; \psi$$

Graphically we can show a meaning of $\phi \; ; \; \psi$ (Fig. 15.4).

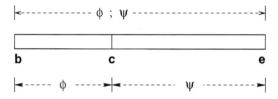

Fig. 15.4. Visualisation of the "Chop" Modality

Sometimes the chop operator, ;, is written as $\frown$. Sometimes we will use one, and sometimes the other form of operator symbol.

Example 15.8 *";": "One Thing at a Time":* Please consider the italicized sentences below as predicates. Then the examples illustrate uses of the chop operator.

- *He spent some time driving* ; *then he walked.*
- *After motoring for some time* ; *he took a short walk* ; *and finally he swam.*
- *She waited for the bus* ; *then the bus arrived* ; *she got on the bus* ; *then she watched the landscape glide by.*

Defining $\Diamond$ in Terms of Chop: ; ($\frown$)

We can then relate the operators: $\Diamond$ and ; ($\frown$):

$$\Diamond \, \phi \equiv (\textbf{true} \, ; \, \phi \, ; \, \textbf{true}) \equiv (\textbf{true} \frown \phi \frown \textbf{true})$$

Since $\Box$ can be defined in terms of $\Diamond$ ($\Box\phi \equiv \neg\Diamond\neg\phi$), and since $\Diamond$ can be defined in terms of 'chop': ';' ($\frown$), we can take 'chop' as the basic "primitive" of an, or the, interval logic.

Definition. By an *interval temporal logic* we shall understand a *temporal logic* whose concepts of time are captured by **Time**, a total partial order over a dense (time) point set, and **ITime**, i.e., time intervals, and whose connectives are those of $\Box$ (always), $\Box_r$ (always in right neighbourhood), $\Box_\ell$ (always in left neighbourhood), $\Diamond$ (sometime), $\Diamond_r$ (sometime in right neighbourhood), $\Diamond_\ell$ (sometime in left neighbourhood), and the chop operator, expressed either by $\frown$ or by ';'. ∎

Definition. By a *linear temporal logic* we shall understand the same as an *interval temporal logic*. ∎

15.2.4 The Classic Temporal Operators: $\Diamond, \Box$

The classical temporal logic basically "makes do" with the following two (interdefinable) modalities:

$\Diamond$: Sometime
$\Box$: Always

To recall, let ϕ, ψ denote any predicates, then:

$\Diamond \, \psi$: Sometime (from now on) ψ will hold.
$\Box \, \phi$: Always (from now on) ϕ will hold.

Definition. By a *classical temporal logic* we shall understand a *temporal logic* whose connectives are those of $\Box$ (always) and $\Diamond$ (sometime). ∎

We now "transfer" into (i.e., move on to) the main part of this chapter, to cover, in some detail, the duration calculus. In so doing we "bring with us", from the present section, the three (interdefinable) modalities:

$\Box \, \phi$: ϕ holds always
$\Diamond \, \psi$: ψ holds sometime
$\phi \, ; \, \psi$: First ϕ holds, for some time; then ψ holds, for some time

15.3 The Duration Calculus

> Just as I consider VDM and RSL, not only two specification languages, but also two strongly related approaches to software development, as being seminal in the current history of software engineering — and, mind you, I was strongly involved in the R&D of both — so I consider the duration calculi as being a similarly important development in our quest to conquer the complexity of systems specification. Hence I shall devote quite some space to covering the duration calculi — while otherwise referring to the seminal monograph [557]. Again, I am grateful to have been instrumental in bringing forth the duration calculi.

The duration calculi is the creation, notably, of:

- Zhou ChaoChen [166,167,169,170,221,438,475,522–524,545,551,552,554–564],

and of his colleagues since 1989:

- Michael Reichhardt Hansen   [166,167,169,170,555–558,562],
- Tony Hoare   [559],
- Dang Van Hung   [78,219–221],
- Anders Peter Ravn   [475,558,559,562,563],
- Hans Rischel   [475,558],
- Pandya K. Paritosh   [166,545],
- Jens Ulrik Skakkebæk   [473–475],
- Wang Ji   [324,521,563],
- Xu QiWen   [412],

and many others — as shown from the citations. Above I have, except for the 2004 monograph,

- [557] by Michael Reichhardt Hansen and Zhou ChaoChen,

listed only publications and reports for the first seven or so years of the duration calculus (actually duration calculi) history. The definitive book on the duration calculi is [557]. It contains an extensive list of references from earliest documents till and including 2003!

15.3.1 Examples, Part I

We show an example to lead the reader in the direction of what the duration calculus is all about. We leave it to you to decipher the below example.

Example 15.9 *Elevator cum Lift: The "Quickie" Version:*
   (1) For a lift system to be adequate it must always be safe and function adequately. There are three functional requirements.
   (2) For the lift system to be safe, then for any duration that the door on floor i is open, the lift must be also at that floor.

(3) The length of time between when someone pushes a button, inside a lift cage, to send it to floor i, and the arrival of that cage at floor i must be less than some time t_s.

(4) The length of time between when someone pushes a button, at floor i, to call it to that floor, and the arrival of a cage at that floor must be less than some time t_c.

(5) The length of time that a door is open when a cage is at floor i must be at least some time t_o.

(1) Req $\equiv$
 $\qquad \square$(SafetyReq $\wedge$ FunctReq1 $\wedge$ FunctReq2 $\wedge$ FunctReq3)

(2) SafetyReq $\equiv$
 $\qquad \lceil$door=i$\rceil$ $\Rightarrow$ $\lceil$floor=i$\rceil$

(3) FunctReq1 $\equiv$
 $\qquad$ ($\lceil$i $\in$ send$\rceil$; **true** $\Rightarrow$ $\ell \leq t_s$) $\vee$ ($\ell \leq t_s$; $\lceil$door=i$\rceil$; **true**)

(4) FunctReq2 $\equiv$
 $\qquad$ ($\lceil$i $\in$ call$\rceil$; **true** $\Rightarrow$ $\ell \leq t_c$) $\vee$ ($\ell \leq t_c$; $\lceil$door=i$\rceil$; **true**)

(5) FunctReq3 $\equiv$
 $\qquad \lceil$door$\neq$i$\rceil$; $\lceil$door=i$\rceil$; $\lceil$door$\neq$i$\rceil$ $\Rightarrow$ $\ell \geq t_o$

A more detailed version of this example is found in Example 15.11.   ∎

Maybe you got the idea? In any case, before going on to further, more extended examples, we bring in what might be called the three cornerstones of the duration calculus. Then we present some more examples. Then we bring in a proper reasonably detailed presentation of the duration calculus. Then, again, some more examples, and finally an axiom system, part of a proper proof system, for the duration calculus.

15.3.2 Some Basic Notions

Boolean States, State Assertions and Characteristic Functions

We model the behaviour of systems by expressing assertions about states and events. (For events we refer to Sect. 15.3.7.) Each state component can be thought of as an assignable (say RSL-declared) variable of some (say RSL-defined) type.

A *Boolean state model* of a system is a set of predicates over its state components. We call these predicates *state assertions*. A *state assertion* is a Boolean-valued function over time. For state component σ the type of the predicate P_σ is:

variable
 $\qquad \sigma$
value
 $\qquad$ P$_\sigma$: $\mathbb{T}$ime $\rightarrow$ **Bool**

Time is the set of real numbers, i.e.:

type
    Time = **Real**

Each such Boolean-valued function (over time) is also called a *Boolean state* (sometimes just a *state*) of the system. It is a *characteristic function* of the particular facet of the system that the state component, i.e., the variable, models. The set of all *Boolean state* functions thus describes the behaviour of the system.

State Durations

By a state duration of a state component, i.e., a state variable, σ, we mean the duration of a Boolean state P_σ (i.e., the state value being truth: **tt**) over a time interval $[b, e]$ as the accumulated presence of that state in the interval:

$$\int_{t=b}^{t=e} (\textbf{if } P(t) = tt \textbf{ then } 1 \textbf{ else } 0 \textbf{ end})\delta t.$$

We shall mostly adopt the (type-incorrect) abbreviation:

$$\int_{t=b}^{t=e} P(t)\delta t,$$

in lieu of the former. It works if you encode **tt** as 1 and **ff** as 0! For the case that $b < e$ and $\int_{t=b}^{t=e} P(t)\delta t > \ell$, we shall abbreviate $\int_{t=b}^{t=e} P(t)\delta t$ by $\lceil P \rceil$, which reads: The duration of P.

    If P is true at some point t, but not in an interval before t, $[b, t)$, nor in an interval after t, $(t, a]$, then $\int P(t)\delta t = 0$, i.e., $\lceil P \rceil = 0$.

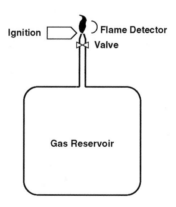

Fig. 15.5. An abstracted gas burner

Example 15.10 *Preliminary Gas Burner Considerations:*

What Is "the" Gas Burner?

A gas burner consists of the following electromechanical components: a pipe leading from a gas reservoir to a valve; a valve which can be in either of four states:

type
    Valve == closed | opening | open | closing;

an ignition apparatus which can be in either of two states:

type
    Ignition == ignite | idle;

and a flame sensor which can be in either of two states:

type
    Flame == flame_on | no_flame

We will presently not need to deal with the ignition; it is included for later reference. We can summarise these components in three state variables:

variable
    valve:Valve
    ignition:Ignition
    flame:FlameSensor

The valve and the flame state components thus define two Boolean state assertions:

value
    valve: **Time** → **Bool**
    flame: **Time** → **Bool**

There is gas flowing iff the valve is opening, open or closing. There is flame burning iff the flamesensor senses flame_on.

Gas Leakage

We can now define a general state assertion, leak:

value
    leak: **Time** → **Bool**
    leak(t) ≡ valve(t) ∧ ∼flame(t)

But what does it mean, with respect to valve(t), when we earlier stated that gas is flowing iff the valve is either opening, open or closing? We will not formally detail this issue here. Instead we appeal to the reader's intuition: When the valve is closed, obviously no gas is flowing. When the valve is opening, and as from some degree of being between closed and open, gas is also flowing, and so on.

Gas Burner Requirements

The real-time requirement for a gas burner is that the proportion of leak time in an interval $[b, e]$ is not more than one twentieth (i.e., $\frac{1}{20}$) of the interval provided the interval $[b, e]$ is at least 60 seconds long:

$$(e - b){\geq}60\sec \Rightarrow \int_{t=b}^{t=e} \text{leak}(t)\delta t{\leq} \tfrac{(e-b)}{20}$$

We rewrite the above into:

$$\text{GasBurnerReq} \equiv \ell \geq 60 \Rightarrow 20*\!\int \text{Leak} \leq \ell$$

∎

15.3.3 Examples, Part II

We bring in one more detailed example before we explain the duration calculus. In Example 15.11 we give a detailing of the above elevator (cum lift) example (Example 15.9). By carefully explaining the application, its safety and functional requirements, and bringing in — so to speak *out of thin air* — the duration calculus formalisations of these requirements, it is hoped that the reader is better motivated for the subsequent systematic, and at times dry, presentation of the syntax and (informal) semantics of the duration calculus.

Example 15.11 *Elevator cum Lift: Function and Safety Requirements, the "Full" Version, Part I:* We refer to the "quickie" version of this example, Example 15.9.

Problem Description

We first give a problem domain description, and then we give a combined set of formal functional and safety requirements, expressed in the duration calculus.

A simple, single lift system allows movement of a single lift cage between a finite number of floors, the starting and stopping of the lift [cage] and the opening and closing of floor doors — all in response to the pressing of floor call and cage send buttons.

Components

The lift system has the following immediate components:

- a lift cage with send buttons, one for each floor, as immediate sub-components
- motor (engine)

- N floors, each with a floor door and a call button as immediate sub-components

In this version we abstract from passengers — assuming that a lift can carry any number of clients!

The *terms* introduced are: *lift system, [lift] cage, send buttons, floor, floor number, [floor] door, call button*. The *taxonomy* is implied by their composition. The system *state* is made up from the above components together with their attributes — which we now detail.

There is a tacit understanding above that might have to be made more explicit: namely that floors are identified by natural numbers, say 0 to N inclusive — and hence that two immediately adjacent floors differ by 1 in their floor number.

Attributes

The system and its components have the following attributes (that is: are of the following types, and have the following values):

- The lift cage is either stopped at floor j for j lying between 0 and N inclusive, or is moving up (or down) between floors i and $i+1$ (i and $i-1$) for i lying between 0 and $N-1$ (N and 1).
- A floor door is either open or closed.
- The motor is either running up (or down) or is stopped.
- The motor, when running, runs at a constant speed — which causes the lift cage to move between immediately neighbouring floors in t_m time units.

The new *terms* introduced are: *stopped, moving, open, close, running, speed, and time unit*. Their *taxonomy* is implied by their interrelations, for example, *motor running* implies *cage moving*, and so on.

Events

We consider only the following events:

- A send button is pressed for floor k, for k in the interval 0 to N inclusive.
- A call button on floor k is pressed.
- The opening (and closing) of floor doors.
- The upward (downward) starting [and stopping] of the motor — implying the same for the cage!

New *terms* are: *[button] pressing, opening, closing, starting, stopping*. As part of what we could call the taxonomy: button pressings are external input events caused by users, whereas motor and (hence) cage starting and stopping, and door opening and closing, are internal events caused by the system (in response to the system state and external events).

Behaviour

A lift journey is behaviourally described:

- Servicing a floor means that the lift cage is stopping at the floor (implying opening and closing of floor doors, etc.).
- There is a request on floor j if floor j has not been serviced since a send button for that floor was last pressed.
- If a lift moves from floor i to floor $i+n$ where $-2 \geq n \geq 2$, and a request is outstanding (pending) for any intermediate floor j (where j lies between i and $i+n$) then the lift will service floor j before proceeding to floor $i+n$.

Invariants

The above plus the invariants fully describe expectations:

- There are at least two floors (a component invariant).
- The cage has exactly one send button for each floor (a component invariant).
- Pressing a call button at floor i causes the lift to service that floor within t_c time units (a procedural, functional requirement).
- Pressing a send button for floor i causes the lift to service that floor within t_s time units (a procedural, functional invariant).
- When a floor is serviced then the floor door is simultaneously open for at least t_o time units (a procedural, functional invariant).
- A floor door may only be open if the lift cage is at that floor (a component [+event] safety invariant).

Requirements: L_Req

The lift system, LS, shall be monitored and controlled by a computing system that shall *respect* the components, *handle* the events and *satisfy* the procedures and invariants enumerated above.

Base Model

type
    LS :: cage:Cages × floors:Floors × motor:Motor
    Cages = Buttons
    bs : Buttons = **Nat** $\overrightarrow{m}$ Button
    fs : Floors = **Nat** $\overrightarrow{m}$ Floor
    Floor :: call:B × door:Door
    Button == Pressed | Off
    Motor == Stopped | Up | Down
    Door == Open | Closed

Formal Requirements

To model that the lift is only at one floor, and the door is only open at, at most, one floor at a time we choose the following state variables:

call: $\{0, \ldots, n\}$–**set**   call buttons pressed
send: $\{0, \ldots, n\}$–**set**   send buttons pressed
floor: $\{0, \ldots, n\}$ lift position
door: $\{0, \ldots, n, \text{closed}\}$ door state

Thus we do not model lift positions between floors. call and send relate to *fs*, and *bs*, respectively.

L_Req $\equiv \Box(\text{SafetyReq} \wedge \text{FunctReq})$

To specify the requirements we introduce a static variable i which ranges over the floors $0, \ldots, n$.

The safety property for the lift control system is:
For every floor the door may only be opened if the lift is at that floor:

SafetyReq $\equiv \lceil\text{door=i}\rceil \Rightarrow \lceil\text{floor=i}\rceil$

Notice, *SafetyReq* is equivalent to stating that "if the lift is not at floor i, then door i must be closed".

In the formulation of the functional requirements we use the phase "to service a floor", which means that the lift is at the floor and that the door is open. As the safety requirement states that a door must only be open if the lift is at the floor, we will formalise servicing a floor by the door being open at that floor.

FunctReq $\equiv$ FunctReq1 $\wedge$ FunctReq2 $\wedge$ FunctReq3

Pressing a send button causes the lift to service the corresponding floor within t_s time units:

FunctReq1 $\equiv$
   $(\lceil i \in \text{send}\rceil \; ; \; \textbf{true} \Rightarrow \ell \leq t_s) \vee (\ell \leq t_s \; ; \; \lceil\text{door=i}\rceil \; ; \; \textbf{true})$

This requirement states that for every observation interval for which $i \in \textit{send}$ holds initially, i.e., the send button for the ith floor is pressed, either the interval is shorter than or equal to t_s or it may be divided into three subintervals where the first lasts at most t_s, in the second the door at floor i is opened, and a final subinterval which is unconstrained.

A similar condition must hold when pressing a call button:
Pressing a call button causes the lift to service the corresponding floor within t_c time units:

FunctReq2 $\equiv$
$\quad$($\lceil i \in$ call$\rceil$; **true** $\Rightarrow \ell \leq t_c$) $\vee$ ($\ell \leq t_c$; $\lceil$door=i$\rceil$; **true**)

The system must guarantee that when a floor is serviced, the doors are open for at least t_o time units:

FunctReq3 $\equiv$
$\quad \lceil$door$\neq$i$\rceil$; $\lceil$door=i$\rceil$; $\lceil$door$\neq$i$\rceil \Rightarrow \ell \geq t_o$

This completes the first part of the *lift system* example. The second part is given in Example 15.12.

$\blacksquare$

15.3.4 The Syntax

The presentation of this part follows that of Skakkebæk et al. [475] (1992).

Simple Expressions

We define simple, i.e., atomic expressions.

$\quad$x,y,...,z:State_Variable
$\quad$a,b,...,c:Static_Variable
$\quad$ff,tt:Bool_Const
$\quad$k,k',...,k'':Const

Static variables designate time-independent values. We assume some context which helps us determine the type of variables.

State Expressions and Assertions

We define state expressions and state assertions. A state assertion is a state expression of type **Bool**, and op is an operator symbol of arity n. We assume a context which helps us determine that an identifier is an op!

$\quad$se:State_Expr ::= Const | Bool_Const | op(se_1,...,se_n)
$\quad$P:State_Asrt ::= State_Expr

We assume a context which helps us determine that a state expression is of type **Bool**, i.e., is a state assertion.

Durations and Duration Terms

If P is a state assertion, then $\int P$ is a duration.
   We define duration terms.

   dt:Dur_Term ::= $\int$ P | **Real** | op(dt_1,...,dt_n) | ℓ

ℓ is an abbreviation for the duration term $\int tt$. op is an n operator symbol of type **Real**. We assume a context which helps us determine that an identifier is an op!

Duration Formulas

We define duration formulas. Let A be any n-ary predicate symbol over real-valued duration arguments. We assume a context which helps us determine that an identifier is an A!

   d:Dur_Form ::= A(dt_1,...,dt_n)
   | **true** | **false** |
   | $\sim d'$ | $d_1 \vee d_n$
   | $d_1;d_n$
   | $d_1 \wedge d_n$
   | $d_1 \Rightarrow d_n$
   | $d_1 \wedge d_n$
   | $\forall$ a: d /* a is */ Static_Variable

Delimiting parentheses can be inserted to clarify precedence.

Common Duration Formula Abbreviations

We make free use of the following common abbreviations:

$\lceil \rceil$	:	$\ell = 0$	: point duration
$\lceil P \rceil$	:	$\int P = \ell \wedge \ell > 0$	: almost everywhere P
$\Diamond d$	:	**true**; d; **true**	: somewhere d
$\Box d$	:	$\neg(\Diamond \neg d)$	: always d
$d_1 \to d_2$	:	d_1; **true** $\Rightarrow d_1 \vee (d:1;d:2;$**true**$)$	: d_2 follows d_1

Precedence Rules:

   First   : $\neg$ $\Box$ $\Diamond$
   Second : $\vee$ $\wedge$;
   Third   : $\Rightarrow$ $\to$

15.3.5 The Informal Semantics

The presentation of this part also follows that of Skakkebæk et al. [475] (1992).

A particular system behaviour $\mathcal{B}$ assigns, for each state variable x, a function from the semi-open time definition set $[0, \infty)^3$ to the type of the values containable in x. For each static variable a the function "selects" a value $\mathcal{V}(a)$. Each state expression then denotes a function obtained by evaluating the state expression for each point of time.

For state assertions, P, we assume *finite variability*, i.e., for any behaviour $\mathcal{B}$, any observation interval can be divided into finitely many sub-intervals with P constant on each open subinterval, not including the interval *begin* and *end* points.

An *observation interval* is an *open* and *bounded* interval: $[b, e]$. For a given interval the duration $\int P$ of a state assertion denotes the real number:

$$\int_{t=b}^{t=e} (\textbf{if } P(t) = tt \textbf{ then } 1 \textbf{ else } 0 \textbf{ end})\delta t.$$

The integral is a measure of the set of points where P has the value tt.

For any behaviour $\mathcal{B}$ and interval $[b, e]$ duration terms denote real values, and atomic duration formulas denote Boolean values. The values of composite duration formulas are obtained by the usual interpretation of the logical operators and quantification. The value of a "chop" formula d_1 ; d_2 is tt iff the interval $[b, e]$ can be divided into $[b, m]$ and $[m, e]$, where $b < m < e$ such that d_1 evaluates to tt in $[b, m]$ and d_2 evaluates to tt in $[m, e]$.

The duration formula d *holds* on the interval $[b, e]$ for the behaviour $\mathcal{B}$ just when d has value tt on $[b, e]$ with any assignment $\mathcal{V}$ of values to the static variables. The duration formula d *holds from start* on the interval $[b, e]$ for the behaviour $\mathcal{B}$ just when it holds on any interval of the form $[0, T]$ for the behaviour $\mathcal{B}$. A duration formula d is *valid* (a *tautology*) just when it holds for every behaviour $\mathcal{B}$ and every interval $[b, e]$. It is sufficient for a formula to be valid, that it holds from start for every behaviour.

Definition. By a *duration calculus* we shall understand a *temporal logic* whose concept of time is captured by **Real**, whose formula connectives include those of $\square$ (always), $\diamond$ (sometime), $\rightarrow$ (follows) and the chop operator, expressed either by $\frown$ or by ';', whose state, P, duration terms include those of $\int P$ (), $o(t_1, ..., t_n)$, and ℓ, and whose formulas further include those of $\lceil\rceil$ (point duration) $\lceil P \rceil$ (almost everywhere P) and whose syntax and semantics is otherwise as stated in Sect. 15.3.4 and in this section.   ■

---

[3]That is: from and including time 0 up to infinity (but, of course, not including infinity)!

15.3.6 Examples, Part III

We bring in a long series of examples that illustrate a number of specification principles and techniques. Notably, they show the decomposition of problems into that of understanding the requirements, that of understanding the application domain (usually abbreviated the domain) and that of recording design decisions. We end this section by expressing some observations.

The Elevator cum Lift Example: Design

Example 15.12 *The Elevator cum Lift Example: The Software Design:*

The Software Design, **L_Design**

The simplest design we can think of is to let the lift service the floors successively, no matter whether they have requested service or not. We start by letting the lift service the ground floor, thereafter it services the first floor, the second floor, and continues in this way, until it reaches the top floor. Having serviced the top floor the lift returns to the ground floor, and the operation cycle is repeated.

The state space for the simple design is the state space for the requirements extended with the variable *move*, which describes where the lift is heading or if it is idle:

$$move : \{0, \ldots, n, \text{idle}\}$$

We define the simple design by the predicate S:

L_Design $\equiv$ SIinit $\wedge$ $\square$ SOperation

Initially the lift is idle at the ground floor with the doors open and no requests for the lift:

SInit $\equiv$
  $\lceil$move=idle$\wedge$floor=0$\wedge$door=0$\wedge$send={}$\wedge$call={}$\rceil$;**true**
  $\vee \lceil\rceil$

SOperation is defined as:

SOperation $\equiv$ SBehaviour $\wedge$ Door $\wedge$ Send $\wedge$ Call $\wedge$ Timing

SBehaviour describes the lift behaviour:

SBehaviour $\equiv$ Up $\wedge$ Down $\wedge$ Stop

If the system is in a state where the lift is idle at floor i, it may proceed to a state where it moves towards the next floor upwards:

$$\text{Up} \equiv \lceil \text{move=idle} \wedge \text{floor=i} \wedge \text{i<n} \rceil \to \lceil \text{move=i+1} \rceil$$

If the lift is at the top floor, it may move towards the ground floor:

$$\text{Down} \equiv \lceil \text{move=idle} \wedge \text{floor=n} \rceil \to \lceil \text{move=0} \rceil$$

If the lift is moving towards a floor, it may reach this floor and become idle:

$$\text{Stop} \equiv \lceil \text{move=i} \rceil \to \lceil \text{move=idle} \wedge \text{floor=i} \rceil$$

Door describes the door behaviour. If the lift is idle and at floor i, the door at floor i is open. Notice that because of the domain of the variable *door* all other doors are closed. If the lift is not idle, all doors are closed:

$$\begin{aligned}
\text{Door} \equiv \\
(\lceil \text{move=idle} \wedge \text{floor=i} \rceil \Rightarrow \lceil \text{door=i} \rceil) \\
\wedge (\lceil \text{move} \neq \text{idle} \rceil \Rightarrow \lceil \text{door=closed} \rceil)
\end{aligned}$$

If the lift is idle at position i, then i does not belong to *send*. At all other times i may belong to *send*:

$$\text{Send} \equiv \lceil \text{door=i} \rceil \Rightarrow \lceil \text{i} \notin \text{send} \rceil$$

The specification of *Call* is similar to the specification of *Send*:

$$\text{Call} \equiv \lceil \text{door=i} \rceil \Rightarrow \lceil \text{i} \notin \text{call} \rceil$$

Timing defines the timing constraints which the system must fulfill.

$$\text{Timing} \equiv \text{MinOpenTime} \wedge \text{MoveTime}$$

MinOpenTime states that when a door is open, it is open for at least t_o time units. If t_o is chosen to be sufficiently large, this assures that people have a chance to get in and out of the lift before the door closes:

$$\text{MinOpenTime} \equiv \lceil \text{door} \neq \text{i} \rceil \, ; \, \lceil \text{door=i} \rceil \, ; \, \lceil \text{door} \neq \rceil \Rightarrow \ell \geq t_o$$

It takes at most t_m time units to move from one floor to another:

$$\text{MoveTime} \equiv \lceil \text{move} \neq \text{idle} \rceil \Rightarrow \ell \leq t_m$$

*Domain Description: Assumptions, **L_Domain***

If we try to prove that the design implies the requirements, i.e., that the design is a correct implementation of the requirements, we find that it is not possible. In order to succeed we need an assumption about the environment, namely that a door is open for at most t_{max} time units:

L_Domain $\equiv$ $\Box$ SMaxOpen
SMaxOpen $\equiv$ $\lceil$door=i$\rceil$ $\Rightarrow$ $\ell \leq t_{max}$

We make this assumption because if something prevents the door from closing we cannot guarantee that a request for the lift will be serviced within t_s time units.

The maximum time it may take before a floor is serviced corresponds to the maximum time it takes to service every other floor before the requested floor:

$$t_s \leq (n+1) \cdot (t_{max} + t_m)$$

The time a door is open is less than or equal to the maximum time the door is open:

$$t_o \leq t_{max}$$

Correctness of Simple Design wrt. Domain and Requirements

In order to check that the simple design, L_Design, is an implementation of the requirements, L_Req (see Page 535), we must prove that:

L_Design $\wedge$ L_Domain $\Rightarrow$ L_Req

We omit the proof. ∎

The Road-Rail Level Crossing Examples

The presentation of this part also follows that of Skakkebæk et al. [475] (1992).

We have chosen a rather large example, but we will present it in parts. In this way the reader can read the first example, or the first two, and so on. The aim of bringing in the examples is to illustrate well-nigh all aspects of the duration calculus, as well as to show a reasonably realistic, i.e., "large", i.e., "industrially scaled" example. We are grateful to Dr. Jens Ulrik Skakkebæk and to Profs. Anders Peter Ravn and Hans Rischel (and the publisher, the IEEE Computer Science Press) for permission to bring in the extensive, albeit substantially edited, quote.

We will "chop" our presentation of the referenced paper [475] up into five parts: Example 15.13 deals with the safety and functional expectations that one should have from a properly designed road-rail level crossing system. The next three examples deal with various assumptions about the domain of road traffic, rail traffic, i.e., trains, and the optical/mechanical devices that are to assist the road-rail level crossing system in achieving required safety and functionality. Example 15.14 deals with assumptions about road traffic. Example 15.15 deals with assumptions about train traffic, and Example 15.16 deals with assumptions about the devices. Finally Example 15.17 outlines the monitoring and control strategy for the computing system, i.e., the machine design.

The real purpose of the paper, i.e., [475], is, additionally, and hence quite importantly, to also show that one can indeed with the duration calculus axiom system prove correctness of a design with respect to the requirements and assumptions.

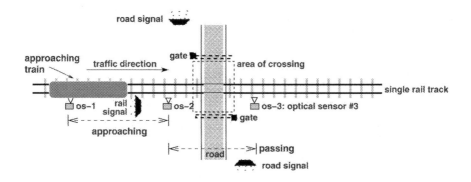

Fig. 15.6. A road-rail level crossing

Example 15.13 *Road-Rail Level Crossing: Function and Safety Require-ments:*

Problem Description

The problem is to describe the *function* and the *safety* of an optical-mechanical traffic system. The problem, in this example, is not to specify how to achieve *function* and *safety*, but only to specify what we mean by *function* and *safety*. Thus the problem is more a domain and a requirements specification than a computing systems design problem.

Consider a road-rail level crossing (Fig. 15.6). All dimensions are rather "out of scale". The road-rail level crossing is for a single track rail with all trains passing only in one direction (left to right on the figure). Many factors determine the monitoring and control of road and rail traffic:

(i) Road traffic is controlled by gates, one on either side of the track.

(ii) The gates close only when road traffic is not "stuck" in the crossing area (shown dashed).

Road traffic is advised of approaching and crossing trains by road signals, one on either side of the track. When the gates are to be lowered these road signals are set to red. When the gates have been fully raised the road signals are set to green.

(iii) Train traffic is controlled (i.e., advised) by a rail signal on the right side of the track of approaching trains, well before the crossing area.

(iv) The rail signal indicates either STOP or GO for oncoming (i.e., approaching) trains.

(v) Optical sensors (os) monitor trains in the vicinity of the crossing area.

(vi) A sensor, os_1, is placed at a reasonable distance from the rail signal such that a train will reach the first sensor before it reaches the rail signal.

(vii) A train enters the system whenever it is so determined by sensor (os_1).

(viii) A train has left the crossing whenever sensor os_3 determines that the rear end of the train has passed the crossing.

(ix) When a train approaches the gates are to be closed — provided there is no traffic "stuck" in the crossing area.

(x) The rail signal is (to be) set to GO after the gates have closed.

(xi) When no trains are approaching or passing, the rail signal must be set to STOP and the gates are to be opened.

The main goal of the combination of optics and mechanics with a computing system monitoring the traffic and controlling the gates and the signal is to ensure *safety*:

(xii) The complete system (optics, mechanics, computing) must never allow road and train traffic to pass the crossing area at the same time.

(xiii) Furthermore, the system must ensure that both road and rail traffic are able to pass the crossing area within some reasonable time.

(xiv) A train is passing whenever it is between sensors os_2 and os_3.

Formalisation

Let us refer to the required system as the Road-Rail Level Crossing System: $\text{R}^2\ell\text{CS}$.

The $\text{R}^2\ell\text{CS}$ accepts inputs from the optical and the gate sensors, and offers output (commands) to the signals and the gates.

[1] State Variables

The *state* consists of a number of variables: (a) one for the *(rail) signal*, (b) one for the two *gates*, (c) one for the road traffic and (d) one for the rail traffic.

type
    Rail_Signal == **stop** | go

Gates == opening | open | closing | closed
Road_Traffic == stopped | stuck_in_cross | free_to_cross
variable
signal:Rail_Signal
gates:Gates
traffic:Road_Traffic

Trains are either *approaching* or *passing*.

variable
approach: **Nat-set**
pass: **Nat-set**

That is, a train is identified by a unique, natural number, i. If some part of train i is between the first two sensors (os_1-os_2), then train i is *approaching*, i.e.,

approach := {i} ∪ approach ;

And, if some part of train i is between the last two sensors (os_2-os_3), then train i is *passing*, i.e.:

pass := {i} ∪ pass ;

Trains are *active* (wrt. crossing) if either approaching or passing (or both). One can define three *state assertions* concerning the state of trains:

value
passing: **Unit → Bool**
passing() ≡ pass ≠ {}

approaching: **Unit → Bool**
approaching() ≡ approach ≠ {}

active: **Unit → Bool**
active() ≡ (approaching ∪ passing) ≠ {}

[2] Requirements

Now we are ready to express requirements:

Req ≡ □(SafeReq∧FunReq$_1$∧FunReq$_2$∧FunReq$_3$)

It turns out that we can express the functional requirements in terms of three state assertions.

[2.1] Safety Requirements

If the gates are not closed or road traffic is "stuck" in the crossing, then the train must not pass:

$$\text{SafeReq} \equiv \lceil ((\text{gates} \neq \text{closed}) \vee (\text{traffic} = \text{stuck})) \rceil \Rightarrow \lceil \sim\text{passing}() \rceil$$

[2.2] Functional Requirements

There are three functional requirements:

1. FunReq_1: The road traffic should maximally be held back for a predefined period of time t_{stop}:

   $$\text{FunReq}_1 \equiv \lceil \text{traffic} = \text{stopped} \rceil \Rightarrow \ell \leq t_{\text{stop}}$$

2. FunReq_2: When all trains have left the crossing, the gates must be open for at least time t_{open}:

   $$\text{FunReq}_2 \equiv$$
   $$\lceil \text{active} \rceil; \lceil \sim\text{active} \rceil; \lceil \text{active} \rceil \Rightarrow \int (\text{gates} = \text{open}) > t_{\text{open}}$$

3. FunReq_3: Provided the road traffic is not stuck, a single train must be able to pass within time t_{active}:

   $$\text{FunReq}_3 \equiv \lceil i \in \text{active} \wedge (\text{traffic} \neq \text{stuck}) \rceil \Rightarrow \ell \leq t_{\text{active}}$$

Example 15.13 illustrated principles and techniques of prescribing requirements, as they were decomposed into those of safety and those of functionality.

In the next three examples, Examples. 15.14–15.16, we "go backwards", as it were, to record the assumptions that any (later) design must (usually) make. That is, we describe (some facets of) the (application) domain. Normally, according to our "dogma", we first establish a domain description, before we, as we have just done, produce a requirements prescription, and, certainly long before we develop a software design specification. The design for the present problem domain of railway level crossings is recorded in Example 15.17.

We somewhat arbitrarily, it may seem, but pragmatically this is very sound, decompose the domain description into three parts: Describing the *road traffic*, i.e., Domain_1, describing the *train traffic*, i.e., Domain_2, and describing the supporting technology, i.e., the *device technology*, i.e., Domain_3. The relevant domain "theory" is the conjunction of these:

$$\text{Domain} \equiv \Box \bigwedge_{i=1}^{3} \text{Domain}_i$$

Example 15.14 *Road-Rail Level Crossing: The Road Traffic Domain:*
We continue the railway level crossing example based on [475].

When running freely, i.e., without control, that is, without proper road signaling and gate control, the road traffic may eventually either stop properly in front of the gates, or get stuck in the crossing. Such stopped or stuck road traffic may subsequently become free, i.e., neither stopped nor stuck:

RoadTrafficAssump$_1$ ≡
  ($\lceil$Traffic=stopped$\rceil$→$\lceil$Traffic=free$\rceil$)
  ∧ ($\lceil$Traffic=free$\rceil$→($\lceil$Traffic=stopped$\rceil$∨$\lceil$Traffic=stuck$\rceil$))
  ∧ ($\lceil$Traffic=stuck$\rceil$→$\lceil$Traffic=free$\rceil$)

Road traffic is stopped iff the gates are not open:

RoadTrafficAssump$_2$ ≡ $\lceil$Traffic=stopped$\rceil$≡$\lceil$Gates≠open$\rceil$

In closing, we record:

$$\text{Domain}_1 \equiv \Box \bigwedge_{i=1}^{2} \text{RoadTrafficAssump}_i$$

■

Example 15.15 *Road-Rail Level Crossing: The Train Traffic Domain:*

Problem Description

We continue the railway level crossing example based on [475].

Trains must only pass if the rail signal is set to GO:

TrainTrafficAssump$_1$ ≡ $\lceil$Passing$\rceil$⇒$\lceil$Signal$\rceil$

An active train travels in one direction only, i.e., initially approaches and finally passes:

TrainTrafficAssump$_2$ ≡
  $\lceil$i ∉ ACt→$\rceil$→$\lceil$i ∈ Appr ∧ i ∉ Pass$\rceil$
  ∧ $\lceil$i ∈ Appr ∧ i ∉ Pass$\rceil$→$\lceil$i ∈ Pass$\rceil$
  ∧ $\lceil$i ∈ Pass$\rceil$→$\lceil$i ∉ Act$\rceil$

The last train in a series of trains passes the crossing before leaving the crossing:

TrainTrafficAssump$_3$ ≡
  ($\lceil$∼Active$\rceil$→$\lceil$Approaching∧∼Passing$\rceil$)

$\wedge$ ($\lceil$Approaching$\wedge\sim$Passing$\rceil\rightarrow\lceil$Passing$\rceil$)
$\wedge$ ($\lceil$Passing$\rceil\rightarrow(\lceil\sim$Active$\rceil\vee\lceil$Active$\rceil$))
$\wedge$ ($\lceil$Active$\rceil\rightarrow\lceil$Passing$\rceil$)

The trains do not hesitate when the rail signal is GO:

$$\text{TrainTrafficAssump}_4 \equiv \lceil\text{Signal}\wedge\text{Active}\rceil\Rightarrow\ell\leq T_{\text{sched}}$$

The railway lines are not overloaded with trains:

$$\text{TrainTrafficAssump}_5 \equiv$$
$$\lceil\text{Active}\rceil;\lceil\sim\text{Active}\rceil;\lceil\text{Active}\rceil$$
$$\Rightarrow \ell > T_{\text{inactive}} + T_{\text{wait}} + T_{\text{gate\_open}} + T_{\text{open}}$$

Assumptions 1, 2 and 4 are really just obvious domain facts.
In closing, we record:

$$\text{Domain}_2 \equiv \square \bigwedge_{i=1}^{5} \text{TrainTrafficAssump}_i$$

■

Example 15.16 *Road-Rail Level Crossing: The Device Domain:*
We continue the railway level crossing example based on [475].
It takes, at most, time $T_{\text{gate\_close}}$ for the gates to close if the road traffic is not stuck in the crossing:

$$\text{DeviceAssump}_1 \equiv$$
$$\lceil\text{Gates}=\text{closing}\wedge\text{Traffic}\neq\text{stuck}\rceil\Rightarrow\ell\leq T_{\text{gate\_close}}$$

It takes, at most, time $T_{\text{gate\_open}}$ for the gates to open:

$$\text{DeviceAssump}_2 \equiv$$
$$\lceil\text{Gates}=\text{opening}\rceil\Rightarrow\ell\leq T_{\text{gate\_open}}$$

The physical properties of *Gates* constrain the value of *gates* to cycle: open, closing, closed, opening, open, ... (in that order):

$$\text{DeviceAssump}_3 \equiv$$
$$(\lceil\text{Gates}=\text{open}\rceil\rightarrow\lceil\text{Gates}=\text{closing}\rceil)$$
$$\wedge (\lceil\text{Gates}=\text{closing}\rceil\rightarrow\lceil\text{Gates}=\text{closed}\rceil)$$
$$\wedge (\lceil\text{Gates}=\text{closed}\rceil\rightarrow\lceil\text{Gates}=\text{opening}\rceil)$$
$$\wedge (\lceil\text{Gates}=\text{opening}\rceil\rightarrow\lceil\text{Gates}=\text{open}\rceil)$$

The rail signal switches between STOP and GO:

$$\text{DeviceAssump}_4 \equiv$$
$$(\lceil\sim\text{Signal}\rceil\rightarrow\lceil\text{Signal}\rceil) \wedge (\lceil\text{Signal}\rceil\rightarrow\lceil\sim\text{Signal}\rceil)$$

In closing, we record:

$$\text{Domain}_3 \equiv \Box \bigwedge_{i=1}^{4} \text{DeviceAssump}_i$$

∎

Finally we are ready to record the design decisions.

Example 15.17 *Road-Rail Level Crossing: The Software Design:*
We continue the railway level crossing example based on [475].

The software design was chosen by the system designers (Skakkebæk, Ravn and Rischel of [475]) to facilitate a proof of correctness with respect to the requirements and the assumptions (i.e., the domain).

The design decisions now presented are a formalisation of a finite state control, one that cycles through phases with inactive, approaching and passing trains. The overall design specification predicate is:

$$\text{Design} \equiv \Box (\bigwedge_{i=1}^{3} \text{ApproachTrains}_i \wedge \bigwedge_{j=1}^{4} \text{PassingTrains}_j)$$

Approaching Trains

The gates will remain open when no trains are present:

ApproachTrains$_1$ ≡
   $(\lceil \sim\text{Active} \rceil \wedge (\lceil \text{Gates=open} \rceil \,;\, \textbf{true})) \Rightarrow \lceil \text{Gates=open} \rceil$

If trains are present, then the gates are open for at most T_{react}:

ApproachTrains$_2$ ≡ $\lceil \text{Gates=open} \wedge \text{Active} \rceil \Rightarrow \ell \leq T_{\text{react}}$

It takes, at most, T_{nts} before the rail signal is GO when the gates have closed:

ApproachTrains$_3$ ≡ $\lceil () \wedge \sim\text{Signal} \wedge \text{Active} \rceil \Rightarrow \ell \leq T_{\text{tnts}}$

Passing Trains

The gates remain closed as long as the rail signal is GO:

PassingTrains$_1$ ≡ $\lceil \text{Signal} \rceil \Rightarrow \lceil \text{Gates=closed} \rceil$

The rail signal remains GO while trains are present:

PassingTrains$_2$ ≡ $\lceil \text{Active} \rceil \wedge (\lceil \text{Signal} \rceil \,;\, \textbf{true}) \Rightarrow \lceil \text{Signal} \rceil$

The rail signal will only indicate GO for at most T_{inactive} after the trains have left:

$$\text{PassingTrains}_3 \equiv \lceil \sim\text{Active}\wedge\text{Signal}\rceil \Rightarrow \ell \leq T_{\text{inactive}}$$

The gates will remain closed for at most T_{wait} after all trains have left:

$$\text{PassingTrains}_4 \equiv$$
$$\lceil (\text{Gates=closed})\wedge\sim\text{Active}\wedge\sim\text{Signal}\rceil \Rightarrow \ell \leq T_{\text{wait}}$$

∎

Some Observations

Comments

Some observations — after a long series of detailed examples — may now be in order:

(1) For the first time, perhaps, in these text books, we have sketched one part of an entire, albeit small, development, reordering a bit: from *domain descriptions* (in the form of assumptions about the environment in which a software design is to serve), via *requirements prescriptions*, to *software design*.

(2) The examples all focused, initially, on requirements. That is to be expected, as real-time applications are typically those related to safety-critical issues.

(3) And those examples have then shown requirements to be expressible in two parts: *safety-critical requirements* issues, and *functional requirements* issues. We shall later, in Vol. 3 of these textbooks, call functional requirements domain requirements.

(4) But there is one issue that we have "skirted": that of actually verifying the software designs that evolved from requirements prescriptions. Two examples illustrated the design versus requirements issue: Example 15.17 versus Example 15.13: The road-rail level crossing; and Example 15.12 versus Example 15.11. So what are we to expect?

Issues of Verification and Model Checking

It was mentioned in Examples 15.17 and 15.12 that given domain assumptions, the design and the requirements, one could now, in the duration calculus, verify the correctness of the design with respect to the requirements and in light of the assumptions. But are we going to do that? No, not in the present three volumes of this series of textbooks!

This requires an explanation! So we shall give one, briefly. As mentioned earlier, the three textbook volumes concentrate on 'formal methods "lite" '. That is, specification. Before we can state theorems to be proven we must master specification. But, of course, a, but not "the", main reason for formal specification is the ability to formally prove properties. We hope to write a volume in this series dedicated to verification and model-checking principles and techniques. These principles and techniques, however, become very much "bound" to the chosen specification language (i.e., tools), whereas the specification principles and techniques "carry over" from one specification language to another. So we claim!

The specificity of the model-checking and theorem-proving principles and techniques for specific specification language(s) is, presently, best covered in user manuals, monographs and textbooks dedicated to these specific notations: Model-checking using SMV [80] or SPIN [149,215], and theorem-proving using HOL [380,393] or PVS [384,385].

A word of caution is, however, needed. Only when actually carrying out proofs of correctness, or only when actually preparing material for model checking can the developer really know how to structure certain specifications: select which parts of a domain to emphasise, and how; formulate certain requirements in one way, rather than another; and, accordingly choose one design over another. So by not covering these aspects here, the developer, you, the reader, has really not (yet) been taught "the final" word. So be it!

To become a full-fledged, professional software engineer, takes more than just the present series of textbooks. For the present we refer to such seminal monographs and textbooks as [131] for RAISE and [557] for the duration calculus.

15.3.7 Transitions and Events

So far, in this chapter, we have considered *states*, assertions about these and their duration. In this brief section we shall consider how we express *transitions* between states — as an extension to the current duration calculus.

Thus, if P is a state assertion which holds in a neighbourhood $[t - \delta_{-t}, t)$ up to time t, and does not hold in a neighbourhood $(t, t + \delta_{+t}]$ after time t, then we say that $\downarrow P$ holds at t. Vice versa, if Q is a state assertion which does not hold in a neighbourhood $[t' - \delta_{-t'}, t')$ up to time t', but which holds in a neighbourhood $(t', t' - \delta_{+t'}]$ after time t', then we say that $\uparrow Q$ holds at t'. Figure 15.7 informally illustrates the issue. We can paraphrase this: $\uparrow P$

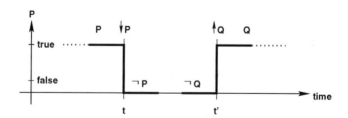

Fig. 15.7. State Transitions

is true at a point, and $\downarrow P$ is true at another point.

More generally, let $[b, e]$ be an interval, and let P be a state assertion that holds for an interval $[b - \delta, b], \delta > 0$ before b, then $\mathrlap{\diagdown}{\kern0.4em\diagdown}P$ holds for the interval $[b, e]$ iff P holds during $[b - \delta, b]$. Conversely, if Q holds for an interval $[b, e + \delta], \delta > 0$ after e, then $\mathrlap{\diagup}{\kern0.4em\diagup}Q$ holds for the interval $[b, e]$ iff Q holds during $[b, e + \delta]$.

Figure 15.8 informally illustrates the issue.

We can paraphrase this: $\mathrlap{\diagdown}{\kern0.4em\diagdown}P$ holds in a non-point interval ($[b, e]$) after P held, and $\mathrlap{\diagup}{\kern0.4em\diagup}Q$ holds in a non-point interval ($[b, e]$) before Q holds.

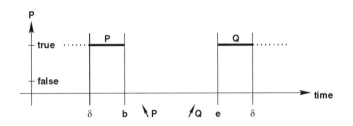

Fig. 15.8. "Single" state transitions

To express that certain before, respectively after, state assertions hold in a point interval, i.e., when (using the above interval notation $[b, e]$) $b = e$, we introduce the variant operator symbols: $\diagdown$, respectively $\diagup$

$$\diagdown P \equiv \mathrlap{\diagdown}{\kern0.4em\diagdown}P \wedge \ell = 0$$

$$\diagup Q \equiv \mathrlap{\diagup}{\kern0.4em\diagup}Q \wedge \ell = 0$$

We can paraphrase this: $\diagdown P$ holds at a point (if P held for some time before that point), and $\diagup Q$ holds at a point (if Q holds for some time after that point).

To express that at some point (b, i.e., also e) a system changes state from σ_P to σ_Q, that is, from P holding to Q holding, we write $\diagdown P \wedge \diagup Q$. Figure 15.9 informally illustrates the issue.

Finally, we introduce temporal operators which shall help us express that a state assertion holds, or does not hold at a point: $\top$, respectively $\bot$. Thus $\top S$ expresses: The state characterised by S holds at a point, and $\bot S$ expresses: The state characterised by S does not hold at a point. Formally:

$$\bot S \equiv \diagdown \neg S \wedge \diagup \neg S$$
$$\top S \equiv \diagdown S \wedge \diagup S$$

Figure 15.10 informally illustrates the issue.

It is high time for an example.

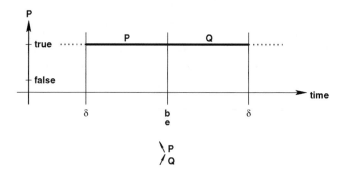

Fig. 15.9. System state transition

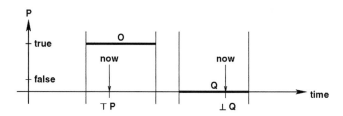

Fig. 15.10. Holds now, does not hold now

Example 15.18 *The Gas Burner State Machine:*

This example and its treatment within the duration calculus has been reported and published in several places: [300, 522, 523]. The proceedings [3] record many other ways of formalising the problem requirements and design solutions. The present exposition is edited from [557].

Example 15.10 stated the gas burner requirements:

GasBurnerReq $\equiv \ell \geq 60 \Rightarrow 20 * \int$ Leak $\leq \ell$

A first design decision is that any leak should last for a period shorter than 1 second:

GasBurnerDesign$_1$ $\equiv \Box(\lceil$Leak$\rceil \Rightarrow \ell < 1)$

And the second design decision is that the distance between any two consecutive leaks must be more than 30 seconds long:

GasBurnerDesign$_2$ $\equiv \Box((\lceil$Leak$\rceil ; \lceil \sim$Leak$\rceil ; \lceil$Leak$\rceil) \Rightarrow \ell > 30)$

Given the axiom system for the duration calculus one can prove:

(GasBurnerDesign$_1$ $\wedge$ GasBurnerDesign$_2$) $\Rightarrow$ GasBurnerReq

In [415, 416] studies are made of the design problem. A finite state machine is suggested. In Fig. 15.11 we show a refinement of that machine.

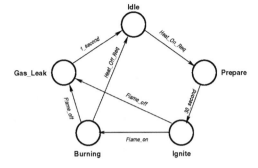

Fig. 15.11. A gas burner finite state control machine

At any one time the gas burner is exactly in one of the five states: Idle: In state Idle gas is off (i.e., is being turned off and kept turned off). The gas burner is willing to accept a *Heat_On_Request*. If such an external event occurs, then the gas burger makes a transition to state **Prepare**. Prepare: The gas burner waits for *30 seconds* after having arrived to state **Prepare**. Then it transitions to state Ignite. Ignite: In state Ignite the gas valve is opened and ignition attempts to set on the flame. If *flame* is detected *on* then the gas burner control transitions to state **Burning**. Otherwise a "flame-on" detector — at some time after ignition and with (still) no flame causes a *Flame_off* event and the gas burner transitions to state Gas_Leak. Burning: In state **Burning** the flame is on. The flame will remain on, either until a flame *Flame_off* is detected, or a *Heat_off_Request* event occurs. In the former case a transition is made to Gas_Leak. State Gas_Leak handles both ignition and flame-off failures. The gas valve is to be closed within one second. Internally a gas burner event *1_second* is issued after at most one second, and the gas burner transitions to state Idle (in which gas is turned off). Now let us examine the properties of the gas burner control machine.

It should now be obvious that the gas burner control machine is in some state:

$$\lceil \rceil \vee \lceil \text{Idle} \vee \text{Prepare} \vee \text{Ignite} \vee \text{Burning} \vee \text{Gas\_Leak} \rceil \qquad (15.1)$$

and is in at most one of these states:

$$\lceil \rceil \wedge \lceil \bigwedge_{s_1 \neq s_2} s_1 \Rightarrow s_2 \rceil \qquad (15.2)$$

where s_i is any of the five states.

There are four events:

$$\text{Heat\_On\_Req} \equiv (\downarrow \text{Idle} \wedge \uparrow \text{Prepare}) \qquad (15.3)$$
$$30\_\text{seconds} \equiv (\downarrow \text{Prepare} \wedge \uparrow \text{Ignite}) \qquad (15.4)$$
$$\text{Flame\_off} \equiv (\downarrow (\text{Ignite} \vee \text{Burning}) \wedge \uparrow \text{Gas\_Leak}) \qquad (15.5)$$
$$\text{Heat\_Off\_Req} \equiv (\downarrow \text{Burning} \wedge \uparrow \text{Idle}) \qquad (15.6)$$

and seven state transitions:

$$\downarrow \text{Idle} \Rightarrow \uparrow \text{Prepare} \qquad (15.7)$$
$$\downarrow \text{Prepare} \Rightarrow \uparrow \text{Ignite} \qquad (15.8)$$
$$\downarrow \text{Ignite} \Rightarrow \uparrow (\text{Burning} \vee \text{Gas\_Leak}) \qquad (15.9)$$
$$\downarrow \text{Burning} \Rightarrow \uparrow (\text{Idle} \vee \text{Gas\_Leak}) \qquad (15.10)$$
$$\downarrow \text{Gas\_Leak} \Rightarrow \uparrow \text{Idle} \qquad (15.11)$$

Event *30_seconds* occurs 30 seconds after the gas burner control machine has entered the **Prepare** state:

$$(\uparrow \text{Prepare} ; (\ell = 30)) \equiv (\uparrow \text{Prepare} ; \lceil \text{Prepare} \rceil ; 30\_\text{second}). \quad (15.12)$$

Flame_off handling must be done within one second:

$$\lceil \text{Flame\_off} \rceil \Rightarrow (\ell \leq 1) \qquad (15.13)$$

Let us name expressions 15.1–15.13 **Gas_Controller**. Given the axiom system for the duration calculus one can deduce:

Gas_Controller $\vdash$ GasBurnerDesign$_1$ $\wedge$ GasBurnerDesign$_2$

In [477] transitions of that machine are subject to probabilities, and a Markov model is studied. We shall content ourselves here with transition probabilities one (i.e., 1) for all transitions.

∎

15.3.8 Discussion: From Domains to Designs

We have covered core aspects of the duration calculus. The duration calculus offers a logic based on intervals and real-time. One can use the duration calculus to abstractly express constraints, i.e., requirements, on the duration of states. This was illustrated in Examples 15.9–15.11 and Example 15.13. One can also use the duration calculus to abstractly express properties of the domain, i.e., of the application area for which software is sought. This was illustrated in Examples 15.14–15.16. And one can finally hint at major design decisions also using the duration calculus. This was illustrated in Examples 15.12, 15.17, and 15.18.

Only in a very implicit sense can duration calculus expressions be said to specify sequential programs — such as we are normally prepared to implement in computing systems: in terms of sequential programs. A duration calculus expression, however, usually implies a sequential program, or a set of cooperating such. RSL specifications, the "closer" we get to software design, i.e., the more "concrete" such specifications become, rather specifically specify sequential programs. At least, it would be a good idea for the developer to make sure that this is so!

Now how can we combine the ability of the duration calculus to express quantitative properties of software (to be designed) and the actual specification of such software?

We turn to this question next. That is, we may seem to completely abandon thoughts and concepts of duration calculus, in favour of rather "down to earth" concepts of explicit timing in what could be considered a specification programming language, Timed RSL, TRSL.

15.4 TRSL: RSL with Timing

In this section we "extend" a subset of RSL with timing. Note, we do not mean the full RSL, just a subset. It is enough, in a textbook like this, to indicate how one might do it in actual software engineering practice.

This section is very much based on [132]. In a sense, we take up where Example 15.2 left us: That example tried, but it did not really achieve anything substantial. It just hinted at something! That "something" will now be put forward. That is, we shall present an extension to RSL which includes real-time facets.

15.4.1 TRSL Design Criteria

We wish to motivate why the extension of RSL is as it is. So we wish to express quantitative aspects of timing in what is basically RSL, i.e., in TRSL. RSL already allows us to express qualitative aspects of time. Notable illustrations are: First, something is specified to occur before something else. This is done using sequencing operators, notably ";". But it is also implied in the let ... in ... end construct. Second, something is specified to occur during the same time interval as something else. This is done using the parallel, ||, and the interlock, $\parallel$, composition of processes (P and Q): $P\|Q$ and $P \parallel Q$. Finally, something is specified to occur at the same time as something else. This is done using the input/output synchronisation and communication actions: c? and $c!v$. The quantitative aspects of timing have to do with *how long things take to do!*

The First TRSL Design Decision

In line with our long-held assumptions that applying a function to an argument and obtaining the result value, and evaluating a composite expression in general, takes no time, that is, it occurs "instantaneously", we make the first design decision.

To do this, we introduce an explicit new, i.e., not RSL, but TRSL construct:

wait (e)

Here e is an expression which yields real number values, t, of type time. If they are integers or natural numbers they are promoted to real values. If they are negative, they are promoted to the zero (real) value (0.0).

The idea is that occurrence of **wait** (e) in some process P:

clause$_{before}$; **wait** (e) ; clause$_{after}$

shall mean that process P waits t time units between evaluation of clause$_{before}$ and evaluation of clause$_{after}$.

The Second TRSL Design Decision

It is only natural to allow such **wait** clauses to occur in texts of process definitions, and of different, i.e., several, such definitions. It is therefore natural to expect that outputs from one process and inputs to another process take time. That is, that processes P and Q which wish to synchronise and communicate via channel c may be delayed, one or the other. In RSL we might schematically write:

type
   V
channel
   c:V
value
   P: **Unit** $\rightarrow$ **out** c **Unit**
   P() $\equiv$ ... c!v ...

   Q: **Unit** $\rightarrow$ **in** c **Unit**
   Q() $\equiv$ ... **let** v = c? **in** ... **end** ...

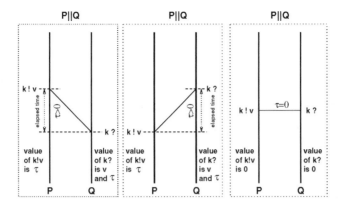

Fig. 15.12. I/O elapsed times: three cases

In reality RSL/CSP output/input may take time as shown in Fig. 15.12:
In TRSL an output is an expression which yields a real-time interval value,
namely, the time it takes from the start of evaluation of the TRSL output
expression till the time that output is being consumed by some other process.
If that other process's TRSL input expression is already ready to engage in the
output/input event the TRSL output expression value is 0.

In TRSL an input is an expression which yields both a value, the usual
input value read from the channel, and a real-time interval value. In balance
with the output expression value, an input expression's real-time interval value
"measures", i.e., represents, the time elapsed from the input being ready and
the communication taking place.

So, only **wait,** output and input clauses when subject to "executions" may
cause or allow time to elapse. In giving precise meaning to the **wait** and the
output/input constructs, we adopt the *maximal progress* assumption: The
time between an input or an output being ready to engage with one another
and the actual communication event taking place is minimised. If an execution,
based on an expression, can evolve without waiting for the environment, it
will not wait.

Consider the following construct:

clause$_1$ $\lceil$ (**wait** r ; clause$_2$).

What do we mean by it? clause$_1$ and clause$_2$ do not initially wait. Taking the
maximal progress assumption literally means that execution would evolve to
be based only on clause$_1$. But this would prevent the possibility of prescribing
an execution that immediately performs clause$_1$, or might wait r time units
and then perform clause$_2$. So we need a new operator (i.e., a new interpretation
of $\lceil$) in the parallel and interlock expansion rules.

Consider:

(**let** v = c ? **in** clause₁ **end**) ▯ (**wait** τ ;)

An execution based on this whole expression waits for its environment to offer an output on channel c.

If the communication of channel c is available within τ time units then the communication must be accepted and execution continues — now based on just clause₁. If an output is not available within τ time units then execution (of this whole expression) continues — now based on just clause₂.

15.4.2 The TRSL Language

We present the syntax and informal semantics of TRSL.

Syntax

We use the following abbreviations:

E: expressions	*c: channels*	τ: *types*
x: variables	*r: reals*	*V:* **value** *definitions*
t,id: identifiers	*T:* **Time**	

We consider all constructs of TRSL to be expressions:

V ::= id:τ	| **skip**	| E ▯ E
| id:τ, V	| **stop**	| E ⊓ E
E ::= ()	| **chaos**	| E ‖ E
| **true**	| x := E	| E ⫲ E
| **false**	| **if** E **then** E **else** E **end**	| E ; E
| r	| **let** id = E **in** E **end**	| λ id:τ • E
| T	| **wait** E	| E(E)
| id	| **let** t = c?x **in** E **end**	| **rec** id:τ • E
| x	| **let** t = c!E **in** E **end**	

Semantics

We need only concern ourselves with the following constructs:

E ::= **wait** E	| E ⊓ E
| **let** t = c?x **in** E **end**	| E ‖ E
| **let** t = c!E **in** E **end**	| E ⫲ E
| E ▯ E	

We explain these constructs:

wait e: The expression e is evaluated. For simplicity we assume a good style of specification, that is, the expression e is a simple expression not involving any of the constructs now covered. Instead, e evaluates either to a real value,

r, or to a natural number, and in both cases a positive such. The natural number value is "promoted" to a real value, r. The behaviour in which **wait** e is being interpreted waits r time units and then proceeds.

let $t = c?x$ **in** e **end**: The behaviour in which this expression is being interpreted, at time t_0, expresses willingness to input a value, v, from channel c. Once it receives a value, ν, at time t_1, ν is assigned to variable x and t is bound, in e, to the time interval value $t_1 - t_0$ promoted to a time value (!).[4] Then e is interpreted in a context that binds t to $t_1 - t_0$ and stores ν in x.

let $t = c!e_o$ **in** e_b **end**: The behaviour in which this expression is being interpreted, at time t_0, expresses willingness to output a value, e_o, to channel c. Once it delivers that value at time t_1, t is bound, in e, to the time interval value $t_1 - t_0$ promoted to a time value (!). Then e_b is interpreted in a context that binds t to $t_1 - t_0$.

$e_1 \;[]\; e_2$: This is external choice between two expression processes. The environment determines whether e_1 or e_2 is chosen, as before.

$e_1 \;\sqcap\; e_2$: This is nondeterministic choice between two expression processes. The environment plays no role in which choice is made. One of the two expressions is selected nondeterministically.

$e_1 \parallel e_2$: This is the usual parallel combination of two expression processes.

$e_1 \;\|\!\!\|\; e_2$: This is the *interlock* expression. It is similar to the parallel expression combination, only more *aggressive* [132]. The two interlocked expression processes will communicate only if they are able to communicate with one another. If they are able to communicate with other concurrent processes, but not with one another, then they *deadlock* — unless one of them can terminate. According to [132], the *interlock* is the main novelty of the RSL/CSP process algebra.

15.4.3 Another Gas Burner Example

For the next example we assume that the reader has followed earlier installments in the "unfolding saga" of gas burners: requirements, design, and so on (that is, Examples 15.10 and 15.18).

Example 15.19 *A Gas Burner Software Design:* Consider a possible system design as shown in Fig. 15.13. The four components have been singled out as follows:

The *gas burner* "mechanics, etc." is the gas burner with gas pipe, valve, ignition and flame detector. We can think of this component as being the environment.

That environment will issue requests for Heat_Off and Heat_On to be considered events that occur spontaneously in the environment. The flame detector similarly issues a Flame_On signal, which is likewise an event.

---

[4]See footnote 1.

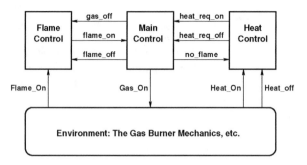

Fig. 15.13. A gas burner system: mechanics and computing system

And that environment will respond to a Gas_On signal from the *Main Controller.*

Let us first recall that the gas burner design decisions were:

GasBurnerDesign$_1$ ≡ □(⌈Leak⌉ ⇒ ℓ<1)
GasBurnerDesign$_2$ ≡ □((⌈Leak⌉ ; ⌈∼Leak⌉ ; ⌈Leak⌉) ⇒ ℓ>30)

as expressed in Example 15.18.

By introducing two state variables, gas and flame, such that:

Leak ≡ gas ∧ ∼flame

(and) into respectively the *Main Controller* and the *Flame Controller* processes, we may eventually be able to reason that the current (i.e., the evolving) design is a correct implementation of the design decisions. This, then, is our reason for the decomposition into the components shown.

The *Flame Controller* monitors the flame — in fact, it "mimics" the flame. It does so by maintaining a state variable flame, set to **true** when the flame is to be on, and to **false** otherwise. It responds to signals from the *Main Controller*: Flame_On, from the environment, sets flame to **true**, informs the *Main Controller* that the flame is on: flame_on, and, when receiving flame_off from the *Main Controller* sets flame to **false.**

The *Heat Controller* senses whether the environment is requesting Heat_On or Heat_Off, and informs the *Main Controller* accordingly: heat_req_on, respectively heat_req_off.

The *Main Controller*, through the *Flame Controller* and *Heat Controller*, monitors the environment, and, through directly issuing Gas_On signals to the environment that valve is to be opened and ignition "fired". The *Main Controller* maintains a variable gas, which is initially **false,** is set to **true** after a heat_req_on request has been received, is reset to **false** heat_req_off request has been received, and so forth!

This prepares us for the TRSL specification of the Gas_Burner_System as consisting of the four processes:

channel
    flame_on, heat_req_on, heat_req_off: **Unit**,
    Flame_On, Heat_On, Heat_Off: **Unit**.
    gas_off, flame_off, no_flame, Gas_On: **Unit**,

variable
    gas:**Bool** := **false**,
    flame:**Bool** := **false**,

value
    Main_Control: **Unit** →
        in heat_req_on,heat_req_off,flame_on
        out gas_off,flame_off,no_flame,Gas_On
        write gas
        Unit

    Flame_Control: **Unit** →
        in gas_off,flame_off,Flame_On
        out flame_on
        write flame
        Unit

    Heat_Control: **Unit** →
        in no_flame,Heat_On,Heat_Off
        out heat_req_on,heat_req_off
        Unit

    Gas_Burner: **Unit** →
        in any
        out any
        write gas,flame
        Unit

    Gas_Burner_System: **Unit** → **write** gas,flame **Unit**

    Gas_Burner_System() ≡
      while true do (Environment() ‖ Gas_Burner()) **end**

    Gas_Burner() ≡
      Flame_Control() ‖ Main_Control() ‖ Heat_Control()

    Flame_Control() ≡
      flame := **false**,
      ((Flame_On?; flame := **true**; flame_on!; flame_off?; flame := **false**)

```
            []
            (gas_off?))

    Heat_Control() ≡
        Heat_On? ; heat_req_on!()
        (no_flame? [] (Heat_Off? ; heat_req_off!()))

    Main_Control() ≡
        gas := false ; heat_req_on? ; wait(30) ; Gas_On!() ; gas := true ;
        ((flame_on? ; heat_req_off? ; gas := false ; flame_off!())
        []
        (wait(1) ; gas_off!() ; gas := false ; no_flame!()))
```

The *Environment* is here modelled in terms of four time durations: $\tau_{\text{initial}}, \tau_{\text{turn\_on}}, \tau_{\text{wait\_for\_flame}}$ and $\tau_{\text{do\_nothing}}$. We do not, i.e., we cannot, prescribe these. The *Environment* is biddable, but is not programmable, as are the other processes.[5]

value
```
    Environment: Unit →
            in Gas_On
            out Heat_On,Heat_Off,Flame_On
            Unit

    Environment() ≡
        wait(τ_initial) ; Heat_On!() ; Gas_On ? ;
        ((wait(τ_turn_on) ; Flame_On!() ; wait(τ_wait_for_flame) ; Heat_Off!())
        []
        wait(τ_do_nothing))
```

∎

15.4.4 Discussion

Example 15.19 was postulated. Although it hinged upon Example 15.18, there really was nothing very explicit about the connection between Examples 15.19 and 15.18. That is, we really ought prove that the Gas_Burner_System of Example 15.19 is correct with respect to the design decisions of Example 15.18. The possibility of, and a reference to such a proof will be given in the next section, which links TRSL with the duration calculus.

---

[5]The terms 'biddable' and 'programmable' will be explained in detail in Vol. 3, Chap. 10.

15.5 RSL with Timing and Durations

This section was written by Chris W. George and Anne E. Haxthausen. It is reproduced here with their kind permissions. It constitutes an excerpt of Sect. 6 of our joint [48].

15.5.1 Review of TRSL

To remind you of TRSL, see the previous section, we give here a few illustrative fragments. First, **wait** may just indicate a delay. Execution of the expression (cf. Sects. 15.4.1–15.4.2 and Example 15.21):

sensor_state := high ; **wait** δ ; sensor_state := low,

will set and keep *sensor_state* high for precisely time δ, and then make it low.

A time out can be modelled by an external choice involving a **wait**. Suppose we need to take some special (abnormal) actions if a signal *normal* does not occur within time t. The expression

normal? ; ...

⌷

wait t ; abnormal!()

will take the first choice provided an output on the channel *normal* occurs within time t. Otherwise, at time t, the wait terminates and the second choice becomes available. Provided there is some process waiting to handle the output *abnormal*, the principle of maximal progress will ensure the second choice occurs, and we would say the normal behaviour has timed out.

Example 15.20 *Train Separation Time:* An example to illustrate the use of time dependence (which is used later in Example 15.21) follows. Suppose the correct behaviour of a system depends on an assumption that trains are separated by more than time δ. It may be safe to just record this as an assumption on our part, because we know it is ensured by other parts of the system, or we may need to specify that if the trains are too close together then an error will be recorded, and some appropriate action taken. In the second case, where we need to record an error, we can specify something like:

value
    detect : **Unit** $\rightarrow$ **in** detect_train **out** train_detected, error **Unit**
    detect() $\equiv$
        while true do
            let t = detect_train? **in**
                if t $\leq$ δ **then** error!()
                else train_detected!()
                end

> **end**
> **end**

An input or output can optionally return the time that it waited for synchronisation: This supports time dependence, i.e., following behaviour can depend on the value of this time. Here the behaviour of *detect* depends on the time *t* that the input *detect_train* (representing the hardware train detection unit) waits. If *t* is too small an error is signalled. Otherwise we pass on the detection event using another channel *train_detected*. Note that correct behaviour of *detect*, in the sense of only reporting actual errors (trains too close together), assumes that the value *t* is the same as the time since the last train, i.e., since the last communication on *detect_train*. This will only be true if there is no wait anywhere in the loop except for the communication on *detect_train*. In particular, we see that the process doing input on *train_detected* must always be ready when *detect* is ready to do output on that channel. This further implies that this other process must have a cycle time of at most δ. This process is described later in Example 15.21.   ∎

In [298, 299] denotational semantics of Timed RSL are given using Duration Calculus, to the combination of which we now turn.

15.5.2 TRSL and Duration Calculus

The Duration Calculi are covered in the seminal work [557]. While TRSL is well-suited for timed design specifications, Duration Calculi is well-suited for timed requirement specifications. This suggests the following development method [204] (illustrated in Fig. 15.14) for real-time systems integrating TRSL and Duration Calculi specifications:

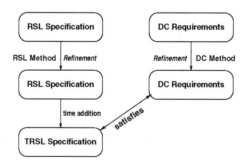

Fig. 15.14. A development method for real-time systems

1. The RAISE method [131] is used for stepwise development of a specification of the untimed properties of the system, starting with an abstract, property-oriented RSL specification and ending with a concrete, implementation-oriented RSL specification.
2. In parallel with the RSL development of the untimed system, a Duration Calculus requirement specification of the real-time properties of that system is developed. State variables in the Duration Calculus specification are variables defined (at least) in the last RSL specification (and in the TRSL specification).
3. Timing information is added to the RSL specification achieving a TRSL specification of a real-time implementation.
4. It must be verified that the TRSL specification satisfies the DC specification.

Hence, there is no syntactic integration between the DC and TRSL specification, but only a consistency requirement that state variables used in the Duration Calculus specification are variables defined in the TRSL specification. The integration is made in the form of a satisfaction (or refinement) relation. The approach for defining this relation has been to make an abstract interpretation within the Duration Calculus formalism of TRSL process definitions. Technically this is done by extending the operational semantics of TRSL [132] with behaviours which are Duration Calculus formulas describing (parts of) the history of the observables of the system. The satisfaction relation between sentences in the two languages is then defined in terms of behaviours. The formal definition and proof rules can be found in [204].

Example 15.21 *Implementation of Train Separation:* We continue Example 15.20.

Problem Description

In some railway control systems sensors are used for train detection. When a train starts passing a sensor, the sensor becomes "high", and after a while it falls back to "low". In order for the control system to be able to detect the high state, the sensor must stay in the high state for a certain minimum of time, δ.

DC Requirements

$$\Box((\lceil\text{sensor\_state=low}\rceil \cdot \lceil\text{sensor\_state=high}\rceil \cdot \lceil\text{sensor\_state=low}\rceil) \Rightarrow \ell \geq \delta)$$

This requirement says that any complete period with high state (i.e., one with a low state before and after) has a duration (ℓ) of at least δ.

TRSL Specification

> **value**
>> δ : Time
>
> **type**
>> SensorState == low | high
>
> **variable**
>> sensor_state:SensorState := low
>
> **channel**
>> train_detected:**Unit**
>
> **value**
>> sensor : **Unit** $\rightarrow$ **in** train_detected **write** sensor_state **Unit**
>> sensor() $\equiv$
>>> sensor_state := low
>>> **while true do**
>>>> train_detected? ;
>>>> sensor_state := high ;
>>>> **wait** δ ;
>>>> sensor_state := low
>>> **end**;

The process *sensor* models the behaviour of a sensor. It ensures the Duration Calculus requirement in terms of the *sensor_state* staying high for exactly δ time units each time.

In order to meet the *system* requirement that the *sensor_state* goes high *after each and every train* (or an error is reported) we also need to use the specification in Example 15.20 of the function *detect* to check that the trains are more than δ apart. Recall that *detect* required that the loop containing the *train_detected* inputs has a delay between such inputs of at most δ, and that is clearly satisfied by *sensor*. (We also need some assurance that every train causes an output on *detect_train*, which is an assumption about the train detection hardware.)

Satisfaction Relation

The following satisfaction relation expresses that the *sensor* process satisfies the previously stated Duration Calculus requirements:

> sensor() **satisfies**
> $\Box((\lceil \text{sensor\_state=low} \rceil \cdot \lceil \text{sensor\_state=high} \rceil \cdot \lceil \text{sensor\_state=low} \rceil) \Rightarrow \ell \geq \delta)$

The satisfaction relation can be proved to hold using proof rules in [204] and the Duration Calculus proof rules given in [557]. ∎

15.6 Discussion

15.6.1 General

We have covered three closely related facets of temporal logics. The classical temporal logic of 'sometimes' and 'always' (derived from Prior's work), the more recent Interval and Linear Temporal Logics (which, for our purposes are the same, i.e., ITL=LTL) and the Duration Calculus (DC). For the latter there were extensions with respect to transition modalities. And for the latter there are further variants, for which we refer to the seminal book on DC [557]. Section 15.7 discusses further aspects of temporal logics.

15.6.2 Principles, Techniques and Tools

We summarise:

Principles. *Quantitative Models of Time:* A main principle concerning the treatment of time appears to be: Try avoid bringing explicit time into your models. When reasoning, in your models, about time-dependent properties of the universe of discourse, avoid establishing (possibly quantified) variables of type time. Instead use the temporal logic modalities (for example, of 'sometimes', 'always', etc.).   ∎

Techniques. *Quantitative Models of Time:* The techniques follow from the explicit choice of which temporal logic is chosen as the medium or tool of expression. With classical temporal logic, using only the 'sometime' ($\Diamond$) and the 'always' ($\Box$) modalities, the techniques can be cumbersome. With the Interval/Linear Temporal Logics the techniques allow for more sophistication. And with Duration Calculus we believe we have a comprehensive and rather satisfactory set of techniques covered in this chapter.   ∎

Tools. *Quantitative Models of Time:* Several tools, i.e., both languages of expression and software tools for supporting the use of these languages, exist:

- (Ana)Tempura: An interpreter for executable Interval Temporal Logic formulae developed over the years [77].
- DCVALID: A suite of tools for Duration Calculus programmed by Paritosh K. Pandya at Tata Institute of Fundamental Research [386].
- TLA+ Tools: A set of tools for TLA+ including syntax analyser, model checker and simulator [283].

There are many more.   ∎

15.7 Bibliographical Notes

We have brought in material on temporal logic based primarily on Bruno Dutertre's Interval Temporal Logic (ITL) [105], and on Zhou ChaoChen and Michael Reichhardt Hansen's Duration Calculus (DC) [557]. Instead of, or as an adjunct to, the Duration Calculus, we could have presented Leslie Lamport's also very elegant and considerably researched and engineered TLA+, Temporal Logic of Actions [281,282,339]. We encourage the reader to study [557] (Duration Calculus) and [282] (TLA+).

• • •

Amir Pnueli first [403], it seems, reported on the idea of using temporal logic to specify properties of certain kinds of programs. Zohar Manna and Amir Pnueli developed this idea into book form: [320,321]. Those books, as well as a third, so far unpublished volume [322] are at the basis of the powerful tool set: STeP, Stanford Temporal Prover [55,56,319].

Manna and Pnueli's approach, as many other verification-based approaches (HOL and Isabelle [380], PVS [384,385,466,467], and SPIN [215]), seems focused, not on specification in the sense of the present volumes, namely of complete domains, complete requirements and complete software designs, but on the specification of a claimed property of some isolated, say crucial part of a domain, of some requirements or of some software design. The HOL, Isabelle, PVS, SPIN, and STeP tools can then support verification of such a property. Linear Temporal Logic, LTL, a predecessor of Dutertre's work on Interval Temporal Logic, ITL, is associated with Ben Moszkowski [372,373]. Sometimes LTL is also referred to as ITL.

15.8 Exercises

These exercises were kindly provided by Dr. Michael Reichhardt Hansen.

Exercise 15.1. *Miscellaneous Small Examples.* Specify the following properties using propositional duration calculus (i.e. $\forall x$ and $\exists x$ must not be used):

1. Pressing the button, a green lamp is on within 3 seconds or a red lamp is on within 7 seconds.
2. Gas is not leaking continuously for more than 5 seconds.
3. An elevator door is open for at least 6 seconds.
4. A light is on at least 15 seconds after the button has been pressed.

Exercise 15.2. *An Inverting C-Gate.* An inverting C-gate is a circuit with two input ports X and Y and with an output port Z. The circuit has a constant delay of $\delta > 0$. The function of the gate is described by:

• If X and Y are different at time t (i.e. $X(t) \neq Y(t)$), then $Z(t+\delta) = Y(t)$.

- If X and Y have the same value at time t (i.e. $X(t) = Y(t)$), then Z does not change its value at time $t + \delta$.

Specify an inverting C-gate in propositional Duration Calculus.

Exercise 15.3. *Scheduling.* Give specifications of the following scheduling disciplines: (1) Round Robin scheduling with a fixed time slice and (2) a first-come first-served scheduling.

Try to avoid using universal and existential quantifications in your specification. Make your specifications as simple as possible.

Part VII

INTERPRETER AND COMPILER
DEFINITIONS

This part will show how to specify compilers and interpreters for various kinds of programming languages.

What do we mean by "specifying compilers and interpreters for a programming language"?

- To specify the semantics of a programming language means to present formulas that ascribe semantic meanings to programs in that language.
- To specify interpreters for a programming language means to present formulas that to each program in that language prescribe computations that yield the same result as if the meaning (function) was applied to program arguments.
- To specify compilers for a (source) programming language, for a given target computer, means to present formulas that to each program in that (source) language prescribes a sequence of instructions of the target computer — a sequence which, when applied to an initial computer state embodying (i.e., encoding) the program arguments, yields the same result as if the meaning (function) was applied to program arguments.

We shall illustrate four kinds of programming language developments:

- SAL: Interpreter and compiler specification of a simple applicative language.
- SIL: Interpreter specification of a simple imperative language.
- SMIL: Interpreter specification of a simple, modular imperative language.
- SPIL: Interpreter specification of a simple parallel, imperative language.

The CHILL [159, 160] and Ada [54, 82] compilers developed in Denmark in the early 1980s were developed using the principles and techniques outlined in the next four chapters.

16

SAL: Simple Applicative Language

- The **prerequisite** for studying this chapter is that you are well familiar with the applicative modelling styles of RSL.
- The **aims** are to introduce a notion of stepwise, informal, but systematic development of compiler specifications from denotational semantics definitions, to do so for a simple applicative, i.e., functional language, and to illustrate classical, yet still fully relevant run-time structures for procedural program execution (stacks, dynamic and static (lexicographic) chains, and the functional result (i.e., the FUNARG) problem.
- The **objective** is to enable you — we claim — to far better understand, and hence far more safely implement, compilers for procedural languages.
- The **treatment** is systematic and ranging informal to formal.

> By applicative programming we shall mean the same as functional programming. Functional programming languages — including LISP [333], and modern ones like SML [168, 359], Miranda [505] and Haskell [503] — focus on programming in terms of (i) function definitions, of (ii) function applications and (iii) functional values. Imperative programming languages inherit two (i–ii) or all of these concepts.

In this section we shall illustrate the development of a requirements for a compiler for a functional language, here referred to as the Simple Applicative Language (SAL). We start with a domain model of SAL in Sect. 16.3. Sections 16.4–16.6 "unravel" that semantics into a semantics definition expressed, not in terms of an abstract specification, but in terms of constructs very close to ordinary (machine) programming. Section 16.7 defines an assembler language, and Sects. 16.8–16.10 define, as compiling algorithms, and in three different ways, the requirements: exactly which assembler language code a compiler must generate for each specific source language, SAL, construct. Section 16.8 does so semi-abstractly, while Sects. 16.9–16.10 do so in terms of what is known as attributed grammars.

This chapter is necessarily detailed. The techniques and the main results of this chapter are those of Sects. 16.6 and 16.8. These results will be applied, amongst others, in Chaps. 17 and 18. There we will present the denotational and the macroexpansion semantics without much detail — relying on the present sections' many such details. Only in this chapter will we present the further development of the macroexpansion semantics into compiling algorithms.

16.1 A Caveat

The formulas in this and the next chapters (Chaps. 17–19) are deliberately expressed in a deterministic subset of RSL, and in such a way that the chosen subset constitutes a general denotational semantics specification language, which allows full recursive map definitions involving recursive functions as range elements. The problem is that "full" RSL cannot handle the recursive definition of maps

let rρ = iρ $\cup$ [n $\mapsto$ f(s(n))(rρ)] **in** rρ **end**

where iρ, n, f and s are some appropriate quantities. By resorting to a severely restricted subset of RSL and endowing that subset with a suitable minimal semantics — commensurate with the full RSL's all fix point semantics — we can meaningfully express such recursively defined maps. We thus take the liberty of doing so in this chapter of these volumes, and otherwise referring the interested reader to any of the standard textbooks on semantics: [93, 158, 432, 448, 499, 533].

16.2 The SAL Syntax

An informal description of a language would ideally consist of four parts: (i) a presentation of the pragmatics, (ii) informal presentation of the semantic types, (iii) informal presentation of the syntactic types, and (iv) informal presentation of the semantics of each syntactic construct — all presented in some possibly interwoven fashion. Recall that we have argued that pragmatics is most important, that the semantic types capture the essence of the semantics, and that it is entities of the syntactic types that denote entities of semantic types.

16.2.1 Informal Exposition of SAL Syntax

SAL is a simple applicative language whose programs are expressions. There are nine expression categories:

Expression Categories	Examples	Abstract Syntax Name
*Const*ants	k	mk_Cst
*Vari*ables	id	mk_Var
Prefix expressions	-e	mk_Pre
Infix expressions	e1 + e2	mk_Inf
*Cond*itional expressions	**if** et **then** ec **else** ea **fi**	mk_If
*Lamb*da Functions	**fun** id.ed	L, mk_Lam
Simple *Let* Blocks	**let** id = ed **in** eb **end**	mk_Let
*Rec*ursive Functions	**letrec** g(id) = ed **in** eb **end**	mk_Rec
*Appl*ications	ef(ea)	mk_App

Most of our RSL elaboration functions, not quite incidentally, will be expressed in a simple language like SAL. Blocks with multiple definitions can be "mimicked" by multiply nested simple (*Let*) blocks. Multiple mutually recursive functions, however, cannot be explicitly defined other than through the use of formal function arguments.

16.2.2 Formal Exposition of SAL Syntax

From Sect. 16.2.1, it should be relatively easy to construct a formal syntax:

type V
   Pro :: E
   E == mk_Cst(i:**Int**)
     | mk_Var(v:V)
⊙ | mk_Pre(po:POp,e:E)
⊘ | mk_Inf(le:E,io:IOp,re:E)
     | mk_If(b:E,c:E,a:E)
     | L
     | mk_Let(v:V,d:E,b:E)
     | mk_Rec(f:V,λe:L,b:E)
     | mk_App(f:E,a:E)
   L == mk_Lam(x:V,e:E)
⊙ POp == minus | factorial | not | ...
⊘ IOp == add | sub | mpy | div | eq | neq | ...

Constants stand for Integer numbers. No provision is made for explicitly representing Booleans. The prefix constant operators, generically referred to as ⊙, are then the usual ones: Arithmetic Minus and Factorial, and the Booleans, the logical Negation; and so are the infix constant operators, generically referred to as ⊘, the arithmetic Addition, Subtraction, Multiply, Divide, etc., and the logical And, Or, Imply, Equal, and Not Equal. Booleans can be represented implicitly as terms involving arithmetics and logical operators.

16.2.3 Comments

SAL may seem awfully trivial to those who are used to programming with an ample supply and type variety of assignable variables, but its realisation, as shown here, illustrates most of the more intricate aspects of interpreter and compiler design. The main reason for this should be seen in SAL's ability to express nested block structures and to yield FUNction VALues out of their defining scope (that, is the so-called FUNARG[1] property [368, 529]). The development thus concentrates on implementing the block structure and function invocation aspects.

16.3 A Denotational Semantics

16.3.1 An Informal Semantics

We suggest that the reader also keep a finger on the formula pages of Sect. 16.3.2 in order to better follow the informal semantics explanation that now follows. Our use of initially capitalised sequences of pronounceable names is meant to refer to identifiers of the formal model.

SAL programs express only three kinds of VALues: integer numbers, truth-valued Booleans, and FUNction VALues. These latter are entities which are functions from VALues to VALues, where these latter VALues again include FUNctions, etc. The VALue of a variable identifier, 'id', is that of the possibly recursively defined defining expression: 'ed' (respectively: 'fixλg.λid.ed') of the lexicographically youngest incarnation, that is, the "outward-going" statically closest embracing block. **fix** is the fix point-finding function which when applied to 'λg.λid.ed' yields the "smallest" solution to the equation: 'g(id)=ed', in which 'g' occurs free in 'ed' (see Vol. 1, Chap. 7, Sect. 7.8.3). Infix and conditional expression VALues are as you expect them to be. The VALue of a block is that of the expression body, 'eb', in which all free occurrences of the 'id' of a **let**, respectively the 'g' of a **letrec**, block header definition have been replaced (or substituted) by their VALues. That is, 'ed' is evaluated in an environment, env$'$, which is exactly that extension of the block-embracing environment, env, which binds 'id' (respectively 'g') to its VALue, and otherwise binds as env. The VALue of a lambda-expression, 'λid.ed', is the FUNction of 'id' that 'ed' denotes in the environment in which it is first encountered, that is, is first defined. Finally: the VALue of an application, 'ef(ea)', is the result of applying the FUNction VALue, that 'ef' designates, to the VALue designated by 'ea'.

---

[1] A specification or a programming language is said to have the FUNARG property if functions are first class values, that is, can be yielded as results of function invocation. See also footnote 5.

16.3.2 A Formal Semantics

This definition expresses the semantics of SAL denotationally, i.e., in terms of mathematical functions, and homomorphically, i.e., the semantics of a compound syntactic object is expressed as the (homomorphic) functional composition of the denotations, i.e., semantics of the individual, proper components. The denoted functions are themselves expressed in terms of semantic types, and these are again functional.

The specification language used in this section is a syntactic subset of RSL whose semantics "subset" is one which allows recursive definition of functional values and which prescribes a minimum fix point semantics. We shall only assume this "subset RSL" in this section.

Semantic Types

We make the distinction between designated values and (denoted) denotations. A value (v:VAL) is the result of an evaluation of an expression in some context which binds identifiers to values. A denotation (D:DEN) is the (usually functional) meaning of an expression, regardless of the environment, i.e., as a function from environments to "something".

type
 ENV = V $\overrightarrow{m}$ VAL
 VAL = Num | Tru | FCT
 Num :: **Int**
 Tru :: **Bool**
 FCT :: VAL $\overset{\sim}{\to}$ VAL
 DEN = ENV $\overset{\sim}{\to}$ VAL

Denotations are the semantic values of expressions. Expression evaluation must refer to values of identifiers, the evaluation of which needs an environment in which to look up these values. Hence the denotation is a function from environments to values. Thus we speak of the denotation of an expression as its "semantic (i.e., denoted) value" and of the value of an expression as the "evaluated (i.e., designated) value".

Operator Meanings

The meanings of the operators are seen, denotationally, as functions from their operand values to result values. These functions are here expressed in terms of the specification language lambda function concept:

value
 M: POp $\to$ (**Int** $\to$ **Int**)
 M(o) $\equiv$ **case** o **of**: minus $\to$ λx • $-$x, ... **end**

M: IOp $\rightarrow$ (**Int** $\times$ **Int** $\rightarrow$ (**Bool** | **Int**))
M(o) $\equiv$
    case o **of**:
        add $\rightarrow$ λx • λy • x+y, ..., eq $\rightarrow$ λx • λy • x=y ...
    end

We shall use the operator meaning function M throughout the many-development-stage treatment of SAL.

Semantic Functions

Programs are expressions to be evaluated in an empty environment. Otherwise we refer the reader to our informal exposition of the semantics of SAL starting in Sect. 16.3.1.

value
    M: Pro $\xrightarrow{\sim}$ VAL, M: E $\xrightarrow{\sim}$ DEN
[0] M(mk_Pro(e)) $\equiv$ M(e)[]
[1] M(mk_Cst(k))ρ $\equiv$ k
[2] M(mk_Var(v))ρ $\equiv$ ρ(v)
[3] M(mk_Pre(o,e))ρ $\equiv$ M(o)M(e)ρ
[4] M(mk_Inf(le,o,re))ρ $\equiv$ M(o)(M(le)ρ,M(re)ρ)
[5] M(mk_If(b,c,a))ρ $\equiv$ **if** M(b)ρ **then** M(c)ρ **else** M(a)ρ **end**
[6] M(mk_Lam(v,e))ρ $\equiv$ λa.(**let** nρ = ρ † [v $\mapsto$ a] **in** M(e)nρ **end**)
[7] M(mk_Let(v,d,b))ρ $\equiv$ **let** nρ = ρ † [v $\mapsto$ M(d)ρ] **in** M(b)nρ **end**
[8] M(mk_Rec(f,mk_Lam(v,e),b))ρ $\equiv$
        let nρ = ρ † [v $\mapsto$ M(e)nρ] **in** M(b)nρ **end**
[9] M(mk_App(f,a))ρ $\equiv$ (M(f)ρ)(M(a)ρ)

Observe the recursion in the definition of nρ in the definition of the meaning of recursive 'let' expressions. (It is the nρ, in the next but last line of the formulas above, which is being recursively defined.) Compare that to the definition of nρ in the two other semantics equations: Those of 'lambda' and simple 'let' expressions.

    By "moving" ($\rightsquigarrow$) the M function argument ρ "over, onto the other side" of the defining equation ($\equiv$) we get:

$$M(e)\rho \equiv \mathcal{E}(\rho) \ \rightsquigarrow\ M(e) \equiv \lambda\rho.\mathcal{E}(\rho)$$

and we see that the meanings of expressions are indeed denotations of the right kind.

16.3.3 Review of SAL Semantics, 1

The reader may feel cheated: We have explained the semantic functions of
SAL in a language reminiscent of a subset of the RSL specification language.
How can we defend this apparent circularity? Well, it is not circular. First,
the two languages are indeed different. SAL has two environment bindings:
one that allows defined (simple) functions to have their free identifiers bound
in the embracing environment, and another that allows defined (recursive)
functions to have free occurrences in the body of their definition of their
function identifier bound in the environment their definition gives rise to,
hence recursive.

```
/* a simple binding */
(let f=4 in
 (let f=λx.a+f
   in f(3) end)
 end)
 ≡
 7

/* in contrast to a recursive binding */
(let f=4 in
 (letrec f=λx.if x=0 then 1 else x*f(n−1) end
   in f(3) end)
 end)
 ≡
 6
```

RSL has only recursive bindings, and since it always has that we leave out the
suffix **rec**. Second, SAL is explained in terms of RSL, and RSL is defined in
terms of mathematics. (We do not show, in these volumes, the RSL semantics
— we only explain it informally!) So they only cosmetically look the same.
In fact, we have indeed cheated: When in the semantics of recursive function
definitions in SAL we defined a new environment recursively, we "went outside
the realm" of RSL. Such recursive definitions of higher-order function types
are, in general, not possible in RSL. So how can we defend that? We cannot,
really, other than by saying: Since the function defined recursively is only
recursive in itself, not by reference to several other functions defined at the
same level — and since this is not possible in SAL, where at most one function
can be defined at every **let • in • end** level, i.e., in each such "block activation"
— one can show that there are indeed solutions to the recursive equations
within the RSL semantics.

   We have, however, achieved a good basis for a development that now
follows: via increasing steps of concreteness to a compiling algorithm for a hypothetical machine. In that sense it is not so important that SAL is a rather

"timid" language. Its concept of function definitions, blocks and function applications is so powerful it can serve as a basis for our subsequent imperative, modular and parallel process language developments.

16.3.4 Two Asides

Of Things to Come!

In subsequent sections we shall follow each example by giving further, increasingly more concrete examples. These definitions are increasingly more 'computational', that is, can best be understood as *specifying sequences of computations* given an input, or, in other words, an initial binding of variables to their meaning. The last definition "unzips" user-defined functions by permitting a *compile-time macro-expansion* of the definition. In doing so it relies on pre-processing SAL program-defined functions into **label** and **goto** "bracketed" metalanguage texts, and calls of these functions into (*branch and link-like*) **goto**s to such texts. The principles of properly *saving, updating* — that is, "setting-up" — and *restoring* — that is, "taking-down" and "reinstalling" — *calling* and *defining environments*, form a detailed description. This description does this more than any of the preceding definitions, and of otherwise published accounts of this so-called *static (environmentally preceding)* and *dynamic (call)* activation chain mechanism.

The Most Recent Error

Consider the following program[2]:

```
1.  (let p = λx.
2.     (let h = λ().
3.        skip
4.     in x(h())
5.     end)
6.  in p(p)
7.  end)
```

We will now assume that the reader has informally learned about implementation of block structures, function definitions and function invocation, for example, in programming courses on functional or imperative programming. If not, then please skip this aside section, and proceed. These volumes, in particular the next sections, will then teach you that! That is, a main purpose of Sect. 16 is to show how informal explications, from [414] via [6,150] to [14], can be sharpened into far more precise descriptions.

---

[2]This example is taken from Hans Langmaack [383]. In that reference Langmaack shows how Edsger W. Dijkstra [100] implemented his Algol 60 compiler for the **X1** machine.

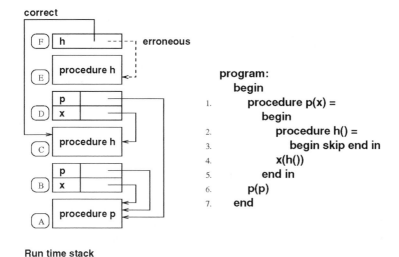

Fig. 16.1. The "most recent error" example

Figure 16.1, in addition to repeating the program text in a slightly different notation, also shows a so-called activation stack for a program execution that has reached program point (3) via program points (6) and (4) in that order. As a result a "bottom-most" activation, $\boxed{\text{A}}$, has been first established, at program point (1). The definition corresponding to program points (1–4) leads to activation $\boxed{\text{A}}$ recording the meaning, $\mathcal{P}$, at this point, of procedure p. At program point (6) invocation (i.e., "call") p(p) results in activation $\boxed{\text{B}}$. It binds both the procedure identifier p and the formal parameter x to $\mathcal{P}$. "Inside" procedure p's definition we note the meaning, $\mathcal{H}$, at this program point (2), of procdure h in activation $\boxed{\text{C}}$. At program point (4) invocation (i.e., "call") x(h) results in activation $\boxed{\text{D}}$. It binds formal procedure identifier x, which has actual argument p, to $\mathcal{P}$, and it binds formal parameter x, which has actual argument h, to $\mathcal{H}$. It is formal parameter x since the (formal) procedure invoked is named p whose formal parameter is x. Eventually program point (2) will be entered — since the actual argument, h(), of x(h()) has to be evaluated. This leads to an activation $\boxed{\text{E}}$ which records a new meaning, $\mathcal{H}'$, for the locally defined procedure h. "Entering" the body of procedure named h, program point (3), leads to a final activation $\boxed{\text{E}}$ which records the bindings of the formal procedure identifier h. The value of h passed as part of the actual argument in x(h()) is, of course, the value that h had at program point (4) — namely the "old", first $\mathcal{H}$ — and not the "most recent" $\mathcal{H}'$.

16.4 A First-Order Applicative Semantics

We continue our use of initially capitalised sequences of pronounceable names which are meant to refer to identifiers of the formal model.

Implementation languages, including hardware machines, usually do not have function values — hence we must "transform" and make more concrete the function VALue, FCT, and the ENVironment concepts of the previous step of development (Sect. 16.3). Thus the abstract VALue of the previous stage of development (Sect. 16.3 Semantic Types) will be implemented in terms of less abstract, but still applicative, values VALa. FunCTion VALues are constructed from lambda expressions, i.e., text values, mk_Lam(v,e) and from ENVironments (Sect. 16.3 Semantic Types). Concrete FunCTion VALues (see Page 577) will be called CLOSures — referring to the "wrapping" of lambda-expression texts with concrete, implemented ENVironments. So we implement FunCTions as CLOSures. ENVironments — which before were maps from identifiers to abstract values — will now be implemented, ENVa, as lists of binding: pairs of identifiers and their now more concrete values, Bind*.

By a first-order (applicative) semantics definition we mean one whose semantic types are nonfunctional, but which is still referentially transparent.[3] Hence, if we were given, as a basis, a denotational semantics we would have to transform its functional components into such objects which by means of suitable "simulations" can mimic the essential aspects of the denotational definition. We now exemplify the notion of transforming functional types into non-functional ones.

16.4.1 Syntactic Types

See Sect. 16.2.2 for the formal SAL syntax.

16.4.2 Semantic Types

From the denotational semantics definition of SAL, two kinds of types are to be transformed: $\text{ENV} = \text{Id} \xrightarrow{m} \text{DEN}$, and among DENotations: $\text{FUN} = \text{DEN} \rightarrow \text{DEN}$.

The former objects were constructed by means of expressions:

let $n\rho = \rho \dagger [v \mapsto a]$ **in** $M(e)n\rho$ **end**
let $n\rho = \rho \dagger [v \mapsto M(d)\rho]$ **in** $M(b)n\rho$ **end**
let $n\rho = \rho \dagger [v \mapsto M(\lambda e)n\rho]$ **in** $M(b)n\rho$ **end**

---

[3] By referential transparency we mean a property that a language may possess or not possess. A language is said to be referentially transparent if the meaning of a composite sentence remains the same whenever any sentence component has been replaced by another sentence component having the same meaning as the replaced component.

The latter objects were denoted by an expression basically of the lambda form:

λa.(**let** nρ = ρ † [v $\mapsto$ a] **in** M(e)nρ **end**)

We shall not motivate the transformation choices further, nor state general derivation principles. Rather we present the transformed objects as "faits accomplis": ENV objects, which are maps ($\rightarrow\!\!\!\!\!m$), as ENVa objects of the tuple type, with extensions (†) accomplished in terms of concatenations (^), and functional application as directed, linear searches (l_search). The mathematical functions, fun, denoted by lambda-expressions are then realized as so-called closures. These are "passive" (i.e., semisyntactic) structures, which pair the (syntactic) expression, d, to be evaluated, with the defining (semantic) environment, env′, so that when fun is to be applied, fun(val), then a simulation of the application of clos to the transformed counterpart, arg, of val, is performed: apply1(clos,arg).

Instead of now presenting the more concrete, first-order functional elaboration functions we first present arguments for why we believe that our choices will do the job. Those arguments are stated as *retrieve*, that is, *abstraction functions* and abs_ENV, abs_DEN, which apply to the transformed objects and yield the more abstract "ancestors" from which they were derived. We next observe that the definition is still functional, as was the denotational. All arguments are explicit, there is no reference to assignable/declared variables. And we finally note that we cannot, given a specific expression, e, "stick" it into the l (function definition together with an initial, say empty environment) and by macrosubstitution eliminate all references to l. The reason for this failure will be seen in our stacking closures, whose subsequent application requires l.

type
    ENVa = Bind*
    Bind == mk_Simp(id:V,den:VALa) | mk_Rec(f:V,λe:L)
    VALa = Num | Tru | CLOS
    CLOS == mk_CLOS(λe:L,env:ENVa)
    DENa = ENVa $\overset{\sim}{\rightarrow}$ VALa

We refer to the introductory parts of this section for a guide to the above definitions.

16.4.3 Abstraction Functions

Whenever a step of development concretises some types wrt. their apparently more abstract, earlier counterparts, it behooves the developer to state in which way the pairs of concrete versus abstract types relate. This is done here in terms of abstraction functions. Two such must be expressed: One that maps concrete (list of pairs) environments to the abstract (map) associations, abs_ENV; and one, abs_VALa, that maps concrete values, VALa, to abstract values, VAL. abs_ENV invokes abs_VALa.

value
   abs_ENV: ENVa → ENV
   abs_ENV(enva) ≡
     if enva = ⟨⟩ **then** [ ] **else**
     let ρ = abs_ENV(**tl** enva) **in**
     case hd enva **of**
       mk_Simp(v,den) → ρ † [v ↦ abs_VAL(den)],
       mk_Rec(f,ℓ) → **let** nρ = ρ † [f ↦ M(ℓ)nρ] **in** nρ **end**
     end end end

Observe how **abs_ENV** makes use of the M function of the previous stage, as does **abs_VAL**:

value
   abs_VAL: VALa → VAL
   abs_VAL(vala) ≡
     case vala **of**
       mk_CLOS(mk_Lam(v,e),enva)
         → λa.(M(e)(abs_ENV(enva)) † [v↦a]),
       _ → vala
     end

16.4.4 Auxiliary Functions

Since the environment is no longer a map to which one can just provide identifiers and obtain, by map application, their values, we must search for it in the list. Since we conjoin new pairs to the list at its head, we search as from the head of the list.[4]

value
   I_search: V × ENVa $\overset{\sim}{\rightarrow}$ VALa
   I_search(v,env) ≡
     if env = ⟨⟩ **then** chaos **else**
     case hd env **of**
       mk_Simp(v,den) → den,
       mk_Rec(v,λe) → mk_CLOS(λe,env),
       _ → I_search(v,**tl** env)
     end end

---

[4]A series of embedded blocks, from outer to inner, may redefine an identifier. That is, an identifier of an embracing block may be redefined by an enclosed block. Identifier value pairs of inner blocks are concatenated to the head, and since they are the lexicographically scoped identifier values bound to inner occurrences of these identifiers we must first retrieve them.

And similarly, since function values are no longer "real" functions, but closures, we must interpret these closures:

value
    apply: CLOS × VALa $\overset{\sim}{\to}$ VALa
    apply(clos,arg) ≡
       case clos **of**
          mk_CLOS(mk_Lam(v,e),env) →
            let env' = ⟨mk_Simp(v,arg)⟩^env **in** I(e)env' **end**,
          _ → **chaos**
       end

16.4.5 Semantic Functions

The reader is well-advised to compare, function definition by function definition, those below, named I, with those, named M, in Sect. 16.3.2.

Semantic Function Signatures

Previous step:
value
    M: Pro $\overset{\sim}{\to}$ VAL, M: E $\overset{\sim}{\to}$ DEN

Present step:
value
    I: Pro $\overset{\sim}{\to}$ VALa, I: E $\overset{\sim}{\to}$ DENa

---

Program Interpretation

Previous step:
[0] M(mk_Pro(e)) ≡ M(e)[ ]

Present step:
[0] I(mk_Pro(e)) ≡ I(e)⟨⟩

Constant Expression Interpretation

Previous step:
[1] M(mk_Cst(k))ρ ≡ k

Present step:

[1] I(mk_ Cst(k))(env) ≡ k

--------- Variable Expression Interpretation ---------

Previous step:

[2] M(mk_ Var(v))ρ ≡ ρ(v)

Present step:

[2] I(mk_Var(v))(env) ≡ I_search(v,env)

--------- Prefix Expression Interpretation ---------

Previous step:

[3] M(mk_ Pre(o,e))ρ ≡ M(o)M(e)ρ

Present step:

[3] I(mk_Pre(o,e))(env) ≡ M(o)(I(e)(env))

--------- Infix Expression Interpretation ---------

Previous step:

[4] M(mk_ Inf(le,o,re))ρ ≡ M(o)(M(le)ρ,M(re)ρ)

Present step:

[4] I(mk_Inf(le,o,re))(env) ≡ M(o)(I(le)(env),I(re)(env))

--------- Conditional Expression Interpretation ---------

Previous step:

[5] M(mk_If(b,c,a))ρ ≡ **if** M(b)ρ **then** M(c)ρ **else** M(a)ρ **end**

Present step:

[5] I(mk_If(b,c,a))(env) ≡ **if** I(b)(env) **then** I(c)(env) **else** I(a)(env) **end**

———————————— Lambda-Expression Interpretation ————————————

Previous step:

[6] M(mk_Lam(v,e))ρ ≡ λa.(**let** nρ = ρ † [v ↦ a] **in** M(e)nρ **end**)

Present step:

[6] I(mk_Lam(v,e))(env) ≡ mk_CLOS(mk_Lam(v,e),env)

It is especially in the above function [re]definition we start to see the development!

———————————— Simple Let Expression Interpretation, 1 ————————————

Previous step:

[7] M(mk_Let(v,d,b))ρ ≡
      let nρ = ρ † [v ↦ M(d)ρ]
      in M(b)nρ **end**

Present step:

[7] I(mk_Let(v,d,b))(env) ≡
      let val = I(d)(env) **in**
      let env′ = ⟨mk_Simp(v,val)⟩^env **in**
      I(b)(env′) **end end**

———————————— Recursive Let Expression Interpretation ————————————

Previous step:

[8] M(mk_Rec(f,mk_Lam(v,e),b))ρ ≡
      let nρ = ρ † [v ↦ M(e)nρ]
      in M(b)nρ **end**

Present step:

[8] I(mk_Rec(f,mk_Lam(v,e),b))(env) $\equiv$
        let env$'$ = $\langle$mk_Rec(f,mk_Lam(v,e))$\rangle\hat{}$env **in** I(b)(env$'$) **end**

─────────── Function Application Expression Interpretation ───────────

Previous step:

[9] M(mk_App(f,a))ρ $\equiv$
        let fct = M(f)ρ, arg = M(a)ρ **in** fct(arg) **end**

Present step:

[9] I(mk_App(f,a))(env) $\equiv$
        let arg = I(a)(env), fct = I(f)(env) **in** apply(fct,arg) **end**

16.4.6 Review

The example development of this section is based on Reynolds [428]. The FUNARG notion[5] is described in [368, 529]. It remains to show that the first-order semantics of this section is correct wrt. the denotational semantics of the previous section. We shall not prove that here, instead we refer to the literature. The theorem to be proved amounts to a recursively defined predicate (see [350, 498]). Early examples of fully rigorous proofs are given in [349, 355, 486, 487]. Standard, more recent textbooks on semantics [93, 158, 432, 448, 499, 533] also give correctness proof examples.

We remind the reader that, in the case of the SAL, SIL and SMIL language definitions of Chaps 16–18, we are relying on a non-standard variant of the RAISE specification language RSL, a variant in which we basically disallow all nondeterminism (incl. sets!) and otherwise constrain RSL in such a way as to obtain a traditional denotational semantics definition language with minimal fix point meanings. In this way we can define functional values recursively, as nρ.

16.4.7 Review of SAL Semantics, 2

In a small step of development we have concretised maps as lists of pairs, and functions as closures of function definitions and the context which binds

─────────

[5]The FUNARG notion is that of being able to pass functions as parameters, and, more particularly, to have functions returned as values of function applications — whereby such returned functions may subsequently be applied "outside" their defining environment.

free identifiers of the function definition text. Simple value bindings are kept simple (mk_Simp), whereas recursively defined value bindings are marked as being so (mk_Rec). We have kept a functional (also known as applicative) definition style.

This means that the semantics definition of this step does not yield functions as values, only closures. But function applications take place as if the applied closures are indeed functions. The definition of this chapter relies on the specification language scope concept to define local environments.

16.5 An Abstract, Imperative Stack Semantics

So far our semantics definitions have been recursively specified: on the inductive structure of the syntax of the object (source) languages, and on the computations they denote. In this section we unravel these recursions by means of stacks. That is, we transform (not necessarily only tail-recursive[6]) function definitions into nonrecursive function definitions plus a stack data structure.

By an abstract state (machine) stack semantics we understand a definition which typically employs globally declared variables of abstract, possibly higher-level, type. It expresses the semantics (not in terms of applicatively defined, "grand" state transformations on this state, but) in terms of statement sequences denoting a computational process of individual, "smaller" state transformations.

16.5.1 Design Decisions — Informal Motivation

In this section we shall state, and informally motivate, our decisions to change the applicative, hence explicitly provided semantic arguments (of semantic functions), to imperative, global state components. Hence these arguments now become implicitly provided.

In the case of SAL we choose to map the semantic ENVa arguments onto a globally declared variable, estk (for environment stack), thereby removing these arguments from the elaboration function references. By doing so we must additionally mimic the metalanguage's own recursion capability. Otherwise we would be cheating by making no progress towards a more concrete definition, one that is expressed in a language more directly mechanisable by a computer without built-in stacks.

Thus the type of estk is to become a stack of stacks. Each estk element is that stack of Vs and their values, which when looked_up properly (cf.

---

[6]By a function being tail-recursively defined we mean that the function definition is, schematically, of the form: **value** f,g: $A \to B$, h: $A \to A$, p: $A \to$ **Bool**, f(a) $\equiv$ **if** p(a) **then** g(a) **else** f(h(a)) **end**. An example of a recursive function definition which is not tail-recursive is: **value** f,g,k: $A \to B$, h: $A \to A$, p: $A \to$ **Bool**, f(a) $\equiv$ **if** p(a) **then** g(a) **else let** $a' = f(h(a))$ **in** k(a') **end end**.

abs_ENV) reflects the bindings of the so-called "lexicographically youngest incarnations" of each identifier in the static scope, that is, in "going outwards" from the identifier-use through embracing blocks towards the outermost program expression level. As long as no **let** or **letrec** defined function is being applied, the estk will contain exactly one ENVa element. As soon as a defined function is applied, the calling environment is dumped on the estk stack. On its top is pushed the ENVa environment current when the function was defined.

In addition, we choose to mechanize the recursive stacking of temporaries, by means of a global value stack, vstk. We could have merged vstk into estk, but at present we decide not to. Hence this abstract machine definition also requires further decomposition of the look_up operation. As before, we state our beliefs as to why we think the present development is on the right track. We do so by presenting retrieve (also known as *abstraction*) *functions*.

16.5.2 Semantics Style Observations

The abstract state machine semantics definition is said to be an operational, or to be a *mechanical* or, which is just a third name for the same idea, a *computational semantics* definition, since it specifies the meaning of SAL by describing the operation of a machine which effects the computation of the desired value.

Such definitions rather directly suggest, or are, realisations. They do not possess or involve implicit, but instead explicit allocation and freeing. The implicit allocations and freeings would have to be done by the implementation language processor (compiler) and its run-time system. The explicit allocations and freeings are determined by the definer, the person who writes down this stage of development. The allocation and freeing is of otherwise recursively nested (that is, stacked) values.

The definition, however, still requires the presence, at run-time, of O — the interpreter. It still cannot be completely factored out of the definition for any given, nontrivial expression. Thus there still cannot be an exhaustive, macrosubstitution process which completely eliminates the interpretive nature of the definition.

The reason is as before: CLOSures are triplets of a function definition bound variable, id, a function body, d, and the recursive, defining environment, env2'. Together they represent, but are not, the function, fun. It must instead be mimicked; hence the required presence of O.

16.5.3 Syntactic Types

See Sect. 16.2.2 for the formal SAL syntax.

16.5.4 Semantic Types

It is always important to fix the semantic types first. But, since we are in a step of development where the syntactic types are fixed throughout most steps, we fix the semantic types second!

type
    ENVi = ENVa*
variable
    e_stk:ENVi := $\langle\langle\rangle\rangle$;
    v_stk:DENa* := $\langle\rangle$;

16.5.5 Abstraction Functions

value
    abs_ENVa: **Unit** $\overset{\sim}{\to}$ ENVa
    abs_ENVa() $\equiv$ **hd c** estk

    abs_DENa: **Unit** $\overset{\sim}{\to}$ DENa
    abs_DENa() $\equiv$ **hd c** vstk

16.5.6 Run-Time Functions

We have the usual push, pop and top functions:

value
    push_e: Bind $\to$ **Unit**
    pop_e: **Unit** $\to$ **Unit**
    push_v: DENa $\to$ **Unit**
    pop_v: **Unit** $\to$ **Unit** DENa

    push_e(bind) $\equiv$ e_stk := $\langle\langle$bind$\rangle$^**hd c** e_stk$\rangle$^**tl c** e_stk
    pop_e() $\equiv$ e_stk := **tl c** e_stk
    push_v(v) $\equiv$ v_stk := $\langle$v$\rangle$^**c** v_stk
    pop_v() $\equiv$ **let** val = **hd c** v_stk **in** v_stk := **tl c** v_stk; val **end**

    top_e: **Unit** $\to$ Bind, top_e() $\equiv$ **hd hd c** e_stk
    top_v: **Unit** $\to$ DENa, top_v() $\equiv$ **hd c** v_stk

as well as some slightly less usual functions on stacks:

    len_e_stk: **Unit** $\to$ **Nat**
    len_e_stk() $\equiv$ **len hd c** e_stk

push_new_e: ENVa → **Unit**
push_new_e(env) ≡ e_stk := ⟨env⟩^**c** e_stk

pop_old_e: **Unit** → **Unit**
pop_old_e() ≡ e_stk := **tl** **c** e_stk

The l_search function (Sect. 16.4.4) was recursively defined. Hence it was a function which returned a value. If a search is attempted for an identifier (id) which is not in the environment, then l_search specified chaos. We now respecify the applicative l_search into an imperative, operational O_search in which we choose to change the recursion to iteration (more specifically, to a while loop search).

We remind the reader that we here use a version of RSL variables in which these designate references. To get at their contained values we apply the contents operator **c**. In proper RSL there is no provision for making the distinction between a variable designating a reference and a variable designating a value. All variables basically designate values. Variable names passed as parameters to functions are passed *by value*, not *by reference*. But we will make the distinction anyway.[7]

value
    O_search: V → **Unit**
    O_search(v) ≡
        variable
            found:**Bool** := **false**,
            index:**Nat** := 1;
        while ∼**c** found **do**
            case (top_e())(index) **of**
                mk_Simp(v,den) → (push_v(den); found := **true**),
                mk_Rec(v,e) →
                    let env = ⟨(top_e())(k) | index≤k≤len_estk()⟩ **in**
                    push_v(mk_CLOS(mk_Lam(v,e),env));
                    found := **true end**,
                _ → **if** index = len_estk()
                        then chaos else index := **c** index + 1 **end**
        end end

16.5.7 Semantic Functions

Two Invariants

The two most important invariant properties to be obeyed by the semantic functions O are:

---

[7]And we may probably miss a few such distinctions, forgetting to use the **c** operator.

1. They "each and all" specify the pushing of a value onto the value stack (i.e., the value stack after (some execution) contains one more element than before (such an execution)).
2. They "each and all" specify that the environment stack is unchanged!

Any stacking (pushing) onto the environment stack, as specified by any of the elaboration functions (O) must be restored (i.e., popped) by that same invocation of the O function.

[0] Interpret Programs

The reader is well-advised to compare function definition by function definition, those below, named O, with those, named I, in Sect. 16.4.5.

_____ Interpret Programs _____

Previous step:

value
    I: Pro $\overset{\sim}{\to}$ VALa
    I(mk_Pro(e)) ≡ I(e)⟨⟩

Present step:

value
    O: Pro → **Unit**
    O(mk_Pro(e)) ≡ O(e)

Recall: I is applicative, hence explicitly shows all arguments. O is imperative and relies on a global state, not shown.

[1] Interpret Constant Expressions

_____ Interpret Constant Expressions _____

Previous step:

value
    I: E $\overset{\sim}{\to}$ DENa
    I(mk_Cst(k))(env) ≡ k

Present step:

value

O: E → **Unit**
O(mk_Cst(k)) ≡ push_v(k)

Recall: I results in a value, O in a side effect on the global state — here explicitly shown.

[2] Interpret Variable Expressions

In both the previous and the present step of development we avail ourselves of the applicative, now imperatively defined search functions.

———————————— Interpret Variable Expressions ————————————

Previous step:

value
    I: E $\overset{\sim}{\to}$ DENa
    I(mk_Var(v))(env) ≡ I_search(v,env)

Present step:

value
    O: E → **Unit**
    O(mk_Var(v)) ≡ O_search(v)

Here the "packaging" of the ("further") evaluation into "similarly" named search functions at least leaves the impression that similar evaluations take place. Only careful comparisons of the I_search and O_search functions — short of formal proofs — will reveal their "equivalence".

[3] Interpret Prefix Expressions

We keep on listing the previous step of development as a back-up for informal derivation.

———————————— Interpret Prefix Expressions ————————————

Previous step:

value
    I: E $\overset{\sim}{\to}$ DENa
    I(mk_Pre(o,e))(env) ≡ **let** val = I(e)(env) **in** M(o)(val) **end**

Present step:

value

O: E → **Unit**
O(mk_Pre(o,e)) ≡ O(e); **let** val = pop_v() **in** push_v(M(o)(val)) **end**

Observe how the O function effects the unstacking of **val** by "overwriting" the
entire stack!

[4] Interpret Infix Expressions

──────────── Interpret Infix Expressions ────────────

Previous step:

value
   I: E $\overset{\sim}{\to}$ DENa
   I(mk_Inf(le,o,re))(env) ≡
     let (rv,lv)=I(le)(env),I(re)(env) **in** M(o)(lv,rv) **end**

Present step:

value
   O: E → **Unit**
   O(mk_Inf(le,o,re)) ≡
     O(le); O(re);
     let rv=pop_v(),lv=pop_v() **in** push_v(M(o)(lv,rv)) **end**

Again, a pair of unstackings is avoided through complete rewrite of, i.e., assignment update to, the entire value stack.

[5] Interpret Conditional Expressions

──────────── Interpret Conditional Expressions ────────────

Previous step:

value
   I: E $\overset{\sim}{\to}$ DENa
   I(mk_If(b,c,a))(env) ≡
     let t = I(b)(env) **in if** t **then** I(c)(env) **else** I(a)(env) **end end**

Present step:

value
   O: E → **Unit**

O(mk_If(b,c,a)) ≡
    O(b); **let** t = pop_v() **in if** t **then** O(c) **else** O(a) **end end**

Definitions [0–5] were the simple semantic functions. Now we move on to the more interesting ones!

[6] Interpret Lambda Expressions

The two **CLOS**ure-taking functions are, of course, different: One is applicatively defined, the other is imperatively defined.

—————————————— Interpret Lambda-Expressions ——————————————

Previous step:

value
    I: E $\overset{\sim}{\to}$ DENa
    I(mk_Lam(v,e))(env) ≡ mk_CLOS(mk_Lam(v,e),env)

Present step:

value
    O: E → **Unit**
    O(mk_Lam(v,e)) ≡ push_v(mk_CLOS(mk_Lam(v,e),top_e()))

In either case, no real evaluation takes place; just the return, respectively the stacking, of a packed closure value.

[7] Interpret Simple Let Expressions

—————————————— Interpret Simple Let Expressions ——————————————

Previous step:

    I(mk_Let(v,d,b))(env) ≡
        let val = I(d)(env) **in**
        let env$'$ = ⟨mk_Simp(v,val)⟩^env **in**
        I(b)(env$'$) **end end**

Present step:

    O(mk_Let(v,d,b)) ≡
        O(d);
        let val = pop_v() **in**
        push_e(mk_Simp(v,val));
        O(b); pop_e(); **end**

Now value stack unstacking must be performed explicitly. Furthermore, the applicative block structure of the specification language means that the locally defined environment, env′, no longer is known once I(b)(env′) has been evaluated. The imperative, global state "stacking-up" to a new environment must, in contrast, be unstacked in order to bring balance, that is, to maintain the invariant.

[8] Interpret Recursive Let Expressions

```
───────────── Interpret Recursive Let Expressions ─────────────

Previous step:

   I(mk_Rec(f,mk_Lam(v,e),b))(env) ≡
      let env′ = ⟨mk_Rec(f,mk_Lam(v,e))⟩^env in
      I(b)(env′) end

Present step:

   O(mk_Rec(f,mk_Lam(v,e),b)) ≡
      push_e(mk_REC(f,mk_Lam(v,e)));
      O(b); pop_e()
```

Again, the local scope of env′ is in contrast to the side effect on the global environment state: The latter stack (on environment activations) must thus be restored. Otherwise we see "practically speaking, the same kind of" recursive function value being bound in the environment before block body evaluation.

[9] Interpret Function Application Expressions

With this interpretation function the difference between the previous and the present step of development becomes obvious.

```
───────────── Interpret Function Application Expressions ─────────────

Previous step:

   I(mk_App(f,a))(env) ≡
      let arg = I(a)(env), fct = I(f)(env) in apply(fct,arg) end

Present step:

   O(mk_App(f,a)) ≡
      O(a); O(f);
      case pop_v() of
         mk_CLOS(mk_Lam(v,e),env) →
```

```
        (push_new_e((mk_Simp(v,pop_v()))^env);
        O(e); pop_old_e()),
  _ → chaos end
```

The first lines of the two function definition bodies "correspond" (an induction hypothesis). The rest of the O body definition "corresponds" to the **apply** function of Sect. 16.4.4.

The reader is kindly invited to follow, for example, using left- and right-hand index fingers, the previous and the present step formulas, clause by clause, in order to, informally, yet systematically, reason why the present step might well be "correct" wrt. the previous step!

16.5.8 Review of SAL Semantics, 3

We have motivated a change from an applicative to an imperative state formulation of our SAL semantics. This change entailed the introduction of two kinds of global variables: a stack for computed expression values, and a stack for deployed environments. The implicit stackings and unstackings of values and environments of a previous definition then had to be done explicitly while preserving respective invariants. We have shown the systematic transcription of previous I functions into the present O functions, and we have carefully related this step of development to a previous step.

The classical example of stack semantics was that of Landin's SECD machine: [284, 286, 288], also treated in Wegner's seminal book [528]. In the 1960s the IBM Vienna group developed elaborate (albeit applicative) stack machine semantics of the PL/I programming language [32, 305, 312]. The locally defined environments of Section 16.4 have been globalised into an imperative environment stack. Similarly for the locally defined expression values: Instead of keeping them locally defined they are pushed onto a value stack, and are unstacked when applied to primitive operations.

From a functional definition we have therefore evolved into an imperative, assignment-oriented definition. This means that the implicit environment extensions and the implicit "reversion" to embracing environments must now be explicitly defined. And this means that the definition of this section is more operational and technically detailed — with such details "clouding" the semantics picture.

16.6 A Macro-expansion Semantics

The idea of macro-expansion semantics seems to have first originated at the IBM Vienna Laboratory — as early as in 1961, with the late Hans Bekič [32], in connection with the development of an Algol 60 compiler for the first Austrian transistorised computer, the Mailüfternl (May breeze).[8] Semantic function definitions are seen as defining compilers from source object languages to the target metalanguage. In this section, as well as in Chaps. 16–17, we deal with the special problems of effecting translations into such simple metalanguage constructs which have a direct counterpart in actual target object languages. Thus the basic idea is that semantic function (i.e., interpreter) definitions can be read as compilers from (as here the SAL) source language constructs into (as here RSL) specification language constructs.

16.6.1 Analysis of Stack Semantics

The unit of binding in the previous SAL definitions is that of a pair: an identifier and its abstract, respectively concrete, value. The abstract values were integers and functions. The concrete values were integers and closures. The bindings were, in the most recent models, kept as elements marked either "simple" or "recursive", and otherwise containing these pairs. Henceforth we shall implement such a pairing element as a so-called *activation*.

An environment, till now, was first modelled as a map from identifiers to abstract values, then as a tuple of elements. Environment maps contained at most one pairing for any given identifier. Environment tuples were searched linearly, from head to tail, for a first occurrence of an identifier pairing — and thus allowed for subsequent, "earlier" bindings of the same identifier. These (earlier) bindings correspond to bindings in Let or Rec blocks embracing a binding of an inner block.

In the abstract state machine stack semantics of SAL we observe a number of storage wise inefficient object representations. These are caused almost exclusively by our choice to stay with the closure representation, CLOS, of functions. Closures "drag" along with them, not only the function body text, but also the entire defining environment. This generally results in extensive duplication of dynamic scope information recorded (i.e., "stored") in ENVi.

Therefore, the basic object transformation objective of this development step is now to keep only nonredundant environment information in the transformed activation stack. We shall achieve this by "folding" the ENVi stack of ENVa stacks "back into" a pointer-based, tree-structured activation stack (STG).

The collection of environment activations are tree-structured because SAL has the FUNARG property. This property is the following: Functions may not only accept, as arguments, but also result in functions. These argument and result functions will normally have been defined in environments different from the one (to and) from which they are (passed, respectively) returned. The previous sentences do not fully argue why the collection of environment activations are tree-structured. Such an explanation is given below.

---

[8] — in poetic naming-contrast to the (imperial) Whirlwind computer designed at MIT (1951)

Each binding, to recall, will now become an activation (record). The linear list of bindings will be effected by augmenting the activation record with pointers.

Let:

$$\langle(idn,vn),(idm,vm),...,(idi,vi),...,(id3,v3),(id2,v2),(id1,v1)\rangle$$

be one such CLOSure (and stack) environment. Then:

[pn $\mapsto$ (pm,idn,vn),
    pm $\mapsto$ (pk,idm,vm),
    ...
    pi $\mapsto$ (pi$-$1,idi,vi),
    ...
    p3 $\mapsto$ (p2,id3,v3),
    p2 $\mapsto$ (p1,id2,v2),
    p1 $\mapsto$ (**nil**,id1,v1)]

could be a naive rendition of the tuple-modelled environment. The pointers pj 'chain' the activation bindings in the order starting with the most recently (dynamically) invoked blocks. (Bindings only — but always — occur in blocks.)

If one of the values, for example, v2:

$$\langle(idn,vn),(idm,vm),...,(idi,vi),...,(id3,v3),(id2,v2),(id1,v1)\rangle$$

describes a closure whose environment part is a copy of the environment tuple as from the ith item:

mk_CLOS(lambda,$\langle$(idi,vi),...,(idm,vm),(idn,vn)$\rangle$)

then the list-modelled environment can be expressed:

$\langle$(idn,vn),
  (idm,mk_CLOS(lambda,$\langle$(idi,vi),...,(id3,v3),(id2,v2),(id1,v1)$\rangle$))),
  ...
  (idi,vi),
  ...
  (id3,v3),
  (id2,v2),
  (id1,v1)$\rangle$

Instead of repeating the closure environment, we replace the environment part of a closure with a pointer whereby the map-modelled environment can be expressed:

[pn $\mapsto$ (pm,idn,vn),
  pm $\mapsto$ (pℓ,idm,mk_CLOS(lambda,pi)),
  ...

pi $\mapsto$ (ph,idi,vi),

...

p2 $\mapsto$ (p1,id2,v2),
p1 $\mapsto$ (**nil**,id1,v1)]

Invoking the closure identified by id2 in the stack model corresponded to pushing an entirely new environment, namely the one starting from position i, as a new stack element.

In the model we are about to decide upon, this will be effected by first introducing an additional pointer into each activation record, i.e., (pc,pe,id,v), such that the existing pointer, as before, designates the dynamic call (hence pc) sequence of activations. The new pointer designates the so-called lexicographically embracing environment chain of activations.

This leads to the following last expression:

[po $\mapsto$ (pn,pi,id,v),
    pn $\mapsto$ (pm,pm,idn,vn),
    pm $\mapsto$ (pℓ,pℓ,idm,mk_CLOS(lambda,pi)),

    ...

    pi $\mapsto$ (ph,ph,idi,vi),

    ...

    p2 $\mapsto$ (p1,p1,id2,v2),
    p1 $\mapsto$ (**nil**,**nil**,id1,v1)]

where v is the value of e.

We can visualise the above. Figure 16.2 does so, and also shows some state components, etc., components whose purpose will be explained now and formalised later.

The six rectangles in the left column of Fig. 16.2 designate six registers. The big "almost" rectangle with the many $(2+\ldots+1+\ldots+2)$ five-component rectangles, labelled DSA0, DSA1, DSAi, DSAm and DSAn, inside it, denotes a storage whose space (cells, bytes, etc.) can be allocated, i.e., "claimed". Each of these 2+1+2 five-component (DSA) rectangles designates a record whose fifth field, the one shown to the right on the figure and labelled stack, designates local stack, i.e., varying space. The other fields are fixed-space record components. The arrows symbolise pointers. Thus the cp register links to the top rectangle: Given cp we can access the contents of that top rectangle. The three-pronged partly solid, partly dashed fork leading out from the ep register designates that the contents of that register successively "traverse" the ep chain. Notice that the traversal follows the (link, i.e., pointer) contents of the record ep fields. Thus it links directly from the top, DSAn, to the middle, DSAi, and onwards (...).

Activations, as we shall see, are never deleted.

Hence, paths via dynamic pointers from activations (i.e., leaves) to the root signify a chain of dynamically preceding (i.e., calling) activations, with one

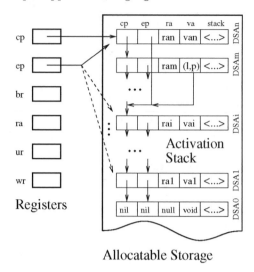

Registers

Allocatable Storage

Fig. 16.2. "Snapshot" of a run-time state

of these chains signifying the current, all other chains those of defining, environment chains of FUNARG functions, i.e., functions having been returned as values of function applications. Each chain is statically and dynamically linked, corresponding to the sub chain of *environmentally preceding, lexicographically youngest*, that is, most recent, *incarnations* of statically embracing blocks; respectively the complete chain of dynamically (call/invocation) preceding activations. We shall later call our activations DSAs (for dynamic storage activations), and the map from pointers to DSAs storage (STG).

We can, however, only succeed in achieving this realisation of activations if, at the same time, we refine CLOSures into pairs of resulting program label points, lfct, and defining environment activation stack pointers, p. From lfct we are able to retrieve the Lambda-expression, and from p we are able to retrieve the defining environment.

Informal Design Description

To realise this goal we also, in this step, refine CLOSures by macro-expansion compilation of SAL texts, e, into extended meta-language texts. By a meta-language, *macro-substitution, compiled* (interpretive) *semantics*, to recall, we basically understand a definition in the metalanguage not containing any references to specifier-defined elaboration functions. We shall, however, widen the above to admit forms which contain such references. These are now thought of as references to *elaboration macros*. Hence they imply a *preprocessing* stage, called compiling, prior to interpretation of "pure" metatext. Pure metatext is a text which is free from references to specifier-defined functions.

We are given input source texts in the form of arguments to elaboration functions. To achieve an extended metalanguage definition, which can be so macro-expanded, recursive definitions of objects must be eliminated. We do so either by taking their fix points, or by "unzipping" them into mechanical constructions.

Taking fix points, for example, results in:

$$\text{env}' = \textbf{fix } \lambda\rho{:}\text{ENV} \bullet (\text{env} \dagger [\text{ id } \mapsto M(d)\rho])$$

but that does not help us very much when we come to actual, effective realisations on computers: Fix points are beautiful in theory, but "costly" in practice. Even though computers may be claimed to possess fix point-finding instructions, **fix**, they would have to be general enough to cater for the most complex case. Instead we unravel each individual use of recursion separately, and so far by hand. In the case of env' we do this by providing suitable stacks, pointer initialisations and manipulations. The guiding principle is to derive, from the more abstract definition to each occurrence of an otherwise recursive definition, a most fitting, efficient and economical realisation. In the next five subsections ([1]–[5]) we now go into a characterisation of the resulting definition at this stage. The definition represents two intertwined efforts: the further concretisation of run-time objects, here the ENVi stack into a further refined state, and the further decomposition of elaboration function definitions so that we can come to the point where C references can be successively eliminated.

[1] The Run-Time State

We refer to Fig. 16.2 which shows a snapshot run-time state.

In the abstract stack rendition of SAL we had separate environment and value stacks. We now merge these two stacks. Thus cstk and vstk are merged into the separately allocated DSAs of a storage (STG). These are chained together: dynamic chains by a CP (for: calling pointer) register, and lexico-graphic chains to (defining) youngest activations (block incarnations) by an EP (for: environment pointer) register. The exact functioning of this scheme is precisely described by the formulae. Hence it will not be informally described here.

[2] Macro-expansion

As outlined above we shall make extensive use of macro substitutions.

Two kinds of text appear in our definitions: text that specifies compile-time (i.e., macro-expansion) actions, and the text being generated. The former is preceded by asterisks (*, one per line of compile time action).

The stacking (pushing) and unstackings (pops) of activations and values will be implemented by two pairs of functions. One may choose to do likewise for these auxiliary functions, pop and push, or one may wish to keep these as standard run-time routines. At this stage we make no decision in this respect.

[3] Realisation of CLOSures

Note the Rec or Lamb cases, "**letrec** g(id)=d **in** b", respectively "λid.ed". Upon evaluation of a Rec or a Lamb their defined function bodies, d, are not elaborated (until actually Applied). Since we have decided to macro-expand these texts "in-line" with the text in which they were defined, and since we are not to execute this text when otherwise elaborating the two definition cases, we shall (i) label their expansions, (ii) label the text immediately following these expansions, (iii) precede the expansion with a (metalanguage) **goto** around the thus expanded text (iv) and terminate the expanded text itself with a **goto** intended to return to the caller. The caller, it is expected, "dropped" a suitable return address in a global **ra** (return address) branch label register before going to the label of the expanded function text. All this is performed in functions C(mk_Lam(...))(...), respectively C(mk_Rec(...))(...). So what is left in the environment of the former CLOSures? The answer is: just the "bare bones", enough to reconstruct (that is, retrieve) the id, the d (text), and their defining environment: the former two from the (fct) label and the environment from contents of cp.

Thus, in this definition, a function CLOSure has been realized as a FCT pair: (fct,ptr). This solution closely mirrors the way in which procedures are realized in actual programming language systems.

[4] The Compile State — Compile-Time Specification

We observe that Labels had to be generated for each Lamb, Appl and Rec (actually its Lamb part). We describe only once (in C(mk_Lam(...))(...) and C(mk_Rec(...))(...)) what metalanguage text to be generated. We shall view semantic function formulas as subject to (as already mentioned) a two phase process: the compile phase which macro-expands the SAL program into "pure" metatext, and the interpretation phase which performs actions as prescribed by the expanded text.

Thus a number of lines of the formulae are executed at *compile-time* (they are marked by a preceding asterisk, *). All dict (in DICT) objects are likewise compile-time computed (marked δ). All references to C functions are eliminated by the compile-time macro-substitution process already mentioned. Remaining lets are then to be executed at run time, that is, in the interpretation phase. In summary, the *abstract compiler*, whose working behaviour will not be formalized, performs three actions: it generates labels; it computes, distributes and uses dictionaries (see next paragraphs, below); and it generates metalanguage (i.e., RSL) texts.

[5] The Compile State — The Dictionary

Whereas in ENV1 and ENV2, VALues of ids were explicitly paired with these, in DSAs only the VALues are left, but in fixed positions (VR).

Consider any variable, id. It is most recently defined at block depth n (respectively at block depths $n, n', \ldots, n''$ since the same identifier may be redefined in embracing or even nonembracing, "disjoint" scopes). And it is used, for example, at block depth ln, where $0 \leq n \leq ln$.

There is thus no need to keep the variable names (i.e., identifiers) in the activation stack. The compile time DICT component thus serves the following, singular purpose (at least in this sample definition): for all ids in some context, to map them into the static block depth, n, at which they were defined. Since the static chain also touches exactly the embracing blocks, the difference ln-n denotes the number of levels one has to chain back to get to the VALue corresponding to id. In fact, that is the whole, singular purpose of the static (EP) chain. Since it is furthermore observed that the only phase dict is used, in the compile phase, any reference to dict is seen also to be eliminated.

Finally, observe that the unique label objects required for naming and by-passing defined function texts and for returning to calling points (designated, respectively, by lfct, lbyp and lret), these unique label objects, once generated, shall be substituted into respective uses.

Execution

We refer — again — to the C function definitions below. The result of executing what a SAL program prescribes is found on top of the temporary list (TL) set aside in each activation (about which — at block exit — we can assert a length of exactly one). So C pushes the result of any expression elaboration on top of the current DSA's TL — with the working register, ur, invariably also holding this result at the instance of pushing.

A simple Let expression is executed by first finding the VALue of the locally defined variable, id, in the environment in which the Let is encountered. Then a new activation is set up to elaborate the body, b, of the Let. Working register ur is used to store the result temporarily while the activation is terminated, but not necessarily disposed of. The result is pushed on the TL of the invoking activation's DSA. Since the VALue so yielded might be a function which was "concocted" by the activation just left, and since that FunCTion may depend on its locally defined Variable VALues, we cannot, in general, dispose of the activation.

This then accounts for our use of the square brackets, [...], around the reclamation of STorage shown. Normally these actions must not be performed unless it can be decided (for example, through some flow analysis means) that the FUNARG property is not used. FunCTion VALues will be realized as pairs: mk_FCT(lfct,ptr), where ptr is a pointer to that, or a contained, activation. This is again the FUNARG situation previously mentioned. By not disposing

of the DSA we are later able to "reactivate" the FunCTion defining activation.
We leave it to the reader to "exercise" remaining aspects of the definition.

16.6.2 Syntactic Types

See Sect. 16.2.2 for a formal definition of syntactic types.

16.6.3 Compile-Time Types

Based on the above informal explanation we can now specify our design:

type
    LN = **Nat**
    DICT = Id $\overrightarrow{m}$ LN
    RSL /* macro-expanded text */
    Lbl
variable
    lbls:Lbl-**set** := {}

value
    get_Lbl: **Unit** → **Unit** Lbl
    get_Lbl() ≡
      let lbl:Lbl • lbl ∉ <u>c</u> lbls **in**
      lbls := {lbl} ∪ <u>c</u> lbls;
      lbl **end**

16.6.4 Run-Time Semantic Types

Figure 16.2 shows a "snapshot" of a run-time state to which, more generally,
correspond the following type and variable definitions:

type
    Ptr, Lbl
    Pt == nil() | ptr(Ptr)
    Lb == null() | lbl(Lbl)
    Va == void() | VAL
    STG = Ptr $\overrightarrow{m}$ DSA
    DSA == mk_DSA(s_cp:CP,s_ep:EP,s_ra:RA,s_va:Va,s_stk:VAL*)
    CP,EP = Pt
    BR,RA = Lb
    VAL = Num | Tru | FCT
    Num :: **Int**
    Tru :: **Bool**
    FCT == mk_FCT(s_br:BR,s_ep:EP)

16.6.5 Run-Time State

The state is initialised to a "bottom" activation with pointer ptr.

value
    ptr:Ptr
variable
    stg:STG := [ptr ↦ mk_DSA(nil(),nil(),null(),void(),⟨⟩)];
    cp,ep:Ptr := ptr;
    br,ra:Lbl := null();
    ur,wr:VAL := void();

16.6.6 Run-Time Stack Operations

The value stack is now "within" each activation. Two operations, therefore, serve to pop and push from, respectively to, that value stack, into, respectively from, a register whose content is of type **VAL**ue, hence we (augmenting the specification language, as we shall be doing quite a lot in this section) express their type in terms of *references* to **VAL**ues.

value
    pop: **ref** VAL → **Unit**
    pop(r) ≡
        let (c,e,a,v,stk) = ($\underline{c}$ stg)(cp) **in**
        stg := $\underline{c}$ stg ∪ [sp ↦ mk_DSA(c,e,a,v,**tl** stk)]
        r := **hd** stk
        end
    push: **ref** VAL → **Unit**
    push(r) ≡
        let (c,e,a,v,stk) = ($\underline{c}$ stg)($\underline{c}$ cp) **in**
        stg := $\underline{c}$ stg ∪ [cp ↦ mk_DSA(c,e,a,v,⟨$\underline{c}$ r⟩^stk)]
        end

16.6.7 Run-Time Stack Search for Variable Values

The C_search operation should be compared, line for line, to the similarly named operation O_search of Sect. 16.5.

value
    C_search: **Nat** → **Unit**
    C_search(n) ≡
        for i=1 **to** n **do** ep := s_ep(($\underline{c}$ stg)($\underline{c}$ ep)) **end**;
        ur := s_va(($\underline{c}$ stg)($\underline{c}$ ep)); push(ur);
        ep := $\underline{c}$ cp

Before, in I_search and O_search, the search was by identifier. Here it is by block depth. Before we had that each iteration of the search had to compare a given identifier to an identifier of the stack. Here there is a "straight chaining back" to the defining activation.

Assertions: The static chain pointer ep has the same value upon invocation of the above macro expanded text as the dynamic chain pointer cp. Search satisfies the invariant: After completion the top of the value stack — as well as register ur — has the value that results from evaluation of any expression.

16.6.8 Macro-expansion Functions

In the definitions that follow we will be using two forms of **let ... in ... end** constructs. One kind is here — extralinguistically — prefixed by asterisks (*), the others not. The former are to be read as directing compile-time generation of **labels**. Once generated, and the appropriately named label values properly substituted into the text following those asterisked **let** constructs, those asterisked **let** constructs can be removed. What remains is the RSL text being generated. Invocations of the macros, C, result in text substitution.

It is now important to observe that we have made all our design decisions: on how to represent environment as a stack of (dynamic save/storage) activations (DSAs), on how to represent CLOSures as pairs, not of text and environments, but as labels (to macro-expanded versions of that text) and pointers (to the top activation of the environment).

Therefore all that remains is to rewrite the I interpretation function of Sect. 16.5.

Invariant: Each invocation of C now leads to RSL text *which interpreted by the RSL (semantics, i.e., by "its") machine* shall lead to the value of the expression being thus evaluated left both on top of the current value stack and the ur register. This is true for all but the C function (etc.) when applied to programs. Here the evaluated value is to be also the value of the RSL clause.

The reader is well-advised in comparing, function definition by function definition, those below, named C, with those, named O, in Sect. 16.5.7.

[0] Program Macro-expansion

```
——————————————— Program Macro-expansion ———————————————

Previous step:

value
    O: Pro → Unit
    O(mk_Pro(e)) ≡ O(e)

Present step:

value
    C: Pro → Unit  RSL
```

$$C(mk\_Pro(e)) \equiv$$
$$C(e)([\,],0);\ ur := \textbf{hd}\ s\_stk((\underline{c}\,stg)(\underline{c}\,cp));\ \textbf{return}\ \underline{c}\,ur$$

Assertion: $C(e)([\,],0)$ leaves the value stack of the activation pointed to by cp with just one value: that of the expression being evaluated. The invariant is satisfied.

[1] Constant Expression Macro-expansion

———————— Constant Expression Macro-expansion ————————

Previous step:

value
$\quad$ O: E $\rightarrow$ **Unit**
$\quad$ O(mk_Cst(k)) $\equiv$ push_v(k)

Present step:

value
$\quad$ C: E $\rightarrow$ (DICT$\times$LN) $\rightarrow$ RSL **Unit**
$\quad$ C(mk_Cst(k))(δ,ln) $\equiv$ (ur := k; push(ur))

Assertion: The invariant is satisfied.

[2] Variable Expression Macro-expansion

———————— Variable Expression Macro-expansion ————————

Previous step:

value
$\quad$ O: E $\rightarrow$ **Unit**
$\quad$ O(mk_Var(v)) $\equiv$ O_search(v)

Present step:

value
$\quad$ C: E $\rightarrow$ (DICT$\times$LN) $\rightarrow$ RSL **Unit**
$\quad$ C(mk_Var(v))(δ,ln) $\equiv$ C_search(ln$-\delta$(v))

Assertion: From the definition of search we see that the invariant is satisfied.

[3] Prefix Expression Macro-expansion

```
_____ Prefix Expression Macro-expansion _____
```

Previous step:

value

    O: E → **Unit**
    O(mk_Pre(o,e)) ≡ O(e); **let** val = pop_v() **in** push_v(M(o)(val)) **end**

Present step:

value

    C: E → (DICT×LN) → RSL **Unit**
    C(mk_Pre(o,e))(δ,ln) ≡ C(e)(δ,ln); ur := M(o)(**c** ur); push(ur)

Assertion: The invariant is satisfied.

[4] Infix Expression Macro-expansion

```
_____ Infix Expression Macro-expansion _____
```

Previous step:

value

    O: E → **Unit**
    O(mk_Inf(le,o,re)) ≡
        O(le); O(re);
        let rv=pop_v(),lv=pop_v() **in** push_v(M(o)(lv,rv)) **end**

Present step:

    C: E → (DICT×LN) → RSL **Unit**
    C(mk_Inf(le,o,re))(δ,ln) ≡
        C(le)(δ,ln); C(re)(δ,ln);
        pop(ur); pop(wr); ur:=M(o)(**c** ur,**c** wr); push(ur)

Assertion: The invariant is satisfied.

[5] Conditional Expression Macro-expansion

```
_____ Conditional Expression Macro-expansion _____
```

Previous step:

value

O: E → **Unit**
O(mk_If(b,c,a)) ≡
    O(b); **let** t=pop_v() **in if** t **then** O(c) **else** O(a) **end end**

Present step:

value
    C: E → (DICT×LN) → RSL **Unit**
    C(mk_If(b,c,a))(δ,ln) ≡
        * **let** l_alt = get_Lbl(), l_out = get_Lbl() **in**
        C(b)(δ,ln); pop(ur); **if** ∼**c** ur **then goto** l_alt **else skip end**;
        C(c)(δ,ln); **goto** l_out; **label** l_alt: C(a)(δ,ln); **label** l_out:
        * **end**

Assertion: The invariant is satisfied: ur and the top of the activation value stack both contain either the value of **c** or the value of **a** — as resulting from the above-specified evaluation.

[6] Lambda-Expression Macro-expansion

————————— Lambda-Expression Macro-expansion —————————

Previous step:

value
    O: E → **Unit**
    O(mk_Lam(v,e)) ≡ push_v(mk_CLOS(mk_Lam(v,e),top_e()))

Present step:

value
    C: E → (DICT×LN) → RSL **Unit**
    C(mk_Lam(v,e))(δ,ln) ≡
        * **let** lbypass = get_Lbl(), lfct = get_Lbl() **in**
        goto lbypass;
        label lfct: B(e)(δ † [v↦ln+1],ln+1); **goto c** ra;
        label lbypass: ur := mk_FCT(lfct,**c** cp); push(ur)
        * **end**

The O definition specifies the value stacking of a CLOSure. Similarly here we value stack a FunCTion. The earlier definition embedded the program text in the value stack. Here that text is macro-expanded "in-line" with the program text with a "jump around" it!

    Assertion: The invariant is satisfied: The CLOSure value, mk_CLOS(mk_Lam(v,e),**hd** $\underline{c}$ cstk),

of the previous step of development is now a FunCTional value

mk_FCT(lfct,$\underline{c}$ cp),

lfct designates the beginning of the macro-expanded text e, and $\underline{c}$ cp designates the top activation of env — with the static chain of the stack of activations designating "the rest". The FunCTional value is both in the working register ur and on top of the current activation's value stack.

[7] Simple Let Expression Macro-expansion

```
──────────── Simple Let Expression Macro-expansion ────────────
```
Previous step:

value
   O: E → **Unit**
   O(mk_Let(v,d,b)) ≡
      O(d);
      let val=pop_v() **in** push_e(mk_Simp(v,val)); O(b);
      pop_e(); **end**

Present step:

value
   C: E → (DICT×LN) → RSL **Unit**
   C(mk_Let(v,d,b))(δ,ln) ≡
      C(d)(δ,ln); pop(ur); B(b)(δ†[v↦ln+1],ln+1)

Assertion: The invariant is satisfied: Line one of the body of C(mk_Let(v,d,b)) above corresponds to line one of O(mk_Let(v,d,b)).

Block Macro-expansion

The B function (below, and as invoked, for example, from C(mk_Let(v,d,b)) above) derives from the last three lines of the O(mk_Let(v,d,b)) function definition. The first and last of these prescribe the environment stacking, respectively environment unstacking, of a simple pairing of a variable to "its value". The first four lines of the body of the B(b)(δ,ln) function definition correspond to line two of the body of the O(mk_Let(v,d,b)) definition. The last five lines of the body below correspond to line four of the body of the O(mk_Let(v,d,b)) definition. See lines two and four of the body of O(mk_Let(v,d,b)) above.

value

B: E → (DICT × LN) → RSL **Unit**

B(b)(δ,ln) ≡

    let ptr:Ptr • ptr ∉ **dom** $\underline{c}$ stg **in**

    stg := $\underline{c}$ stg ∪ [ptr ↦ mk_DSA($\underline{c}$ cp,$\underline{c}$ ep,$\underline{c}$ ra,$\underline{c}$ ur,⟨⟩)];

    cp,ep := ptr;

    C(b)(δ,ln);

    pop(ur);

    ep := s_ep(($\underline{c}$ stg)($\underline{c}$ cp));

    ra := s_ra(($\underline{c}$ stg)($\underline{c}$ cp));

    cp := s_cp(($\underline{c}$ stg)($\underline{c}$ cp));

    [stg := $\underline{c}$ stg \ {ptr};]

    push(ur) **end**

The following assumptions are made about the auxiliary function B — invoked both in C(mk_Lam(v,e))(δ,ln) and C(mk_Let(v,d,b))(δ,ln): When invoked from C(mk_Lam(v,e))(δ,ln) register ur contains a function argument value. See C(mk_App(f,a))(δ,ln), the last pop(ur) below (subsection [9]). When invoked from C(mk_Let(v,d,b))(δ,ln) register ur contains simply bound values. In either case the B(b)(δ,ln) function definition specifies the copying of that register content onto the activation stack.

We observe that the 'removal' of the DSA established upon block entry is put in square brackets ([...])! If the language (SAL) being modelled has the FUNARG property then (usually) we cannot remove activations as they may be referred to by ["returned"] function values.

Let us consider the following SAL program fragment:

(**let** f=λa.G(a) **in** f(3) **end**)

The first occurrence of f is a defining occurrence; the last occurrence is a using occurrence. The second occurrence of f is bound to the first. Let us assume the environment before entry to this fragment to be ρ. Let us annotate (to the left of the first and to the right of the second vertical divides) the above program with its environment bindings in the style of Section 16.3:

ρ | (**let** f=λa.G(a) **in** | ρ' =ρ † [f ↦ M(λa.G(a))ρ]

ρ' | f(3) | ρ'

ρ' | **end**) | ρ

Here we have been a little lax in allowing ourselves to express the syntactic argument to M "as the text" rather than as the corresponding abstract value mk_Lam(a,G(a)). C(mk_Let(v,d,b)) places the function f value on top of the current activation's value stack as well as in working register ur. The body of B(b) places the ur content in the variable location (f) of the new activation — colloquially speaking in ρ', the one "on top of" ρ. ("Colloquially" since we are no longer working with ρ's but with DSA activations.)

[8] Recursive Function/Let Expression Macro-expansion

```
_____ Recursive Function/Let Expression Macro-expansion _____

Previous step:
value
    O: E → Unit
    O(mk_Rec(f,mk_Lam(v,d),b)) ≡
        push_e(mk_REC(f,mk_Lam(v,d))); O(b); pop_e()


Present step:
value
    C: E → (DICT×LN) → RSL  Unit
    C(mk_Rec(f,mk_Lam(v,e),b))(δ,ln) ≡
        * let lfct = get_Lbl(), lbypass = get_Lbl() in
        goto lbypass;
        label lfct: B(e)(δ † [f↦ln+1,v↦ln+2],ln+2); goto c ra;
        label lbypass:
        let ptr:Ptr • ptr ∉ dom c stg in
        ur := mk_FCT(lfct,ptr);
        stg := c stg ∪ [ptr ↦ mk_DSA(c cp,c ep,c ra,c ur,⟨⟩)];
        cp,ep := ptr;
        C(b)(δ † [f↦ln+1],ln+1);
        pop(ur);
        ep := s_ep((c stg)(c cp)); ra := s_ra((c stg)(c cp));
        cp := s_cp((c stg)(c cp)); [ stg := c stg \ {ptr}; ]
        push(ur)
        end
        * end
```

Assertion: The invariant is satisfied: The interpretation of a block with a recursively defined procedure is the composition of the interpretation of an ordinary block and a function definition — with the proviso that the DSA pointer is also contained in the function closure. The above remark on the FUNARG property also applies here.

Let us, in the style of the simple definition of f above, in the annotations after definition of the B function, as invoked by the C(mk_Let(v,d,b) function definition body, consider the following recursive program:

(**letrec** f = λn.**if** n=0 **then** 1 **else** n∗f(n−1)
in f(3) **end end**)

Inspecting C(mk_Rec(f,mk_Lam(v,e),b)) we see that the f function value is "concocted" in the next, not the previous activation, and placed on this next activation.

[9] Function Application Expression Macro-expansion

```
_____ Function Application Expression Macro-expansion _____

Previous step:
value
    O: E → Unit
    O(mk_App(f,a)) ≡
        O(a); O(f);
        case pop_v() of
            mk_CLOS(mk_Lam(v,e),env) →
                (push_new_e(⟨mk_Simp(v,pop_v())⟩^env);
                 O(e); pop_old_e()),
            _ → chaos end


Present step:
value
    C: E → (DICT×LN) → RSL  Unit
    C(mk_App(f,a))(δ,ln) ≡
        * let lret = get_Lbl() in
        C(a)(δ,ln); C(f)(δ,ln);
        case c ur of
            mk_FCT(lfct,ptr) →
                {ep:=ptr,br:=lfct,ra:=lret,(pop(ur);pop(ur))};
                goto c br; label lret:,
            _ → chaos
        end * end
```

Assertion: The invariant is satisfied:

- The value stack unstacking O: vstk := tl tl c vstk; corresponds to C: (pop(ur);pop(ur)).
- The function body evaluation O: O(e); corresponds to C: br:=lfct; ...; goto c br;.
- The C: ra:=lret, and the C: label lret:, "balance" the function definition C(mk_Lam(v,e))(δ,ln)'s C: goto c ra;.
- Otherwise stacking and unstacking of activations takes place inside B as invoked in C(mk_Lam(v,e))(δ,ln).

16.6.9 Review of SAL Semantics, 4

Function values of earlier steps of development so to speak embodied the function definition texts (and their defining context, the environment). They did so either very implicitly, as in the "real" function values, FCT of Section 16.3, or they "packed" the function values into pairs of explicit text and concrete environments, as in the closures, CLOS of Sects. 16.4–16.5. In this section function values were finally implemented in terms of concepts close to actual (machine) programming: labels prefixing program texts and pointers to environment stack records. In Sects. 16.3–16.5 the function definitions can be viewed as interpreters. The M, I and O function definitions interpret syntactic "things", that is, they express their values (or denotations). In this section C defines a compiler from source language texts into specification (viz.: RSL) texts — where the latter texts are void of any reference to interpretation and compilation functions. To do so it was necessary to extend RSL beyond proper RSL (!) by introducing labels and gotos. The result is a definition, C, which uses concepts very close to those of low-level (machine) programming languages.

In the next section we shall postulate and define a computer architecture in terms of its machine programming concepts: registers, storage, storage addresses, machine instructions and code (as sequences of instructions). Then, in the three subsequent sections, we end our development of SAL by presenting three algorithms for compiling SAL expressions into machine code. In the section on the denotational semantics of SAL we laid down a *domain model* of SAL. The sections on first-order applicative, imperative stack and macro-expansion semantics of SAL serve to develop part of a *domain requirements* for SAL. The compiling algorithms express those requirements.

16.7 ASM: An Assembler Language

In this section we illustrate the definition of a hardware computer, and its derivation from a macro-expansion semantics. The hardware computer definition is in the form of an assembler language, that is, uses symbolic identifiers rather than absolute bit patterns.

The structure of the hardware computer is solely determined by what we can "read off" from the macro-expansion semantics of Section 16.6.

16.7.1 Semantic Types

We systematically relate types and state variables of the macro-expansion semantics presented earlier to types and state variables of the hardware computer; we refer to Sect. 16.6.4 and to the formulas below. Labels correspond to labels. The DSA structured storage is mapped onto a "flat" storage: Pointers become locations. A DSA becomes a sequence of words: The first four words are fixed, and are expected to be compiled so, and to contain two location values, a label value and an expression value. The next words are to act as a value stack for intermediate expression evaluation values.

The fixed environment pointer registers, cp and ep, branch and return label registers, br and ra, and the intermediate expression evaluation value registers, uw and wr, will be mapped onto a group, reg, of general-purpose registers. Functions were pairs of a branch label and an environment pointer and become pairs of an instruction list label and a storage location. Values are type marked.

value
    n,r:**Nat axiom** n$\geq$32,r$\geq$5
type
    Lbl
    LBL == mkLbl(lbl:Lbl)
    LOC == mkLoc(loc:Loc)
    Loc = {| 0..2^n-1 |}
    RNO == mkRno(rno:Rno)
    Rno = {| 0..2^r-1 |}
    STG = Loc $\overrightarrow{m}$ VAL
    REG = Rno $\overrightarrow{m}$ VAL
    VAL = **Int** | **Bool** | LBL | LOC | FCT
    FCT == mkFct(lbl:LBL,loc:LOC)
    OUT = VAL*

OUT shall, primitively, model computer output.

16.7.2 The Computer State

The basic state components are the storage, the group of registers and the output list.

variable
    stg:STG := [...]
    reg:REG := [...]
    out:OUT := $\langle$ ... $\rangle$

16.7.3 The Address Concept

An address is a syntactic quantity consisting of a base register designator, and an integer displacement. An address denotes a location.

type
    Adr = Bas × Dis
    Bas = Rno

Dis = **Int**

value
    A: Adr → Loc
    A(b,d) ≡ loc((**c** reg)(b)) + d
       pre ∃ lo:Loc • (**c** reg)(b)=mkLoc(lo)
       post $0 \le loc((\mathbf{c}\,reg)(b)) + d < 2^n$

16.7.4 Machine Instructions

The computer performs actions on the state as prescribed by code. The code is a linear, indexed sequence of instructions, kept separately from storage, with some instructions being (symbolic) labels, designated by unconditional and conditional jump instructions.

type
    Lbl
    Code = Ins*
    Ins = Sim | Sto | Lim | Lod | Fct | Jmp | Cjp |
          Mov | Adj | Pck | Unp | Out | Sto

In detail:

type
    Sim == mkSim(a:Adr,v:SiVal)
    Sto == mkSto(a:Adr,r:Rno,n:**Nat**)
    Lim == mkLim(r:Rno,v:LiVal)
    Lod == mkLod(r:Rno,n:**Nat**,a:Adr)
    mFct == mkmFct(r:Rno,uo:mOp)
    dFct == mkdFct(r:Rno,bo:dOp,ra:(RNO|Adr))
    Jmp == mkJmp(tar:Tar)
    Cjp == mkCjp(r:Rno,c:Cmp,tar:Tar)
    Cmp == truth | falsity | zero | not_fct | ...
    Mov == mkMov(fr:Rno,tr:Rno)
    Adj == mkAdj(r:Rno,i:**Int**)
    Pck == mkPck(fr1:Rno,fr2:Rno,tr:Rno)
    Unp == mkUnp(fr:Rno,tr1:Rno,tr2:Rno)
    Out == mkOut(sou:Sou)
    Sou == RNO | mkTxt(t:**Text**)
    Sto == finish

Storable and loadable values, monadic (unary) and dyadic (binary) operators, and jump target labels are:

type

    SiVal = **Int** | **Bool** | ...

    LiVal = **Int** | **Bool** | LBL | ...

    mOp == minus|not|...

    dOp == add|sub|mpy|div|and|or|not|xor|lo|leq|eq|neq|geq|hi|...

    Tar = LBL | RNO

Annotations:

- Sim designates the "store immediate" instruction. Sim is motivated by evaluation of constants. See the right hand side of C(mk_Cst(k))(δ,ln). We have, rather conservatively, decided to maintain any (intermediate) expression value both in a working register and "on top" of the ("DSA" local) evaluation stack.
- Sto designates the "store" instruction. Sto is motivated by the "end" of any expression evaluation. See the right hand side of C(mk_Cst(k))(δ,ln) and the ur := ...; push(ur) lines of the C_search(n) variable stack search, and the C(mk_Pre(...))(δ,ln), the C(mk_Inf(...))(δ,ln), and the C(mk_Lam(...))(δ,ln) interpretation functions. See also the "conservative" remark above (under Sim).
- Lim designates the "load immediate" instruction. Lim is motivated by evaluation of constants. (See the "conservative" decision remark just above, and at the right-hand side of C(mk_Cst(k))(δ,ln) $\equiv$.)
- Lod designates the "load" instruction. Lod is motivated in the same way as was the store instruction.
- mFct, dFct designates the monadic, respectively the dyadic, operation "apply function" instructions. They are motivated by prefix and infix operator applications. See the M(o)(...) clauses of the C(mk_Pre(o,_))(δ,ln) and C(mk_Inf(_,o,_))(δ,ln) functions.
- Jmp designates the "unconditional jump" instruction. Jmp is motivated by the **goto** lbypass and the **goto** $\underline{c}$ra lines of the C(mk_Lam(...))(δ,ln) and C(mk_Rec(...))(δ,ln) functions.
- Cjp designates the "conditional jump" instruction. Cjp is motivated by the **if** $\sim\underline{c}$ ur **then goto** l_alt **else skip end** line of the C(mk_If(b,c,a))(δ,ln) function.
- Mov designates the "move" instruction. Mov is motivated by the ep := $\underline{c}$ cp line of the C_search(n) function and the cp,ep := ptr line of the interpreter function C(mk_Rec(...))(...).
- Adj designates the "adjust" (increment) instruction. It is motivated by the loop decrements (or, vice versa, increments) expressed in the **for** i=1 **to** n **do** ... **end** line of the C_search(n) function, as well as by the need to set aside sufficient storage, in each DSA-like invocation, for the local evaluation stack. Its size can be calculated, depth, from the expression, e, being evaluated. Stack DSA's are prescribed to be set aside in the two functions, B(b)(δ,ln) and the C(mk_Rec(f,mk_Lam(v,e),b))(δ,ln) functions

which handle blocks, hence stacking of DSA's: stg := $\underline{c}$ stg $\cup[$ ptr$\mapsto$dsa $]$ — where dsa = mk_DSA($\underline{c}$ cp,$\underline{c}$ ep,$\underline{c}$ ra,$\underline{c}$ ur,$\langle\rangle$).

- Pck designates the "pack" instruction. It is motivated by the use of the mk_CLOS and mk_FCT (injector) functions of the O_search(...) and O(mk_Lam(...)), respectively the C(mk_Lam(...)) and C(mk_Rec(...)) interpreter function definitions.
- Unp designates the "unpack" instruction. It is motivated by the use of the mk_CLOS and mk_FCT (projector) functions of the O(mk_App(f,a)), respectively the C(mk_App(f,a)), interpreter functions.
- Out designates the "output" (print) instruction. It is motivated by the **return** clause of the C(mk_Pro(e)) interpreter function.

16.7.5 Machine Semantics

Our semantics of ASM is (thus) expressed imperatively.

Interpreting Code

A main function, Ic, applies to code, i.e., sequences of instructions. Ic invokes cue_Iil, which is given all of the code, and is provided with a cue as to which instruction of code to interpret. For Ic(code) the cue is 1. For cue_Iil each instruction interpretation yields, besides a state change, the index, the cue, of the next instruction to be interpreted.

value
    Ic: Code $\to$ **Unit**
    Ic(code) $\equiv$ cue_Iil(code)(1)

    cue_Iil: Code $\to$ **Nat** $\to$ **Unit**
    cue_Iil(code)(i) $\equiv$
      if i$\geq$**len** code
        then skip
        else
          let j = Ii(code(i))(i) **in**
          let cue = **if** j=i+1 **then** j **else** idx(code)(j) **end**
          cue_Iil(code)(cue) **end end**
      end

Find Label Index

A "link and load" time function converts symbolic labels to natural number list indices:

value
    idx: Code $\rightarrow$ Lbl $\rightarrow$ **Nat**
    idx(code)(l) $\equiv$
        let cue:**Nat** • cue $\in$ **inds** code $\wedge$ code(cue)=mkLbl(l)
        in cue **end**

The Store Immediate and Store Instructions

type
    Sim == mkSim(a:Adr,v:SiVal)
    SiVal = **Int** | **Bool** | ...
    Sto == mkSto(a:Adr,r:Rno,n:**Nat**)
value
    Ii: Ins $\rightarrow$ **Nat** $\rightarrow$ **Nat Unit**

    Ii(mkSim((b,d),v))(i) $\equiv$
        let loc = A(b,d) **in** stg := $\underline{c}$ stg † [loc $\mapsto$ v] **end** ; i + 1

    Ii(mkSto((b,d),r,n))(i) $\equiv$
        let loc = A(b,d) **in**
        for j = 0 **to** n−1 **do** stg := $\underline{c}$ stg † [loc+j $\mapsto$ ($\underline{c}$ reg)(r+j)] **end end** ;
        i + 1

The Load Immediate and Load Instructions

type
    Lim == mkLim(r:Rno,v:LiVal)
    LiVal = **Int** | **Bool** | LBL | ...
    Lod == mkLod(r:Rno,n:**Nat**,a:Adr)
value
    Ii: Ins $\rightarrow$ **Nat** $\rightarrow$ **Nat Unit**

    Ii(mkLim(r,v))(i) $\equiv$
        reg := $\underline{c}$ reg † [r $\mapsto$ v]; i + 1

    Ii(mkLod(r,n,(b,r)))(i) $\equiv$
        let loc = A(b,d) **in**
        for j = 0 **to** n−1 **do** reg := $\underline{c}$ reg † [r+j $\mapsto$ ($\underline{c}$ stg)(loc+j)] **end end** ;
        i + 1

The Apply Function Instructions

For the apply functions we get down to the "nitty-gritty" details of the representation of bits in machine words. We abstract, obviously, leaving it to the reader to decipher the below:

type
 BITS = (**true**|**false**)^w
value
 alltrue = $\langle$ **true** | i **in** $\langle$ 1..w $\rangle$ $\rangle$
 allfalse = $\langle$ **false** | i **in** $\langle$ 1..w $\rangle$ $\rangle$

 Val2Bits: VAL $\rightarrow$ BITS
 bits: **Bool** $\rightarrow$ BITS, bits(b) $\equiv$ $\langle$ b | i **in** $\langle$ 1..w $\rangle$ $\rangle$

type
 mFct == mkmFct(r:Rno,uo:mOp)
value
 Ii: Ins $\rightarrow$ **Nat** $\rightarrow$ **Nat Unit**
 Ii(mkmFct(r,o))(i) $\equiv$
  case o **of**
   minus $\rightarrow$ $\underline{c}$ reg † [r $\mapsto$ − ($\underline{c}$ reg)(r)],
   not $\rightarrow$ $\underline{c}$ reg † [r $\mapsto$ Not(($\underline{c}$ reg)(r))],
   ...
  end

 Not: BITS $\rightarrow$ BITS
 Not(w) $\equiv$ $\langle$ ∼w(i) | i **in** $\langle$ 1..w $\rangle\rangle$

type
 dFct == mkdFct(r:Rno,bo:dOp,ra:(RNO|Adr))
value
 Ii: Ins $\rightarrow$ **Nat** $\rightarrow$ **Nat Unit**
 Ii(mkdFct(r,o,ra))(i) $\equiv$
  let val1 = ($\underline{c}$ reg)(r),
    val2 = **case** ra **of**
       mkAdr(b,d) $\rightarrow$ ($\underline{c}$ stg)(A(b,d)),
       mkRno(rn) $\rightarrow$ ($\underline{c}$ reg)(rn)
     end in
  reg := ($\underline{c}$ reg) † [r $\mapsto$
  case bo **of**
   add $\rightarrow$ val1+val2, sub $\rightarrow$ val1−val2, mpy $\rightarrow$ val1*val2,
   div $\rightarrow$ Div(val1,val2), and $\rightarrow$ And(val1,val2), or $\rightarrow$ Or(val1,val2),
   xor $\rightarrow$ Xor(val1,val2), lo $\rightarrow$ bits(val1<val2), leq $\rightarrow$ bits(val1≤val2),

eq → bits(val1≥val2), neq → bits(val1≠val2), geq → bits(val1≥val2),
hi → bits(val1>val2), ... **end**] **end** ;
i + 1

value
Div: **Int** × **Int** → **Int**
Div(i,j) **as** q
  pre i ≥ 0 ∧ j > 0
  post ∃ m,r:NAT • i = m*j+r

And: BITS × BITS → BITS
And(w1,w2) ≡ ⟨ w1(i) ∧ w2(i) | i **in** ⟨ 1..w ⟩ ⟩

Or: BITS × BITS → BITS
Or(w1,w2) ≡ ⟨ w1(i) ∨ w2(i) | i **in** ⟨ 1..w ⟩ ⟩

Xor: BITS × BITS → BITS
Xor(w1,w2) ≡ ⟨ w1(i) **xor** w2(i) | i **in** ⟨ 1..w ⟩ ⟩

The Unconditional Jump Instruction

type
  Jmp == mkJmp(tar:Tar)
  Tar = LBL | RNO
value
  Ii: Ins → **Nat** → Lbl **Unit**
  Ii(mkJmp(target))(i) ≡
    case target **of**
      mkLbl(lbl) → lbl,
      mkRno(rno) → (**c** reg)(rno)
    end

The Conditional Jump Instruction

type
  Cjp == mkCjp(r:Rno,c:Cmp,tar:Tar)
  Cmp == truth | falsity | zero | not_fct | ...
  Tar == LBL | RNO
value
  Ii: Ins → **Nat** → **Nat** **Unit**
  Ii(mkCjp(rno,cond,target))(i) ≡
    let l = **case** target **of** mkLbl(l′) → l′, mkRno(rno′) → reg(rno′) **end in**

if case cond **of**

    truth → (**c** reg)(rno)=alltrue,

    falsity → ~((**c** reg)(rno))=allfalse,

    zero → (**c** reg)(rno)=0,

    not_fct → ~is_fct((**c** reg)(rno)),

    ... **end**

  then l **else** i+1 **end end**

value

  is_fct: VAL → **Bool**

  is_fct(val) ≡ **case** val **of** mkFct(r,o,ra) → **true**, _ → **false end**

The Register Move and Adjust Instructions

type

  Mov == mkMov(fr:Rno,tr:Rno)

  Adj == mkAdj(r:Rno,i:Intg)

value

  Ii: Ins → **Nat** → **Nat Unit**

  Ii(mkMov(fr,tr))(i) ≡ reg:=**c** reg†[tr↦(**c** reg)(fr)] ; i+1

  Ii(mkAdj(r,i))(i) ≡ reg:=**c** reg†[r↦(**c** reg)(r)+i] ; i+1

The Pack and Unpack Instructions

type

  Pck == mkPck(fr1:Rno,fr2:Rno,tr:Rno)

  Unp == mkUnp(fr:Rno,tr1:Rno,tr2:Rno)

value

  Ii: Ins → **Nat** → **Nat Unit**

  Ii(mkPck(r,l,a))(i) ≡

    reg := **c** reg † [r ↦ mkFCT((**c** reg)(l),(**c** reg)(a))] ; i + 1

    pre ∃ lbl:Lbl • (**c** reg)(l)=lbl ∧ ∃ loc:LOC • (**c** reg)(a)=loc

  Ii(mkUnp(l,a,r))(i) ≡

    reg := **c** reg † [l↦lbl(reg(r)),a↦loc((**c** reg)(r))] ; i + 1

    pre ∃ la:Lbl,lo:LOC • (**c** reg)(r)=mkFCT(la,lo)

The Output Instruction

type
    Out == mkOut(sou:Sou)
    Sou == RNO | mkTxt(t:**Text**)
    Sto == **stop**
value
    Ii: Ins → **Nat** → **Nat Unit**

    Ii(mkOut(sou))(i) ≡
        out:=c̲ out^**case** sou **of** mkRno(r)→⟨(c̲ reg)(r)⟩,mkTxt(txt)→⟨txt⟩ **end**;
        i + 1

The Finish Instruction

    Ii: Ins → **Nat** → **Nat Unit**
    Ii(finish)(i) ≡ **stop** ; 0

16.7.6 Review of ASM

We have suggested a machine language, i.e., a computer architecture. The data structures and the instruction repertoire of this computer were argued to "fit" the imperative and other constructs of the previous section's macro-expanded expressions. Thus it is claimed that this machine language will prove to be an effective target language into which to compile source language programs. This, therefore, is our next task: to show so.

16.8 A Compiling Algorithm

In Section 16.7 we developed the architecture of a machine, ASM, a computer, based on the macro-expansion semantics of Section 16.6. In the present section we shall demonstrate how one, informally, yet systematically and formally documented, can derive a compiling algorithm from SAL expressions to ASM code. By a compiling algorithm we understand a prescription that specifies which machine code to generate from any (SAL) expression (or, as we shall later indicate, from any imperative language program phrase). A compiling algorithm is thus a requirements prescription.

    We shall make use of the *dictionary* and *lexicographic level number* constructs dict and ln as before. An extra argument, stk, is passed to any compiling function. It represents the current stack index to the target machine realisation of the TLs of the DSAs.

Since storage can, in general, not be reclaimed when a block body value has been computed (i.e., when a block expression has been evaluated), and since, in this version, we have decided to stick with the merge of the control information of the activations (cp, ep, ra) and the local variable (vr), with temporaries (tl:TL), we set aside, for the "linearly addressed" storage, the maximum amount of storage cells needed in any expression evaluation, and let that be an overcautious realisation, at this stage, of the TL components of DSAs.

To that end a crude compiler function, depth, is defined. depth computes the number of temporaries, d, needed to compute any expression value, but takes into account that embedded *Let* and *Recursive* function definition blocks lead to new activations for which separate stacks, TL, are set aside. We say that depth is crude since optimising versions are relatively easy to formulate, but would, in this example, lead to excessive numbers of formula lines. The disjoint DSAs of the macro-expansion semantics definition are now mapped onto a linear ("cell") storage. Each "new" DSA realisation consists of 4+d storage cells and the temporary stack, that is, cp, ep, ra, vr and tl:TL.

16.8.1 Syntactic Types

See Sect. 16.2.2 for a formal definition of syntactic types.

16.8.2 Compile-Time Types and State

type
    LN = **Nat**
    DICT = Id $\overrightarrow{m}$ LN
    RSL /∗ macro-expanded text ∗/
    Lbl
variable
    lbls:Lbl-**set** := {}

16.8.3 Compile-Time Dynamic Function

As before, we need to generate labels "on the fly":

value
    get_Lbl: **Unit** → Lbl
    get_Lbl() ≡
        let lbl:Lbl • lbl $\notin$ **c** lbls **in**
        lbls := {lbl} ∪ **c** lbls;
        lbl **end**

16.8.4 Compile-Time Static Function

depth was explained in the introduction above.

value
   depth: Expr → **Nat**
   depth(e) ≡
      case e **of**
         mk_Cst(_) → 1,
         mk_Var(_) → 1,
         mk_Pre(_,e′) → depth(e′),
         mk_Inf(le,_,re) → **max**{depth(le),depth(re)}+1,
         mk_If(b,c,a) → **max**{depth(b),depth(c),depth(a)}+1,
         mk_Lam(_,_) → 1,
         mk_Let(_,d,_) → depth(d),
         mk_Rec(_,_,_) → 1,
         mk_App(f,a) → **max**{depth(f),depth(a)}+1
      end
   max: **Nat-set** → **Nat**
   max(ns) ≡ **let** n:**Nat** • n ∈ ns ∧ ~∃ j:**Nat** • j ∈ ns ∧ j>i **in** n **end**
      pre ns≠{}

16.8.5 Run-Time Constant Values

The label lerror is global: Whenever evaluation fails, a jump is made to this label (an error message is output, and further evaluation stops). We shall refer to the constant identifiers cp, ep, ra, vr, pm, u, j, top, t, br repeatedly. Identifiers vr, pm, u and j designate "the same thing": the placeholder for local variables, function parameters, temporary values, and the **for** loop step-counter value introduced below. Identifiers top and t designate "the same thing": The placeholder for the first (i.e., bottom) stack value.

variable
   lerror:Lbl := get_Lbl()
value
   cp:**Nat** = 0,
   ep:**Nat** = 1,
   ra:**Nat** = 2,
   vr,pm,u,j:**Nat** = 3,
   top,t:**Nat** = 4,
   br:**Nat** = 5

The cp, ep, ra, vr (u) values index the first four registers as well as the first four cells of any DSA realisation. Register indices top and br designate the current evaluation stack top register, respectively the branch (forward) register.

These constants (cp, ep, ra, vr, pm, u, j,top, t and br) will be used in this section and in Sects. 16.9 and 16.10 in corresponding compilation algorithms (pages 638–640 and 648–651).

16.8.6 Compilation Functions

In the development below we show first the macro-expansion function definitions, and then the compiling specifications, SAL construct by construct.

[0] Program Compilation

```
─────────────────── Program Compilation ───────────────────

Previous step:

    C: Pro → RSL  Unit
    C(mk_Pro(e)) ≡ C(e)([ ],0); ur := hd
    s_stk((c stg)(c cp));return c ur


Previous step:

    CA: Pro → Unit  Code
    CA(mk_Pro(e)) ≡
      * let lexit = get_Lbl(), de = depth(e) in
      ⟨ mkLim(cp,0), mkLim(ep,0), mkLim(top,t+de) ⟩
      ⌃ CA(e)([ ],0,t) ⌃
      ⟨ mkLod(u,1,mkAdr(p,t)), mkOut(u), mkJmp(lexit),
        lerror, mkOut("error"), lexit, finish ⟩
      * end
```

[1] Constant Expression Compilation

```
──────────────── Constant Expression Compilation ────────────────

Previous step:

    C: E → (DICT×LN) → RSL  Unit
    C(mk_Cst(k))(δ,ln) ≡ (ur := k; push(ur))


Previous step:

    CA: E → DICT × LN × STK → Code  Unit
    CA(mk_Cst(k))(_,_,stk) ≡ ⟨mkLim(u,k),mkSim(mkAdr(cp,stk),k)⟩
```

[2] Variable Expression Compilation

—————————— Variable Expression Compilation: *Previous step:* ——————————

Previous Step:

C(mk_Var(v))(δ,ln) ≡ C_search(δ(id))

C_search: **Nat** → **Unit**
C_search(n) ≡
    for i=1 **to** n **do** ep := s_ep((**c** stg)(**c** ep)) **end**;
    ur := s_va((**c** stg)(**c** ep));
    push(ur);
    ep := **c** cp

For such statements, $S(i)$, which do not change the step counter value j, it is immaterial whether we count up or down. The RSL **for** loop can also be expressed using the second and last clause below.

    assert:
      /* for certain kinds of $S(i)$ */

      for j **in** ⟨ 1..n ⟩ **do** $S(j)$ **end**
      ≡
      for j = 1 **to** n **do** $S(j)$ **end**
      ≡
      for j **in** ⟨ n..1 ⟩ **do** $S(j)$ **end**
      ≡
      for j = n **by** −1 **to** 1 **do** $S(j)$ **end**
      ≡
      variable j:**Nat** := n;
      while **c** j ≠ 0 **do** $S(j)$; j := **c** j − 1 **end**
      ≡
      variable j:**Nat** := 1;
      while **c** j ≠ n+1 **do** $S(j)$; j := **c** j + 1 **end**

So, when at lexicographic level n, searching the stack of DSAs for the value of the variable defined at level ln, we count "backwards", from ln-n to 0.

—————————— Variable Expression Compilation: *Present step:* ——————————

Present Step:

CA(mk_Var(v))(δ,ln,stk) ≡

```
 * let n = δ(v),
 *    lloop = get_Lbl(),
 *    lload = get_Lbl() in
⟨ mkLim(j,ln−n),
  lloop,
  mkCjp(j,zero,lload),
  mkLod(ep,1,mkAdr(ep,ep)),
  mkAdj(j,−1),
  mkJmp(lloop),
  lload,
  mkLod(u,1,mkAdr(ep,vr)),
  mkSto(mkAdr(cp,stk),u,1),
  mkMov(ep,cp) ⟩
 * end
```

[3] Prefix Expression Compilation

_____ Prefix Expression Compilation _____

Previous step:

$$C(mk\_Pre(o,e))(\delta,ln) \equiv$$
$$C(e)(\delta,ln);$$
$$ur := M(o)(\underline{c}\,ur);$$
$$push(ur)$$

Previous step:

$$CA(mk\_Pre(o,e))(\delta,ln,stk) \equiv$$
$$CA(e)(\delta,ln,stk) \,\widehat{}$$
$$⟨ mkmFct(u,o),$$
$$mkSto(mkAdr(cp,stk),u,1) ⟩$$

[4] Infix Expression Compilation

_____ Infix Expression Compilation _____

Previous step:

$$C(mk\_Inf(le,o,re))(\delta,ln) \equiv$$
$$C(le)(\delta,ln); C(re)(\delta,ln); pop(ur); pop(wr);$$
$$ur := M(o)(\underline{c}\,ur,\underline{c}\,wr);$$

push(ur)

Previous step:

CA(mk_Inf(le,o,re))(δ,ln,stk) ≡
  CA(re)(δ,ln,stk) ⌢ CA(le)(δ,ln,stk+1) ⌢
  ⟨ mkLod(u,1,mkAdr(cp,stk+1)),
    mkdFct(u,o,mkAdr(cp,stk)),
    mkSto(mkAdr(cp,stk),u,1)⟩

[5] Conditional Expression Compilation

────────────── Conditional Expression Compilation ──────────────

Previous step:

C(mk_If(b,c,a))(δ,ln) ≡
  * **let** l_alt = get_Lbl(), l_out = get_Lbl() **in**
  C(b)(δ,ln);
  pop(ur);
  if ∼**c** ur
      then goto l_alt
      else skip end
  C(c)(δ,ln); **goto** l_out;
  label l_alt: C(a)(δ,ln);
  label l_out:
  * **end**

Present step:

CA(mk_If(b,c,a))(δ,ln,stk) ≡
  * **let** lalt = get_Lbl(), lout = get_Lbl() **in**
  CA(b)(δ,ln,stk) ⌢
  ⟨ mkLod(u,1,mkAdr(cp,stk)),
    mkCjp(u,falsity,lalt) ⟩ ⌢
  CA(c)(δ,ln,stk) ⌢
  ⟨ mkJmp(lout),
    lalt ⟩ ⌢
  CA(a)(δ,ln,stk) ⌢
  ⟨ lout ⟩
  * **end**

[6] Lambda-Expression Compilation

```
_____ Lambda-Expression Compilation _____
```

Previous step:

C(mk_Lam(v,e))(δ,ln) ≡
  * **let** lbypass = get_Lbl(), lfct = get_Lbl() **in**
  goto lbypass;
  label lfct: B(e)(δ † [v↦ln+1],ln+1);
    goto <u>c</u> ra;
  label lbypass: ur := mk_FCT(lfct,<u>c</u> cp); push(ur)
  * **end**

Present step:

CA(mk_Lam(v,e))(δ,ln,stk) ≡
  * **let** lbypass = get_Lbl(), lfct = get_Lbl() **in**
  ⟨ mkJmp(lbypass), lfct ⟩ ⌢
  CA(e)(δ † [v ↦ ln+1],ln+1,stk) ⌢
  ⟨ mkJmp(ra),
    lbypass,
    mkLim(u,lfct), mkPck(u,u,p), mkSto(mkAdr(cp,stk),u,1) ⟩
  * **end**

[7] Simple Let Expression Compilation

```
_____ Simple Let Expression Compilation _____
```

Previous step:

C(mk_Let(v,d,b))(δ,ln) ≡
  C(d)(δ,ln); pop(ur);
  B(b)(δ†[v↦ln+1],ln+1)

Previous step:

CA(mk_Let(v,d,b))(δ,ln,stk) ≡
  CA(d)(δ,ln,stk) ⌢
  ⟨ mkLod(u,1,mkAdr(cp,stk)) ⟩ ⌢
  CB(b)(δ † [v ↦ ln+1],ln+1,stk)

[*] Block Expression

```
_____ Block Expressions _____

Previous step:

    B: E → (DICT × LN) → RSL Unit
    B(b)(δ,ln) ≡
        let ptr:Ptr • ptr ∉ dom c̲ stg in
        stg := c̲ stg ∪ [ ptr ↦ mk_DSA(c̲ cp,c̲ ep,c̲ ra,c̲ ur,⟨⟩) ];
        cp,ep := ptr;
        C(b)(δ,ln);
        pop(ur);
        ep:=s_ep((c̲ stg)(c̲ cp));
        ra:=s_ra((c̲ stg)(c̲ cp));
        cp:=s_cp((c̲ stg)(c̲ cp));
        [ stg := c̲ stg \ {ptr}; ]
        push(ur)
        end


Present step:

    CB(b)(δ,ln,stk) ≡
        * let dbl = depth(b) in
        ⟨ mkSto(mkAdr(top,cp),cp,t),
          mkMov(cp,top),
          mkMov(ep,top),
          mkAdj(top,t+dbl) ⟩ ⌢
        CA(b)(δ,ln+1,stk) ⌢
        ⟨ mkLod(u,1,mkAdr(cp,t)),
          mkLod(p,t−1,mkAdr(cp,cp)),
          mkSto(mkAdr(cp,stk),u,1) ⟩
        * end
```

[8] Recursive Function/Let Expression Compilation

```
_____ Recursive Function/Let Expression Compilation _____

Previous step:

    C(mk_Rec(f,mk_Lam(v,e),b))(δ,ln) ≡
        * let lfct = get_Lbl(), lbypass = get_Lbl() in
        goto lbypass;
        label lfct:
```

```
        B(e)(δ † [f↦ln+1,v↦ln+2],ln+2);
        goto c ra;
    label lbypass:
        let ptr:Ptr • ptr ∉ dom c stg in
        ur := mk_FCT(lfct,ptr);
        stg := c stg ∪ [ ptr ↦ mk_DSA(c cp,c ep,c ra,c ur,⟨⟩) ];
        cp,ep := ptr;
        C(b)(δ † [f↦ln+1],ln+1);
        pop(ur);
        ep:=s_ep((c stg)(c cp));
        ra:=s_ra((c stg)(c cp));
        cp:=s_cp((c stg)(c cp));
        [ stg := c stg \ {ptr}; ]
        push(ur)
    end * end
```

Present step:

```
  CA(mk_Rec(f,mk_Lam(v,e),b))(δ,ln,stk) ≡
    * let lfct = get_Lblb(), lbypass = get_Lbl(), db = depth(b) in
    ⟨ mkJmp(lbypass), lfct ⟩ ⌃
    CB(d)(δ † [f ↦ ln+1,v ↦ ln+2],ln+2,stk)
    ⟨ mkJmp(ra),
        lbypass,
        mkLim(u,lfct),
        mkSto(mkAdr(top,cp),cp,t−1),
        mkPck(u,u,top),
        mkSto(mkAdr(top,u),u,1),
        mkMov(cp,top),
        mkMov(ep,top),
        mkAdj(top,t+db) ⟩ ⌃
    CA(b)(δ † [f ↦ ln+1],ln+1,stk) ⌃
    ⟨ mkLod(u,1,mkAdr(cp,t)),
        mkLod(cp,t−1,mkAdr(cp,cp)),
        mkSto(mkAdr(cp,stk),u,1) ⟩ * end
```

[9] Function Application Expression Compilation

────────── Function Application Expression Compilation ──────────

Previous step:

```
  C(mk_App(f,a))(δ,ln) ≡
```

```
    * let lret = get_Lbl() in
  C(a)(δ,ln); C(f)(δ,ln);
  case c̲ ur of
     mk_FCT(lfct,ptr) →
         {ep:=ptr,
          br:=lfct,
          ra:=lret,
          (pop(ur);pop(ur))};
         goto c̲ br;
         label lret:,
     _ → chaos
  end
  * end
```

Present step:

```
  CA(mk_App(f,a))(δ,ln,stk) ≡
     * let lret = get_lbl() in
  CA(a)(δ,ln,stk) ⌢ CA(f)(δ,ln,stk+1) ⌢
  ⟨ mkLod(u,1,mkAdr(cp,stk+1)),
     mkCjp(u,non_function,lerror),
     mkUnp(br,ep,u),
     mkLim(ra,lret),
     mkLod(pm,1,mkAdr(cp,stk)),
     mkJmp(br),
     lret ⟩
     * end
```

16.8.7 Review of Compiling Algorithm

Lest one should miss sight of it, it may be important to remind the reader of what we have done. We shall do it in the following fashion. The compiling function, CA, is just another functional program. It applies, at the root, to a complete SAL program represented in abstract form. And it applies, recursively, to subparts of that SAL program, and to sub-subparts, etc. The result of "performing" CA on a complete SAL program is an ASM program, i.e., ASM code. That code can then be submitted to an ASM computer, i.e., an an ASM interpreter.

The above kind of review is "repeated" for the next two kinds of compiling algorithms. Those compiling algorithms are, however, expressed in terms of what is known as attribute semantics. The reviews are found in Sects. 16.9.7 and 16.10.7.

16.9 An Attribute Grammar Semantics

By an attribute grammar semantics of a source language we understand (i) a set of usually concrete, BNF, grammar syntax rules defining the source language's character string representations; (ii) an association of what we shall call attributes, named and typed variables, to each syntactic category; and (iii) to each rule, i.e., to each pairing of a left-hand side nonterminal with a right-hand side alternative, i.e., a finite sequence of zero, one or more nonterminals (and terminals), a set of actions: one per attribute associated with either the left- or the right-hand side nonterminal. The actions are statement sequences. Their role is to assign values to the attributes.

In Sect. 7.7.2 we gave a brief introduction to attribute grammar semantics, so we shall now assume the concept reasonably well known [45, 128, 262, 270, 272, 304, 328, 532, 541].

Let us, anyway, refresh our memory. The meaning of an attribute grammar semantics is as follows: Consider a source text and its corresponding (cum "annotated") parse tree. To each tree node allocate a variable for each attribute associated with that node's syntactic category. Then compute the values of these according to the action sets. Two extreme cases arise: The value of an attribute is a function solely of the attribute values of the attributed variables of the immediate descendant, or of the immediate ascendant nodes. In the former case we say that the attribute variable assigned to is synthesised, while in the latter case we say it is inherited.

We first choose the same basic run-time realisation as propagated till now. For the sake of notational variety, and perhaps also your increased reading ability, we express the compiled target code in "free form". Hence the meaning is intended to be identical, down to the individual computation sequences. Thus the reader will observe a close resemblance between the example now given and that of the previous section. In fact, their main difference is one of style.

To compute depth, see Sect. 16.8.4, we observe that it is computed from the leaves of the parse tree "up", i.e., it is a synthesized attribute. Following the depth function definition we therefore ascribe a depth attribute of type natural number to each of the syntactic categories and follow the specification given in the depth function definition to determine the specific assignment right-hand sides. We refer to each attribute grammar rule for details.

stack (stk), level number (ln) and dictionary (dict) attributes are all "passed down" from the parse tree root, and are thus inherited. Finally the code attribute is synthesized. It "stores" the so-far generated code text strings. We have not shown a formal BNF grammar for those strings, but leave that as an exercise for the reader.

16.9.1 Abstract Syntactic Types

The concrete grammar presented in Sect. 16.9.2 is based on the abstract syntax of Sect. 16.2.2.

16.9.2 SAL BNF Grammar, 1

The concrete grammar chosen, at this stage, for SAL is LR(1). That is: proper SAL text strings need to look ahead, left-to-right, only one token (a keyword, a "k"onstant, an "id"entifier, a parenthesis, etc.), to determine the phrase structure.

```
Pro ::= Exp
Exp ::= k                                   |
    ::= id                                  |
    ::= ⊙ Exp                               |
    ::= ( Exp ⊘ Exp )                       |
    ::= if Exp then Exp else Exp end |
    ::= let Id = Exp in Exp end             |
    ::= Lam                                 |
    ::= rec Id = Lam in Blk end             |
    ::= apply Exp ( Exp )
Lam ::= fun ( Id ) = Blk end
Blk ::= Exp
```

BNF Grammar 16.1. A first one for SAL

We omit giving syntax for constants (k) and identifiers (id), and for monadic (⊙) and dyadic (⊘) operators.

16.9.3 Node Attributes

Syntax category	Attribute		Type	Kind
Pro	code		Code	synthesised
Exp, Lam	code		Code	inherited
	ln	(level number)	**Nat**	inherited
	dict	(dictionary)	Id $\overrightarrow{m}$ **Nat**	inherited
	stk	(stack index)	**Nat**	inherited
	d	(depth)	**Nat**	synthesised
Blk	code		Code	inherited
	ln	(level number)	**Nat**	inherited
	dict	(dictionary)	Id $\overrightarrow{m}$ **Nat**	inherited

16.9.4 Constants

As before, we need a single, hence global, program point to where jumps can be made in case of erroneous computation situations:

global lerror = get_Lbl()

In the compilation algorithms below we refer to some of the constants cp, ep, ra, vr, pm, u, j, top, t and br. Their natural number values were defined is Sect. 16.8.5.

16.9.5 Some Typographical Distinctions

In the compilation sections which now follow we have adopted some conventions concerning the use of roman and *italic* texts. Roman text designates auxiliary quantities whose values are to be evaluated in the code attribute computation process. *Italic* text designates code text to be generated. Since the code to be generated is text we surround it by double quotes as follows: "code".

16.9.6 Compilation Functions

[0] Program Compilation

The final code text to be generated for an entire SAL program emerges from the $code_p$ attribute variable at the program root.
   We refer to Compiling Algorithm 16.1.

[1] Constant Expression Compilation

We refer to Compiling Algorithm 16.2.

[2] Variable Expression Compilation

We refer to Compiling Algorithm 16.3.

[3] Prefix Expression Compilation

We refer to Compiling Algorithm 16.4.
Here $\odot$ is used both to designate (denote) the source language monadic operator as well as the target language's same! Just for convenience!

[4] Infix Expression Compilation

We refer to Compiling Algorithm 16.5.
Here $\oslash$ is used as was $\odot$ above, for prefix expressions.

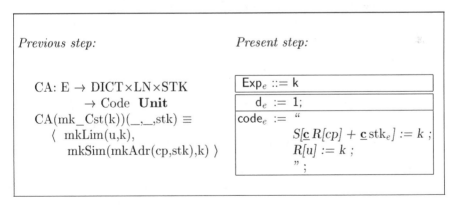

Compiling Algorithm 16.1. Program compilation

Previous step:

CA: E → DICT×LN×STK
        → Code **Unit**
CA(mk_Cst(k))(_,_,stk) ≡
  ⟨ mkLim(u,k),
    mkSim(mkAdr(cp,stk),k) ⟩

Present step:

$Exp_e ::= k$
$d_e := 1;$
$code_e :=$ "
$S[\underline{c}\,R[cp] + \underline{c}\,stk_e] := k ;$
$R[u] := k ;$
" ;

Compiling Algorithm 16.2. Constant expression compilation

[5] Conditional Expression Compilation

We refer to Compiling Algorithm 16.6.

Previous step: *Present step:*

$$CA(mk\_Var(v))(\delta,ln,stk) \equiv$$

$*$ **let** n $= \delta(v)$,

$*$ lloop $=$ get_Lbl(),

$*$ lload $=$ get_Lbl() **in**

$\langle$ mkLim(j,ln$-$n),

    lloop,

    mkCjp(j,zero,lload),

    mkLod(ep,1,mkAdr(ep,ep)),

    mkAdj(j,-1),

    mkJmp(lloop),

    lload,

    mkLod(u,1,mkAdr(ep,vr)),

    mkSto(mkAdr(cp,stk),u,1),

    mkMov(ep,cp) $\rangle$

$*$ **end**

Exp_e ::= id
local
lloop $=$ get_Lbl() **in**
lload $=$ get_Lbl() **in**
d_e := 1 ;
$code_e$:= "
$\quad R[j]:=\underline{\mathbf{c}}\, ln_e\text{-}\underline{\mathbf{c}}\, dict_e\,(id);$
$\quad lloop:$
$\quad \underline{if}\ \underline{\mathbf{c}}\ R[j]=0$
$\quad \underline{then}\ goto\ lload;$
$\quad R[ep]:=\underline{\mathbf{c}}\, S[\underline{\mathbf{c}}\, R[ep]]+ep;$
$\quad R[j]\ :=\underline{\mathbf{c}}\, R[j]\text{-}1;$
$\quad \underline{goto}\ lloop\ ;$
$\quad lload:$
$\quad R[u]:=\underline{\mathbf{c}}\, S[\underline{\mathbf{c}}\, R[ep]]+vr;$
$\quad S[\underline{\mathbf{c}}\, R[cp]+\underline{\mathbf{c}}\, stk_e]:=\underline{\mathbf{c}}\, R[u];$
$\quad R[ep]:=\underline{\mathbf{c}}\, R[cp];$
$\quad "\ ;$

Compiling Algorithm 16.3. Variable expression compilation

[6] Lambda-Expression Compilation

We refer to Compiling Algorithm 16.7.

[7] Simple Let Expression Compilation

We refer to Compiling Algorithm 16.8.

[*] Block Expression Compilation

We refer to Compiling Algorithm 16.9.

[8] Recursive Function/Let Expression Compilation

We refer to Compiling Algorithm 16.10.

[9] Function Application Expression Compilation

We refer to Compiling Algorithm 16.11.

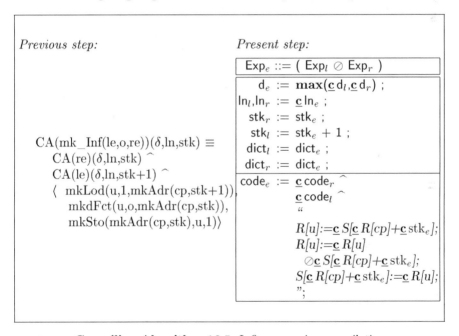

Previous step:

$$\begin{array}{l} \mathrm{CA}(\mathrm{mk_Pre}(o,e))(\delta,\mathrm{ln},\mathrm{stk}) \equiv \\ \quad \mathrm{CA}(e)(\delta,\mathrm{ln},\mathrm{stk})\ \frown \\ \quad \langle\ \mathrm{mkmFct}(u,o), \\ \qquad \mathrm{mkSto}(\mathrm{mkAdr}(cp,\mathrm{stk}),u,1)\ \rangle \end{array}$$

Present step:

$$\mathsf{Exp}_e ::= \odot\ \mathsf{Exp}_a$$

$$\begin{array}{rcl} \mathsf{d}_e &:=& \underline{\mathsf{c}}\,\mathsf{d}_a; \\ \mathsf{ln}_a &:=& \underline{\mathsf{c}}\,\mathsf{ln}_e; \\ \mathsf{stk}_a &:=& \underline{\mathsf{c}}\,\mathsf{stk}_e; \\ \mathsf{dict}_a &:=& \underline{\mathsf{c}}\,\mathsf{dict}_e; \end{array}$$

$$\begin{array}{rcl} \mathsf{code}_e &:=& \underline{\mathsf{c}}\,\mathsf{code}_a\ \frown \\ && \text{``} \\ && \quad R[u]{:=}\odot\ \underline{\mathsf{c}}\ R[u]; \\ && \quad S[\underline{\mathsf{c}}\ R[cp]{+}\underline{\mathsf{c}}\,\mathrm{stk}_e]{:=}\underline{\mathsf{c}}\ R[u]; \\ && \text{''}; \end{array}$$

Compiling Algorithm 16.4. Prefix expression compilation

Previous step:

$$\begin{array}{l} \mathrm{CA}(\mathrm{mk_Inf}(le,o,re))(\delta,\mathrm{ln},\mathrm{stk}) \equiv \\ \quad \mathrm{CA}(re)(\delta,\mathrm{ln},\mathrm{stk})\ \frown \\ \quad \mathrm{CA}(le)(\delta,\mathrm{ln},\mathrm{stk}{+}1)\ \frown \\ \quad \langle\ \mathrm{mkLod}(u,1,\mathrm{mkAdr}(cp,\mathrm{stk}{+}1)), \\ \qquad \mathrm{mkdFct}(u,o,\mathrm{mkAdr}(cp,\mathrm{stk})), \\ \qquad \mathrm{mkSto}(\mathrm{mkAdr}(cp,\mathrm{stk}),u,1)\rangle \end{array}$$

Present step:

$$\mathsf{Exp}_e ::= (\ \mathsf{Exp}_l \oslash \mathsf{Exp}_r\ )$$

$$\begin{array}{rcl} \mathsf{d}_e &:=& \mathbf{max}(\underline{\mathsf{c}}\,\mathsf{d}_l,\underline{\mathsf{c}}\,\mathsf{d}_r)\ ; \\ \mathsf{ln}_l,\mathsf{ln}_r &:=& \underline{\mathsf{c}}\,\mathsf{ln}_e\ ; \\ \mathsf{stk}_r &:=& \mathsf{stk}_e\ ; \\ \mathsf{stk}_l &:=& \mathsf{stk}_e + 1\ ; \\ \mathsf{dict}_l &:=& \mathsf{dict}_e\ ; \\ \mathsf{dict}_r &:=& \mathsf{dict}_e\ ; \end{array}$$

$$\begin{array}{rcl} \mathsf{code}_e &:=& \underline{\mathsf{c}}\,\mathsf{code}_r\ \frown \\ && \underline{\mathsf{c}}\,\mathsf{code}_l\ \frown \\ && \text{``} \\ && \quad R[u]{:=}\underline{\mathsf{c}}\ S[\underline{\mathsf{c}}\ R[cp]{+}\underline{\mathsf{c}}\,\mathrm{stk}_e]; \\ && \quad R[u]{:=}\underline{\mathsf{c}}\ R[u] \\ && \qquad \oslash\underline{\mathsf{c}}\ S[\underline{\mathsf{c}}\ R[cp]{+}\underline{\mathsf{c}}\,\mathrm{stk}_e]; \\ && \quad S[\underline{\mathsf{c}}\ R[cp]{+}\underline{\mathsf{c}}\,\mathrm{stk}_e]{:=}\underline{\mathsf{c}}\ R[u]; \\ && \text{''}; \end{array}$$

Compiling Algorithm 16.5. Infix expression compilation

16.9.7 Review of Attribute Semantics, 1

The below review should be compared to the review given, in Sect. 16.8.7, of the compiling algorithm of Sect. 16.8.

Lest one should miss sight of it, it may be important to remind the reader of what we have done. We shall do it in the following fashion. Assume a SAL

Previous step:	Present step:
	$\mathsf{Exp}_e ::=$ **if** Exp_b
	then Exp_c
	else Exp_a **end**
	local
	lalt $=$ get_Lbl()
	lout $=$ get_Lbl() **in**
	$d_e := \mathbf{max}(\underline{\mathbf{c}}\, d_b, \underline{\mathbf{c}}\, d_c, \underline{\mathbf{c}}\, d_a) + 1$;
CA(mk_If(b,c,a))(δ,ln,stk) $\equiv$	$\mathsf{ln}_b := \underline{\mathbf{c}}\, \mathsf{ln}_e$;
$*$ **let** lalt $=$ get_Lbl(),	$\mathsf{ln}_c := \underline{\mathbf{c}}\, \mathsf{ln}_e$;
$*$ lout $=$ get_Lbl() **in**	$\mathsf{ln}_a := \underline{\mathbf{c}}\, \mathsf{ln}_e$;
CA(b)(δ,ln,stk) $\widehat{}$	$\mathsf{stk}_b := \underline{\mathbf{c}}\, \mathsf{stk}_e$;
$\langle$ mkLod(u,1,mkAdr(cp,stk)),	$\mathsf{stk}_c := \underline{\mathbf{c}}\, \mathsf{stk}_e$;
mkCjp(u,falsity,lalt) $\rangle$ $\widehat{}$	$\mathsf{stk}_a := \underline{\mathbf{c}}\, \mathsf{stk}_e$;
CA(c)(δ,ln,stk) $\widehat{}$	$\mathsf{dict}_b := \underline{\mathbf{c}}\, \mathsf{dict}_e$;
$\langle$ mkJmp(lout),	$\mathsf{dict}_c := \underline{\mathbf{c}}\, \mathsf{dict}_e$;
lalt $\rangle$ $\widehat{}$	$\mathsf{dict}_a := \underline{\mathbf{c}}\, \mathsf{dict}_e$;
CA(a)(δ,ln,stk) $\widehat{}$	$\mathsf{code}_e := \underline{\mathbf{c}}\, \mathsf{code}_b$ $\widehat{}$
$\langle$ lout $\rangle$	"
$*$ **end**	$R[u]:=\underline{\mathbf{c}}\, S[\underline{\mathbf{c}}\, R[cp]+\underline{\mathbf{c}}\, \mathsf{stk}_e$];
	$\underline{if} \sim\underline{\mathbf{c}}\, R[u]\ \underline{then}\ \underline{goto}\ lalt$;
	" $\widehat{}$ $\underline{\mathbf{c}}\, \mathsf{code}_c$ $\widehat{}$ "
	$\underline{goto}\ lout$;
	$\underline{lalt:}$
	" $\widehat{}$ $\underline{\mathbf{c}}\, \mathsf{code}a$ $\widehat{}$ "
	$\underline{lout:}$
	" ;

Compiling Algorithm 16.6. Conditional expression compilation

program. Assume that it has been properly parsed, and that the parse tree, with all its nodes, is somehow represented as a data structure in storage. What the attribute semantics given in this section prescribes is the following: To each node, the root and all the internal nodes, are associated the prescribed variables. Thus a variable declaration mentioned one time in the above definition, for a given syntactic category, is repeated for all nodes of that prescribed category. And all the parse tree nodes are further decorated with all the assignment texts of attributes semantics rules [0–9] for each given syntax rule. That is, they are repeated for each occurrence of subparse tree corresponding to that rule. Now, when all that has been done, an execution takes place. All the assignments are now to be effected. Some can be done

Previous step:	Present step:

<table>
<tr><td rowspan="12">

$CA(mk\_Lam(v,e))(\delta,ln,stk) \equiv$
 * **let** lbypass = get_Lbl(),
 *   lfct = get_Lbl() **in**
 $\langle$ mkJmp(lbypass),
     lfct $\rangle$ ^
 $CA(e)(\delta \dagger [v \mapsto ln+1],ln+1,stk)$ ^
 $\langle$ mkJmp(ra),
     lbypass,
     mkLim(u,lfct),
     mkPck(u,u,p),
     mkSto(mkAdr(cp,stk),u,1) $\rangle$
 * **end**

</td></tr>
<tr><td>$Exp_e ::= Lam_l$</td></tr>
<tr><td>

$d_e := d_l$
$ln_l := ln_e$
$stk_l := stk_e$
$dict_l := dict_e$

</td></tr>
<tr><td>$code_l := code_e$</td></tr>
<tr><td>$Lam_e ::= \textbf{fun} (\text{ id }) = Blk_b \textbf{ end}$</td></tr>
<tr><td>

local =
 lfct = get_Lbl() **in**
lbypass = get_Lbl() **in**

</td></tr>
<tr><td>

$d_e := 1$;
$ln_b := \underline{\textbf{c}} \, ln_e + 1$;
$dict_b := \underline{\textbf{c}} \, dict_e \dagger [\text{ id } \mapsto \underline{\textbf{c}} \, ln_e + 1]$;

</td></tr>
<tr><td>

$code_e :=$ "goto lbypass;
     lfct:
     "^$\underline{\textbf{c}}\,code_b$ ^ "
     goto $\underline{\textbf{c}}\,R[ra]$;
     lbypass:
     $R[u]:=lfct$;
     $R[u]:=$
       $mkFct(\underline{\textbf{c}}\,R[u],\underline{\textbf{c}}\,R[cp])$;
     $S[\underline{\textbf{c}}\,R[cp]+\underline{\textbf{c}}\,stk_e]:=\underline{\textbf{c}}\,R[u]$;
     " ;

</td></tr>
</table>

Compiling Algorithm 16.7. Lambda-Expression compilation

right away: the inherited assignments at those nodes just "below", i.e., immediately next to, the root, the synthesised at those nodes that are just "above",
i.e., immediately next to, a leaf. Once those assignments have been done additional assignments to synthesised and inherited attributed variables can be
made, and so on. When no more assignments can be made, the root node code
text variable contains the resulting ASM-like program, and that program, i.e.,
code, can now be executed.

The above kind of review is repeated for the next kind of attribute semantics. That review is found in Sect. 16.10.7.

16.10 Another Attribute Grammar Semantics

The BNF grammar of Sect. 16.9.2 is both 'bottom-up' and 'top-down' analyz-
able. That did not matter very much in Section 16.9, since attribute variable

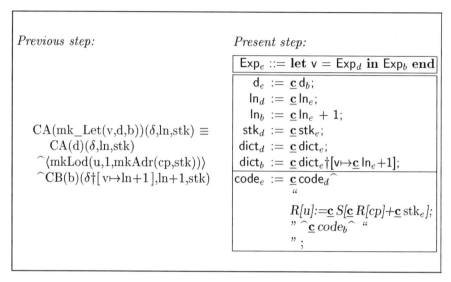

Compiling Algorithm 16.8. Simple let expression compilation

value computations, that is, the computation based on attribute action cluster interpretations, still required the presence of the entire parse tree before any code text could be generated. In the present section we present an attribute grammar semantics specification of another compiling algorithm. The new compiling algorithm is based solely on a top-down parse of SAL expressions. That new algorithm is capable of generating code text simultaneously with parsing. Again we shall not argue how we choose a solution. Such arguments are left to proper, specialised texts on attribute grammar semantics [94, 260, 531].

Instead, we ask you to recall the twin stack abstract machine of Section 16.6. In the implementation of the DSA stack we shall let DSAs fit exactly four t positions: cp, ep, ra and vr. Temporaries are now to be allocated to a global, contiguous stack, STK. Since SAL is simply applicative, it permits, e.g., no GOTOs. This poses no problems as concerns correct indices into STK positions, i.e., the stack top. The STK is realised in the storage "below" the activation stack. Think of the target machine addressing being "wrapped around" the address zero to a maximum available storage address — and you get a scheme that was at least quite common in the early days of computing.

To cope with known code text to be "delay generated" a global attribute, also called code, is introduced. It is treated like a stack. Pushing onto the stack corresponds to concatenation; pop to removing the head, the top element code, from the stack, and top to yielding that code. Pushing occurs for all code texts known when recognising the initial prefix string, as one does in top-down parsing, of a composite expression, to wit: ⊙, ⊘, (, **if**, **let**, **rec**,

<table>
<tr><td>

Previous step:

</td><td>

Present step:

</td></tr>
</table>

| | $\mathsf{Blk}_b ::= \mathsf{Exp}_e$ |

$\mathsf{In}_e := \underline{\mathbf{c}}\,\mathsf{In}_b + 1 ;$
$\mathsf{dict}_e := \mathsf{dict}_b ;$
$\mathsf{stk}_e := \mathsf{t} ;$

$\mathsf{code}_b :=$

$CB(b)(\delta,\mathrm{ln},\mathrm{stk}) \equiv$
   $*$ **let** $\mathrm{dbl} = \mathrm{depth}(b)$ **in**
   $\langle$ mkSto(mkAdr(top,cp),cp,t),
     mkMov(cp,top),
     mkMov(ep,top),
     mkAdj(top,t+dbl) $\rangle$ $\widehat{\ }$
   $CA(b)(\delta,\mathrm{ln}+1,\mathrm{stk})$ $\widehat{\ }$
   $\langle$ mkLod(u,1,mkAdr(cp,t)),
     mkLod(p,t$-$1,mkAdr(cp,cp)),
     mkSto(mkAdr(cp,stk),u,1) $\rangle$
   $*$ **end**

"
$S[\underline{\mathbf{c}}\,R[top]+cp]:=\underline{\mathbf{c}}\,R[cp];$
$S[\underline{\mathbf{c}}\,R[top]+ep]:=\underline{\mathbf{c}}\,R[ep];$
$S[R[top]+ra]:=\underline{\mathbf{c}}\,R[ra];$
$S[R[top]+vr]:=\underline{\mathbf{c}}\,R[u];$
$R[cp]:=\underline{\mathbf{c}}\,R[top];$
$R[ep]:=\underline{\mathbf{c}}\,R[cp];$
$R[top]:=$
   $\underline{\mathbf{c}}\,R[top]+(t+\underline{\mathbf{c}}\,d_e);$
" $\widehat{\ }\underline{\mathbf{c}}\,\mathsf{code}_e\widehat{\ }$"
$R[ep]:=\underline{\mathbf{c}}\,S[\underline{\mathbf{c}}\,R[cp]+ep];$
$R[ra]:=\underline{\mathbf{c}}\,S[\underline{\mathbf{c}}\,R[cp]+ra];$
$R[u]:=\underline{\mathbf{c}}\,S[\underline{\mathbf{c}}\,R[cp]+t];$
$R[cp]:=\underline{\mathbf{c}}\,S[\underline{\mathbf{c}}\,R[cp]+cp];$
$S[\underline{\mathbf{c}}\,R[cp]+\underline{\mathbf{c}}\,\mathsf{stk}_e]:=\underline{\mathbf{c}}\,R[u];$
" ;

Compiling Algorithm 16.9. Block expression compilation

fun and **apply.** Popping of one part occurs when any expression has been completely analysed: k, id, $)$ and **end.**

16.10.1 Abstract Syntactic Types

The concrete grammar presented in Sect. 16.9.2 is (still) based on the abstract syntax of Sect. 16.2.2.

16.10.2 SAL BNF Grammar, 2

To be able to have the full advantage of top-down parsing, we introduce the slight complication of representing infix *(operand operator operand)* expressions in prefix Polish form: *operator(operand,operand)*. Other than this one complication the grammars look identical. We refer to Fig. 16.2.

We omit giving syntax for constants (k) and identifiers (id), and for monadic ($\odot$) and dyadic ($\oslash$) operators.

<table>
<tr><td>

Previous step:

The formulas in this and the next compiling algorithm have been provided with let (de)compositions and otherwise typed in a smaller font so as to make the formulas fit within the paper margins.

$$CA(mk\_Rec(f,\ell,b))(\delta,ln,stk) \equiv$$
$*$ **let** $mk\_Lam(v,e) = \ell$ **in**
$*$ **let** $ln' = ln+1,\ ln'' = ln'+1,$
$*$ $d = [f{\mapsto}ln',v{\mapsto}ln'']$ **in**
$*$ **let** $lfct = get\_Lbl(),$
$*$ $lbypass = get\_Lbl(),$
$*$ $db = depth(b)$ **in**
   $\langle\ mkJmp(lbypass),lfct\ \rangle\ \widehat{\ }$
   $CB(d)(\delta{\dagger}d,ln'',stk)$
   $\langle\ mkJmp(ra),$
     $lbypass, mkLim(u,lfct),$
     $mkSto(mkAdr(top,cp),cp,t{-}1),$
     $mkPck(u,u,top),$
     $mkSto(mkAdr(top,u),u,1),$
     $mkMov(cp,top),$
     $mkMov(ep,top),$
     $mkAdj(top,t{+}db)\ \rangle\ \widehat{\ }$
   $CA(b)(\delta{\dagger}[f{\mapsto}ln{+}1],ln{+}1,stk)\ \widehat{\ }$
   $\langle\ mkLod(u,1,mkAdr(cp,t)),$
     $mkLod(cp,t{-}1,mkAdr(cp,cp)),$
     $mkSto(mkAdr(cp,stk),u,1)\ \rangle$
$*$ **end end end**

</td><td>

Present step:

$Exp_e ::= \textbf{rec } f = Lam \textbf{ in } Blk_b \textbf{ end}$
$Lam ::= \textbf{fun } (\ id\ ) = Blk_d \textbf{ end}$

local
   $lfct\ =\ get\_Lbl(),$
$lbypass\ =\ get\_Lbl()\ \textbf{in}$

$d_e\ :=\ 1\ ;$
$ln_d\ :=\ \underline{c}\,ln_e{+}2;$
$ln_b\ :=\ \underline{c}\,ln_e{+}1;$
$dict_d\ :=\ \underline{c}\,dict_e$
     $\dagger[f{\mapsto}\underline{c}\,ln_e{+}1,id{\mapsto}\underline{c}\,ln_e{+}2];$
$dict_b\ :=\ \underline{c}\,dict_e\dagger[f{\mapsto}\underline{c}\,ln_e{+}1];$

$code_e\ :=\ ``\ \underline{goto}\ lbypass;$
   $lfct:$
   $"\ \widehat{\ }\ code_d\widehat{\ }\ ``$
   $\underline{goto}\ \underline{c}\,R[ra];$
   $lbypass:$
   $R[u]{:=}lfct;$
   $R[u]{:=}$
     $mkFct(\underline{c}\,R[u],\underline{c}\,R[top]);$
   $S[\underline{c}\,R[top]{+}cp]{:=}\underline{c}\,R[cp];$
   $S[\underline{c}\,R[top]{+}ep\ ]{:=}\underline{c}\,R[ep];$
   $S[\underline{c}\,R[top]{+}\ ra\ ]{:=}\underline{c}\,R[ra];$
   $S[\underline{c}\,R[top]{+}\ vr\ ]{:=}\underline{c}\,R[u];$
   $R[cp]{:=}\underline{c}\,R[top];$
   $R[ep]{:=}\underline{c}\,R[top];$
   $R[top]{:=}\underline{c}\,R[top]{+}(t{+}\underline{c}\,d_e);$
   $"\ \widehat{\ }\ code_b\widehat{\ }\ ``$
   $R[ep]{:=}\underline{c}\,S[\underline{c}\,R[cp]{+}ep];$
   $R[ra]{:=}\underline{c}\,S[\underline{c}\,R[cp]{+}ra];$
   $R[u]{:=}\underline{c}\,S[\underline{c}\,R[cp]{+}t\ ];$
   $R[cp]{:=}\underline{c}\,S[\underline{c}\,R[cp]{+}cp];$
   $S[\underline{c}\,R[cp]{+}\underline{c}\,stk_e]{:=}\underline{c}\,R[u];";$

</td></tr>
</table>

Compiling Algorithm 16.10. Recursive function/let expression compilation

16.10.3 Global Variables

There will thus be two global variables: code, which is treated like a stack, and output, which is treated as an **out** channel. Sometimes stacked code will be output.

variable
   code:Code
value

Previous step:	*Present step:*

$$\text{Exp}_e ::= \underline{\text{apply}}\ \text{Exp}_f\ (\ \text{Exp}_a\ )$$

$$\textbf{local}\ \text{lret}\ =\ \underline{\text{get\_Lbl}()}\ \textbf{in}$$

Previous step:

$$\begin{aligned}
&\text{CA}(\text{mk\_App(f,a)})(\delta,\text{ln,stk}) \equiv \\
&* \textbf{let}\ \text{lret} = \text{get\_lbl}()\ \textbf{in} \\
&\quad \text{CA}(a)(\delta,\text{ln,stk}) \\
&\quad \hat{\ }\ \text{CA}(f)(\delta,\text{ln,stk+1})\ \hat{\ } \\
&\quad \langle\ \text{mkLod}(u,1,\text{mkAdr(cp,stk+1)}), \\
&\qquad \text{mkCjp}(u,\text{non\_function,lerror}), \\
&\qquad \text{mkUnp}(\text{br,ep,u}), \\
&\qquad \text{mkLim}(\text{ra,lret}), \\
&\qquad \text{mkLod}(\text{pm,1,mkAdr(cp,stk)}), \\
&\qquad \text{mkJmp}(\text{br}), \\
&\qquad \text{lret}\ \rangle \\
&* \textbf{end}
\end{aligned}$$

Present step:

$$\begin{aligned}
d_e &:= \textbf{max}\{\ \underline{\textbf{c}}\,d_f,\underline{\textbf{c}}\,d_a\ \}; \\
\text{ln}_f,\text{ln}_a &:= \underline{\textbf{c}}\,\text{ln}_e; \\
\text{stk}_a &:= \underline{\textbf{c}}\,\text{stk}_e; \\
\text{stk}_f &:= \underline{\textbf{c}}\,\text{stk}_e+1; \\
\text{dict}_f,\text{dict}_a &:= \underline{\textbf{c}}\,\text{dict}_e; \\
\text{code} &:= \underline{\textbf{c}}\,\text{code}_a\ \hat{\ } \\
&\quad \underline{\textbf{c}}\,\text{code}_f\ \hat{\ } \\
&\quad \text{``}R[u]:= \\
&\qquad \underline{\textbf{c}}\,S[\underline{\textbf{c}}\,R[cp]+\underline{\textbf{c}}\,\text{stk}_e+1]; \\
&\quad \underline{if} \sim \underline{no\_fct}\ \underline{\textbf{c}}\,R[u]; \\
&\quad \underline{then}\ \underline{goto}\ \text{lerror}; \\
&\quad R[br]:=Lbl(\underline{\textbf{c}}\,R[u]); \\
&\quad R[ep]:=Loc(\underline{\textbf{c}}\,R[u]); \\
&\quad R[ra]:=\text{lret}; \\
&\quad R[pm]:= \\
&\qquad \underline{\textbf{c}}\,S[\underline{\textbf{c}}\,R[cp]+\underline{\textbf{c}}\,\text{stk}_e]; \\
&\quad \underline{goto}\ \underline{\textbf{c}}\,R[br]; \\
&\quad \text{lret:''};
\end{aligned}$$

Compiling Algorithm 16.11. Function application expression compilation

```
Pro ::= Exp
Exp ::= k                                    |
    ::= id                                   |
    ::= ⊙ Exp                                |
    ::= ⊘( Exp , Exp )                       |
    ::= if Exp then Exp else Exp end         |
    ::= let Id = Exp in Exp end              |
    ::= Lam                                   |
    ::= rec Id = Lam in Blk end              |
    ::= apply Exp ( Exp )
Lam ::= fun ( Id ) = Blk end
Blk ::= Exp
```

BNF Grammar 16.2. Another one for SAL

$$\text{push: } \textbf{Code}^* \rightarrow \textbf{Unit},\ \ \text{push(cl)} \equiv \text{code} := \text{cl}\ \hat{\ }\ \underline{\textbf{c}}\,\text{code}$$
$$\text{top: } \textbf{Unit} \rightarrow \textbf{Code},\ \ \text{top()} \equiv \textbf{hd}\,\underline{\textbf{c}}\,\text{code}$$
$$\text{pop: } \textbf{Unit} \rightarrow \textbf{Unit},\ \ \text{pop()} \equiv \text{code} := \textbf{tl}\,\underline{\textbf{c}}\,\text{code}$$
channel

output:Code*

16.10.4 Constants

There is only one run-time constant: the label of the instruction as from where error situations are to be handled.

global lerror = get_Lbl()

In the compilation algorithms below we refer to some of the constants cp, ep, ra, vr, pm, u, j, top, t and br. Their natural number values were defined is Sect. 16.8.5.

16.10.5 Node Attributes

All attributes are now inherited.

Syntax category	Attribute		Type	Kind
Exp, Lam, Blk	ln	(level number)	**Nat**	inherited
	dict	(dictionary)	Id $\overrightarrow{m}$ **Nat**	inherited

16.10.6 Compilation Functions

[0] Program Compilation

We refer to Compiling Algorithm 16.12.

[1] Constant Expression Compilation

We refer to Compiling Algorithm 16.13.

[2] Variable Expression Compilation

We refer to Compiling Algorithm 16.14.

[3] Prefix Expression Compilation

We refer to Compiling Algorithm 16.15.

[4] Infix Expression Compilation

We refer to Compiling Algorithm 16.16.

Previous step:

CA: Pro → **Unit** Code
CA(mk_Pro(e)) ≡
  * **let** lexit = get_Lbl(),
  *   de = depth(e) **in**
  ⟨ mkLim(cp,0),
        mkLim(ep,0),
        mkLim(top,t+de) ⟩
  ⌒ CA(e)([ ],0,t) ⌒
  ⟨ mkLod(u,1,mkAdr(p,t)),
        mkOut(u),
        mkJmp(lexit),
        lerror,
        mkOut("error"),
        lexit, finish ⟩
  * **end**

Present step:

Pro ::= Exp$_e$
local lexit = get_Lbl() **in**
In$_e$:= 0 ; dict$_e$:= [ ] ;
output ! " R[cp] := 0 ; R[ep] := 0 ; R[top] := t ; R[stk] := -1 ; ";
push (⟨ " R[u] := **c** S[-1] ; out := **c** R[u] ; <u>goto</u> lexit ; lerror: out := "error" ; lexit: <u>finish</u> ; " ⟩   ) ;

Compiling Algorithm 16.12. Program compilation

Previous step:

CA: E → DICT×LN×STK
              → Code **Unit**
CA(mk_Cst(k))(_,_,stk) ≡
  ⟨ mkLim(u,k),
      mkSim(mkAdr(cp,stk),k) ⟩

Present step:

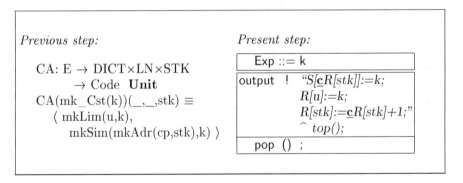

Exp ::= k
output ! "S[**c**R[stk]]:=k; R[u]:=k; R[stk]:=**c**R[stk]+1;"   ⌒ top();
pop () ;

Compiling Algorithm 16.13. Constant expression compilation

[5] Conditional Expression Compilation

We refer to Compiling Algorithm 16.17.

[6] Lambda-Expression Compilation

We refer to Compiling Algorithm 16.18.

Previous step:	Present step:
	$Exp_e ::= id$
CA(mk_Var(v))(δ,ln,stk) ≡	**local**
* **let** n = δ(v),	lloop = get_Lbl(),
* lloop = get_Lbl(),	lload = get_Lbl() **in**
* lload = get_Lbl() **in**	output ! "
⟨ mkLim(j,ln−n),	$R[j]:=\underline{c} \, ln_e\text{-}(\underline{c} \, dict_e)(id);$
lloop,	*lloop:*
mkCjp(j,zero,lload),	*if* $\underline{c} \, R[j]=0$
mkLod(ep,1,mkAdr(ep,ep)),	*then goto lload;*
mkAdj(j,−1),	$R[ep]:=\underline{c} \, S[\underline{c} \, R[ep]]+ep;$
mkJmp(lloop),	$R[j]:=\underline{c} \, R[j]\text{-}1;$
lload,	*goto lloop;*
mkLod(u,1,mkAdr(ep,vr)),	*lload:*
mkSto(mkAdr(cp,stk),u,1),	$R[u]:=\underline{c} \, S[\underline{c} \, R[ep]]+vr;$
mkMov(ep,cp) ⟩	$S[\underline{c} \, R[stk]]:=\underline{c} \, R[u];$
* **end**	$R[stk]:=\underline{c} \, R[cp];$
	"
	^ top()
	pop () ;

Compiling Algorithm 16.14. Variable expression compilation

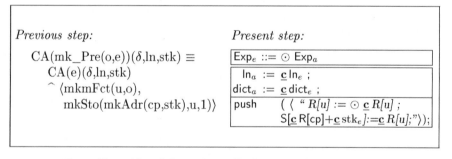

Compiling Algorithm 16.15. Prefix expression compilation

[7] Simple Let Expression Compilation

We refer to Compiling Algorithm 16.19.

[•] Block Compilation

We refer to Compiling Algorithm 16.20.

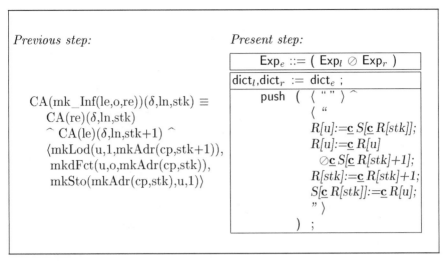

Compiling Algorithm 16.16. Infix expression compilation

[8] Recursive Function/Let Expression Compilation

We refer to Compiling Algorithm 16.21.

[9] Function Application Expression Compilation

We refer to Compiling Algorithm 16.22.

16.10.7 Review of Attribute Semantics, 2

We refer the reader to the review of the attribute semantics of Sect. 16.9.7. That review can serve, inter alia, also as a review of the present attribute semantics with the following exception: A special traversal of the tree is prescribed: from the root towards the leaves, and left-to-right. That is, from subtrees associated with early SAL program text "towards" subtrees associated with later SAL program texts. In the present attribute semantics all attributed variables are inherited and there is an auxiliary stack. In descending down the parse tree of any SAL program, output of code is made at each node. Some output includes code text popped from that stack. Some node actions, during descent, push code "fragments" onto the stack. When rightmost, i.e., "last" leaves have been traversed, then the output code can be executed.

16.11 Discussion

16.11.1 General

We have covered the, perhaps most crucial, stages of development of a compiler for a functional programming language. From a most abstract, yet model-

Previous step:	Present step:
	$\text{Exp}_e ::= \textbf{if } \text{Exp}_b$ $\quad\quad \textbf{then } \text{Exp}_c \textbf{ else } \text{Exp}_a \textbf{ end}$
	local $\quad$ lalt $=$ get_Lbl() $\quad$ lout $=$ get_Lbl() **in**
$\text{CA}(\text{mk\_If}(b,c,a))(\delta,\text{ln},\text{stk}) \equiv$ $\quad * \textbf{ let } \text{lalt=get\_Lbl}(),$ $\quad * \quad \text{lout=get\_Lbl}() \textbf{ in}$ $\quad \text{CA}(b)(\delta,\text{ln},\text{stk})\;\hat{}$ $\quad \langle\; \text{mkLod}(u,1,\text{mkAdr}(cp,\text{stk})),$ $\quad\quad \text{mkCjp}(u,\text{falsity},\text{lalt})\;\rangle\;\hat{}$ $\quad \text{CA}(c)(\delta,\text{ln},\text{stk})\;\hat{}$ $\quad \langle\; \text{mkJmp}(\text{lout}),$ $\quad\quad \text{lalt}\;\rangle\;\hat{}$ $\quad \text{CA}(a)(\delta,\text{ln},\text{stk})\;\hat{}$ $\quad \langle\; \text{lout}\;\rangle$ $\quad * \textbf{ end}$	$\text{ln}_b := \underline{\mathbf{c}}\,\text{ln}_e\;;$ $\text{ln}_c := \underline{\mathbf{c}}\,\text{ln}_e\;;$ $\text{ln}_a := \underline{\mathbf{c}}\,\text{ln}_e\;;$ $\text{dict}_b := \underline{\mathbf{c}}\,\text{dict}_e\;;$ $\text{dict}_c := \underline{\mathbf{c}}\,\text{dict}_e\;;$ $\text{dict}_a := \underline{\mathbf{c}}\,\text{dict}_e\;;$
	push $(\;\langle$ " $\quad R[u] := \underline{\mathbf{c}}\,S[\underline{\mathbf{c}}\,R[\text{stk}]\,]\;;$ $\quad R[\text{stk}] := \underline{\mathbf{c}}\,R[\text{stk}] + 1\;;$ $\quad \underline{if} \sim\!\underline{\mathbf{c}}\,R[u]\;\underline{then}\;\underline{goto}\;\text{lalt}\;;$ $\quad$ " $\rangle\hat{}\;\langle$ " $\quad \underline{goto}\;\text{lout}\;;$ $\quad \text{lalt}:$ $\quad$ " $\rangle\hat{}\;\langle$ " $\quad \text{lout}:$ $\quad$ " $\rangle$ $\quad)\;;$

Compiling Algorithm 16.17. Conditional expression compilation

oriented, denotational semantics, via steps of increasingly more operational, cum computational semantics to a compiling algorithm specification for that functional programming language. We presented three compiling algorithm models: An abstract compiling algorithm specification, and two attributed grammar compiling algorithm specifications.

The transition from the semantics specification to the compiling algorithm specification represented the transition from domain description, to requirements prescription. In this example that transition was just hinted at. In Vol. 3, Chap. 28, Sect. 28.2, we present some of the principles and techniques for that transition for realistic compiler development.

We find that most, if not all, textbooks on compiler development fail in not presenting the kind of material here presented.

Those 'textbooks on compiler development', to us, "jump" right into the middle of how proper compiler development can, or even ought, take place. To us, by omitting a serious and substantial treatment of exactly how to develop

Previous step:

$CA(mk\_Lam(v,e))(\delta,ln,stk) \equiv$
* **let** lbypass = get_Lbl(),
*   lfct = get_Lbl() **in**
⟨ mkJmp(lbypass),
   lfct ⟩ ⌢
$CA(e)(\delta\dagger[v\mapsto ln+1],ln+1,stk)$⌢
⟨ mkJmp(ra),
   lbypass,
   mkLim(u,lfct),
   mkPck(u,u,p),
   mkSto(mkAdr(cp,stk),u,1) ⟩
* **end**

Present step:

$\text{Lam}_e ::= \textbf{fun} \ (\ \text{id} \ ) = \text{Blk}_b \ \textbf{end}$

local
lfct = get_Lbl()
lbypass = get_Lbl() **in**

$\text{ln}_b := \underline{c}\ \text{ln}_e + 1 \ ;$
$\text{dict}_b := \underline{c}\ \text{dict}_e\dagger[\text{id}\mapsto\underline{c}\ \text{ln}_e +1];$

push (" ⟨
        <u>goto</u> <u>c</u> R[ra] ;
        lbypass:
        R[u]:=lfct;
        R[u]:=
          mkFct(<u>c</u> R[u],<u>c</u> R[cp]);
        S[<u>c</u> R[stk]]:=<u>c</u> R[u];
        R[stk]:=<u>c</u> R[stk]-1;
        ")) ;

output !   " *<u>goto</u> lbypass ; lfct:*" ;

Compiling Algorithm 16.18. Lambda-Expression compilation

the specification for a compiling algorithm, of exactly which target machine code the compiler shall generate for each source language construct in the program being compiled, those 'textbooks' skirt the most crucial issue, at least to us.

But now, here, in this chapter, You have gotten it. Now you can much better exploit those other 'textbooks'. They are usually very good at covering syntactic issues: lexical scanning, and error correcting parsing. And, from textbook to textbook, some focus on code optimisation (albeit, as we claim, without a proper treatment of which code to generate, and why), and some focus on compiler dictionary techniques, and some on attribute grammars. All depending on their authors' own specialty.

With the present chapter you can now much better exploit the better of 'those other textbooks'.

16.11.2 Principles, Techniques and Tools

We summarise:

Principles. *Functional Programming Language Implementations:* The development of interpreters and compilers for functional (and other) programming languages rests on a number of principles: (i) That denotations semantics specifications can be understood also as specifying translations from source

Previous step:	Present step:
	$\boxed{\text{Exp}_e ::= \textbf{let } v = \text{Exp}_d \textbf{ in } \text{Exp}_b \textbf{ end}}$
$\begin{aligned}&\text{CA(mk\_Let(v,d,b))}(\delta,\text{ln,stk}) \equiv \\ &\quad \text{CA(d)}(\delta,\text{ln,stk})\widehat{} \\ &\quad \langle\text{mkLod(u,1,mkAdr(cp,stk))}\rangle\widehat{} \\ &\quad \text{CB(b)}(\delta\dagger[\,v\!\mapsto\!\text{ln+1}\,],\text{ln+1,stk})\end{aligned}$	$\begin{aligned}\text{ln}_d &:= \underline{c}\,\text{ln}_e; \\ \text{ln}_b &:= \underline{c}\,\text{ln}_e+1; \\ \text{stk}_d &:= \underline{c}\,\text{stk}_e; \\ \text{dict}_d &:= \underline{c}\,\text{dict}_e; \\ \text{dict}_b &:= \underline{c}\,\text{dict}_e\;\underline{c}\,\text{dict}_e \\ &\quad\dagger[v\!\mapsto\!\underline{c}\,\text{ln}_e+1]; \end{aligned}$
	$\text{push } (\quad \langle \text{ `` } \\ \qquad R[u]:=\underline{c}\,S[\underline{c}\,R[stk]]; \\ \qquad R[stk]:=\underline{c}\,R[stk]+1; \\ \qquad \text{'' } \rangle\widehat{\phantom{x}} \\ \qquad \langle \text{ `` '' } \rangle \\ \quad) \;;$

Compiling Algorithm 16.19. Simple let expression compilation

language constructs to specification (here RSL) constructs; (ii) that functional values constructed from, say, environments and source language constructs, can be redefined as closures of pairs of these; and (iii) that the specification language formulations can, eventually, be expressed in a variant that is close to machine language constructs. ∎

Techniques. *Functional Programming Language Implementation:* The techniques, as also outlined in this chapter, involve (i) stepwise transformation of denotational specifications via first-order functional and first-order imperative constructions, to macro-expansion semantics; these intertwined with (ii) stepwise transformation of higher-order functional types into first-order data structures, eventually into simple pairs of stack pointers and program point labels; and these again intertwined with (iii) stepwise transformation of recursive run-time computational structures to stack-based such — in addition to several other techniques. ∎

Tools. *Functional Programming Language Implementation:* As for other kinds of programming languages, tools applicable to the development of interpreters and compilers for functional languages are covered in the following textbooks: Lex (lexical scanners) and Yacc ("Yet Another Compiler Compiler") [211, 297], Attribute Grammars & Their Applications, [94], and the Cornell Synthesizer Generator (of interpreters and compilers), [424–426]. All books are essentially based on the attribute grammar idea of Donald E. Knuth [128, 262, 270, 272, 304, 328, 376, 532, 541]. ∎

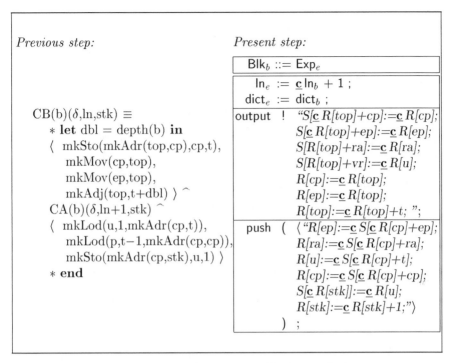

Previous step: *Present step:*

	$Blk_b ::= Exp_e$	
	$In_e := \underline{c}\, In_b + 1$; $dict_e := dict_b$;	

$CB(b)(\delta,ln,stk) \equiv$
  * **let** dbl = depth(b) **in**
  ⟨ mkSto(mkAdr(top,cp),cp,t),
    mkMov(cp,top),
    mkMov(ep,top),
    mkAdj(top,t+dbl) ⟩ ⌢
  CA(b)(δ,ln+1,stk) ⌢
  ⟨ mkLod(u,1,mkAdr(cp,t)),
    mkLod(p,t−1,mkAdr(cp,cp)),
    mkSto(mkAdr(cp,stk),u,1) ⟩
  * **end**
	output !	*"S[**c** R[top]+cp]:=**c** R[cp]*;
		*S[**c** R[top]+ep]:=**c** R[ep]*;
		*S[R[top]+ra]:=**c** R[ra]*;
		*S[R[top]+vr]:=**c** R[u]*;
		*R[cp]:=**c** R[top]*;
		*R[ep]:=**c** R[top]*;
		*R[top]:=**c** R[top]+t; "*;

	push (	⟨ *"R[ep]:=**c** S[**c** R[cp]+ep]*; *R[ra]:=**c** S[**c** R[cp]+ra]*; *R[u]:=**c** S[**c** R[cp]+t]*; *R[cp]:=**c** S[**c** R[cp]+cp]*; *S[**c** R[stk]]:=**c** R[u]*; *R[stk]:=**c** R[stk]+1;"*⟩) ;

Compiling Algorithm 16.20. Block compilation

We also refer to the useful URL: `http://dinosaur.compilertools.net/` which informs on syntax handling tools (viz.: LEX, YACC, and related or similar tools).

16.12 Review and Bibliographical Notes

This chapter presents a major set of principles and techniques for compiler development: From denotational descriptions (Sect. 16.3), via increasingly more concrete, computational descriptions (Sects. 16.4–16.5), including a macro-expansion description (Sect. 16.6), and via a formalisation of a target machine, to two forms of compiling algorithms (Sects. 16.8–16.10).

The present chapter covered principles and techniques for describing what a compiler, for a functional programming language, should generate of machine code. The first functional programming language was John McCarthy's LISP [333].

Current functional programming languages include Miranda [505], Haskell [503], and, notably SML [168, 359]. We remind the reader that the terms 'applicative programming' and 'functional programming', in this book, are treated synonymously.

Previous step:	Present step:

<table>
<tr><td colspan="2">

Previous step:

The formulas in this and the next compiling algorithm have been provided with let (de)compositions and otherwise typed in a smaller font so as to make the formulas fit within the paper margins.

</td></tr>
</table>

Present step:

$\mathrm{Exp}_e ::= $ **rec** f = Lam **in**
$\qquad\qquad$ Blk$_b$ **end**
Lam ::= **fun** (id) = Blk$_d$ **end**

---

local
$\quad$ lfct $=$ get_Lbl(),
lbypass $=$ get_Lbl() **in**

$\mathrm{ln}_d := \underline{c}\,\mathrm{ln}_e + 2$;
$\mathrm{ln}_b := \underline{c}\,\mathrm{ln}_e + 1$;
$\mathrm{dict}_d := \underline{c}\,\mathrm{dict}_e \dagger[\mathrm{f}\mapsto\underline{c}\,\mathrm{ln}_e+1,$
$\qquad\qquad \mathrm{id}\mapsto\underline{c}\,\mathrm{ln}_e+2];$
$\mathrm{dict}_b := \underline{c}\,\mathrm{dict}_e\dagger[\mathrm{f}\mapsto\underline{c}\,\mathrm{ln}_e+1];$

---

output ! " *goto lbypass* ;
$\qquad$ *lfct:* " ;

---

push ($\langle$ " *goto* $\underline{c}\,R[ra]$;
$\qquad$ *lbypass:*
$\qquad R[u] := $ lfct ;
$\qquad R[u] := $
$\qquad\qquad mkFct(\underline{c}R[u],\underline{c}R[top]);$
$\qquad S[\underline{c}R[top]+cp]:=\underline{c}R[cp];$
$\qquad S[\underline{c}\,R[top]+ep]:=\underline{c}R[ep];$
$\qquad S[\underline{c}R[top]+ra]:=\underline{c}R[ra];$
$\qquad S[\underline{c}\,R[top]+vr]:=\underline{c}R[u];$
$\qquad R[cp] := \underline{c}R[top];$
$\qquad R[ep] := \underline{c}R[top]$;
$\qquad R[top] := \underline{c}R[top] + t$;
$\qquad$ " $\rangle \,\widehat{}\, \langle$ "
$\qquad R[ep]:=\underline{c}S[\underline{c}R[cp]+ep];$
$\qquad R[ra]:=\underline{c}S[\underline{c}R[cp]+ra];$
$\qquad R[u]:=\underline{c}S[\underline{c}R[cp]+t];$
$\qquad R[cp]:=\underline{c}S[\underline{c}R[cp]+cp];$
$\qquad S[\underline{c}R[stk]]:=\underline{c}R[u];$
$\qquad R[stk]:=\underline{c}R[stk]+1;")$
) ;

Previous step continued (left column):

$\mathrm{CA}(\mathrm{mk\_Rec}(\mathrm{f},\ell,\mathrm{b}))(\delta,\mathrm{ln},\mathrm{stk}) \equiv$
$*$ **let** mk_Lam(v,e) $= \ell$
$* \quad \mathrm{ln}' = \mathrm{ln}+1,\ \mathrm{ln}''=\mathrm{ln}'+1,$
$* \quad \delta' = [\mathrm{f}\mapsto\mathrm{ln}',\mathrm{v}\mapsto\mathrm{ln}''] $ **in**
$*$ **let** lfct $=$ get_Lblb(),
$* \quad$ lbypass $=$ get_Lbl(),
$* \quad$ db $=$ depth(b) **in**
$\langle$ mkJmp(lbypass),lfct $\rangle\,\widehat{}\,$
$\mathrm{CB}(\mathrm{d})(\delta\dagger\delta',\mathrm{ln}'',\mathrm{stk})$
$\langle$ mkJmp(ra),
lbypass,
mkLim(u,lfct),
mkSto(mkAdr(top,cp),cp,t-1),
mkPck(u,u,top),
mkSto(mkAdr(top,u),u,1),
mkMov(cp,top),
mkMov(ep,top),
mkAdj(top,t+db) $\rangle\,\widehat{}\,$
$\mathrm{CA}(\mathrm{b})(\delta\dagger[\mathrm{f}\mapsto\mathrm{ln}'],\mathrm{ln}+1,\mathrm{stk})\,\widehat{}\,$
$\langle$ mkLod(u,1,mkAdr(cp,t)),
mkLod(cp,t-1,mkAdr(cp,cp)),
mkSto(mkAdr(cp,stk),u,1) $\rangle$
$*$ **end end**

Compiling Algorithm 16.21. Recursive function/let expression compilation

Classical texts of compiler writing are: Randell and Russells's [414], Gries's [150], and Aho and Ullman's [6]. To us Randell and Russells's [414] and then Gries's [150] are acceptable: Focus on the run-time structures of compiled programs. Aho and Ullman's [6], also seminal, focuses more on lexical scanning and parsing — the authors having made substantial contributions to automata and formal language theory. Appel's [14] is, to us, not acceptable: Fails, in

Previous step:	Present step:

Present step:

$Exp_e ::= \underline{apply}\ Exp_f\ (\ Exp_a\ )$
local lret $=$ get_ Lbl() **in**
$In_f, In_a := \underline{c}\ In_e\ ;$
$dict_f, dict_a := \underline{c}\ dict_e\ ;$
push ($\langle$ " " $\rangle$ ^
$\langle$ "
$R[u] := \underline{c}\ S[\underline{c}\ R[stk] - 1\ ];$
$\underline{if} \sim \underline{non\_function}\ \underline{c}\ R[u]$
$\underline{then}\ \underline{goto}\ lerror;$
$R[br] := Lbl(\underline{c}\ R[u]);$
$R[ep] := Loc(\underline{c}\ R[u]);$
$R[ra] := lret;$
$R[pm] := \underline{c}\ S[\underline{c}\ R[stk]];$
$R[stk] := \underline{c}\ R[stk]-2;$
$\underline{goto}\ \underline{c}\ R[br];$
lret:
" $\rangle$
) ;

Previous step:

$CA(mk\_App(f,a))(\delta,ln,stk) \equiv$
  * **let** lret = get_lbl() **in**
  $CA(a)(\delta,ln,stk)$ ^
  $CA(f)(\delta,ln,stk+1)$ ^
  $\langle$ mkLod(u,1,mkAdr(cp,stk+1)),
    mkCjp(u,non_function,lerror),
    mkUnp(br,ep,u),
    mkLim(ra,lret),
    mkLod(pm,1,mkAdr(cp,stk)),
    mkJmp(br),
    lret $\rangle$
  * **end**

Compiling Algorithm 16.22. Function application expression compilation

our opinion, to properly explain semantic issues — yet [14] has some rather worthwhile features: Techniques for program flow analysis being one of them.

In our approach, of the present and the next chapters, we focus on semantics, and hence also on run-time structures of compiled programs.

All of the above textbooks fail to cover what we have referred to as the *FUNARG* property of some programming languages [368, 529].

Landin introduced the *SECD* machine concept [284, 286, 288]. Reynolds [428] provided beautiful insight into interpreters for higher-order functional programming languages, i.e., languages in which functions are "first-class citizens", i.e., can have functions as ordinary values.

The IBM Vienna (Austria) Laboratory's work, in the 1960s and early 1970s, on providing semantics for a rather unwieldy programming language, i.e., PL/I [110,111], and of relating this to effective implementations — notably that of Bekič, Jones, Lucas and Walk [32,33,305,312] — serves as a foundation for our treatment of the present chapter.

The "great, seminal epic" on denotational semantics and congruent, i.e., "correct" interpreter (and hence compiler) implementations is Milne and Strachey's [350].

Attribute semantics was introduced by Knuth, propagated by Wirth, and otherwise studied by many others [45, 128, 262, 270, 272, 304, 328, 532, 541].

Tools for handling attribute semantics were developed by Kastens, Hutt, Zimmermann, Wilhelm, Deransart and Jourdan [94, 260, 531].

Wand [518, 520] investigates the transition from denotational semantics descriptions of programming languages to suitable computer architectures, i.e., machines "into" which effective compilations, and "on which" effective executions, can take place.

The compiler textbook by Wilhelm can be recommended [531].

16.13 Exercises

Exercise 16.1 *Case Expression.* Postulate a simple case expression:

case expr_0 **of**
    constant_1 → expr_1,
    constant_2 → expr_2,
    ... → ...,
    others → expr_n,
end

Base expressions, expr_0, evaluate to either integer values, or Boolean values; constant_i designate corresponding values; expr_i are ordinary expressions; and the literal **others** serve to designate a "catch all other values constant!"

Now, give a syntax for this kind of case expression, assume well-formedness, and define extensions to the four semantics of respective sections: 16.3 (denotational), 16.4 (first-order applicative), 16.5 (abstract imperative stack), and 16.6 (macro-expansion) — where these extensions define the semantics of the above kind of case expressions.

Exercise 16.2 *Macro-expansion Example.* Let two typical SAL programs be:

letrec f = λn.**if** n=0 **then** 1 **else** n∗f(n−1) **end in** f(5) **end**
letrec f = λn.**case** n **of** 0 → 1, **others** → n∗f(n−1) **end in** f(5) **end**

Now you are to recast the above two expressions into the abstract syntax values of SAL, given in Sect. 16.2.2, and to macro-expand both as per the definition given in Sect. 16.6 (for the first of the above expressions), and that you have given for the simple case expression in Exercise 16.1 for the second of the above expressions.

Exercise 16.3 *ASM': Assembler Machine.* Does the macro-expansion of case expression that you have given in Exercise 16.2 give cause for additional machine language instructions? If so, suggest such (one or more) and extend the machine language presented in Sect. 16.7 accordingly.

Exercise 16.4 *Code Generation Example.* For the two examples of Exercise 16.2 show their compilation into ASM (of Sect. 16.7), respectively ASM' (of Exercise 16.3, if relevant).

17

SIL: Simple Imperative Language

- The **prerequisite** for studying this chapter is that you are well familiar with the imperative modelling styles of RSL.
- The **aims** are to show the applicability of the compiler development principles and techniques of Chap. 16, and to do so for a simple imperative language, but only in a phasewise transition from a denotational semantics to a macro-expansion semantics.
- The **objective** is to enable you — we claim — to far better understand, and hence far more safely implement, compilers for procedural languages.
- The **treatment** is systematic and from informal to formal.

The computer is an imperative machine, one may claim. Its code specifies: *"Do this, then do that"* — as if they were imperial commands. Naturally the first programming languages, e.g., Fortran [13], were imperative languages. Hence, to understand the very essence of how imperative programs can be represented "inside" the computer is essential.

17.1 The Background

In the semantics of the simple applicative language, SAL, in Chap. 16, we got many seemingly tricky details reasonably straight: dynamic allocation and linking of block (and procedure) activations, and text (i.e., macro) expansion with insertion of labels and jumps to these. The same ideas can now be applied to SIL, the simple imperative language of the present chapter. We will apply them again, in Chap. 17, to a modular language[1], SMIL, whose run-time activation stack resembles a cactus stack!

In the semantics of SAL, in Chap. 16, we additionally showed how to transform a macro-expansion semantics, based on the design of a computer (cum

---

[1]By a modular language we mean one which offers modules of a kind similar to the scheme concept of RSL, cf. Chap. 10.

machine) language, into a compiling algorithm. Chapter 16 further showed the transformation of the compiling algorithm into either of two attribute grammar semantics. We shall not show the steps to compiling algorithms and attribute grammars in this chapter. The same principles and techniques as applied in Chap. 16 apply to the language developments of this chapter and Chap. 18.

In this chapter we now illustrate the development of a pair of semantics: a denotational semantics and, in one "straight" step of development, a macro-expansion semantics for a simple imperative language, SIL. The step from denotational to macro-expansion semantics can be made since we have already illustrated the essential facets, namely that of implementing the block (including procedure) concept in terms of an activation stack.

17.2 Syntactic Types

The simple applicative language, SAL, of the previous chapter embodies all interesting aspects of expressions: constants, simple (unassignable) variables, prefix and infix expressions, conditional expressions, blocks, simple and recursive function definitions and function applications. Therefore in the exposition of SIL, we concentrate on the imperative features: declared and assignable variables, assignment statements, iterations (while loops) and calls of procedures as statements. Now also blocks will be considered statements. A block consists of zero, one or more (typeless) variable declarations; zero, one or more statement and parameterless procedure definitions (which are themselves blocks); and a statement list. A while loop has a conditional expression and otherwise consists of a statement list.

17.2.1 Concrete, Schematic Syntax

We first show schematic examples of the various syntactic constructs: Fig. 17.1.

17.2.2 Abstract Syntax

Then we show the usual kind of RSL abstract syntax.

type
    P, V, E
    Stm == Blk | Asg | Whi | Call | StmL
    Blk = mk_Blk(vs:V-**set**,pros:(P $\overrightarrow{m}$ Blk),s:Stm)
    StmL = mkSL(sl:Stm*)
    Asgn = mk_Asg(v:V,e:E)
    Whi = mk_Whi(e:E,s:Stm)
    Call = mk_Call(p:P)

We do not define expressions, e:E, but could, for example, assume those of SAL.

17.3 Imperative Denotational Semantics

We present the denotational semantics in the traditional style. First we present the semantic types, then the (usually auxiliary) functions (i.e., functions which are defined over values of semantics types only) and, finally, the semantic functions.

17.3.1 Semantic Types

Assignable variables, v:V, designate locations, l:LOC, of storage, stg:STG. And storage maps locations to values, val:VAL. We do not further specify any value, location, and therefore not any storage structuring — as was done in Sect. 8.7.1 (specifically subsection "Values and Value Types") onwards. An imperative metastate variable, 'stg', contains the storage.

An applicative argument to all semantic functions is the environment, ρ, which binds visible (i.e., "in scope") variable identifiers to locations and visible (i.e., "in scope") procedure identifiers to their denotations, In other words, it binds functions from, in this simplifying case, no arguments, i.e., (), to partial, state-to-state changing functions, i.e., **Unit** $\xrightarrow{\sim}$ **Unit**.

variable
    stg:STG := [ ];
type

STATEMENT CATEGORIES	EXAMPLES	CONSTRUCTOR

Block	**begin**
	  variables v,v',...,v";
	  procedures
	    p = block,
	    p' = block',
	    ...
	    p" = block";
	  s; s'; ...; s"
	end
		mk_Blk

Assignment	v := e	mk_Asgn
While loop	**while** e **do** s; s'; ...; s" **end**	mk_Whi
Call	**call** p()	mk_Call

Fig. 17.1. Syntactic constructs of SIL

LOC, VAL
ρ:ENV = (V $\underset{\overrightarrow{m}}{}$ LOC) $\cup$ (P $\underset{\overrightarrow{m}}{}$ FCT)
STG = LOC $\underset{\overrightarrow{m}}{}$ VAL
FCT = () $\rightarrow$ **Unit** $\overset{\sim}{\rightarrow}$ **Unit**

The $\cup$ operator is, strictly speaking, not an RSL type constructor. But it could be, informally, so defined:

$$(A \underset{\overrightarrow{m}}{} B) \cup (C \underset{\overrightarrow{m}}{} D) \equiv \{| \ m \bullet m:(A \underset{\overrightarrow{m}}{} B) \lor m:(C \underset{\overrightarrow{m}}{} D) \ |\}$$

When a procedure is called, its value, fct:FCT, is applied to an empty argument, (), and implicitly to the imperative metastate. This effects a state change, which in an imperative RSL definition is expressed as a **Unit** to **Unit** function.

17.3.2 Auxiliary Semantic Functions

Upon block entry, locations are allocated, one distinct location, per declared variable.

value
    Alloc: **Unit** $\rightarrow$ LOC **Unit**
    Alloc() $\equiv$
        let loc:LOC $\bullet$ loc $\notin$ **dom** $\underline{c}$ stg **in**
        stg := $\underline{c}$ stg $\cup$ [loc $\mapsto$ undefined];
        return loc **end**

17.3.3 Semantic Functions

Since we express the semantic meaning function, M, in terms of operations upon an imperative metastate we have that the signature of M includes **Unit** to **Unit** functionality.

Procedure Denotations

Procedure values, i.e., procedure denotations, are constructed from their defining block, b:B, and environment, ρ:ENV, as the function, λ, of no arguments, (), which when applied to such 'no arguments' behaves as does the interpretation, M, of the procedure block in the defining environment.

value
    Den(b)ρ $\equiv$ λ().M(b)ρ

Statement and Expression Function

value
   M: Stm → ENV → **Unit** → **Unit**
   M: Exp → ENV → **Unit** VAL

   M(mk_Blk(vs,pm,s))ρ ≡
      let mρ = ρ † [v ↦ Alloc()|v:V • v ∈ vs] **in**
      let nρ = mρ † [p ↦ Den(pm(p))nρ | p:P•p ∈ **dom** pm] **in**
      M(s)nρ;
      stg := $\underline{c}$ stg \ {nρ(v) | v:V • v ∈ vs} **end end**

   M(mkSL(sl))ρ ≡ **for** i=1 to **len** sl **do** M(sl(i))ρ **end**

   M(mk_Asg(v,e))ρ ≡ stg := $\underline{c}$ stg ∪ [ρ(v) ↦ M(e)ρ]

   M(mk_Whi(e,s))ρ ≡
      let b = M(e)ρ **in**
      if b
         then (M(s)ρ; M(mk_Whi(e,s))ρ)
         else skip
      end end

   M(mk_Call(p))ρ ≡ (ρ(p))()

Note how the meaning of the while loop mirrors the following source (i.e., SIL) text to source text transformation — had SIL had a conditional, i.e., an **if then else** statement:

while e **do** sl **end**
≡
if e **then** (sl; **while** e **do** sl **end**) **else skip end**

In other words, one of the two conditional statement forms suffices.

17.4 Macro-expansion Semantics

We also present the macro-expansion semantics in the usual style. First, we present the syntactic types, then the compile-time semantics types, then the run-time semantic types, followed by abstraction functions (that relate run-time semantics values to semantic values of the denotational semantics) and finally the semantic functions, i.e., the macros.

17.4.1 Syntactic Types

See Section 17.2 for a discussion of syntactic types.

17.4.2 Compile-Time Semantic Types

The RSL specification language is ad hoc extended to include labels and gotos. Labels are further unanalysed atomic entities. No two labels of any RSL Text are alike. At compile-time labels are "drawn" (get_Lbl) from a potentially infinite set of labels, Lbl. A compile-time (i.e., a meta-) variable contains those labels already inserted into expanded metatext.

type
    Lbl
    $\Psi = \{ls\} \xrightarrow{\sim}_m$ Lbl-**set**
variable
    ls:Lbl-**set** := {}
value
    get_Lbl: **Unit** → Lbl
    get_Lbl() ≡
        let lbl:Lbl • lbl ∉ <u>c</u> ls **in**
        ls := {lbl} ∪ <u>c</u> ls;
        return lbl **end**

17.4.3 Run-Time Semantic Types

"Snapshot" of a Run-Time State

Figure 17.2 shows a "snapshot" of a run-time state:

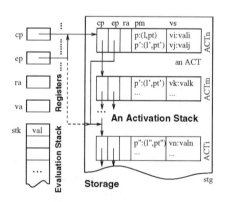

Fig. 17.2. "Snapshot" of a SIL run-time state

Figure 17.2 is reminiscent of Fig. 16.2. The four rectangles in a left column of the figure designate four registers. The big "almost" rectangle with the many (2+... +1) five-component rectangles, labelled ACTm, ACTn, and ACTi, inside it denotes a storage whose space (cells, bytes, etc.) can be allocated, i.e., "claimed". Each of these 2+... +1 five-component (ACT) rectangles designates a record whose fourth and fifth fields, the ones shown to the right on the figure and labelled pm and vs, designate procedure map (pm), respectively variable allocation space (vs). The pm field of the top ACTn "contains" two procedure name-labelled procedure closures (pairs of program point labels and environment stack activation pointers). The vs field of the top ACTn "contains" two variable bindings: from variable names to variable values. The other fields, cp, ep and ra (calling pointer (dynamic chain), static pointer (environment chain), and return address) values, are fixed space record components. The arrows symbolise environment stack activation pointers. Thus the cp register links to the top rectangle: Given cp we can access the contents of that top rectangle. The two-pronged, partly solid, partly dashed, arrow leading out from the ep register designates that the contents of that register successively "traverse" the ep chain. Notice that the traversal follows the (link, i.e., pointer) contents of the record ep fields. Thus it links directly from the top, DSAn, to a "lower", ACTi, and onwards (...).

Semantic Types

type
    Ptr
    mSTG = Ptr $\overrightarrow{m}$ ACT
    ACT == mk_ACT(s_ep:EP,s_cp:CP,s_ra:RA,s_pm:PM,s_vs:VS,...)
    CP, EP == mk_nil() | PT
    RA == mk_null() | LB
    PT :: Ptr
    LB :: Lbl
    PM = P $\overrightarrow{m}$ CLOS
    CLOS == mk_CLOS(lb:Lbl,pt:Ptr)
    VS = V $\overrightarrow{m}$ VAL

17.4.4 Run-Time State Declaration and Initialisation

The run-time state resembles the state of a target machine — on which compiled SIL programs are executed. Such a machine has a storage, stg, an evaluation stack, stk, two environment pointer registers (cp, ep), a return address register (ra) and value register (va).

value
    ptr:Ptr

variable
    stg:STG := [ptr↦mk_ACT(mk_nil(),mk_nil(),mk_null(),[ ],[ ])]
    cp:CP := ptr;
    ep:EP := ptr;
    ra:RA := mk_null();
    va:VAL := undefined;
    stk:VAL* := ⟨⟩

17.4.5 Abstraction Functions

It is always a good idea, before proceeding too deeply into macro function definitions, to try express how one can abstract from the concrete run-time state the denotation semantics storage, environment and functions. Below we sketch such an attempt.

value
    abs_STG: **Unit** → dSTG
    abs_STG() ≡ merge{
        [**let** mk_ACT(_,_,_,_,vm)=($\underline{c}$ stg)(pt) **in**
        makeLOC(pt,v)↦vm(v) **end**|v:V•v ∈ **dom** vm]|pt ∈ **dom**($\underline{c}$ stg)}

    makeLOC: Ptr × V → LOC

    abs_ENV: P → **Unit** ENV
    abs_ENV(ep) ≡
        if $\underline{c}$ ep = mk_nil() **then** [ ] **else**
        let mk_ACT(_,ep′,_,pm,vm) = ($\underline{c}$ stg)(ep) **in**
        let ρ = abs_ENV(ep′) **in**
        ρ † [p ↦ abs_FCT(pm(p)) | p:P • p ∈ **dom** pm]
            † [v ↦ makeLOC(ep,v) | v:V • v ∈ **dom** vm]
        end end end

    abs_FCT: CLOS → **Unit** → FCT
    abs_FCT(mk_CLOS(lb,ep)) ≡ ...
        /* from lb to construct source text: Blk */
        /* from ep to construct ENV: abs_ENV(ep) */

We remind the reader that the above sketches at most constitute rather informal reasoning. But perhaps this is enough in a compiler engineering environment, where the compiler writers have otherwise gone through a proper semantics course, for example, one based on any of [93,158,432,448,499,533].

17.4.6 Macros

value

C: Stm → **Unit** → RSL
C(mk_Blk(vs,pm,s)) ≡
*   **let** lmap = [p ↦ get_Lbl() | p:P • p ∈ **dom** pm], lout = get_Lbl() **in**
     let pt:Ptr • p ∉ **dom** **c** stg **in**
     let act = mk_ACT(**c** cp,**c** ep,**c** ra,
        [p ↦ mk_CLOS(lmap(p),pt) | p:P • p ∈ **dom** pm],
        [v ↦ undefined | v:V • v ∈ vs]) **in**
     stg := **c** stg ∪ [pt ↦ act]; cp := pt;
     C(s);
     ep := s_ep((**c** stg)(**c** cp));
     ra := s_ra((**c** stg)(**c** cp));
     cp := s_cp((**c** stg)(**c** cp));
     stg := **c** stg \ {pt}
     goto lout;
     ⟨ **label** lmap(p): M(pm(p)); **goto** **c** ra; | p:P • p ∈ **dom** pn ⟩
     label lout:
     end end * **end**

The metalinguistic pointed brackets, ⟨...⟩, surrounding the text of the second-to-last line express the compile-time distributed expansion of as many triplets

    label lmap(p): M(pm(p)); **goto** **c** ra;

as there are procedures in the procedure map.

    Above we assumed that SIL does not have the FUNARG property.

    The "Chain" function links back through the environment chain of pointers until an activation is found in which the Chain argument, name, is found, either as a variable name or as a procedure name.

Chain: P|V → **Unit**
Chain(name) ≡
    let mk_ACT(_,ep,_,pm,vm) = (**c** stg)(**c** ep) **in**
    if name ∈ **dom** pm ∪ **dom** vm **then skip else**
    (ep := e; Chain(name)) **end end**

The next three macros define the text to be generated for simple statements:

value
    C(mk_SL(sl)) ≡ ⟨ C(sl(i)); | 1 ≤ i ≤ **len** sl ⟩

    C(mk_Asg(v,e)) ≡
       C(e); Chain(v);
       let mk_ACT(cp,ep,pm,vm) = (**c** stg)(**c** ep) **in**
       let act = mk_ACT(cp,ep,pm,vm † [v ↦ **c** va]) **in**
       stg := **c** stg † [**c** ep ↦ act] **end end**;
       ep := **c** cp

C(mk_Whi(e,sl)) ≡
  * **let** lloop = get_Lbl() **in let** lout = get_Lbl() **in**
  label lloop: C(e);
  if ~**hd** $\underline{c}$ stk **then goto** lout **else skip end**;
  ⟨ C(sl(i)); | 1 ≤ i ≤ **len** sl ⟩
  goto lloop; **label** lout: * **end end**

C(mk_Call(p)) ≡
  Chain(p);
  let mk_ACT(_,_,_,pm,) = ($\underline{c}$ stg)($\underline{c}$ ep) **in**
  let mk_CLOS(lfct,eptr) = pm(p) **in**
  * **let** lout = get_Lbl() **in**
  ra := lout; ep := eptr;
  goto lfct;
  label lout: * **end**
  end end

17.5 Discussion

17.5.1 General

We have briefly outlined a macro-expansion semantics based on a conventional denotational semantics of a simple imperative language, SIL. Only four kinds of statements were exemplified: blocks, assignments, while loops and subroutine invocation. The interesting statements are, of course, the block and the procedure (i.e., subroutine) invocation statements. The rest are "fillers". They are included to make the simple imperative language reasonably representative.

We observe that the basic principles of activation stacks, and of static and dynamic chains, are the same as for the simple applicative language, SAL, of Chap. 16. And that, of course, is the whole idea. We leave as exercises the inclusion of more statements in SIL, and of expressions and their evaluation.

17.5.2 Principles, Techniques and Tools

We summarise:

Principles. *Imperative Programming Language Implementations:* The development of interpreters and compilers for imperial (and other) programming languages rests on basically the same principles as were outlined in Sect. 16.11.2 on a principle of functional programming language implementation. ∎

Techniques. *Imperative Programming Language Implementation:* The techniques, as also outlined in this chapter, again, are very much the same as were outlined in Sect. 16.11.2 on techniques of functional programming language implementation. ∎

Tools. *Imperative Programming Language Implementation:* Again we refer to Sect. 16.11.2 on functional programming language implementation tools. ∎

17.6 Bibliographical Notes

Two seminal books, long since out of print, on compiler construction must be mentioned:

[414]: B. Randell, L. Russell: *ALGOL 60 Implementation, The Translation and Use of* ALGOL 60 *Programs on a Computer* (Academic Press, A.P.I.C. Studies in Data Processing, Vol.5., New York and London, 1964); and
[150]: D. Gries: *Compiler Construction for Digital Computers* (John Wiley and Sons, New York, 1971).

Both were very careful in presenting and motivating the compiling algorithm choices wrt. run-time stacks — in both cases for the Algol 60 programming language [24].

17.7 Exercises

Exercise 17.1 *Macro-expansion Example.* Exemplify a very small SIL program. That is, please come up with one yourself. (i) Show it as a concrete text; (ii) then as an abstract syntax value as per the syntax given in Sect. 17.2.2; and finally (iii) macro expand this program as per the macro-expansion semantics of Sect. 17.4.

Exercise 17.2 *Assembler Language.* Recall ASM, the assembler machine language of Sect. 16.7. It was "geared", i.e., fitted to cope with SAL. Now, based, for example, on your solution to Exercise 17.1, (i) does ASM have a sufficient instruction repertoire to cope with translations of SIL programs into ASM code? If so, argue that. If not, first argue why, and (ii) then suggest appropriate new, simple instructions along the line of ASM, Sect. 16.7 (i.e., add to the syntax of ASM, Sect. 16.7.4). Finally, (iii) extend the machine state of Sect. 16.7.2 (you may have to add new semantic types, cf. Sect. 16.7.1), if needed, and extend the semantics definition (as given in Sect. 16.7.5).

Exercise 17.3 *SIL′: Expressions.* Extend SIL into SIL′ by detailing a (small) variety of expression forms (as per SAL, as given in Sect. 16.2). Then extend the syntax and denotational semantics definitions given in this chapter. Define also the corresponding macro-expansion semantics.

Exercise 17.4 *SIL": Additional Statements.* Extend SIL' into SIL", by adding new statements, for example, conditional (e.g., **if .. then .. else .. fi** and **case .. of .. end**), skip (i.e., **do nothing**) and iterative, say **loop .. until .. end,** statements. Then extend the syntax and denotational semantics definitions given in this chapter. Define also the corresponding macro-expansion semantics.

Exercise 17.5 *SIL'": Function Procedures.* Allow as part of block definitions those of function procedures, i.e., procedures which can be invoked in expression forms and which result in values. That is:

    function f(a_1,a_2,...,a_n) ≡ $\mathcal{E}$(a_1,a_2,...,a_n)
    ... f(e_1,e_2,...,e_n) ...

Define SIL'" as an extension to SIL" by adding the function procedure definition clause and the function invocation expression. Then extend the syntax and denotational semantics definitions given in this chapter. Define also the corresponding macro-expansion semantics.

SMIL: Simple Modular, Imperative Language

- The **prerequisite** for studying this chapter is that you are familiar with the modularity concepts as introduced in Chap. 10.
- The **aims** are to show the applicability of the compiler development principles and techniques of Chaps. 16–17, and to do so for a simple modular, imperative language, but only in a phase-wise transition from a denotational semantics to a macro-expansion semantics.
- The **objective** is to enable you — we claim — to far better understand, and hence far more safely implement, compilers for object-oriented languages.
- The **treatment** is systematic and from informal to formal.

Object-oriented languages are usually modular. Simula-67 [41], Modula (2 and 3) [171, 377, 536], Oberon [418, 537–540], Eiffel [344, 345], C++ [492] and Java [8, 15, 146, 301, 465, 513] are modular languages. The RAISE specification language, RSL, can be claimed to be object-oriented [130]. Modules are like abstract data types. In principle they can form a lattice of multiple inheritance-defined types, syntactically speaking. Semantically speaking, or more colloquially, operationally speaking, modules can be thought of as usually dormant coroutines having own states. That is, modules denote a kind of objects. In this section we shall define an interesting, nontrivial modular and imperative language, SMIL.

18.1 Syntactic Types

SMIL programs consist of one main and an unordered collection of uniquely named submodules. All modules contain definition parts. Main modules, in addition, contain a statement list. Definition parts consist of unordered collections of variable and/or possibly recursive procedure definitions. Definitions are either local, imported or exported.

Variable definitions consist in this (untyped) language of just variable identifiers. Local and exported procedure definitions consist of unique procedure identifiers, parameter lists and bodies. Imported procedure definitions consist of just procedure identifiers. In what follows, we concentrate on modelling the modularity of the example language. We therefore leave unspecified statements, procedure parameter lists and procedure bodies.

Since (as we shall later see) we need to allocate all variables "globally", i.e., also local ones, with possibly identically named local variables in distinct modules, we need to make all variable identifiers distinct. The nondistinctness is, of course, a *static feature* offered by the modular language, but it has no consequence for the dynamic semantics. So we choose to use the following syntactic types, where all submodules are uniquely named, and all imported variables are associated with their module of origin:

type
    M, Stmt, Proc
    Mn = {main} | M
    Prgr :: Main × (M $\xrightarrow{m}$ Sub)
    Main :: Defs × Stmt*
    Sub = Defs
    Defs :: Vars × Procs
    Vars == mk_Vars(xvs:V-**set**,ivs:(Mn $\xrightarrow{m}$ V-**set**),lvs:V-**set**)
    Procs == mk_Procs(xps:Prom,ips:(Mn $\xrightarrow{m}$ P-**set**),lps:Prom)
    Prom = P $\xrightarrow{m}$ Proc

xvs [*xps*] identify exported variables [procedures]; *ivs* [*ips*] identify, by module name, imported variables [procedures]. A static semantics, which we do not show, ensures that there are indeed such named modules in which these imported variables [procedures] are declared; *lvs* [*lps*] declare local variables [respectively procedures].

18.2 A Denotational Semantics

18.2.1 Semantic Types

Variable identifiers designate locations, and procedure identifiers designate functions. Designations are semantic type entities and are recorded in environments. Storages are likewise semantic entities.

type
    ENV = (V $\xrightarrow{m}$ LOC) $\cup$ (P $\xrightarrow{m}$ FCT)
    STG = LOC $\xrightarrow{m}$ VAL
    FCT = VAL* $\rightarrow$ **Unit** × VAL

Here, we have foreseen and defined a global state for the semantic functions. That is, we model storage using an imperative formulation. Accordingly, side effects of procedures are modelled as transformations on the global state of the model. The choice of an imperative modelling technique is, however, only dictated by convenience, not by necessity.

The total environment, ρ, has two parts: one, an incoming, structured in two levels and records all variable denotations, and another, an incoming and resulting, is structured in one level and records all exported denotations only:

$$\text{TENV} = \text{MENV} \cup \text{ENV}$$
$$\text{MENV} = \text{Mn} \underset{m}{\rightarrow} \text{LENV}$$
$$\text{LENV} = \text{V} \underset{m}{\rightarrow} \text{LOC}$$

18.2.2 Auxiliary Functions

Static Functions

'Export' is a compile-time function:

value
    Export: Defs $\rightarrow$ (V|P)-**set**
    Export(mk_Defs(mk_Vars(xvs,_,_),mk_Procs(xmp,_,_))) $\equiv$
        xvs $\cup$ **dom** xpm

Temporal Functions

As before, we need to allocate (and free) variable locations:

value
    Alloc: **Unit** $\rightarrow$ **Unit** $\times$ LOC
    Alloc() $\equiv$
        let loc:LOC • loc $\notin$ **dom** stg **in**
        stg := stg $\cup$ [loc $\mapsto$ undefined];
        loc **end**

18.2.3 Semantic Functions

The statement list of the main module is to be interpreted in an environment, $mm\rho$, which, besides its own local and exported variables and procedures also must record the designations of imported variables and procedures. To construct their designation the total environment, ρ, of all exported such is initially required. The contributions, $m\rho$ and $sms\rho$, to the total ρ come from the exports of the main, respectively all the submodules.

First we compute variable locations, then procedure denotations. The reason for this "split" is the following. In computing locations we simultaneously allocate new such, i.e., perform side effects. In computing procedure denotations we need to know the denotations of all other procedures which can potentially be mutually recursively invoked. But no new allocations are effected. Both computations are recursively defined, but only the latter is genuinely recursive in that it recursively uses the environment which it constructs. It turns out that if we combined the variable location computation into the set of recursive definitions, then the totally undefined environment would be their minimal fix point solution — due to the side effect aspects.

Semantic Function Types

value

    I_prgr: Prgr $\rightarrow$ **Unit**
    I_sl: Stmt $\rightarrow$ ENV $\rightarrow$ **Unit**
    C_Ldp: Defs $\rightarrow$ **Unit** $\times$ LENV
    C_Lsms: (M $\xrightarrow{m}$ Sub) $\rightarrow$ **Unit** $\times$ (M $\xrightarrow{m}$ LENV)
    C_mm: Defs $\times$ Sub-**set** $\rightarrow$ TENV $\rightarrow$ ENV $\times$ ENV
    C_sms: (M $\xrightarrow{m}$ Sub) $\rightarrow$ TENV $\rightarrow$ ENV
    C_dp: Mn $\rightarrow$ TENV $\rightarrow$ ENV
    Proc_Den: Proc $\rightarrow$ ENV $\rightarrow$ FCT

We start, here, by stating the type of all needed functions. This is a good way to structure or organize definition work: First the "interesting" types (the semantic types) are settled upon; next the type (i.e., signature) of the functions needed to create and manipulate them are settled upon and, finally, the bodies of the functions are "filled in".

Semantic Function Definitions

value

    I_prg(mk_Prgr(mk_Main(dp,sl),sms)) $\equiv$
      let mlρ = C_Ldp(dp),
          slρ = C_Lsms(sms) **in**
      let (mmρ,dmmρ) = C_mm(dp,sms)ρ,
          smsρ = C_sms(sms)ρ,
          ρ = [main $\mapsto$ mlρ] $\cup$ slρ $\cup$ smsρ **in**
      I_sl(sl)(mmρ) **end end**

    C_Ldp(mk_Defs(mk_Vars(xvs,_,lvs),_)) $\equiv$
      [v $\mapsto$ Alloc() | v:V • v $\in$ xvs $\cup$ lvs]

    C_Lsms(sms) $\equiv$ [m $\mapsto$ C_Ldp(sms(m)) | m:M • m $\in$ **dom** sms]

C_mm(dp,sms)ρ $\equiv$
   let mk_Defs(mk_Vars(xvs,_,_),mk_Procs(xpm,_,_)) = dp **in**
   let mmρ = C_dp(dp,main)ρ **in**
   (mmρ,mmρ $\cup$
      $\bigcup${C_dp(sms(m),m)ρ / Export(sms(m))
      | m:M•m $\in$ **dom** sms})
   end end

C_sms(sms)ρ $\equiv$
   if sms = [ ] **then** [ ] **else let** m:M • m $\in$ **dom** sms **in**
   C_dp(sms(m))ρ $\cup$ Csms(sms \ {m})ρ **end end**

C_dp(mk_Defs(mk_Vars(xvs,ivs,),mk_Procs(xpm,ips,lpm)),m)ρ $\equiv$
   let pm = xpm $\cup$ lpm **in**
   let nρ = ρ(m)
     $\cup$ [v$\mapsto$$\rho$(v)|m:Mn,v:V • m $\in$ **dom** ivs$\wedge$v $\in$ ivs(m)]
     $\cup$ [p$\mapsto$Proc_Den(pm(p))(nρ) | p:P • p $\in$ **dom** pm]
     $\cup$ [p$\mapsto$$\rho$(p) | p:P • p $\in$ ips] **in** nρ **end end**

18.3 A Macro-expansion Semantics

We now develop the denotational semantics of Sect. 18.2 into a macro-substitution semantics. We decide on realizing the combined (ENV,STG) complex in terms of a complex of so-called activations: one for the main module, and one for each of the submodules. All these activations are allocated simultaneously.

Each activation is uniquely designated by a pointer. Each activation contains allocations for all exported and local variables, and closures for all procedures, whether exported, imported or local.

18.3.1 Run-Time Semantic Types

type
   ENV_STG = Ptr $\underset{\overrightarrow{m}}{}$ ACTV
   ACTV == mk_ACTV(ssta:Pt,sdy:Pt,sra:Lbl,senv:sENV,sstg:sSTG,...)
   sENV = (V $\underset{\overrightarrow{m}}{}$ Ptr) $\cup$ (P $\underset{\overrightarrow{m}}{}$ CLOS)
   sSTG = V $\underset{\overrightarrow{m}}{}$ VAL
   CLOS :: Ptr $\times$ Lbl

The idea of the macro-expansion stage is (also) to expand the procedure body text into RSL (metalanguage) text "in-line" with the macro-expanded text which, through calls, refers to those procedures.

Suffice it here to summarize that invocations of procedures in a denotational definition are effected by finding the procedure designation in the environment, and then applying this function to an evaluated argument list. In the macro-expanded, operational semantics version we have compiled all the source-language program text into metalanguage text; and procedure calls are effected by jumping to an appropriate metatext point, i.e., a label (in Lbl). The denotational procedure designation embodies the defining environment. Now the operational procedure closure contains, besides a label, a pointer to the appropriate activation. Procedure invocations occur in the calling environment, i.e., lead to an activation stacked on top of the calling activation and chained to it by a dynamic pointer. Since procedures may possibly be passed as parameters to other procedures (i.e., to their invocation), or since procedure bodies may contain nested procedure definitions where inner ones may refer to outer ones, we also need to chain back to defining environments, i.e., we need, finally, in our activations, a static pointer (chain). All this pointer chaining is nothing new. We first introduced it in the operational semantics of SAL, then SIL!

For each of the functions of Sect. 18.2 we have to redefine a corresponding set of macro-expansion functions. We now outline our design decisions. Our point is to illustrate a technique of going from abstract, denotational, to less abstract, more concrete operational definitions, and of how to relate them in an attempt to convince the reader of the possible correctness of the realization. In the following we refer to the denotational semantics (DS) formulae of Sect. 18.2.3 as (DS ...) and to those of this subsection as (MS ...) (mechanical, or macro-expansion semantics).

We leave it to the reader to further study our solution below.

In constructing the macro-expansion semantics the following auxiliary name suffix conventions are applied: macro-expansion (compile-time) suffix c and (metatext interpretation run-time) suffix r.

18.3.2 Compile/Run-Time Semantic Types

type
> Lbl, Ptr
> PT == mk_nil | Ptr
> LB == mk_null | Lbl
> VA == mk_void | VAL
> LblM = M $\overrightarrow{m}$ PLM
> PLM = P $\overrightarrow{m}$ Lbl
> PtrM = M $\overrightarrow{m}$ Ptr
> VarM = V $\overrightarrow{m}$ Ptr

value
> undefined:VAL

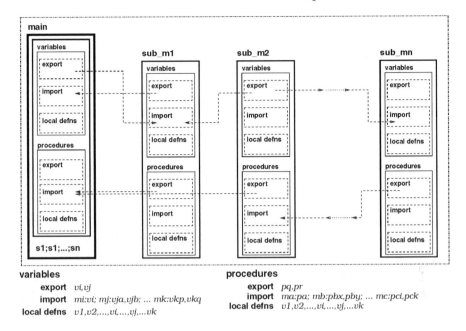

Fig. 18.1. A cactus stack run-time state for modular programs

18.3.3 Compile-Time Semantic Types

variable
    ls:Lbl-**set** := {}
value
    get_Lbl: **Unit** → **Unit** Lbl
    get_Lbl() ≡ **let** lbl:Lbl • lbl ∉ **c** ls **in** ls := **c** ls ∪ {lbl}; **return** lbl **end**

    GLdp: Dp → **Unit** × PLM
    GLdp(mk_Defs(_,mk_Procs(xpm,_,lpm))) ≡
        [p ↦ get_Lbl() | p:P • p ∈ **dom**(xpm ∪ lpm)]

    GLsmm: (M $\overrightarrow{m}$ Sub) → **Unit** LblM
    GLsmm(smm) ≡ [n ↦ GLdp(smm(n)) | n:M • n ∈ **dom** smm]

18.3.4 Semantic Functions

value
    M_prgr: Prgr → **Unit**
    M_prgr(mk_Prgr(mk_Main(mm,sl),smm)) ≡
        ∗ **let** plm = G_Ldp(mm) **in**

$*$ **let** nplm$'$ = G_Lsmm(smm) **in**
$*$ **let** lout = get_Lbl() **in**
let (xvm,mp) = M_Ldp(mm) **in**
let (sxvm,snpm) = M_Lsmm(smm) **in**
let vpm = sxvm $\cup$ xvm,
      npm = snpm $\cup$ [main $\mapsto$ mp] **in**
let nplm = nplm$'$ $\cup$ [main $\mapsto$ mp] **in**
I_ns(mm,nplm,main)(mp,vpm);
$\langle$ I_ns(smm(n),nplm,n)(npm(n),vpm); | n:Mn $\bullet$ n $\in$ **dom** smm $\rangle$
cp := mp; ep := mp;
Msl(sl);
goto lout;
E_P(mm,nplm(main));
$\langle$ E_P(smm(n),nplm(n)); | n:M $\bullet$ n $\in$ **dom** smm $\rangle$
label lout: **end end end end** $*$ **end end end**

M_Ldp: Defs $\rightarrow$ **Unit** $\times$ (VarM $\times$ Ptr)
M_Ldp(mk_Defs(mk_Vars(xvs,_,lvs),_)) $\equiv$
  let ptr:Ptr $\bullet$ ptr $\notin$ **dom** $\underline{c}$ stg **in**
  let actv = mk_ACTV(mk_nil,mk_nil,mk_null,
               [v $\mapsto$ ptr | v $\in$ xvs $\cup$ lvs],
               [v $\mapsto$ undefined | v $\in$ xvs $\cup$ lvs],...) **in**
  stg := $\underline{c}$ stg $\cup$ [ptr $\mapsto$ actv];
  return ([x $\mapsto$ ptr | x:V $\bullet$ s $\in$ xvs],ptr)
  end end

M_Lsms: (M $\overrightarrow{m}$ Sub) $\rightarrow$ **Unit** $\times$ (VarM $\times$ Ptr)
MLsms(smm) $\equiv$
  case smm **of**:
    [] $\rightarrow$ ([],[]), _ $\rightarrow$
    let n:M $\bullet$ n $\in$ **dom** smm **in**
    let (xvm,ptr) = M_Ldp(smm(n)) **in**
    let (rxvm,rnpm) = M_Lsms(smm $\setminus$ {n}) **in**
    return (xvm $\cup$ rxvm,rmp $\cup$ [n $\mapsto$ ptr])
    end end end end

I_ns: Defs $\times$ LblM $\times$ Mn $\rightarrow$ (Ptr$\times$VarM) $\rightarrow$ **Unit**
I_ns(mk_Defs(mk_Vars(_,ivs,_),
    mk_Procs(xpm,ips,lpm)),nplm,n)(mpm,vpm) $\equiv$
  let mk_ACTV(sta,dyn,ra,env,stg,...) = ($\underline{c}$ stg)(mpm(n)) **in**
  let env$'$ = env
    $\cup$ [v $\mapsto$ vpm(v) | v:V $\bullet$ v $\in$ ivs]
    $\cup$ [p $\mapsto$ mk_CLOS(mpm(n),(nplm(n))(p))
        | p:P $\bullet$ p $\in$ **dom**(xmp $\cup$ lpm)]
    $\cup$ [p $\mapsto$ mk_CLOS(mpm(n$'$),(nplm(n$'$))(p))

| p:P,n′:M • p ∈ ips ∧ n′ ∈ **dom** nplm ∧ p ∈ nplm(n′)] **in**
  stg := **c** stg ∪ [(mpm(n)) ↦ mk_ACTV(sta,syn,ra,env′,stg,...)]
  end end

M_sl: Stm* → **Unit**
M_sl(sl) ≡ ⟨ M_c(sl(i)) | 1 ≤ i ≤ **len** sl ⟩

E_P: Defs → PLM → **Unit**
E_P(mk_Defs(_,mk_Procs(xpm,_,lpm)))(plm) ≡
  ⟨ **label** plm(p):
      M_proc((xmp ∪ lpm)(p));
      goto c ra; | p:P • p ∈ **dom**(xmp ∪ lpm) ⟩

18.4 Discussion

18.4.1 General

We remind the reader that the presentation given in this chapter, as well as the presentations given in Chaps. 16–17, assumes a deterministic subset of RSL, one for which the recursive definitions of environment (ρ) have minimal fix point solutions. Otherwise the definitions do not make any sense. We refer to standard textbooks [93, 158, 432, 448, 499, 533] on denotational semantics for the full story.

18.4.2 Principles, Techniques and Tools

We summarise:

Principles. *Modular Programming Language Implementations:* The development of interpreters and compilers for modular (and other) programming languages rests on basically the same principles as were outlined in Sect. 16.11.2 on principles of functional programming language implementation. ■

Techniques. *Modular Programming Language Implementations:* The techniques, as also outlined in this chapter, again, are very much the same as were outlined in Sect. 16.11.2 on techniques of functional programming language implementation. ■

Tools. *Modular Programming Language Implementations:* Again we refer to Sect. 16.11.2 on 'functional programming language implementation tools. ■

18.5 Bibliographical Notes

Modular languages are usually object-oriented (OO). Simula-67 [41], Modula
(2 and 3) [171,377,536], Oberon [418,537–540], C++ [492], Eiffel [344,345],
Java [8,15,146,301,465,513], and C# [207,346,347,401] are such OO languages.

18.6 Exercises

Exercise 18.1 *Syntactic Types for OO Languages.* Select one of the OO
programming languages: Modula (2 and 3) [171,377,536] or Oberon [418,537–
540] or Eiffel [344,345] or C++ [492] or Java [8,15,146,301,465,513] or C#
[207,346,347,401] and develop type definitions and syntactic well-formedness
for programs in the chosen OO language.

Exercise 18.2 *SMIL' Expressions.* As for Exercise 17.3 extend SMIL with
suitable expressions and define both a denotational and a macro-expansion
semantics.

Exercise 18.3 *Additional SMIL'' Statements.* As for Exercise 17.4 extend
SMIL with suitable statements and define both a denotational and a macro-
expansion semantics.

Exercise 18.4 *SMIL''' Function Procedures.* As for Exercise 17.5 extend
SMIL with suitable function procedures and further expressions, and define
both a denotational and a macro-expansion semantics.

SPIL: Simple Parallel, Imperative Language

- The **prerequisite** for studying this chapter is that you are well familiar with RSL's CSP (Communicating Sequential Processes) language constructs, such as covered in Vol. 1, Chap. 21.
- The **aims** are to introduce a special style of defining functions, to use this style in giving an "interleave" semantics to a CSP-like language, and to thus illustrate the flexibility of the RSL specification language.
- The **objective** is to ensure that the reader becomes a versatile professional software engineer.
- The **treatment** ranges from intuitive via semiformal to almost formal.

This section is structured as follows. First we state, in Sect. 19.1, the **problem** to be solved — while motivating why we wish to solve that problem. Then we outline, in Sect. 19.2, the **syntax** of programs in the chosen language. This is not always the best way to start when designing a new language. Usually it is better to start with decisions on what the basic concepts of the language should denote. In the Simple Parallel Imperative Language, SPIL, they — most abstractly — could be claimed to denote traces of input/output events. For illustrative purposes, that is, in order to bring in an example of a state transition system, we have here chosen a structural operational semantics-like definition. Some of the design, therefore, of the **semantic types** is arrived at, in Sect. 19.3, after an analysis of some of the more conventional process concepts. The rest of the design of the **semantic types** is finalised in Sect. 19.4, after an analysis of some of the special, technical process concepts. Finally, in Sect. 19.6 we present the detailed **semantic functions**.

19.1 The Problem

We face the problem of delineating a suitable variant of the syntax of an imperative version of a CSP-like [119, 212, 213, 436] language — such as it, for example, is present in the RAISE Specification Language, RSL, [130, 131], and to give this language a semantics. In particular we must show principles and techniques for the design of a structural operational semantics [252, 402].

We have chosen an imperative version of a CSP-like language for educational reasons. It is close to occam [225,327], and its imperativeness is close to C [263], Modula (2 and 3) [171,377,536], Oberon [418,537–540], Eiffel [344,345] or C++ [492], Java [8, 15, 146, 301, 465, 513], and C# [207, 346, 347, 401]. Hence, due to its resemblance to CSP, it is relatively easy to learn, and interesting parallel programs can thus quickly be established.

19.2 Syntax

We assume general familiarity with the concepts of CSP [119, 212, 213, 436].

19.2.1 Informal Syntax

Process Expressions

With that familiarity — see Vol. 1, Chap. 21 — we shall just present an informal, schema-like syntax and shall only comment on the system definition.

<u>p</u>rocess (command) <u>e</u>xpressions
  pe : st
    | io
    | **call** pn(arl)
    | pq_1 ‖ pq_2 ‖ ... ‖ pq_p
    | pq_1 ⌐ pq_2 ⌐ ... ⌐ pq_i
    | (io_1 → pq_1) [] ... [] (io_n → pq_n)
    | sy

<u>io</u> (input/output) commands
  io : c_i ? v
    | c_j ! e

<u>p</u>rocess (command) <u>e</u>xpression se<u>q</u>uence
  pq : pe_1; pe_2; ...; pe_q

Process expressions are either statements, or channel input/output commands, or are process invocation commands, or are structured, i.e., are parallel, ‖, nondeterministic internal choice, ⌐, or input/output guarded nondeterministic external choice, [], commands, or are system commands. Input/output commands name a channel and specify a variable or an expression, respectively. Structured process commands contain lists of process commands.

Expressions and Statements

expressions
    e: k | v | id | ...

expression (argument) lists
    arl : e_1, e_2, ..., e_m

statements
    st : v := e
    | **case** e **of**:
            val_1 ↦ **do** pq_1 **end**
            val_2 ↦ **do** pq_2 **end**
            ...
            val_n ↦ **do** pq_n **end**
        end
    | **while** e **do** pq **end**
    | **do** pq **until** e **end**

Expressions are simple expressions, either constants, or variable names or formal identifiers (of procedure definitions), or are further unspecified. Process invocation argument lists are lists of simple expressions. Statements are either assignment statements, or are cases (i.e., multiway switch) conditional statements, or are repetitive (iterative) loop statements, either while or repeat.

System Processes

    sy: **system**
        variables: v_1, v_2, ..., v_w;
        channels: c_1, c_2, ..., c_s;
        process definitions:
            pn_1(fpl_1): pq_1;
            pn_2(fpl_2): pq_2;
            ...
            pn_q(fpl_q): pq_q;
        initial process invocations:
            call pn_i(arl_i)
            || **call** pn_j(arl_j)
            || ...
            || **call** pn_k(arl_k)
    end

    fpl : id_1, id_2, ..., id_m

A program specification is a system specification. A system specification declares variables, introduces channels and defines processes. A system specification ends with specifying the (**call**) invocation of a subset of the defined processes.

19.2.2 Formal Syntax

type

Cn, Vn, Pn, Id, VAL	$\mid$ output(o:Cn,e:E)
P = S $\mid$ IO $\mid$ C $\mid$ Q	C == call(pn:Pn,al:E*)
S == asg(lhs:Vn,rhs:E)	Q == pal(ps:P*-**set**)
$\mid$ cas(b:E,switch(VAL $\overrightarrow{m}$ P*))	$\mid$ ind(ps:P*-**set**)
$\mid$ whi(b:E,seq:P*)	$\mid$ xnd(ps:(IOPl-**set**))
$\mid$ rep(seq:P*,b:E)	$\mid$ sys(s:Sys)
E == ...	Sys = Vn-**set**
$\mid$ cst(val:VAL)	$\times$ Cn-**set**
$\mid$ fp(id:Id)	$\times$ (Pn $\overrightarrow{m}$ PD)
$\mid$ var(v:Vn)	$\times$ C-**set**
IO == input(i:Cn)	PD = Id* $\times$ P*
	IOPl = IO $\times$ P*

Channel, variable and process names as well as process definition (formal parameter) identifiers are further unspecified atomic quantities. We do not specify what values are.

We have arbitrarily chosen to model the system body of process invocations as a map from distinct process definition names to process definitions. This pragmatic choice disallows the same process to be invoked more than once in a system body. One can easily remodel this part of the definition into one allowing such parallel invocations of identical processes. For our purpose, which is that of illustrating how we give an operational semantics to a process language, the present choice avoids complications that are not germane to the main purpose.

19.3 Process Concepts and Semantic Types

It is quite customary to hear the following being said by practicing programmers and even computer programming lecturers: "and here the program calls a procedure", and other such anthropomorphisms. Programs do not do anything! They are innate texts. They prescribe that a suitable machine performs a number of actions.

In this section, as well as throughout this technical note, we shall try avoid, as best we can, the above kind of anthropomorphisms. But we do not guarantee this! It has become an almost acceptable, yet unfortunate habit. It is acceptable when we are aware of the problem. Unfortunate, since this erroneous use of language may hide some deeper lack of understanding, and may reveal a lack of proper abstraction. It is desirable, we firmly believe, that we in general make clear distinctions between syntactics, semantics and pragmatics matters.

19.3.1 Syntactic Notions

Textual

By a *process definition* we understand a syntactic construct (a syntactic structure), *pd:PD*. By a *process name* we understand a syntactic construct, *pn:Pn*, which names a process definition. By a *process expression* we mean the same as a *process command*, namely a syntactic construct, *p:P*. Statements are either simple (i.e., atomic) or composite (or structured) — as are process commands. The *assignment* statement is a simple statement. The **case, while** and **until** statements are structured statements. The *sequential* (;), *parallel,* (||) *internal nondeterministic choice* (⌐), *guarded external nondeterministic choice* (⌐), the global, "outermost" and the inner, embedded *system* process commands are structured process commands. That is, a *parallel program* is a system process command, called the *outermost global system process command.* Any system process command properly contained in a process command, i.e., a system process command other than the global command, is said to be *embedded,* or *inner.*

By *prologue* we understand either the *formal parameter list* of a procedure definition, or the variable and channel declarations and the process definitions of a system process command. By body we understand either the remaining part of respective process constructs: the list of process commands of a procedure definition, the parallel (the **call**) invocation expression of a system command and the set of alternative process command lists of a parallel or of a nondeterministic command — whether internal or external choice.

Contextual: Scope and Binding

The notion of scope is a static notion to be obeyed by processes. A scope defines which variable names, channel names, formal parameter identifiers and process definition names may be referred to. That is, a scope statically delineates a program text, "from this line of program text to this line of program text, except those embedded lines" (where inner system commands redefine scope).

System commands define the binding of these names and identifiers to their syntactic meaning: variable names to the fact that they are variables, channel names to the fact that they are channels, formal parameter identifiers to the fact that they are formal parameters and process names to their process definitions. The binding is effective in the scope of the names and identifiers.

Contained, local system commands may redefine some or all of these names and/or may introduce new names. Redefinition allows a channel name in one scope to be a variable name in another scope. Those names and identifiers not redefined are inherited and thus are ported to the inner scope — for as long as further local system expressions do not redefine (syntactic) scope meanings.

Contextual: Hiding and Modularisation

A process definition body, i.e., its sequence of process commands, is allowed to be just one command, and that command could be a system command. In this way the programmer is free to choose a set of local variables, local channels and local process definitions for each process definition (and none, if so decided, for the global system).

In any case, system commands allow the declaration of variables private to the processes invoked by the system command — as well as the introduction of channels and definition of processes. Entities (variables, channels and processes) which are declared, introduced, respectively defined in a system command, are said to be hidden from the outside. They are not part of the surrounding scope, are not visible outside the system command. (System commands are like ordinary blocks in ordinary programming languages.)

Process definitions can be said to define modules, i.e., object classes. This may be especially clear when their body consists of exactly one process command which is a system command. These process definition modules can be invoked any number of times: in parallel, albeit, requiring, for technical reasons, just a tiny variation in actual argument lists, so as to make the process (the **call**) invocations distinct.

So our language has several of the capabilities. The properties of a modular, or object-oriented programming language. That is, system command process definitions constitute modules and their (the **call**) invocation constitutes objects. Output/input synchronisation and communication between processes, i.e., objects, can be used to implement methods. Since we have not imposed any type discipline on our language we cannot talk about inheritance, let alone multiple inheritance, but the possibility of introducing such a type concept is straightforward.

19.3.2 Machines and Interpreters

Programs specify processes. Machines carry out processes: They provide resources to follow the prescriptions of a program. Amongst resources we mention storage for program variables, "stacks" of environments to handle process-related scope matters. A machine which carries out the prescriptions of a program does so according to a prescription of the semantics of the programming language of that program. Such a prescription, when operational, is here called an interpreter for the programming language.

19.3.3 Semantic Notions and Types

Actions

By a *process action* we understand a smallest, indivisible atomic, step of a machine when following the prescription of a process command. Examples of process actions are: following the prescription of an assignment statement, or a pair of input/output commands, or a call command.

Processes

By a *process* we understand a semantic construct: that which is prescribed (to be, and now being) executed by a machine — a possibly infinite sequence of *process actions*. By a *process invocation* we understand a semantic construct, the process action that obeys the prescription of a *process* **call** command. Examples of (usually) nonatomic processes are those that result from a machine following the prescriptions of structured (i.e., composite) statements, and those that result from a machine following the prescriptions of structured (i.e., composite) process commands.

Objects

In general an object is here considered to be the (the **call**) invocation of a process definition. Its object-orientedness becomes all the more clear when one considers those of process definitions whose bodies are single system commands. It will, in general, prescribe its own variables — i.e., the object state. If the system processes do not refer to any variables declared in embracing system commands, then we see that object-orientedness is more transparent.

Environments ρ :ENV — I

The semantic type of environments is a "classical" type that has been conventionally used since the early 1960s. Environments are the semantic counterpart to syntactic scopes (and syntactic scope bindings). A system process establishes an environment: It inherits any surrounding environment, which is empty (nil, void) in the case of the global system process, and overrides (†) this with the operational semantic meaning of the names (re)defined by the system process (Sects. 19.5.1 and 19.6.13). A process definition when invoked also establishes an environment: It inherits the environment of the scope in which the process is defined, and overrides † this with the binding of formal parameter identifiers to actual argument values, position by position (Sects. 19.4.4 and 19.6.9).

Storages σ : Σ

The semantic type of storages is a "classical" type that has been conventionally used since the early 1960s. Each system process may contain processes that operate only on the system-declared variables. Different systems will then each have their own set of variables, i.e., their own storage.

In the semantic model of this chapter we model the system storage concept in terms of a single, global metastorage, σ : Σ.

type
$$\sigma{:}\Sigma = \text{LOC} \xrightarrow{m} \text{VAL}$$

Since we do not detail a type concept, we shall say nothing about locations and values.

19.4 Process-Oriented Semantic Types

In addition to the conventional semantic types of environments and storages the operational semantics definition of this technical note makes use of additional semantic types: the type of unique process identifiers (not to be confused with process names[1]); the extension of the conventional environment to record bindings of (sets of) channels to the (singleton set of) process identifier created during prologue execution of system process in which they were introduced; and a heap for recording process continuations. In addition we also make use of process states, $\gamma : \Gamma$, which record the state of a process that is subject to (eligible for) interpretation actions; the totality, i.e., the set, $\psi : \Psi$, of all "currently eligible" process states, referred to as the process state configuration; and the composition of all three: process state configuration, heap and storage into the program state, $\omega : \Omega$, which the Next-state ("one-step" transition) function possibly transforms.

19.4.1 Unique Process Identifiers $\pi : \Pi$

With every process we associate a unique process identifier, $\pi : \Pi$.

type Π

When a set of parallel processes, pqs, of process π are started, whatever sequence of zero, one or more processes, pl, follows after this set (pqs), it cannot begin executing before the started processes have all terminated.

Operationally we handle this as follows. Each started process, pq_1, pq_2, $\ldots$, pq_q, is given a globally unique identification, π_i, for $i = 1$ to n, and its own list of process commands, pq_i, is affixed a **stop**(π_i) process (command). The "continuation" process structure

$$\theta : (\{\pi_1, \pi_2, \ldots, \pi_q\}, ((pl, `rho), \pi s))$$

is put on a heap (ξ of "to be executed" processes) — where πs is the set of all process identifiers mentioned above, that is, initially πs. Once any of the processes pq from pqs terminates, then its process marker, **stop**(π_i), causes the removal of π_i from the unique continuation structure. Emptiness of the set $\{\pi_1, \pi_2, \ldots, \pi_q\}$ means that all of the parallel processes pqs have terminated. It is then time to restore pl and to convert the heap "continuation" θ. Conversion is explained below.

Similarly for process (the **call**) invocation. And, each set of channels allocated upon entry to a system process is marked in the heap by a likewise unique process identifier: $(\pi, \{c_1, c_2, \ldots, c_k\})$. See Sects. 19.5.1, 19.6.7, 19.6.9 and 19.6.13 for allocation to the heap, and Sect. 19.6.8 for updates to, incl. conversions of the heap.

We summarise:

---

[1] A process definition has one name, but, depending on its number of possibly recursive (the **call**) invocations, may have many process identifications.

- With every syntactically defined contiguous sequence of process actions we associate a unique process identifier.
- That is:
  ⋆ A process definition body gives rise to a unique process identifier.
  ⋆ Each process command list of a set of process command lists of a parallel process command gives rise to a unique process identifier.
  ⋆ A system process command gives rise to a unique process identifier.
- Each channel is associated with the unique process identifier of the system process in which it is defined.

19.4.2 The Heap $\xi : \varXi$

Processes may (via the **call**) invoke processes defined in environments different from the one current at the place of invocation. A sequence of process commands may, properly within it, contain parallel process commands:

pe_1; (pe_21 ∥ pe_22 ∥ ... ∥ pe_2n); pe_3

Execution as prescribed by process expression pe_3 does not commence before all of pe_2i, for all i from 1 to n, have properly terminated.

A heap is an abstract data structure to which arbitrary substructures can be allocated and from which they can be removed (freed). Furthermore, one can update these substructures.

We introduce a heap state component, $\xi : \varXi$. The data structures allocated to the heap stand for process continuations: pairs of a sequence of process commands and the environment in which they are to be interpreted. Such pairs designate the program text after a process (the **call**) invocation, respectively after a parallel process command.

type

$\xi{:}\varXi = (\varPi\text{-set} \xrightarrow{\;\overrightarrow{m}\;} (\varTheta|\textbf{terminated})) \cup (\varPi \mapsto \text{Cn-set}) \text{ /* the heap */}$

$\theta{:}\varTheta = (\text{P}^* \times \text{ENV}) \times \text{Pi-set}$

The heap, rather arbitrarily, is also used to keep the bindings of sets of system local channel names to unique process identifiers. See Sects. 19.4.1 and 19.4.3.

The heap also conveniently records all process identifiers ever allocated, whether still in use (associated with a still visible channel, or a process that is still running) or out of service (because the channel is no longer visible or the process has terminated or finished).

──────────── Model Assertions ────────────

(i) The sets of πs allocated to the heap on behalf of process continuations, θ, are all disjoint, **and** (ii) the singleton sets, likewise of πs allocated to the heap on behalf of channels, are likewise disjoint from any process continuation πs, **and** (iii) the sets [known as process history identifiers] of πs′ paired with pairs of process continuation and environments (i.e., process closures) include the πs of its map inverse, **and** (iv) the union set of all the channel binding singleton π sets ($\{\pi\}$) and the union set of all process history identifier sets πs', at any point in the interpretation of a parallel program, identify the set of all so far allocated channels and processes.[2] We define, in Sect. 19.5.4, a function, *Bound*, which retrieves all these π's from the heap.

We summarise:

- A heap is a global state component.
- It records all channels ever allocated by their unique process identifier.
- It also records all process continuations, that is, the rest of a process definition body's process command list after a **call** command or a parallel process command — as a process closure:
  - ⋆ together with a defining environment,
  - ⋆ and the set of process identifiers of the **call**ed process (a singleton set) or the parallel command's parallel processes process command.
- If a process has, or a set of parallel processes have all, **terminated** then it is, resp. they are, marked so in the heap.

19.4.3 Input/Output Channel Bindings

type

$\quad$ QS == stop(π:Π)
$\quad$ QI == in(cπ:(c:Cn,pi:Π),v:Vn)
$\quad$ QO == out(cπ:(c:Cn,pi:Π),e:E)
$\quad$ QIO = QI | QO
$\quad$ QIOPl = QIO × Psl
$\quad$ Psl = {| pl | pl:(P|QS)* •
$\qquad\qquad$ ∀ i:**Nat**•i ∈ **inds** pl \ {**len** pl}
$\qquad\qquad\qquad$ ⇒ pl(i)∉ QIO ∧ pl(**len** pl)∈ QIO |}

Syntactically input and output process commands name channels. Since system process definitions may redefine channels an environment (ρ) is established that binds, amongst others, channel names to the pair of these channel names and the unique process identifier of the composite parallel process in which they occur.

We summarise:

- Input and output commands may be encoded: QIO.
- An encoded guarded command list, QIOPl, has its guard being an encoded input or output command and its last command being a **stop** marker.

---

[2] Some of these channels and processes may have been abandoned, respectively terminated. A channel is abandoned when it is no longer in the scope of a running process.

19.4.4 Environments ρ : ENV

Variables are bound to their locations. Formal parameter identifiers of an invoked procedure (definition) are bound to the actual argument values. Process names are bound to their closure, a pair of the process definition and the environment in which it was defined. Σ is the global storage; it binds locations to values. We only allow simple values: process and channel "denotations" (also a form of closures) are not allowed to be values. But one could think of another parallel, imperative language of so-called mobile processes [119,358,446] where such values are allowed. Each continuation, θ, process structure also contains the environment current at the instance the set, pqs, of parallel processes was first encountered.

type
$$\rho: \text{ENV} = (\text{Vn} \xrightarrow{m} \text{LOC})$$
$$\cup \ (\text{C} \xrightarrow{m} \Pi)$$
$$\cup \ (\text{Id} \xrightarrow{m} \text{VAL})$$
$$\cup \ (\text{Pn} \xrightarrow{m} \text{CLOS})$$
$$\text{CLOS} = \text{PD} \times \text{ENV}$$

We summarise:

- Environments provide for binding of
  - ⋆ variables to locations,
  - ⋆ channels to process identifiers,
  - ⋆ formal parameter identifiers to argument values and
  - ⋆ process definition names to process closures.

19.4.5 State Composition $\Psi, \Gamma, \Xi, \Sigma, \Omega$

The operational semantics is expressed as a (*Next*) state transition function, that is, as a structural operational semantics, but is written in a variant of RSL. The crucial issue is: What is the state of a process?

To keep track of all the varying number of specified processes at widely different levels of definition, some deeply embedded in surrounding ("outer") process commands, others less deeply we introduce a state component, ψ, which is a set of individual process states γ. The state γ is like a continuation (θ). The difference is that a state γ may have translated some of its leading input/-output process commands of its program text components, pl:SeqP, from the purely syntactical representational form (including an ordinary input/output process command, IO) to some internal, the QIO, forms (Sect. 19.6.6). Also, a state γ may have translated some of its leading nondeterministic external choice process commands in a certain way, for instance, from the IOPl form to the QIOPl form, and from there to the NonPs forms (Sect. 19.6.11).

type
  IOsPl = SeqPl | NonPs
  SeqPl′ = P′*
  P′ = QIO | P | Stop
  Stop == stop(pi:Π)
  SeqPl = {| pl | pl:SeqPl′ •
      ∀ x:**Nat** • x ∈ **inds** pl \ {1} ⇒ pl(x)∉ QIO
      ∀ x:**Nat** • x ∈ **inds** pl \ {**len** pl} ⇒ ∀ π:Π • pl(x) ≠ stop(π) |}
  NonPs = ((IO|QIO) × P*)-**set** × SeqPl
  γ:Γ = IOsPl × ENV
  ψ:Ψ = Γ-**set**
  Ω = (Ψ × Ξ × Σ) | {finish}

The Global State

We summarise:

- The global state consists of three state components:
  1. a storage, $\sigma : \Sigma$
  2. a heap, $\xi : \Xi$
  3. a set of candidates for next actions, $\psi : \Psi$
- Each next action candidate, $\gamma : \Gamma$, consists of two parts:
  1. a possibly encoded textual part:
     - ⋆ either a simple process command list
     - ⋆ or a set of pairs of a guard and a command list, which stands for a nondeterministic external choice command
  2. and an environment.

A γ pair (iospl,ρ)

- is either of the form (pl,ρ), where *pl* is a list of encoded process expressions (in SeqPl),
- or of the form (((ioqios,pl′),pl″),ρ) where pl′, pl″ are lists of process expressions (in respectively P* and SeqPl) and ioqios is a set of pairs (ioqio$_i$,pl$_i$) (in NonPs) where pl$_i$ is a list of process expressions and ioqio$_i$ is a set of pairs of possibly encoded input/output clauses and lists of ordinary (un-encoded) process expressions.

───────────────────── Model Assertions ─────────────────────

No two elements of ψ derive from the same process, i.e., all their encoded π's are distinct.

19.5 Initial and Auxiliary Semantic Functions

19.5.1 Start Function

value
  Start: Sy → **Unit**
  Start(sys(vs,cs,pdm,ps)) ≡
    let $(\psi,\pi,\pi s,\sigma)$ = System(vs,cs,pdm,ps)([ ])([ ])([ ]) **in**
    NextCont(ψ,[{π} ↦ cs,πs ↦ ⟨finish⟩],σ)
    end
    assert card ψ = **card** ps = **card** πs
          ∧ **card dom** σ = **card** vs
          ∧ **card dom** ρ
              = **card dom** vs + **card** cs + **card dom** pdm

19.5.2 System Function

The *System* function prepares a set, ψ, of process continuations: pairs of program texts (lists of process commands) and environments; a set, ψ's, of unique process identifiers, one for each process (the **call**) invocation (found in ps); and (updates) the storage, σ. The environment, ρ, that is also (update) constructed by *System* is used in (is put into) the process closures of ψ. All channel names are bound, in ρ, to a unique process identifier. It really doesn't matter which, as long as all channel names of a system receive the same identifier and that identifier is never bound to other systems' channel names.

  System(vs,cs,pdm,ps)(ρ)(ξ)(σ) ≡
    let (ρ',σ') = BindAndAlloc(vs)(ρ)(σ),
          π:Π,πs:Π-**set** • **card** πs = **card** ps ∧ Free({π}∪ πs,ξ) **in**
    let ρ'' = ρ' ∪ [c ↦ π | c:Cn • c ∈ cs] ∪
                [pn ↦ (pdm(pn),ρ'') | pn:Pn • pn ∈ **dom** pdm] **in**
    let ψ = Distribute(πs,ps,ρ) **in**
    $(\psi,\pi,\pi s,\sigma')$ **end end end**
    assert card ψ = **card** ps

Observe that the definition of ρ'' is recursive. This recursion allows defined processes to invoke one another or themselves recursively. If such recursion, for some pragmatic reason or other, is not required, then the process definition closure need not be given the same environment to which it contributes (ρ' suffices). RSL [130, 131], strictly speaking, does not permit us to express, in general, such recursive definitions. In the case of the semantics of this chapter, one can, however, show that there is indeed a suitable solution to the recursive definition of ρ''.

19.5.3 Bind and Allocate Functions

The *BindAndAlloc* function is a "classical" variable binding and storage allocation function: To each variable a distinct location is found in storage and a binding provided in the environment.

> BindAndAlloc: Vn-set $\rightarrow$ ENV $\rightarrow$ Σ $\rightarrow$ Σ × ENV
> BindAndAlloc(vs)(ρ)(σ) $\equiv$
>   **if** vs = {}
>   **then** (ρ,σ)
>   **else let** v:Vn • v $\in$ vs, loc:LOC • loc $\notin$ **dom** σ **in**
>   **let** ρ' = ρ † [v $\mapsto$ loc],
> σ' = σ ∪ [loc $\mapsto$ **chaos**] **in**
>   BindAndAlloc(vs \ {v})(ρ')(σ') **end end**
>   **end**

19.5.4 Free and Bound Functions

The *Free* function checks that a set of process identifiers have never been allocated to the heap.

> Free: Π-set × Ξ $\rightarrow$ **Bool**
> Free(πs,ξ) $\equiv$ Bound(ξ) $\cap$ πs' = {}

> Bound: Ξ $\rightarrow$ Π-set
> Bound(ξ) $\equiv$
>   **let** πs' = { π | π:Π • π $\in$ **dom** ξ },
> πs'' = ∪ { πs | πs:Π-set • (,πs'') $\in$ **rng** ξ } **in**
> πs' ∪ πs'' **end**
>   **assert dom** ξ $\subseteq$ πs' ∪ πs''

Free, *Bound* express whether a set of unique process identifiers are free, i.e., not used, not *Bound*, in the heap. *Bound* computes all process identifiers ever (i.e., so far) bound to channels (πs'), respectively processes (πs'').

Model Assertions

(i) If a π is in the definition set, i.e., the **dom**ain of the heap map, then it designates a set of channel names, **and** (ii) if a set $\{\pi_1, \pi_2, \ldots, \pi_n\}$ is in the **dom**ain of the heap map then it designates a pair of a process closure and a set, πs of process identifiers such that $\{\pi_1, \pi_2, \ldots, \pi_n\} \subseteq \pi$s.

19.5.5 Distribute Function

The *Distribute* function creates a set of process continuations, γ. These are pairs of process command sequences ending in a **stop**(π) clause. The *Next*-state transition function will inspect the head of these command lists of the continuation in ψ. The **stop**(π) clause, when encountered, shall contribute to the eventual removal from the heap, ξ, of the process closure allocated there when certain process commands were first encountered. In the case of the initial system initialisation the clause **finish** is being retrieved — signifying that the whole program has terminated (Sects. 19.5.6 and 19.6.14).

> Distribute: Π-**set** $\times$ P-**set** $\times$ ENV $\rightarrow \Psi$
> Distribute$(\pi s, pqs, \rho) \equiv$
>   **if** $\pi s=\{\}$ /* assert: */ $pqs=\{\}$
>   **then let** $\pi:\Pi \bullet \pi \in \pi s$, pq:P* $\bullet$ pq $\in$ pqs **in**
> $\{(pq\hat{\ }\langle stop(\pi)\rangle, \rho)\} \cup$ Distribute$(\pi s \setminus \{\pi\}, pqs \setminus \{pq\}, \rho)$ **end**
>   **else** $\{\}$
>   **end**
>   **pre card** $\pi s =$ **card** pqs

The *Distribute* and the *BindAndAlloc* functions, as a technicality, are expressed using recursive descent on finite sets.

19.5.6 Transition Loop

> NextCont: $\Omega \rightarrow$ **Unit**
> NextCont$(\psi, \xi, \sigma) \equiv$
>   **let** $\omega =$ Next(ψ, ξ, σ) **in**
>   **if** $\omega =$ finish **then skip else** NextCont(ω) **end end**

The *NextCont* function has the **Unit** type since it may never terminate! We often define processes to willfully never terminate.

─────────────── Model Assertion ───────────────

> If the interpreter encounters **finish** then the global system program has terminated.

19.6 Semantic Functions

19.6.1 The *Next*-State Transition Function

The *Next*-state transition function inspects an ω state and delivers, always, an ω state.

> Next: $\Omega \rightarrow \Omega$
> Next$(\psi, \xi, \sigma) \equiv$ ... /* defined case by case */ ...

Thus, in RSL, we write a structural operational semantics, i.e., a transition system definition of "mechanical", step-by-step executions of parallel programs.

    The idea is that the combined, i.e., the total state, ψ, of all processes is investigated by inspecting an arbitrary component, γ, (of interest) "each time round the *Next* loop" (where *NextCont* defines that loop):

Next({⟨⟨cmd⟩^pl,ρ⟩} ∪ ψ,ξ,σ) ≡ ...
Next({⟨⟨(nd,pq),pl⟩,ρ⟩} ∪ ψ,ξ,σ) ≡ ...
assert ∃ π:Π • pl(**len** pl) = stop(π)

There are, as shown, two forms potentially subject to inspection. Here pl stands for encoded process expression lists (always ending with a **stop(π)** command); pq stands for ordinary unencoded process expression lists; cmd stands for a single, possibly encoded process expression; and nd for a set of possibly encoded input/output ("guard") commands.

The reader is directed towards the special, not strictly "RSL kosher(!)", use of formal parameter expressions as indicated above. The union of one (or, as for the input/output rendezvous, two) process states, σ, with a "remaining" process state configuration, ψ, expresses a suitable nondeterminism by the program interpreter: namely that process "progress" is arbitrary. Which of the many processes makes "next" steps depends on so many other circumstances than those explicit from the program text: the availability of machine resources, the degree to which "real" concurrency can be provided for in the actually executing programs, etc.

19.6.2 The Assignment Statement

Such a component, amongst many others, but one which is ready for execution, could be the "atomic" assignment statement:

Next({⟨⟨asgn(v,e)⟩^pl,ρ⟩} ∪ ψ,ξ,σ) ≡
    let loc = ρ(v), val = Eval_Expr(e)(ρ)(σ) **in**
    let σ' = σ † [loc ↦ val] **in**
    ({⟨pl,ρ⟩} ∪ ψ,ξ,σ') **end end**
    pre v ∈ **dom** ρ ∧ loc ∈ **dom** σ ∧ pl ≠ ⟨⟩

We see that the assignment statement is executed and disappears from the Ψ component.

We also get the meaning of an assignment: that of evaluating its "right-hand side" expression and binding its value to the location of the "left-hand side" variable.

—————————— Language Assertion ——————————

If evaluation of the expression terminates then the assignment statement will terminate. (It is here assumed that the variable is known.)

19.6.3 The case Statement

Now to the structured statements. First, the **case** switch:

Next({(⟨cas(e,sw)⟩^pl,ρ)} ∪ ψ,ξ,σ) ≡
   let val = Eval_Expr(e)(ρ)(σ) **in**
   if val ∈ **dom** sw
      then let pq = sw(val) **in** ({(pq^pl,ρ)} ∪ ψ,ξ,σ) **end**
      else chaos
   end end
   pre pl ≠ ⟨⟩

It generalises the two-way **if then else end** switch. The *Next* transition is from the structured **cases** switch, if applicable, by replacing that statement by the selected list of process commands.

The essential aspect of the **case** statement has been specified: the selection, if possible, of a continuation amongst a set of alternative such. If no *case*-list "guard" matches the *case*-expression value then **chaos** ensues: what happens next is left undefined!

─────────── Language Assertion ───────────

If evaluation of the expression terminates and if interpretation of the selected case branch terminates then the case statement will terminate.

19.6.4 The *while* Loop

A transition involving the **while** loop:

Next({(⟨whi(e,pq)⟩^pl,ρ)} ∪ ψ,ξ,σ) ≡
   let val = Eval_Expr(e)(ρ)(σ) **in**
   if val
      then ({(pq^⟨whi(e,pq)⟩^pl,ρ)} ∪ ψ,ξ,σ)
      else ({(pl,ρ)} ∪ ψ,ξ,σ)
   end end
   pre pl ≠ ⟨⟩

also results in either removing it altogether from the Ψ state component, or in prefix-appending its body to the process command list whose first element was that **while** loop. This essentially expresses the meaning of a **while** loop through its rewriting!

─────────── Language Assertion ───────────

If the evaluation of the while expression when first encountered terminates, and if every subsequent interpretation of the while body of process expressions terminates, then the while clause terminates.

19.6.5 The *repeat until* Loop

Similarly for the repeat **until** loop:

$\text{Next}(\{(\langle\text{rep(pq,e)}\rangle\widehat{\ }\text{pl},\rho)\} \cup \psi,\xi,\sigma) \equiv$
$\quad(\{(\text{pq}\widehat{\ }\langle\text{whi(e,pq)}\rangle\widehat{\ }\text{pl},\rho)\} \cup \psi,\xi,\sigma)$
pre pl $\neq \langle\rangle$

which likewise leads to a rewrite, i.e., a reshuffling of an appropriate state Ψ component.

────────────────── Language Assertion ──────────────────

A language semantics assertion similar to that for the while loop can be formulated.

──

19.6.6 Simple Input/Output Processes

Transitions involving the simple, atomic process synchronisation and communication commands, either **input** or **output**, result in their replacement by almost similar **in**, respectively **out**, commands. The replacements encode the proper, unique process identifier to which the command name is bound in the environment. The issue here is that one and the same channel name may have been declared in two different contexts which might bind these names to different process identifiers — hence they are not designating the same, but instead different channels.

$\text{Next}(\{(\langle\text{input(c,v)}\rangle\widehat{\ }\text{pl},\rho)\} \cup \psi,\xi,\sigma) \equiv$
$\quad(\{(\langle\text{in}((c,\rho(c)),v)\rangle\widehat{\ }\text{pl},\rho)\} \cup \psi,\xi,\sigma)$
$\quad\textbf{pre } \text{pl} \neq \langle\rangle \wedge v \in \textbf{dom } \rho \wedge \rho(v) \in \textbf{dom } \sigma$
$\quad\quad\wedge\ c \in \textbf{dom } \rho \wedge c \in \textbf{dom } \xi$

$\text{Next}(\{(\langle\text{output(c,e)}\rangle\widehat{\ }\text{pl},\rho)\} \cup \psi,\xi,\sigma) \equiv$
$\quad(\{(\langle\text{out}((c,\rho(c)),e)\rangle\widehat{\ }\text{pl},\rho)\} \cup \psi,\xi,\sigma)$
$\quad\textbf{pre } \text{pl} \neq \langle\rangle \wedge c \in \textbf{dom } \rho \wedge c \in \textbf{dom } \xi$

If we are in a Ψ state where there is a "match", that is, one process wishes to input on a channel and another wishes to output on that channel, then the communication may take place. The value of the expression is communicated by being assigned to the receiving process's variable v.

$\text{Next}(\{(\langle\text{in}((c,\pi),v)\rangle\widehat{\ }\text{pl},\rho),(\langle\text{out}((c,\pi),e)\rangle\widehat{\ }\text{pl}',\rho')\} \cup \psi,\xi,\sigma) \equiv$
$\quad\textbf{let } \text{loc} = \rho(v), \text{val} = \text{Eval\_Expr(e)}(\rho')(\sigma) \textbf{ in}$
$\quad(\{(\text{pl},\rho),(\text{pl}',\rho')\} \cup \psi,\xi,\sigma \dagger [\text{loc} \mapsto \text{val}]) \textbf{ end}$
$\quad\textbf{pre } \text{pl} \neq \langle\rangle \wedge v \in \textbf{dom } \rho$
$\quad\quad\wedge\ \rho(v) \in \textbf{dom } \sigma \wedge c \in \textbf{dom } \rho$
$\quad\quad\wedge\ \pi \in \textbf{dom } \xi \wedge c \in \xi(\pi)$

This last transition rather neatly expresses why one refers to the input/output process commands as defining a rendezvous of two processes: their handshake synchronisation and communication (of a value from one process to a location of the local storage of another process). The output clause expression is not evaluated till the rendezvous actually takes place.

―――――――――― Model Assertion ――――――――――

The two process states represent different processes: A process cannot synchronise and communicate with itself.

19.6.7 The Parallel Process Command, ||

$Next(\{((\langle par(pqs)\rangle\hat{}pl,\rho)\} \cup \psi,\xi,\sigma) \equiv$
    let $\pi s:\Pi\text{-set} \bullet \textbf{card } \pi s = \textbf{card } pqs \wedge Free(\pi s,\xi)$ **in**
    let $\psi' = Distribute(\pi s,pqs,\rho),$
        $\xi' = \xi \cup [\pi s \mapsto ((pl,\rho),\pi s)]$ **in**
    $(\psi' \cup \psi,\xi',\sigma)$ **end end**
    pre $pl \neq \langle\rangle \wedge ...$

The *Distribute* function yields a process continuation, γ, for each of the parallel process expressions in *pqs*, and assigns it to the set, the Ψ component, of all such process continuations. The rest of the process expression, *pl*, after the parallel process expression (essentially after *pqs*) is temporarily allocated to the heap. This models the semantics of the parallel process expression: Only after all of the parallel processes, now in ψ', have terminated, will the process expression *pl* be honoured.

19.6.8 The *stop* Process Technicality

When the interpreter encounters a **stop**(π) clause then the heap is inspected. If the process identified by the π was the last of a set of one or more parallel processes or was that of a process (**call**) invocation, then the invoking process continuation is restored and the original set of processes (represented by their identifiers) is marked as having **terminated**.

$Next(\{((\langle stop(\pi)\rangle,\rho)\} \cup \psi,\xi,\sigma) \equiv$
    let $\pi s:\Pi\text{-set} \bullet \pi s \in \textbf{dom } \xi \wedge \pi \in \pi s$ **in**
    let $((pq,\rho'),\pi s') = \xi(\pi s)$ **in**
    let $\xi' = \textbf{if } \pi s=\{\pi\}$
                then $\xi(\{\pi\}) \cup [\pi s' \mapsto \textbf{terminated}]$
                else $\xi\backslash\pi s \cup [\pi s\backslash\{\pi\} \mapsto ((pq,\rho'),\pi s')]$ **end in**
    if $\pi s=\{\pi\}$ **then** $(\{(pq,\rho')\} \cup \psi,\xi',\sigma)$ **else** (ψ,ξ',σ) **end**
    end end end
    assert $\pi s \subseteq \pi s'$

It is emphasized that the use of the **stop**(π) clause is a technicality. Other means, other encodings could have been defined. In an operational semantics there usually are several such rather detailed and somewhat ad hoc technical choices.

19.6.9 The Process *call* Command

Invoking a defined process is treated like starting a single parallel process. This is so since a defined process may have been defined in a scope, i.e., with an environment (ρ'), different from that of the invoking process (ρ).

Next({(($\langle$call(pn,el)$\rangle$)^pl,ρ)} $\cup$ ψ,ξ,σ) $\equiv$
    let ((idl,pq),ρ') = ρ(pn) **in**
    let ρ'' = ρ'†[idl(i)$\mapsto$Eval_Expr(el(i))(ρ)(σ)|i:**Nat**•i $\in$ **inds** el] **in**
    let π:Π • Free({π},ξ) **in**
    ({(pq^$\langle$stop(π)$\rangle$),ρ'')} $\cup$ ψ,ξ $\cup$ [{π} $\mapsto$ ((pl,ρ),{π})],σ)
    end end end
    pre pl $\neq$ $\langle\rangle$ $\wedge$ pn $\in$ **dom** ρ $\wedge$ **len** el = **len** idl $\wedge$ ...

Actual arguments are bound to formal parameters, resulting in ρ''.

19.6.10 Internal Nondeterministic Processes, $\sqcap$

The definition of the internal nondeterministic process command is simple. The **let** clause expresses the internal nondeterministic choice: An arbitrary process expression, *pq*, from amongst *pqs* is chosen.

Next({(($\langle$ind(pqs)$\rangle$)^pl,ρ)} $\cup$ ψ,ξ,σ) $\equiv$
    let pq:P* • pq $\in$ pqs **in** ({(pq^pl,ρ)} $\cup$ ψ,ξ,σ) **end**
    pre pl $\neq$ $\langle\rangle$ $\wedge$ ...

19.6.11 External Nondeterministic Processes, $\square$

The *Next* transition on external nondeterministic process command processes has to prepare for the eventuality that any number of the external nondeterministic alternative process potentialities is or will be ready to either input or output from ("completely") other processes. So all alternative process commands must, somehow, have their first, an input or an output command, be prepared, as were "ordinary" input/output commands, by finding the appropriate channel bindings. This is done by the *MakeIO* function. Then we prepare a set of potential alternative process potentialities, one of which will eventually be selected and all the others discarded.

Next({(($\langle$xnd(gs)$\rangle$^pl,ρ)} $\cup$ ψ,ξ,σ) $\equiv$
    let g = { MakeIOpq(io)(ρ) | io:IOPl • io $\in$ gs } **in**
    ({((g,pl),ρ)} $\cup$ ψ,ξ,σ) **end**

MakeIO: IOPl $\to$ ENV $\to$ QIOPl
MakeIO((io,pq))(ρ) $\equiv$
    case io **of**:

input(c,v) → (in((c,ρ(c)),v),pq),
output(c,e) → (out((c,ρ(c)),e),pq)
end

assert v $\in$ **dom** ρ $\wedge$ $\exists$ π:Π • π $\in$ **dom** ξ $\wedge$ c $\in$ $\xi(\pi)$

19.6.12 Nondeterministic Input/Output Processes

There are now three possibilities of synchronisation and communication involving external nondeterministic process alternatives:

- A potential external nondeterministic process alternative (of one process, π) is enabled to input from another potential external nondeterministic process alternative (of another process, π'), which is enabled for output.

  Next({((({(in((c,π),v),pq)} $\cup$ iopqps,pl),ρ),
  (((({(out((c,π),e),pq')} $\cup$ iopqps'),pl'),ρ')} $\cup$ ψ,ξ,σ) $\equiv$
  let loc = ρ(v), val = Eval_Expr(e)(ρ')(σ) **in**
  ({(pq$\hat{\ }$pl,ρ),(pq'$\hat{\ }$pl',ρ')} $\cup$ ψ,ξ,σ † [loc $\mapsto$ val]) **end**
  pre π $\in$ **dom** ξ $\wedge$ c $\in$ $\xi(\pi)$ $\wedge$ v $\in$ **dom** ρ $\wedge$ loc $\in$ **dom** σ $\wedge$
  ρ $\neq$ ρ' $\wedge$ pl $\neq$ $\langle\rangle$ $\wedge$ pl' $\neq$ $\langle\rangle$
  assert {(pq$\hat{\ }$pl,ρ),(pq'$\hat{\ }$pl',ρ')} $\cap$ ψ = {}

- A potential external nondeterministic process alternative (of one process, π) is enabled to input from another (not nondeterministic) process (π'), which is enabled for output.

  Next'({((({(in((c,i),v),pq)} $\cup$ iopqps,pl),ρ),
  (($\langle$out((c,i),e)$\rangle\hat{\ }$pl',ρ')} $\cup$ ψ,ξ,σ) $\equiv$
  let loc = ρ(v), val = Eval_Expr(e)(ρ')(σ) **in**
  ({(pq$\hat{\ }$pl,ρ),(pq'$\hat{\ }$pl',ρ')} $\cup$ ψ,ξ,σ † [loc $\mapsto$ val]) **end**
  pre /* similar to above */
  assert /* similar to above */

- And vice versa wrt. input and output.

  Next({((({(out((c,i),e),pq)} $\cup$ iopqps,pl),ρ),
  (($\langle$in((c,i),v)$\rangle\hat{\ }$pl,ρ')} $\cup$ ψ,ξ,σ) $\equiv$
  let val = Eval_Expr(e)(ρ)(σ), loc = ρ'(v) **in**
  ({(pq$\hat{\ }$pl,ρ),(pl',ρ')} $\cup$ ψ,ξ,σ † [loc $\mapsto$ val]) **end**
  pre /* similar to above */
  assert /* similar to above */

Again we see the rendezvous of two distinct (hence parallel) processes over a channel, a "handshake" synchronising and communicating, as mentioned in Sect. 19.6.6.

19.6.13 The Embedded System Process Command

The embedded system process is very much like the global system process (Sect. 19.5.1).

Next({(⟨sys(vs,cs,pdm,ps)⟩ˆpl,ρ)} ∪ ψ,ξ,σ) ≡
    let (ψ′,π,πs,σ′) = System(vs,cs,pdm,ps)(ρ)(ξ)(σ) **in**
    (ψ′ ∪ ψ,ξ ∪ [{π} ↦ cs,πs ↦ ((pl,ρ),ψ′)],σ′) **end**
    pre pl ≠ ⟨⟩ ∧ ...
    assert ψ′ ∩ ψ={}∧{π}∪πs ∩ Bound(ξ)={}∧**card** ψ′=**card** ps∧...

The auxiliary function *System* was defined in Section 19.5.1.

19.6.14 A *finish* Process Technicality

If when inspecting a process continuation in the Ψ component the interpreter finds a `finish` clause, then we can assert that the program is terminating.

Next({(⟨finish⟩,ρ)} ∪ ψ,ξ,σ) ≡ finish
    assert: ξ = [ ] ∧ ψ = {}

――――――――――――― Model Assertion ―――――――――――――
When a `finish` clause is encountered then the process state configuration is just a singleton set. That is, ψ is empty. And the heap type will consist only of the process identifiers of (all) processes ever activated (but now terminated) and those of all channels ever instantiated.

19.7 Discussion

19.7.1 General

We have defined the syntax of a nontrivial CSP-like language. And we have given an operational, i.e., a computational style semantics of this language. To do so we contrived a rather complicated notion of configuration. The main idea of this chapter was to introduce the reader to this kind of structural operational semantics. We find it a useful exercise to understand this semantics. The semantics definition style of this chapter offers one way of defining concurrent systems and languages. Although unwieldy, it may serve well in smaller applications than the one shown here.

    Use of the structural operational semantics definition techniques of Plotkin [402] is advised since it lends itself more to a proof-oriented specification. We refer to current textbooks on semantics covering the operational semantics definition style [93, 158, 432, 448, 499, 533].

19.7.2 Principles, Techniques and Tools

We summarise:

Principles. *Parallel Programming Language Definitions:* Concurrent programs are best characterised, it appears, by their transitions: from program point to program point, usually from points of interactions between threads of programs, i.e., processes, or between the concurrent program and its environment. As a result, it is advisable to model concurrent programs, and hence parallel programming languages, by the kind of structural operational semantics exemplified in this chapter. ∎

Techniques. *Parallel Programming Language Definitions:* A first decision that has to be made wrt. the definition of the semantics of a parallel programming language is that of the "atomicity" language constructs: The "coarsest atomicity" is that of assembling all internal actions between synchronisation and/or communication points of a process into one atomic step. The "finest atomicity" is that of considering the smallest possible evaluation step of also the declarations, expressions and statements between synchronisation and/or communication points as "atomic steps". From the decision of what constitutes an atomic step follows decisions wrt. configurations. ∎

Tools. *Parallel Programming Language Definitions:* Since structural operational semantics can often be written in the form of algebraic semantics rewrite rules [63,340], tools like interpreters for such algebraic semantic specification languages as `CafeOBJ` [123], `Casl` [40,371], and, especially, `Maude` [81], are interesting for checking out consistency and (relative) completeness of a structural operational semantics. ∎

19.8 Bibliographical Notes

The language of this chapter is a variant of CSP: Communicating Sequential Processes. In [213] the semantics of CSP is given in terms of a number of laws, i.e., axioms that determine properties of CSP programs. In [436] the semantics of CSP is given in a variety of ways: operationally, à la Plotkin [402], denotationally, where the semantic types are traces (of behaviours), and algebraically, i.e., in terms of laws. Kahn's approach to language design and language definition is also appealing [252].

In [119] we give a hybrid way of defining a semantics for a variant of CSP. A proper theoretical foundation for this approach has yet to be given. The language defined in [119] allows for the dynamic creation of processes, and for certain forms of process "mobility". By a *mobile process* we shall understand a process which can be communicated via channels — and thus which resides on a variety of processors. The π-calculus [358,446] provides an exciting theory for studying process mobility.

19.9 Exercises

Exercise 19.1 *Multiple Client/Single Server Connectors.* There is given a very simple parallel programming language, C_nS_1L, whose only programs are of the following multiple client/single server kind:[3]

type Cldx, M, Γ, Σ, Γ_C=Cldx $\overrightarrow{m}$ Γ
value γ_C:Γ_C, σ:Σ
channel {cs[c]:M|c:Cldx}
value
    system: **Unit** $\rightarrow$ **Unit**
    client: c:Cldx $\rightarrow$ Γ $\rightarrow$ **write,read** cs[c] **Unit**
    server: Σ $\rightarrow$ **read,write** {cs[c]|c:Cldx} **Unit**

    system() $\equiv$ ||{client(c)(γ_C(c))|c:Cldx} || server(σ)

    client(c)(γ) $\equiv$
        let m = some_c_value(γ) **in**
        cs[c]!m;   /* request service */
        let m' = cs[c]? **in**   /* service delivered */
        client(c)(next_c_state(m')(γ)) **end end**

    server(σ) $\equiv$
        []{**let** m = cs[c]? **in**   /* receive service request */
        let m' = some_s_value(c,m)(σ) **in**   /* perform service */
        cs[c]!m';   /* deliver service result */
        server(next_s_state(i,m')(σ)) **end end** | c:Cldx}

Assume the "some" and "next" functions. Programs c_ns_1p in C_nS_1L are connectors between multiple clients and a single server communicating over simply multiplexed channels.

19.1.1 Formalise a syntax for C_nS_1L programs. Assume the "some" and "next" functions.
19.1.2 Define a predicate which expresses that C_nS_1L programs are well formed.
19.1.3 Define appropriate semantic types of run-time contexts and states and a set of next state functions that specify an elaboration of C_nS_1L programs in the style of this chapter.

C_nS_1L programs differ only in the abstract "some" and "next" functions for which you can postulate two sets of semantic elaboration functions Val_fcts and Int_fcts.

---

[3]C_nS_1L programs are here expressed in a syntax similar to RSL. But C_nS_1L programs are not to be considered RSL programs.

Exercise 19.2 *Multiple Client/Multiple Server Connectors.* There is given a very simple parallel programming language, C_mS_nL, whose only programs are of the following multiplexed client/server kind:

type M, Γ, Σ, CIdx, SIdx, Γ_C=CIdx $\overrightarrow{m}$ Γ, Σ_S=SIdx $\overrightarrow{m}$ Σ
value γ_C:Γ_C, σ_S:Σ_S
channel {cs[c,s]:M|c:CIdx,s:SIdx}
value
    system: **Unit** $\rightarrow$ **Unit**
    client: c:CIdx $\rightarrow$ Γ $\rightarrow$ **read,write** {cs[c,s]|s:SIdx} **Unit**
    server: s:SIdx $\rightarrow$ Σ $\rightarrow$ **write,read** {cs[c,s]|c:CIdx} **Unit**

    system() $\equiv$ ($\|$ {client(c)(γ_C(c))|c:CIdx}) $\|$ ($\|$ {server(s)(σ_S(s))|s:SIdx})

    client(c)(γ) $\equiv$
        let m = some_c_value(γ) **in**
        $[]$ {cs[c,s]!m;   /* send service request */
            let m' = cs[c,s]? **in**   /* receive service result */
            client(c)(next_c_state(s,m')(γ)) **end** | s:SIdx}
        end

    server(s)(σ) $\equiv$
        $[]$ {**let** m = cs[c,s]? **in**   /* receive service request */
            let m' = some_s_value(c,m)(σ) **in**   /* perform service */
            cs[c,s]!m';   /* deliver service result */
            server(s)(next_c_state(c,m')(γ)) **end end** | c:CIdx}

Assume the "some" and "next" functions. Thus programs c_ms_np in C_mS_nL are very simple connectors between multiple clients and multiple servers communicating over doubly multiplexed channels. Thus we assume that all servers can perform all the desired functions for any of the multiple clients.

19.2.1 Formalise a syntax for C_mS_nL programs. Assume the "some" and "next" functions.
19.2.2 Define a predicate which expresses that c_ms_np programs in C_mS_nL are well formed.
19.2.3 Define appropriate semantic types of run-time contexts and states and a set of next state functions that specify an elaboration of C_mS_nL programs in the style of this chapter.

C_mS_nL programs differ only in the abstract "some" and "next" functions for which you can postulate two sets of semantic elaboration functions Val_fcts and Int_fcts.

Exercise 19.3 *Mobile Processes.* There is given a "funny little, unstructured" parallel programming language, MΠL, with the following constructs:

1. **process type** Π
2. **process definition** p() $\equiv$ body ;
3. **process variable** process_var[0..]:Π
4. process_var[i] := **start** p() ;
5. **send** value_expression **to process** process_var[j] ;
6. **receive** ordinary_var **from process** process_var[k] ;

i,j,k are natural number-valued expressions. p stands for a variety of **process** names: p, p1, ..., pn, q, ... process_var likewise for a variety of **process variable** names. The idea of this language is that a program consists of a single definition of a process identification type (item 1.), of a number of process definitions (item 2.), and a process variable declaration (item 3.). Process variable declarations designate flexible vectors of an indefinite number of atomic type Π-valued variables. (For simplicity you need only one such process variable declaration.) The process definition bodies consist of a sequence of ordinary variable declarations and of a statement sequence. Statements are either the usual complement of ordinary assignment, while-loop, if-then-else and other such statements — containing a usual complement of expressions. Statements are, additionally, selected from the three statements shown in items 4.–6. A program consists of one, an initialising process statement, for example process_var[0] := **start** p() (item 4.). Finally the idea is that every process — once started — is assigned a unique process identifier being also the value of the **start** p() expression. Execution of a start clause (item 4.) in a process leads to the start up of a new process of the designated kind, the allocation of a fresh, that is, unique process identification to this process and the assignment of that identification to the designated process variable cell. Execution of a send clause (item 5.) first leads to the evaluation of the value expression, resulting in a value, v, then to the offering of output v to the process identified by the designated process variable cell. Execution of the send clause only completes once the identified process has accepted v. Execution of a receive clause (item 6.), by some process, π, proceeds as follows. Process π, in a sense, by attempting to elaborate the receive clause, declares itself willing to receive any value from any (other) process. If no process is offering a value for process π then execution of the receive clause waits until such a value is offered, if ever.

19.3.1 Narrate and formalise a syntax for MΠL programs. Assume a category of ordinary statements.

19.3.2 Narrate and define a predicate which express that mπp programs in MΠL are well formed.

19.3.3 Narrate and define appropriate semantic types of run-time contexts and states and a set of next state functions that specify an interpretation of MΠL programs in the style of this chapter.

State all appropriate assumptions.

(MΠL is a simplified version of the language presented in [119].)

Part VIII

CLOSING

20

Closing

- The **prerequisite** for studying this chapter is that you have now ended the study of this, the second, volume in our series of three volumes on software engineering.
- The **aims** are to present a conclusion that covers Vols. 1 and 2 of these textbooks on software engineering, and to present a preliminary answer to *What's Next?*
- The **objective** is to properly conclude Vol. 2, and to properly link Vols. 1 and 2 to Vol. 3.
- The **treatment** is discursive.

20.1 A Summary

Volume 1 of this series of textbooks on software engineering focused on three aspects: (i) on the basic discrete mathematics used in most model-oriented formal specification languages, (ii) on the basic principles and techniques of abstraction and formal modelling, and (iii) on propagating, hand-in-hand with material on abstraction and modelling, the RAISE Specification Language, RSL.

The present volume has focused on four aspects: (iv) further principles and techniques of abstraction and formal modelling (specification facets: hierarchies and compositions, denotations and computations, and a crucial concept, which then is treated in various other guises in several chapters of this volume, that of time, space and time/space), (v) linguistics (pragmatics, semantics, syntax, and their summary in semiotics), (vi) diagrammatic and temporal specification techniques (modularity, automata and machines, Petri nets, message and live sequence charts, statecharts, and temporal logics [quantitative models of time]), and (vii) language definitions (of applicative [i.e., functional], imperative, modular and parallel programming languages) and how to develop prescriptions for what and how compilers should translate.

20.2 Conclusion: Volumes 1 and 2

The division of topics covered by Vols. 1 and 2 was determined on pragmatic grounds: between what could be considered basic principles and techniques and what could be considered more advanced principles and techniques. With the basic ones the software engineer can specify simple abstract software designs. With the advanced principles and techniques the software engineer can specify requirements and domains.

So, in one sense, we are, at the completion of Vol. 2, at *road's end!* We have presented, and expectedly you have learned, a necessary and, with the formal specification languages known today, sufficient set of tools. We have also presented principles and techniques for the abstract, formal modelling of such phenomena as are encountered when embarking upon software development, and such concepts as are "put inside" computers, i.e., when concluding software development.

The hedge above, "with the formal specification languages known today", forewarns the reader that the immediate and the longer term futures will offer new specification paradigms and new specification languages. Some of these will be cleaner and more elegant than what we have today. Most others will not. Yet other proposals will offer means to abstractly model facets of phenomena and, notably, concepts for which we today seem not to have proper tools. We are thinking, as an example, of modelling (autonomous) agents which communicate messages of *knowledge and belief* of, and in, one another's knowledge (i.e., state), or of *promise and commitment*, and so on.

So be prepared to look around. With the ballast provided by Vols. 1 and 2 it should not be difficult for the practicing software engineer to keep abreast.

20.3 Preview of Volume 3

And, in another sense, at the completion of Vol. 2, we are *at another road's start!*

Common to both Vols. 1 and 2 is that these two volumes focus on formal modelling and formal specification. Nothing substantial was said about informal, i.e., natural and professional language informal specification.

The crucial points of Vol. 3 are summarised by these questions

1. *How does one start?*
2. *How does one make formal models readable by everyone concerned?*
3. *How does one decompose overall software development into manageable and believable parts?*

We shall try address these three issues below.

1. 'Start' is meant in at least two ways.

(a) One starts, ideally, with the development of a model of the domain, then goes on to model the requirements, and finally one designs (and hence implements, i.e., "codes") the software.

(b) And, one starts by rough sketching, i.e., by informally describing (prescribing, specifying) phenomena and concepts (of the domain, the requirements, the software). One then proceeds to analyse these sketches, forming concepts, and establishing terminologies (of the domain, of the requirements, and of the software — three different sets of terms), and proceeds further to precisely narrate, i.e., again informally describe (prescribe, specify) the domain, the requirements, the software — the latter possibly hand-in-hand with their formalisation.

(c) Finally, one really starts by identifying phenomena and concepts, by analysing these into entities, functions, events and behaviours.

2. Item 1 contained the answer to the second question above: *How does one make formal models readable by everyone concerned?* One does so by carefully constructing informal descriptions (prescriptions, specifications) of the formal models.

3. Items 1 and 2 also contained the answer to the third question above: *How does one decompose overall software development into manageable and believable parts?* One does so by phasing the development into three well- and predefined phases, and each of these into well- and predefined stages, and these stages into steps. The latter are well-defined, but not predefined: arising, as they do, out of the specifics of the problem at hand.

Some comments may be in order:

3. Item 3 above, then, basically, announced a main purpose of Vol. 3: to bring in material that covers in "excruciating" details, the principles, techniques and tools of three phases of software development: domain model development, requirements model development, and software design, and within these a great number of mandatory stages, and optional and mandatory steps.

2. Item 2 above implies that Vol. 3, after an introductory chapter on the domain/requirements/design triptych, restarts with six chapters on subjects that "cut across", i.e., are common to, the three parts on domain engineering, requirements engineering, and computing systems (i.e., notably software) design. This preamble covers documentation principles and techniques (documents), methods and methodology, models and modelling, descriptions (theory and practice), on defining and on definitions, and Michael Jackson's description principles. (The last two uses of the term descriptions also comprise prescriptions and specifications.)

1. Statement 1(c) implies Vol. 3's Part III: *Descriptions: Theory and Practice* with its Chaps. 5, 6 and 7: *Phenomena and Concepts, On Defining and On Definitions*, and *Jackson's Description Principles*. Here are shown — from very basic principles — how one really "starts"!

Welcome to Vol. 3. Have as much fun reading it as we had in writing it!

20.4 "UML"-ising Formal Techniques

The present volume deviates from Vols. 1 and 3 in having three chapters and a crucial part of yet another chapter authored by former students of mine. Thereby this volume is able to show how many important formal specification techniques can be, as we term it, "UML"-ised. Rather than trying to formalise UML, we have taken the original notational subsystems, variants of which are claimed to have been incorporated into UML, under other names, and then we show how (yet other) variants can be used in conjunction with model-oriented formal specifications — as here, expressed in RSL.

We find it futile to try formalise UML, for several reasons.

- First, because UML initially did not build on sound foundations. When UML first came out it did not reflect 20–30 years of painstaking advances in programming methodology. Where it seemingly did, for example, inclusion of entity set relations (ER), it was not, as is ER, based on simple, yet sufficient foundations. Petri nets, in some shape or other, appear in UML, but it was not clear which variants of Petri nets, or whether the semantics of Petri nets was being followed. Similar to message sequence charts and statecharts — "by any other name they did not smell as sweet" in UML, and that is somehow rather unfortunate — because whatever UML was trying to achieve, *Broadness of application, convenience of notation, and multiplicity of views,*[1] was, we believe, somewhat compromised. The diagrammatic notations of the ER's class diagrams, of Petri nets, of message and live sequence charts and of statecharts are important. Not all software engineers "think" or "read-consume" textually. Some are aided, significantly, by reasoning over diagrams.
- Second, because UML lacks abstraction, it has no reasoning "power" (no logic, i.e., no proof system), and it has no way of relating two different class diagrams — is one an implementation of the other? That is, it has no notion of refinement or transformation, and has no precise language for expressing the nondiagrammatic parts of a specification (save those of the object constraint language, OCL).
- Third, UML is a moving, unpredictable target: It makes little sense to follow on the heels of, or to try influence language design decisions made by the Object Management Group, OMG, which has been charged with that responsibility.

We are quite confident that the "UML"-ised formal combinations of RSL with class diagrams, Petri nets, message or live sequence charts, and with statecharts that you find in the present volume are, relatively speaking, far more

---

[1] This positive phrase is due to Chris George.

precise and cover as much ground as one can possibly expect. Where UML's class diagrams may have a few more twists (i.e., associations, etc.) to them, we find that, for example, RSL can easily express these for every specific instance. (But we find it increasingly cumbersome to formalise several of these associations, etc.)

Part IX

APPENDIXES

A

Naming Convention

Throughout the three volumes of this book we reasonably consistently use the following naming conventions.

1. **Names:** Names serve to identify. In order to discuss matters one must identify phenomena and concepts, that is, give them names.

   (a) **Categories of specification concepts:** Specifications always conceptualise. Even when we name phenomena, these names represent not the phenomena but concrete concepts thereof.

   In specifications (descriptions and prescriptions) we make use of the following specification concepts:

   - types and values of types,
   - functions,
   - variables,
   - channels,
   - schemes,
   - objects and
   - parameters of types, values, functions and classes.

   (b) **Choice of identifiers:** The specifier is free to choose how to spell names. But generally it seems to be a good idea to deploy a consistent and known naming scheme. In the following sections we bring in the convention that has been employed in these volumes.

   (c) **Mnemonics:** We try to use such abbreviations of full names that are easy to remember yet do not fill up text and formula lines. Thus Stmt stands for the syntactic type of statements and stmt for a particular value of that type.

   (d) **Identifiers:** Names are expressed in terms of identifiers. Identifiers are finite, usually short sequences of one or more alphanumeric characters. Sometimes we use infix underscore, __, to help compose names into memorisable identifiers. By an alphanumeric character we mean either one of the 26 Roman letters, or some Greek letter, or a digit. Sometimes a succession of definitions of similarly typed value identifications has the first be an ordinary identifier, say id, as described above, while subsequent identifications are primed versions of the identifier, that is, id′, id″, id‴, etcetera.

2. **Type names:** There are basically three kinds of types:
   - syntactic types,
   - semantic types and
   - pragmatic types.

   All our type names start with a capital letter.

   (a) **Syntactic types:** Letters of syntactic type names, except the initial letter, are usually spelled in lowercase. Sometimes syntactic type names are composed from two or rarely three sub-names, each starting with a capital letter: GotoStmt.

   (b) **Semantic types:** Letters of semantic type names are usually all spelled in uppercase.

   (c) **Pragmatic types:** We usually treat pragmatic types, i.e., types of practical convenience, as syntax types.

3. **Value names:** We spell all letters of all identifiers of values in lowercase. And we usually try define such names that are lowercase, usually abbreviated versions of the names of the type of these values. Thus if the type name is PartNumTbl then a value name of that type might well be pnt.

   If a value identifier names a set of element values of type B then we usually use the identifier bs. If it names a list of elements then bℓ (or bl) is used. If it names map values (from type B to C) then bmc may be used. And so on.

4. **Special semantic type and value names:** We consider the names of three kinds of semantic types and their corresponding values:
   - contexts or environments,
   - states and
   - configurations of contexts (or environments) and states.

   (a) **Context or environment names:** For contexts we normally use the value and type name abbreviations: ctx:CTX or decorated versions thereof. For environments we normally use the value and type name abbreviations: ρ:ENV or decorated versions thereof.

   (b) **State names:** For states we normally use the value and type name abbreviations: σ:Σ or decorated versions thereof.

   (c) **Configuration names:** For configurations we normally use the value and type name abbreviations: γ:Γ or θ:Θ or decorated versions thereof.

5. **Function names:** Function names range over a widest possible variety of identifiers. Special categories of functions are listed below.

6. **Auxiliary function names:** Auxiliary functions are introduced in order to express main function definitions as succinctly as possible. Some auxiliary function categories, but far from all, are mentioned next.

(a) **Observer functions:** Observer functions, obs_B, apply to entities of type sorts, say of type A, and yield attributes or subentities of type B of these. Observer functions are postulated. They cannot be defined.

(b) **Is functions:** Is functions, is_A, apply to entities of type sorts and yield truth values: **true** if the entity is of type A, **false** otherwise. Is functions are postulated. They cannot be defined.

(c) **Well-formedness functions:** Well-formedness functions usually have their function names composed from a wf_ prefix. Well-formedness functions apply to values of concrete types to define those values which belong to a desired, i.e., well-formed, subtype. See also the next item: invariant functions.

(d) **Invariant functions:** Invariant functions usually have their function names composed from an inv_ prefix. Invariant functions apply to values of concrete types to define those values which belong to a desired, i.e., invariant, subtype. The distinction between well-formed and invariant functions is pragmatic: By well-formedness we express a desired property of a usually composite value. By invariance we express that functions yielding values are expected to yield such which satisfy the invariance criterion.

(e) **Abstraction functions:** Abstraction functions usually have their function names composed from an abs_ prefix. Abstraction functions apply to values of some concrete type and yield values of a claimed more abstract, yet concrete type.

(f) **Retrieve functions:** Retrieve functions usually have their function names composed from a retr_ prefix. Retrieve functions apply to values of some concrete type, A_{i+1}, and yield values of a claimed more abstract, yet concrete type, A_i — where type A_{i+1} is said to be an implementation, a data reification, of A_i.

(g) **Injection functions:** Injection functions usually have their function names composed from an inj_ prefix. Injection functions apply to values of some type, A_i, and yield values of a claimed more concrete type, A_{i+1}. A_{i+1} is said to be an implementation, a data reification, of A_i.

7. **Semantic function names:** There are basically four kinds of semantic functions.

- Evaluation functions apply to expressions and configurations (environments and states) and yield values.
- Interpretation functions apply to statements and configurations (environments and states) and yield state changes.
- Elaboration functions apply to clauses (sometimes just expressions) and configurations (environments and states) and yield values and state changes.
- A fourth category of semantic functions apply to declarations and configurations (environments and states) and yield environment and state changes.

- Meaning functions comprise the above: evaluation, interpretation and elaboration functions.
- Compilation functions which apply to syntactic source language constructs and compilation configurations (environments and states) and yield syntactic target language constructs.

With the first three and the last two categories above we normally use the following varieties of semantic function names.

(a) **Evaluation function names:** Either we name these functions by just the identifier V (or $\mathcal{V}$), or by that identifier and some suffix, according to the syntactic category, say Expr (V_Expr), or we name these functions by just identifier eval (or val) — again possibly composed with some appropriate suffix (val_Expr).

(b) **Interpretation function names:** Either we name these functions by just the identifier I (or $\mathcal{I}$), or by that identifier and some suffix, according to the syntactic category, say Stmt (I_Stmt), or we name these functions by just identifier int — again possibly composed with some appropriate suffix (int_Stmt).

(c) **Elaboration function names:** Either we name these functions by just the identifier I (or $\mathcal{E}$), or by that identifier and some suffix, according to the syntactic category, say Clause (E_Clause), or we name these functions by just identifier elab — again possibly composed with some appropriate suffix (elab_Clause).

(d) **Meaning function names:** Are either of the three kinds of names introduced above: evaluation, interpretation or elaboration function names — but sometimes we just "spell" the meaning function name as M (or M, M, or even $\mathcal{M}$).

(e) **Compilation function names:** These names we usually spell with an initial, capitalised C (or C, C, or even $\mathcal{C}$), sometimes followed by a suffix which usually designates (abbreviates) the name of the syntactic category (i.e., the name of the type) of its arguments.

8. **Variable names:** Variable names usually follow the naming convention of value names, see item 3 — possibly with the exception that the character v is (or characters var are) prefixed by the base stem of the value identifier.

9. **Channel names:** Channel names usually are composed from two or three parts, optionally the character c, for channel, and two abbreviations, say c and s, of the names, say client and server, of the definitions of the processes between which the channels communicate.

10. **Scheme names:** Scheme names are usually spelled in all capitals.

11. **Object names:** Object names are usually spelled like are the schemes from which the objects are instantiated.

12. **Parameter names:** Parameter names are usually spelled like are the values of the types designated.

B

Indexes

- The **prerequisite** for studying this chapter is that you need look up where a term has been defined or is used.
- The **aim** is to illustrate the breadth and depth, the variety and multitude of terms used in these volumes.
- The **objective** is to satisfy your needs.
- The **treatment** is systematic.

Volume 1 Appendix B contains an extensive glossary.

B.1 Symbols Index

Symbol, Greek: Mark, token, ticket, watchword, outward sign, covenant.

Symbol, Meaning: Something that stands for, represents, or denotes something else; a material object representing, or taken to represent, something immaterial or abstract (1590); a written character or mark used to represent something; a letter, figure, or sign conventionally standing for some object, process, etc. (1620)

The SHORTER OXFORD ENGLISH DICTIONARY
On Historical Principles [303]

An attempt has been made to structure the symbols index. You may have to look in more than one place to find a cross-reference to the first appearances of the symbol, literal or abbreviation that you are looking for,

Volume 1 has an extensive symbols index covering RSL. We refer to that index.

B.1.1 Time/Space

$=$ equality (time, space), 129
$\geq$ greater than or equal (time), 129
$>$ greater than (time), 129
$\cap$ common space, 129
$\{\}=$ empty space predicate, 129
$\{\}\neq$ non-empty space predicate, 129
$\leq$ less than or equal (time), 129
$<$ less than (time), 129
$\neq$ nonequality (time, space), 129
$\cup$ union (space), 129

$\mathcal{CONTINUOUS}$ continuity of functions, 130

A_p^t entity A at location p at time t, 136

B.1.2 Modular RSL

class as in **class ... end**, 248

class class definition literal, 253–257
end as in **class ... end**, 248
extend ... with class extension, 259–260
hide scheme hiding, 260–262
in as in **hide ... in class ... end**, 261, 262
object object declaration literal, 253, 257
scheme scheme definition literal, 257–265

B.1.3 Petri Nets

$\bigcirc$ state, 316
$[]$ transition, 316
$\rightarrow$ arrow, links transitions to states and states to transitions, 316
• Petri net token, 317

B.1.4 Message Sequence Charts

B.1.5 Live Sequence Charts

B.1.6 Statecharts

B.1.7 Temporal Logics

B.1.8 Duration Calculus

B.1.9 Timed RSL: TRSL

B.1.10 Abbreviations

B.2 Concepts Index

> **Conceive:** To grasp with the mind.
>
> **Conception:** The act of conceiving, apprehension, imagination.
>
> **Concept:** The product of the faculty of conception, an idea of a class of objects, a general notion.
>
> *The SHORTER OXFORD ENGLISH DICTIONARY*
> *On Historical Principles [303]*

The terms: a concept, an idea, a notion, an apprehension and an imagination are treated as similar terms. The concept index also lists common abbreviations.

B.3 Characteriations and Definitions Index

Definition: The setting of bounds, limitation.
The action of determining a question at issue, of defining.
A precise statement of the essential nature of a thing.
A declaration of the signification of a word or phrase.
The SHORTER OXFORD ENGLISH DICTIONARY
On Historical Principles [303]

We shall list both characterisations and definitions. The latter are usually more formally expressed than the former.

B.4 Authors Index

> **Author:** The person who originates or gives existence to anything;
> an inventor, constructor, or founder.
> He who gives rise to an action, event, circumstance, or state of things.
> One who sets forth written statements;
> the writer or composer of a treatise or book.
>
> The SHORTER OXFORD ENGLISH DICTIONARY
> On Historical Principles [303]

The authors listed here (many with [references] to (usually) their main books) are (co)authors of publications cited on the referenced page(s). Not all referenced publications have their authors listed here — but a very high proportion have been listed here! There are 196 such authors listed here!

References

1. M. Abadi, L. Cardelli: *A Theory of Objects* (Springer, NY, USA 1996)
2. J.-R. Abrial: *The B Book: Assigning Programs to Meanings* (Cambridge University Press, Cambridge, UK 1996)
3. J.-R. Abrial, E. Börger, H. Langmaack, editors. *Formal Methods for Industrial Applications: Specifying and Programming the Steam Boiler Control*. Springer, Lecture Notes in Computer Science, Vol. LNCS 1165, 1997.
4. J.-R. Abrial, L. Mussat. *Event B Reference Manual (Editor: Thierry Lecomte)*, June 2001. Report of EU IST Project Matisse IST-1999-11435.
5. ACM (special issue of): *Programming Languages and Pragmatics*. Communications of the ACM **9**, 6 (1966)
6. A.V. Aho, R. Sethi, J.D. Ullman: *Compilers: Principles, Techniques, and Tools* (Addison-Wesley, Mass., USA, January 1986)
7. J. Allen: *Natural Language Understanding* (Benjamin/Cummings, CA, USA 1987)
8. J. Alves-Foss (ed.): *Formal Syntax and Semantics of Java* (Springer, 1998)
9. S. Andersen, S. Holmslykke: Analysis: Integrating UML Class Diagrams, and Message and Live Sequence Charts into the RAISE Specification Language. MSc Thesis, Informatics and Mathematical Modelling, Technical University of Denmark (2004)
10. S. Andersen, S. Holmslykke: Implementation: Integrating UML Class Diagrams, and Message and Live Sequence Charts into the RAISE Specification Language. MSc Thesis, Informatics and Mathematical Modelling, Technical University of Denmark (2005)
11. ANSI X3.23-1974: The COBOL Programming Language. Technical Report, American National Standards Institute, Standards on Computers and Information Processing (1974)
12. ANSI X3.53-1976: The PL/I Programming Language. Technical Report, American National Standards Institute, Standards on Computers and Information Processing (1976)
13. ANSI X3.9-1966: The FORTRAN Programming Language. Technical Report, American National Standards Institute, Standards on Computers and Information Processing (1966)
14. A.W. Appel: *Modern Compiler Implementation in Java* (Cambridge University Press, 1998)

15. K. Arnold, J. Gosling, D. Holmes: *The Java Programming Language* (Addison-Wesley, USA 1996)

16. K. Åström, B. Wittenmark: *Adaptive Control* (Addison-Wesley, 1989)

17. R. Audi: *The Cambridge Dictionary of Philosophy* (Cambridge University Press, The Pitt Building, Trumpington Street, Cambridge CB2 1RP, UK 1995)

18. J. Austin: *How to Do Things with Words* (Harvard University Press, 1 Jan 1975)

19. F. Baader, D. Calvanese, D. McGuinness, D. Nardi, P. Patel-Schneider: *The Description Logic Handbook: Theory, Implementation and Applications* (Cambrige University Press, 2003)

20. R.-J. Back, J. von Wright: *Refinement Calculus: A Systematic Introduction* (Springer, Heidelberg, Germany 1998)

21. R. Backhouse: *Syntax of Programming Languages: Theory and Practice* (Prentice Hall, 1979)

22. J.W. Backus: The Syntax and Semantics of the Proposed International Algebraic Language of the Zürich ACM-GAMM Conference. In: *ICIP Proceedings, Paris 1959* (Butterworths, London, 1960) pp 125–132

23. J.W. Backus: *Can Programming Be Liberated from the von Neumann Style? A Functional Style and Its Algebra of Programs.* Communications of the ACM **21**, 8 (1978) pp 613–641

24. J.W. Backus, P. Naur: *Revised Report on the Algorithmic Language ALGOL 60.* Communications of the ACM **6**, 1 (1963) pp 1–1

25. J.C.M. Baeten, C. Verhoef: A congruence theorem for structured operational semantics with predicates. In: *Proceedings CONCUR 93, Hildesheim, Germany*, vol 715 of *Lecture Notes in Computer Science* (Springer, 1993) pp 477–492

26. J.C.M. Baeten, C. Verhoef: Concrete Process Algebra. In: *Handbook of Logic in Computer Science*, vol 4: Semantic Modelling, ed by S. Abramsky, D.M. Gabbay, T.S.E. Maibaum (Oxford University Press, 1995)

27. J.C.M. Baeten, W.P. Weijland: *Process Algebra*, no 18 of *Cambridge Tracts in Theoretical Computer Science* (Cambridge University Press, 1990)

28. J. Barnes (ed.): *The Complete Works of Aristotle; I and II* (Princeton University Press, USA 1984)

29. D. Beech: On the Definitional Method of Standard PL/I. In: *Principles of Programming Languages, SIGPLAN/SIGACT Symposium, ACM Conference Record/Proceedings* (ACM, NY, USA, 1973) pp 87–94

30. H. Bekič: Towards a Mathematical Theory of Processes. TR 25.125, IBM Laboratory, Vienna (1971)

31. H. Bekič: *An Introduction to ALGOL 68.* Annual Review in: 'Automatic Programming', Pergamon Press **7** (1973)

32. H. Bekič: Programming Languages and Their Definition. In: *Lecture Notes in Computer Science, Vol. 177*, ed by C.B. Jones (Springer, 1984)

33. H. Bekič, D. Bjørner, W. Henhapl, C.B. Jones, P. Lucas: A Formal Definition of a PL/I Subset. Technical Report 25.139, Vienna, Austria (1974)

34. H. Bekič, P. Lucas, K. Walk et al.: Formal Definition of PL/I, ULD Version I. Technical Report, IBM Laboratory, Vienna (1966)

35. H. Bekič, P. Lucas, K. Walk et al.: Formal Definition of PL/I, ULD Version II. Technical Report, IBM Laboratory, Vienna (1968)

36. H. Bekič, P. Lucas, K. Walk et al. Formal Definition of PL/I, ULD Version III. IBM Laboratory, Vienna, 1969.

37. H. Bekič, K. Walk: Formalization of Storage Properties. In: *Symposium on Semantics of Algorithmic Languages*, vol LNM 188 (Springer, 1971)

38. H. Ben-Abdallah, S. Leue: Expressing And Analyzing Timing Constraints in Message Sequence Chart Specifications. Technical Report 97-04, Electrical and Computer Engineering, University of Waterloo, Canada (1997)

39. S. Bennett, S. McRobb, R. Farmer: *Object-Oriented Systems Analysis And Design Using UML*, 2nd edn (McGraw-Hill, 2002)

40. M. Bidoit, P.D. Mosses (eds.): CASL *User Manual* (Springer, 2004)

41. G. Birtwistle, O.-J. Dahl, B. Myhrhaug, K. Nygaard: *SIMULA* begin (Studentlitteratur, Lund, Sweden, 1974)

42. D. Bjørner: *Flowchart-Machines*. BIT **10**, 4 (1970) pp 415–442

43. D. Bjørner: Folded Syntax- and Recursive Flowchart-Machines. In: *HICSS (Hawaii Int'l. Conf. Sys. Sci.)* (1970) pp 415–453

44. D. Bjørner: Programming in the Meta-Language: A Tutorial. In: *The Vienna Development Method: The Meta-Language, [51]*, ed by D. Bjørner, C.B. Jones (Springer, 1978) pp 24–217

45. D. Bjørner: The Systematic Development of Compiling Algorithm. In: *Le Point sur la Compilation*, ed by M. Amirchahy, D. Neel (INRIA Publ. Paris, 1979) pp 45–88

46. D. Bjørner (ed.): *Abstract Software Specifications*, vol 86 of *LNCS* (Springer, 1980)

47. D. Bjørner: Stepwise Transformation of Software Architectures. In: *[52]* (Prentice Hall, 1982) pp 353–378

48. D. Bjørner, C.W. George, A.E. Haxthausen et al.: "UML"-ising Formal Techniques. In: *INT 2004: Third International Workshop on Integration of Specification Techniques for Applications in Engineering*, vol 3147 of *Lecture Notes in Computer Science* (Springer, 2004, ETAPS, Barcelona, Spain) pp 423–450

49. D. Bjørner, J. Goossenaerts, S. Prehn: Enterprise Modelling. Technical Report 17, UNU/IIST, Macau (1994)

50. D. Bjørner, C.A.R. Hoare, H. Langmaack (eds.): *VDM & Z — Formal Methods in Software Development, Proc. of VDM-Europe Symposium '90*, vol 428 of *Lecture Notes in Computer Science* (Springer, 1990)

51. D. Bjørner, C.B. Jones (eds.): *The Vienna Development Method: The Meta-Language*, vol 61 of *LNCS* (Springer, 1978)

52. D. Bjørner, C.B. Jones (eds.): *Formal Specification and Software Development* (Prentice Hall, 1982)

53. D. Bjørner, C.B. Jones, M. Mac an Airchinnigh, E. Neuhold, editors. *VDM – A Formal Method at Work*. Proc. VDM-Europe Symposium 1987, Brussels, Belgium, Springer, Lecture Notes in Computer Science, Vol. 252, 1987.

54. D. Bjørner, O. Oest (eds.): *Towards a Formal Description of Ada*, vol 98 of *LNCS* (Springer, 1980)

55. N. Bjørner, A. Browne, M. Colon et al.: *Verifying Temporal Properties of Reactive Systems: A STeP Tutorial*. Formal Methods in System Design **16** (2000) pp 227–270

56. N. Bjørner, Z. Manna, H. Sipma et al.: The Stanford Temporal Prover. In: *Internet* (Published: http://www-step.stanford.edu/, 1994–2005)

57. W.D. Blizard: *A Formal Theory of Objects, Space and Time*. The Journal of Symbolic Logic **55**, 1 (1990) pp 74–89

58. Y. Bontemps, P. Heymans, H. Kugler: Applying LSCs to the Specification of an Air Traffic Control system. In: *Proc. of the 2nd Int. Workshop on "Scenarios and State Machines: Models, Algorithms and Tools" (SCESM'03), at the 25th Int. Conf. on Soft. Eng. (ICSE'03)*, ed by S. Uchitel, F. Bordeleau (2003)

59. G. Booch, J. Rumbaugh, I. Jacobson: *The Unified Modeling Language User Guide* (Addison-Wesley, 1998)

60. P. Borst, H. Akkermans, J.L. Top: *Engineering Ontologies*. Submitted to: International Journal of Human-Computer Studies (Special issue on Using Explicit Ontologies in KBS Development) (1996)

61. P. Branquart, J. Lewi, M. Sintzoff, P. Wodon: *The Composition of Semantics in ALGOL 68*. Communications of the ACM **14**, 11 (1971) pp 697–708

62. M. Broy, K. Stølen: *Specification and Development of Interactive Systems — Focus on Streams, Interfaces and Refinement* (Springer, Heidelberg, Germany 2001)

63. R. Bruni, J. Meseguer: Generalized Rewrite Theories. In: *Automata, Languages and Programming. 30th International Colloquium, ICALP 2003, Eindhoven, The Netherlands, June 30 – July 4, 2003. Proceedings*, vol 2719 of *Lecture Notes in Computer Science*, ed. by Jos C.M. Baeten, J.K. Lenstra, J. Parrow and G.J. Woeginger (Springer, 2003) pp 252–266

64. A. Bunker, G. Gopalakrishnan: Using Live Sequence Charts for Hardware Protocol Specification and Compliance Verification. In: *IEEE International High Level Design Validation and Test Workshop* (IEEE Computer Society Press, 2001)

65. A.W. Burks, H. Wang: *The Logic of Automata — Part I*. Journal of ACM **4**, 2 (1957) pp 193–218

66. A.W. Burks, H. Wang: *The Logic of Automata — Part II*. Journal of ACM **4**, 3 (1957) pp 279–297

67. F. Burns, A. Koelmans, A. Yakovlev: *Analysing superscalar processor architectures with Coloured Petri Nets*. International Journal on Software Tools for Technology Transfer **2**, 2 (1998) pp 182–191

68. R. Burstall, J. Goguen: Putting Theories together to Make Specifications. In: *Proc. of (IJCAI) Int'l. Joint Conf. on AI* (Boston, 1977)

69. R. Burstall, J. Goguen: *The Semantics of CLEAR: A Specification Language*. [46] (1980) pp 292–332

70. R. Burstall, J. Goguen: Algebras, Theories and Freeness: An Introduction for Computer Scientists. In: *Proc. Marktoberdorf Summer School on Theoretical Foundations of Programming Meth.* (Springer, 1981)

71. F. Buschmann, R. Meunier, H. Rohnert, P. Sommerlad, M. Stal: *Pattern-Oriented Software Architecture: A System Of Patterns* (John Wiley, UK 1996)

72. M. Carey. Statecharts: Permutation City. Electronically, on the Web: http://www.permutationcity.co.uk/alife/statecharts.html, 2004.

73. R. Carnap: *The Logical Syntax of Language* (Harcourt Brace and Co., N.Y. 1937)

74. R. Carnap: *Introduction to Semantics* (Harvard Univ. Press, Mass. 1942)

75. R. Carnap: *Meaning and Necessity, A Study in Semantics and Modal Logic* (University of Chicago Press, 1947 (enlarged edition: 1956))

76. R. Carnap: *The Logical Structure of the World and Pseudo-problems in Philosophy* (R.A. George (tr.), London, UK 1967)

77. A. Cau, B. Moszkowski: AnaTempura: Runtime Verification & Animation Toolkit. In: *Internet* (Published: www.cse.dmu.ac.uk/STRL/research/-software/index.html#tempura, 18 October 2004)

78. P. Chan, D.V. Hung: Duration Calculus Specification of Scheduling for Tasks with Shared Resources. Research Report 44, UNU/IIST, Macau (1995)

79. P.P. Chen: *The Entity-Relationship Model — Toward a Unified View of Data.* ACM Trans. Database Syst **1**, 1 (1976) pp 9–36

80. E.M. Clarke, O. Grumberg, D.A. Peled: *Model Checking* (The MIT Press, MA, USA 2000)

81. M. Clavel, F. Durán, S. Eker et al.: The Maude 2.0 System. In: *Rewriting Techniques and Applications (RTA 2003)*, no 2706 of *Lecture Notes in Computer Science*, ed by Robert Nieuwenhuis (Springer, 2003) pp 76–87

82. G. Clemmensen, O. Oest: Formal Specification and Development of an Ada Compiler – A VDM Case Study. In: *Proc. 7th International Conf. on Software Engineering, 26.-29. March 1984, Orlando, Florida* (IEEE Press, 1984) pp 430–440

83. P. Constantin: *Navier–Stokes Equations* (University of Chicago Press, 1988)

84. D. Crystal: *The Cambridge Encyclopedia of Language* (Cambridge University Press, 1987, 1988)

85. O.-J. Dahl: Object Orientation and Formal Techniques. In: *see [50]*, vol 428 of *Lecture Notes in Computer Science* (Springer, Heidelberg, Germany, 1990) pp 1–11

86. O.-J. Dahl, E.W. Dijkstra, C.A.R. Hoare: *Structured Programming* (Academic Press, 1972)

87. O.-J. Dahl, C.A.R. Hoare: Hierarchical Program Structures. In: *[86]* (Academic Press, 1972) pp 197–220

88. O.-J. Dahl, K. Nygaard: *SIMULA – An ALGOL-Based Simulation Language.* Communications of the ACM **9**, 9 (1966) pp 671–678

89. W. Damm, D. Harel: *LSCs: Breathing Life into Message Sequence Charts.* Formal Methods in System Design **19** (2001) pp 45–80

90. O. Danvy: A Rational Deconstruction of Landin's SECD Machine. Research RS 03–33, BRICS: Basic Research in Computer Science, Dept. of Comp. Sci., University of Århus, Denmark (2003)

91. J. Darlington, P. Henderson, D. Turner: *Functional Programming and Its Applications* (Cambridge Univ. Press, 1982)

92. J. de Bakker: *Mathematical Theory of Programming Correctness* (Prentice Hall, 1980)

93. J. de Bakker: *Control Flow Semantics* (The MIT Press, Mass., USA, 1995)

94. P. Deransart, M. Jourdan: *Attribute Grammars and Their Applications*, vol 461 of *Lecture Notes in Computer Science* (Springer, 1990)

95. N. Dershowitz, J.-P. Jouannaud: Rewrite Systems. In: *Handbook of Theoretical Computer Science*, vol B: Formal Models and Semantics, ed by J. van Leeuwen (Elsevier, 1990) pp 243–320

96. R. Diaconescu, K. Futatsugi, K. Ogata: *CafeOBJ: Logical Foundations and Methodology.* Computing and Informatics **22**, 1–2 (2003)

97. E. Dijkstra: *A Discipline of Programming* (Prentice Hall, 1976)

98. E. Dijkstra, W. Feijen: *A Method of Programming* (Addison-Wesley, 1988)

99. E. Dijkstra, C. Scholten: *Predicate Calculus and Program Semantics* (Springer: Texts and Monographs in Computer Science, 1990)

100. E.W. Dijkstra: *An ALGOL 60 Translator for the X1*. Annual Review in: 'Automatic Programming', Pergamon Press **3** (1962) pp 329–356
101. E.W. Dijkstra: *Go To Statement Considered Harmful*. Communications of the ACM **11**, 3 (1968) pp 147–148
102. E.W. Dijkstra: *Hierarchical Ordering of Sequential Processes*. Acta Informatica **1** (1971) pp 115–138
103. V. Donzeau-Gorge, G. Kahn, B. Lang: Formal Definition of the Ada Programming Language. Technical Report, INRIA (1980)
104. R. Dorf: *Modern Control Systems* (Addison-Wesley, 1967 (fifth ed. 1989))
105. B. Dutertre: Complete Proof System for First-Order Interval Temporal Logic. In: *Proceedings of the 10th Annual IEEE Symposium on Logic in Computer Science* (IEEE CS, 1995) pp 36–43
106. S. Efroni, D. Harel, I. Cohen: *Towards Rigorous Comprehension of Biological Complexity: Modeling, Execution and Visualization of Thymic T Cell Maturation*. Genome Research **13** (2003) pp 2485–2497
107. S. Efroni, D. Harel, I. Cohen: *Reactive Animation: Realistic Modeling of Complex Dynamic Systems*. Computer **38**, 1 (2005) pp 38–47
108. S. Efroni, D. Harel, I. Cohen: A Theory for Complex Systems: Reactive Animation. In: *Multidisciplinary Approaches to Theory in Medicine (R.C. Paton, ed.)* (Elsevier, 2005 (to appear))
109. E. Engeler: *Symposium on Semantics of Algorithmic Languages*, vol 188 of *Lecture Notes in Mathematics* (Springer, 1971)
110. ECMA (European Computer Manufacturers Assoc.): PL/I BASIS/I. ECMA/TC10 and ANSI X3J1 (1974)
111. ECMA (European Computer Manufacturers Assoc.): PL/I. ECMA/TC10 and ANSI X3.53-1976, (1976)
112. D.J. Farmer: *Being in time: The nature of time in light of McTaggart's paradox* (University Press of America, Maryland 1990)
113. W. Feijen, A. van Gasteren, D. Gries, J. Misra, editors. *Beauty is Our Business*, Texts and Monographs in Computer Science, NY, USA, 1990. Springer. A Birthday Salute to Edsger W. Dijkstra.
114. A. Field, P. Harrison: *Functional Programming* (Addison-Wesley, 1988)
115. J. Fisher, D. Harel, E. Hubbard et al.: Combining State-based and Scenario-based Approaches in Modeling Biological Systems. In: *Proc. Computational Methods in Systems Biology (CMSB'04)*, vol 3082 of *(Lecture Notes in Bioinformatics)* (Springer, 2004) pp 236–241
116. J. Fisher, N. Piterman, E. Hubbard, M. Stern, D. Harel: Computational Insights into C. elegans Vulval Development. In: *Proc. Natl. Acad. Sci.*, vol 102, 1 (2005) pp 1951–1956
117. W.J. Fokkink: The *tyft/tyxt* format reduces to tree rules. In: *Proceedings 2nd International Symposium on Theoretical Aspects of Computer Science (TACS'94), Sendai, Japan*, vol 789 of *Lecture Notes in Computer Science* (Springer, 1994) pp 440–453
118. FOLDOC: The free online dictionary of computing. Electronically, on the Web: http://wombat.doc.ic.ac.uk/foldoc/foldoc.cgi?ISWIM, 2004
119. P. Folkjær, D. Bjørner: A Formal Model of a Generalised CSP-like Language. In: *Proc. IFIP'80*, ed by S. Lavington (North-Holland, Amsterdam, 1980) pp 95–99
120. G. Franklin, J. Powell, M. Workman: *Digital Control of Dynamic Systems* (Addison-Wesley, 1980 (second ed. 1990))

121. R. Frost: *Mountain Interval* (Henry Holt and Company, New York, USA 1920 (online edition: Bartleby, 1995-9. www.bartleby.com/119/1.html))

122. A. Funes, C.W. George: Formal Foundations in RSL for UML Class Diagrams. Research Report 253, UNU/IIST, Macau (2002)

123. K. Futatsugi, R. Diaconescu: *CafeOBJ Report. The Language, Proof Techniques and Methodologies for Object-Oriented Algebraic Specification* (World Scientific Publishing)

124. K. Futatsugi, J. Goguen, J.-P. Jouannaud, J. Meseguer: Principles of OBJ-2. In: *12th Ann. Symp. on Principles of Programming* (ACM, 1985) pp 52–66

125. K. Futatsugi, A. Nakagawa, T. Tamai, editors. *CAFE: An Industrial-Strength Algebraic Formal Method.* Elsevier 2000. Proceedings from an April 1998 Symposium, Numazu, Japan.

126. A. Galton: Temporal Logic. In: *The Stanford Encyclopedia of Philosophy* (Published: http://plato.stanford.edu/archives/win2003/entries/logic-temporal/, Winter 2003)

127. A.L. Gançarski, P.R. Henriques: Interactive information retrieval from XML documents represented by attribute grammars. In: *Proceedings of the 2003 ACM Symposium on Document Engineering, [512]* (2003) pp 171–174

128. H. Ganzinger: Transforming Denotational Semantics into Practical Attribute Grammars. In: *[249]* (1980) pp 1–69

129. H. Garcia-Molina, J.D. Ullman, J.D. Widom: *Database System Implementation* (Pearson, June 11, 1999)

130. C.W. George, P. Haff, K. Havelund et al.: *The RAISE Specification Language* (Prentice Hall, UK 1992)

131. C.W. George, A.E. Haxthausen, S. Hughes et al.: *The RAISE Method* (Prentice Hall, UK 1995)

132. C.W. George, Y. Xia: An Operational Semantics for Timed RAISE. In: *FM'99 — Formal Methods*, ed by J.M. Wing, J. Woodcock, J. Davies (Springer, 1999) pp 1008–1027

133. E. Gery, D. Harel, E. Palatshy: A Complete Lifecycle Model-Based Development System. In: *Proc. 3rd Int. Conf. on Integrated Formal Methods (IFM 2002)* (Springer, May 2002)

134. J. Goguen: Some Ideas in Algebraic Semantics. Technical Report, Naropa Inst., Boulder, Co., UCLA Dept. of Comp. Sci., CA, USA (1978)

135. J. Goguen: Some Design Principles and Theory for OBJ-0. In: *Lecture Notes in Computer Science, Vol. 75* (Springer, 1979) pp 425–471

136. J. Goguen, J. Meseguer: Order-Sorter Algebra I. Technical Report SRI-CSL-89-10, SRI CSL Technical Report, Naropa Inst., Boulder, Co., UCLA Dept. of Comp. Sci., (1989)

137. J. Goguen, K. Parsaye-Ghomi: Algebraic Denotational Semantics Using Parameterized Abstract Modules. In: *Lecture Notes in Computer Science, Vol. 107* (Springer, 1981) pp 292–309

138. J. Goguen, J. Thatcher, E. Wagner, J. Wright: Abstract Data Types as Initial Algebras and Correctness of Data Representations. In: *ACM Conf. on Computer Graphics* (1975) pp 89–93

139. J. Goguen, J. Thatcher, E. Wagner, J. Wright: *Initial Algebra Semantics and Continuous Algebras.* Journal of the ACM **24**, 1 (1977) pp 68–95

140. J. Goguen, J. Thatcher, E. Wagner, J. Wright: An Initial Algebra Approach to the Specification, Correctness and Implementation of Abstract Data Types.

In: *Current Trends in Programming Methodology*, ed by R. Yeh (Prentice Hall, 1978)

141. A. Goldberg, D. Robson: *Smalltalk-80: the Language and Its Implementation* (Addison-Wesley, 1983)

142. I. Goldstein, D. Bobrow: Extending Object-Oriented Programming in Smalltalk. In: *Proceedings of the 1980 Lisp Conference* (1980) pp 75–81

143. J. Goossenaerts: Generic Models for Manufacturing Industry. Technical Report 32, UNU/IIST, Macau (1994)

144. J. Goossenaerts, D. Bjørner: An Information Technology Framework for Lean/Agile Supply-based Industries in Developing Countries. Technical Report 30, UNU/IIST, Macau (1994)

145. J. Goossenaerts, D. Bjørner: Interflow Systems for Manufacturing: Concepts and a Construction. Technical Report 31, UNU/IIST, Macau (1994)

146. J. Gosling, F. Yellin: *The Java Language Specification* (ACM Press Books, 1996)

147. J. Gray: Notes on database operating systems. In: *Operating Systems – An Advanced Course*, vol 60 of *Lecture Notes in Computer Science*, ed. by R. Bayer et al. (Springer, 1978) pp 393–481

148. J. Gray, A. Reuter: *Transaction Processing: Concepts and Techniques* (Morgan Kaufmann, 1993)

149. J.-C. Grégoire, G.J. Holzmann, D. Peled, editors. *The SPIN Verification System*, volume 32 of *DIMACS series*. American Mathematical Society, 1997, 203p.

150. D. Gries: *Compiler Construction for Digital Computers* (John Wiley, NY, 1971)

151. D. Gries: *The Science of Programming* (Springer, 1981)

152. D. Gries, F.B. Schneider: *A Logical Approach to Discrete Math* (Springer, 1993)

153. M. Große-Rhode: *Semantic Integration of Heterogeneous Software Specifications* (Springer, Heidelberg and Berlin, Germany 2004)

154. J.F. Groote: Transistion Systems Specification with Negative Premises. Technical Report, CWI, Amsterdam (1990)

155. J.F. Groote, F.W. Vaandrager: *Structured Operational Semantics and Bisimulation as a Congruence*. Information & Computation **100**, 2 (1992) pp 202–260

156. C. Gunther, J. Mitchell: *Theoretical Aspects of Object-Oriented Programming* (MIT Press, Mass., USA, 1994)

157. C. Gunther, D. Scott: Semantic Domains. In: *[509] — vol.B.*, ed by J. Leeuwen (North-Holland, Amsterdam, 1990) pp 633–674

158. C. Gunther: *Semantics of Programming Languages* (MIT Press, Mass., USA, 1992)

159. P. Haff (ed.): *The Formal Definition of CHILL* (ITU (Intl. Telecomm. Union), Geneva, Switzerland 1981)

160. P. Haff, A. Olsen: Use of VDM within CCITT. In: *[53]* (Springer, 1987) pp 324–330

161. A.M. Hagalisletto, I.C. Yu: Large Scale Construction of Railroad Models from Specification. In: *International Conference on Systems, Man and Cybernetics* (IEEE, October 10-13, 2004)

162. L.H. Hamel: Towards a Provably Correct Compiler for OBJ3. Technical Report TR-1-94, Programming Research Group, Oxford University, UK (1994)

163. E. Hamilton, H. Cairns (eds.): *The Collected Dialogues of Plato* (Princeton University Press, NJ 1961)

164. K.M. Hansen: Validation of a Railway Interlocking Model. In: *FME'94: Industrial Benefit of Formal Methods*, ed by M. Naftalin, B.T. Denvir (Springer, 1994) pp 582–601

165. K.M. Hansen: Linking Safety Analysis to Safety Requirements. PhD Thesis, Department of Computer Science, Technical University of Denmark (1996)

166. M.R. Hansen, P. Paritosh, C.C. Zhou: Finite Divergence. Research Report 15, UNU/IIST, Macau (1993)

167. M.R. Hansen, A.P. Ravn, H. Rischel, C.C. Zhou: Duration Specifications for Shared Processors. *School & Symposium:* Formal Techniques in Real-Time and Fault-Tolerant Systems, *January 1992, Nijmegen, The Netherlands*, Dept. of Computer Science, Technical University of Denmark (1991)

168. M.R. Hansen, H. Rischel: *Functional Programming in Standard ML* (Addison-Wesley, 1997)

169. M.R. Hansen, C.C. Zhou: Semantics and Completeness of Duration Calculus. Technical Report ID/DTH MRH 6, ProCoS, ESPRIT BRA 3104, Dept. of Computer Science, Technical University of Denmark (1991)

170. M.R. Hansen, C.C. Zhou, J. Staunstrup: A Real-Time Duration Semantics for Circuits. *Submitted to Workshop on* Timing Issues in the Specification and Synthesis of Digital Systems, *March 1992, Princeton, NJ, USA*, Dept. of Computer Science, Technical University of Denmark (1991)

171. S. Harbinson: *Modula 3* (Prentice Hall, NJ, USA 1992)

172. D. Harel: *On a Folklore Theorem.* Communications of the ACM (1978)

173. D. Harel: *Algorithmics — The Spirit of Computing* (Addison-Wesley, 1987)

174. D. Harel: *Statecharts: A Visual Formalism for Complex Systems.* Science of Computer Programming **8**, 3 (1987) pp 231–274

175. D. Harel: *On Visual Formalisms.* Communications of the ACM **33**, 5 (1988)

176. D. Harel: On the Behavior of Complex Object-Oriented Systems. In: *Proc. Conf. on Object-Oriented Modeling of Embedded Real-Time Systems (OMER '99; Peter P. Hofmann and Andy Schurr, eds.)* (Springer, 2002) pp 11–15

177. D. Harel: *A Grand Challenge for Computing: Full Reactive Modeling of a Multicellular Animal.* Bulletin of the EATCS, European Association for Theoretical Computer Science **81** (2003) pp 226–235

178. D. Harel: From Play-In Scenarios to Code: Capturing and Analyzing Reactive Behavior. In: *Proc. NATO Advanced Study Institute on Models, Algebras and Logic of Engineering Software* (IOS Press, 2003) pp 317–350

179. D. Harel: A Grand Challenge for Computing: Full Reactive Modeling of a Multi-cellular Animal. In: *Current Trends in Theoretical Computer Science: The Challenge of the New Century, Algorithms and Complexity, Vol I, (Eds. G. Paun, G. Rozenberg and A. Salomaa)* (World Scientific, Singapore, 2004) pp 559–568

180. D. Harel: *A Turing-Like Test for Biological Modeling.* Nature Biotechnology **23** (2005) pp 495–496

181. D. Harel: *The Science of Computing — Exploring the Nature and Power of Algorithms* (Addison-Wesley, April 1989)

182. D. Harel: *From Play-In Scenarios To Code: An Achievable Dream.* Computer **34**, 1 (January 2001) pp 53–60

183. D. Harel: From Play-In Scenarios To Code: An Achievable Dream. In: *Proc. Fundamental Approaches to Software Engineering, FASE*, vol 1783 (Tom Maibaum, ed.) of *Lecture Notes in Computer Science* (Springer, March 2000) pp 22–34

184. D. Harel, S. Efroni, I. Cohen: Reactive Animation. In: *Proc. 1st Int. Symposium on Formal Methods for Components and Objects (FMCO 2002)*, vol 2852 of *Lecture Notes in Computer Scienc* (Springer, 2003) pp 136–153

185. D. Harel, E. Gery: *Executable Object Modeling with Statecharts*. IEEE Computer **30**, 7 (1997) pp 31–42

186. D. Harel, H. Kugler: Synthesizing State-based Object Systems from LSC Specifications. In: *Proc. 5th Int. Conf. on Implementation and Application of Automata, CIAA 2000*, vol 2088 of *Lecture Notes in Computer Science* (Springer, 2001) pp 1–33

187. D. Harel, H. Kugler: *Synthesizing State-based Object Systems from LSC Specifications*. International Journal of Foundations of Computer Science **13**, 1 (2002) pp 5–51

188. D. Harel, H. Kugler: *Synthesizing State-based Object Systems from LSC Specifications*. Int. J. of Foundations of Computer Science **13**, 1 (2002) pp 5–51

189. D. Harel, H. Kugler, R. Marelly: The Play-in/Play-out Approach and Tool: Specifying and Executing Behavioral Requirements. In: *Proc. Israeli Workshop on Programming Languages & Development Environments (PLE'02)* (July 2002)

190. D. Harel, H. Kugler, R. Marelly, A. Pnueli: Smart Play-Out of Behavioral Requirements. In: *Proc. 4th Int. Conf. on Formal Methods in Computer-Aided Design (FMCAD 2002)* (November 2002) pp 378–398

191. D. Harel, H. Kugler, A. Pnueli: Smart Play-Out Extended: Time and Forbidden Elements. In: *Proc. 4th Int. Conf. on Quality Software (QSIC'04)* (IEEE Computer Society Press, 2004) pp 2–10

192. D. Harel, H. Kugler, A. Pnueli: Synthesis Revisited: Generating Statechart Models from Scenario-Based Requirements. In: *Formal Methods in Software and System Modeling (H.-J. Kreowski et al., eds.)* (Springer, 2005) pp 309–324

193. D. Harel, H. Lachover, A. Naamad et al.: *STATEMATE: A Working Environment for the Development of Complex Reactive Systems*. Software Engineering **16**, 4 (1990) pp 403–414

194. D. Harel, R. Marelly: Playing with Time: On the Specification and Execution of Time-Enriched LSCs. In: *Proc. 10th IEEE/ACM Int. Symp. on Modeling, Analysis and Simulation of Computer and Telecommunication Systems* (ACM Press, 2002)

195. D. Harel, R. Marelly: *Come, Let's Play — Scenario-Based Programming Using LSCs and the Play-Engine* (Springer, 2003)

196. D. Harel, R. Marelly: *Specifying and Executing Behavioral Requirements: The Play In/Play-Out Approach*. Software and System Modeling (SoSyM) **2** (2003) pp 82–107

197. D. Harel, A. Naamad: *The STATEMATE Semantics of Statecharts*. ACM Transactions on Software Engineering and Methodology (TOSEM) **5**, 4 (1996) pp 293–333

198. D. Harel, M. Politi: *Modelling Reactive Systems with Statecharts: The Statemate Approach* (McGraw-Hill, 1998)

199. D. Harel, P. Thiagarajan: Message Sequence Charts. In: *UML for Real: Design of Embedded Real-time Systems*, ed by Luciano Lavagno and Grant Martin and Bran Selic (Kluwer Academic, 2003)

200. M. Harrison: *Introduction to Formal Language Theory* (Addison-Wesley, MA, USA 1978)

201. K. Havelund, R. Milne: The Semantics of RSL. Technical Report RAISE/-DDC/KH/43/V2, CRI: Computer Resources International, Denmark (1989)
202. K. Havelund, K.R. Wagner: Kentrikos. Technical Report RAISE/DDC/KH/-27/V5, Dansk Datamatik Center (1987)
203. A.E. Haxthausen: Some Approaches for Integration of Specification Techniques. In: *Proceedings of INT'00 — Integration of Specification Techniques with Applications in Engineering* (Technical Report 2000/04, Technical University of Berlin, 2000) pp 33–40
204. A.E. Haxthausen, Y. Xia: Linking DC together with TRSL. In: *Proceedings of 2nd International Conference on Integrated Formal Methods (IFM 2000), Schloss Dagstuhl, Germany, November 2000*, no 1945 of *Lecture Notes in Computer Science* (Springer, 2000) pp 25–44
205. E. Hehner: *The Logic of Programming* (Prentice Hall, 1984)
206. E. Hehner: *A Practical Theory of Programming*, 2nd edn (Springer, 1993)
207. A. Hejlsberg, S. Wiltamuth, P. Golde: *The C# Programming Language* (Addison-Wesley, MA, USA)
208. M. Hennessy: *Algebraic Theory of Processes* (MIT Press, Mass., USA, 1988)
209. M. Hennessy, T. Regan: *A process algebra for timed systems.* Information and Computation **117** (1995) pp 221–239
210. M.C. Henson, S. Reeves, J.P. Bowen: *Z Logic and Its Consequences.* Computing and Informatics **22**, 1–2 (2003)
211. H. Herold: *lex und yacc.* (Addison-Wesley, MA, USA 2003)
212. C.A.R. Hoare: *Communicating Sequential Processes.* Communications of the ACM **21**, 8 (1978)
213. C.A.R. Hoare: *Communicating Sequential Processes* (Prentice Hall, 1985)
214. C.A.R. Hoare, J.F. He: *Unifying Theories of Programming* (Prentice Hall, 1997)
215. G.J. Holzmann: *The SPIN Model Checker, Primer and Reference Manual* (Addison-Wesley, Mass., 2003)
216. T. Honderich (ed.): *The Oxford Companion to Philosophy* (Oxford University Press, UK 1995)
217. J. Hopcroft, J. Ullman: *Introduction to Automata Theory, Languages and Computation* (Addison-Wesley, 1979)
218. P. Øhrstrøm, P.F.V. Hasle: *Temporal Logic, from Ancient Ideas to Artificial Intelligence*, vol 57 of *Studies in Linguistics and Philosophy* (Kluwer Academic, The Netherlands 1995)
219. D.V. Hung, P.H. Giang: A Sampling Semantics of Duration Calculus. Research Report 50, UNU/IIST, Macau (1995)
220. D.V. Hung, K.K. Il: Verification via Digitized Model of Real-Time Systems. Research Report 54, UNU/IIST, Macau (1996)
221. D.V. Hung, C.C. Zhou: Probabilistic Duration Calculus for Continuous Time. Research Report 25, UNU/IIST, Macau (1994)
222. J. Ichbiah et al.: *Preliminary Ada Reference Manual & Rationale for the Design of the Ada Programming Language, Parts A and B.* SIGPLAN **14**, 6 (1979)
223. J. Ichbiah et al.: Requirements for Ada Programming Support Environments, "Stoneman". Technical Report, US Department of Defense, Research and Engineering (1980)
224. IEEE LAN and MAN Standards Committee: *Part 11: Wireless LAN Medium Access Control (MAC) and Physical Layer (PHY) Specifications* (IEEE, 1999)

225. Inmos Ltd.: Specification of instruction set & Specification of floating point unit instructions. In: *Transputer Instruction Set – A compiler writer's guide* (Prentice Hall UK 1988) pp 127–161

226. International Telecommunication Union (ITU, 1995-2004). ITU, SDL and MSC related Web pages:
    - www.sdl-forum.org,
    - www.sdl-forum.org/Events/SAM03.htm,
    - www-i2.informatik.rwth-aachen.de/Research/AG/MCS/MSC/index.html
    - www.sdl-forum.org/Tools

    and SDL conferences
    - 11th International SDL Forum, Stuttgart, Germany, July 1-4, 2003. Proceedings. Lecture Notes in Computer Science 2708 Springer 2003.
    - 10th International SDL Forum Copenhagen, Denmark, June 27-29, 2001, Proceedings. Lecture Notes in Computer Science 2078 Springer 2001.
    - 9th International SDL Forum, Montréal, Québec, Canada, 21-25 June, 1999, Proceedings. Elsevier 1999.
    - 8th International SDL Forum, Evry, France, 23-29 September 1997, Proceedings. Elsevier 1997.
    - 7th International SDL Forum, 26-29 September 1995, Oslo, Norway. Elsevier Science 1995.

227. International Telecommunication Union (ITU-T). CCITT Recommendation Z.120: Message Sequence Chart (MSC), 1992.

228. International Telecommunication Union (ITU-T). ITU-T Recommendation Z.120: Message Sequence Chart (MSC), 1996.

229. International Telecommunication Union (ITU-T). ITU-T Recommendation Z.120: Message Sequence Chart (MSC), 1999.

230. D. Jackson: *Structuring Z Specifications with Views*. ACM Transactions on Software Engineering and Methodology 4, 4 (1995) pp 365–389

231. M.A. Jackson: *Principles of Program Design* (Academic Press, 1969)

232. M.A. Jackson: *System Design* (Prentice Hall, 1985)

233. M.A. Jackson: *Software Requirements & Specifications: a lexicon of practice, principles and prejudices* (Addison-Wesley, UK 1995)

234. M.A. Jackson: *Software Hakubutsushi: Sekai to Kikai no Kijutsu (Software Requirements & Specifications: a lexicon of practice, principles and prejudices)* (Toppan, Japan 1997)

235. M.A. Jackson: *Problem Frames — Analyzing and Structuring Software Development Problems* (Addison-Wesley, UK 2001)

236. M.A. Jackson, G. Twaddle: *Business Process Implementation — Building Workflow Systems* (Addison-Wesley, 1997)

237. I. Jacobson, G. Booch, J. Rumbaugh: *The Unified Software Development Process* (Addison-Wesley, 1999)

238. K. Jensen: *Coloured Petri Nets*, vol 1: Basic Concepts (234 pages + xii), Vol. 2: Analysis Methods (174 pages + x), Vol. 3: Practical Use (265 pages + xi) of *EATCS Monographs in Theoretical Computer Science* (Springer, Heidelberg 1985, revised and corrected second version: 1997)

239. K. Jensen, F. Heitmann, M. Weber et al. (1995-2005) Miscellaneous Petri Net Web pages:
    - http://www.daimi.au.dk/PetriNets/: Coloured Petri Nets (Editor: Kurt Jensen).

- `http://www.informatik.hu-berlin.de/top/pnml/about.html`: Petri Net XML Markup Language (Editor: Frank Heitmann).
- `http://petri-net.sourceforge.net/`: Platform Independent Petri Net Editor (Editor: Michael Weber).
- `http://pdv.cs.tu-berlin.de/~azi/petri.html`: What is a Petri Net? (Editor: (Editor: Armin Zimmermann)).
- `http://www.informatik.uni-hamburg.de/TGI/pnbib/`: The Petri Nets Bibliography (Editor: Heiko Rölke).
- `http://www.informatik.uni-hamburg.de/TGI/pnbib/newsletter.html`: Petri Net Newsletter (Editors: Jörg Desel, Kurt Lautenbach, Gabriel Juhás (executive editor), Karsten Schmidt, Peter Kemper, Peter H. Starke, Ekkart Kindler (executive editor), Rüdiger Valk).

240. K. Jensen, N. Wirth: *Pascal User Manual and Report*, vol 18 of *LNCS* (Springer, 1976)

241. O. Jespersen: *Essentials of English Grammar* (University of Alabama Press, 1964)

242. O. Jespersen: *Modern English Grammar on Historical Principles* (London: Allen & Unwin, Copenhagen: Einar Munksgaard, 1909–1949)

243. O. Jespersen: *Essentials of English Grammar* (Routledge, an imprint of Taylor & Francis Books Ltd, 1933)

244. O. Jespersen: *Essentials of English Grammar* (HarperCollins, 1933)

245. Jin Au Kong: *Maxwell Equations* (EMW Publishing, June 2002)

246. C.B. Jones: *Systematic Software Development Using VDM* (Prentice Hall, 1986)

247. C.B. Jones: *Systematic Software Development Using VDM*, 2nd edn (Prentice Hall, 1990)

248. C.B. Jones, P. Lucas: Proving Correctness of Implementation Techniques. In: *A Symposium on Algorithmic Languages, Vol. 188 of Lecture Notes in Computer Science*, ed by E. Engeler (Springer, 1971) pp 178–211

249. N.D. Jones: Flow Analysis of Lambda Expressions. In: *International Colloquium on Automata, Languages and Programming, European Association for Theoretical Computer Science* (Springer, 1980)

250. N.D. Jones, C. Gomard, P. Sestoft: *Partial Evaluation and Automatic Program Generation* (Prentice Hall, 1993)

251. J.-P. Jouannaud: Rewrite Proofs and Computations. In: *Proof and Computation*, vol 139 of *Computer and Systems Sciences*, ed by H. Schwichtenberg (Springer, 1995)

252. G. Kahn: Natural Semantics. In: *4th Ann. Symposium on Theoretical Aspects of Computer Science (STACS)* (ACM, NY, USA, 1987) pp 22–39

253. N. Kam, I. Cohen, D. Harel: The Immune System as a Reactive System: Modeling T Cell Activation with Statecharts, Extended abstract. In: *Proc. Visual Languages and Formal Methods (VLFM'01), part of IEEE Symp. on Human-Centric Computing (HCC'01)* (IEEE Press, 2001) pp 15–22

254. N. Kam, I. Cohen, D. Harel: *The Immune System as a Reactive System: Modeling T Cell Activation with Statecharts*. Bulletin of Mathematical Biology (To appear)

255. N. Kam, D. Harel, I. Cohen: Modeling Biological Reactivity: Statecharts vs. Boolean Logic. In: *2nd Int. Conf. on Systems Biology (ICSB 2001)* (2001) pp 301–310

256. N. Kam, D. Harel, I. Cohen: Modeling Biological Reactivity: Statecharts vs. Boolean Logic. In: *Proc. Working Conf. on Advanced Visual Interfaces (AVI'02), Trento, Italy, May 2002* (2002) pp 345–353

257. N. Kam, D. Harel, H. Kugler et al.: Formal Modeling of C. elegans Development: A Scenario-Based Approach. In: *Modeling in Molecular Biology (G. Ciobanu and G. Rozenberg, eds.)* (Springer, 2004) pp 151–173

258. N. Kam, D. Harel, H. Kugler et al.: Formal Modeling of C. elegans Development: A Scenario-Based Approach. In: *Proc. 1st Int. Workshop on Computational Methods in Systems Biology (ICMSB 2003)*, vol 2602 of *Lecture Notes in Computer Science* (Springer, February 2003) pp 4–20

259. S. Kamin, J.-J. Lévy: Two Generalizations of the Recursive Path Ordering. Unpublished manuscript, Department of Computer Science, University of Illinois, Urbana, IL (1980)

260. U. Kastens, B. Hutt, E. Zimmermann: *GAG: A Practical Compiler Generator*, vol 141 of *Lecture Notes in Computer Science* (Springer, 1982)

261. M.H. Kay: XML five years on: a review of the achievements so far and the challenges ahead. In: *Proceedings of the 2003 ACM Symposium on Document Engineering, [512]* (2003) pp 29–31

262. K. Kennedy, S. Warren: Automatic Generation of Efficient Evaluators for Attribute Grammars. In: *Proc. ACM National Conference* (1974) pp 32–49

263. B. Kernighan, D. Ritchie: *C Programming Language*, 2nd edn (Prentice Hall, 1989)

264. T. King: Formalising British Rail's Signalling Rules. In: *FME'94: Industrial Benefit of Formal Methods*, ed by M. Naftalin, B.T. Denvir (Springer, 1994) pp 45–54

265. S. Kleene: Representation of Events in Nerve Nets and Finite Automata. In: *see [468]* (Princeton University Press, 1956) pp 3–42

266. S.C. Kleene: *Introduction to Meta-Mathematics* (Van Nostrand, New York and Toronto, 1952)

267. J.W. Klop: Term Rewriting Systems. In: *Handbook of Logic in Computer Science*, vol 2: Background: Computational Structures, ed by S. Abramsky, D. Gabbay, T. Maibaum (Oxford University Press, 1992) pp 1–116

268. J. Klose, H. Wittke: An Automata Based Interpretation of Live Sequence Charts. In: *TACAS 2001*, ed by T. Margaria, W. Yi (Springer, 2001) pp 512–527

269. D. Knuth: *The Art of Computer Programming, Vol.1: Fundamental Algorithms* (Addison-Wesley, Mass., USA, 1968)

270. D. Knuth: *Semantics of Context-Free Languages*. Math. Sys. Theory 2 and 5 (1968. Corrigenda, 5, p. 95, 1971) pp 127–145 and 95–96 (errata)

271. D. Knuth: *The Art of Computer Programming, Vol.2.: Seminumerical Algorithms* (Addison-Wesley, Mass., USA, 1969)

272. D. Knuth: Examples of Formal Semantics. In: *[109]* (1971) pp 178–211

273. D. Knuth: *The Art of Computer Programming, Vol.3: Searching & Sorting* (Addison-Wesley, Mass., USA, 1973)

274. D.E. Knuth: *Structured Programming with goto Statements*. Computing Surveys **6**, 4 (1974) pp 261–301

275. L.M. Kristensen, S. Christensen, K. Jensen: *The practitioner's guide to Coloured Petri Nets*. International Journal on Software Tools for Technology Transfer **2**, 2 (1998) pp 98–132

276. T. Kristoffersen, A.M. Hagalisletto, H.A. Hansen: Simulating the Oslo subway by hierarchic, coloured, object-oriented, timed Petri Nets with viewpoints. In: *14th Nordic Workshop on Programming Theory, NWPT 2002* (20-22 November)

277. T. Kristoffersen, A. Moen, H.A. Hansen: Extracting High-Level Information from Petri Nets: A Railroad Case. In: *Proceedings of the Estonian Academy of Sciences*, vol 52 of *Physics and Mathematics* (December 2003)

278. I. Krüger, R. Grosu, P. Scholz, M. Broy: From MSCs to Statecharts. In: *Distributed and Parallel Embedded Systems*, ed by F.J. Rammig (Kluwer Academic, 1999) pp 61–71

279. H. Kugler, D. Harel, A. Pnueli, Y. Lu, Y. Bontemps: Temporal Logic for Scenario-Based Specifications. In: *Proc. 11th Int. Conf. on Tools and Algorithms for the Construction and Analysis of Systems (TACAS'05)* (Springer, 2005)

280. P.B. Ladkin, S. Leue: Analysis of Message Sequence Charts. Technical Report IAM 92-013, Institute for Informatics and Applied Mathematics, University of Berne, Switzerland (1992)

281. L. Lamport: *The Temporal Logic of Actions*. Transactions on Programming Languages and Systems **16**, 3 (1995) pp 872–923

282. L. Lamport: *Specifying Systems* (Addison-Wesley, Mass., USA 2002)

283. L. Lamport: TLA+ Tools. In: *Internet* (Published: research.microsoft.com/users/lamport/tla/tools.html, 2004)

284. P. Landin: *The Mechanical Evaluation of Expressions*. Computer Journal **6**, 4 (1964) pp 308–320

285. P. Landin: *A Correspondence Between ALGOL 60 and Church's Lambda-Notation (in 2 parts)*. Communications of the ACM **8**, 2-3 (1965) pp 89–101 and 158–165

286. P. Landin: A Generalization of Jumps and Labels. Technical Report, Univac Sys. Prgr. Res. Grp., NY (1965)

287. P. Landin: An Analysis of Assignment in Programming Languages. Technical Report, Univac Sys. Prgr. Res. Grp., NY (1965)

288. P. Landin: Getting Rid of Labels. Technical Report, Univac Sys. Prgr. Res. Grp., NY (1965)

289. P. Landin: A Formal Description of ALGOL 60. In: *[484]* (1966) pp 266–294

290. P. Landin: A Lambda Calculus Approach. In: *Advances in Programming and Non-numeric Computations*, ed by L. Fox (Pergamon, 1966) pp 97–141

291. P. Landin: *The Next 700 Programming Languages*. Communications of the ACM **9**, 3 (1966) pp 157–166

292. P. Landin. Histories of discoveries of continuations: Belles-lettres with equivocal tenses, 1997. In O. Danvy, editor, ACM SIGPLAN Workshop on Continuations, Number NS-96-13 in BRICS Notes Series, 1997.

293. P. Leinonen: Automating XML document structure transformations. In: *Proceedings of the 2003 ACM Symposium on Document Engineering, [512]* (2003) pp 26–28

294. H. Leonard, N. Goodman: *The Calculus of Individuals and Its Uses*. Journal of Symbolic Logic **5** (1940) pp 45–55

295. M.E. Lesk, E. Schmidt, S.C. Johnson et al. The LEX and YACC Page. Electronically, on the Web: http://dinosaur.compilertools.net/, 2003.

296. S. Leue: Methods and Semantics for Telecommunications Systems Engineering. PhD Thesis, Philosophisch-naturwissenschaftlichen Fakultät, University of Berne, Switzerland (1995)

297. J.R. Levine, T. Mason, D. Brown: *Lex & Yacc* (O'Reilly & Associates, October 1992)

298. L. Li, J. He: A Denotational Semantics of Timed RSL using Duration Calculus. Research Report 168, UNU/IIST, Macau (1999)

299. L. Li, J. He: Towards a Denotational Semantics of Timed RSL using Duration Calculus. Research Report 161, UNU/IIST, Macau (1999)

300. X. Li, J. Wang: Specifying Optimal Design of a Steam-boiler System. In: *Formal Methods for Industrial Applications: Specifying and Programming the Steam Boiler Control* (Springer, Lecture Notes in Computer Science, Vol. LNCS 1165, Berlin Heidelberg, Germany 1997)

301. T. Lindholm, F. Yellin: *The Java Virtual Machine Specification* (ACM Press Books, 1996)

302. B. Liskov, S. Zilles: *Programming with Abstract Data Types.* 'Very High Level Languages', SIGPLAN **9**, 4 (1974) pp 59–59

303. W. Little, H. Fowler, J. Coulson, C. Onions: *The Shorter Oxford English Dictionary on Historical Principles* (Clarendon Press, Oxford, UK, 1987)

304. B. Lorho, C. Pair: Algorithms for Checking Consistency of Attribute Grammars. In: *Proving and Improving Programs* (INRIA Publ., 1975)

305. P. Lucas: Two Constructive Realizations of the Block Concept and Their Equivalence. Technical Report 25.085, IBM Laboratory, Vienna (1968)

306. P. Lucas: Formal Definition of Programming Languages and Systems. In: *Proc. IFIP'71* (Springer, 1971)

307. P. Lucas: On the Semantics of Programming Languages and Software Devices. In: *Formal Semantics of Programming Languages*, ed by Rustin (Prentice Hall, 1972)

308. P. Lucas: On the Formalization of Programming Languages: Early History and Main Approaches. In: *[51]*, ed by D. Bjørner, C.B. Jones (Springer, 1978)

309. P. Lucas: *Formal Semantics of Programming Languages: VDL.* IBM Journal of Devt. and Res. **25**, 5 (1981) pp 549–561

310. P. Lucas: Main Approaches to Formal Specification. In: *[47]* (Prentice Hall, 1982) pp 3–24

311. P. Lucas: Origins, Hopes, and Achievements. In: *[53]* (Springer, 1987) pp 1–18

312. P. Lucas, K. Walk: *On the Formal Description of PL/I.* Annual Review Automatic Programming Part 3 **6**, 3 (Elsevier Science 1969)

313. E. Luschei: *The Logical Systems of Leśniewski* (North Holland, Amsterdam, The Netherlands 1962)

314. G. Lüttgen, M. van der Beeck, R. Cleaveland: Statecharts via Process Algebra. Technical Report ICASE Report No. 99-42, Institute for Computer Applications in Science and Engineering, NASA Langley Research Center, Hampton, Virginia, USA (1999)

315. C. Lutz. The Description Logics Web Page. Electronically, on the Web: http://dl.kr.org/, 2004. Dresden University of Technology, Department of Computer Science, Institute for Theoretical Computer Science, Germany.

316. C.K. Madsen: Integration of Specification Techniques. MSc Thesis Report, Institute of Informatics and Mathematical Modelling, Technical University of Denmark (2003)

317. C.K. Madsen: Study of Graphical and Temporal Specification Techniques. Pre-MSc Thesis Report, Institute of Informatics and Mathematical Modelling, Technical University of Denmark (2003)

318. Z. Manna: *Mathematical Theory of Computation* (McGraw-Hill, 1974)

319. Z. Manna, A. Anuchitanukul, N.S. Bjørner et al.: STeP: The Stanford Temporal Prover. Technical Report, STAN-CS-TR-94-1518, Computer Science Department, Stanford University, CA, USA (1994)

320. Z. Manna, A. Pnueli: *The Temporal Logic of Reactive Systems: Specifications* (Addison-Wesley, 1991)

321. Z. Manna, A. Pnueli: *The Temporal Logic of Reactive Systems: Safety* (Addison-Wesley, 1995)

322. Z. Manna, A. Pnueli: Temporal Verification of Reactive Systems: Progress. In: *Internet* (Published: http://theory.stanford.edu/~zm/tvors3.html, 1996)

323. Z. Manna, R. Waldinger: *The Logical Basis for Computer Programming, Vols.1-2* (Addison-Wesley, 1985–90)

324. X. Mao, Q. Xu, J. Wang: Towards a Proof Assistant for Interval Logics. Research Report 77, UNU/IIST, Macau (1996)

325. R. Marelly, D. Harel, H. Kugler: Multiple Instances and Symbolic Variables in Executable Sequence Charts. In: *Proc. 17th Ann. ACM Conf. on Object-Oriented Programming, Systems, Languages, and Applications (OOPSLA 2002)* (ACM Press, November 2002) pp 83–100

326. S. Mauw, M.A. Reniers: *An Algebraic Semantics of Basic Message Sequence Charts.* The Computer Journal 37, 4 (1994) pp 269–277

327. D. May: *occam* (Prentice Hall, UK 1982)

328. B. Mayoh: *Attribute Grammars and Mathematical Semantics.* SIAM J. of Comp. 10 (1981) pp 503–518

329. J. McCarthy: *Recursive Functions of Symbolic Expressions and Their Computation by Machines, Part I.* Communications of the ACM 3, 4 (1960) pp 184–195

330. J. McCarthy: Towards a Mathematical Science of Computation. In: *IFIP World Congress Proceedings*, ed by C. Popplewell (North-Holland, Amsterdam, 1962) pp 21–28

331. J. McCarthy: A Basis for a Mathematical Theory of Computation. In: *Computer Programming and Formal Systems* (North-Holland, Amsterdam, 1963)

332. J. McCarthy. Common Business Communication Language. Electronically, on the Web: http://www-formal.stanford.edu/jmc/cbcl.html, 1982.

333. J. McCarthy, P.W. Abrahams, D.J. Edwards, T.P. Hart, M.I. Levin: *LISP 1.5 Programmer's Manual* (MIT Press, Mass. 1962)

334. J. McCarthy, J. Painter: Correctness of a Compiler for Arithmetic Expressions. In: *[451]* (1966) pp 33–41

335. W. McCulloch, W. Pitts: *A logical calculus of the ideas immanent in nervous activity.* Bulletin of Mathematical Biophysics 5 (1943) pp 115–133

336. H.V. McIntosh. Notes on Cellular Automata, Department of Microprocessor Applications, Institute of Science, Autonomous University of Puebla, Mexico. Published on the Internet, originally from 1987.

337. P. McKerrow: *Introduction to Robotics* (Addison-Wesley, 1990)

338. J.M.E. McTaggart: *The Unreality of Time.* Mind 18, 68 (October 1908) pp 457–84

339. S. Merz: *On the Logic of TLA+.* Computing and Informatics 22, 1–2 (2003)

340. J. Meseguer: Software Specification and Verification in Rewriting Logic. NATO Advanced Study Institute (2003)
341. Meta Software Corporation. Design/CPN Reference Manual. Available at http://www.daimi.au.dk/designCPN/man/Reference/Reference.All.pdf, 1993.
342. J. Mey: *Pragmatics: An Introduction* (Blackwell, 2001)
343. B. Meyer: *Object-Oriented Software Construction* (Prentice Hall, 1988)
344. B. Meyer: *Eiffel: The Language*, second revised edn (Prentice Hall, NJ, USA 1992)
345. B. Meyer: *Object-Oriented Software Construction*, second revised edn (Prentice Hall, NJ, USA 1997)
346. Microsoft Corporation: *MCAD/MCSD Self-paced Training Kit: Developing Web Applications with Microsoft Visual Basic .NET and Microsoft Visual C# .NET* (Microsoft Corporation, Redmond, WA, USA 2002)
347. Microsoft Corporation: *MCAD/MCSD Self-paced Training Kit: Developing Windows-Based Applications with Microsoft Visual Basic .NET and Microsoft Visual C# .NET* (Microsoft Corporation, Redmond, WA, USA 2002)
348. D. Miéville, D. Vernant: *Stanisław Leśniewski aujourd'hui* (Grenoble October 8-10, 1992)
349. R. Milne: The Formal Semantics of Computer Languages and Their Implementation. PhD Thesis, Programming Research Group, PRG 13, Oxford Univ., UK (1974)
350. R. Milne: Transforming Predicate Transformers. In: *[378]* (1978)
351. R. Milne: The Sequential Imperative Aspects of the RAISE Specification Language. Technical Report RAISE/STC/REM/2/V1, STC/STL, Harlow, UK (1987)
352. R. Milne: The Concurrent Imperative Aspects of the RAISE Specification Language. Technical Report RAISE/STC/REM/–/V1, STC/STL, Harlow, UK (1988)
353. R. Milne: The RSL Proof Rules. Technical Report LACOS/CRI/DOC/5, CRI A/S, Birkerød, Denmark (1990)
354. R. Milne: The Semantic Foundations of the RAISE Specification Language. Technical Report RAISE/STC/REM/11, CRI: Computer Resources International, Denmark (1990)
355. R. Milne, C. Strachey: *A Theory of Programming Language Semantics* (Chapman and Hall, London, Halsted Press/John Wiley, NY 1976)
356. R. Milner: *Calculus of Communication Systems*, vol 94 of *Lecture Notes in Computer Science* (Springer, 1980)
357. R. Milner: *Communication and Concurrency* (Prentice Hall, 1989)
358. R. Milner: *Communicating and Mobile Systems: The π-Calculus* (Cambridge University Press, 1999)
359. R. Milner, M. Tofte, R. Harper: *The Definition of Standard ML* (MIT Press, Mass., USA and London, UK, 1990)
360. M. Minsky: Some Universal Elements for Finite Automata. In: *Automata Studies (Editors Claude E. Shannon and John McCarthy) [468]*, no 34 of *Annals of Mathematical Studies* (Princeton University Press, NJ, 1956) pp 117–128
361. M. Minsky: *Computation: Finite and Infinite Machines* (Prentice Hall, NJ, USA, 1967)
362. M. Minsky: A Framework for Representing Knowledge. Reprinted in The Psychology of Computer Vision, P. Winston (Ed.), McGraw-Hill, 1975. Technical Report 306, MIT AI Laboratory, Mass., USA (1974)

363. C.C. Morgan: *Programming from Specifications* (Prentice Hall, UK 1990)
364. C. Morris: Foundations of the Theory of Signs. In: *International Encyclopedia of Unified Science* (Univ. of Chicago Press, 1938)
365. C. Morris: *Signs, Languages and Behaviour* (G. Brazillier, NY, 1955)
366. L. Morris: The Next 700 Programming Language Descriptions. Unpubl. ms., Univ. of Essex, Comp. Ctr., UK (1970)
367. L. Morris: Advice on Structuring Compilers and Proving them Correct. In: *Principles of Programming Languages, SIGPLAN/SIGACT Symposium, ACM Conference Record/Proceedings* (1973) pp 144–152
368. J. Moses: *The Function of FUNCTION in LISP*. ACM SIGPLAN Notices (1970) pp 13–27
369. T. Mossakowski, A.E. Haxthausen, D. Sanella, A. Tarlecki: *CASL — The Common Algebraic Specification Language: Semantics and Proof Theory*. Computing and Informatics **22**, 1–2 (2003)
370. P.D. Mosses: *Action Semantics* (Cambridge University Press: Tracts in Theoretical Computer Science, UK 1992)
371. P.D. Mosses (ed.) CoFI (The Common Framework Initiative): CASL *Reference Manual*, vol 2960 of *Lecture Notes in Computer Science (IFIP Series)*, (Springer, 2004)
372. B.C. Moszkowski: *Executing Temporal Logic Programs* (Cambridge University Press, UK 1986)
373. B.C. Moszkowski: A Complete Axiomatization of Interval Temporal Logic with Infinite Time. In: *LICS'00: 15th Annual IEEE Symposium on Logic in Computer Science* (IEEE Press, CA, USA 2000) p 241
374. Y. Nakamura: *Theory of Robotics* (Addison-Wesley, 1990)
375. National Institute of Standards and Technology (NIST). International System of Units. Electronically, on the Web: http://physics.nist.gov/cuu/Units/, 2000. NIST Web address: http://www.nist.gov.
376. D. Neel, M. Amirchahy: Semantic Attributes and Improvement of Generated Code. In: *ACM Nat. Conf.* (1974) pp 1–10
377. G. Nelson (ed.): *Systems Programming in Modula 3* (Prentice Hall, NJ, USA 1991)
378. E.J. Neuhold (ed.): *Formal Description of Programming Concepts (I)* (North-Holland, Amsterdam, Proc. of IFIP TC-2 Aug. 1977 Work. Conf., St. Andrews, Canada, 1978)
379. N. Nikitchenko: *Towards Foundations of a General Theory of Transport Domains*, Research Report 88, UNU/IIST, P.O.Box 3058, Macau (1996).
380. T. Nipkow, L.C. Paulson, M. Wenzel: *Isabelle/HOL, A Proof Assistant for Higher-Order Logic*, vol 2283 of *LNCS* (Springer, Heidelberg, Germany, 2002)
381. Object Management Group: The CORBA Home Page. Electronically, on the Web: http://www.corba.org/, 1997–2005.
382. Object Management Group: *OMG Unified Modeling Language Specification*, version 1.5 edn (OMG/UML, http://www.omg.org/uml 2003)
383. E.-R. Olderog, editor. *Festschrift to Hans Langmaack*, Lecture Notes in Computer Science. Springer, October 1999. The cover of this volume shows a fictitious program. It illustrates the problem of 'The Most Recent Error': (**let** p = λx•(**let** h = λ()•() **in** x(h()) **end**) **in** p(p) **end**) — the described implementation of which was wrong in [100].
384. S. Owre, N. Shankar, J.M. Rushby, D.W.J. Stringer-Calvert. *PVS Language Reference*. Computer Science Laboratory, SRI International, CA, 1999.

385. S. Owre, N. Shankar, J.M. Rushby, D.W.J. Stringer-Calvert. *PVS System Guide.* Computer Science Laboratory, SRI International, CA, 1999.

386. P.K. Pandya: DCVALID: Duration Calculus Validator. In: *Internet* (Published: www.tcs.tifr.res.in/~pandya/dcest.html, 2003)

387. D. Park: A Predicate Transformer for Weak Fair Iteration. In: *6th IBM Symp. on Math. Found. of Comp. Sci.* (1981)

388. D.L. Parnas: *On the Criteria to Be Used in Decomposing Systems into Modules.* Communications of the ACM **15**, 12 (1972) pp 1053–1058

389. D.L. Parnas: *A Technique for Software Module Specification with Examples.* Communications of the ACM **14**, 5 (1972)

390. D.L. Parnas: *Software Fundamentals: Collected Papers, Eds.: David M. Weiss and Daniel M. Hoffmann* (Addison-Wesley, 2001)

391. D.L. Parnas, P.C. Clements, D.M. Weiss: Enhancing reusability with information hiding. In: *Tutorial: Software Reusability (Ed.: Peter Freeman)* (IEEE Press, 1986) pp 83–90

392. R. Paul: *Robot Manipulators: Mathematics, Programming, and Control* (MIT Press, Mass. and London, UK, 1981)

393. L. Paulson: *Logic and Computation: Interactive Proof with Cambridge LCF* (Cambridge University Press, 1987)

394. C.S. Peirce: *Reasoning and the Logic of Things, Edited by Kenneth Laine Ketner* (Harvard University Press, 1993)

395. C.S. Peirce: *Pragmatism as a Principle and Method of Right Thinking: The 1903 Harvard Lectures on Pragmatism* (State Univ. of N.Y. Press, and Cornell Univ. Press, 1997)

396. C.S. Peirce: *Peirce on Signs: Writings on Semiotics* (Univ. of North Carolina Press, Editor: James Hoopes, 1991)

397. C.S. Peirce: *Writings: A Chronological Edition* (Indiana University Press, 15 Jan 1994)

398. M. Pěnička: Theories of Transportation: Domain and Requirements. PhD Thesis, Faculty of Transportation, Czech Technical University, Prague, Czech Republic (2005)

399. J.L. Peterson: *Petri Net Theory and the Modeling of Systems* (Prentice Hall, NJ 1981)

400. C.A. Petri: *Kommunikation mit Automaten* (Bonn: Institut für Instrumentelle Mathematik, Schriften des IIM Nr. 2, 1962)

401. C. Petzold: *Programming Windows with C# (Core Reference)* (Microsoft Corporation, Redmond, WA, USA 2001)

402. G.D. Plotkin: *A Structural Approach to Operational Semantics.* Journal of Logic and Algebraic Programming **60–61** (2004) pp 17–139

403. A. Pnueli: The Temporal Logic of Programs. In: *Proceedings of the 18th IEEE Symposium on Foundations of Computer Science* (IEEE CS, 1977) pp 46–57

404. A. Pnueli, M. Shalev: What is a step: on the semantics of Statecharts. In: *Theoretical Aspects of Computer Software (TACS'91)*, vol 526 of *Lecture Notes in Computer Science*, ed by T. Ito, A.R. Meyer (Springer, 1991) pp 244–264

405. R.L. Poidevin, M. MacBeath (eds.): *The Philosophy of Time* (Oxford University Press, UK 1993)

406. A. Prior. *Changes in Events and Changes in Things*, chapter in [405]. Oxford University Press, UK 1993.

407. A.N. Prior: *Logic and the Basis of Ethics* (Clarendon Press, Oxford, UK 1949)

408. A.N. Prior: *Formal Logic* (Clarendon Press, Oxford, UK 1955)
409. A.N. Prior: *Time and Modality* (Oxford University Press, Oxford, UK 1957)
410. A.N. Prior: *Past, Present and Future* (Clarendon Press, Oxford, UK 1967)
411. A.N. Prior: *Papers on Time and Tense* (Clarendon Press, Oxford, UK 1968)
412. X. Qiwen: Semantics and Verification of the Extended Phase Transition Systems in the Duration Calculus. Research Report 72, UNU/IIST, Macau (1996)
413. M.O. Rabin, D. Scott: *Finite automata and their decision problems*. IBM Journal of Research and Development **3** (1959) pp 115–125
414. B. Randell, L. Russell: *ALGOL 60 Implementation, The Translation and Use of ALGOL 60 Programs on a Computer* (Academic Press, 1964)
415. A. Ravn, H. Rischel, K. Hansen: *Specifying and Verifying Requirements of Real-Time Systems.* IEEE Trans. Software Engineering **19** (1992) pp 41–55
416. A. Ravn, H. Rischel, E. Sørensen: Control Program for a Gas Burner: Requirements, ProCoS Case Study 0. Technical Report, Dept. of Computer Science, Technical University of Denmark (1989)
417. E.T. Ray: *Learning XML, Guide to Creating Self-describing Data* (O'Reilly, UK, January 2001)
418. M. Reiser: *The Oberon System, User Guide and Programmer's Manual* (Addison-Wesley, 1991)
419. W. Reisig: *Petri Nets: An Introduction*, vol 4 of *EATCS Monographs in Theoretical Computer Science* (Springer, 1985)
420. W. Reisig: *A Primer in Petri Net Design* (Springer, 1992)
421. W. Reisig: *Elements of Distributed Algorithms: Modelling and Analysis with Petri Nets* (Springer, 1998)
422. M. Reniers: Static Semantics of Message Sequence Charts. In: *Proceedings of the 7th SDL Forum* (1995)
423. M. Reniers: Syntax Requirements of Message Sequence Charts. In: *Proceedings of the 7th SDL Forum*, ed by R. Braek, A. Sarma (1995)
424. T.W. Reps: *Generating Language-Based Environments* (MIT Press, Mass., USA 1984)
425. T.W. Reps, T. Teitelbaum: *The Synthesizer Generator: A System for Constructing Language-Based Editors* (Springer, NY, USA 1988)
426. T.W. Reps, T. Teitelbaum: *The Synthesizer Generator Reference Manual*, 3rd edn (Springer, NY, USA 1988)
427. J.C. Reynolds: *GEDANKEN – A Simple Type-less Language based on the Principle of Completeness and the Reference Concept.* Communications of the ACM **13**, 5 (1970) pp 308–319
428. J.C. Reynolds: Definitional Interpreters for Higher-Order Programming Languages. In: *Proc. 25th ACM Nat'l. Conf.* (1972) pp 717–740
429. J.C. Reynolds: *The Craft of Programming* (Prentice Hall, 1981)
430. J.C. Reynolds: *The Discoveries of Continuations.* LISP and Symbolic Computation **6**, 3–4 (1993) pp 233–247
431. J.C. Reynolds: *Theories of Programming Languages* (Cambridge University Press, UK 1998)
432. J.C. Reynolds: *The Semantics of Programming Languages* (Cambridge University Press, 1999)
433. J.G. Riecke, H. Thielecke: *Typed Exceptions and Continuations Cannot Macro-Express Each Other.* Lecture Notes in Computer Science **1644** (1999) p 635
434. G. Rochelle: *Behind time: The incoherence of time and McTaggart's atemporal replacement* (Ashgate, Vt., USA 1998)

435. A.W. Roscoe (ed.): *A Classical Mind: Essays in Honour of C.A.R. Hoare* (Prentice Hall, 1994)
436. A.W. Roscoe: *Theory and Practice of Concurrency* (Prentice Hall, 1997)
437. A.W. Roscoe, J.C.P. Woodcock (eds.): *A Millennium Perspective on Informatics* (Palgrave, 2001)
438. S. Roy, C.C. Zhou: Notes on Neigborhood Logic. Research Report 97, UNU-IIST, Macau (1997)
439. A. Roychoudhury, P. Thiagarajan: Communicating Transaction Processes. In: *Proc. of the 3rd IEEE International Conference on Application of Concurrency in System Design (ACSD'03)* (IEEE Press, 2003)
440. J. Rumbaugh, I. Jacobson, G. Booch: *The Unified Modeling Language Reference Manual* (Addison-Wesley, 1998)
441. R. Rustin: *Formal Semantics of Programming Languages* (Prentice Hall, 1972)
442. P. Ryan, S. Schneider, M. Goldsmith et al.: *Modelling and Analysis of Security Protocols* (Addison-Wesley, December 2000)
443. K.B. Sall: *XML Family of Specifications* (Pearson, 2002)
444. A. Salomaa: *Formal Languages* (Academic Press, NY, USA 1973)
445. B.-Z. Sandler: *Robotics: Designing the Mechanisms for Automated Machinery* (Prentice Hall, 1991)
446. D. Sangiorgio, D. Walker: *The π-Calculus* (Cambridge University Press, 2001)
447. R. Schilling: *Fundamentals of Robotics, Analysis and Control* (Prentice Hall, 1990)
448. D.A. Schmidt: *Denotational Semantics: a Methodology for Language Development* (Allyn & Bacon, 1986)
449. D.A. Schmidt: *The Structure of Typed Programming Languages* (MIT Press, 1994)
450. S. Schott, M.L. Noga: Lazy XSL transformations. In: *Proceedings of the 2003 ACM Symposium on Document Engineering, [512]* (2003) pp 9–18
451. J. Schwartz: *Mathematical Aspects of Computer Science, Proc. of Symp. in Appl. Math.* (American Mathematical Society, RI, USA, 1967)
452. D. Scott: Continuous Lattices. In: *Toposes, Algebraic Geometry and Logic*, ed by F. Lawvere (Springer, Lecture Notes in Mathematics, Vol. 274 1972) pp 97–136
453. D. Scott: Data Types as Lattices. Unpublished Lecture Notes, Amsterdam (1972)
454. D. Scott: Lattice Theory, Data Types and Semantics. In: *Symp. Formal Semantics*, ed by R. Rustin (Prentice Hall, 1972) pp 67–106
455. D. Scott: Mathematical Concepts in Programming Language Semantics. In: *Proc. AFIPS, Spring Joint Computer Conference, 40* (1972) pp 225–234
456. D. Scott: Lattice-Theoretic Models for Various Type Free Calculi. In: *Proc. 4th Int'l. Congr. for Logic Methodology and the Philosophy of Science*, Bucharest (North-Holland, Amsterdam, 1973) pp 157–187
457. D. Scott: *Data Types as Lattices*. SIAM Journal on Computer Science **5**, 3 (1976) pp 522–587
458. D. Scott: *Logic and Programming Languages*. Communications of the ACM **20**, 9 (1977) pp 634–641
459. D. Scott: Relating Theories of the Lambda Calculus. In: *To H.B. Curry: Essays on Combinatory Logic, Lambda Calculus and Formalism*, ed by J. Hindley (Academic Press, 1980) pp 403–450

460. D. Scott: Lectures on a Mathematical Theory of Computation. Techn. Monograph 19, Programming Research Group (1981)

461. D. Scott: Domains for Denotational Semantics. In: *International Colloquium on Automata, Languages and Programming, European Association for Theoretical Computer Science*. M. Nielsen, E. Meineche Schmidt (eds.), LNCS Vol. 140 (Springer, 1982) pp 577–613

462. D. Scott: Some Ordered Sets in Computer Science. In: *Ordered Sets*, ed by I. Rival (Reidel, 1982) pp 677–718

463. D. Scott, C. Strachey: Towards a Mathematical Semantics for Computer Languages. In: *Computers and Automata*, vol 21 of *Microwave Research Inst. Symposia*, Polytechnic Inst. of Brooklyn, NY, USA (1971) pp 19–46

464. J.R. Searle: *Expression and Meaning: Studies in the Theory of Speech Acts* (Cambridge University Press, 1985)

465. P. Sestoft: *Java Precisely* (MIT Press, 2002)

466. N. Shankar, S. Owre, J.M. Rushby. *PVS Tutorial*. Computer Science Laboratory, SRI International, Menlo Park, CA, 1993.

467. N. Shankar, S. Owre, J.M. Rushby, D.W.J. Stringer-Calvert. *PVS Prover Guide*. Computer Science Laboratory, SRI International, Menlo Park, CA, Sept. 1999.

468. C.E. Shannon, J. McCarthy: *Automata Studies*, no 34 of *Annals of Mathematical Studies*, 2nd printing 1958 edn (Princeton University Press, NJ, USA 1956)

469. R. Sharp: *Principles of Protocol Design* (Prentice Hall, 1994)

470. P.M. Simons. *Foundations of Logic and Linguistics: Problems and Their Solutions*, chapter Leśniewski's Logic and Its Relation to Classical and Free Logics. New York, 1985. Georg Dorn and P. Weingartner (eds.). Plenum Press, NY, 1985.

471. A. Simpson, J. Woodcock, J. Davies: The mechanical verification of solid state interlocking geographic data. In: *Proceedings of Formal Methods Pacific*, ed by L. Groves, S. Reeves (Springer, Wellington, New Zealand 1997) pp 223–242

472. Simula: Simula Research Laboratory. In: *Internet* (Published: http://www.simula.no/, 2004)

473. J.U. Skakkebæk: A Verification Assistant for a Real-Time Logic. PhD Thesis, Department of Computer Science, Technical University of Denmark (1994)

474. J.U. Skakkebæk: Development of Provably Correct Systems. Dept. of Computer Science, Technical University of Denmark (MSc. Thesis)

475. J.U. Skakkebæk, A.P. Ravn, H. Rischel, C.C. Zhou: Specification of Embedded, Real-Time Systems. In: *Proceedings of 1992 Euromicro Workshop on Real-Time Systems* (IEEE Computer Society Press, 1992) pp 116–121

476. Smalltalk: smalltalk.org Internet Home Page. In: *Internet* (Published: http://www.smalltalk.org/, 2004)

477. E. Sørensen, N. Hansen, J. Nordahl: *From CSP Models to Markov Models: A Case Study*. IEEE Trans. Software Engineering **19** (1993) pp 554–570

478. C.M. Sperberg-McQueen, H. Thompson. XML Schema. Electronically, on the Web: http://www.w3.org/XML/Schema, April 2000.

479. J.M. Spivey: *Understanding Z: A Specification Language and Its Formal Semantics*, vol 3 of *Cambridge Tracts in Theoretical Computer Science* (Cambridge University Press, 1988)

480. J.M. Spivey: *The Z Notation: A Reference Manual*, 2nd edn (Prentice Hall, 1992)

481. J.T.J. Srzednicki, Z. Stachniak (eds.): *Leśniewski's Lecture Notes in Logic* (Dordrecht, 1988)

482. J.T.J. Srzednicki, Z. Stachniak: *Leśniewski's Systems Protothetic* (Dordrecht, 1998)

483. Merriam–Webster. Online Dictionary: http://www.m-w.com/home.htm, 2004. Merriam–Webster, Inc., 47 Federal Street, P.O. Box 281, Springfield, MA 01102, USA

484. T.B. Steel (ed.): *Formal Language Description Languages*, IFIP TC-2 Work. Conf., Baden (North-Holland, Amsterdam, 1966)

485. J. Stein (ed.): *The Random House American Everyday Dictionary* (Random House, NY, USA 1949, 1961)

486. J. Stoy: *Denotational Semantics: The Scott-Strachey Approach to Programming Language Theory* (MIT Press, 1977)

487. J. Stoy: *The Congruence of Two Programming Language Definitions.* Theoretical Comp. Science **13** (1981) pp 151–174

488. C. Strachey: Fundamental Concepts in Programming Languages. Unpubl. Lecture Notes, NATO Summer School, Copenhagen, 1967, and Programming Research Group, Oxford Univ., UK (1968)

489. C. Strachey: The Varieties of Programming Languages. Techn. Monograph 10, Programming Research Group, Oxford, UK (1973)

490. C. Strachey: Continuations: A Mathematical Semantics Which Can Deal with Full Jumps. Techn. Monograph, Programming Research Group, Oxford, UK (1974)

491. C. Strachey, D. Scott: Mathematical Semantics for Two Simple Languages. Technical Report, Princeton Univ., NJ, USA (1970)

492. B. Stroustrup: *C++ Programming Language* (Addison-Wesley, 1986)

493. J. Sun, J.S. Dong: Live Sequence Charts as Communicating Sequential Processes. Technical Report, School of Computing, Dept. of Computer Science, National University of Singapore (2004)

494. Sun Microsystems. Java Jini. Electronically, on the Web: http://www.sun.com/software/jini/, 1997–2005.

495. S.J. Surma, J.T. Srzednicki, D.I. Barnett, V.F. Rickey (eds.): *Stanisław Leśniewski's: Collected Works (2 Vols.)* (Dordrecht, Boston, New York 1988)

496. R. Temem: *Navier–Stokes Equations* (Oxford University Press, 2001)

497. R. Tennent: *Principles of Programming Languages* (Prentice Hall, 1981)

498. R. Tennent: The Semantics of Inference Control. In: *International Colloquium on Automata, Languages and Programming, European Association for Theoretical Computer Science.* M. Nielsen, E. Meineche Schmidt (eds.), LNCS Vol. 140 (Springer, 1982) pp 532–545

499. R. Tennent: *The Semantics of Programming Languages* (Prentice Hall, 1997)

500. H. Thielecke: *Using a Continuation Twice and Its Implications for the Expressive Power of Call/CC.* Higher-Order and Symbolic Computation **12**, 1 (1999) pp 47–73

501. H. Thielecke: *On Exceptions Versus Continuations in the Presence of State.* Lecture Notes in Computer Science **1782** (2000) pp 397–411

502. E. Thomas: *Maxwell's Equations and Their Applications* (Adam Hilger, June 1985)

503. S. Thompson: *Haskell: The Craft of Functional Programming*, 2nd edn (Addison-Wesley, 1999)

504. S. Tsohadtzidis: *Foundations of Speech Act Theory, Philosophical and Linguistic Perspectives* (Taylor & Francis, 1994)

505. D. Turner: Miranda: A Non-strict Functional Language with Polymorphic Types. In: *Functional Programming Languages and Computer Architectures*, no 201 of *Lecture Notes in Computer Science*, ed by J. Jouannaud (Springer, Heidelberg, Germany, 1985)

506. UDDI. Oasis UDDI. Electronically, on the Web: http://www.uddi.org/, 2005.

507. J.D. Ullman, J. Widom: *A First Course in Database Systems* (Prentice Hall, 2001)

508. J. van Benthem: *The Logic of Time*, vol 156 of *Synthese Library: Studies in Epistemology, Logic, Methhodology, and Philosophy of Science (Editor: Jaakko Hintika)*, 2nd edn (Kluwer Academic, The Netherlands 1991)

509. J. van Leeuwen (ed.): *Handbook of Theoretical Computer Science, Volumes A and B* (Elsevier, 1990)

510. P. van Roy, S. Haridi: *Concepts, Techniques and Models of Computer Programming* (MIT Press, Mass., USA 2004)

511. A. van Wijngaarden: Report on the Algorithmic Language ALGOL 68. Acta Informatica **5** (1975) pp 1–236

512. C. Vanoirbeek, editor. *Proceedings of the 2003 ACM Symposium on Document Engineering*, New York, NY, USA (ACM Press, 2003)

513. B. Venners: *Inside the Java 2.0 Virtual Machine (Enterprise Computing)* (McGraw-Hill, 1999)

514. C. Verhoef: *A congruence theorem for structured operational semantics with predicates and negative premises*. Nordic Journal of Computing **2**, 2 (1995) pp 274–302

515. J.-Y. Vion-Dury: XPath on left and right sides of rules: toward compact XML tree rewriting through node patterns. In: *Proceedings of the 2003 ACM Symposium on Document Engineering, [512]* (2003) pp 19–25

516. W3.   Web Services Activity, SOAP.   Electronically, on the Web: http://www.w3.org/2002/ws/, http://www.w3.org/2000/xp/Group/, http://www.w3.org/2000/xp/Group/xmlp-rec-issues.html http://www.w3.org/2000/xp/Group/2/03/soap1.2implementation.html, http://www.w3.org/2000/xp/Group/4/08/implementation.html, 2005.

517. W3.   Web Services Definition Language.   Electronically, on the Web: http://www.w3.org/TR/wsdl, 2005.

518. M. Wand: Deriving Target Code as a Representation of Continuation Semantics and Different Advice on Structuring Compilers and Proving them Correct. Techn. Repts. 94-95, Dept. of Comp. Sci., Indiana State Univ., Bloomington (1980)

519. M. Wand: *Induction, Recursion and Programming* (North-Holland Publ. Co., Amsterdam, 1980)

520. M. Wand: Semantics-Directed Machine Architecture. In: *Principles of Programming Languages, SIGPLAN/SIGACT Symposium, ACM Conference Record/Proceedings* (1982)

521. J. Wang, W. He: Formal Specification of Stability in Hybrid Control Systems. Research Report 56, UNU/IIST, Macau (1995)

522. J. Wang, X.S. Li, C.C. Zhou: A Duration Calculus Approach to Specifying the Steam-boiler Problem. Technical Report 38, UNU/IIST, Macau (1995)

523. J. Wang, X.S. Li, C.C. Zhou: Specifying Optimal Design of the Steam-boiler System. Technical Report 39, UNU/IIST, Macau (1995)

524. J. Wang, X. Yu, C.C. Zhou: Hybrid Refinement. Research Report 20, UNU/IIST, Macau (1994)

525. T. Wang, A. Roychoudhury, R.H.C. Yap, S.C. Choudhary: Symbolic Execution of Behavioral Requirements. In: *PADL: Practical Aspects of Declarative Languages*, vol 3057 of *Lecture Notes in Computer Science* (Springer, 2004)

526. J. Warmer, A. Kleppe: *The Object Constraint Language: Precise Modeling with UML* (Addison-Wesley, 1998)

527. J. Warmer, A. Kleppe: *The Object Constraint Language: Getting Your Models Ready for MDA*, 2nd edn (Addison-Wesley, 2003)

528. P. Wegner: *Programming Languages, Information Structures, and Machine Organization* (McGraw-Hill, 1968)

529. J. Weizenbaum: The FUNARG Problem Explained. unpubl. note, Proj. MAC, MIT, Mass., USA (1968)

530. Wikipedia: Bisimulation. In: *Internet* (Published: http://www.answers.com/-topic/bisimulation, 2005)

531. R. Wilhelm: *Compiler Design* (Addison-Wesley, 1995)

532. W. Wilner: Formal Semantics Definition Using Synthesized and Inherited Attributes. In: *[441]* (1972)

533. G. Winskel: *The Formal Semantics of Programming Languages* (MIT Press, Mass., USA, 1993)

534. N. Wirth: *Systematic Programming* (Prentice Hall, 1973)

535. N. Wirth: *Algorithms + Data Structures = Programs* (Prentice Hall, 1976)

536. N. Wirth: *Programming in Modula-2* (Springer, Heidelberg, Germany, 1982)

537. N. Wirth: *From Modula to Oberon*. Software — Practice and Experience **18** (1988) pp 661–670

538. N. Wirth: *The Programming Language Oberon*. Software — Practice and Experience **18** (1988) pp 671–690

539. N. Wirth, J. Gutknecht: *The Oberon System*. Software — Practice and Experience **19**, 9 (1989) pp 857–893

540. N. Wirth, J. Gutknecht: *The Oberon Project* (Addison-Wesley, 1992)

541. N. Wirth, H. Weber: *EULER: A Generalization of ALGOL, and Its Formal Definition*. Communications of the ACM **9**, 1-2 (1966) pp 13–23, 89–99

542. J.C.P. Woodcock: *Using Standard Z* (Prentice Hall, UK 1993)

543. J.C.P. Woodcock, J. Davies: *Using Z: Specification, Proof and Refinement* (Prentice Hall, UK, 1996)

544. Xerox Learning Research Group: *The Smalltalk-80 system*. Byte **1981**, 6 (1981) pp 36–48

545. Y. Xinyao, W. Ji, C.C. Zhou, P.K. Pandya: Specification of an Adaptive Control System. Research Report 19, UNU/IIST, Macau (1994)

546. XML. Then XML Home Page. Electronically, on the Web: http://www.xml.com/, 2005.

547. S. Yang, D. Bjørner: A Formal Specification of CTP: Communicating Transaction Processes (see [439]). Technical Report, School of Computing, National University of Singapore (2005)

548. W. Yang: *Mealy Machines are a Better Model of Lexical Analyzers*. Computer Languages **22**, 1 (1996) pp 27–38

549. K.C. Yeager: *The MIPS R10000 Superscalar Microprocessor*. IEEE Micro **40**, 2 (1996) pp 28–40

550. T. Yoshikawa: *Foundations of Robotics* (MIT Press, 1990)

551. H. Yu, P.K. Pandya, Y. Sun: A Calculus of Sampled Data Systems. Research Report 21, UNU/IIST, Macau (1994)

552. Z. Yuhua, C.C. Zhou: A Formal Proof of a Deadline Driven Scheduler. Research Report 16, UNU/IIST, Macau (1994)

553. H. Zemanek: Semiotics and Programming Languages. In: *[5]* (1966) pp 139–143

554. C.C. Zhou: Duration Calculi: An Overview. Research Report 10, UNU/IIST, Macau (1993)

555. C.C. Zhou, M.R. Hansen: Lecture Notes on Logical Foundations for the Duration Calculus. Lecture Notes, 13, UNU/IIST, Macau (1993)

556. C.C. Zhou, M.R. Hansen: An Adequate First Interval Order Logic. Research Report 91, UNU/IIST, Macau (1996)

557. C.C. Zhou, M.R. Hansen: *Duration Calculus: A Formal Approach to Real-Time Systems* (Springer, 2004)

558. C.C. Zhou, M.R. Hansen, A.P. Ravn, H. Rischel: Duration Specifications for Shared Processors. In: *Proceedings Symp. on Formal Techniques in Real-Time and Fault-Tolerant Systems, Nijmegen 6-10 Jan. 1992*, Vol. 571 of Lecture Notes in Computer Science, Springer (1992)

559. C.C. Zhou, C.A.R. Hoare, A.P. Ravn: *A Calculus of Durations*. Information Proc. Letters **40**, 5 (1992)

560. C.C. Zhou, D.V. Hung, X.S. Li: A Duration Calculus with Infinite Intervals. Research Report 40, UNU/IIST, Macau (1995)

561. C.C. Zhou, X. Li: A Mean Value Duration Calculus. Research Report 5, UNU/IIST, Macau (1993)

562. C.C. Zhou, A.P. Ravn, M.R. Hansen: An Extended Duration Calculus for Real-Time Systems. Research Report 9, UNU/IIST, Macau (1993)

563. C.C. Zhou, J. Wang, A.P. Ravn: A Formal Description of Hybrid Systems. Research Report 57, UNU/IIST, Macau (1995)

564. C.C. Zhou, H. Yu: A Duration Model for Railway Scheduling. Technical Report 24b, UNU/IIST, Macau (1994)

565. K. Zimmerman: Outline of a Formal Definition of FORTRAN. Technical Report LR.25.3.053, IBM Laboratory, Vienna (1969)

Monographs in Theoretical Computer Science · An EATCS Series

Texts in Theoretical Computer Science · An EATCS Series